MW01050715

Get started with your **Connected Casebook**

Redeem your code below to access the **e-book** with search, highlighting, and note-taking capabilities; **case briefing** and **outlining** tools to support efficient learning; and more.

1. Go to www.casebookconnect.com
2. Enter your access code in the box and click **Register**
3. Follow the steps to complete your registration and verify your email address

If you have already registered at CasebookConnect.com, simply log into your account and redeem additional access codes from your Dashboard.

ACCESS CODE:
Scratch off with care.

Is this a used casebook? Access code already redeemed? Purchase a digital version at **CasebookConnect.com/catalog**.

If you purchased a digital bundle with additional components, your additional access codes will appear below.

"I liked being able to search quickly while in class."

"Being able to highlight and easily create case briefs was a fantastic resource and time saver for me!"

"I loved it! I was able to study on the go and create a more effective outline."

For technical support, please visit http://support.wklegaledu.com.

ENTREPRENEURSHIP LAW

ASPEN CASEBOOK SERIES

ENTREPRENEURSHIP LAW: CASES AND MATERIALS

Second Edition

STEPHEN F. REED

Assistant Director, Donald Pritzker
Entrepreneurship Law Center
Clinical Professor of Law
Northwestern Pritzker
School of Law

ESTHER S. BARRON

Director, Donald Pritzker
Entrepreneurship Law Center
Clinical Professor of Law
Northwestern Pritzker
School of Law

Wolters Kluwer

Published by Wolters Kluwer in New York.

Wolters Kluwer Legal & Regulatory U.S. serves customers worldwide with CCH, Aspen Publishers, and Kluwer Law International products. (www.WKLegaledu.com)

To contact Customer Service, e-mail customer.service@wolterskluwer.com, call 1-800-234-1660, fax 1-800-901-9075, or mail correspondence to:

Wolters Kluwer
Attn: Order Department
PO Box 990
Frederick, MD 21705

Printed in the United States of America.

1 2 3 4 5 6 7 8 9 0

ISBN 978-1-4548-9973-0

Library of Congress Cataloging-in-Publication Data

Names: Reed, Stephen F., author. | Barron, Esther, author.
Title: Entrepreneurship law : cases and materials / Stephen F. Reed (Assistant Director, Entrepreneurship Law Center, Clinical Associate Professor of Law, Northwestern University School of Law), Esther S. Barron (Director, Entrepreneurship Law Center, Clinical Professor of Law, Northwestern University School of Law).
Description: Second edition. | New York : Wolters Kluwer, 2021. | Series: Aspen casebook series | Includes index. | Summary: "This comprehensive book by two former private practitioners covers the emerging field of Entrepreneurship Law"—Provided by publisher.
Identifiers: LCCN 2020054645 (print) | LCCN 2020054646 (ebook) | ISBN 9781454899730 (hardcover) | ISBN 9781543817539 (epub)
Subjects: LCSH: Business enterprises—Law and legislation—United States. | Entrepreneurship—United States. | LCGFT: Casebooks (Law)
Classification: LCC KF1355 .R445 2021 (print) | LCC KF1355 (ebook) | DDC 346.73/065—dc23
LC record available at https://lccn.loc.gov/2020054645
LC ebook record available at https://lccn.loc.gov/2020054646

About Wolters Kluwer Legal & Regulatory U.S.

Wolters Kluwer Legal & Regulatory U.S. delivers expert content and solutions in the areas of law, corporate compliance, health compliance, reimbursement, and legal education. Its practical solutions help customers successfully navigate the demands of a changing environment to drive their daily activities, enhance decision quality and inspire confident outcomes.

Serving customers worldwide, its legal and regulatory portfolio includes products under the Aspen Publishers, CCH Incorporated, Kluwer Law International, ftwilliam.com and MediRegs names. They are regarded as exceptional and trusted resources for general legal and practice-specific knowledge, compliance and risk management, dynamic workflow solutions, and expert commentary.

To my beloved dad, the original entrepreneur in my life, my greatest inspiration and the commissioner of all good things. No one could have set the bar higher than you did, and you will always be my model for how to live as an attorney, a professor, an entrepreneur and a human being.

— **Esther S. Barron**

To Zella and Bennett, who work hard, love to laugh, and make me proud: follow your heart, and if your heart leads you to law school, take Entrepreneurship Law and buy a copy of this book.

— **Stephen F. Reed**

SUMMARY OF CONTENTS

CONTENTS

CHAPTER III

ORGANIZING THE NEW VENTURE   75

CHAPTER V

FINANCING   183

CHAPTER VI

EMPLOYMENT LAW   249

CHAPTER VII

OPERATIONAL CONTRACTS   287

CHAPTER VIII

CONDUCTING BUSINESS ONLINE   317

CHAPTER IX

RISK MANAGEMENT   355

CHAPTER X

EXIT STRATEGIES   383

PREFACE

Entrepreneurship classes have traditionally been reserved for MBA and undergraduate business programs. In past years, law students interested in this area might be lucky enough to enroll in a business school class as an elective to get some insight into this world, but would miss exposure to the underlying legal doctrine. Even as more forward thinking and innovative law schools incorporated entrepreneurship into law school curricula, law professors were forced to use books designed for business students and supplement readings to make the material appropriate for a law school class. This casebook attempts to build a bridge between the study of the entrepreneur and the legal rules that apply to the venture.

In this casebook, we will meet hypothetical entrepreneurs, Andrew Orlando and Olivia Gold, who are based on the hundreds of entrepreneurs we have represented over the past decade. Andrew and Olivia will face many of the legal issues that we have helped our clients tackle. And similar to the real world practice of law, the situations that students will encounter as the entrepreneurs' legal counsel will provide meaningful opportunities to strategize and consider implications of various potential actions and decisions. We have also attempted to weave in aspects of the entrepreneurs' personalities that we have experienced and which add layers of complexity to the representation and relationships involved.

This casebook is designed to provide a solid background in the legal doctrine applicable in entrepreneurship, and a simulated experience of what legal counsel for entrepreneurs manage over the course of representation of a new company from inception through initial growth. We hope you all are counsel to the next Google, but keep in mind that it may be just as exciting and impactful to represent entrepreneurs who achieve their success on a smaller scale. One by one, successful new ventures are strengthening our nation and the globe, changing how we live and interact with one another and delivering opportunity and success to countless entrepreneurs – and the lawyers who work with them.

Esther S. Barron
Stephen F. Reed

April 2021

ACKNOWLEDGMENTS

We are grateful for the support of our colleagues at Northwestern Pritzker School of Law, particularly Tom Morsch, who founded the Donald Pritzker Entrepreneurship Law Center in 1999 as the Small Business Opportunity Center, and gave us opportunity and inspiration. We also recognize Northwestern Law students in our Entrepreneurship Law course, who have provided an invaluable testing ground for the cases, materials and problems in the book.

Our research assistants over the years have also made valuable contributions to the work, including Bill Benitez, Peter Hanoian, Dylan Hanson, Jonathan Hillel, Bharat Kejriwal, Jonathan Man, Huy Pham, Heather Scheiwe, and Melissa Tilney, all of whom were Northwestern students, and Allen Mendenhall, who came to us courtesy of Ilya Shapiro and the Cato Institute. Our former colleague Sheila Simhan was very helpful in gathering material for the book, as were our assistants Lauren Sosin Bender and Alyssa Huff. We also appreciate the faculty at other law schools who gave and continue to give us feedback, particularly those who use this book in their classes and have shared the results.

Finally, we are grateful for the love, encouragement and support we have received from our families and friends.

American Bar Association. Model Rules of Professional Conduct and Official Comments Rules 1.7 and 1.13. American Bar Association. Copyright © 2012. Reprinted with Permission.

American Bar Association. Model Rules of Professional Conduct Rule 1.1. American Bar Association. Copyright © 2020. Reprinted with permission.

Bernard, G. Wogan. Using Forms for Drafting Help – Tips for Young Lawyers. Probate and Property. American Bar Association. Copyright © 2011. Reprinted with permission.

Bernthal, J. Brad. The Evolution of Entrepreneurial Finance: A New Typology. 2018 Brigham Young University Law Review 775. Brigham Young University Law Review. Copyright © 2019. Reprinted with permission.

Chesler, Susan M. Drafting Effective Contracts: How to Revise, Edit and Use Form Agreements. Business Law Today, Vol. 19. No. 2. American Bar Association. Copyright © 2009. Reprinted with permission.

Coyle, John F. and Joseph M. Green. Essay: The Safe, the Kiss, and the Note: A Survey of Startup Seed Financing Contracts. 103 Minnesota Law Review Headnotes 42. Minnesota Law Review Headnotes. Copyright © 2018. Reprinted with permission.

Davis, Christine Spinella. Liability Insurance 101 for Business Litigators. The Young Lawyer. American Bar Association. Copyright © 2009. Reprinted with permission.

Eyal-Cohen, Mirit. Through the Lens of Innovation. 43 Florida State University Law Review 951. Florida State University. Copyright © 2016. Reprinted with permission.

Fleischer, Victor. The Rational Exuberance of Structuring Venture Capital Start-Ups. 55 Tax Law Review 137. New York University School of Law. Copyright © 2003. Reprinted with permission.

Gilson, Ronald J. Engineering a Venture Capital Market: Lessons from the American Experience. 55 Stanford Law Review 1067, 1071-1072. Stanford University School of Law. Copyright © 2003. Reprinted with permission.

Goldberg, Daniel S. Choice of Entity for a Venture Capital Start-Up: The Myth of Incorporation. 55 Tax Law 923. American Bar Association. Copyright © 2002. Reprinted with permission.

Heminway, Joan MacLeod. Lawyering for Social Enterprise. 20 Transactions: Tennessee Journal of Business Law 797. The University of Tennessee College of Law. Copyright © 2019. Reprinted with permission.

Hwang, Cathy. Faux Contracts. 105 Virginia Law Review 1025. Copyright © 2019. Copyright for the material used is owned by the Virginia Law Review Association and used by permission of the Virginia Law Review Association.

Klar, Manuel. Binding Effects of the European General Data Protection Regulation (GDPR) On U.S. Companies. 11 Hastings Science and Technology Law Journal 101. University of California, Hastings College of the Law. Copyright © 2020. Reprinted with permission.

Linfield, James. Founder Basics: Founder's Stock, Vesting and Founder Departures. Cooleygo.com (accessed July 2020). Copyright © Cooleygo.com. Reprinted with permission.

Molot, Jonathan T. A Market in Litigation Risk. 76 University of Law Review 367. The University of Chicago Press. Copyright © 2009. Reprinted with permission.

Pozen, David E. We Are All Entrepreneurs Now. 43 Wake Forest Law Review 283. Wake Forest Law Review Association. Copyright © 2008. Reprinted with permission.

Schouest, Brett. Limit Transaction Risks by Using Indemnity Agreements, Insurance. San Antonio Business Journal. American City Business Journals. Copyright © 2007. Reprinted with permission.

I

INTRODUCTION TO ENTREPRENEURSHIP LAW

Whether an attorney sees entrepreneurship as a philosophically essential aspect of "The American Dream," an important engine in the economy, or simply a good opportunity for client development, the impact of entrepreneurs and entrepreneurial ventures in the United States is undeniable. Occasionally entrepreneurs themselves, lawyers who represent new or small ventures are faced with a unique set of issues not always seen in other areas of practice. While some clients are "social entrepreneurs" — who work with a social purpose through a for-profit or nonprofit venture — and others are traditional business-minded entrepreneurs, all entrepreneurs present lawyers with distinct substantive and interpersonal challenges.

Attorneys who represent entrepreneurs and entrepreneurial ventures need at least a basic comprehension of a myriad of legal disciplines: employment law, intellectual property law, contract law, corporate and agency law, finance law, e-commerce law, and securities law, to name just a few. Throughout this casebook, we introduce the most common doctrinal areas faced by lawyers who represent entrepreneurs. Recognizing that representing entrepreneurial ventures and entrepreneurs is practically different from representing large corporations and their stockholders, we look through the lens of the entrepreneur's lawyer.

Key to understanding the approach lawyers take when representing entrepreneurs is an understanding of some basic characteristics of entrepreneurs as individuals, and the special problems that arise when a person and her business seem to be one and the same being. In this chapter, we introduce some ways of thinking about entrepreneurship and entrepreneurs, including an exploration of a few substantive and ethical aspects of being engaged as counsel to an entrepreneur or an entrepreneurial venture.

A. ENTREPRENEURS AND LAWYERS

On a basic level, we all understand that an entrepreneur is a person who starts a new business. Given the place of entrepreneurs in the economy, the historical and current value of innovation and entrepreneurship in helping the nation and

1

the world to overcome crises of all types, and the prominence of entrepreneurs in popular culture, we probably also believe entrepreneurship is a pretty big deal. We may even think of entrepreneurs as heroes, or at least celebrities — think of Mark Zuckerberg (of Facebook), or Sergey and Larry (of Google), or the late Steve Jobs (of Apple, NeXT, Pixar, and Apple (again)). We may think of entrepreneurs as brave or foolish, clever or opportunistic, or as possessing any other number of characteristics. As lawyers, however, we need to think about entrepreneurs as clients with goals, and try to help the clients achieve the goals. To be effective at these tasks, a lawyer must understand each client's style and personality so that she can tailor and deliver legal advice in a way that will be constructive.

The first two readings of this chapter will help to frame our conception of the complex meaning of "entrepreneur" and the associated characteristics these clients may possess. In the process, you will learn of a few historical approaches to thinking about entrepreneurs, and also to some current thinking on lawyers as entrepreneurs. As you read, try to think practically about how a client's personality traits can affect a lawyer's approach to practicing law.

WE ARE ALL ENTREPRENEURS NOW
David E. Pozen, 43 Wake Forest L. Rev. 283 (2008)

Everyone, it seems, is an entrepreneur these days. People who tackle civic problems through innovative methods are "social entrepreneurs." Those who promote new forms of legislation or government action are "policy entrepreneurs." Those who seek to change the way society thinks or feels about an issue are "norm entrepreneurs." Those who try to alter the boundaries of altruism or deviance are "moral entrepreneurs." Martin Luther King, Jr., it turns out, was a social, policy, norm, and moral entrepreneur all at the same time. And then, of course, there are the capitalist entrepreneurs, starting for-profit ventures and transforming economic markets as usual. Capitalist entrepreneurship no longer ends at the founding, though: once those ventures become settled concerns, employees may become "intrapreneurs" by pioneering an initiative or subsidiary within the existing corporate structure.

. . .

Theories of entrepreneurship have a long and rich history in Western economic thought. Numerous influential economists have proffered definitions of entrepreneurship as an aspect of their broader positive or normative projects, in which they identify core traits of the entrepreneur and explain his or her role in a market economy. There is a "dis-jointed nature" to this body of work, some have pointed out, because entrepreneurship has been from the start an extremely capacious concept, and commentators have invoked it for a variety of ends. Theories of entrepreneurship abound, but we have no completely satisfying synthetic account of the practice, and we probably never will.

Modern dictionary definitions of entrepreneurship tend to emphasize three interrelated functions. First, the entrepreneur initiates and organizes a business venture, identifying an opportunity and assembling the necessary tools, skills, and personnel to pursue it. Second, the entrepreneur manages the venture, overseeing its efforts to attract customers and generate revenues, at least for an initial period. And third, the entrepreneur assumes the risk of the venture, generally by investing his or her own capital and reputation and by forsaking a guaranteed income. Implicit in this last function is a tradeoff between the promise of economic gain and the potential for economic loss — a tradeoff that is dramatically exemplified in real life. The majority of new businesses in the United States will fail within their first several years, but some succeed spectacularly, and many of America's wealthiest individuals made their fortunes as entrepreneurs.

Linked to the functional characteristics of the entrepreneur is a set of personal traits that also plays an important role in defining the term. Entrepreneurs, in the American imagination, are leaders, innovators, pioneers, problem solvers, and risk takers; they are diligent, persistent, charismatic, dynamic, imaginative, and resourceful, the bricoleurs of the capitalist marketplace. The term's connotations are not wholly positive, however. Entrepreneurs can be greedy, cunning, opportunistic, and self-interested, possessed of a kind of Nietzschean will to power that may lead to domination and destruction as well as to value creation.[5]

The etymology of "entrepreneur" is tightly bound up with the history of economic theorizing about capitalism. The term derives from the French entreprendre, which translates roughly as to undertake or to embark upon. It came into being in the early fifteenth century and crossed the Channel around 1475 but did not stick. It was not until the mid-1750s, in an essay published posthumously, that the Irish economist Richard Cantillon introduced the term into mainstream economic discourse. Cantillon divided economic actors into two broad camps, those who receive assured incomes and those who do not. The latter, Cantillon explained, are the entrepreneurs, and he gave as an example the merchants who bought goods from country farmers at a fixed price to sell to city dwellers at a price that could not be known in advance. Cantillon's key contribution to the theory of entrepreneurship was to invest it with some substantive economic content and to identify risk bearing as a constitutive element.

The next major thinker to explore entrepreneurship, and the one most often credited with elevating the concept to prominence in economic theory, was the French economist Jean-Baptiste Say. Say went beyond Cantillon's focus on uncertainty of income to develop an account of the entrepreneur who "shifts economic resources out of an area of lower and into an area of higher productivity and greater yield." In his pursuit of profit, according to Say, the entrepreneur figures out how to satisfy a greater number of human needs and wants. Entrepreneurship therefore involves not only the reallocation of existing economic resources but also the generation of new resources; it is a positive-sum, not a zero-sum, game. Being an entrepreneur — or a "master-agent," as Say sometimes described it — "requires a combination of moral qualities, that are not often found together," such as "judgment, perseverance, and a knowledge of the world, as well as of business." Say's work was instrumental in identifying the entrepreneur as both a maker of markets and a creator of economic value, and in painting a picture of the entrepreneur as a rare, exceptionally talented and motivated individual. To this day, Say's basic insights on entrepreneurship continue to frame much of the academic and popular discussion on the subject.

---

5. Reflecting these two sides to the entrepreneurial profile, my thesaurus tells me that entrepreneurs are explorers, heroes, knights, organizers, pioneers, producers, romantics, undertakers, venturers, and voyagers; and yet entrepreneurs are also synonymous with charlatans, gamblers, madcaps, mercenaries, opportunists, pirates, rogues, speculators, swashbucklers, and wheeler dealers. . . .

Economic theory, however, has not always assigned a place of prominence to the entrepreneur, and for the most part it still does not. From Adam Smith and David Ricardo on, a venerable line of classical and neoclassical economists have developed market models that assign little to no special significance to the entrepreneur. Entrepreneurs are largely absent from the economic theory of Smith — he never uses the term — who elided the distinction between creators of businesses and owners of businesses and whose depiction of an "invisible hand" leading to market equilibrium drew attention away from the entrepreneur's self-consciously generative role. Neoclassical economists such as Alfred Marshall and A.C. Pigou, writing at the turn of the twentieth century, and Milton Friedman and George Stigler, writing in the mid-to-late twentieth century, have likewise tended to trivialize entrepreneurship in their formal models of a steady-state economy. They have done this, William Baumol observes, partly because innovation is an entirely heterogeneous output that does not lend itself to formal mathematical description and, more basically, because in the neoclassical world of perfect information, perfect competition, negligible transaction costs, and homogeneous goods, entrepreneurs would have nothing to offer; the concept of entrepreneurship would not even make much sense.

The real world is a rather messy place, though, and the absence of entrepreneurship certainly looks like a phenomenological lacuna in the neoclassical view. As neoclassical theory has grown more sophisticated throughout recent decades — spurred by econometric and behavioral evidence to recognize the importance of norms and institutions and the possibilities for imperfect competition, incomplete information, temporary disequilibria, and irrational decision making — there are signs that it has begun to reacquaint itself with the entrepreneur. Still, it remains deeply ironic that the academic discipline most focused on the capitalist process has so marginalized the entrepreneur, while lawyers, sociologists, and political scientists cannot stop talking about her.

. . .

After the early interventions of scholars such as Richard Cantillon and Jean-Baptiste Say, it was the great Austrian economist Joseph Schumpeter who made the most profound contribution to the theory of entrepreneurship and to the public's appreciation of the concept. Schumpeter built on Say in developing the idea of the entrepreneur as innovator, forcing major structural changes across markets and industries in a process of "creative destruction" vital for sustaining a dynamic economy and long-run economic growth. "The function of entrepreneurs," Schumpeter maintained, "is to reform or revolutionize the pattern of production" by exploiting a new technology, developing a new source of supply, reorganizing an industry, or the like. For Schumpeter, the economy did not tend naturally toward stability and growth through the workings of an invisible hand, but rather was propelled forward in sudden leaps by the endogenous innovations of key entrepreneurs. His was a story not of harmonious stasis but of evolution through punctuated equilibria. Yet while Schumpeter wrote with great admiration about "the entrepreneurial type," motivated primarily not by profit but by the "desire to found a private dynasty, the will to conquer in a competitive battle, and the joy of creating," like Weber he recognized that societies often resist the changes that entrepreneurs induce, sometimes violently. . . . As his paradoxical label "creative destruction" captured so sharply, Schumpeter too saw the fundamental public ambivalence that will attach to entrepreneurship on account of its destabilizing power.

Writing around the same time as Schumpeter, the American economist Frank Knight conceptualized the entrepreneur's contribution in very different and nearly as influential terms. Whereas Schumpeter largely excluded the assumption of risk and the duties of ownership from his account of entrepreneurship, Knight drew on Cantillon in emphasizing the entrepreneur's role as a bearer of market uncertainty, as a manager as well as a creator. Knight famously distinguished between risk, which is related to recurring events and is insurable, and uncertainty, which derives from unique events and cannot, Knight claimed, be estimated with any precision. In an economy characterized by changing consumer tastes and purchasing power, Knight argued, adventurous entrepreneurs are needed to create, own, and control business enterprises, guaranteeing wages to their employees in return for the potential of monetary gain. In an economy riven with uncertainty, that is, entrepreneurs must address "the primary problem or function [of] deciding what to do and how to do it." Entrepreneurship, for Knight, was a kind of profession and a public service as well as a disposition and a skill set.

. . .

To sum up: although economic theory has been sporadic in its concern for entrepreneurship, a significant and rapidly growing body of scholarship has interrogated the subject conceptually and empirically. Many have linked entrepreneurship to economic growth and to a characteristic menu of personality traits. Some theorists of the entrepreneur, such as Cantillon and Knight, have emphasized her role in taking on economic risk; others such as Kirzner and Say her role in making and perfecting markets; others such as Baumol and Schumpeter her role in generating innovation and economic value. These theories intersect at many points, clash at others, and do not form a unified whole. . . .

THROUGH THE LENS OF INNOVATION
Mirit Eyal-Cohen, 43 Fla. St. U. L. Rev. 951 (2016)

The American economy is at a critical moment in history. The aftermath of the latest downturn reveals that we have experienced one the deepest recessions in recent times. Yet, our economy has not yet regained its full strength. Now, more than ever, there is a need for economic renewal and mobility. Entrepreneurship is essential for revitalization, economic growth, job creation, and technological renewal. These elements are the driving force behind improvements in well-being and standards of living. Governments have long realized that continuous growth depends upon a vibrant society of entrepreneurs. While the current global pressure to capture entrepreneurship is strong, our competitive edge is being diminished by countries that have developed superior ways to attract intellectual wealth. Accordingly, entrepreneurship warrants distinct legal attention.

Law plays a significantly active role in creating an environment in which entrepreneurs can successfully act. Lawmakers can utilize law to encourage entrepreneurs to create opportunities by reducing transaction and information costs. Law can function as a stabilizing force that allows private actors to contract about future market conditions and reduce their uncertainty. It has the power to increase or reduce the regulatory costs of pursuing entrepreneurship.

Law can also impose rules that obstruct entrepreneurial opportunities. For example, patent laws ensure that entrepreneurs retain control of their discoveries and entrepreneurial gains. They facilitate risk-taking by ensuring that entrepreneurs reap the benefits of successful speculation. Nevertheless, if taken to the extreme, patent laws can hamper entrepreneurship by generating monopoly positions over discoveries and preventing other entrepreneurs from developing and improving them.

Congress has frequently declared that enticing entrepreneurship is a fundamental value in American society. Yet, our laws are not compatible with current economic and technological advances. Recent literature has begun to investigate the ways in which the law can improve production of goods and labor expansion. Legal reform proposals have suggested ways in which the legal system — the contents of specific laws, judicial doctrines, regulations, and legal processes — can be improved to spur production and growth. These proposals have outlined changes in the laws governing immigration, taxation and financial institutions, as well as contracts, torts, patents, education, land use, and other concerns. They have focused on improving the range of property rights and the rule of law. Yet, the question remains: To what degree are they successful in capturing the phenomenon?

All of these reform discussions lack something fundamental: they fail to recognize the contradicting nature of their topics. Legal rules impose duties and establish rights. The practice of law seeks order and authority and the continuity of tradition. Through causal reasoning, it advances an aim and pursues the means to achieve that aim. Using logical deductions lawyers create legal models and doctrinal rules to apply to complex circumstances. Law denotes the existence of norms that deliver sanctions and remedies when certain conditions hold. It enforces rules and creates classifications that aim to direct behavior in a uniform manner.

Entrepreneurship thrives on freedom and creativity. Its essence is making judgments about the unknown. Entrepreneurs make their decisions in a state of uncertainty, without being able to calculate the likelihood or probabilities of an imminent sequence of events. Therefore, entrepreneurship involves the creative reading of the present and the imaginative prediction of the future. It prospers on deviations as opposed to traditional causation, and it involves adapting to disarray. In a state of disequilibrium, the entrepreneur's alertness discovers profitable opportunities to match unmet demand with untapped supply. Therefore, entrepreneurs prefer legal structures that provide them with greater autonomy.

This Article argues that these differences matter. The nature of a legal solution is essentially cognitive and causal; it does not address the effectual aspects of entrepreneurship. The friction between law and entrepreneurship creates significant distortionary effects. Through theoretical discourse, this Article maintains that a new approach is necessary. It contends that a legal culture that wishes to entice greater innovation is one that requires its legal agents to think like entrepreneurs. While some scholars have developed frameworks for crafting laws that facilitate entrepreneurship, they have mostly focused on theories of risk. However, there is more to entrepreneurship than taking risks.

. . .

III. THE ENTREPRENEURSHIP PROCESS

Innovation is a function of economic evolution. Over the last few decades, a vast amount of literature has been developed that establishes the characteristics of individual entrepreneurs, especially from a psychological perspective. This type of scholarship portrays entrepreneurs as special individuals who tend to exhibit a particular combination of traits that enable them to assume the role of innovators. Such literature has emphasized that entrepreneurs are better able to understand and evaluate certain risks and their returns. Factors such as independence, creativity, confidence, and resilience were found to affect an entrepreneur's decision to take risks and be innovative. Yet to date, there is no agreement on the qualities that are necessary for entrepreneurs to be successful.

It is difficult to isolate human actions that fully capture entrepreneurial elements. Behind every entrepreneurial firm are individuals or groups of people with unique characteristics and entrepreneurial spirits. Regulating the commercialization of entrepreneurial opportunities is mostly administrable at the entity level. Actions, rather than psychological attributes, are what give meaning to the entrepreneurship process. Accordingly, this Part will consider entrepreneurship from the womb to the tomb. It will unfold the entrepreneurship process and frame it in four main stages: discovery, concept development, implementation, and harvesting success or failure.

A. Discovery of Opportunities

The main element that distinguishes the entrepreneurship process from other business undertakings is novelty. Decision making in the business context involves entrepreneurial and non-entrepreneurial actions. The latter usually entails the task of calculation, the deployment of production factors that happen to be unused, or the readjustment of production means. The entrepreneurial aspect of decision making is discovery. Innovative ideas challenge the current body of knowledge and eventually push society forward by destroying old premises. Discovery is a self-determining decision to carry out "new combinations" by introducing new products, new markets, or deploying existing means of production in a unique way.

Kirzner developed the notion of entrepreneurial "alertness" to denote the quest for innovative knowledge. He argued that entrepreneurs are often dissatisfied with the current available knowledge. That dissatisfaction inspires them to be alert to changing conditions and overlooked possibilities. Entrepreneurial discovery ensues when entrepreneurs believe they have revealed possibilities for innovation that actual or potential competitors had hitherto not seen.

Some entrepreneurial discoveries may also generate negative externalities. Creativeness at its peak can also create societal harms or wasteful, inefficient, or destructive outcomes. Nevertheless, when used in a positive manner, entrepreneurship overall improves the efficiency of our lives. The first step in the entrepreneurship process, then, is the search for the discoveries or new combinations that will achieve a constructive effect. This entails observing current opportunities and studying inefficiencies, wasteful processes, or failed projects with the aim of improving them or creating new ones. It could yield either valuable or useless results that will lead to entrepreneurial success or failure.

At this critical stage of discovery, entrepreneurs heavily invest in knowledge procurement, more so than others, in observing their environment, collecting market research data, and determining current and future resources required to develop the opportunities. Next, entrepreneurs conceptualize the idea. This is far from being an easy task. Doubts and uncertainties are inevitable elements of this process. Entrepreneurs need to overcome the uncertainty hurdle and proceed with developing what they perceive as the future.

B.   Resourcing and Concept Development

Following the discovery stage, the entrepreneurship process proceeds to conceptualizing and planning. This stage entails evaluating the discovery, looking at available resources, calculating the return on investment, the real and perceived value of the opportunity, and its risks and rewards. It includes establishing the goals of the project and identifying its uniqueness and competitive advantage over existing rivals. Entrepreneurs do so in the shadow of uncertainty lacking future market information.

The business model and strategy are essentially the entrepreneurs' theory regarding how they will make money from their idea. It involves an assumption of a market need and a hypothesis about how much customers would be willing to pay for the product. Entrepreneurs design for the target consumer market by envisioning the buyers of the new product. At this stage, establishing an organization is a way to gather resources and express their creativity and autonomy. Once a sufficient amount of planning has been conducted, entrepreneurs will choose the organizational form they see as the best fit for their venture and goals.

C.   Realization and Implementation

Innovation is distinct from invention. Innovation and "economic leadership" are more relevant to the economy than invention. Inventions are economically insignificant if they are not successfully delivered to the market. The task of the entrepreneur is to carry the invention into practice. The entrepreneurship process takes the previously unnoticed opportunities that entrepreneurs discovered and translates them into profitable exchanges. Production begins and creates new demand in the market that rapidly generates large revenues and sustainable profits by successfully transforming knowledge into economic value.

Entrepreneurs need to carefully and surreptitiously develop their product. They need to navigate their way through this process without losing control over the essence of the entrepreneurial action. They have to create demand that will transport that sought-after, supra-competitive entrepreneurial gain. They need to make decisions while assessing market uncertainties and taking risks. The presence of specialists and departments may restrict entrepreneurs' thought processes and key decisions. At this crucial point, entrepreneurs may realize their interests have separated from that of their organization. The implementation of the entrepreneurial idea can result in a successful process that yields quick but substantial entrepreneurial gains. However, it can also result in failure, as the next Section reveals.

D.   Harvesting Entrepreneurial Success or Recognizing Failure

Entrepreneurs create economic value by successfully pulling together a unique package of resources that exploit untapped opportunities. They infuse economic value into the market by creatively securing and allocating the necessary skills and resources. This economic value is what Schumpeter called "entrepreneurial gains" — the outcome of a successful delivery of the discovery to the market recognized via upsurge in the firm's growth. This reflects the firm's ability to convert valuable knowledge into superior economic performance.

Following the moment when entrepreneurs realize success, they begin to reap "supra-competitive gains." These gains are pure profits emanating from the creation of new market demand and the absence of competitors. What makes entrepreneurial gains uniquely different? Schumpeter distinguished between entrepreneurial gains and ordinary business profits by emphasizing the scope and timing of their onset. Entrepreneurial gains are the portion over and above a normal profit. They follow innovation and do not arise as a response to preexisting demand in the market. The prospect of receiving large rewards and personal gains leads to and maintains alertness to potential economically or socially significant opportunities. Nevertheless, as will be further discussed, entrepreneurial profits are only temporary premiums of successful innovation.

Not all entrepreneurs succeed. The implementation stage can also result in entrepreneurial failure. But entrepreneurial failure is an important part of the entrepreneurship process. Kirzner argued that when there is no room for error, there is no room for opportunities for entrepreneurial discovery. Entrepreneurs often tend to be over-optimistic about the outcomes or the availability of production means. They may also miscalculate the market reaction to their innovation. Making "correct" decisions requires more than reaching an accurate mathematical answer. It involves a detailed assessment of current and future realities and anticipating changes in market conditions in an uncertain environment.

Entrepreneurial failure is economically and culturally valuable. It signals to the market what ideas do not work and provides lessons about new possibilities for improving the process. Entrepreneurial failure is a vital element of the entrepreneurship process and a catalyst for growth. Entrepreneurial failure diffuses knowledge among entrepreneurs and points to other solutions that may lead to entrepreneurial success. Knowledge spillover occurs when failure is followed by entrepreneurial actions of others. Learning from entrepreneurial errors increases the competitiveness of the market. Some entrepreneurs are quick to spot unnoticed opportunities, while others notice only those revealed by the errors of others. Some succeed in pursuing entrepreneurship while others produce waste and fail.

The scope of entrepreneurship, therefore, must include the possibility of discovering errors. Studies on economic growth demonstrate that the benefits of entrepreneurial success outweigh the cost of entrepreneurial failure. Overall, society reaps more benefits from entrepreneurial action. Accordingly, entrepreneurship requires distinct legal considerations. . . .

V.   LEGAL CLASSIFICATION FROM THE POINT OF VIEW OF ENTREPRENEURS

The key function of the entrepreneur is to implement innovations effectively. The entrepreneur "is the man who gets things done," and the "enterprise" is the conduit for implementing the entrepreneur's novel ideas and discoveries. Entrepreneurs are people who possess the power to set things into motion. They do not act in a void. Law governs transactions. It administers exchanges between the entrepreneur and other market players, such as vendors, investors, employees, and the government. Law imposes order and directs the entrepreneurs' ability to execute innovations. It provides entrepreneurs with advantages; it also presents them with hurdles. . . .

Entrepreneurs are heavily invested in the unknown. They constantly make judgments about contingencies, such as cash flow problems, partner breakups, natural disasters, loss of a major customer, new competition, industry change, loss of key personnel, etc. All of these matters require entrepreneurs to make decisions in the shadow of uncertainty. At each stage of the transient entrepreneurship process, the entrepreneur faces ambiguity regarding future market conditions. In the discovery stage, the focus is on trying to predict future market conditions and the market reaction to the newly discovered opportunity. In the resourcing and concept development stage, uncertainty about obtaining funding looms. In the realization stage, the entrepreneur is uncertain about whether the opportunity will lead to a success or a failure. The uncertainty that surrounds the new discovery differs from business risk because it stems from newly created market conditions and it is difficult to identify or measure.

Unpredictable, changing circumstances benefit from a stable legal order. Yet, setting strict legal rules can lead to stagnation, among other things, and can restrain entrepreneurs from adjusting the process to meet unanticipated developments. The recent development of sharing economy is one example that highlights the dissonance between law and entrepreneurship. In the past few years, new Internet-based platforms have been shaping a new consumer culture, lowering transaction costs and improving accessibility to shared goods and services on a previously unimaginable scale. Companies such as Uber, Zipcar, Airbnb and TaskRabbit developed new ways to allow greater access to services, accommodation, and transportation. The hotel, taxi, and other industries as well as many state regulators responded by demanding that the new sharing economy comply with existing occupancy, consumer, and taxi regulations, including entry controls and price-fixing.

Likewise, a recent California case required the court to decide whether the sharing economy can fit within labor law's classification of employee or independent contractor. The Northern District of California court applied the California independent contractor test and the "right of control" test, which are descendants of traditional legal doctrines that determine whether the law may hold an employer liable for the tortious conduct of an employee. If indeed drivers ultimately succeed in receiving employee status, the sharing economy model could face a serious challenge.

In this sharing economy example, instead of applying existing classifications from old laws that fail to account for challenges presented by the new sharing economy, the law can be better designed to ensure regulatory objectives of safety and consumer protection. The regulator could create new experimental regulations for sharing economy that will allow more flexibility and further evaluation of the effectiveness of such regulations as more information on these services becomes available. The new sharing economy is one of many examples of the dissonance between law and innovation. Different areas of the law such as intellectual property, telecommunication law, securities law, immigration, taxation, labor laws, etc. consist of similar "friction points" with innovation.

. . .

ENTREPRENEURSHIP AND LAW: ACCESSING
THE POWER OF THE CREATIVE IMPULSE
Steven H. Hobbs, 4 Entrepren. Bus. L. J. (2009)

The process of change has shaped the perceptions and realities of how people interact in a world that has become a much smaller place. We find ourselves in an era of global marketplaces that include mega-corporations not bound by national borders or allegiances, as well as the local, small villages where internet access makes it possible for even the smallest business to access the wide world of trade. Entrepreneurship allows us to create new ways of providing innovative services and products to diverse markets and consumers.

Consequently, the creation of entrepreneurial ventures calls for imaginative methods of structuring laws and legal relationships that increase the chance of successfully bringing new services and products to the market. The legal advocate who assists entrepreneurs must become conversant in the theory and application of the entrepreneurial process. This is especially true for lawyers who represent the wide variety of stakeholders in economic, social, educational, and political enterprises, from family businesses, to venture capitalists, to social service providers in nonprofit organizations, to government entities engaged in economic and community development. The skill sets of lawyers must include strategic planning, leadership qualities, and creative problem solving.

. . .

As an initial matter, one should consider the definition of entrepreneurship, especially as it relates to law. . . .

[T]he entrepreneurial process is fundamentally about dynamic change in the manner in which services and products are created and/or re-created. The entrepreneur recognizes possibilities for building a business or organization, seeks the resources necessary for bringing the enterprise into existence, and successfully develops plans for bringing the service or product to market. A broader definition, developed by Jeffrey A. Timmons and James Spinelli, posits a comprehensive method of conceptualizing the process:

> Entrepreneurship is a way of thinking, reasoning, and acting that is opportunity obsessed, holistic in approach, and leadership balanced. Entrepreneurship results in the creation, enhancement, realization, and renewal of value, not just for owners, but for all participants and stakeholders. At the heart of the process is the creation and/or recognition of opportunities, followed by the will to seize these opportunities. It requires a willingness to take risks — both personal and financial — but in a very calculated fashion in order to constantly shift the odds of success, balancing the risk with the potential reward. Typically, entrepreneurs devise ingenious strategies to marshal limited resources.

This definition takes a holistic approach to the process by entailing creativity, strategic planning, the varied participants, risk, and reward. Understanding entrepreneurship as a multi-variant, dynamic process informs the advisors to entrepreneurs of how best to facilitate the enterprise's growth and development.

From a lawyer's perspective, this requires new ways of adapting our legal system to facilitate the entrepreneurial process. For example, one tends to focus on how the entrepreneurial process is carried out in a start-up business or venture, although entrepreneurial functions can occur in an established firm. The form of the business — sole proprietorship, various partnership forms, various corporate forms, or joint ventures — must be tailored to the nature of the enterprise. Various stakeholders, including employees, managers, and investors, must be accommodated. Other legal issues may arise, demanding creative solutions. For example, the service or product may need protection through licensing and intellectual property law. Due diligence requires a legal analysis of the systems of law which must be accommodated in order for the enterprise to function lawfully. A host of regulatory and tax laws may need to be considered and analyzed from the point-of-view of the new service or product. Thought must also be given to new legal risks and liabilities that may not be readily apparent in the first observation and usage of the service or product.

. . .

[T]he entrepreneurial lawyer will need skill sets that include strategic planning, leadership, and creative problem solving. At the heart of these skills will be a need to foster imagination and innovation in the manner in which we advise entrepreneurs and aid in shaping their enterprises. Just as small businesses are forming strategic alliances with larger businesses to achieve efficiency in bringing services and products to market, so too will lawyers have to conceive of new ways of doing business.

First, an essential, innovative tool and skill for lawyers is to understand the development and use of business plans. They are designed to provide a roadmap for the enterprise, an assessment of the financial, legal and marketing issues, and a resource through which the entrepreneur can attract both human and financial capital. The business plan presents a description of the stakeholders, the needed resources, financial statements, plans for achieving the production of the service or product, and a projection of the business's estimated point of profitability. The plan is designed to take a creative business idea from conception to operational reality. It affords the advisors to the entrepreneur, such as lawyers, venture capitalists, and accountants, a chance to make suggestions and give input on how to maximize the chances of success.

A business plan also tells the story of the entrepreneurial client's enterprise. It offers insight into that client's hopes and dreams. This knowledge allows the entrepreneurial lawyer to tell the client's story to other stakeholders, including potential key employees, financial investors, and government officials who may need to grant regulatory approval. Storytelling, according to Pink, is one of the aptitudes that we will need in this world of rapid change. An entrepreneurial lawyer is an advocate for a client in a crowded marketplace and when time is of the essence, the lawyer must be able to articulately state the client's case and get to the essence of the business proposal. Of course, lawyers have always been known as great storytellers.

Second, the power of the creative impulse is multiplied exponentially when expressed in collaboration with others. Here is where leadership skills will become important when working with a team. Kuratko & Hodgett describe this phenomenon as follows:

> If you wish to become innovative and creative, you need to visualize yourself in complementary relationships to the things and people of the world. You must learn to look at them in terms of how they complement you in your attempts to satisfy your own needs and to complete your projects. You must begin to look at people in nonconventional ways and from a different perspective.

Many minds acting together can solve a problem, improve the efficiency of a service or product, or make a service or product available to more people, cheaply, and with added value. Here is where entrepreneurship, as an expression of the creative impulse, and the law, as a system that facilitates the functioning of enterprises, intersect. New creations and changing market conditions change business and commercial relationships and create heretofore unimaginable risks and dangers. New legal relationships create new legal responsibilities, which in turn create new risk of loss. Here, risk of loss can either be financial (investments of venture capital) or tortious (such as when a new wonder drug later proves to cause unacceptable risks). The lawyer's task is to aid in the identification and structuring of the new relationships and in the minimization and spreading of the risk of loss.

. . .

And finally, the entrepreneurial lawyer must both be imaginative and innovative in crafting creative solutions to legal practice problems. . . .

Our challenge, as lawyers, is both to understand how the creative impulse animates our clients who engage in service or product enterprises, and to tap into the creative impulse in the design and provision of legal services. Lawyers should both assist and serve entrepreneurs animated by a creative impulse and, concurrently, become entrepreneurial in the manner and methods in which we practice law. Daniel Pink notes that information technology has forever changed the way people access legal services and products. There are do-it-yourself websites and internet services where lawyers offer advice in a limited fashion. Pink is certainly correct when observing that new ways of legal practice will be informed by those who can tackle far more complex problems and those who can provide something that databases and software cannot — counseling, mediation, courtroom storytelling, and [other services]. For the entrepreneurial lawyer, this will mean recognizing that being creative will give him or her an edge in the global marketplace for legal services. Furthermore, by paying attention to how we practice, we might just discover, as the lawyers who do collaborative work, that the practice of law can be personally satisfying and rewarding.

. . .

Notes and Questions

1. The stereotypical entrepreneur is a risk-taker, and the stereotypical attorney is risk averse. As one might imagine, these differing approaches to life and business can have an impact on the attorney-client relationship. Suppose a client wants to take a risk that the attorney feels is too great. Who makes the final call? If you are the attorney and a client is making a move you feel introduces too significant a legal risk, should you attempt to end the representation, or assist the client in moving forward? For example (and as we will see in later chapters), clients can ask attorneys to draft contracts that the attorneys know are unlikely to be enforceable. Should attorneys agree to draft unenforceable contracts?

2. Consider the notion, explored by Pozen, that entrepreneurs are

> leaders, innovators, pioneers, problem solvers, and risk takers; they are diligent, persistent, charismatic, dynamic, imaginative, and resourceful, the bricoleurs of the capitalist marketplace. . . . Entrepreneurs can be greedy, cunning, opportunistic, and self-interested, possessed of a kind of Nietzschean will to power that may lead to domination and destruction as well as to value creation.

If Pozen is right about entrepreneurs, there will be a temptation for attorneys representing (or trying to represent) entrepreneurs to cater to strong entrepreneurial personalities. How might a lawyer giving good or bad news to an entrepreneurial client deliver the message differently than a lawyer giving similar news to in-house counsel at a large corporation? What risks might this style of communication introduce for the lawyer?

3. Eyal-Cohen contrasts entrepreneurship and the law as being quite opposite and potentially incompatible with each other — at least as they exist today. At a minimum, "law" and "entrepreneurship" have processes and approach problem solving in very different ways. What challenges does this present for a lawyer representing entrepreneurs?

4. Hobbs suggests that lawyers can learn from entrepreneurs and harness their own creative impulses. For example, entrepreneurial lawyers can seek to develop innovative solutions to legal problems. Is this kind of risk-taking compatible with your conception of what it is to be an attorney and counselor? How might you expect a sole practitioner's tolerance for risk would compare with a large law firm's tolerance?

5. Think about entrepreneurs you know, either personally or through reading about them in the media. Do they have personality characteristics in common with each other? Do you have traits in common with them? In what ways are you different?

6. Hobbs stresses the importance of business plans. Recently, venture capitalists and other sophisticated investors have made light of overly complex and lengthy business plans as a waste of time, and seem to be more impressed by prototypes and other more tangible evidence of potential success. In addition, investors can lose respect for entrepreneurs that seem to believe there is certainty and predictability that can be neatly laid out in a business plan. Instead, they prefer nimble entrepreneurs who are willing to adapt and "pivot" in response to customer preferences and market changes. Why do you think there is a trend away from lengthy business plans and toward "investor decks" among certain sophisticated outside investors?

B.   STRUCTURING THE ATTORNEY-CLIENT RELATIONSHIP

If we accept that stereotypical attorneys and stereotypical entrepreneurs are different in outlook and approach when it comes to taking risks and addressing problems, we can imagine how this culture clash will permeate the lawyer-entrepreneur relationship. For both attorney and client, structuring the relationship properly from the beginning is helpful in reducing later misunderstandings. The attorney will prepare a written engagement letter, discussed at the end of the chapter, in which the terms of the business and legal relationship between the attorney and the client are explained. Prior to the engagement letter stage, however, the lawyer and entrepreneur must first clearly communicate as to who the client will be: the entrepreneur as an individual, or the new venture. Lawyers must then separate, in their minds and in their counsel, the individuals from the entity. All parties need to understand the dynamic and structure of this relationship and continue to respect it appropriately throughout the engagement. This issue can become complicated and misunderstandings regarding the relationship can be the source for liability and litigation between attorney and client.

In the next readings, you will first read one perspective on the ever-present question "who is the client?" Next, we have included selected rules and official comments from the Model Rules of Professional Conduct addressing the potential conflicts of interest when representing multiple clients. As you read both the article and the Model Rules, try to make the abstract practical by imagining yourself in the shoes of the attorney described in the first paragraph of the Ibrahim piece. At the end of the chapter, we introduce two additional ethical issues: competence — an ever-present issue for the attorney representing an entrepreneurial venture in all its complexity; and conflicts of interest between attorney and client — an issue with direct impact on the ways entrepreneurs can pay for legal services.

SOLVING THE EVERYDAY PROBLEM OF CLIENT IDENTITY IN THE CONTEXT OF CLOSELY HELD BUSINESSES
Darian M. Ibrahim, 56 Ala. L. Rev. 181 (2004)

Consider a seemingly simple dilemma that virtually all practicing lawyers face at some point in their careers and that many practitioners face daily. The lawyer receives an all-too-familiar visit from two friends who together ask the lawyer to form a legal entity for their new business. (Assume, for the purposes of this hypothetical, that the business form chosen is a corporation.) In this initial meeting, the friends ask the lawyer to prepare the necessary organizational documents. This task, which lawyers engage in daily, sounds simple enough, and there would be near universal agreement that the lawyer may undertake this representation. But numerous conflicts of interest are certain to arise between the friends, if not during formation then during the operation of the corporation, and these are often ignored or deemed unimportant by the lawyer. Indeed, . . . even if the lawyer appreciates these conflicts, she has no — or conflicting — guidance in resolving them.

For example, consider some common questions that arise during formation. To issue stock to the friends, the lawyer must know whether they will be equal owners or majority-minority owners. If the latter, does the lawyer have a duty to advise the minority shareholder that, without contractual protections, he could be outvoted on all matters? Without legal guidance, an unsophisticated minority shareholder would not know that his appointments as an initial officer and director of the corporation are subject to the majority shareholder choosing not to remove him from these positions.

The lawyer's dilemma, in its most-stripped-down form, is this: Who is the lawyer's client? Simply the corporation as an entity? Both shareholders? One shareholder to the exclusion of the other? Or some combination of the foregoing? Lawyers have faced potential civil liability and disciplinary actions for failing to appreciate the entity-owner distinction, and clients are usually even more confused.

Assume the client is the corporation as an entity. This would provide no guidance for the lawyer when determining whether to advise the minority shareholder of the possible perils of this status. It would be impossible for the lawyer to know at the time of incorporation whether it would be better for the corporation if the majority shareholder could effectively eliminate the minority shareholder's management rights. Maybe the majority shareholder is more business-savvy, or perhaps the majority shareholder will prove too impetuous in his decision-making and the minority shareholder's veto power on important decisions will keep him in check. In short, the lawyer will most likely be unable to predict which shareholder will be the better decision-maker at the outset. Moreover, even if the lawyer could hazard a guess, it is unadvisable to put the lawyer in the position of having to make subjective decisions that involve business, rather than legal, judgment.

Assume the client is only the majority shareholder. If the lawyer advises the minority shareholder to prospectively guard against oppressive conduct, the majority shareholder may have a cause of action against the lawyer. Now assume the client is only the minority shareholder. If the lawyer did not advise the minority shareholder of the dangers of this status, the lawyer could be liable to the shareholder for inadequate representation. If both shareholders are deemed the lawyer's clients, the lawyer will face ethical conflicts of interest problems.

To complicate matters, a lawyer forming a closely held corporation is usually asked to prepare a shareholders agreement to govern internal matters between the shareholders. The shareholders agreement should provide, at the very least, a restriction on the transferability of shares. Such a provision prevents one shareholder from selling his shares to a third party without first giving the remaining shareholder the right to buy them (commonly referred to as a "right of first refusal" provision). This gives shareholders the right to choose with whom they do business.

Often shareholders will instruct the lawyer to "prepare your standard shareholders agreement." The lawyer should respond that "there is no standard shareholders agreement" because each business and each set of shareholder relationships is unique. Moreover, almost every drafting choice the lawyer makes will favor one shareholder over the other. This is easy to see when considering the majority-minority ownership situation. For instance, shareholders agreements commonly divide decisions into those that can be made by a mere majority and those that require the unanimous approval of the shareholders. Lawyers representing majority shareholders prefer that no decisions require unanimous consent — that way, their clients ultimately make all decisions. Conversely, lawyers representing minority shareholders would prefer that a broad range of decisions require unanimous consent, thus giving their clients more of a voice in the operation and affairs of the corporation. It is difficult to see how the lawyer who represents only the corporation, or both shareholders, or who does not appreciate the subtleties of client identity, can adequately draft a shareholders agreement. Yet lawyers do it daily.

. . .

The foregoing discussion may lead the reader to conclude that these problematic drafting choices only present themselves in the majority-minority situation, and that representation of the nebulous "corporation," or even co-representation of the shareholders, is a harmless fiction in the equal ownership situation. Although client identity may be less of a concern in the equal ownership situation, important drafting choices benefiting one shareholder over another still exist. How the lawyer drafts the corporation's internal documents again depends on who is classified as the lawyer's client. The foregoing discussion focuses on potential conflicts during the corporation's initial stages, but lawyers will continue to encounter these ethically gray issues once the corporation is up and running.

. . .

SELECTIONS FROM MODEL RULES OF PROFESSIONAL CONDUCT AND OFFICIAL COMMENTS
American Bar Association (2012)

Rule 1.7 Conflict of Interest: Current Clients

(a) Except as provided in paragraph (b), a lawyer shall not represent a client if the representation involves a concurrent conflict of interest. A concurrent conflict of interest exists if:

(1) the representation of one client will be directly adverse to another client; or

(2) there is a significant risk that the representation of one or more clients will be materially limited by the lawyer's responsibilities to another client, a former client or a third person or by a personal interest of the lawyer.

(b) Notwithstanding the existence of a concurrent conflict of interest under paragraph (a), a lawyer may represent a client if:

(1) the lawyer reasonably believes that the lawyer will be able to provide competent and diligent representation to each affected client;

(2) the representation is not prohibited by law;

(3) the representation does not involve the assertion of a claim by one client against another client represented by the lawyer in the same litigation or other proceeding before a tribunal; and

(4) each affected client gives informed consent, confirmed in writing.

Comment

General Principles

. . .

[2] Resolution of a conflict of interest problem under this Rule requires the lawyer to: 1) clearly identify the client or clients; 2) determine whether a conflict of interest exists; 3) decide whether the representation may be undertaken despite the existence of a conflict, i.e., whether the conflict is consentible; and 4) if so, consult with the clients affected under paragraph (a) and obtain their informed consent, confirmed in writing. The clients affected under paragraph (a) include both of the clients referred to in paragraph (a)(1) and the one or more clients whose representation might be materially limited under paragraph (a)(2).

. . .

[4] If a conflict arises after representation has been undertaken, the lawyer ordinarily must withdraw from the representation, unless the lawyer has obtained the informed consent of the client under the conditions of paragraph (b). . . .

[5] Unforeseeable developments, such as changes in corporate and other organizational affiliations or the addition or realignment of parties in litigation, might create conflicts in the midst of a representation, as when a company sued by the lawyer on behalf of one client is bought by another client represented by the lawyer in an unrelated matter. Depending on the circumstances, the lawyer may have the option to withdraw from one of the representations in order to avoid the conflict. . . .

Identifying Conflicts of Interest: Directly Adverse

. . .

[7] Directly adverse conflicts can . . . arise in transactional matters. For example, if a lawyer is asked to represent the seller of a business in negotiations with a buyer represented by the lawyer, not in the same transaction but in another, unrelated matter, the lawyer could not undertake the representation without the informed consent of each client.

Identifying Conflicts of Interest: Material Limitation

[8] Even where there is no direct adverseness, a conflict of interest exists if there is a significant risk that a lawyer's ability to consider, recommend or carry out an appropriate course of action for the client will be materially limited as a result of the lawyer's other responsibilities or interests. For example, a lawyer asked to represent several individuals seeking to form a joint venture is likely to be materially limited in the lawyer's ability to recommend or advocate all possible positions that each might take because of the lawyer's duty of loyalty to the others. The conflict in effect forecloses alternatives that would otherwise be available to the client. The mere possibility of subsequent harm does not itself require disclosure and consent. The critical questions are the likelihood that a difference in interests will eventuate and, if it does, whether it will materially interfere with the lawyer's independent professional judgment in considering alternatives or foreclose courses of action that reasonably should be pursued on behalf of the client.

. . .

Personal Interest Conflicts

[10] The lawyer's own interests should not be permitted to have an adverse effect on representation of a client. . . . [A] lawyer may not allow related business interests to affect representation, for example, by referring clients to an enterprise in which the lawyer has an undisclosed financial interest. . . .

. . .

Nonlitigation Conflicts

. . .

[28] Whether a conflict is consentable depends on the circumstances. For example, a lawyer may not represent multiple parties to a negotiation whose interests are fundamentally antagonistic to each other, but common representation is permissible where the clients are generally aligned in interest even though there is some difference in interest among them. Thus, a lawyer may seek to establish or adjust a relationship between clients on an amicable and mutually advantageous basis; for example, in helping to organize a business in which two or more clients are entrepreneurs, working out the financial reorganization of an enterprise in which two or more clients have an interest or arranging a property distribution in settlement of an estate. The lawyer seeks to resolve potentially adverse interests by developing the parties' mutual interests. Otherwise, each party might have to obtain separate representation, with the possibility of incurring additional cost, complication or even litigation. Given these and other relevant factors, the clients may prefer that the lawyer act for all of them.

Special Considerations in Common Representation

[29] In considering whether to represent multiple clients in the same matter, a lawyer should be mindful that if the common representation fails because

the potentially adverse interests cannot be reconciled, the result can be additional cost, embarrassment and recrimination. Ordinarily, the lawyer will be forced to withdraw from representing all of the clients if the common representation fails. In some situations, the risk of failure is so great that multiple representation is plainly impossible. For example, a lawyer cannot undertake common representation of clients where contentious litigation or negotiations between them are imminent or contemplated. Moreover, because the lawyer is required to be impartial between commonly represented clients, representation of multiple clients is improper when it is unlikely that impartiality can be maintained. Generally, if the relationship between the parties has already assumed antagonism, the possibility that the clients' interests can be adequately served by common representation is not very good. Other relevant factors are whether the lawyer subsequently will represent both parties on a continuing basis and whether the situation involves creating or terminating a relationship between the parties.

[30] A particularly important factor in determining the appropriateness of common representation is the effect on client-lawyer confidentiality and the attorney-client privilege. With regard to the attorney-client privilege, the prevailing rule is that, as between commonly represented clients, the privilege does not attach. Hence, it must be assumed that if litigation eventuates between the clients, the privilege will not protect any such communications, and the clients should be so advised.

[31] As to the duty of confidentiality, continued common representation will almost certainly be inadequate if one client asks the lawyer not to disclose to the other client information relevant to the common representation. This is so because the lawyer has an equal duty of loyalty to each client, and each client has the right to be informed of anything bearing on the representation that might affect that client's interests and the right to expect that the lawyer will use that information to that client's benefit. See Rule 1.4 ["Communications"]. The lawyer should, at the outset of the common representation and as part of the process of obtaining each client's informed consent, advise each client that information will be shared and that the lawyer will have to withdraw if one client decides that some matter material to the representation should be kept from the other. In limited circumstances, it may be appropriate for the lawyer to proceed with the representation when the clients have agreed, after being properly informed, that the lawyer will keep certain information confidential. For example, the lawyer may reasonably conclude that failure to disclose one client's trade secrets to another client will not adversely affect representation involving a joint venture between the clients and agree to keep that information confidential with the informed consent of both clients.

[32] When seeking to establish or adjust a relationship between clients, the lawyer should make clear that the lawyer's role is not that of partisanship normally expected in other circumstances and, thus, that the clients may be required to assume greater responsibility for decisions than when each client is separately represented. Any limitations on the scope of the representation made necessary as a result of the common representation should be fully explained to the clients at the outset of the representation. See Rule 1.2(c).

. . .

Organizational Clients

. . .

[35] A lawyer for a corporation or other organization who is also a member of its board of directors should determine whether the responsibilities of the two roles may conflict. The lawyer may be called on to advise the corporation in matters involving actions of the directors. Consideration should be given to the frequency with which such situations may arise, the potential intensity of the conflict, the effect

of the lawyer's resignation from the board and the possibility of the corporation's obtaining legal advice from another lawyer in such situations. If there is material risk that the dual role will compromise the lawyer's independence of professional judgment, the lawyer should not serve as a director or should cease to act as the corporation's lawyer when conflicts of interest arise. The lawyer should advise the other members of the board that in some circumstances matters discussed at board meetings while the lawyer is present in the capacity of director might not be protected by the attorney-client privilege and that conflict of interest considerations might require the lawyer's recusal as a director or might require the lawyer and the lawyer's firm to decline representation of the corporation in a matter.

Rule 1.13 Organization As Client

(a) A lawyer employed or retained by an organization represents the organization acting through its duly authorized constituents.

(b) If a lawyer for an organization knows that an officer, employee or other person associated with the organization is engaged in action, intends to act or refuses to act in a matter related to the representation that is a violation of a legal obligation to the organization, or a violation of law that reasonably might be imputed to the organization, and that is likely to result in substantial injury to the organization, then the lawyer shall proceed as is reasonably necessary in the best interest of the organization. Unless the lawyer reasonably believes that it is not necessary in the best interest of the organization to do so, the lawyer shall refer the matter to higher authority in the organization, including, if warranted by the circumstances to the highest authority that can act on behalf of the organization as determined by applicable law.

(c) Except as provided in paragraph (d), if

(1) despite the lawyer's efforts in accordance with paragraph (b) the highest authority that can act on behalf of the organization insists upon or fails to address in a timely and appropriate manner an action, or a refusal to act, that is clearly a violation of law, and

(2) the lawyer reasonably believes that the violation is reasonably certain to result in substantial injury to the organization,

then the lawyer may reveal information relating to the representation whether or not Rule 1.6 ["Confidentiality of Information"] permits such disclosure, but only if and to the extent the lawyer reasonably believes necessary to prevent substantial injury to the organization.

(d) Paragraph (c) shall not apply with respect to information relating to a lawyer's representation of an organization to investigate an alleged violation of law, or to defend the organization or an officer, employee or other constituent associated with the organization against a claim arising out of an alleged violation of law.

(e) A lawyer who reasonably believes that he or she has been discharged because of the lawyer's actions taken pursuant to paragraphs (b) or (c), or who withdraws under circumstances that require or permit the lawyer to take action under either of those paragraphs, shall proceed as the lawyer reasonably believes necessary to assure that the organization's highest authority is informed of the lawyer's discharge or withdrawal.

(f) In dealing with an organization's directors, officers, employees, members, shareholders or other constituents, a lawyer shall explain the identity of the client when the lawyer knows or reasonably should know that the organization's interests are adverse to those of the constituents with whom the lawyer is dealing.

(g) A lawyer representing an organization may also represent any of its directors, officers, employees, members, shareholders or other constituents, subject to the provisions of Rule 1.7 ["Conflict of Interest: Current Clients"]. If the organization's consent to the dual representation is required by Rule 1.7, the consent shall be given by an appropriate official of the organization other than the individual who is to be represented, or by the shareholders.

Comment

The Entity as the Client

[1] An organizational client is a legal entity, but it cannot act except through its officers, directors, employees, shareholders and other constituents. Officers, directors, employees and shareholders are the constituents of the corporate organizational client. The duties defined in this Comment apply equally to unincorporated associations. "Other constituents" as used in this Comment means the positions equivalent to officers, directors, employees and shareholders held by persons acting for organizational clients that are not corporations.

[2] When one of the constituents of an organizational client communicates with the organization's lawyer in that person's organizational capacity, the communication is protected by Rule 1.6. Thus, by way of example, if an organizational client requests its lawyer to investigate allegations of wrongdoing, interviews made in the course of that investigation between the lawyer and the client's employees or other constituents are covered by Rule 1.6. This does not mean, however, that constituents of an organizational client are the clients of the lawyer. The lawyer may not disclose to such constituents information relating to the representation except for disclosures explicitly or impliedly authorized by the organizational client in order to carry out the representation or as otherwise permitted by Rule 1.6.

[3] When constituents of the organization make decisions for it, the decisions ordinarily must be accepted by the lawyer even if their utility or prudence is doubtful. Decisions concerning policy and operations, including ones entailing serious risk, are not as such in the lawyer's province. Paragraph (b) makes clear, however, that when the lawyer knows that the organization is likely to be substantially injured by action of an officer or other constituent that violates a legal obligation to the organization or is in violation of law that might be imputed to the organization, the lawyer must proceed as is reasonably necessary in the best interest of the organization. As defined in Rule 1.0(f), knowledge can be inferred from circumstances, and a lawyer cannot ignore the obvious.

. . .

Clarifying the Lawyer's Role

[10] There are times when the organization's interest may be or become adverse to those of one or more of its constituents. In such circumstances the lawyer should advise any constituent, whose interest the lawyer finds adverse to that of the organization of the conflict or potential conflict of interest, that the lawyer cannot represent such constituent, and that such person may wish to obtain independent representation. Care must be taken to assure that the individual understands that, when there is such adversity of interest, the lawyer for the organization cannot provide legal representation for that constituent individual, and that discussions between the lawyer for the organization and the individual may not be privileged.

[11] Whether such a warning should be given by the lawyer for the organization to any constituent individual may turn on the facts of each case.

Dual Representation

[12] Paragraph (g) recognizes that a lawyer for an organization may also represent a principal officer or major shareholder.

. . .

Notes and Questions

1. Prof. Ibrahim describes a very common situation encountered by lawyers who represent entrepreneurs. In a situation with multiple founders with potentially divergent interests, is it better for the attorney to choose one entrepreneur as a client or to represent the new venture being created? Does your analysis change if the lawyer has a preexisting professional relationship with one of the founders?

2. Model Rule 1.7(b) seems to suggest that a conflict between clients can be acceptable if certain requirements are met. Is it likely that two co-founders could both be represented by the attorney under the exception described in the Rule? Does the exception change your response to Question 1? How does Model Rule 1.13 complicate this relationship?

3. Even if a lawyer and entrepreneur agree that the lawyer will represent the new business and not the individual founder, the entrepreneur will often refer to — and think of — the attorney as "my lawyer" rather than "the organization's lawyer." Does a lawyer need to do anything to work against this kind of perception by the entrepreneur and third parties? What are the consequences, positive and negative, of taking any such actions?

4. Model Rule 1.13 says a lawyer working for an entity "represents the organization acting through its duly authorized constituents." The official comment sheds further light on what the Rule means, making the (perhaps) obvious point that lawyers who represent entities take direction from the officers, directors, and owners of their client. Put another way, the way a lawyer knows what his entity client wants him to do is to ask the officers, directors, and owners of the client.

Some lawyers and scholars worry that by representing an entity, rather than its founders, the attorney may face a conflict where he needs to tell his human "client" that the instruction is counter to the best interest of his entity client. Subpart (b) of Rule 1.13 and the associated official comment address what to do in this situation. If the client is a small entrepreneurial venture with one shareholder who is also the sole director and officer, can a situation ever arise in which the human "client" gives an instruction that is counter to the desires of the entity client? What if the lawyer concludes the instruction from the human client is very likely to destroy the business? Furthermore, what if the human client admits that the instruction is intended to destroy the business? To the extent you feel there is a potential conflict, would it be appropriate to raise this issue with your client, or would it fall into the category of "theoretically interesting but not practical or relevant"?

5. Imagine two entrepreneurs arrive at an attorney's door with a business plan and a prototype. They say they are just two people with a great idea who are looking to start a business but haven't yet formed a company. Assume a search of relevant databases reveals that they have not filed any paperwork with the secretary of state of any state to form a legal entity. Do they have a legal entity now? Who owns the intellectual property they have created? Is there any person other than the two individual entrepreneurs or the "entity yet-to-be-formed" who the attorney can represent in this context?

SELECTIONS FROM MODEL RULES OF PROFESSIONAL CONDUCT
American Bar Association (2020)

Rule 1.1 Competence

A lawyer shall provide competent representation to a client. Competent representation requires the legal knowledge, skill, thoroughness and preparation reasonably necessary for the representation.

Comment
Legal Knowledge and Skill

[1] In determining whether a lawyer employs the requisite knowledge and skill in a particular matter, relevant factors include the relative complexity and specialized nature of the matter, the lawyer's general experience, the lawyer's training and experience in the field in question, the preparation and study the lawyer is able to give the matter and whether it is feasible to refer the matter to, or associate or consult with, a lawyer of established competence in the field in question. In many instances, the required proficiency is that of a general practitioner. Expertise in a particular field of law may be required in some circumstances.

[2] A lawyer need not necessarily have special training or prior experience to handle legal problems of a type with which the lawyer is unfamiliar. A newly admitted lawyer can be as competent as a practitioner with long experience. Some important legal skills, such as the analysis of precedent, the evaluation of evidence and legal drafting, are required in all legal problems. Perhaps the most fundamental legal skill consists of determining what kind of legal problems a situation may involve, a skill that necessarily transcends any particular specialized knowledge. A lawyer can provide adequate representation in a wholly novel field through necessary study. Competent representation can also be provided through the association of a lawyer of established competence in the field in question.

[3] In an emergency a lawyer may give advice or assistance in a matter in which the lawyer does not have the skill ordinarily required where referral to or consultation or association with another lawyer would be impractical. Even in an emergency, however, assistance should be limited to that reasonably necessary in the circumstances, for ill-considered action under emergency conditions can jeopardize the client's interest.

[4] A lawyer may accept representation where the requisite level of competence can be achieved by reasonable preparation. This applies as well to a lawyer who is appointed as counsel for an unrepresented person. See also Rule 6.2 ["Accepting Appointments"].

Thoroughness and Preparation

[5] Competent handling of a particular matter includes inquiry into and analysis of the factual and legal elements of the problem, and use of methods and procedures meeting the standards of competent practitioners. It also includes adequate preparation. The required attention and preparation are determined in part by what is at stake; major litigation and complex transactions ordinarily require more extensive treatment than matters of lesser complexity and consequence. An agreement between the lawyer and the client regarding the scope of the representation may limit the matters for which the lawyer is responsible. See Rule 1.2(c)

[stating "A lawyer may limit the scope of the representation if the limitation is reasonable under the circumstances and the client gives informed consent"].

. . .

Maintaining Competence

[8] To maintain the requisite knowledge and skill, a lawyer should keep abreast of changes in the law and its practice, engage in continuing study and education and comply with all continuing legal education requirements to which the lawyer is subject.

Rule 1.8 Conflict Of Interest: Current Clients: Specific Rules

(a) A lawyer shall not enter into a business transaction with a client or knowingly acquire an ownership, possessory, security or other pecuniary interest adverse to a client unless:

(1) the transaction and terms on which the lawyer acquires the interest are fair and reasonable to the client and are fully disclosed and transmitted in writing in a manner that can be reasonably understood by the client;

(2) the client is advised in writing of the desirability of seeking and is given a reasonable opportunity to seek the advice of independent legal counsel on the transaction; and

(3) the client gives informed consent, in a writing signed by the client, to the essential terms of the transaction and the lawyer's role in the transaction, including whether the lawyer is representing the client in the transaction.

. . .

(k) While lawyers are associated in a firm, a prohibition in the foregoing paragraphs (a) through (i) that applies to any one of them shall apply to all of them.

Comment
Business Transactions Between Client and Lawyer

[1] A lawyer's legal skill and training, together with the relationship of trust and confidence between lawyer and client, create the possibility of overreaching when the lawyer participates in a business, property or financial transaction with a client, for example, a loan or sales transaction or a lawyer investment on behalf of a client. The requirements of paragraph (a) must be met even when the transaction is not closely related to the subject matter of the representation, as when a lawyer drafting a will for a client learns that the client needs money for unrelated expenses and offers to make a loan to the client. The Rule applies to lawyers engaged in the sale of goods or services related to the practice of law, for example, the sale of title insurance or investment services to existing clients of the lawyer's legal practice. See Rule 5.7 ["Responsibilities Regarding Law-related Services"]. It also applies to lawyers purchasing property from estates they represent. It does not apply to ordinary fee arrangements between client and lawyer, which are governed by Rule 1.5, although its requirements must be met when the lawyer accepts an interest in the client's business or other nonmonetary property as payment of all or part of a fee. In addition, the Rule does not apply to standard commercial transactions between the lawyer and the client for products or services that the client generally markets to others, for example, banking or brokerage services, medical services, products manufactured or distributed by the client, and utilities' services. In such transactions, the lawyer has no advantage in dealing with the client, and the restrictions in paragraph (a) are unnecessary and impracticable.

[2] Paragraph (a)(1) requires that the transaction itself be fair to the client and that its essential terms be communicated to the client, in writing, in a manner that can be reasonably understood. Paragraph (a)(2) requires that the client also be advised, in writing, of the desirability of seeking the advice of independent legal counsel. It also requires that the client be given a reasonable opportunity to obtain such advice. Paragraph (a)(3) requires that the lawyer obtain the client's informed consent, in a writing signed by the client, both to the essential terms of the transaction and to the lawyer's role. When necessary, the lawyer should discuss both the material risks of the proposed transaction, including any risk presented by the lawyer's involvement, and the existence of reasonably available alternatives and should explain why the advice of independent legal counsel is desirable. See Rule 1.0(e) (definition of informed consent).

[3] The risk to a client is greatest when the client expects the lawyer to represent the client in the transaction itself or when the lawyer's financial interest otherwise poses a significant risk that the lawyer's representation of the client will be materially limited by the lawyer's financial interest in the transaction. Here the lawyer's role requires that the lawyer must comply, not only with the requirements of paragraph (a), but also with the requirements of Rule 1.7. Under that Rule, the lawyer must disclose the risks associated with the lawyer's dual role as both legal adviser and participant in the transaction, such as the risk that the lawyer will structure the transaction or give legal advice in a way that favors the lawyer's interests at the expense of the client. Moreover, the lawyer must obtain the client's informed consent. In some cases, the lawyer's interest may be such that Rule 1.7 will preclude the lawyer from seeking the client's consent to the transaction.

[4] If the client is independently represented in the transaction, paragraph (a)(2) of this Rule is inapplicable, and the paragraph (a)(1) requirement for full disclosure is satisfied either by a written disclosure by the lawyer involved in the transaction or by the client's independent counsel. The fact that the client was independently represented in the transaction is relevant in determining whether the agreement was fair and reasonable to the client as paragraph (a)(1) further requires.

. . .

Notes and Questions

1. As you will see throughout this casebook, effective representation of entrepreneurs requires competence in a large number of legal areas. Start-ups need assistance in employment law, intellectual property law, business organization law, dispute resolution, contract law, product liability law, e-commerce law, the Uniform Commercial Code, securities law, tax law, and many other areas. How can an attorney effectively represent an entrepreneur in light of Rule 1.1? When a client has a specific and specialized legal need, such as the desire to prosecute a patent, and the attorney does not have the relevant expertise, what should the attorney do (i) from a legal ethics perspective, (ii) from a business development perspective, and (iii) from a client relations perspective?

2. Entrepreneurial clients often lack cash to pay service providers, including their lawyers. Imagine an entrepreneur offers you an ownership stake in the new business in exchange for your legal services. In light of Rule 1.8, can you accept? Should you accept? What benefits, in financial and non-financial terms, might an attorney receive in this situation? What risks? If you accept that lawyers are risk adverse, can you imagine what reaction large law firms have to this kind of offer?

Can you imagine what reaction they had to this kind of offer during the internet boom of the late 1990s or the tech entrepreneurship resurgence in the 2010s?

INTRODUCTION TO HYPOTHETICAL CLIENTS

Dr. Olivia M. Gold, a research scientist, has developed an innovative new method of analyzing and detecting bacteria growth in food. The new technology is faster, more accurate, and less expensive than previous technology in this area. Olivia developed the process in her free time, and not during the hours she was supposed to be working her regular job in the "Gene Lab" of Kramer BioGenetics, Inc. Olivia has not discussed her discovery with any of her supervisors or co-workers at Kramer.

Andrew Orlando is an old college buddy of Olivia's. Andrew is a brand manager at a health care company, Life Line, Inc. He works on the brand "Clean Machine," which is primarily comprised of a line of antibacterial kitchen soaps. He recently convinced Olivia that they should form a new, jointly owned business to exploit Olivia's discovery.

Andrew and Olivia believe that they can use Olivia's technology to create a food testing probe that will be able to analyze the bacteria level in food and indicate on a small LCD display whether the food is safe to eat. Rather than trying to sell Olivia's technology to an established medical or other health care company, they intend to design the product themselves, and then their new business will market the product directly to consumers as well as to stores such as Wal-Mart. Although Olivia has some questions about Andrew's judgment and maturity, she knows that Andrew's marketing expertise, outgoing personality, and connections in the health care world will be essential to the success of the new business. They have not yet had a discussion about how much of the company they will each own, or how they will ultimately make decisions. In fact, they already have had one significant disagreement: Andrew would like to call the product "General Germ," whereas Olivia prefers the name "Germ Genie."

Olivia and Andrew are each prepared to invest $125,000 to get the new business going, but they realize they will need a lot more than $250,000 to make it through the research and development phases of their business before they have a product ready to launch. If they can raise sufficient capital, their projections show that their business will be "cash-flow positive" within 18 months of the product launch.

Olivia and Andrew have come to you looking for help with their new venture. We will be considering various issues faced by the intrepid entrepreneurs in problems at the end of every chapter of this book.

PROBLEM

You work for attorney Jessica Leigh, a partner in the successful Wildcat Firm. Jessica is a rainmaker, and her newest catch is the venture to be started by Olivia Gold and Andrew Orlando. Prior to commencing the representation, Jessica had the clients sign the engagement letter below.

September 5, 2020

Germ Genie
Attn: Olivia M. Gold and Andrew Orlando
4101 N. Western Ave, Unit 5B
Chicago, Illinois 60622

Dear Dr. Gold and Mr. Orlando:

We are pleased that you have asked the Wildcat Firm to act as legal counsel for the company you intend to form, Germ Genie (the "Company"), in connection with the Company's formation, the protection of its trademarks and patents, the preparation of customer and vendor contracts, and any other matter that you and we may specifically agree to be subject to such representation. The purpose of this letter is to set forth the terms and conditions of our relationship.

Our fees will be determined in accordance with our normal billing practices, taking into account the various factors we normally consider in determining our fees, and will be billed on a monthly basis.

Our normal billing practice is to determine fees by multiplying the number of hours spent working on a matter by our regular and customary billing rates for similar services performed by the firm. The minimum billing increment is ordinarily 1/10 hour. As we discussed, my current billing rate is $400. Hourly rates for attorneys currently range from $100 to $700. These rates may be changed by the firm in the future, in which case new rates will apply to all work performed thereafter.

In addition to our fees described above, you will be responsible for all out-of-pocket expenses incurred. Statements for out-of-pocket expenses will be submitted monthly or at other appropriate intervals. These will be paid promptly unless other arrangements are made. Large expenditures like government filing fees, taxes, and the like will be discussed with the Company before they are incurred. In circumstances where a third party provider or government agency is involved, we may ask that you pay these expenses directly.

It must be understood that we represent the Company only, and not either of you as individuals or as owners or employees of the Company. Accordingly, our representation of the Company does not create any fiduciary relationship between the Wildcat Firm and either of you. You should consider retaining separate counsel to advise you on issues affecting you as individuals. Additionally, it should be understood that we have the right to discuss with both of you any information provided to us by one of you.

Periodically, we distribute materials that include listings of representative clients and a basic description of the legal services performed for each client. We may refer in those materials to our representation of the Company and the work we have performed for the Company.

It is the Company's right as a client to terminate this engagement at any time on reasonable notice and upon the payment of all expenses incurred to the date of termination. Upon the termination of our engagement or completion of the matters set forth above, the Wildcat Firm will have no obligation to provide further legal assistance or advice or to inform the Company of changes in the law that could affect it. All files will be turned over to the Company on its written request except internal documents and drafts of documents, which we may retain.

We know of no engagements for other clients of the Wildcat Firm that would prevent us from representing the Company. However, if a situation should arise in which it becomes appropriate to take a position adverse to one of our other clients, we reserve the right to withdraw from this engagement.

Please sign and return a copy of this letter to confirm that the Company agrees with the terms and conditions of our engagement. We look forward to working with you.

Very truly yours,
Jessica Leigh

Agreed and accepted:
Germ Genie
By: _____
    Olivia M. Gold
And: _____
    Andrew Orlando

1. Suppose that the client asks you to assist with preparing documents for the investment in the Company by an unrelated angel investor. Can you do so under the terms of the existing engagement letter? What steps might you take to ensure that the new project is covered by the same terms as the other projects you have agreed to complete?

2. Over drinks one night, you tell a friend of yours that you now are working on the "Germ Genie" client, and that you are excited because "they have a neat new technology that could revolutionize food safety." You do not say anything specific about the projects you are working on for the client, nor do you name the individual founders. Unbeknownst to you, Olivia and Andrew are two tables away and hear everything you have said, which they angrily tell Jessica the next day. Have you violated your ethical duties or breached your engagement letter? What strategy will you use in discussing the issue with Jessica? With the client?

3. Imagine that on a Monday you call the client to discuss an issue. The client does not answer the call and you leave a voicemail. On Tuesday, you try again and have a four-minute conversation with the receptionist who answers the phone. On Wednesday, you send an email to the client requesting a return phone call and you briefly explain the issue in the message. Finally, on Thursday, you hear back from the client and speak for exactly one hour. What is the maximum amount of time you would feel justified in billing the client? What is the minimum amount of time you would need to charge to be fair to the Wildcat Firm? What amount of time would you charge?

4. Suppose a prominent venture capitalist in town is a longstanding client of the Wildcat Firm. Jessica introduces the venture capitalist to Olivia and Andrew, and the venture capitalist wants to invest in Germ Genie.

(a) Would Jessica overstep her place, or violate any ethical rules, by introducing the venture capitalist to Germ Genie?

(b) Assume the clients have negotiated the salient business terms on their own without legal representation. Can the Wildcat Firm draft the documents, and if so, who will be the client?

(c) Assume the venture capitalist wants the Wildcat Firm to represent her in a contentious negotiation over the terms of her investment in Germ Genie. Must the Wildcat Firm withdraw from representing Germ Genie?

5. Imagine that only Andrew signs the engagement letter. The client relationship, including billing and collections, proceeds normally, and Andrew is your primary point of contact. Six months into the engagement, you get a call from Andrew, telling you that Olivia has agreed to sell her interest in Germ Genie to Andrew for a nominal amount, and he asks you to prepare the necessary paperwork. What responsibilities do you have to Olivia, to Andrew, and to Germ Genie? Can you just complete the work Andrew requested and send it to him without contacting anyone else?

6. Assume that, as with the Model Rules of Professional Conduct, your state code of ethics does not require engagement letters between attorneys and clients. Do you think that Jessica made a good or bad choice in having the client sign an engagement letter? Are there circumstances you can imagine that would make an engagement letter more advisable with an entrepreneurial client than with a large established company? Less advisable?

II

THE TRANSITION FROM EMPLOYEE TO ENTREPRENEUR

This chapter explores the issues that arise when an entrepreneur conceives and decides to begin pursuing an idea for a new business while still an employee of another organization. The entrepreneur must be aware that the planning and launching of a new venture may be subject to legal restrictions. These restrictions can apply to the entrepreneur's activities both while still employed and after the employment relationship terminates. Under state law, the entrepreneur owes an employer fiduciary duties — chiefly a duty of loyalty — notwithstanding the desire to launch a new venture. The duty to be loyal to the employer can prevent the entrepreneur from launching a competing business while still employed, and from usurping a corporate opportunity in the process of starting a business. At the same time, the entrepreneur may have entered into an employment contract that could severely limit the ability to commence a competing business even after the employment relationship and the related fiduciary duties have terminated. Intellectual property concerns are also at play: the entrepreneur may also find she does not own the innovation, invention, or other intellectual property necessary to start the business, even if she invented it on her own time. In addition, the entrepreneur needs to be wary of violating Federal and state trade secrets statutes when founding and building a business.

A. CONCERNS ARISING SEPARATELY FROM ANY CONTRACTUAL RELATIONSHIP

In Section B of this chapter, we explore the duties that can arise between a worker and her employer because of a written contract. In this Section A, we explore legal obligations that exist whether or not there is a written contract between the worker and the existing employer. These concerns are in three primary categories: fiduciary duty concerns, unfair competition concerns, and trade secret concerns.

1. Fiduciary Duties

Broadly put, a fiduciary relationship is a relationship in which parties place trust and confidence in each other. A "fiduciary duty" is an embodiment of that relationship in a legal or ethical rule the parties are expected to follow in their course of conduct. While students who have taken a Business Associations or Corporations course have been exposed to fiduciary duties in the context of a director or officer of a corporation, or a partner in a partnership, fiduciary duties extend some distance down into the hierarchy of a business organization. An employee who is categorized as a "key" or "skilled" employee will owe duties of loyalty and care similar to the duties owed by a director of the same organization.

When it comes to a client looking to leave her current employer to start a new business, duty of loyalty issues are paramount. The lawyer must help to determine whether the employee is the type that owes a duty of loyalty — understanding that a key employee like a high-ranking vice president likely will owe such a duty, a skilled employee like a technical designer will likely owe such a duty, but a rank-and-file employee like a mailroom worker likely will not owe such a duty. As a public policy matter, our laws reflect an interest in providing lower-level employees (who have less responsibility and receive less compensation) with more latitude to change jobs.

Having determined whether the client owes a duty to the current employer, the lawyer then must explore whether the client has done — or intends to do — anything that violates the duty of loyalty. Directly competing while still an employee is disloyal; directly competing after termination of employment (which terminates the fiduciary relationship) is permissible since no duty of loyalty is owed after the termination of the fiduciary relationship. Sharing or use of confidential information learned while the fiduciary relationship existed is disloyal, even if the sharing or use occurs after the termination of the fiduciary relationship. Preparation for competition is not in and of itself disloyal when conducted while the employment relationship exists, suggesting an employee can work on a business plan for a competing business or even explore renting office space, provided such efforts do not interfere with the employee's job responsibilities. The moment the employee begins to offer a competing product or service, however, the employee is competing and the duty of loyalty has been breached.

2. Trade Secrets

Federal and state trade secret statutes apply to workers with access to trade secrets. A trade secret is any information of value to the company (often stated as information that gives the company a competitive advantage), which the company has taken steps to keep confidential. If an entrepreneur takes confidential information — such as a password-protected customer list, an internal business strategy document, or private marketing data — from his current employer and uses it for his new venture, the entrepreneur has likely violated the state trade secret law. (Note that this is in addition to any duty of loyalty violation that may occur from using the information.) In addition to the civil penalties that the entrepreneur may face under trade secret statutes, these statutes typically give rise to criminal liability. A lawyer representing an entrepreneur must counsel the client to avoid taking any sensitive information from the current employer. Trade secrets are discussed in greater detail in Chapter 4.

3.   Unfair Competition

The tort of unfair competition — which is born largely out of state common law — addresses economic harm resulting from unfair business practices. An employee can commit this tort easily by violating the fiduciary duty of loyalty, or infringing a trademark, or misappropriating confidential information (including misappropriation of information that violates trade secret statutes). In short, anything dishonest or unjust is a possible claim under an unfair competition theory. Employers typically include unfair competition claims in actions against former employees, and when advising entrepreneurs the lawyer must look out for anything that "smells bad" and warn the client of this possible tort.

The following cases involve employees who have taken a variety of actions that potentially implicate the duty of loyalty, trade secret law, and the tort of unfair competition. As you read them, keep the basic premises summarized above in mind, and notice the ways in which the court expresses the legal rules and applies them to the specific, nuanced facts of the cases.

REHABILITATION SPECIALISTS, INC. v. KOERING
Court of Appeals of Minnesota 404 N.W.2d 301 (1987)

Rehabilitation Specialists, Inc. ("RSI") appeals from a summary judgment for Nancy Koering, an ex-employee who started a competing business, on its suit for breach of her duty of loyalty, as well as unfair competition and misappropriation of confidential business information. We reverse and remand for trial.

FACTS

RSI provides physical therapy, occupational therapy and related therapy services to health care facilities in Minnesota and several other states. In 1982, RSI hired Koering as its director of occupational therapy. In January, 1984, Koering was promoted to assistant administrator, and in November, 1984, she was promoted to administrator. Koering's responsibilities included soliciting business and negotiating contracts for RSI.

In May, 1985, Koering considered starting her own therapy business. On June 13, 1985, she told this to Robert Schuchman, vice-president of operations for Beverly Enterprises ("Beverly"), a company which owns and operates over 1200 long-term care facilities nationally. Beverly is one of RSI's major customers. Schuchman dealt almost exclusively with Koering while she was at RSI.

Koering described her June 13 meeting with Schuchman in an answer to an interrogatory, as follows:

> Nancy informed Mr. Schuchman that she was thinking about beginning her own business and inquired about possible opportunities for contracting for new business.

Her affidavit states that during the meeting they

> generally discussed the likelihood of success for my business. At no time during our conversation did I inquire about any specific contracts with Beverly. I did not attempt to solicit any business from Beverly nor did I encourage Beverly to break any of its present contracts with RSI.

Schuchman's affidavit describes the meeting like this:

> Nancy Koering . . . informed me that she was thinking about beginning her own therapy business. I offered my encouragement and informed her that there would probably be some new contracting opportunities available with Beverly.
>
> At no time during our conversation did Nancy Koering suggest that Beverly sever its ties with RSI and divert its business to her.

After this meeting, Schuchman contacted Koering and told her that, if she began her own business, Beverly would offer her two nursing home contracts, with the Bloomington and Lake Ridge nursing homes. A few weeks later, Schuchman again contacted Koering and offered her contracts with three additional facilities: the Excelsior Health Care Center, the Long Lake Nursing Home and the Hillcrest Health Center.

In a letter dated July 23, 1985, Koering wrote to Schuchman:

> I will be meeting with my bank within the next week. It would be advantageous to be able to present the contracts for Bloomington and Lake Ridge and a letter of intent concerning Excelsior, Long Lake and Hillcrest. For this reason I have enclosed contracts for Bloomington and Lake Ridge in Beverly format. . . .
>
> I am prepared to resign July 31 and will look forward to beginning in Bloomington September 1.

At the time Schuchman made his offers to Koering, RSI did not have contracts with any of the five facilities (although it had contracted with Excelsior and Long Lake in the past). Koering's affidavit states that the Bloomington contract was executed on July 31, 1985, to be effective September 1, 1985; the Lake Ridge contract was not executed until after she left RSI; and the other three contracts were not negotiated or executed until after she left RSI. The record indicates that Koering signed the Bloomington contract at a so-called "50 percent fee for service" rate.

Koering and RSI's president, Jeffrey Anlauf, had previously negotiated, on behalf of RSI, with Beverly for the Bloomington contract and others. Her affidavit states:

> Beverly offered the contracts to RSI at a 50 percent fee for service rate but Jeffrey Anlauf rejected this offer. He then directed me to inform Beverly that RSI was not willing to accept the contracts at a rate less than 65 per cent for two specific homes and 60 per cent for the remaining two homes. Beverly was unwilling to agree to RSI's terms and awarded the contracts to another therapy service provider.

Anlauf's affidavit states that he never rejected the Bloomington contract, or any of the other four contracts secured by Koering, and that RSI desired the Bloomington contract and would have wanted the others as well. At his deposition, he testified that he had instructed Koering to offer to do all of Beverly's contracts for 50 percent.

On July 26, 1985, Koering notified Anlauf that she intended to leave RSI to begin her own therapy business, and that she believed she would have five therapy contracts. They discussed the possibility of her conducting her business using RSI's offices and staff, for a six percent management fee; she later declined the offer. Anlauf testified he did not know then that Koering's five contracts were with Beverly.

Koering ended her employment with RSI August 31, 1985. She did not have a written employment contract with RSI, nor had she signed a covenant not to compete.

Prior to leaving, Koering filed corporate documents for her new business, met with a bank to obtain financing and applied for business insurance. When she left RSI, she took with her the sole copy (according to Anlauf) of its policy and procedure manual, a list of its employees and several sample contracts. Two of the first three employees she hired left RSI to work for her; the third had stopped working at RSI approximately one year earlier.

RSI sued Koering alleging: breach of her duty of loyalty as an employee, unfair competition and misappropriation of confidential business information. The trial court granted Koering's motion for summary judgment on all three grounds.

ISSUE

Did the trial court err in granting summary judgment for respondent on appellant's claims for breach of duty of loyalty, unfair competition and misappropriation of confidential business information?

ANALYSIS

. . .

2. Duty of Loyalty

RSI alleges that Koering violated the implied common law duty of loyalty in her oral employment contract by soliciting customers and employees for herself while still employed by RSI.

An employee's duty of loyalty prohibits her from soliciting the employer's customers for herself, or from otherwise competing with her employer, while she is employed. Employees who wish to change jobs or start their own businesses, however, should not be unduly hindered from doing so. An employee has the right, therefore, while still employed, to prepare to enter into competition with her employer.

There is no precise line between acts by an employee which constitute prohibited "solicitation" and acts which constitute permissible "preparation." Because of the competing interests, the actionable wrong is a matter of degree. Whether an [employee's] actions constituted a breach of her duty of loyalty is a question of fact to be determined based on all the circumstances of the case.

The trial court found that Koering did not breach her duty of loyalty to RSI because while she "did discuss her intention to leave, she did not solicit the plaintiff's customers."

Even if the characterization of her conduct as passive were accurate, it would not necessarily shield her from liability. See Community Counselling Service, Inc. v. Reilly, 317 F.2d 239, 244 (4th Cir. 1963) ("If prospective customers undertake the opening of negotiations which the employee could not initiate, he must decline to participate in them.")[.]

We believe a fact issue exists as to whether her conduct crossed the line from preparation to solicitation. Koering admits she told RSI's customer "she was thinking about beginning her own business and inquired about possible opportunities for contracting for new business." While still employed by RSI, she tentatively secured five contracts from him. She sent him two draft contracts and requested letters of intent regarding the three others. . . .

The fact that RSI did not have contracts with the five facilities Koering contracted for does not preclude a finding that she was competing with her employer in violation of her duty of loyalty. Beverly was a customer of RSI, and it was Koering's duty to attempt to secure additional contracts from it for RSI, not for herself.

. . .

3.   Unfair Competition

Count two of RSI's complaint charges Koering with unfair competition, based on the same facts alleged in its first count for breach of contract, i.e., her solicitation of RSI's customers and employees.

Unfair competition is not a tort with specific elements; it describes a general category of torts which courts recognize for the protection of commercial interests.

An employee's breach of his duty of loyalty may constitute unfair competition.

Since we hold that there is an issue of fact as to whether Koering solicited RSI's customer in violation of her duty of loyalty, she is not entitled to summary judgment on RSI's unfair competition claim.

4.   Misappropriation of Confidential Information

Count three of RSI's complaint alleges Koering misappropriated certain confidential business information.

Minnesota has adopted the Uniform Trade Secrets Act, which provides a cause of action for "misappropriation" of "trade secrets." The statute defines trade secrets as follows:

"Trade secret" means information, including a formula, pattern, compilation, program, device, method, technique, or process, that:

(i) derives independent economic value, actual or potential, from not being generally known to, and not being readily ascertainable by proper means by, other persons who can obtain economic value from its disclosure or use, and

(ii) is the subject of efforts that are reasonable under the circumstances to maintain its secrecy.

Minn. Stat. § 325C.01, subd. 5 (1986).

Koering admits having taken from RSI its policy and procedures manual. Anlauf states in his affidavit:

> The manual was prepared by a committee of RSI employees who spent numerous hours over an extended period of time drafting a manual designed to fulfill the needs of a company involved in the provision of rehabilitation therapy services. . . . The cost of preparing this manual to RSI was over $20,000.
>
> . . . The value this manual would confer upon a competitor is substantial. As a result, only one copy of the working draft was printed, which Nancy Koering took with her without permission. . . . Great efforts are made to keep this document confidential and its distribution limited. . . . The first page of the manual indicates that distribution of this manual is controlled and that "manuals must be returned upon termination." . . . RSI's offices are . . . secure and important documents such as this are frequently stored in locked employee offices within our main office area and are, at times, also locked within lockable furniture in my office.

Although she argues that the manual is not protected because it was a form purchased from a company, Koering admits "the management staff of RSI changed the form to meet RSI's needs," at Anlauf's direction.

Koering also argues there was no "misappropriation" of confidential information because there is no evidence that she actually "used or disclosed" any of the items she took. The trade secrets act, however, defines "misappropriation" as the "acquisition of a trade secret of another by a person who knows . . . the trade secret was acquired by improper means." Minn. Stat. § 325C.01, subd. 3(i). It defines "improper means" as including "theft" or "breach . . . of a duty to maintain secrecy."

The act also provides for injunctive relief against "threatened misappropriation" of trade secrets. Minn. Stat. § 325C.02(a). It defines "misappropriation" alternatively as the "use of a trade secret of another without . . . consent by a person who used improper means to acquire knowledge of the trade secret."

The evidence raises issues of fact as to whether the manual was a "trade secret" and whether it was acquired by "improper means."

DECISION

Koering is not entitled to summary judgment on RSI's claims for breach of her duty of loyalty, unfair competition and misappropriation of confidential information.

Reversed and remanded.

ALTERG, INC. v. BOOST TREADMILLS LLC

United States District Court for the Northern District of California, 388 F. Supp. 3d 1133 (2019)

Plaintiff AlterG, Inc. ("AlterG") brings this action against three of its former employees, Sean Whalen, Thomas Allen, and Michael James Bean (the "Individual Defendants") and the competing company they founded, Boost Treadmills LLC

("Boost") (collectively, "Defendants"). AlterG alleges that Defendants infringed its patents and misused its trade secret information to create Boost products. AlterG's complaint pleads ten causes of action: (1) patent infringement; (2) breach of contract; (3) trade secret misappropriation; (4) breach of fiduciary duty; (5) interference with contract; (6) interference with prospective economic advantage; (7) false advertisement; (8) trade libel; (9) unfair competition; and (10) conspiracy. Pending before the Court is Defendants' motion to dismiss all counts of the complaint.

For the reasons stated on the record at the hearing on May 9, 2019, and discussed below, the motion to dismiss is GRANTED.

I. FACTUAL AND PROCEDURAL BACKGROUND

The complaint alleges the following. Plaintiff AlterG is a "medical device company" that is the "leading provider of impact reduction treadmills," also known as "Anti-Gravity Treadmills," that are used for "orthopedic rehabilitation and training." "One of the keys [sic] drivers of AlterG's success is its patented Differential Air Pressure ('DAP') technology," which works by "us[ing] a pressurized bag to provide a counterforce to the subject's body weight, reducing their effective weight on the treadmill surface." From 2012 to 2015, AlterG devoted substantial resources to develop "a lower cost, bare bones AlterG machine" in response to "potential competitors who wanted to develop anti-gravity training and rehab machines using mechanical unweighting and other options, and at a lower price point than AlterG." AlterG calls this project the "Low-Cost Platform Project," or "LCPP." AlterG ultimately decided not to commercialize or sell any products developed as part of the LCPP.

The Individual Defendants are three former employees of AlterG. "Whalen was the founder of AlterG" as well as "the initial and primary inventor . . . principally involved in developing the technology and products of the company." He therefore "had intimate access to and knowledge of AlterG products, technology, business plans, intellectual property strategy, marketing strategy, financial data, vendors, suppliers, customers, and confidential research and development." Whalen relinquished his former positions at AlterG but continued working for the company as a consultant until he stopped working for AlterG altogether on March 31, 2015. During this consultancy period, "Whalen was the principal consultant and engineer" on the LCPP.

Allen joined AlterG in 2007 and has "held numerous jobs at AlterG in sales, business development, and in international sales." Through those positions, he became "intimately familiar with the products of AlterG and specifically the costing, bill of materials (BOM), sales and financial information, customer acquisition, marketing projections, and business strategy for AlterG products." Like Whalen, Allen worked closely with the LCPP team from 2012 through 2015. Allen was also AlterG's "principal liaison" to Woodway USA ("Woodway"), a longtime supplier of treadmills for AlterG. He resigned from AlterG on April 28, 2015.

Bean joined AlterG in 2008 and worked in various sales roles at the company. He resigned from AlterG in April 2017. "Since Bean's departure from AlterG in April 2017, AlterG has discovered communications between Bean and Allen about Allen's work on a competing anti-gravity unit while Bean was still an employee of AlterG."

Each of the Individual Defendants signed various confidentiality and nondisclosure agreements with AlterG during their employment with the company, which provided that they would "not use or disclose AlterG's proprietary and confidential information in any way contrary to the benefit of AlterG." AlterG and Woodway also "entered into various confidentiality agreements whereby AlterG would provide to Woodway proprietary and confidential information to assist Woodway to build and supply AlterG with anti-gravity units."

Boost was formed at the end of 2016 and registered in April 2017. Allen and Bean are founders of Boost, and Whalen worked for the company in product development. AlterG believes that "Defendants conspired almost immediately [upon leaving AlterG] to create a competing machine incorporating AlterG intellectual property," and that "Boost was developing an unweighting treadmill well prior to the company's registration." As part of this process, Whalen and Allen started "secretly" working with Woodway and "utilized confidential, proprietary, and trade secret information from the [LCPP], and other AlterG intellectual property, to shortcut the research and development time to come to market with a lower cost unweighting treadmill." "At the end of 2017, Boost introduced its first product — the Boost One," which "infringes AlterG patents" and "incorporates numerous technology features developed by AlterG in connection with the [LCPP]."

AlterG further alleges that Defendants "falsely claim that the problematic Boost One is a superior product over the AlterG DAP systems 'at a fraction of the cost.'" Defendants have also "told customers and prospects false statements to denigrate AlterG and its superior technology, falsely claiming that AlterG was going out of business, is in poor financial health and will not be able to get Woodway treadmills anymore." The upshot of Defendants' allegedly unlawful practices is that Defendants have been able to "sell over 20 units [of Boost products] to date to customers considering an AlterG unit."

. . .

III. DISCUSSION

. . .

B. Trade Secret Misappropriation

AlterG's third cause of action is trade secret misappropriation. To state a claim for trade secret misappropriation under the [Defend Trade Secrets Act, the Federal trade secrets statute], a plaintiff must allege that: "(1) the plaintiff owned a trade secret; (2) the defendant misappropriated the trade secret; and (3) the defendant's actions damaged the plaintiff."

1. Alleging Trade Secrets with Sufficient Particularity

Defendants argue that AlterG fails to identify its allegedly misappropriated trade secrets with sufficient particularity to state a claim under the DTSA. The Court agrees.

"A plaintiff need not spell out the details of the trade secret," but must "describe the subject matter of the trade secret with sufficient particularity to separate it from matters of general knowledge in the trade or of special persons who are skilled in the trade, and to permit the defendant to ascertain at least the boundaries within which the secret lies." Alta Devices, 343 F. Supp. 3d at 881 (citations, internal quotation marks and alterations omitted). *Alta Devices* provides helpful guidance as to the degree of particularity that is required. The court there found that the plaintiff, a manufacturer of thin-film solar technology, adequately pleaded its trade secret claim based on a combination of factors. First, the plaintiff identified "the exact technology in question: thin-film GaAs solar technology." Second, the plaintiff listed with specificity the types of trade secrets relating to the "thin-film GaAs solar technology": "[m]ethods of[] high throughput thin-film deposition; epitaxial lift-off of the thin-film; and GaAs substrate maintenance and re-use," as well as "confidential cost analysis; proofs and tests of manufacturing concepts and techniques; tool roadmaps; manufacturing process flows; and identification of equipment and equipment vendors; and information related to the foregoing." Id. In addition to the fact that the technology was described with specificity, a non-disclosure agreement between the parties described with further particularity the confidential information that was imparted to defendants, for example, "CVD technology and its commercial viability," including the "CVD (Alta 2T) chamber scheme," "growth rate," "thin film quality," "uniformity," "gas utilization efficiency," and "scalability and short cycle time feasibility." Id. Because the plaintiff's trade secret claims were based on the confidential information exchanged pursuant to the non-disclosure agreement, the court concluded that the defendant had fair notice of the scope of the trade secrets asserted.

In contrast, the court in Vendavo, Inc. v. Price f(x) AG, No. 17-CV-06930-RS, 2018 U.S. Dist. LEXIS 48637, 2018 WL 1456697 (N.D. Cal. Mar. 23, 2018) found that the plaintiff failed to allege its trade secret claim with sufficient particularity. The plaintiff, a provider of business software, claimed that the defendant had misappropriated trade secrets including "source code, customer lists and customer related information, pricing information, vendor lists and related information, marketing plans and strategic business development initiatives, 'negative know-how' learned through the course of research and development, and other information related to the development of its price-optimization software, including ideas and plans for product enhancements." 2018 U.S. Dist. LEXIS 48637, [WL] at *3. The court determined that the plaintiff had "set out its purported trade secrets in broad, categorical terms, more descriptive of the types of information that generally *may* qualify as protectable trade secrets than as any kind of listing of particular trade secrets [it] has a basis to believe actually were misappropriated here." 2018 U.S. Dist. LEXIS 48637, [WL] at *4 (emphasis in original).

Here, AlterG alleges that Defendants misappropriated the following trade secrets:

- "[N]umerous learnings from AlterG's Low-Cost Platform Project that explored market alternatives that included positive and negative learnings of low cost mechanical unweighted systems, air pressure systems, and Differential Air Pressure systems under strict confidentiality and non-disclosure agreements."
- Trade secrets "related to AlterG's development of anti-gravity rehabilitation products" and "mechanical unweighting mainframes," including "technology and negative information and learnings."
- "[T]rade secret information related to AlterG's design and development of its anti-gravity rehabilitation and training units, including, but not limited to its marketing and product strategy, cost strategies, customer needs, material selection

and fabrication techniques, engineering and structural technology, selection and qualification of components, knowledge [**18] of vendors with appropriate, specialized skills, and technology innovation."

These allegations more closely resemble the broad categories of information in *Vendavo* than the specific descriptions provided in *Alta Devices*. The references in [the complaint] to "positive and negative learnings" and "technology and negative information and learnings" are vague. The types of information listed ... are somewhat more concrete, but are not tethered to a specific technology; it cannot be discerned which aspects of AlterG's "anti-gravity rehabilitation and training units" the information pertains to. And although AlterG, like the plaintiff in *Alta Devices*, has alleged that the trade secrets at issue are covered by confidentiality agreements between the parties, AlterG only summarizes rather broadly the categories of information protected by the agreements. See Compl. at 5 n.2 (defining "Confidential Information" to include "techniques, sketches, drawings, models, inventions, know-how, processes, apparatus, equipment, algorithms, software programs, software source documents, and formulae related to the current, future and proposed products and services of the Company, and includes, without limitation, its respective information concerning research, experimental work, development, design details, and specifications, engineering, financial information, procurement requirements, purchasing manufacturing, customer lists, business forecasts, sales, and merchandising and marketing plans and information"). AlterG has not attached the agreements to the complaint, and its allegations fail to "describe the subject matter of the trade secret with sufficient particularity to separate it from matters of general knowledge in the trade or of special persons who are skilled in the trade." *Alta Devices*, 343 F. Supp. 3d at 881.

Accordingly, Defendants' motion to dismiss AlterG's trade secret claim is GRANTED. AlterG is granted leave to amend its complaint to allege with greater specificity the types of trade secrets that were misappropriated and the exact technology to which they pertain. Such allegations may be enhanced if the confidentiality agreements between the parties detail the protected information that AlterG imparted to Defendants. In amending its trade secret claim, AlterG should also take care to delineate the boundaries between its trade secrets and its information that has been made public through patents and patent applications.

. . .

D. Breach of Fiduciary Duty

AlterG's fourth cause of action alleges that Whalen breached the fiduciary duty he owed to AlterG by using AlterG's proprietary and confidential information to benefit Boost. To state a claim for breach of fiduciary duty, a plaintiff must allege: (1) the existence of a fiduciary duty; (2) breach of the fiduciary duty; and (3) damage proximately caused by the breach. Here, Defendants do not dispute that Whalen owed a fiduciary duty to AlterG while he was serving as its director, but contends that the duty ended when he joined Boost, because by that point he was no longer a director of AlterG.

Defendants are correct that, as a general matter, an officer's fiduciary duty to their employer ends upon their resignation. However, "[c]ourts addressing the issue have rejected an expansive reading of the decision in GAB Bus. Servs. and appropriately recognized that officers are also charged with a continuing duty to protect privileged and confidential information, which continues even after they leave the company." This means that Whalen owed a continuing fiduciary duty to AlterG not to use its confidential information to its detriment, even after he joined Boost.

However, the breach of fiduciary duty claim arises from the same confidentiality agreements underlying AlterG's breach of contract claim. . . . AlterG needs to describe the terms of the confidentiality agreements and the trade secrets they protect with more particularity so that it can be ascertained whether Whalen's disclosures constituted a breach of his fiduciary duty. Accordingly, Defendants' motion to dismiss AlterG's breach of fiduciary duty claim is GRANTED, and AlterG may amend its complaint to either attach the relevant confidentiality agreements or to allege their essential terms.

E.   Interference with Contract

AlterG's fifth cause of action is interference with contract. "The elements which a plaintiff must plead to state the cause of action for intentional interference with contractual relations are (1) a valid contract between plaintiff and a third party; (2) defendant's knowledge of this contract; (3) defendant's intentional acts designed to induce a breach or disruption of the contractual relationship; (4) actual breach or disruption of the contractual relationship; and (5) resulting damage." Here, the complaint alleges that Defendants interfered with three sets of contracts: the confidentiality agreements between AlterG and Woodway; contracts between AlterG and its vendors, suppliers, and customers; and the confidentiality agreements between each Individual Defendant and AlterG. Defendants argue that AlterG's allegations are deficient as to all three.

1.   Confidentiality Agreements between AlterG and Woodway

Defendants claim that the complaint fails to specify what agreements between AlterG and Woodway were interfered with. Defendants also argue that the complaint "presents no facts that support a possible breach of such agreements."

The first argument in unpersuasive. The complaint specifies that the contracts at issue are two confidentiality agreements between AlterG and Woodway: "a Master Agreement signed May 30, 2007, and a subsequent agreement signed in 2012." The essential terms of the agreements are also specified: "AlterG would provide to Woodway proprietary and confidential information to assist Woodway to build and supply AlterG with anti-gravity units," including "all specifications, drawings, files, instructions, and other documents," and this information was "not to be shared or used with or on behalf of any other person or entity."

However, Defendants' second argument has merit. The complaint states that "Whalen and Allen started secretly working with Woodway on developing a low-cost anti-gravity unit," and "utilized confidential, proprietary, and trade secret information from the [LCPP], and other AlterG intellectual property, to shortcut the research and development time to come to market with a lower cost unweighting treadmill utilizing a Woodway treadmill." This does not mean, however, that

Whalen and Allen induced or caused Woodway to disclose AlterG's confidential information to them. In fact, the complaint does not even allege that Woodway in fact disclosed any information; it merely states that Whalen and Allen "utilized" information. It is difficult to imagine that Woodway possessed any confidential information from the LCPP that Whalen and Allen did not already have, given that "Whalen was the principal consultant and engineer" on the LCPP and Allen was also heavily involved in the LCPP. If anything, as AlterG's "principal liaison" to Woodway, Allen may have been the one who conveyed AlterG's information to Woodway in the first place.

Thus, AlterG has failed to adequately allege that Defendants induced Woodway to breach its contracts with AlterG.

2.   *Contracts with Vendors, Suppliers, and Customers*

AlterG's allegations with respect to its vendors, suppliers, and customers are wholly lacking. The complaint states only that "[c]ontracts existed between AlterG . . . and AlterG vendors, suppliers, and customers" and that "Defendants have . . . interfered with contracts between AlterG and its vendors, suppliers, and customers." AlterG does not identify any of these "vendors, suppliers, and customers," nor provide any details about the contracts and contractual provisions with which Defendants allegedly interfered. AlterG has therefore failed to state a claim with respect to these contracts.

3.   *Confidentiality Agreements between Individual Defendants and AlterG*

AlterG alleges that Defendants interfered with each other's confidentiality agreements with AlterG. Defendants counter that "[t]here is not a single statement, allegation, or fact set forth in the complaint regarding Defendant inducing another Defendant to breach" these agreements. It is true that while the complaint alleges that the Individual Defendants disclosed confidential information to each other, it stops short of explicitly stating that they intentionally induced each other to disclose this information. See, e.g., Compl. ¶ 36 ("Bean . . . disclosed confidential and proprietary information about AlterG technology, marketing strategy, and prospective and actual customers and test sites to his friends at Boost" while he was still working at AlterG.). Nevertheless, a reasonable inference in AlterG's favor can be drawn that Defendants encouraged each other's disclosure. The allegation that they "conspired . . . to create a competing machine incorporating AlterG's intellectual property" undercuts the possibility that Whalen, Allen, and Bean each made the independent decision to disclose AlterG's information to each other without any prompting.

However, because AlterG needs to allege with more specificity the essential terms of the confidentiality agreements underlying this contractual interference claim, the Court will dismiss this claim pending AlterG's amendment.

Accordingly, Defendants' motion to dismiss the interference with contract claim is GRANTED with leave to amend.

F. Interference with Prospective Economic Advantage

AlterG's sixth cause of action alleges that Defendants interfered with its prospective economic advantage with Woodway and with AlterG's vendors, suppliers, and prospective and current customers. The elements of a claim for intentional interference with prospective economic advantage are: "(1) an economic relationship between the plaintiff and some third person containing the probability of future economic benefit to the plaintiff; (2) knowledge by the defendant of the existence of the relationship; (3) intentional acts on the part of the defendant designed to disrupt the relationship; (4) actual disruption of the relationship; and (5) damages to the plaintiff proximately caused by the acts of the defendant." Blank v. Kirwan, 39 Cal. 3d 311, 330, 216 Cal. Rptr. 718, 703 P.2d 58 (1985). "The chief practical distinction between interference with contract and interference with prospective economic advantage is that a broader range of privilege to interfere is recognized when the relationship or economic advantage interfered with is only prospective." Pac. Gas, 50 Cal. 3d at 1126. Nevertheless, courts have made clear that "[t]he law precludes recovery for overly speculative expectancies by initially requiring proof" that it is "reasonably probable that the prospective economic advantage would have been realized but for defendant's interference." Westside Ctr. Assocs. v. Safeway Stores 23, Inc., 42 Cal. App. 4th 507, 522, 49 Cal. Rptr. 2d 793 (1996).

AlterG's vague allegations are insufficient to state a claim for interference of prospective economic advantage. With respect to Woodway, the complaint explains that Woodway supplies treadmills to AlterG and has long worked with AlterG to build treadmills "using AlterG's proprietary designs." Thus, it can be reasonably inferred that this established commercial relationship contains the probability of future economic benefit to AlterG as Woodway continues to supply AlterG with treadmills. However, AlterG wholly fails to explain how Defendants' actions have jeopardized the ongoing supplier relationship between Woodway and AlterG. The complaint does not allege that Defendants intentionally acted to disrupt Woodway's supply of treadmills to AlterG, or that the supply was actually disrupted. Indeed, "[t]o this day, Woodway continues to supply treadmills to AlterG."

The allegations are even more lacking when it comes to AlterG's relationship with its "vendors, suppliers, and prospective and current customers." Nowhere does the complaint identify these entities or allege any facts to explain their economic relationship with AlterG, much less suggest that such relationships contain[s] the probability of future economic benefit to [AlterG]." Without any facts, it is impossible for the Court to determine whether it is reasonably probable that the prospective economic advantage would have been realized but for Defendants' interference.

Accordingly, Defendants' motion to dismiss Plaintiff's interference with prospective economic advantage claim is GRANTED with leave for AlterG to amend.

. . .

J. Conspiracy

AlterG's tenth cause of action alleges that Defendants entered into a conspiracy "to interfere with and damage AlterG's business and misappropriate AlterG's intellectual property and confidential information." Defendants argue this claim must be dismissed because conspiracy cannot be pled as a standalone cause of action.

Defendants are correct that "[c]onspiracy is not a cause of action, but a legal doctrine that imposes liability on persons who, although not actually committing a tort themselves, share with the immediate tortfeasors a common plan or design in its perpetration." Here, AlterG may be able to state viable tort claims, such as for breach of fiduciary duty and interference with contract, via amendment. Accordingly, Defendants' motion to dismiss the conspiracy claim as an independent cause of action is GRANTED, but AlterG can amend its complaint to state the viable tort claim and to make clear that it is alleging that the Individual Defendants conspired to commit tortious acts and are therefore each liable for those acts under a theory of conspiracy liability.

. . .

Notes and Questions

1. Employees owe their employers certain fiduciary duties even in the absence of a written employment agreement. Courts must balance an individual's ability to earn a living against an employer's right to have an employee act in the employer's interest. An employee's position within an organization determines the level of the duty owed, and skilled and key employees owe employers a higher duty. The court in Burbank Grease Services, LLC v. Sokolowski, 717 N.W.2d 781 (Sup. Ct. Wis. 2006) explains:

> A claim for the breach of an agent's duty of loyalty may sound both in tort and in contract. . . . When such a claim is made against an employee, the first question is whether the agent has a fiduciary relationship with the employer. . . . If the employee is a "key employee," then a fiduciary duty of loyalty will exist. . . . Whether an employee is a "key employee" depends on the precise nature of his or her employment duties, which determination requires a factual inquiry.

In *Koering*, RSI hired Koering as its director of occupational therapy. She was subsequently promoted to assistant administrator, and then to administrator. Koering's responsibilities were fairly high level and included soliciting business and negotiating contracts on behalf of RSI. In *AlterG*, the departing employees were the founder and lead inventor, a person who worked in domestic and international sales and in business development, and as a salesperson. What if the workers in *Koering* and *AlterG* had been receptionists? How would this have impacted the plaintiffs' arguments in the two cases? Under current law, some employees have more latitude in their activities while others are subject to heightened restrictions. Should this be the case, and why or why not?

2. The court in *Koering* emphasizes that the defendant crossed the line from preparation to solicitation. If Koering had merely begun planning the business, but had not communicated any such intentions to customers of her employer until after she terminated her employment, would the result have been different? What if she had communicated her intentions to RSI's customers that she eventually intended to leave RSI and start a competing business, but did not begin a dialogue about whether such customers would do business with her new company in the future? What are factors a court should consider in determining whether behavior has moved from preparation to solicitation, where is the "line," and why should it matter?

3. Koering and the defendants in *AlterG* started their new businesses in the same industry as their former employers. What if they had started unrelated businesses while still employed by RSI and AlterG? Would this be a breach of any duties owed to their employers?

4. The court quotes the Uniform Trade Secrets Act (which Minnesota has adopted), which defines a trade secret as

> information, including a formula, pattern, compilation, program, device, method, technique, or process, that:
>
> (i) derives independent economic value, actual or potential, from not being generally known to, and not being readily ascertainable by proper means by, other persons who can obtain economic value from its disclosure or use, and
>
> (ii) is the subject of efforts that are reasonable under the circumstances to maintain its secrecy.

In analyzing whether taking RSI's manual setting forth company policies and procedures constituted misappropriation of trade secrets, the court focused on the time spent by RSI employees working on the manual and the ultimate cost of the manual to RSI. If Koering had been the only RSI employee to work on the manual and then she took a copy of "her work" when she left RSI, do you think the court would be less likely to consider this action to rise to the level of misappropriation of a trade secret? What if Koering simply made a copy of the manual to take with her when she left RSI, but had left the original manual with her former employer? Do you think this would have affected the court's analysis? Why did the court focus on where RSI kept the manual and what measures RSI used to protect it?

5. The Federal Defend Trade Secrets Act defines a trade secret as

> all forms and types of financial, business, scientific, technical, economic, or engineering information, including patterns, plans, compilations, program devices, formulas, designs, prototypes, methods, techniques, processes, procedures, programs, or codes, whether tangible or intangible, and whether or how stored, compiled, or memorialized physically, electronically, graphically, photographically, or in writing if — (A) the owner thereof has taken reasonable measures to keep such information secret; and (B) the information derives independent economic value, actual or potential, from not being generally known to, and not being readily ascertainable through proper means by, another person who can obtain economic value from the disclosure or use of the information.

Does it strike you that the Uniform Trade Secrets Act and the Defend Trade Secrets Act have a meaningful difference in the scope of secrets they protect? Why do you imagine the federal government adopted this statute, which explicitly does not preempt state law, rather than leaving this matter to the states?

6. The court in *AlterG* dismisses the company's causes of action because they failed to state a claim. Assuming that AlterG would have excellent lawyers who would have a good sense of what was necessary in a complaint, why do you think they filed a complaint that was lacking in specifics?

7. In Pepsico, Inc. v. Redmond, 54 F.3d 1262 (7th Cir. 1995), an employee of Pepsico who had worked on Pepsico's "All Sport" beverage left Pepsico to work for Quaker Oats Company in the Gatorade division. Pepsico argued there would be trade secret misappropriation by the employee in the new job, because the employee had intimate knowledge of Pepsico's All Sport business and it was inevitable that

Pepsico trade secrets would be used in his new job. The Seventh Circuit agreed and enjoined the employee from taking the job at Quaker. This so-called inevitable disclosure doctrine is another tool in an employer's arsenal when seeking to stop an employee who works with trade secrets from taking a closely related job or starting a competing business. Can you think of other situations in which the "inevitable disclosure" doctrine would be implicated?

COMEDY COTTAGE, INC. v. BERK
Appellate Court of Illinois 495 N.E.2d 1006 (1986)

Plaintiffs, Edward Hellenbrand and Comedy Cottage, Inc., operate a comedy club known as the Comedy Cottage at 6350 North River Road in Rosemont, Illinois. They brought this injunctive action against Jay Berk, a former vice-president and general manager of the club. Among other things, the complaint alleged that Berk breached his fiduciary duty by acquiring a lease to the premises after the corporation's lease had been terminated and establishing a rival club there. . . .

Hellenbrand began leasing the premises in 1975. He operated a restaurant and lounge which began presenting comedy acts produced by an agency known as the Comedy College. After a dispute with the owner of the Comedy College, Hellenbrand changed the name of the club to the Comedy Cottage and began presenting comedy acts on his own. The Comedy Cottage, Inc., was incorporated soon afterwards. Hellenbrand and his wife were the sole directors and stockholders of the corporation.

In 1978, Hellenbrand hired defendant Jay Berk as general manager of the Comedy Cottage. In 1979 or 1980, Berk was given 10% of the shares and made vice-president of Comedy Cottage. Experiencing health problems, Hellenbrand moved to Nevada and left Berk to manage the daily affairs of the business. For the next five or six years, Berk acted as general manager and Hellenbrand made periodic visits to the club.

In 1984, Hellenbrand and Berk discussed making Berk a 50% shareholder of the corporation. At trial Berk testified that Hellenbrand promised to make him a half owner but later reneged on his promise. However, Hellenbrand testified that he offered the stock to Berk but Berk rejected the offer because the corporation was involved in a dispute regarding alleged lease arrearages with a former landlord. Hellenbrand testified that he decided not to reoffer the stock on the advice of family and friends. Berk was never made a 50% shareholder in the corporation.

In June 1984, the ownership of the premises changed hands and the Comedy Cottage's lease expired. Hellenbrand directed Berk to obtain a new lease for the premises. Berk negotiated with the new owner, defendant Carl Swanson, and entered into a written month-to-month lease for the premises. This lease listed Berk as lessee and not the corporation, but was signed by Berk as vice-president and general manager of the Comedy Cottage, Inc. Apparently, Hellenbrand was unaware of the month-to-month lease because he continued to direct Berk to obtain a new lease. In February of 1985, Berk sent Hellenbrand a proposed lease for a term of 1½ years. Again, the proposed lease listed Berk as lessee and not the Comedy Cottage, Inc.

Upon receiving the proposed lease, Hellenbrand became upset and called Berk to berate him for having the lease drawn up in his own name. Afterward

Hellenbrand sent a letter to Berk informing him that he would never be made a 50% shareholder of Comedy Cottage, Inc. Hellenbrand also contacted Swanson to find why the Comedy Cottage, Inc., was not listed as lessee. Swanson told him to change the signatory portion of the lease as he saw fit. Hellenbrand changed the named lessee on the proposed lease to the Comedy Cottage, Inc., and signed it without removing Berk's name from the signatory portion of the lease. He sent the proposed lease back to Berk who was to sign it "if he wanted to." Berk then forwarded it to Swanson who never signed the proposed lease.

Shortly thereafter, Swanson decided not to lease the premises to Hellenbrand and delivered a notice to Berk terminating the month-to-month tenancy of Comedy Cottage. The notice was dated March 30, 1985. Berk testified that he immediately called Hellenbrand in Nevada to inform him of the notice of termination. During that conversation he resigned as an employee of the corporation. However, he agreed to continue running the club until Hellenbrand could take over. On March 30, 1985, Berk sent a formal letter of resignation by certified mail to Hellenbrand in Nevada and enclosed the notice of termination of the lease. Hellenbrand's wife signed for the letter on April 1, 1985. Although Hellenbrand claimed that he had already left for Chicago by the time the letter arrived, he testified that he telephoned Swanson from Nevada on April 2, 1985. During their conversation Swanson said that he did not want to do business with Hellenbrand and that he had relet the premises to a new tenant who was not identified to Hellenbrand. Hellenbrand testified that he learned Berk was the new tenant of the premises when he arrived in Chicago on April 4, 1985.

After resigning from the Comedy Cottage, Inc., Berk formed a new corporation known as the Comedy Company, Inc., and began negotiating for a lease of the premises. On April 1, 1985, Berk contacted the insurance agent for the Comedy Cottage to have the corporation's group insurance policy transferred to his new corporation, the Comedy Company. However, the policy was never changed. On April 5 or 6, 1985, Berk executed a lease of the premises on behalf of the Comedy Company, Inc. During this period of time, Berk also attempted to get a liquor license for the premises in the name of the Comedy Company.

Subsequently, Hellenbrand placed a sign on the premises that stated, "Guess what? After ten years our landlord does not want us to live here anymore. So what? Neither do we. We do not need this building. Our Shows are great anywhere. We are expanding to the following locations . . . ." Another sign was also posted in the club that made a derogatory comment about Berk.

. . .

The principal issue before us is whether defendant breached his fiduciary duty of loyalty to the Comedy Cottage. Defendant asserts that he did not breach his fiduciary duty because: (1) he resigned his position with the corporation before entering into competition; and (2) any corporate opportunity regarding a lease of the premises was terminated by the owner.

An officer of a corporation owes a fiduciary duty of loyalty to his corporate employer. An officer's duty of loyalty includes the obligation to disavow any corporate opportunity where the officer's private interest would conflict with those of the corporation. In determining whether an officer may take advantage of a business opportunity in which a corporation is interested, courts consider whether the corporation had an interest, actual or in expectancy, in the opportunity and whether the acquisition thereof by the officer would hinder or defeat plans and purposes of the corporation in carrying on or developing legitimate business for which it was created.

It must be recognized that at least initially the Comedy Cottage possessed a protectable property interest in the expectancy that the lease of its place of business would be renewed. (Patient Care Services, S.C. v. Segal (1975), 32 Ill. App. 3d 1021, 1029-30, 337 N.E.2d 471 (renewal of contract for services at hospital constituted corporate opportunity).) The acquisition of a lease of the premises by defendants hindered corporate plans to utilize the goodwill and public patronage built up during its many years of operation at the same location. Thus, Berk had a duty to refrain from acquiring the lease at the expense of the corporation.

Defendant's duty is not inconsistent with his right to enter into competition with a former employer upon leaving such employment (absent a restrictive contractual provision to the contrary). However, the resignation of an officer will not sever liability for transactions completed after the termination of the party's association with the corporation if the transactions began during the existence of the relationship or were founded on information acquired during the relationship.

As vice-president and general manager of the Comedy Cottage, defendant was in charge of running the day-to-day operations of the corporation. He was personally entrusted with the negotiations for the renewal of the lease. Because of his confidential position, defendant had knowledge of the prior negotiations with the landlord, the prior month-to-month lease and the circumstances surrounding its termination. In particular, Berk was still general manager when he received notice of termination of the corporation's lease. Berk then used the knowledge gained as a result of his position with the corporation as an opportunity to resign and obtain a lease for himself without competition or disclosure. Even assuming arguendo that defendant did not begin competing for the lease until after his resignation, defendant remained bound by his fiduciary duty because his acquisition of the lease was based upon knowledge acquired during his employment. The fact that the information involved in this case does not rise to the level of a trade secret does not negate the existence of a fiduciary duty with respect to this transaction.

In addition, Berk contends that because the corporation sought to obtain the lease without success, he could acquire the lease even though the corporation was more or less interested in it, citing Northwestern Terra Cotta Corp. v. Wilson (1966), 74 Ill. App. 2d 38, 219 N.E.2d 860. However, Northwestern Terra Cotta is distinguishable. There, a corporate director paid $7 per share for stock which his corporation had unsuccessfully sought to purchase for $5 per share. No breach of fiduciary duty occurred because the court found no support for the claim that the corporation was interested in acquiring the stock for the higher price paid by the director. Here, in contrast, the corporation remained interested in the property acquired by its former officer, and no evidence indicated that he acquired the lease for a price higher than the corporation was willing to pay.

Defendant claims that any opportunity for the corporation to obtain a renewal of the lease was eliminated when the owner of the premises terminated the prior month-to-month lease and announced that he would no longer deal with Hellenbrand. However, Hellenbrand entered the negotiations only after Berk forwarded without explanation a proposed lease that listed Berk as lessee and president of Comedy Cottage, Inc. It appears from the record, therefore, that the personality conflict between Hellenbrand and the owner arose, in part, because Berk failed to clarify his actions to his employer or the owner of the premises. Moreover, once Berk learned of the termination of the corporation's lease, he did little or nothing to rectify the situation despite his special responsibilities in this matter.

Under these circumstances, we cannot say that the trial court erred in finding that Berk breached his fiduciary duty.

. . .

Notes and Questions

1. Because fiduciary duties arise out of the relationship between employee and employer, they terminate upon termination of employment. How do you then explain the court's statement that "the resignation of an officer will not sever liability for transactions completed after the termination of the party's association with the corporation if the transactions began during the existence of the relationship or were founded on information acquired during the relationship"? Are there other situations where a court could justify extending the fiduciary obligation of an employee beyond the employment term?

2. The court seemed to rely heavily on the fact that Berk leased the same location used by his former employer, Comedy Cottage. Do you think the outcome of the case would have been different if Berk terminated his employment and then negotiated and signed a lease for the Comedy Company at a location across the street? What if he had begun negotiating the lease for the location across the street several weeks prior to giving notice of his intent to terminate his employment?

3. Berk contacted the insurance agent for the Comedy Cottage to have the corporation's group insurance policy transferred to his new corporation, the Comedy Company. What significance do you think this point may have had to the court?

4. If Berk had not named himself as lessee in the original month-to-month lease, do you think the court would have been more sympathetic to his position?

B.   CONTRACTUAL DUTIES

In this part of the chapter, we explore the kinds of promises employees and independent contractors make in typical employment or engagement contracts — it being understood that the non-contractual issues discussed in Section A apply regardless of whether the worker has a contract with the company. The contracts workers sign typically contain at least three types of provisions that are significant to the budding entrepreneur: "no moonlighting" provisions, non-competition and non-solicitation covenants, and provisions protecting the company's intellectual property.

1.   No Moonlighting Provisions

Employees may be asked to sign contracts in which they agree not to work on any outside businesses, even those that do not compete with the employer. These restrictions are generally enforced by courts and represent a significant challenge to entrepreneurs who have signed them. After all, if the entrepreneur has agreed not to work on any outside businesses, she is contractually prohibited from devoting time toward developing or launching any business.

2. Non-Competition and Non-Solicitation Restrictive Covenants

Understanding that the non-competition rules implied by the duty of loyalty terminate at the end of employment, employers often ask employees to agree not to compete with the business for some period following termination of employment. Historically, courts and lawmakers have favored policies that permit or encourage free competition, and discourage restraints on trade — and covenants not to compete fly in the face of this tradition. At the same time, we recognize that employers have legitimate interests that can be jeopardized when employees leave a business to compete. Thus, with important exceptions discussed in the Notes and Questions after these cases, covenants not to compete are enforceable in most jurisdictions if they are reasonable in geographic scope and duration and if they protect a legitimate business interest of the employer. A lawyer representing an entrepreneur must carefully advise the client on two matters: first, whether the covenant is in fact enforceable, and second, whether the former employer is likely to sue the entrepreneur or the new venture, thereby crippling it, regardless of whether the covenant is enforceable.

Non-solicitation covenants generally prohibit the solicitation of customers or employees after the worker ceases working for the company. Since non-solicitation covenants do not restrict a worker's ability to make a living, these clauses are much more certain to be enforced by courts than non-competition clauses.

3. Protection of Intellectual Property

Although companies are protected by state trade secret statutes and general statutory principles giving them ownership over workers' intellectual property (all of which are discussed in more detail in Chapter 4), they often seek to protect intellectual property by contract as well. Workers are often asked to sign confidentiality covenants in which they agree to keep an employer's information confidential — often forever — and these agreements are generally enforced. Workers also may agree to assign to the employer all intellectual property they create while engaged by the company. For an entrepreneur seeking to leave her current employment, these "assignment of inventions" provisions are of particular concern because they often reach to things the worker does on her own time and using her own resources. State statutes discussed below seek to protect employees from overreaching by employers on this front, but the fact remains that entrepreneurs are often surprised at how little of their creative efforts is owned by them. Since intellectual property is often the lifeblood of a new business, lawyers advising entrepreneurs need to help clients determine whether their current or former employers will have ownership claims on the intellectual property they intend to use for the new business. If it turns out a former employer does have a claim on some of the new business's intellectual property, the subsequent litigation, arbitration, or even threatened litigation can lead to significant expenses for the new business.

On all of these contractual issues, lawyers must also be sensitive to the fact that the entrepreneur may not be aware of what his employment contract says — or what it means for the new business. Clients take bad news in this area very personally, particularly if it makes them feel trapped in their current job or if it means they may not be able to start their new business at all. From a counseling perspective, the lawyer must treat these issues carefully and help the client to find solutions to what often are difficult problems. Occasionally, a lawyer may find herself advising a client to approach the current employer for permission to start the business, or for an assignment of intellectual property necessary to start the business. These conversations, in turn, can be difficult, and their success depends as much on the entrepreneur's relationship with his immediate supervisors and higher-ranked officers as it does on the legal merits to the entrepreneur's position.

GENZYME CORPORATION v. BISHOP
United States District Court for the Western District of Wisconsin
460 F. Supp. 2d 939 (2006)

. . .

BACKGROUND

Plaintiff Genzyme Corporation is a Massachusetts corporation with its principal place of business in Cambridge, Massachusetts. Plaintiff is a biotechnology company whose products and services are focused on rare inherited disorders[,] kidney disease, orthopedics, transplant and immune disease, cancer, and diagnostic testing. On July 1, 2005 plaintiff completed its acquisition of Bone Care International (hereinafter Bone Care) a company specializing in Vitamin D products.

Defendant Charles Bishop [is a] citizen of the State of Wisconsin residing in Mt. Horeb, Wisconsin. He is Bone Care's former President, Chief Executive Officer, Director and Chief Scientific Officer. Defendant Keith Crawford is likewise a citizen of the State of Wisconsin residing in Fitchburg, Wisconsin. He is Bone Care's former Senior Director of Medical Marketing and Scientific Affairs. Defendant Eric Messner is a citizen of the State of Illinois residing in Lake Forest, Illinois. Defendant Messner served as Bone Care's Director of Marketing.

In March of 2005 defendant Bishop became Bone Care's Executive Vice-President and Chief Scientific Officer. On March 18, 2005 defendant Bishop entered into an Employee Agreement with Bone Care which became effective on April 25, 2005. Said agreement contained [a covenant not to compete, among other disputed provisions.]

Additionally, defendants Crawford and Messner entered into Employee Agreements containing identical provisions. When plaintiff acquired Bone Care it became the successor to said agreements.

In July and August of 2005 defendants Bishop, Crawford, and Messner (hereinafter collectively referred to as individual defendants) all terminated their employment with Bone Care/Genzyme. In September of 2005 the individual defendants formed defendant Proventiv Therapeutics LLC (hereinafter Proventiv.) Defendant Proventiv is a Delaware limited liability company with its principal place of business in Madison, Wisconsin. [Preventiv specializes in Vitamin D products and is a direct competitor of Bone Care.]

In June of 2006 the individual defendants sold defendant Proventiv to defendant Cytochroma, Inc. (hereinafter Cytochroma.) Defendant Cytochroma is a

Canadian corporation with its headquarters in Markham, Ontario. Defendant Cytochroma purchased defendant Proventiv in part for its drug pipeline and patent applications covering new Vitamin D uses. The individual defendants currently serve as defendant Cytochroma's executive officers.

. . .

B. Defendants' Motion to Dismiss [Contract Claims]

Defendants assert several of the restrictive covenants contained within the individual defendants' Employee Agreements are overbroad and unenforceable as a matter of law. Additionally, defendants assert said agreements fail in their entirety because the restrictive covenants contained within them are all interdependent and indivisible. Accordingly, defendants argue their motion to dismiss plaintiff's breach of contract claims should be granted.

It is important to note that all parties agree Wisconsin law governs this controversy. Generally, Wisconsin law disfavors covenants not to compete. This is because Wisconsin law favors the mobility of workers and "therefore, a contract that operates to restrict trade or competition is prima facie suspect." Accordingly, such restrictions must withstand close scrutiny to pass legal muster as being reasonable; they will not be construed to extend beyond their proper import or further than the language of the contract absolutely requires. Additionally, such restrictions are to be construed in favor of the employee. The legislature codified this policy in Wis. Stat. § 103.465 which provides as follows:

> A covenant by an assistant, servant or agent not to compete with his or her employer or principal during the term of the employment or agency, or after the termination of that employment or agency, within a specified territory and during a specified time is lawful and enforceable only if the restrictions imposed are reasonably necessary for the protection of the employer or principal. Any covenant, described in this subsection, imposing an unreasonable restraint is illegal, void and unenforceable even as to any part of the covenant or performance that would be a reasonable restraint.

Accordingly, to be enforceable a restrictive covenant must: (1) be necessary for the protection of the employer, (2) provide a reasonable time restriction, (3) provide a reasonable territorial limit, (4) not be harsh or oppressive as to the employee[,] and (5) not be contrary to public policy. However, the "validity of a restrictive covenant is to be established by examination of the particular circumstances which surround it." Accordingly, whether the reasonableness determination is characterized as either a question of law or one of fact "it still remains one which can be made only upon a consideration of factual matters."

. . .

[After considering various aspects of the contract, the court turns to analyzing the plaintiff's claim based on violations of the covenant not to compete in the employment agreements of the defendants.] Said provision provides as follows:

> That during the term of his . . . employment by Bone Care and for a period of six months after the termination of such employment . . . Employee will not directly or indirectly own, operate, manage, consult with regarding matters related to those exposed to during your employment with Bone Care, control, participate in the

management or control of, be employed by in a position comparable to that occupied during your employment with Bone Care, or maintain or continue any interest whatsoever in any enterprise that competes with Bone Care in the development and or sale of vitamin D compounds as therapies for certain diseases in competition with Bone Care in pharmaceutical research and development . . . without the written consent of Bone Care . . . . This restriction applies whether termination is voluntary, requested by the employee, or initiated by the employer.

Defendants' attacks on said covenant are multiple. Defendants argue the covenant not to compete is unenforceable as a matter of law because: (1) it is not necessary for plaintiff's protection, (2) it is harsh and oppressive to employees, (3) it does not contain a reasonable territorial limit[,] and (4) it is contrary to public policy. Additionally, defendants argue the covenant not to compete is indivisible from the non-disclosure agreement which is unenforceable under Wisconsin law because it contains neither temporal nor geographic limitations. However, the "validity of a restrictive covenant is to be established by examination of the particular circumstances which surround it." The Court does not possess any information concerning the circumstances surrounding the covenant not to compete. . . . Accordingly, the court cannot grant defendants' motion to dismiss [this count] of plaintiff's complaint.

First, Wisconsin courts have held that a determination whether a covenant not to compete is reasonably necessary for an employer's protection cannot be intelligently made without considering the nature and character of information to which an employee had access during the course of employment, the extent to which such information is vital to an employer's ability to conduct its business, and the extent to which such information could be obtained through other sources. The Court cannot make such an intelligent determination on a motion to dismiss. Plaintiff's complaint alleges that the individual defendants were high-level management employees. Accordingly, it is possible they had access to a wide variety of confidential and proprietary information concerning Vitamin D development. As such, the covenant not to compete may be reasonably necessary for plaintiff's protection because "what may be unreasonable in one instance may be very reasonable in another." However, such a determination does not lend itself to a motion to dismiss.

Additionally, Wisconsin courts have held that a determination concerning whether a restraint is harsh or oppressive to an employee cannot be made without considering "the extent to which the restraint on competition actually inhibits the employee's ability to pursue a livelihood in that enterprise, as well as the particular skills, abilities, and experience of the employee sought to be restrained." The Court is not privy to such information in connection with defendants' motion to dismiss. Accordingly, the Court cannot conclude that as a matter of law the covenant not to compete is harsh or oppressive to employees.

Next, concerning defendants' territorial limitation argument, Wisconsin courts have held that a territorial limitation need not be expressed in geographic terms as an absolute prerequisite to a valid and enforceable agreement. The covenant not to compete at issue restricts employees from competing in the area of pharmaceutical research and development. This may "more closely approximate [] the area of the employer's vulnerability to unfair competition by a former employee." Accordingly, the Court cannot conclude that as a matter of law the absence of an express geographic territorial limitation renders the covenant not to compete invalid and unenforceable.

Finally, the Court cannot conclude that as a matter of law the non-disclosure agreement contained within the individual defendants Employee Agreements is a restraint on trade. In Sysco Food Servs. of E. Wis., LLC v. Ziccarelli, 445 F. Supp. 2d 1039 (E.D. Wis. 2006) (applying Wisconsin law), a case relied on by defendants, the Court held that a confidentiality covenant which prohibited defendants from using information about plaintiff's customers in order to compete against it was a restraint on trade because it governed similar types of activities as would a covenant not to compete and it served to restrict competition from plaintiff's former employees. However, the non-disclosure agreement at issue states in relevant part as follows:

> That during the term of employment with Bone Care and thereafter, Employee will not . . . disclose or authorize or permit anyone under his or her direction to disclose to anyone not properly entitled thereto . . .

Said provision does not contain the use restriction which the Court in *Sysco Food Servs. of E. Wis., LLC* found to be outcome determinative and defendants failed to demonstrate how their mobility is affected by such a provision. In the end, the non-disclosure provision may be a restraint on trade.[5] However, without a showing as to how such a provision affects the individual defendants' mobility the Court cannot determine that as a matter of law it is subject to the requirements of Wis. Stat. § 103.465. Accordingly, defendants' motion to dismiss [this count] is denied.

[Defendants also argued for the dismissal of various tort claims based on breach of the duty of loyalty, usurpation of corporate opportunity, and conspiracy. Defendants' motion was denied on the grounds that the court lacked sufficient facts to grant the motion as a matter of law.]

MAGIC LEAP, INC. v. XU

United States District Court for the Northern District of California
2020 U.S. Dist. LEXIS 106093 (2020)

. . .

I. BACKGROUND

Plaintiff Magic Leap, Inc. ("Magic Leap") is a Delaware corporation with its principal place of business in Plantation, Florida. Plaintiff specializes in the field of "spatial computing, which encompasses augmented, virtual and hybrid (or mixed) reality technology." Defendant Chi Xu ("Xu") resides in Beijing, China. Defendant Hangzhou Tairuo Technology Co., Ltd. (d/b/a "Nreal"), is a Chinese business entity established in or about early 2017.

---

5. If the non-disclosure provision is found to be a restraint on trade plaintiff bears a heavy burden of proving it is reasonable considering it has no time limitation and it applies to information which is not considered a trade secret.

Plaintiff alleges that Xu "formerly worked for Magic Leap in its Sunnyvale, California, facilities from July 27, 2015, until August 15, 2016." As a condition of his employment, Xu signed a Proprietary Information and Inventions Agreement (the "PIIA"), which "contains a broad prohibition against the use or disclosure of the defined confidential and proprietary information both during and after Mr. Xu's employment" with Plaintiff ("PIIA"). Plaintiff further alleges that, during Xu's employment with Plaintiff, Xu "had access to much of Magic Leap's Confidential Information spanning all phases of its research and development efforts."

In August 2016, Xu ended his employment with Plaintiff. In 2017, Xu subsequently formed Nreal, a company that quickly released a competing prototype of "lightweight, ergonomically designed, mixed reality glasses," called the Nreal Light. Plaintiff alleges that the Nreal Light is "strikingly similar to confidential Magic Leap designs and confidential and proprietary information to which [Xu] had access as an employee."

Accordingly, on June 17, 2019, Plaintiff filed suit in this Court and named Xu and Nreal as Defendants. . . .

III. DISCUSSION

. . .

A. *Claim One: Breach of Contract*

Plaintiff's first claim, which is asserted against Xu, alleges that Xu breached the parties' Proprietary Information and Inventions Agreement ("PIIA"). Defendants argue that the Court should dismiss this breach of contract claim for two reasons. First, Defendants argue that the breach of contract claim fails as a matter of law because the contract is an unenforceable restraint against trade [under California law]. Second, Defendants argue that Plaintiff has not adequately pleaded any breach. The Court addresses each argument in turn.

1. *The PIAA Is Plausibly Enforceable*

Defendants argue that the Court must dismiss Plaintiff's breach of contract claim because it is unenforceable as an unlawful "restraint of trade" pursuant to California Business and Professions Code section 16600. The Court disagrees that the PIIA is an unenforceable restraint against trade as a matter of law.

Section 16600 states that "every contract by which anyone is restrained from engaging in a lawful profession, trade, or business of any kind is to that extent void," subject to statutory exceptions not relevant here. Cal. Bus. & Profs. Code § 16600; see also Cal. Bus. & Profs. Code § 16601-07 (codifying exceptions for non-compete agreements associated with the sale or dissolution of certain businesses and addressing other special circumstances). Thus, pursuant to section 16600, courts regularly void nonsolicitation and no-hire agreements. See, e.g., Edwards v. Arthur Andersen LLP, 44 Cal. 4th 937, 948, 81 Cal. Rptr. 3d 282, 189 P.3d 285 (2008) (holding nonsolicitation provision void); VL Systems, Inc. v. Unisen, Inc., 152 Cal. App. 4th 708, 61 Cal. Rptr. 3d 818 (2007) (holding no-hire provision void). Specifically, in *Edwards*, the California Supreme Court confirmed the continued viability and breadth of Section 16600. The Court explained that by enacting section 16600, the California legislature intended to further "a settled legislative policy in favor of open competition and employee mobility." Thus, section 16600 is a broad prohibition on "every contract by which anyone is restrained from engaging in a lawful profession, trade, or business of any kind." Cal. Bus. & Profs. Code § 16600.

Here, Defendants only challenge Section 2 of the PIIA, which governs an employee's use of confidential information, based upon the broad way that Plaintiff defined "confidential information." For example, Defendants note that the PIIA defines confidential information "to include 'products, 'processes,' 'technology,' 'customer lists and customers,' and 'services,' as well as broader concepts such as 'know-how,' 'business information,' 'processes,' and 'ideas.'" The PIIA requires Xu to "hold in strictest confidence, and not to use except for the benefit of [Plaintiff]" any of these broad categories of confidential information, both during and after his employment. Defendants thus argue that the contract constitutes a restraint on trade because the confidentiality agreement is not sufficiently tailored to protect Plaintiff's trade secrets.

However, unlike the confidentiality agreement at issue here, the cases cited by Defendants in their motion all considered explicit nonsolicitation or noncompete agreements. For example, in *Dowell*, the court considered a noncompete clause that "prohibited an employee from rendering services, directly or indirectly, to a competitor where those services could enhance the use or marketability of a conflicting product through the use of confidential information to which the employee had access." Dowell v. Biosense Webster, Inc., 179 Cal. App. 4th 564, 578, 102 Cal. Rptr. 3d 1 (2009). Similarly, Defendants' citation to this Court's decision in *Richmond Technologies, Inc.* is inapt, because in that case, the Court found that "the nonsolicitation and non-interference provisions in the Non-Disclosure Agreement are likely to be found unenforceable under California law." (quoting Richmond Techs., Inc. v. Aumtech Bus. Sols., No. 11-CV-02460-LHK, 2011 U.S. Dist. LEXIS 71269, 2011 WL 2607158, at *18 (N.D. Cal. July 1, 2011)). In that same decision, this Court also found that the provision barring "the use of confidential source code, software, or techniques . . . is likely enforceable." 2011 U.S. Dist. LEXIS 71269, [WL] at *19. Finally, on reply, Defendants also cite *Western Air*, in which a court found unlawful an employment provision entitled "Restrictions on Competition" that included both a nonsolicitation clause and a noncompete clause. W. Air Charter, Inc. v. Schembari, No. 2:17-cv-00420-AB (KSx), 2017 U.S. Dist. LEXIS 217520, 2017 WL 7240775, at *1 (C.D. Cal. Dec. 14, 2017). None of these cases apply here because they all involve explicit restraints on trade, such as nonsolicitation and noncompete agreements, rather than run-of-the-mill confidentiality provisions.

As a result, the Court finds that this case is more analogous to SPS Technologies, LLC v. Briles Aerospace, Inc., No. CV 18-9536-MWF (ASX), 2019 U.S. Dist. LEXIS 219610, 2019 WL 6841992 (C.D. Cal. Oct. 30, 2019). There, in response to a plaintiff's claim that the defendant breached his employment agreement, the defendant argued that the agreement's broadly worded confidentiality provisions were void under section 16600. The SPS court acknowledged that even though the contract did not contain any express noncompete agreement, the agreement could nonetheless be invalid under section 16600 if it "imposed a restraint of a substantial character." The SPS court would therefore have to assess whether the "restraining effect [is] significant enough that its enforcement would implicate the policies of open competition and employee mobility that animate section 16600." However, because such an analysis would involve a "fact-intensive inquiry" in that case, the Court could not determine as a matter of law whether section 16600 applied and denied the defendant's motion to dismiss that count.

So too here. Unlike cases that considered express restraints on trade, including noncompete provisions or nonsolicitation provisions, the instant breach of contract claim merely covers a confidentiality agreement. Although the Ninth Circuit has held that application of section 16600 does not require any express restraints of trade, the Ninth Circuit has also acknowledged that whether such a provision "impose[s] a restraint of a substantial character" may require "fact-finding" or further development of the record.

Accordingly, the Court declines to hold as a matter of law that the confidentiality provisions of the PIIA are unenforceable pursuant to section 16600.

2. Plaintiff Fails to Plead the Element of Breach

Defendants next argue that the Court must dismiss Plaintiff's breach of contract claim because Plaintiff failed to adequately plead the element of breach. The Court agrees.

To state a claim for breach of contract under California law, a plaintiff must plead facts establishing the following elements: "(1) existence of the contract; (2) plaintiff's performance or excuse for nonperformance; (3) defendant's breach; and (4) damages to plaintiff as a result of the breach." CDF Firefighters v. Maldonado, 158 Cal. App. 4th 1226, 1239, 70 Cal. Rptr. 3d 667 (2008). As to the third element, Defendants' breach, Plaintiff merely alleges that Xu "breached the PIIA through his unauthorized use of Magic Leap's Confidential Information in starting Nreal as a business and creating and promoting Nreal Light products." Elsewhere in the complaint, Plaintiff also alleges that, "[o]n information and belief, Mr. Xu used his knowledge of Magic Leap's Confidential Information, including but not limited to the Confidential Designs, to make production and design decisions at Nreal and to guide the development of spatial computing products intended for sale." Although these allegations explain why Xu allegedly breached the PIIA, these allegations fail to explain how Xu breached the PIAA. In fact, Plaintiff's complaint is devoid of any allegation as to what specific "confidential information" Plaintiff believes that Xu used to start Nreal or to create and promote the Nreal Light. In the absence of any specific allegation, the Complaint conclusorily recites the "breach" element of Plaintiff's breach of contract claim, which is inadequate to state a claim for breach of contract.

. . .

Plaintiff's overly broad allegation that Xu misused "Confidential Information, including but not limited to the Confidential Designs," contains even less factual substance than the complaint in *Sricom.*

Nor do Plaintiff's excuses for inadequately pleading breach withstand scrutiny. Plaintiff argues that the Complaint need not "identify [Plaintiff's] confidential code-named projects in a publicly filed complaint." Although Plaintiff need not spell out the exact details of Plaintiff's confidential designs in order to adequately plead breach, Plaintiff must do more than simply state that Xu breached the confidentiality agreement by disclosing confidential information. . . .

Accordingly, the Court GRANTS Defendants' motion to dismiss Plaintiff's claim for breach of contract. . . .

Notes and Questions

1. In considering the covenant not to compete, the *Genzyme* court refers to Wis. Stat. § 103.465, which states:

> A covenant by an assistant, servant or agent not to compete with his or her employer or principal during the term of the employment or agency, or after the termination of that employment or agency, within a specified territory and during a specified time is lawful and enforceable only if the restrictions imposed are reasonably necessary for the protection of the employer or principal. Any covenant, described in this subsection, imposing an unreasonable restraint is illegal, void and unenforceable even as to any part of the covenant or performance that would be a reasonable restraint.

Although a covenant not to compete that falls outside the restrictions of the statute will be unenforceable as a contract in restraint of trade, Wisconsin does enforce covenants that fall within the statutory boundaries. By contrast, consider California's approach to the same issue, as set forth in the *Magic Leap* case and in Cal. Bus. & Prof. Code § 16600:

> Except as provided in this chapter, every contract by which anyone is restrained from engaging in a lawful profession, trade, or business of any kind is to that extent void.

California will enforce certain covenants not to compete, but only those made in connection with an owner's sale of a business (or all of her ownership in the business) or made in connection with the dissolution of a partnership or limited liability company.

Taking another example, Colorado courts view non-compete agreements with considerable suspicion. Covenants not to compete are discussed in the same statutory section that discusses worker intimidation, and are generally forbidden except contracts made in connection with the sale of a business and contracts made with executive and management personnel (Colo. Rev. Stat. § 8-2-113):

> (1) It shall be unlawful to use force, threats, or other means of intimidation to prevent any person from engaging in any lawful occupation at any place he sees fit.
> (2) Any covenant not to compete which restricts the right of any person to receive compensation for performance of skilled or unskilled labor for any employer shall be void, but this subsection (2) shall not apply to:
>> (a) Any contract for the purchase and sale of a business or the assets of a business;
>> (b) Any contract for the protection of trade secrets;
>> (c) Any contractual provision providing for recovery of the expense of educating and training an employee who has served an employer for a period of less than two years;
>> (d) Executive and management personnel and officers and employees who constitute professional staff to executive and management personnel.

Why might the Wisconsin, California, and Colorado legislatures have come to such varying approaches to covenants not to compete? In a factual situation like the one in *Genzyme*, would a California court enforce the covenant not to compete? A Colorado court?

2. In *Magic Leap*, the agreement in question did not contain a non-compete, or even a nonsolicitation, clause (which California attorneys will sometimes include as a hopefully enforceable attempt to get some non-compete-like protection). Instead, the issue concerned a confidentiality provision. How might a confidentiality provision accomplish some of the same goals as a non-compete in a jurisdiction where non-competes will not be enforced?

3. Companies often ask their employees to sign unenforceable covenants not to compete. In some situations, the covenants are unenforceable by their mere existence (such as in California); in other situations, the covenants protect an overly large geographic territory; and in other situations, the covenants are overbroad in terms of the industry they cover, leading to the conclusion that they are not reasonably necessary for the employer's protection. Why might counsel to a company recommend that its client have employees sign a non-compete provision that counsel knows or strongly suspects is unenforceable?

4. Given the roles of the various defendants with Bone Care, the business they started, and the timing of their departure, do you think the former employer had a legitimate fiduciary duty claim in addition to its contract claim?

5. The decision of whether to enforce a covenant not to compete against a departing employee can hinge on both business and personal motivations. Keep in mind that high-level executives who make this determination may have their own egos at play and may be angered or hurt by an employee who leaves in a manner that smacks of betrayal. Consider ways you as the attorney for an entrepreneur could counsel your client on preferred exit strategies that would minimize potential ill will and foster a more positive departure.

ICONIX, INC. v. TOKUDA

United States District Court for the Northern District of California
457 F. Supp. 2d 969 (2006)

. . .

Plaintiff Iconix, Inc. ("Plaintiff" or "Iconix") is a corporation organized and existing under the laws of the state of Delaware with its principal place of business in Mountain View, California.

Defendants in this matter are Lance Tokuda, Jia Shen, and netPickle, Inc. (collectively, "Defendants").

Defendant Lance Tokuda ("Tokuda") is a former employee and officer of Iconix; Tokuda resides in Foster City, California.

Defendant Jia Shen ("Shen") is a former employee of Iconix; Shen resides in East Palo Alto, California.

Defendant netPickle, Inc. ("Netpickle") is a corporation organized and existing under the laws of the State of Delaware and has its principal place of business in Foster City, California.

Plaintiff provides email identity services that proactively combat email fraud spawned by phishing. Phishing is a form of email fraud where senders impersonate legitimate businesses and organizations to try to get recipients to divulge personal information such as passwords and account numbers so the senders can steal the recipient's identity and/or funds from the recipient's account.

Tokuda and Shen began their employment at Iconix in December of 2004. Tokuda was the Vice President of Engineering and Chief Technology Officer at Iconix and was in charge of setting the engineering and development direction for Iconix and for managing the engineering team. Among other things, Tokuda supervised the development of Iconix's new intellectual property and ideas. Shen was the Manager of Client Development at Iconix, and his responsibilities included overseeing the work of software development.

As employees of Iconix, Tokuda and Shen both signed contracts entitled, "Proprietary Information and Inventions Assignment Agreement." These contracts are quoted in pertinent part below.

In the fall of 2005, Plaintiff was actively generating, developing, and evaluating ideas for increasing traffic to Plaintiff's website. This activity included developing new features that would entice consumers to download Iconix's email identity product ("email ID product"). Of particular interest to Iconix was the ability to penetrate community websites such as www.myspace.com, where web users create profiles and socially network with one another. To implement this marketing strategy, Plaintiff created a separate website, called Uberfuze.com ("Uberfuze"), that was targeted directly at social networking users.

In the fall of 2005, Iconix engineers, including Tokuda, discussed the idea of creating a feature that would rotate through a user's pictures. The user would download Iconix's email ID product and then be able to use the feature. Iconix continued to evaluate the feature and began to test it as a marketing strategy by the beginning of 2006.

In late December of 2005, Tokuda gave notice to Iconix. Tokuda's last day of employment was January 23, 2006.

On or about January 20, 2006, Iconix discovered that in or around October 2005, while he was still an officer of Iconix, Tokuda secretly registered the domain name rockmyspace.com. Prior to that time, Tokuda had covertly been developing a customizable slideshow feature for his own personal benefit. While an Iconix officer, Tokuda also secretly formed his own company, Netpickle, for the purpose of exploiting the customizable slideshow feature for his own benefit. Tokuda also began soliciting other Iconix personnel, including Shen, to join him in creating his own customizable slideshow business. Tokuda's solicitation of Iconix employees and the Defendants' development of a competing customizable slideshow feature occurred on Iconix's company time and through the use of Iconix's computers. Shen and Tokuda launched rockmyspace.com on the night of November 13-14, 2005.

Since January, 2006, Tokuda and NetPickle registered the domain name rockyou.com. Defendants currently market their customizable slideshow feature using the www.rockyou.com website. (Defendants' slideshow technology and website are referred to collectively as "rockmyspace," "rock-myspace.com," "RockYou," and "rockyou.com." These terms are used interchangeably.) By February 19, 2006, rockmyspace had already exceeded 1.1 million registered users.

When Iconix found out that Shen helped Tokuda take Iconix's ideas and property to form his own customizable slideshow business, Iconix was forced to terminate Shen's employment.

On March 13, 2006, Iconix sent Defendants a letter requesting that they return the customizable slideshow program and source code to its rightful owner, Iconix, and that they cease and desist all other activity in which they are engaged that uses software or derivative works owned by Iconix. Defendants refused to do so. On

March 27, 2006, Plaintiff filed the original Complaint in this matter. On May 4, 2006, Plaintiff filed the instant Motion for Preliminary Injunction.

   . . .

ANALYSIS

   . . .

1. Merits of the Claims

Plaintiff shows probable success on the merits of its claims.

   . . .

b. *Breach of Contract*

Plaintiff argues that Tokuda and Shen breached their Proprietary Agreements by failing to disclose, assign, and transfer the work they developed for implementing an animated slideshow tool and the website that they developed, launched, and operated while in Plaintiff's employ. Tokuda's and Shen's Proprietary Agreements both state:

> a. Assignment of Inventions. I agree to assign and transfer to the Company, without further consideration, my entire right, title and interest (throughout the United States and in all other countries or jurisdictions), free and clear of all liens and encumbrances, in and to all Inventions. Such assignment and transfer to the Company shall be continuous during my employment as of the relevant time of development of each such Invention. The Company may, in [its] sole discretion, agree to provide consideration for certain Inventions through a written agreement between the Company and the undersigned which specifically provides for such consideration; in all other cases, no consideration shall be paid. The Inventions shall be the sole property of the Company, whether or not copyrightable or patentable or in a commercial stage of development. In addition, I agree to maintain adequate and current written records on the development of all Inventions, which shall also remain the sole property of the Company.
>
> b. Inventions. "Inventions" collectively means any and all ideas, concepts, inventions, discoveries, developments, know-how, structures, designs, formulas, algorithms, methods, products, processes, systems and technologies in any stage of development that are conceived, developed or reduced to practice by me alone or with others; any and all patents, patents pending, copyrights, moral rights, trademarks and any other intellectual property rights therein; and any and all improvements, modifications, derivative works from, other rights in and claims related to any of the foregoing under the laws of any jurisdiction, except Inventions excluded in Schedule A[5] and to the extent that California Labor Code Section 2870 lawfully prohibits assignment. I understand that Section 2870(a) provides as follows:

---

5. Schedule A was left blank for both Tokuda and Shen. Thus, no Inventions were excluded as having been listed on Schedule A. . . .

Any provision in an employment agreement which provides that an employee shall assign, or offer to assign, any of his or her rights in an invention to his or her employer shall not apply to an invention that the employee developed entirely on his or her own time without using the employer's equipment, supplies, facilities, or trade secret information except for those inventions that either: (1) Relate at the time of conception or reduction to practice of the invention to the employer's business, or actual and demonstrably anticipated research or development of the employer or (2) Result from any work performed by the employee for the employer.

. . .

f. Disclosure. I agree to disclose promptly to the Company all Inventions and relevant records. I further agree to promptly disclose to the Company any idea that I do not believe to be an Invention, but is conceived, developed, or reduced to practice by me (alone or with others) while I am employed by the Company. I will disclose the idea, along with all information and records pertaining to the idea, and the Company will examine the disclosure in confidence to determine if in fact it is an Invention subject to this Agreement.

Plaintiff argues that all of the work that Tokuda and Shen did relating to rockmyspace while employed by Iconix falls under the Proprietary Agreement. Plaintiff cites to Shen's deposition, in which he testified that he conceived of the idea for rockmyspace in the fall of 2005, based on his work at Iconix around that time. . . . Plaintiff argues that Defendants developed rockmyspace into a thriving website with hundreds of thousands of registered users by the time they left. . . . [Shen and Tokuda testified that they did not disclose rockmyspace to Plaintiff until January 2006, when Tokuda asked Ames to help rockmyspace get funding and asked Ames not to tell Iconix about the meeting.]

Plaintiff argues that the exception provided by California Labor Code § 2870 (quoted as part of the above excerpt from the Proprietary Agreements) does not apply. Section 2870 provides an exception to assignment of the rockmyspace invention, only if Tokuda and Shen developed rockmyspace 1) entirely on their own time, 2) entirely without use of Iconix's equipment, supplies, or facilities; and 3) rockmyspace did not relate to Iconix's business, or actual or demonstrably anticipated research or development, or result from any work that Tokuda and Shen performed for Iconix. Plaintiff argues that section 2870 does not apply as an exception to assignment because "[t]here is overwhelming evidence that Defendants used Iconix company equipment and resources to develop and operate rockmyspace." Moreover, Plaintiff argues that even if there is such a thing as "entirely on his or her own time," within the meaning of California Labor Code § 2870, for senior start-up company employees like Tokuda and Shen, this work, using Iconix equipment and resources, was completed, in part, during the regular workday — sometimes for the entire day, and even in the middle of meetings. Plaintiff argues that this work cannot be construed as "entirely" on the employee's own time.

First, in providing evidence of the usage of Iconix company equipment and resources, Plaintiff cites to the Declaration of Eric Lindblom, the Director of Information Technology at Iconix, which states that Lindblom's examination of the company computer used by Shen revealed that the computer contained the "source code for the [rockmyspace] website and the related applications used by the website, including the customizable slideshow application." . . . Lindblom also discovered a database of users of the rockmyspace service on Shen's company computer, as well as a bridge loan term sheet and a taxpayer identification form for Netpickle that had been filled out. On Tokuda's company computer, Lindblom found a PowerPoint presentation for investors labeled "netPickle.ppt." . . . On Shen's computer, Lindblom also discovered logs of instant messaging conversations, held between individuals logged in using the instant messaging identities of Tokuda and Shen; the messages sent from the user logged in with Shen's instant messaging username were sent from Shen's company computer. Many of these conversations were held on weekdays, between the hours of 9:00 a.m. and 5:00 p.m., and featured discussion of the conceptualization, design, software, operation, and business of rockmyspace.com. In particular, some of these conversations described and facilitated Tokuda's and Shen's actions in debugging and installing code for rockmyspace.com. One such instant messaging conversation was held while the user logged in as Tokuda was attending a meeting of Iconix executives ("hey jia, in exec meeting").

Even putting aside use of Plaintiff's equipment and resources, Plaintiff argues that the exception provided by California Labor Code § 2870 does not apply because, for reasons explained in the section regarding Breach of Fiduciary Duty above, the animated slideshow tool and the website targeting social website users were "directly related to business Iconix was pursuing and to Iconix's anticipated research or development."

In their Opposition, Tokuda and Shen raise a variety of arguments against a finding of breach of their Proprietary Agreements. First, Tokuda and Shen argue section 2(f) of the Proprietary Agreements (quoted above) stands for the proposition that if Plaintiff determined that it did not wish to pursue its broadly coined definition of "Invention," no "assignment" under section 2(a) of the Proprietary Agreements was necessary. However, this construction is not supported by the language of the Proprietary Agreement. The Proprietary Agreements request disclosure in order to determine whether an idea is an "Invention subject to this Agreement." The Proprietary Agreements do not suggest that assignment is unnecessary if the company does not wish to a pursue a particular "Invention." Far from challenging Plaintiff's argument that Tokuda and Shen failed to disclose rockmyspace to Plaintiff, Tokuda and Shen argue that they "only retained those things that were not usable in email and were directed at social networking, things that Iconix made clear it did not want." The clear terms of the Proprietary Agreements indicate that Tokuda and Shen did not have the discretion to retain any ideas. Pursuant to section 2(f) of the Proprietary Agreements, they had to disclose not only all Inventions, but also "any idea" that they did not believe to be an Invention so that Plaintiff could determine whether or not the idea qualified as an Invention. Thus, Tokuda and Shen's alternate argument that rockmyspace is not an "Invention" because it is not original is also unavailing. Tokuda and Shen were still required to disclose rockmyspace. Apart from the fact that the Proprietary Agreement does not require that an Invention be original, section 2(f) specifically states that Tokuda and Shen were required to disclose "any idea" that they "do not believe to be an Invention."

Further, Defendants argue that the rockmyspace slideshow and website cannot be claimed under the Proprietary Agreement given the circumstances surrounding their limited use of Plaintiff's equipment: 1) Shen used his Iconix computer on vacation to program the [site] and 2) Iconix computers were used to handle minor operational issues. Tokuda and Shen argue that Shen "programmed using the Iconix laptop on vacation as a dumb terminal to his server and only used the Iconix laptop because Iconix asked him to take the laptop on vacation." Tokuda and Shen also argue that "using Iconix computers for personal purposes was allowed and Iconix never said it would lay title to such things." Tokuda and Shen cite to Shen's Declaration in which he states,

> I did a lot of personal activities, including work on my websites, on my Iconix laptop, because I did not have a laptop of my own. I stored photos, video games, music, personal finance information, passwords, and many other personal files on the Iconix laptop. I carried my laptop at all times because I was always on call for any website emergencies. Mr. Picazo and Mr. Zager were aware of my use of the laptop for personal purposes and encouraged me having my laptop with me at all times. In addition, Eric Lindblom, Iconix's Director of Information Technology, knew from November 2005 that I was doing some maintenance of the RockMySpace (later renamed Rockyou) website through the Iconix laptop I used. No one ever raised an objection or said I couldn't use the laptop for personal purposes.

Tokuda and Shen's argument is unavailing. Regardless of whether use of Iconix computers for personal purposes was considered acceptable, the Proprietary Agreements clearly require that Tokuda and Shen assign and transfer all inventions to Plaintiff, unless those inventions were developed entirely on the employee's own time, without using the employer's equipment, supplies, facilities, or trade secret information. Even then, as discussed above, the Proprietary Agreements provide an exception to this exception, requiring assignment and transfer of those inventions that either: (1) Relate at the time of conception or reduction to practice of the invention to the employer's business, or actual and demonstrably anticipated research or development of the employer or (2) Result from any work performed by the employee for the employer. Thus, even if it was considered acceptable for Shen to use his Iconix computer for personal use, any Inventions developed using that computer had to be assigned and transferred. To the extent that Tokuda and Shen believed that the rockmyspace slideshow and website were not Inventions, they still had to disclose those ideas to Plaintiff, pursuant to section 2(f) of the Proprietary Agreements.

In response to Plaintiff's arguments that Tokuda and Shen worked on rockmyspace during business hours, Tokuda and Shen concede that they sometimes worked on maintenance of rockmyspace between the hours of 9:00 A.M. and 5:00 P.M. They argue however, that given that the two often worked 14-16 hour days for Iconix or worked through the night, the idea that something was done on "work time" simply because it happened between 9:00 A.M. and 5:00 P.M. is artificial. To clarify, in his Declaration, Shen does not speak in terms of working between 9:00 A.M. and 5:00 P.M., but states specifically that, "[s]ometimes, the operational work [on rockmyspace] spilled into work hours at Iconix." Further, as noted above, Plaintiff presents evidence that Tokuda was having an instant messenging [sic] conversation about rockmyspace while participating in an Iconix executive meeting. Even if "work time" is not properly circumscribed by the hours of 9:00 A.M. and 5:00 P.M., Tokuda and Shen fail to convincingly rebut Plaintiff's allegations that they worked on rockmyspace during work hours. As noted above, the exception to the assignment and transfer provision of the Proprietary Agreements provided by California Labor Code section 2870 only applies to "an invention that the employee developed entirely on his or her own time."

Finally, Tokuda and Shen argue that the Proprietary Agreements are unenforceable as against public policy, because they are open-ended, allowing any idea to be claimed as owned by Iconix, even if the idea is not within Iconix's anticipated line of business and was developed during the employee's free time. This argument is unavailing. As Plaintiff argues, the Proprietary Agreements are not open-ended and are not against public policy. To the contrary, the scope of the Proprietary Agreements are limited by their explicit incorporation of California Labor Code § 2870, which provides the standard for the public policy of California on issues of invention assignment contracts. Cal. Lab. Code § 2870(b) ("To the extent a provision in an employment agreement purports to require an employee to assign an invention otherwise excluded from being required to be assigned under subdivision (a), the provision is against the public policy of this state and is unenforceable."). Even Tokuda and Shen's example is unavailing: by explicitly incorporating section 2870 in the Proprietary Agreements, Plaintiff relies on the explicit public policy of California in determining not to claim — contrary to Tokuda and Shen's argument — those ideas developed during the employee's free time so long as those ideas do not fall within the exceptions set forth in section 2870.

Instead of furthering their position, Tokuda and Shen's arguments, discussed above, merely provide further evidence that the rockmyspace slideshow and website were subject to the disclosure, assignment, and transfer provisions of the Proprietary Agreements because they were "conceived, developed, or reduced to practice by" Tokuda and Shen while they were "employed by the Company." On balance, Plaintiff provides convincing evidence that section 2870 does not apply to excuse Tokuda and Shen's failure to assign and transfer rockmyspace to Iconix, and that Tokuda and Shen breached the terms of their Proprietary Agreements.

c.   Copyright Infringement

Plaintiff argues that the copyright in the rockmyspace software developed by Tokuda and Shen, while working for Plaintiff, is Plaintiff's property under the terms of the Proprietary Agreements signed by Tokuda and Shen. Mot. at 15. Plaintiff argues that Netpickle has infringed and will continue to infringe this copyright.

i.   Copyright Ownership

On February 16, 2006, Plaintiff filed for an expedited copyright registration on the software code for the rockmyspace.com website that Plaintiff obtained from Shen's company computer. On March 6, 2006, Plaintiff received the certificate of copyright registration. As quoted above, the Proprietary Agreements explicitly assign copyrights in Defendants' inventions to Iconix. As discussed above, the only exception to this assignment is provided by California Labor Code § 2870, which for the reasons stated above, does not apply in the instant case.

In its Opposition, Netpickle ignores this argument and argues at length that the software cannot be owned by Plaintiff because it does not satisfy the "work for hire" doctrine. Pursuant to 17 U.S.C. § 201(b), "In the case of a work made for hire, the employer or other person for whom the work was prepared is considered the author for purposes of this title, and, unless the parties have expressly agreed otherwise in a written instrument signed by them, owns all of the rights comprised in the copyright."

. . .

While Plaintiff argues, in turn, that it does satisfy the "work for hire" standard, the "work for hire" standard is irrelevant, where the Proprietary Agreements assign ownership of the Netpickle claims that Tokuda and Shen transferred all assets related to the rockmyspace website — including the disputed software code — to Netpickle, as part of the incorporation of copyright to Plaintiff. Although the Ninth Circuit has not addressed this issue, the leading copyright treatise and other Circuits agree that "the parties may expressly agree that all works produced by the employee during the period of the employment relationship shall belong entirely to the employer" and that the "work for hire" doctrine applies only in the absence of such express agreement. Therefore, Plaintiff has presented convincing evidence that the copyright was assigned to Plaintiff.

. . .

ii. Copyright Infringement

Plaintiff observes that Netpickle does not challenge that Netpickle's use of Iconix-registered code or insubstantial variants of that code continued through at least mid-May 2006. Plaintiff argues that using the code to operate and further develop the website necessarily involves making infringing copies of the software. Indeed, according to the Ninth Circuit, running copyrighted software, without ownership of the copyright or a license to run the software, constitutes copyright infringement: "[T]he loading of copyrighted computer software from a storage medium (hard disk, floppy disk, or read only memory) into the memory of a central processing unit ('CPU') causes a copy to be made. In the absence of ownership of the copyright or express permission by license, such acts constitute copyright infringement." Netpickle does not challenge this proposition. Thus, Plaintiff has provided convincing evidence that Netpickle has infringed copyrighted software owned by Plaintiff.

. . .

2. Irreparable Harm

For the reasons stated above, Plaintiff has shown probable success on the merits of it's [sic] various claims. [Here the court concludes that Plaintiff also succeeds in showing irreparable harm under a copyright law concept that says irreparable harm is presumed for copyright plaintiffs who have successfully made prima facie cases of infringement. Plaintiff thus prevails and is entitled to a preliminary injunction preventing Defendants from using intellectual property that Plaintiff contends belongs to Iconix. Plaintiff does not succeed in preventing Defendants from using a later generation of the software because Plaintiff did not show that the later software incorporates Iconix property.]

. . .

Notes and Questions

1. Employers often ask workers to sign Assignment of Inventions clauses along the same lines as the contract signed by the. individual defendants in the *Iconix* case. Particularly important when employees or independent contractors are being engaged to invent or develop products, the clauses give the employer ownership of intellectual property developed by workers if the property is developed using company equipment or if it relates to the employer's business or projects the worker

is pursuing for the employer. States have enacted statutory limits on this type of clause, such as the California Labor Code section discussed in the case. Why might state legislatures have an interest in limiting Assignment of Inventions clauses? Why might employers desire more broadly drafted Assignment of Inventions clauses?

2. Toy inventor Carter Bryant was a product designer for Mattel, Inc. working on the Barbie doll line. In a 2004 lawsuit, Mattel alleged that while employed by Mattel (and while subject to an inventions assignment agreement) Bryant designed the product line that became Bratz dolls. Rather than giving this design to Mattel, Bryant sold it to MGA Entertainment Inc., a small rival toy manufacturer. Mattel, Inc. v. Bryant, 441 F. Supp. 2d 1081, 1085 (C.D. Cal. 2005). Mattel ultimately agreed to settle its breach of contract and copyright infringement suit against Bryant. At the same time, it vigorously pursued MGA. While Mattel won its copyright infringement lawsuit at trial, it ultimately lost and was ordered to pay MGA over $300 million in connection with a trade secret-based counterclaim and associated punitive damages. The Chief Executive of MGA, Isaac Larian, reacted to the decision by saying, "The American dream lives. . . . This is a victory for all entrepreneurs, immigrants who came here." Andrea Chang, *Bratz Doll Maker MGA Wins Court Battle with Mattel*, Los Angeles Times, Apr. 22, 2011.

(a) Why would Mattel drop its suit against the former employee who stole its intellectual property but maintain the suit against the Bratz manufacturer?

(b) The Mattel/MGA litigation is estimated to have cost in the hundreds of millions of dollars in legal fees. Even though MGA won, is there a cautionary tale here for entrepreneurs?

3. As demonstrated in *Iconix*, an employer is not limited to contractual Assignment of Inventions clauses when seeking to establish ownership of intellectual property developed by former workers. Where the product developed by the worker-turned-entrepreneur is copyrightable, like the software in this case, an employer can use copyright theories to pursue workers. Of course, this strategy only works if the employer owns the copyright in the created material. As discussed in Chapter 4, copyrightable works created by employees are generally the property of their employers, whereas copyrightable works created by independent contractors, absent a written contract, remain the property of the independent contractor. Does *Iconix* give any guidance about what constitutes an employee's "own time" for purposes of determining whether an invention will be assigned?

4. As an attorney representing an inventor-turned-entrepreneur, what questions should you ask, and what documents should you review, in giving advice about the ownership of the intellectual property your client intends to use as the basis for the new venture? What strategies might you recommend to address concerns about ownership of the property?

PROBLEM

Your clients from Chapter 1, Olivia and Andrew, have contacted you with some questions about legal restrictions they may face in starting their new business. Andrew has no written contracts with Life Line, but Olivia signed an offer letter and the following additional contract:

KRAMER BIOGENETICS, INC.
STANDARD RESEARCH EMPLOYEE FORM 2.07:
EMPLOYEE NON-DISCLOSURE, NON-COMPETITION,
AND DEVELOPMENTS AGREEMENT

In consideration and as a condition of my employment or continued employment by Kramer Biogenetics, Inc. or one of its subsidiaries (collectively, the "Company"), I hereby agree with the Company as follows:

1. During the period of my employment by the Company (the "Employment Period") and for a period of one (1) year thereafter, I agree that I will not, directly or indirectly, alone or as a partner, officer, director, employee, stockholder, or creditor of any entity, (a) engage in any business activity that competes with the Company in the United States, or (b) solicit or do any business with any customer of the Company or any potential customer of the Company if such solicitation or business relates to products similar to or competitive with products manufactured, marketed, or sold by the Company. During the Employment Period and for a period of one (1) year thereafter, I agree that I will not, directly or indirectly, alone or as a partner, officer, director, employee, stockholder, or creditor of any entity, solicit, interfere with, or endeavor to entice any employee of the Company to leave the Company.

2. I have not revealed, and I will not at any time whether during or after the Employment Period reveal, to any person or entity, any of the trade secrets or confidential information concerning the organization, business, or finances of the Company or of any third party which the Company is under an obligation to keep confidential (including, without limitation, trade secrets or confidential information respecting inventions, products, designs, formulae, methods, know-how, techniques, systems, processes, software programs, works or authorship, customer lists, projects, plans, and proposals) except as may be required in the ordinary course of performing my duties as an employee of the Company, and I have kept secret and will keep secret all matters entrusted to me and shall not use or attempt to use any such information in any manner which may injure or cause loss or may be calculated to injure or cause loss, whether directly or indirectly, to the Company. Further, I agree that during and after the Employment Period I shall not make, use, or permit to be used any notes, memoranda, reports, lists, records, drawings, sketches, specifications, software programs, data, documentation, or other materials of any nature relating to any matter within the scope of business of the Company or concerning any of its dealings or affairs other than for benefit of the Company, it being agreed that all of the foregoing shall be and remain the sole and exclusive property of the Company, and that immediately upon termination of my employment I shall deliver all of the foregoing, and all copies thereof, to the Company at the facility where I was employed, together with a written certification that I have fully complied with such obligation.

3. If at any time or times during the Employment Period, I (either alone or with others) have made, conceived, created, discovered, invented, or reduced to practice, or shall make, create, discover, invent, or reduce

to practice, any invention, modification, discovery, design, development, improvement, process, software program, work of authorship, documentation, formula, data, technique, know-how, trade secret, or other intellectual property right whatsoever or any interest therein (whether or not patentable or registrable under copyright, trademark, or similar statutes) (herein called "Developments"), then:

> (a) such Developments and the benefits thereof are and shall immediately become the sole and absolute property of the Company and its assigns, as works made for hire or otherwise;
>
> (b) I shall promptly disclose to the Company (or any persons designated by it) each such Development;
>
> (c) as may be necessary to ensure the Company's ownership of such Developments, I hereby assign any and all rights (including, without limitation, any copyrights, patents, and trademarks) I may have or acquire in the Developments and benefits and/or rights resulting therefrom to the Company and its assigns without further compensation; and
>
> (d) I shall communicate, without cost or delay, and without disclosing to others the same, all available information relating thereto (with all necessary plans and models) to the Company.

The Company has informed me, and I hereby agree, that as provided in the Illinois Employee Patent Act, the requirement to assign Developments hereunder shall not apply to a Development that I develop entirely on my own time without using the Company's equipment, supplies, facilities, or trade secret information, except for those Developments that either (i) relate at the time of conception or reduction to the Company's business, or actual or demonstrably anticipated research or development of the Company; or (ii) result from any work performed by me for the Company. Without limiting the generality of paragraphs 3(b) and 3(d) above, I will disclose to the Company all discoveries and intellectual property rights conceived during the Employment Period which I believe meet the criteria set forth in the Illinois Employee Patent Act, whether or not the property of the Company under the terms of the preceding sentence, provided that such disclosure shall be received by the Company in confidence to the extent it pertains to discoveries and intellectual property rights which are not the property of the Company under this paragraph 3. In addition, this paragraph does not apply to Developments developed by me prior to the Employment Period.

4. I will, during and after the Employment Period, at the request and cost of the Company, promptly sign, execute, make, and do all such deeds, documents, acts, and things as the Company and its duly authorized agents may reasonably require:

> (a) to apply for, obtain, register, and vest in the name of the Company alone (unless the Company otherwise directs) letters patent, copyrights, trademarks, or other analogous protection in any country throughout the world and when so obtained or vested to renew and restore the same; and

(b) to defend any judicial, opposition, or other proceedings in respect of such applications and any judicial, opposition, or other proceedings or petitions or applications for revocation of any such letters patent, copyright, trademark, or other analogous protection.

In the event the Company is unable, after reasonable effort, to secure my signature for any letters patent, copyright, or trademark registration or other documents regarding any legal protection relating to a Development, whether because of my physical or mental incapacity or for any other reason whatsoever, I hereby irrevocably designate and appoint the Company and its duly authorized officers and agents as my agent and attorney-in-fact, to act for and in my behalf and stead to execute and file any such application or applications or other documents and to do all other lawfully permitted acts to further the prosecution and issuance of letters patent, copyright, or trademark registrations or any other legal protection thereon with the same legal force and effect as if executed by me.

5. I agree that any breach of this Agreement by me would cause irreparable damage to the Company and that in the event of such breach the Company shall have, in addition to any and all remedies of law, the right to an injunction, specific performance, or other equitable relief to prevent the violation of my obligations hereunder, without the necessity of a bond or other security.

6. I represent that the Developments identified in the pages, if any, attached hereto as Exhibit A comprise all the unpatented and unregistered copyrightable Developments which I have made, conceived, or created prior to the Employment Period, which Developments are excluded from this Agreement. I understand that it is only necessary to list the title and purpose of such Developments but not the details thereof.

7. I represent that, except as disclosed on the pages, if any, attached hereto as Exhibit B, I am not a party to, or bound by the terms of, any agreement or obligation to any previous employer or other party to refrain from using or disclosing any trade secret or confidential or proprietary information in the course of my employment by the Company or to refrain from competing, directly or indirectly, with the business of such previous employer or any other party. I further represent that my performance of all the terms of this Agreement and as an employee of the Company does not and will not breach any agreement or obligation for me to keep in confidence proprietary information, knowledge, or data acquired by me in confidence or in trust prior to or during my employment with the Company, and I will not disclose to the Company or induce the Company to use any confidential or proprietary information or material belonging to any previous employer or others. I have not entered into, and I agree I will not enter into, any agreement, either written or oral, in conflict with the terms of this Agreement.

8. I agree that each provision herein shall be treated as a separate and independent clause, and the unenforceability of any one clause shall in no way impair the enforceability of any other clauses herein. Moreover, if one or more of the provisions contained in this Agreement shall for any reason

be held to be excessively broad as to scope, activity, subject, or otherwise so as to be unenforceable, such provision or provisions shall be construed by the appropriate judicial body by limiting or reducing it or them, so as to be enforceable to the maximum extent compatible with the applicable law as it shall then appear.

9. My obligations under this Agreement shall survive the termination of my employment regardless of the manner of such termination and shall be binding on my heirs, executors, administrators, and legal representatives.

KRAMER BIOGENETICS, INC.
By: /s/ JANET PATEL
       Janet Patel
       General Counsel

EMPLOYEE:

/s/ OLIVIA M. GOLD

DATE:_____

. . .

EXHIBIT A
None.

. . .

EXHIBIT B
None.

Notes and Questions

1. Considering both the contract above and the other concepts in this chapter, what steps can Olivia take toward starting her new venture during the period she is still employed by Kramer? What can she do after she leaves? Assume the common law of restrictive covenants in the applicable jurisdiction follows the national consensus also followed in the cases in this chapter.

2. What steps can Andrew take while still employed by Life Line? What can he do after he leaves?

3. How will your answer to Question 1 change if Olivia and Andrew are in California and Olivia's contract is governed by California law? Will your answer to Question 2 change?

4. Olivia and Andrew both want to recruit a few of their best former colleagues to work for the new venture. What advice should you give them?

5. Andrew's iPhone was paid for by Life Line during the term of his employment. In addition to his personal contacts, the iPhone contains contact information for (a) several service providers who did contract work for Life Line, and (b) several large customers of Life Line. Can Andrew contact people from either of these two groups as necessary in developing and operating the new business? What advice do you have for him as to this information?

6. Olivia learned a tremendous amount about product development while working at Kramer. She now understands, better than before she worked for Kramer, how theory and practice work together to create new consumer products. Olivia assures you that she does not intend in any way to copy or pirate any product development procedures from Kramer, but you are concerned that her entire approach may have been influenced by Kramer's processes and other trade secrets. What advice can you give your client on this issue?

III

ORGANIZING THE NEW VENTURE

Entrepreneurs have a lot on their minds. In the midst of conceiving and consistently refining an idea, assembling a team, choosing a name, creating a logo and website, finding money to pay for development, and designing a product or service offering, many entrepreneurs view the legal organization of their new venture as a low priority. To the lawyer, and any law student who has taken a Business Associations or Corporations course, it may seem foolish to ignore one of the greatest benefits of forming a business entity, namely, shielding the entrepreneur from personal liability for the debts of the business. To the entrepreneur, forming an entity may seem like a legal nicety that can wait until later — after all, if the entrepreneur does not focus on developing the product, there will not be any business at all. Even once the entrepreneur has been convinced of the value of forming an entity, she must be convinced of the value of a written agreement among co-founders.

In this chapter, we explore the various business forms available to entrepreneurial ventures. Lawyers working with entrepreneurs must be able to move beyond the client-treasured clichés of entity selection ("we should just form an LLC like everybody else," "we have to form a C-corp to get VC financing," "everyone incorporates in Delaware") and give nuanced, personalized counseling applicable for each business venture. By helping clients to craft a solid legal foundation, attorneys can significantly contribute to a business's future success.

A. ENTITY CHARACTERISTICS AND APPLICABLE STATE LAW

A new business can be structured in any number of ways, and a key early task of the entrepreneur's lawyer is helping the client to choose the optimal structure. Before we get to entity choice, which is covered in Section B, we will first outline the various entity types and their characteristics. We will also briefly address transferability of ownership interests in business entities and the choice of state of formation.

1. Sole Proprietorship

If your client is already conducting business on his own without any formal structure, he is a sole proprietorship. While the sole proprietorship is unincorporated and is not technically an "entity," it is likely the most common structure for small businesses, particularly in the early stages. In a sole proprietorship, the business is a mere extension of the entrepreneur himself. As such, all liabilities and risks associated with the business rest with the entrepreneur as an individual, and likewise all assets of the business are really just assets owned by the individual. The entrepreneur pays taxes on his income (which includes all income of the business, of course, since the business's income is really just the entrepreneur's income). The business can be sold, like any other piece of personal property owned by the individual, and the sole proprietorship dies when the entrepreneur dies. If the sole proprietor uses a business name for writing or receiving checks or otherwise conducting business, the name should be registered with the applicable secretary of state, typically by filing a simple form and, if required, publishing a legal notice in a local newspaper. Other than that particular formality, there are no special filings associated with creating a sole proprietorship — it is created automatically when the individual begins to conduct business.

2. General Partnership

Unlike a sole proprietorship, which is typically not governed by any specialized statutes since it is really just an individual person conducting business on her own, partnerships are governed by state statutes. Under state law, a general partnership is formed automatically when two or more persons come together as co-owners to conduct a business for profit. Typically, there are two indicia of "co-ownership": shared profit and shared control of the business. Notice that no formal partnership agreement is required, nor is there any requirement that the partners intend to form the partnership — thus, entrepreneurs who seek legal assistance after they have started working together are typically already a general partnership, even though they may not know it. Many entrepreneurs are quite surprised to learn that they are already operating as a general partnership.

Absent an agreement to the contrary, state statutes will say that partners share control and profits equally, regardless of how much capital they have invested in the business or how much time they devote to the business. An entrepreneur who has funded 100 percent of a two-partner business may not expect to only own 50 percent of the partnership. For those reasons and others, it is important to establish the ground rules for the partnership in a written partnership agreement early on.

Although under modern statutes a partnership is considered to be an entity separate from its owners, a partnership is not taxed as a separate legal person. Rather, the income or losses of the business "flow through" to the partners in equal proportions (or as otherwise set forth in a written partnership agreement) and the partners individually pay the partnership's income tax. Similarly, each partner remains personally liable for all debts of the business. Thus, if a business is sued over a contract signed by one partner as agent for the partnership, all partners are personally liable. This outcome may surprise entrepreneurs, particularly if they haven't realized they are in a state law general partnership.

From a fiduciary duty standpoint, partners owe duties of care and loyalty to the partnership as well as the other partners. These duties can be modified if permitted by state statute, but typically the duty of loyalty cannot be eliminated.

3. Limited Partnership

Unlike a general partnership, a limited partnership is not created automatically. Rather, it is created by filing with the secretary of state of the state in which the partnership is created. A limited partnership has two types of partners: "general partners," who have control of the business and have unlimited personal liability for the debts of the partnership; and "limited partners" (typically outside investors), who have no control over the business and have no liability for the partnership's debts. Limited partnerships are governed by state limited partnership statutes, and almost always have a written partnership agreement to govern such matters as the sharing of profits and losses and the authority of the general partner. As with a general partnership, the taxes of the limited partnership are paid by the partners in proportion to their share of the partnership income.

4. Limited Liability Partnership

A limited liability partnership (known as a "limited liability limited partnership" in some states) is created by filing with the secretary of state of the state of formation and is governed by a state statute. In many states, LLPs are limited to certain service-providing professions, such as attorneys or accountants. LLPs are taxed like general partnerships with each partner having to pay tax on her share of the partnership's income, but liability is treated quite differently from a general partnership. States vary on this matter, but under a common approach, each partner is individually liable for his own malpractice or other bad acts, but not for the misconduct or negligence (such as professional malpractice) of his partners. In addition, each partner is liable for all other general business debts of the partnership that are not related to any individual partner's provision of services.

5. Corporation

A corporation is formed by filing Articles of Incorporation with the secretary of state of the state of formation (as further described below in Section C). A corporation is a separate legal person, distinct from its owners. The units of ownership in a corporation are called "shares," and the owners of a corporation are called "shareholders." The shareholders elect a board of directors, who are responsible for the corporation and have fiduciary duties of care and loyalty to the corporation and its shareholders. (Note that the shareholders, in their role as shareholders, do not owe fiduciary duties to the corporation or other shareholders unless they are subject to specialized state law rules for dominant shareholders.) Directors choose officers, such as a president, secretary, and treasurer, who run the corporation on a day-to-day basis.

In a corporation, shareholders are shielded from liability for the debts of the business — it is a so-called limited liability entity. The exception to this liability shield, which is covered extensively in a typical Business Associations or Corporations class, is when conduct of a shareholder leads to "piercing the corporate veil" for that shareholder. Piercing the veil is rare, but is justified where a shareholder has ceased to treat the corporation as a separate legal person, but rather treats it as an extension of the shareholder himself. In extreme examples, shareholders may use the business bank account as a personal account, sign contracts under the shareholder's personal name rather than the corporate name, fail to follow corporate formalities concerning required meetings of the board or shareholders, and bend the corporation to only serve the shareholder's individual interests. If an entrepreneurial venture is organized as a corporation, the lawyer must counsel the entrepreneur to avoid veil-piercing by taking simple steps like establishing a separate corporate bank account and holding and taking minutes at regular board and shareholder meetings.

Income from businesses organized as corporations is taxed in two different ways. A traditional or "C" corporation (named for the subchapter of the Internal Revenue Code that governs this type of entity) is taxed as a separate legal person on its income at the corporate tax rate. Shareholders do not pay tax on the corporation's income. However, if the corporation then declares a dividend and distributes cash or other assets to the shareholders, those shareholders need to pay tax on the income they receive. This phenomenon — where the entity pays tax on its income and then the owners pay tax on the income they receive from the entity in the form of a dividend — is referred to as "double taxation."

If an entrepreneur wants to form a corporation but does not want to be subject to double taxation, she can form the corporation under state law and, if it meets the criteria to do so, file a form with the Internal Revenue Service electing to be taxed as a so-called S-corporation. S-corporations are taxed like partnerships, meaning that the corporation itself does not pay taxes, but rather the income flows through to the shareholders who then each pay tax on their share of the corporation's income. To be classified as an S-corporation, a corporation must have no more than 100 shareholders, all of whom must be individual human beings (and certain rare, specialized entities) who are legal residents of the United States. S-corporations can only issue one class of stock, meaning that the kinds of preferred stock required by many investors and discussed in Chapter 5 are not permissible.

6. Limited Liability Company

A limited liability company is formed by filing Articles of Organization with the secretary of state (as further described below in Section C). An LLC is a separate legal person, distinct from its owners. The owners are called "members." Members are shielded from liability in a similar manner to shareholders of a corporation. Members owe fiduciary duties to the entity and to the other members, but these duties can be cut back significantly in the written document governing the LLC, which is called an "Operating Agreement" or "Limited Liability Company Agreement."

State LLC statutes can vary broadly, but they typically all contain significant opportunity for flexible customization of the entity's governance in an Operating

Agreement. LLCs are often categorized as "member-managed," meaning the entity is run directly by its owners like a general partnership, or "manager-managed," meaning the entity is run by a manager or group of managers elected by the members. There are few limits to the ways in which LLCs are run — some are set up with formal board structures, officers, and members who have limited voting rights other than selecting the board; and others are set up as casual collectives run by a majority who are never really required to have formal meetings. The flexibility of LLCs extends beyond management style and includes the ability to structure different kinds of equity ownership, arguably with even more creativity than equity structures in corporations (see Chapter 5 for a discussion of equity types).

From a tax perspective, LLCs have a choice: they can be taxed on a flow-through basis like a partnership, or they can elect to be taxed as a C-corporation and be subject to double taxation. This flexibility is called "check the box" tax treatment because they can literally check a box on a form filed with the Internal Revenue Service to select their tax treatment.

7. *Benefit Corporations and Low Profit Limited Liability Companies*

Benefit corporations (called "public benefit corporations" in Delaware) are created the same way traditional corporations are — by a filing with the secretary of state. Indeed, benefit corporations are similar to regular corporations in almost every way — they have shareholders who elect directors, directors who choose officers, their corporate veil can be pierced, they can be taxed as "C" or "S" corporations, and so on. The key difference between a benefit corporation and other corporations has to do with their purpose and priorities. The purpose of a regular corporation is to generate profit for the benefit of shareholders. If boards fail to prioritize profit, shareholders can bring a lawsuit against the directors for breach of duty. The purpose of a benefit corporation, on the other hand, is to pursue a mission that is acceptable under the applicable state's benefit statute. If the board of a benefit corporation fails to prioritize its stated purpose — while also balancing the financial interests of the company and shareholders — shareholders can bring a lawsuit against the directors for breach of duty.

The types of purposes that are permissible for benefit corporations vary from state to state. In Delaware, the definition is broad and defines public benefit as "a positive effect (or reduction of negative effects) on one or more categories of persons, entities, communities or interests (other than stockholders in their capacities as stockholders) including, but not limited to, effects of an artistic, charitable, cultural, economic, educational, environmental, literary, medical, religious, scientific or technological nature." In New York, the requirements are slightly tighter, where benefit corporations can have a "general public benefit" that — unlike in Delaware — is required to be measured against a third-party standard, or a "specific public benefit" of the type that a charity would provide.

Like benefit corporations — which are essentially regular corporations with a different guiding purpose than regular corporations — low profit limited liability companies (L3Cs) are regular limited liability companies with a different purpose. Whereas LLCs are generally supposed to prioritize profit over social mission, L3Cs prioritize mission over profit. In all other respects, L3Cs are just like LLCs: members can draft operating agreements to customize economics and governance, the L3C veil can be pierced, L3Cs can be taxed as partnerships or corporations on a check-the-box basis, and so on.

One important note about both benefit corporations and L3Cs is that the statutes governing the entities vary across states and, unlike traditional corporations and LLCs, not every state has such entity types. As of 2020, less than two-thirds of states had benefit corporation statutes, and fewer than that had L3C statutory provisions. Coupled with the statutory variations among states that have those entities, this lack of homogeneity makes lawyers wonder how states will treat other states' benefit corporations or L3Cs, and creates uncertainty and risk that clients will find themselves unable to achieve the goals that led them to choose these entity types to begin with.

When working with social entrepreneurs, lawyers may need to educate their clients about the differences between benefit corporations and B Corps. While benefit corporations are the entities formed under state law and described in this chapter, "B Corp" is a certification applied to companies that seek and are granted the certification from a nonprofit called B Lab. To be certified as a B Corp, a company must meet a variety of standards about its mission and activities, and meet the requirement that it be incorporated as a benefit corporation or organized as a L3C if it is in a state that has one of those entity types.

8. *Nonprofit Corporations and Tax-Exempt Entities*

A nonprofit or "not-for-profit" corporation is formed the same way traditional corporations and public benefit corporations are created: by filing articles of incorporation with the secretary of state of the state in which the corporation is to be created. Nonprofit corporations are governed by a board of directors and have officers, but nonprofits do not have shareholders. No one owns a nonprofit corporation. In most nonprofits, the board of directors is elected annually by the board who is in office at the time of the election; the board, in essence, elects itself and its own successors. (In some nonprofits, there is a small group of people called "members" whose function is to elect the board — but this governance structure is relatively rare. Note that "members" of nonprofits like museums, for example, are generally not members for board election purposes but are just donors.) Nonprofit corporations cannot declare dividends to make distributions to their owners because, as mentioned above, they do not have owners. Similarly, an entrepreneur cannot take equity investors in a nonprofit, since nonprofits do not sell equity securities.

Nonprofits, when created, are still responsible for taxes as C or S corporations. Typically, though, when an entrepreneur establishes a nonprofit corporation, they also want it to become exempt from paying tax on its earnings. Under Section 501(c)(3) of the Internal Revenue Code, nonprofit corporations can apply to become tax exempt entities. To achieve this status, a nonprofit has to meet several criteria including, importantly, that they have an exempt purpose. In a portion of its website with resources for tax exempt entities, the Internal Revenue Service explains that

> [t]he exempt purposes set forth in section 501(c)(3) are charitable, religious, educational, scientific, literary, testing for public safety, fostering national or international amateur sports competition, and preventing cruelty to children or animals.

The term charitable is used in its generally accepted legal sense and includes relief of the poor, the distressed, or the underprivileged; advancement of religion; advancement of education or science; erecting or maintaining public buildings, monuments, or works; lessening the burdens of government; lessening neighborhood tensions; eliminating prejudice and discrimination; defending human and civil rights secured by law; and combating community deterioration and juvenile delinquency.

A nonprofit corporation can apply for tax exempt status with the IRS after being incorporated. If the company is determined by the IRS to be exempt, then it is not required to pay federal tax on income it makes that is importantly related to its purpose, and donors to the organization are generally entitled to a tax deduction in the amount of their donation.

9.   Transferability of Interests in a Business Entity

A traditional way attorneys sought to differentiate entity types has been on the ease with which ownership interests in the entity can be transferred. Under state corporate law, shares of a corporation can be transferred without the approval of the corporation or other shareholders. Under state partnership and LLC law, the economic benefits of ownership in the entity (such as the right to receive profits distributions) can be transferred, but voting and other management rights can only be transferred with the approval of the other partners or members. For an entrepreneurial venture with legal representation, however, this distinction is artificial; a good lawyer will always put a contract into place that governs transferability of equity in the way the client chooses. For a corporation, this may mean restricting the transferability of shares (which would be freely transferable by statute in the absence of a written agreement), and for an LLC, this may mean permitting free transfers of membership interests without other members' approval (which would be restricted by statute in the absence of a written agreement). No matter what the entity type, a contract among members can deliver the desired result, and we see little reason this factor should weigh into decision making on entity choice.

Note that with a nonprofit corporation, there are no shares or shareholders, and so there is no ownership stake to be transferred under state law. Nonprofits can merge with other nonprofits — but again, there is no equity interest to be transferred with nonprofit corporations.

10.   State Variations and Choosing a State of Formation

In determining the specific default rules applicable to the various entity types, lawyers consult applicable state statutes. Although law school Corporations and Business Associations classes may use the Uniform Partnership Act of 1997, the Model Business Corporations Act, or the Model Limited Liability Company Act for instructional purposes, lawyers in practice must look to the current law of their state — which may follow the model or uniform acts closely or may depart significantly. Sometimes, the applicable vocabulary varies by state; for example, the equity owners of a corporation in Delaware are called "stockholders" in the statute, whereas the equity owners of a corporation in California are called "shareholders." Sometimes, more important governance principles are different; for example, a limited liability company member in Delaware does not have the right to withdraw from the LLC unless permitted to do so in the operating agreement, whereas a limited liability company member in Illinois has the right to withdraw from the LLC even if the operating agreement prohibits withdrawal. That said, some state law differences that seem significant can be easily eliminated by contract or in the articles of incorporation; for example, a few states mandate a particular type of weighted director election procedure known as "cumulative voting" but permit corporations to opt out of cumulative voting in their articles of incorporation.

The statutory variations described above are occasionally sufficiently significant that they drive the selection of the state in which an entity is to be formed. Other times, aesthetics will drive state selection — notably the perception that "sophisticated" businesses that are "going places" always form in Delaware. While lawyers may reject this kind of fashion-based state selection, if a start-up is seeking funding from investors who are swayed by such things, it is not illogical to cater to your audience. (That said, we have yet to find a venture capitalist (VC) who walked away from a desirable deal based on state of formation. It is much more common for a VC who has particular state preferences to require the relatively straightforward process of moving the entity to another state immediately prior to the VC investment.)

Lawyers may also feel — correctly — that the corporate law in Delaware is more developed, predictable and robust than that of other states. Lawyers must take the analysis to a deeper level, however, and ask whether the enhanced predictability will make any difference to a business at the start-up phase. While it could be argued that publicly traded companies find recognizable value in a somewhat more predictable set of corporate law outcomes, it doesn't seem that this commonly cited advantage of Delaware law makes a difference to the average start-up.

Oftentimes, new ventures are driven by a more immediate reality when it comes to state selection: cost. When forming in a "foreign" jurisdiction (meaning a state in which the company is not a resident), the venture needs to pay the cost of formation and also the cost of a local "resident agent." In addition, the venture will likely also have to become "qualified to do business" in its actual state of operation, often at the same price it would have paid had it initially just organized in that state — and will have to pay annual fees in both states to keep the entity in good standing. These costs — which can amount to hundreds or more extra dollars each year in filing fees, accountant fees, and attorney fees — make foreign formation a pricey option for smaller start-ups.

Notes and Questions

1. The following chart lays out, in summary form, some of the basic vocabulary and substantive legal differences among the entity types.

Entity Type	Sole Proprietorship	General Partnership	Limited Partnership	Limited Liability Partnership	Limited Liability Company	C-Corporation	S-Corporation	Benefit Corporation	Low Profit Limited Liability Company	Nonprofit Corporation
How to form	Begin operations	Forms automatically under state law when two or more individuals associate to carry on, as co-owners, a business for profit	File Certificate of Limited Partnership or similar document with secretary of state of formation	File Statement of Registration or similar document with secretary of state of formation	File Articles of Organization (aka Certificate of Formation) with secretary of state of formation	File Articles of Incorporation (aka Certificate of Incorporation) with secretary of state of state of formation (known as the "Charter")	File Articles of Incorporation (aka Certificate of Incorporation) with secretary of state of state of formation AND make S-election with IRS	File Articles of Incorporation (aka Certificate of Incorporation) with secretary of state of state of formation	File Articles of Organization (aka Certificate of Formation) with secretary of state of state of formation	File Articles of Incorporation (aka Certificate of Incorporation) with secretary of state of state of formation; apply for federal and state tax exemptions if desire to be tax exempt
Owners	The sole proprietor	Partners	Partners (General Partner and Limited Partners)	Partners	Members	Shareholders	Shareholders	Shareholders	Members	None
Liability	Unlimited personal liability	Unlimited	General Partner has unlimited liability; Limited Partners have limited liability	Each partner's liability generally limited to liabilities arising out of the acts of that partner alone, not acts by other partners	Limited	Limited	Limited	Limited	Limited	Limited

(Continued)

Entity Type	Sole Proprietorship	General Partnership	Limited Partnership	Limited Liability Partnership	Limited Liability Company	C-Corporation	S-Corporation	Benefit Corporation	Low Profit Limited Liability Company	Nonprofit Corporation
Who runs it	The sole proprietor	Partners — each has equal vote and majority rules unless Partnership Agreement says otherwise	General Partner (Limited Partners must have very limited control)	Partners — each has equal vote and majority rules unless Partnership Agreement says otherwise	Flexible — Members or Manager, depending on whether member- or manager-managed, or could have "Board of Managers"	Shareholders elect Board of Directors who in turn elect officers	Shareholders elect Board of Directors who in turn elect officers	Shareholders elect Board of Directors who in turn elect officers	Flexible — Members or Manager, depending on whether member- or manager-managed, or could have "Board of Managers"	Board typically elects its own successors, board also elects officers
Basic governance rules	Whatever sole proprietor desires	Statutory default, as modified by written Partnership Agreement	Statutory default, as modified by written Partnership Agreement	Statutory default, as modified by written Partnership Agreement	Statutory default, as modified by written Operating Agreement	Statutory default, as modified by Bylaws	Statutory default, as modified by Bylaws	Statutory default, as modified by Bylaws	Statutory default, as modified by written Operating Agreement	Statutory default, as modified by Bylaws
Other agreements among equity holders	N/A	Partnership Agreement	Partnership Agreement	Partnership Agreement	Operating Agreement	Shareholders Agreement	Shareholders Agreement	Shareholders Agreement	Operating Agreement	
Tax treatment	Personal	Flow-through	Flow-through	Flow-through	Check the box	Double taxation	Flow-through	Double taxation or flow through depending on if C or S	Check the box	Either taxed as C- or S-corporation or, if apply for tax exempt status, then tax exempt as to income related to purpose

2. Consider the section above on choice of state of formation. How would you communicate with an entrepreneur with visions of grandeur who wants to form a corporation in Delaware when you have determined there are noticeable savings to remaining domestic in your state? What if, like Nevada, your state has a substantively similar statute to Delaware and courts that use Delaware law as precedent? Do you find the appearance-based argument in favor of Delaware persuasive, and how does your answer change if potential investors are experienced?

3. As discussed above, limited liability companies can opt to be taxed as corporations or as flow-through entities. When might you counsel an entrepreneur to form an LLC taxed as a C-corporation, instead of just forming a C-corporation to begin with?

4. The economic and voting rights attached to the equity securities of a corporation (known as "shares" or "stock" and described further in Chapter 5) are generally required to be part of the Articles of Incorporation, which are filed with the secretary of state and are part of the public record. The economic and voting rights attached to the equity securities of a limited liability company (known as "membership units" or "membership interests") are generally part of the Operating Agreement, which (like a Partnership Agreement for a partnership) are not filed and are not part of the public record. What might be some advantages of having the characteristics of an entrepreneurial venture's equity securities remain confidential?

5. Imagine two entrepreneurs come to your office with a business plan and a prototype, and they say they have not yet formed an entity but they want your advice on how to start their business. Is their assumption that they have not formed an entity correct? If not, what complications might arise for their business — or for you as their counsel — as a result of their inadvertent entity selection? Now imagine that these same entrepreneurs have actually begun to sell a small number of products. If one of the entrepreneurs becomes overly optimistic based on limited initial success and signs (i) a five-year lease for office space, and (ii) a purchase order for significant inventory, who is on the hook for these agreements and obligations? If the business fizzles out shortly after these agreements are signed, what happens?

B. CHOOSING THE BEST ENTITY FOR AN ENTREPRENEURIAL VENTURE

As discussed above, if a start-up operates as a sole proprietorship or any type of partnership, the founders will face unlimited liability for the debts of the venture. For this reason, lawyers are loathe to recommend these entity types for clients except in the earliest stages of a business's development, notwithstanding the possible tax advantages offered by flow-through tax treatment. S-corporations, which are state law corporations to which the Internal Revenue Service gives flow-through tax treatment similar to a partnership, are typically not favored for fast-growing start-ups because they include the limitations on ownership and equity issuances discussed above.

The choice for many entrepreneurial ventures, then, is between a C-corporation and a limited liability company. As a threshold matter, we note that clients often find it helpful to group the differences between corporations and LLCs into two categories: financial and economic aspects, and management and governance aspects.

On the financial side, the key difference is that C-corporations are subject to the so-called double taxation discussed above, and limited liability companies benefit from flow-through taxation. In terms of capital structure, both entity types can have multiple classes of ownership interest (see Chapter 5 for a full discussion of equity types) with varying economic rights, so the desire to have, say, "preferred securities," is generally not a differentiating factor between the entities.

On the governance side, corporations have formal governance structures put in place by statute — as noted above, shareholders elect the board of directors, who in turn elect the officers, and officers run the day-to-day business of the corporation. Limited liability companies are significantly more flexible — if desired, they can mimic the corporate governance structure with members electing a board that elects officers; or, if desired, an LLC can operate more like a partnership with members directly running the business; or, if desired, an LLC can be something in between, with members electing a manager who runs the business. From a fiduciary duty standpoint, corporate directors' and officers' duties are clear (they owe duties of loyalty and due care to the corporation and its shareholders), and in most circumstances shareholders are permitted to operate selfishly without regard to other shareholders. For members of an LLC, the duties are more akin to the duties a partner has toward the partnership and her other partners, but can be modified significantly in the operating agreement to more closely match the duties in a corporation.

For social entrepreneurs, the choices are somewhat more daunting. Many mission-driven founders assume they should form tax-exempt nonprofits, and feel bashful at the idea that they may want to later sell their business when they are ready to exit the venture. Others may feel that a benefit corporation or L3C structure best matches their goals, even if warned of the potential uncertainty associated with these choices. Still other social entrepreneurs may be comfortable with traditional entity types, believing they can achieve their goals and possibly reap other benefits from a predictable, established structure.

In the following readings, various commentators disagree as to the optimal structure for an entrepreneurial venture, underscoring the difficulty of reaching the right decision and the need to develop advice tailored to the particular venture.

STARTING FROM SCRATCH: A LAWYER'S GUIDE TO REPRESENTING A START-UP COMPANY

Richard A. Mann, Michael O'Sullivan, Larry Robbins & Barry S. Roberts
56 Ark. L. Rev. 773 (2004)

. . .

In a 1994 article examining the choice of entity by high-tech start-ups, Professor Joseph Bankman argued that, because of tax advantages, using an entity with pass-through taxation is a better choice than using a corporation. Given that the start-up costs of a high-tech company are tax deductible, his premise was that a partnership structure would allow the inevitable losses in the early stages of the start-up to pass through to each individual partner. These losses could be used to offset income from other sources and reduce the partner's tax liability. On the other hand, if the new entity is a corporation, only the corporation can deduct the losses. As Bankman points out, "the newly-formed company, however, has no material source of present or past income against which to deduct the expense." Yet, Bankman found that most start-ups incorporate and thereby forego many of the tax advantages that partnerships receive. While the theory regarding the value of losses is interesting, as a practical matter, these losses have little if any value to the traditional venture fund supported by institutional investors.

By mid-1996 every state had enacted an LLC statute. LLCs became popular because they combined the best attribute of partnerships, pass-through taxation, with the best attribute of corporations, limited liability. Therefore, some commentators have argued that the LLC is the best initial choice for entrepreneurs. On the other hand, one of the advantages of incorporating is separating equity ownership from control, an attribute not always present with an LLC. LLCs are specifically designed to be more flexible than corporations and can be organized as manager-managed entities. However, venture capitalists appear to be cool to this approach: "Conventional wisdom holds that venture capital firms generally do not invest in limited liability companies."

Not surprisingly, the choice of entity for high-tech start-ups often is driven by their subsequent need for additional money from venture funding. Venture capitalists invest in companies that statistically are likely never to go public. As private company investors, the venture capitalist seeks as much certainty as possible in an investment. In this respect corporations have the advantage because they have many years of case law providing much greater predictability relating to shareholder rights and director duties. Furthermore, even those arguing that the LLC should be the entity of choice, acknowledge that if the start-up ever goes public, the market will require it to incur the costs of restructuring as a corporation. Nevertheless, they contend that the transaction costs associated with a restructuring are less than the tax benefits derived from starting out as an LLC.

In explaining the higher incidence of incorporation over partnership formation, despite the theoretical tax advantages of not incorporating, Bankman suspected that entrepreneurs simply did not value tax savings as a priority. Some entrepreneurs were not even aware of the tax consequences of incorporating. Since Bankman's study, LLCs have become more widely accepted as a viable start-up entity choice. Nevertheless, corporations remain the preferred vehicle for high-tech start-ups. The following is an explanation for the persistence of incorporation despite the tax advantages of an LLC:

> To the extent participants in this market continue to choose the corporate form over theoretically available LLC structures, it may be because innovation may not promise sufficient advantages over the customary structure. . . . Venture capital firms structure investment relationships through legal forms that create significant rights in firm governance. If these rights are valuable, sophisticated investors are not likely to experiment with organizational innovations that carry uncertain consequences.

In addition to corporate governance issues, most venture capital firms have restrictions in their fund documents that prohibit investing in flow-through entities due to certain adverse income tax consequences to their limited partners. Further, the flow through of losses to pension plans and other tax-exempt entities is in most cases meaningless, so there may be no tax advantage ever under any circumstances. In addition, the body of case law available to interpret stockholder rights, and director duties is well established for corporations but virtually barren for partnerships and LLCs. Finally, venture investors look for methods to enhance cash flow after a start-up reaches profitability. If net operating losses have flowed through to investors, the losses are no longer available to the enterprise. For corporations, the incurred losses are available to shelter future taxable income and support future tax-free growth of the enterprise.

An entrepreneur should weigh the advantages and disadvantages of each business entity, taking into account whether the nature of the entity matches the type of investor that is being targeted. For example, a venture that can be financed by a few high net worth investors may be a candidate for operating as an LLC, but a biotechnology company requiring institutional investors would not typically be a candidate.

. . .

CHOICE OF ENTITY FOR A VENTURE CAPITAL START-UP: THE MYTH OF INCORPORATION
Daniel S. Goldberg, 55 Tax Law. 923 (2002)

Most tax professionals would advise entrepreneurs to commence their start-up business as a limited liability company (LLC), which, absent an election, is treated as a partnership for federal tax purposes. That advice reflects the notion that tax considerations are among the most important in choosing an entity form, and LLCs offer the advantages of partnership treatment yet provide the limited liability of corporations.

In the high-tech start-up industry, however, entrepreneurs are often advised to begin business as a corporation, albeit sometimes an S corporation if the entity can qualify. This advice is based largely on several perceived operating advantages which are either more easily achieved by or require the corporate form.

Most important of these perceived advantages, perhaps, is the need for the corporate form to achieve the most sought after exit strategies of a public offering or a tax-free acquisition by a public company, sometimes referred to as the "home run" exit strategies. Another perceived advantage of the corporate form is its facility to allow for stock options to employees, giving them additional work incentives through compensation that does not deplete the start-up company's cash resources. Another commonly perceived corporate advantage lies in satisfying the desire of investors to invest in corporations rather than other types of entities. These investors may be early stage investors, sometimes referred to as "angel investors" or simply "angels," or later stage investors, sometimes referred to as "venture capitalists." Venture capitalists sometimes form investment funds with several participating investors, called "venture capital funds." Finally, advisors appear to view the tax advantages of LLCs as more theoretical than real, neither of great magnitude nor importance to any of the participants in the venture.

This article asserts that advisors who advise immediate incorporation are relying largely on myths that the corporation, rather than the LLC, is the more desirable entity for a start-up seeking venture capital funding. This article will review briefly the most important federal tax advantages enjoyed by the LLC over the corporation and then set forth, examine, and debunk the myths of incorporation.

II. TAX CONSIDERATIONS IN CHOICE OF ENTITY, IN GENERAL

A. Net Profits

The most salient aspect of partnership taxation, which includes the tax treatment of LLCs that are treated as partnerships for tax purposes, is the fact that only a single level of tax is incurred when operating in a partnership structure. The partnership itself is not subject to tax. Rather the structure involves what is generally referred to as pass-through treatment. Thus, if a partnership has income, the income is taxed at the partner level only. And, if a partnership has losses, the losses pass through to the partners, to offset partners' other income (subject to outside basis limitations, at-risk rules, and passive activity loss rules). In the discussion that follows, the terms partnership and limited liability company are used interchangeably.

In contrast to the single tax, pass-through character of partnership taxation, a corporation (other than an electing S corporation) is treated as an entity for tax purposes. As such, a corporation's income is subject to a corporate level tax, and distributions of that income are subject, in general, to a shareholder level tax as dividend income, unless otherwise excused under the Code.

. . .

B. Net Losses

The partnership/LLC structure also facilitates the pass-through of losses incurred in the business to the partners. Each partner includes on his tax return his distributive share of the partnership's losses from operations.

In contrast, losses incurred by a corporation (other than an electing S corporation) remain in the corporation to be carried back or carried forward to the extent there is income to offset in past or future years. But the losses are not available for use by the shareholders themselves. This carryover rule, however, is subject to some qualifications. The most important qualification for start-up companies is the application of the corporate change of ownership rules. While in theory the loss carries over to offset future income of the corporation, the change of ownership rules could cause the loss to become useless after a few rounds of new equity financing, thereby potentially causing the corporate losses to be largely wasted if no income is earned by the corporation in the interim.

. . .

For an owner of an equity interest in the business enterprise, choosing the partnership structure over the corporate form can result in substantial current tax savings. The pass-through of losses to partners should make the partnership/LLC form attractive to U.S. domestic angel (early stage) investors, particularly individuals and closely held entities. From a financial reporting standpoint, however, it may involve a disadvantage for many venture capital investors and venture capital investment funds which would prefer not to show losses for financial reporting purposes.

III. FREQUENTLY STATED REASONS TO USE CORPORATE FORM FOR VENTURE CAPITAL START-UP: THE MYTHS

As set forth in Part II, comparison of the partnership/LLC and corporate forms generally would lead one to choose the partnership/LLC form at the early stages of a business. At a later time, when one of the home run exit strategies comes within reach, conversion to a corporation could be desirable and indeed could be accomplished at that point.

Nevertheless, planners have frequently advised, and entrepreneurs have frequently chosen, to commence their enterprises as corporations rather than as LLCs. There are several reasons generally given for this choice of entity. The material that follows examines those often-stated reasons for incorporation at commencement of the enterprise.

A. *"To Go Public or Merge with a Public Corporation, You Must Eventually Convert to a Corporation. Might as Well Start There and Avoid the Potential Tax Problems and Expenses of Later Incorporation."*

The argument proceeds that the optimal exit strategies, the home run strategies of going public or engaging in a merger, require the use of the corporate structure. Accordingly, because the business entity needs to adopt the corporate form eventually, it might as well incorporate at the start. An alternate form of this argument is that a start-up business needs to incorporate to attract venture capital funding because incorporating demonstrates that the entity is serious about quickly achieving one of the home run exit strategies.

The tax advantage of incorporation lies largely in the ability of the shareholders of a corporation to achieve greater liquidity and risk diversification in their investment without incurring immediate tax. These objectives can be achieved by either exit strategy: (1) becoming a public company, a status available only to entities treated as corporations for tax purposes, or (2) being acquired in a tax-free reorganization, also a type of transaction reserved for corporations under the tax law.

1. *Going Public*

Developing a public market for a corporation's shares is easily accomplished from a tax point of view; a corporation becomes a public company by issuing shares in an initial public offering for cash. Thereafter, sales by the founder shareholders of a portion of their stock, within the limits allowed under the securities law, permits the founder shareholders to diversify their investment by incurring gain and paying tax only with respect to the shares that are sold. Beginning the business under a corporate structure facilitates this process because the entity that will be public is already in existence.

Beginning the business's operational existence as a partnership or an LLC, however, does not create insurmountable hurdles for the business or its owners. It is a rather simple matter to convert the partnership/LLC to a corporation either before or as a part of the public offering of a newly formed corporation's shares under section 351. An incorporation of an LLC can follow three forms: (1) the LLC can transfer its assets to the corporation in exchange for stock; (2) the LLC can distribute its assets to its members who then contribute those assets to the corporation in exchange for stock and; (3) the members can contribute their interests to the corporation in exchange for stock. . . .

The incorporation of the LLC can also take place as part of the initial public offering. . . .

2.   *Tax-Free Reorganization*

The other sought-after exit strategy is the acquisition of the corporation by a public company whose shares are readily saleable because they have a public market. The acquisition would be tax free to the corporation and to its shareholders[.] . . .

In the merger, the shareholders of the merged corporation, sometimes referred to as the target, receive their acquiring company shares tax free. But those shareholders take a basis in the shares they receive equal to the basis they had in the target company's shares. In that sense, the tax on the disposition is deferred until sale or other taxable disposition of those shares. Those shares, presumably, can now be sold piecemeal, so that the target company's shareholders will have achieved liquidity and the opportunity to diversify their investment. Moreover, in the event the target company's shareholders receive some cash (but not so much cash as to disqualify the transaction from reorganization treatment), the shareholders will recognize gain (or sometimes dividend income) to the extent of the cash received.

In contrast, the acquisition by an acquiring corporation of the assets of an LLC or of all of the members' interests in the LLC for stock may or may not be tax free to the members, depending upon whether, immediately after the transaction, the target LLC or its members control (own at least 80% of the stock of) the acquiring corporation. If they do, the transaction will qualify under section 351 for the LLC or the members, as the case may be, as transferors. Such control by the target LLC or its members would be unusual indeed, so that in general, the LLC transaction will constitute a taxable exchange for the members.

[The author concludes that, with planning, this obstacle can be overcome as follows:]

[T]he cautious advisor could recommend incorporation once the business reached sufficient size or profitability to be an attractive acquisition candidate. Admittedly, in that case an incorporation decision would have to be faced with no assurance that a reorganization or public offering would follow. Subsequent liquidation of the corporation with high value, low basis assets could be costly if the exit scenario never develops because there would be no corporate net operating loss carryover to shield the corporate level gain on liquidation. As a result, choosing the right time to incorporate will be something of a balancing act and require careful judgment, knowledge of the market, and perhaps a willingness to take some tax risk. These tax risks can be minimized with appropriate foresight, however, and should not constitute a serious impediment to operating the business as an LLC until an incorporation decision becomes appropriate.

. . .

Thus, the incorporation phase of the life cycle of a putative public company or tax-free acquisition target need not begin at the inception of the business. Incorporation can be accomplished before or as part of a public offering or in advance of acquisition discussions with a potential acquiring corporation. The extra expense involved in forming an LLC is minimal for an enterprise that will be going public or the target of a lucrative merger offer. If neither opportunity develops, however, then the costs of incorporation will be saved, which will offset the costs of formation of an LLC, and in the interim, the tax advantages of LLC treatment will be enjoyed — a benefit that may very well be substantial.

. . . If, on the other hand, incorporation at the inception of the business is chosen and neither home run exit strategy becomes viable and the start-up business must be disposed of in some other way, incorporation will result in substantial and expensive tax disadvantages. . . .

[I]f the exit strategy involves a taxable sale, the partnership structure is likely to be less expensive from a tax perspective than the corporate structure. More importantly, the parties can get themselves out of a partnership or LLC structure often without tax and always without entity level tax. This is not so with a corporation. Finally, if it becomes desirable for a business begun as a partnership to be a corporation, either to raise money or in order to participate in a tax-free acquisition with another corporation, then a conversion to a corporation can generally be accomplished without incurring tax. The reverse is not true. One cannot convert a corporation into an LLC tax-free.

B. *"We Need Stock and Options to Compensate Our New Employees."*

Stock options, whether nonqualified or qualified incentive stock options (ISOs), have been a useful tool in attracting talented employees to work for cashpoor but prospect-rich high-tech and not so high-tech Internet start-up companies. Being able to offer a software developer 10,000 stock options, allowing the employee to share in the good fortune of the company when the home run scenario occurs, can be important to a cash-strapped start-up.

Corporate stock options are well understood by both the grantor corporations that issue them and the grantees. They can take the form of either non-qualified options (sometimes called non-statutory options) or ISOs. If the options are non-statutory or nonqualified options, then in general, the recipient does not realize income when he receives them. Rather, income is realized when the options are exercised by the recipient and the measure of that income is the so-called spread — the difference between the exercise price and value of the stock at the time of exercise. At that time, however, the corporation will be entitled to deduct that same amount in computing its taxable income.

On the other hand, if the options are statutory or ISOs, then no income is realized by the service provider either upon receipt or exercise of the option for regular tax purposes. . . . Further, gain on sale of the stock received upon exercise of an ISO is eligible for long-term capital gain rates if the stock is held for the requisite long-term holding period. No deduction, however, is allowed to the corporation upon exercise of the ISO or upon sale by the option holder of the stock. To qualify as an ISO, certain statutory requirements must be satisfied, including the requirements that the strike price must be at the fair market value of the stock determined at the time of grant and the employee must actually pay for the shares at exercise.

One could fashion a similar plan creating options (nonqualified only) to purchase partnership/LLC interests. The exercise of the option, as in the case of a corporation, will result in income to the option holder in the amount of the spread (the excess of the value of the partnership interest over the option exercise price) and a deduction to the partnership[.] . . .

Alternatively, in lieu of options, the LLC could grant actual profits interests in the LLC to the service providers (as distinguished from interests in the capital of the LLC). The profits interests could take the form of Class B Member Units with zero beginning capital account balances. As such, the Class B units would have no claim on the assets of the LLC if the LLC were liquidated immediately.

Under this scenario, a new service provider member should have no income as a result of receiving the profits interest. This result stems from the theory that an interest in future profits has only speculative and undeterminable value at the time of receipt and therefore does not constitute income upon receipt. Upon hypothetical liquidation of the LLC at the time of the service provider's receipt of the profits interest, all of the LLC's property would be distributed to the capital contributor members who have capital accounts in the newly formed LLC equal to the value of their contributions or their restated capital account balances if the LLC's assets have been revalued. The capital contributor members have priority and would receive the first amount of liquidation proceeds up to the amount of their capital account balances in the LLC, which would be equal to the value of the LLC's property at that time, leaving no liquidation proceeds for distribution to holders of a profits interest.

The Service generally accepts this theory and result[.] . . . Although granting of a profits interest has different economic consequences than the granting of a capital interest, it generally accomplishes the parties' objectives and has substantially more benign tax consequences.

. . .

It cannot be gainsaid that partnership/LLC interests are more difficult to understand and their tax treatment is subject to more uncertainty than corporate stock. Moreover, a profits interest in such an entity or a phantom interest, both alternatives to actual options to purchase partnership interests, may very well be regarded suspiciously by the prospective employee. Employees are likely to be predisposed toward stock options, like Microsoft millionaires received. Founders may also be more comfortable with stock and stock options. Even a unitized partnership or LLC, having units instead of bare percentage interests, may prove unsatisfactory to prospective employees. In sum, the corporate structure does carry the advantage of simplicity if ownership options for employees are a significant factor in choosing a structure.

. . .

C. "Venture Capitalists Demand to Invest in Corporations."

This third, often-cited reason for choosing the corporate structure has some currency. It is grounded in the fact that venture capitalists are typically investment fund partnerships which invest their constituent partners' money. The real investors are the partners in the fund and they may be pension funds and other non-tax-paying entities like university endowments or foreign investors.

Tax-exempt investors tend to prefer the corporate form for their investments in order to avoid unrelated business income. Also, foreign investors tend to prefer the corporate form for their U.S. investments in order to avoid being deemed to be engaged in a U.S. trade or business through a permanent establishment, which is generally the situation for foreign partners of a partnership engaged in

U.S. business. Such a status for the foreign investor would require U.S. tax filings and possibly tax payments.

1. Tax-Exempt Investors

A tax-exempt organization's distributive share of income from an LLC is treated like income from the LLC's underlying activities for purposes of the unrelated business income tax (UBIT), as if the income were earned directly by the organization. The tax-exempt organization's distributive share of the trade or business income of an LLC is characterized as trade or business income of the tax-exempt organization, therefore, and is subject to income tax as unrelated business taxable income under UBIT. As such, it is taxable to those otherwise tax-exempt entities and requires the filing of special income tax returns by them. This treatment is in contrast to dividends, interest, gains from sale of stock and other portfolio (non-business) income, which are tax free to them.

Many tax-exempt investors demand that any venture capital fund in which they invest avoids generating income that would subject them to UBIT on the income from the fund and will decline to invest without assurance of this protection. If the fund intends to invest in LLCs, these organizations will not invest in the venture capital fund.

While the reaction described above by tax-exempt entities exists, it tends to be exaggerated. With some advance planning, the tax-exempt entities themselves can overcome the UBIT problems. The UBIT issue only becomes a problem if and when operating income is earned by the portfolio company of the fund. At the point that a portfolio company turns the corner and begins to earn a profit, it can incorporate and avoid the realization of UBIT income for its tax-exempt fund investors.

Choosing the correct point in time for incorporation may be problematic. . . .

A [more] dependable method for avoiding UBIT problems resulting from the venture capital fund partnership investing in LLCs is the creation for the venture capital fund of a corporate entity as one of its partners. UBIT-shy investors can invest in the corporation, which in turn will invest those funds in the venture capital fund partnership. Operating income earned by a portfolio company would pass through to the investor corporation, incur a tax at that level (in lieu of UBIT at the tax-exempt entity's level) and be passed through again to the tax-exempt entity, less income tax paid by the corporation, as dividend income, which is not subject to UBIT. Alternatively, the tax-exempt entity can create a corporation itself to invest in the venture capital fund or several such funds.

Economically, this plan is roughly comparable to the tax-exempt entity paying the tax on the UBIT income, but without having to keep track of that income itself or file the special forms required by the UBIT regime. . . .

2. Foreign Investors

In general, foreign investors do not want to be engaged in business in the U.S. because it subjects them to U.S. tax on their U.S. source business income and other income effectively connected with the U.S. business. A foreign investor in a venture capital fund partnership that invests in portfolio companies formed as

LLCs is deemed to be engaged in the underlying business of the LLCs. The consequence of this rule is that a foreign partner's distributive share of a partnership's U.S. business income is subject to U.S. tax to the foreign partner as U.S. effectively connected income. Moreover, the Service has ruled that even the foreign partner's sale of his partnership interest will be subject to U.S. tax if the partnership or any of its portfolio LLCs had a U.S. office or other fixed place of business in the U.S.

The solution to the problem, however, is not to restrict the fund's investments to corporations, but rather to have foreign investors invest in the fund through a special purpose foreign or domestic corporation. This will insulate the foreign investor from being deemed to engage in U.S. business.

. . .

E. *"The Path for Venture Capital Investments in Corporations Is Well Plowed, with Certain Arrangements During Various Rounds of Financing Becoming Standard. To Use an LLC for This Purpose Would Require Reinvention of the Wheel."*

The merit of this argument derives largely from the fact that a venture capital investor focuses much of his interest on the home run exit strategies — the public offering and merger scenarios. The familiar venture capital investment documents therefore contain detailed provisions for conversion of the investor's preferred stock to common, dilution, and anti-dilution and registration rights, concepts often regarded as relevant only to corporations.

In fact, provision for these eventualities can be incorporated in an LLC operating agreement to mirror the terms of a typical corporate agreement. For example, the LLC operating agreement can provide for classes of units (like stock) instead of percentage interests and governance with a board of directors and corporate type officers such as president, vice-president, and secretary. Also, provision can be made for conversion to a corporation by means of incorporation, pursuant to which classes of units are converted to corresponding classes of stock. In sum, the type of entity used should not necessarily restrict the type of deals that can be struck by the parties. Indeed, in many respects, the LLC allows for greater flexibility than the corporate structure, especially with regard to distributions and the allocation of tax attributes during operations as an LLC.

F. *"Venture Capitalists Are Used to the Corporate Form and Are Largely Unaware of and Unconcerned with the Tax Advantages of LLCs over Corporations."*

As the economic world changes, the players must adapt. If LLCs offer significant tax advantages over corporations to the owners of those entities, then the market will favor businesses that adopt the LLC structure over those that adopt the corporate structure. Successful venture capitalists in start-up situations will recognize this and presumably gravitate toward that structure. One should therefore expect that over time, the LLC structure will become a familiar one to investors, and the tax advantages will become widely known and sought.

IV. CONCLUSION

The principal lesson to be taken from this article is that the choice of entity in a start-up situation should be made with care, taking into account the advantages of each available structure. It is likely that upon full consideration of the issues discussed in this article and the probable short-term and long-term outcomes for the business, the LLC will prove to be the best choice in most start-up situations, particularly where a hybrid structure is not feasible or is too expensive to institute. Even if the LLC structure is chosen at inception and it proves to be inferior to the corporate structure in a particular situation, the parties can change the structure to a corporate one, or a hybrid, with relative ease and cost efficiency. It is this flexibility of the LLC that is one of its most significant advantages. In contrast, it is generally very costly to go from a corporation to an LLC.

THE RATIONAL EXUBERANCE OF STRUCTURING VENTURE CAPITAL START-UPS
Victor Fleischer, 57 Tax L. Rev. 137 (2003)

The venture capital market imploded in 2001. It was a devastating year for VC investors; the average portfolio lost nearly one-third of its value. With losses, not gains, now on everyone's mind, this Article takes the bursting of the dot com bubble as an opportunity to reevaluate the tax structure of venture capital start-ups. Prior commentators have pointed out that venture capital start-ups are structured in a tax-inefficient manner, particularly with respect to losses. A typical start-up is organized as a corporation under state law, which means that it is treated as a separate entity from its owners for tax purposes. If a start-up instead were organized as a partnership or limited liability company (LLC), it could elect pass-through treatment for tax purposes. The gains or (more likely) the losses of the new business would flow through to the investors, with each investor recognizing its share of taxable income or loss. A start-up's tax losses are potentially very valuable to certain investors. Because a start-up typically is organized as a corporation, however, its tax losses get trapped at the entity level and only can be carried forward as a net operating loss (NOL), which is less valuable. Lawyers who advise venture capital professionals understand the tax effects of structuring a start-up as a corporation. The corporate law differences between an LLC and a privately-held corporation are relatively minor. Why, then, do nearly all start-ups choose the seemingly less tax-efficient structure? Should post-bubble deal planners revise the standard deal structure to better account for losses?

Conventional wisdom attributes the choice of deal structure to a kind of "irrational exuberance." People are foolishly biased towards thinking about gains, not losses. Entrepreneurs and venture capitalists, dreaming of gains, discount the value of tax losses generated by a start-up. . . .

This Article argues that even in the post-bubble era the exuberance of venture capital deal planners is rational, or, at least, that there is a method to the madness. There is surely some truth in the observation that start-ups are organized in a tax-inefficient manner: Partnerships are, on paper, more tax-efficient than corporations. But various "frictions" — nontax business costs such as transaction costs, information problems, reputational concerns, and adverse accounting treatment — currently prevent deal planners from using the theoretically tax-favorable form. If these frictions wear down over time, there may well be more start-ups organized as partnerships. But for now I think it is a mistake to conclude that start-ups are organized irrationally, or to accept the conventional wisdom that a casino mentality or some other cognitive bias explains the behavior of deal planners.

I make four main points. First, the tax losses are not as valuable as they might seem; tax rules prohibit many investors from capturing the full benefit of the losses. Second, the venture capital professionals who structure the deals do not share personally in the losses, so they have little reason to care about the tax effects of the losses. Third, gains are taxed more favorably if the start-up is organized as a corporation from the outset, and again, this favorable treatment of gains is especially attractive to the venture capital professionals — further evidence that agency costs may be playing a role. Fourth, corporations are less complex than partnerships: Organizing as a corporation minimizes legal costs and simplifies employee compensation and exit strategy.

. . .

II.   THE PUZZLE

Entrepreneurs are optimists. They believe that their ideas, like the children of Lake Wobegon, are all better than average. This cognitive bias leads to a heightened sense of confidence and control, blunting the perception of risk and masking the likelihood of failure. In a recent study, more than one-third of Silicon Valley engineers rated their performance among the top 5% of all engineers, and nearly 90% placed their performance in the top 25%. Given this cognitive bias, the gambler's mentality of Silicon Valley would appear to be a plausible explanation for why start-ups are organized as corporations. A behavioral law and economics approach would suggest that entrepreneurs and venture capitalists are foolishly optimistic and should pay more attention to losses. Should sober-minded and dispassionate lawyers throw a wet blanket over this irrational exuberance?

In fact, while it may be true that entrepreneurs and venture capitalists are overly optimistic, it does not follow necessarily that this cognitive bias drives the choice of organizational form. Optimism in the venture capital industry can be a conversation-stopper, just as risk aversion can be used improperly as an intellectual crutch to explain institutional arrangements like hedging or insurance. If anything, recent data show a lack of correlation between optimism bias and deal structure: Post-bubble investors have displayed signs of pessimism, not optimism, and yet deal structures largely remain the same. Optimism bias is an unsatisfying explanation, and the importance of the puzzle — millions of dollars of tax losses left on the table, year after year — warrants a closer look.

A.   The Alternative Structures: C Corp and Pass-Throughs

The choice of whether to incorporate a business venture sometime turns on the so-called "double tax" of corporate earnings, once at the entity level and again at the shareholder level when earnings are distributed. In the discussion that follows, however, the double tax is a minor issue, as most start-ups do not have income (and thus no taxable income) in the first few years of existence. For start-ups, the treatment of losses is the key to the puzzle. It should be noted, however, that the double taxation of gains can impact the tax liability of investors on exit. In particular, using a pass-through structure has the distinct advantage of allowing a buyer to get a step-up in basis on an asset sale while the seller pays only one level of tax, while a C corporation's shareholders would face a second level of tax on liquidation. . . . For the most part, however, the main advantage of the pass-through structure is the pass-through of losses, and that is where the discussion below focuses.

. . .

III.   WHY PARTNERSHIP TAX LOSSES ARE LESS ATTRACTIVE THAN THEY SEEM

The value of tax losses generated by a start-up organized as a partnership depends on whether the LP investors [meaning passive investors who are not actively participating in the business] have taxable income to offset and whether the LPs can use the losses immediately. Of the four major classes of venture capital investors — U.S. individuals, U.S. corporations, tax-exempt investors, and foreign investors — only a subset of one class, widely-held U.S. corporations with current tax liability, can use the losses fully and is likely to prefer the pass-through structure. For other investors, the pass-through structure is actually disadvantageous, as it either creates new tax liabilities or eliminates tax benefits available in the C corp structure. Moreover, the venture capital professionals who structure the deals do not share in the losses, so they have little reason to pay attention to the tax effects of losses.

. . .

There is one key class of investors not subject to any significant tax law restrictions: corporate LPs. The tax losses generated by the pass-through structure are potentially valuable to corporate LPs; widely-held corporations are not subject to the passive loss rules, and many corporations have current tax liability that they would like to shelter. Some corporations do invest in start-ups, and one would expect such investors to push for the investment to be structured in the most tax-efficient form. For example, Intel owns several funds that invest strategically in start-ups. When Intel invests in a start-up organized as a partnership, and the start-up generates tax losses in the early years of the venture, Intel may use the tax losses generated from that investment to offset taxable income from its normal business operations. If, on the other hand, the start-up is organized as a corporation, and Intel's investment falls short of the 80% threshold needed to bring the start-up within Intel's consolidated tax return, Intel cannot benefit from the start-up's losses. Why, then, are corporate LPs content with the C corp structure?

Three nontax factors explain why corporate investors traditionally play a small role in venture capital investing and why, when they do invest in venture capital, they prefer the C corp structure: (1) accounting treatment, (2) the passive nature of the relationship between the LPs and the start-up, and (3) the networking bond between the venture capitalists and tax-exempt LPs.

Corporate managers focus heavily on reported GAAP earnings, not after-tax returns. A corporate taxable investor in the pass-through structure would see an increase in after-tax earnings compared to the C corp structure, but the losses that generate tax savings would depress reported earnings on the corporate investor's income statement to shareholders. If the start-up is organized as a corporation, a minority investor must use the "equity method" — where losses are immediately reflected on the income statement — only if the interest exceeds 20%. But if the corporate investor's interest is less than 20%, as would usually be the case for a corporate LP investing in a start-up though a venture capital fund, the corporate LP may use the "cost method," in which gains or losses are not recognized on the income statement until the investment is sold. And so in the usual case where a start-up suffers early losses that may be offset by later gains, the cost method results in a prettier picture for shareholders and analysts. If, on the other hand, the start-up is organized as a partnership, then an interest of just 3-5% requires use of the equity method. The start-up's losses depress reported earnings even though the true value of the investment is the same regardless of form.

. . .

The passive nature of the relationship between the LPs and the start-up is a second nontax factor that discourages corporate investors from entering venture capital-managed funds. Corporate managers like to take an active role in their investments, based on their expertise in the corporation's underlying business. Corporations invest in start-ups only when they believe they can create value by taking on an active role in advising the start-up, thus assuming a role usually performed by the venture capitalists. The presence of the venture capitalists then makes little sense, as it simply adds another layer of complexity to the management structure. Empirical results show that this logic holds up in the real world. Corporate venture investments perform on par with noncorporate investments only when there is a strategic fit between the corporate investor and the start-up.

A third nontax factor that discourages venture capitalists from courting corporate LPs is the value of the networking bond between the venture capitalists and tax-exempt LPs. Venture capital professionals often have close relationships with the tax-exempt investors in their funds. Tax exempts are long-term relationship investors likely to make repeat investments with the same professionals over time. Venture capitalists like the passive approach that tax-exempts take to their investments, leaving the professionals with broad discretion over the management of the investments in portfolio companies.

Corporate LPs, on the other hand, are meddlesome. As noted above, they are more likely to seek an active role (or at least a monitoring role) with respect to the portfolio companies. There may even be an increased risk that the corporate LP may appropriate the intellectual property of the portfolio company. Moreover, it is difficult for venture capital professionals to develop relationships with corporate managers, even over the 10-year period of a fund, as turnover rates are much higher at corporations than at tax-exempts like CalPERS or TIAA-CREF.

Finally, corporate LPs have a well-earned reputation for being fickle investors who do not always live up to their funding commitments. When a venture fund is formed, the LPs do not contribute cash up front. Rather, each LP makes a commitment to contribute cash when a capital call is issued, which occurs over a period of two to four years as the venture capital fund identifies worthy investments. Default rates among corporate LPs are higher than among tax-exempts; this has been especially true in recent years.

In sum, key tax and nontax factors make the tax losses — the central advantage of the pass-through structure — worth less than they appear. The lack of attention paid to tax losses is not irrational or based on myth, but rather makes sense in the context of the current tax rules, accounting rules, and institutional investment market.

. . .

V.   COMPLEXITY AND THE C CORP ADVANTAGE

It has been easier, historically, to create and run a start-up organized as a corporation rather than as a partnership or LLC. Lawyers and deal planners are becoming more adept at addressing the complexities associated with pass-through entities, but some tricky issues remain. It is worth highlighting three areas that illustrate how the corporate form is simpler and easier: employee compensation, corporate governance, and exit strategy.

A.   Compensating Employees Is Simpler

For an entrepreneur thinking about forming or joining a new business, compensation issues make the C corp structure more attractive than the pass-through structure. Partnership tax law treats any employee with an equity stake as a partner, complicating compensation issues and increasing tax liabilities for the employees. The chief obstacle relates to the tax treatment of partnership options[.]

. . .

A venture capital start-up using the C corp structure typically creates an option pool to entice talented employees and reduce the amount of cash compensation necessary to hire competitively. It generally is assumed that partnership options are taxed much the same as stock options, but there is little authority and much uncertainty surrounding this area.

The granting of a partnership option is relatively unproblematic, as it is accepted that the grant of the option is not a taxable event to either the entrepreneur or the partnership, unless the option has a "readily ascertainable fair market value" when granted, which normally will not be the case. . . .

There are additional complications when the employee exercises the option. If the option gives the holder the right to acquire a profits interest, it is unclear what amount, if any, is taxable at exercise. If the option gives the holder the right to acquire a capital interest, then it is clear that some amount should be taxable at exercise, but it is unclear how this amount should be measured. Moreover, assuming some amount is taxable to the holder, then the partnership should receive a deduction, but it is unclear how the deduction may be allocated among the various existing and incoming partners. It is also unclear whether the exercise is a taxable event to the historic partners as a deemed sale of a portion of partnership assets to the incoming partner. As the assets of the start-up will have appreciated in value at the time of the exercise, the historic partners risk accelerating a tax bill at a time when they are unlikely to have cash with which to pay the tax. Finally, it is also worth noting that partnership options make it more difficult to maintain proper capital accounts.

Partnership options may also have "bad" accounting treatment, meaning that it may be necessary for companies to treat partnership options as a current expense on the income statement, thereby depressing reported earnings. . . .

Finally, the complexity of drafting partnership options cannot be dismissed. Although the theory is relatively simple for those familiar with partnership tax principles, the mechanics are difficult. In particular, the flexibility and variability of partnership agreements with regard to the allocation of income and loss and the maintenance of capital accounts makes the drafting extremely tricky. . . .

This complexity not only increases legal costs, it could make it more difficult to attract talented employees. Unlike executives of public companies, start-up employees often do not retain counsel, instead relying on the company to explain the employment compensation package. Employees may be suspicious of the more complicated nature of partnership options and discount the value of the proposed compensation package accordingly.

B.   Corporate Governance and Drafting

Corporate law differences between a closely-held corporation and a limited liability company generally are thought to be insignificant. In practice, however, there is enough uncertainty about how corporate governance provisions will apply, and there are enough difficult drafting issues, so that even today clients are sometimes wary about using a non-corporate entity. LLCs are somewhat new. Although the first LLC statute was passed in 1977, they did not become commonplace until the 1990's. As a result, there is little case law outlining the rights and obligations of LLC members. In general, LLCs offer flexibility with respect to management of the company, the rights and obligations from one member to another, and disclosure obligations. Some states, including Delaware, even permit members to waive fiduciary duties. Flexibility brings uncertainty, both in terms of determining what rights LLC agreements confer and whether the agreements will be enforceable in court.

Uncertainty creates a significant information cost. When a start-up is organized as a corporation, it is easy for the parties to understand and value their rights and obligations. For example, when the venture capital fund in the C corp structure receives preferred stock, it is understood, without even looking at the charter, that no dividend may be paid to the common stockholders so long as the preferred's dividend is outstanding, and if the start-up is liquidated, the fund will receive all of the proceeds until its liquidation preference is satisfied. Under the pass-through structure, on the other hand, there are no such limitations on distributions until the parties agree to them in the LLC operating agreement. A "capital interest" in an LLC has no meaning other than what the parties assign to it. Another example is fiduciary duty. Under the C corp structure, venture capital fund managers who sit on the board of the start-up have a fiduciary duty of care and duty of loyalty to the start-up's founders and managers. If an LLC is used, it is unclear what duties, if any, the venture capitalists owe to the founders and managers; a venture capital director may be free to divert corporate opportunities away from the LLC startup to other portfolio companies. To ensure that the founders and managers of the start-up are protected, the start-up's lawyers have to draft appropriate protections in the LLC operating agreement. Other commentators have noted that the lack of well-established practices and default rules for LLCs increases transaction costs in the venture capital context.

Granted, these differences in corporate governance are relatively minor and can be addressed in the drafting process. Moreover, parties might be more concerned with their reputation than with their legal rights and obligations. Indeed, in recent years, outside the context of venture capital-managed funds, deal planners have developed a hybrid structure that uses both an LLC and a corporation.

Nevertheless, the uncertainty of the LLC form increases legal costs and is an unwelcome addition to a negotiating atmosphere already laden with uncertainty and distrust. In particular, entrepreneurs who are accustomed to running corporations might resist trying out a new and unfamiliar entity. For start-ups that hope to incorporate within a few years anyway, adding an extra layer of legal costs, complexity, and uncertainty is unappealing, creating another reason why entrepreneurs and venture capital professionals prefer the C corp structure.

C. Smoother Exit Strategy

Corporate governance and employee compensation issues make the C corp structure advantageous for creating and running a start-up. It is also vital to examine exit strategy, where — in most cases — it is also easier for investors to sell their stake in a venture capital start-up if it has been structured as a corporation from the beginning.

Of course, partnerships and LLCs may legally convert into corporations, and often do. The incorporation process is not as easy as it might seem, however, particularly when a sale or reorganization is close at hand. [T]he transition from partnership to corporation is expensive. . . . [T]he transaction costs cannot fully explain the structuring choice, since the conversion costs amount to only a small percentage of the value of the tax deductions lost.

But neither should one dismiss the complexity of conversion right before exit. A successful exit is always possible, but exiting is simpler and cheaper if the start-up has been organized as a corporation from the outset. Incorporating a business just before selling or going public can cause unwanted delays. It requires management to face further complicating an already cumbersome process at the most sensitive time for a start-up — when it has finally turned the corner and may be sold to a third party or shopped to investment bankers for a potential IPO. Specifically, incorporation introduces an opportunity for holdup, as each manager will be asked to exchange her partnership interest (or option) for stock or options in the new entity. Because the enthusiastic participation of management is essential to a successful road show, managers may be in a position to extract additional value from the company at this sensitive time. This could happen, even if management continues to hold shares in the same company. But by forcing management into an exchange, incorporation encourages managers to engage their attorneys and renegotiate their own personal deals with the company.

. . .

VI. CONCLUSION

This Article has argued that the seemingly irrational decision to organize a start-up as a corporation is, in fact, quite rational. The key factors are the limited ability of investors to use tax losses, agency costs, the tax treatment of gains, and the complexity of the pass-through structure. This Article also has demonstrated the value of avoiding the behavioral phenomena of optimism bias as a simple explanation for seemingly irrational behavior — at least in the context of sophisticated investors with a great deal of money at stake. Optimism plays a role, to be sure, but it is not the wild-eyed optimism of a naive entrepreneur. Rather, the venture capitalist's rational emphasis on the tax treatment of gains, not losses, and the various tax and nontax advantages of the corporate form make the corporation the preferred vehicle for financing a venture capital start-up. And so tax plumbing ends up providing a workable, if inelegant, solution to this wonderful puzzle.

LAWYERING FOR SOCIAL ENTERPRISE

Joan MacLeod Heminway, 20 Transactions: Tennessee Journal
of Business Law 797 (2019)

. . .

II.   CHOOSING THE RIGHT BUSINESS ENTITY FOR SOCIAL ENTERPRISES

How do social enterprises organize themselves, from a legal standpoint? There are many options. Each has its advantages and disadvantages. In the current social enterprise environment, specific areas of tension in corporate law compound this general complexity. Having said that, it seems wise to start with the general issues in entity selection and work our way toward the specific, contentious corporate law issues. Social enterprise entity formation issues test a lawyer's duty of competence — "legal knowledge, skill, thoroughness and preparation" — in multiple ways.

Of course, founders and promoters of social enterprise can remain sole proprietors or, if desired, form unincorporated business associations (i.e., partnerships, limited liability partnerships, limited partnerships, limited liability companies, or where available, low-profit limited liability companies — a specialized form of limited liability company designed for use by social enterprises) or incorporate in one of several forms. New corporate forms have proliferated in the past ten years, making corporate choices more textured (and, for some, more confusing or contentious). In essence, the traditional choice of incorporating as a non-profit corporation or a for-profit corporation has expanded to include, in a majority of states, a third (and sometimes a fourth) option to incorporate as one of several different types of for-profit social enterprise corporation. Accordingly, while the spectrum of organizational choices still extends from sole proprietorships through unincorporated business associations to nonprofit and for-profit corporations, the range of options in that spectrum has increased.

This wider variety of choices makes the lawyer's task in assisting the client more demanding. In an earlier essay, I noted the challenges that alternative entities bring to choice of entity decisions in general. I stated there that "[t]he substantial change and complexity presented to legal counsel by the introduction of alternative forms of business entity over the past quarter century test a business lawyer's ability to exercise ethical professional judgment at multiple junctures and in myriad ways." Add to the evolution and intricacy of legal rules that I noted in that essay both the new corporate law options for organizing social enterprise firms and . . . multi-faceted social enterprise business models . . . , and the professional stresses mount.

Although various state laws offer a number of distinctive, specialized social enterprise corporate forms, most states offer three principal options for the incorporation of a social enterprise: a conventional non-profit corporation and a traditional for-profit corporation, as well as a benefit corporation, a for-profit corporation that operates under tailored, narrow management and governance constraints geared to a public purpose. Some commentators contextualize the benefit corporation (among other social enterprise forms of entity) as a hybrid form of corporation, inhabiting a place somewhere between the customary non-profit and for-profit corporate forms.

This relative positioning of the benefit corporation form between the non-profit and traditional for-profit corporate forms is accurate but incomplete. Indeed, benefit corporations are for-profit corporations under both federal tax law and state corporate law (enabling them to offer pecuniary gain — a private benefit — to funders through the ownership of an equity interest in the business) with public-facing aims like that of a non-profit corporation. But it is not quite that simple.

The core distinctive legal rules governing benefit corporation law are novel and unique to the benefit corporation form. Professor Brett McDonnell succinctly explains the characteristic governance norms in benefit corporation law in a recently published article:

> [B]enefit corporations . . . impose fiduciary duty . . . requirements. The directors and officers of a benefit corporation must consider the effects of their actions on a variety of specified interests, including employees, customers, the community, the environment, and the ability of the company to generate a general public benefit. Shareholders may sue if they believe a company's directors and officers have violated this duty, although their remedies are limited. Nonshareholder constituencies (e.g. employees or customers) do not have the right to sue to enforce the duty to consider their interests, although companies may grant standing by agreement.

In most states, benefit corporations also have a state-law filing requirement additional to the required filing of an annual report. They must file a "benefit report." "In these reports, companies must say what they have done to pursue general public benefit, along with any specific public purpose they may have. This must be measured against an independent third-party standard. . . ." Lawyers offering advice on business entity choice must be conversant with and competent in advising on these innovative benefit corporation rules as well as the formation, structure, governance, financing, and third-party liability rules of conventional non-profit corporations and traditional for-profit corporations.

That general depiction of a benefit corporation also may understate the level of knowledge required to engage in capable representation of a social enterprise or its constituents. Of course, not all state non-profit or traditional for-profit corporation laws are the same. Perhaps it is not surprising, then, that within the benefit corporation form, there also are a number of different state statutory models. In other words, different states have adopted different forms of benefit corporation, magnifying further the number of options a social entrepreneur or business promoter has for legally organizing a social enterprise business. A business lawyer must understand the individual state law similarities and differences in all three types of corporation, as well as the similarities and differences in all applicable unincorporated business forms in order to offer professionally responsible legal advice on entity formation in a social enterprise context. And the lawyer must then be able to use this knowledge in context to advise the principals of the social enterprise in the selection of a business form based on the then available facts.

Assuming formation and maintenance costs can be managed, the lawyer's contextual analysis typically focuses on three key potential points of difference that may distinguish the reasonable expectations of principals of one social enterprise from those of another in a way that is determinative of the lawyer's recommendation on choice of entity:

- Entity-level federal and state income tax obligations and benefits (which may depend on, e.g., whether the social enterprise is anticipated to operate exclusively for religious, charitable, scientific, or educational purposes, whether the activities of the social enterprise are expected to include influencing legislation or participating or intervening in any political campaign for or against any candidate for public office, and whether the business model proposed for the social enterprise incorporates the possibility of paying federal or state taxes on business income — all of which help distinguish a non-profit social enterprise exempt from federal and state income taxation from an income-tax-paying for-profit corporate social enterprise);

- Benefits available to presumed funders (including whether prospective funders may want a tax deduction, credit, or other tax benefit or whether they may desire to share in the profits of the venture, which would promote or preclude organization of the social enterprise as a tax-exempt non-profit corporation); and

- Management governance obligations, including fiduciary duties (for instance, whether corporate directors and officers will expect or require flexibility in determining the nature and objectives of their decision making, which provides insights into whether the structured decision making and management duties of a benefit corporation may make that for-profit corporate form a beneficial choice in organizing under an individual state's corporate law).

A significant level of diligence is required to obtain the relevant facts — information sufficient to perform the required analysis. "A lawyer shall act with reasonable diligence . . . in representing a client."

Yet, even a lawyer who can effectively access and acquire accurate and complete information from social enterprise entrepreneurs, founders, or promoters relating to these three matters may find it difficult to offer definitive advice to social enterprise venturers. The three areas of inquiry may point in different directions, and while the first two areas of inquiry may offer relatively clear solutions, the vagaries of the law on social enterprise decision-making in the corporate form raise particularly thorny choice-of-entity issues.

Notes and Questions

1. In considering entity choice for a new entrepreneurial venture, what factors might lead a lawyer to recommend — or at least accept — a sole proprietorship or general partnership?

2. The Mann et al., Goldberg, and Fleischer articles provide three perspectives on the corporation versus LLC debate. To what extent do you find each persuasive? If a client comes to you looking for help with entity selection, what questions will you ask to get at the key issues in choosing between a C-corporation and a limited liability company?

3. In the August 2003 issue of The Business Lawyer (58 Bus. Law. 1433), Richard A. Booth makes the following observation about entity choice in entrepreneurial ventures:

> It is difficult to believe that an entrepreneur does not think about how choice of entity will help the business succeed. Indeed, many say that venture capital firms prefer to deal with corporations. Although there are several technical reasons offered for this preference (such as worries about unrelated business income for nonprofit investors), most have been debunked. In the end, however, it may be

that investors are simply worried that there may be too many surprises lurking in the customized structure of alternative forms such as LLCs. Thus, it may be that one function of the corporate form is to provide a more or less standardized package of rights (or at least parameters) that can be more easily and reliably understood by potential investors and other third parties. As it turns out, this is nothing new. The stock exchanges have always imposed listing standards, presumably for similar reasons. And recent events notwithstanding, one of the essential functions of generally accepted accounting principles (GAAP) is to foster comparability across companies. Although one might question the need for standardization, it seems clear that in a world of innumerable investment opportunities, a firm can compete better for capital if it is more easily understood by potential investors. In other words, it costs less for investors to invest in a familiar form of organization. That is not to say that a new control feature of some sort might not be attractive and indeed afford the firm an edge from time to time. But that does not mean that it makes sense to reinvent the wheel with every deal. Boiler plate has its value.

Do you agree with Prof. Booth? Is predictability a relevant concept for all types of start-ups?

4. Imagine a client who is a social entrepreneur. What considerations might drive you to recommend that the client form a tax-exempt nonprofit, or a benefit corporation, or a traditional entity like a corporation or LLC?

C.   ORGANIZING THE NEW ENTITY

Once the entrepreneur and her counsel have agreed upon an entity type, the next task for the lawyer is to form the new entity. As noted in the entity type chart above, forming a limited liability company, low profit limited liability company, corporation, benefit corporation, nonprofit corporation, limited partnership, or limited liability partnership requires a filing with the secretary of state of the state in which the entity is being organized.

In the case of a corporation, benefit corporation, or nonprofit corporation, the document filed with the secretary of state is typically called "Articles of Incorporation" (or, in some states, the Certificate of Incorporation). Form articles of incorporation are typically available on the website of the secretary of state. The person who files the articles of incorporation is called the "incorporator." The incorporator might be a founder of the business, or a lawyer, or a paralegal, or any person authorized to make the filing. After filing the articles of incorporation, the incorporator typically adopts bylaws and hands the corporation over to the board of directors in a document called the "Action by Incorporator." Neither the bylaws nor the action by incorporator are filed with the secretary of state, but they are added to the corporate records of the corporation maintained by the secretary of the corporation. Once the board receives the corporation from the incorporator, the board has an initial or "organizational" meeting, during which it sells shares to the initial shareholders (if it is a traditional corporation or a benefit corporation) and elects officers, among other things. The board is able to act in a writing signed by all directors, and oftentimes the organizational meeting is handled by written consent, rather than with an in-person meeting.

NEW YORK STATE OF OPPORTUNITY.	Division of Corporations, State Records and Uniform Commercial Code

New York State
Department of State
DIVISION OF CORPORATIONS,
STATE RECORDS AND
UNIFORM COMMERCIAL CODE
One Commerce Plaza
99 Washington Ave.
Albany, NY 12231-0001
www.dos.ny.gov

CERTIFICATE OF INCORPORATION
OF

(Corporation Name)

Under Section 402 of the Not-for-Profit Corporation Law

FIRST: The name of the corporation is:

SECOND: The corporation is a corporation as defined in subparagraph (5) of paragraph (a) of Section 102 of the Not-for-Profit Corporation Law.

THIRD: _(Select all that apply)_

The purpose(s) for which the corporation is formed is:

☐ any purpose for which corporations may be organized under the Not-for-Profit Corporation Law as a charitable corporation.

☐ any purpose for which corporations may be organized under the Not-for-Profit Corporation Law as a non-charitable corporation.

☐ any purpose for which corporations may be organized under the Not-for-Profit Corporation Law as a charitable corporation or as a non-charitable corporation. (_Note: Checking this box results in the corporation being categorized as a charitable corporation in paragraph FIFTH._)

☐ the following specific purpose(s):

FOURTH: *(Check the appropriate statement)*

☐ The corporation is not formed to engage in any activity or for any purpose requiring consent or approval of any state official, department, board, agency or other body. No consent or approval is required.

☐ The corporation is formed to engage in an activity or for a purpose requiring consent or approval of a state official, department, board, agency or other body. Such consent or approval is attached.

FIFTH: The corporation is a: ☐ charitable corporation ☐ non-charitable corporation under Section 201 of the Not-for-Profit Corporation Law.

SIXTH: The office of the corporation is to be located in the County of _____, State of New York.

SEVENTH: The names and addresses of the initial directors of the corporation are:
(A minimum of three is required)

Name: _____

Address: _____

Name: _____

Address: _____

Name: _____

Address: _____

EIGHTH: The Secretary of State is designated as agent of the corporation upon whom process against it may be served.

The address to which the Secretary of State shall mail a copy of any process accepted on behalf of the corporation is: _____

_____

_____ .

NINTH: *(Optional – Corporations seeking tax exempt status may include language required by the Internal Revenue Service in this paragraph. See Not-for-Profit Incorporation Instructions.)*

The following language relates to the corporation's tax exempt status and is not a statement of purposes and powers. Consequently, this language does not expand or alter the corporation's purposes or powers set forth in paragraph THIRD.

NAME, SIGNATURE & ADDRESS OF INCORPORATOR:

_____   **X** _____
(Print or Type Name of Incorporator)   *(Signature of Incorporator)*

_____
(Address of Incorporator)

_____
(City, State, Zip Code)

CERTIFICATE OF INCORPORATION
OF

_____
(Corporation Name)

Under Section 402 of the Not-for-Profit Corporation Law

Filer's Name and Mailing Address:

_____
Name:

_____
Company, if Applicable:

_____
Mailing Address:

_____
City, State and Zip Code:

NOTES:
1. §301 of the Not-for-Profit Corporation Law requires that the name contain "Incorporated" or "Inc." or one of the other words or abbreviations indicative of corporate character unless the corporation qualifies for one of the exceptions in §301.
2. This sample form is provided by the New York State Department of State for filing a certificate of incorporation.
3. This form is designed to satisfy the minimum filing requirements pursuant to the Not-for-Profit Corporation Law. The Department of State will accept any other form which complies with the applicable statutory provisions.
4. The Department of State recommends that this legal document be prepared under the guidance of an attorney.
5. The Department of State does not provide legal, accounting or tax advice.
6. This certificate must be submitted with a **$75 filing fee** made payable to the Department of State.

_____

For DOS use only

A limited liability company is organized (notice we do not use the word "incorporated," which is reserved for forming corporations) when Articles of Organization (or a "Certificate of Formation") are filed with the secretary of state of the state in which the LLC is organized. The same process applies to a low profit limited liability company. The person who files the articles of organization is typically called the "authorized person" and, like an incorporator, might be a founder, or a lawyer, or a paralegal. The authorized person typically does not sign any further documents after the filing — instead, the members of the LLC or L3C execute an Operating Agreement. The election to be manager-managed or manager-managed must be made in the articles of organization in some states. The operating agreement then sets forth the governance and other aspects of the LLC or L3C.

Notes and Questions

1. In regard to choosing the name for a corporation or other entity, the secretary of state will generally require that the chosen name be "distinguishable" from the names of other entities on file. While some states, like California, approach this issue from a trademark-law-like perspective (see Chapter 4 for discussions of the concept of consumer confusion), most states ask a simpler question: can the proposed name be distinguished from other names on file, even if they are similar? Thus, a person could form a business called "John's General Store, Inc." even if there were already a corporation in that state called "General Store, Inc." — the distinguishing factor is the addition of the word "John's." Of course, that is not to say that a name considered "distinguishable" by the secretary of state is an advisable choice from a trademark or marketing perspective. A name that is distinguishable could still be considered confusingly similar. Therefore, it is conceivable that the secretary of state would permit the formation of a corporation with a particular name and the company would later be successfully sued for trademark infringement.

Lawyers generally check name availability before organizing a new venture by calling the secretary of state or searching the name on the secretary of state's website. Why do secretaries of state require distinguishability in a business name rather than some greater — or lesser — standard?

2. The broadly worded purpose clause in the second paragraph of the New York State Certificate of Incorporation is typical for most states. Oftentimes, an entrepreneur will suggest revising the standard language to include a more specific corporate purpose — much to the chagrin of her attorney, who doesn't want to limit the new venture's corporate charter in that way. What might be a good reason to limit corporate purpose, and are there ways — other than a limitation in the publicly filed charter document — that might be alternatives a lawyer can present to a client?

3. The term "authorized shares" means the total number of shares of capital stock a corporation is permitted to issue under the terms of its articles of incorporation. The number of authorized shares can be increased after the articles of incorporation are initially filed by amending the articles in accordance with the statute. To the extent a corporation is authorized to issue preferred shares, which are a class

of shares that have special management or economic rights, that fact will also be disclosed in the articles. (See Chapter 5 for a discussion of preferred stock.) In some states, the articles of incorporation will also include information about the number of shares being issued at the time of formation; other states follow the New York model and only require the listing of the number of authorized shares. Some states also require that shares have a "par value" associated with them. All "par value" means is "minimum issue price," and to ensure a corporation has maximum flexibility in future issuances of stock, attorneys typically recommend extremely low par values (such as $0.0001). What might be the policy behind requiring corporations to disclose the number of authorized shares and the characteristics of preferred shares in the articles of incorporation?

4. Entrepreneurs will often want to have a large number of authorized shares so that, when they sell shares to investors or grant options to employees, the recipient will feel they are getting something significant. It seems nicer to say to an investor "you are receiving 100,000 shares in exchange for your $15,000 investment" rather than "you are receiving 1 share in exchange for your $15,000 investment" even if the percentage ownership in the company is the same. Entrepreneurs may also feel that a higher number of authorized shares gives them more shares to sell to sophisticated investors as the business grows and attracts more capital. While generally share numbers are like points on a pinball machine in that they don't matter except in relation to each other, in some states it is administratively more difficult to avoid paying high franchise taxes when the number of authorized shares is high. For example, in Delaware, the franchise tax is calculated based on authorized shares rather than amount of capital in the business, unless a corporation affirmatively requests an alternative method of calculating franchise tax based on the size of the business. As a general rule, a start-up can be well served at formation with anywhere from 1,000 to 10,000,000 shares of capital stock. As noted above, this number can be amended — and will be amended — from time to time as needed (for example, a venture capitalist will require an amendment to the articles of incorporation to establish the series of preferred stock it is purchasing and to ensure adequate authorized shares for employee equity plans). The corporation should be careful at the time of formation to issue only a portion of the total authorized capital, leaving some authorized shares available for later investors or workers.

5. Unlike corporations, limited liability companies are not required to disclose information about their equity securities in their articles of organization. What might be the policy behind not requiring LLCs to disclose the number of authorized membership units and their economic and management rights in the articles of organization?

6. Amendments to the articles of incorporation require the approvals set forth in state law — typically the approval of the board and the shareholders. The articles of incorporation for a start-up — especially a fast-growing, well-funded start-up — will often include a so-called blank check preferred stock provision, in which a number of shares of preferred stock are authorized but not yet assigned any rights. The board is then given the power to assign rights to the so-called undesignated preferred in the future without the need for a shareholder vote, in a provision like this:

> The Board of Directors shall have authority by resolution to issue the undesignated Preferred Stock from time to time on such terms as it may determine and to divide the undesignated Preferred Stock into one or more series and, in connection with the creation of any such series, to determine and fix by the resolution or resolutions providing for the issuance of shares thereof:

(a) the distinctive designation of such series, the number of shares which shall constitute such series, which number may be increased or decreased (but not below the number of shares then outstanding) from time to time by action of the Board of Directors.

(b) the dividend rate, the times of payment of dividends on the shares of such series, whether dividends shall be cumulative, and, if so, from what date or dates, and the preference or relation which such dividends will bear to the dividends payable on any shares of stock of any other class or any other series of Preferred Stock;

(c) the price or prices at which, and the terms and conditions on which, the shares of such series may be redeemed;

(d) whether or not the shares of such series shall be entitled to the benefit of a retirement or sinking fund to be applied to the purchase or redemption of such shares and, if so entitled, the amount of such fund and the terms and provisions relative to the operation thereof;

(e) whether or not the shares of such series shall be convertible into, or exchangeable for, any other shares of stock of the Corporation or any other securities and, if so convertible or exchangeable, the conversion price or prices, or the rates of exchange, and any adjustments thereof, at which such conversion or exchange may be made, and any other terms and conditions of such conversion or exchange;

(f) the rights of the shares of such series in the event of voluntary or involuntary liquidation, dissolution or winding up, or upon any distribution of the assets, of the Corporation;

(g) whether or not the shares of such series shall have priority over or parity with or be junior to the shares of any other class or series in any respect, or shall be entitled to the benefit of limitations restricting (i) the creation of indebtedness of the Corporation, (ii) the issuance of shares of any other class or series having priority over or being on a parity with the shares of such series in any respect, or (iii) the payment of dividends on, the making of other distributions in respect of, or the purchase or redemption of shares of any other class or series on a parity with or ranking junior to the shares of such series as to dividends or assets, and the terms of any such restrictions, or any other restriction with respect to shares of any other class or series on a parity with or ranking junior to the shares of such series in any respect;

(h) whether such series shall have voting rights, in addition to any voting rights provided by law and, if so, the terms of such voting rights, which may be general or limited; and

(i) any other powers, preferences, privileges, and relative, participating, optional, or other special rights of such series, and the qualifications, limitations or restrictions thereof, to the full extent now or hereafter permitted by law.

The powers, preferences and relative, participating, option and other special rights of each series of Preferred Stock, and the qualifications, limitations or restrictions thereof, if any, may differ from those of any and all other series at any time outstanding. The shares of any one series shall have the same voting, conversion and redemption rights and other rights, preferences, privileges and restrictions.

Why might a lawyer representing a founding entrepreneur be suspicious of an investor's request for a blank check preferred? In what circumstances might a founder support blank check preferred?

7. Business entities filing with the secretary of state are generally required to have an authorized agent in their state of formation. This "registered agent" or "agent for service of process" can be an individual with an address in the state (not a post office box), or a company in the state that is specifically approved by

the secretary of state to receive service of process. If an entrepreneur hires a professional agent for service of process, she will be required to pay an annual fee to the agent — typically a few hundred dollars. The agent must receive service of process or other official communications on behalf of the corporation and must forward those documents along in a timely manner. Lawyers will occasionally act as agents for service of process for their clients. What advantages and disadvantages— to the lawyer and the client — arise from the lawyer taking on that role?

D.   AGREEMENTS AMONG OWNERS

An early and essential task facing an entrepreneur's lawyer is to persuade the client that preparing a written agreement among co-founders is important. Oftentimes clients will avoid the subject because it is inherently awkward: how does one go to one's future business partner (especially if the person is a friend or family member) in the earliest, trust-building moments of a business relationship, and demand a written record of the deal? The division of equity among founders winds up being a particularly difficult issue to negotiate, particularly if the founders are still figuring out their roles within the business. The lawyer must convince the client that the best time to put a business relationship in writing is at the early stages when everyone agrees and the business has not yet gained enough value to be worth a protracted negotiation.

Even when clients see the value in putting their relationship in writing, they will see a written founders' agreement as being a low priority, especially when compared with the exciting and essential task of developing the product and building the business. Clients may be inclined to avoid this step because they are anxious to devote their time to working on the business rather than "mundane" legal exercises. They may feel they don't know enough about the business to determine how much of it each of them should own, and when. Also, they may be less willing to allocate precious resources away from the business to pay a lawyer. The logical argument runs as follows: "why should I spend money and time developing a founders' agreement for a business that doesn't even exist, and can't exist unless I prioritize building it?" Lawyers with experience in representing entrepreneurs have seen multiple good businesses fail — or result in protracted legal battles — and can give a good counter argument: "why should you bother building a successful business just so you can fight about it and drive it into the ground later?"

1.   Shareholders Agreements

Typically, the agreement among founders is memorialized in a "Shareholders Agreement" (for a corporation) or the Operating Agreement (for a limited liability company). As the company grows and takes on more equity holders (such as friends and family, or angel investors, or venture capitalists, all as discussed in Chapter 5), the shareholders agreement or operating agreement will be amended to account for the rights and restrictions applicable to all shareholders. The difficult issues of relative ownership of equity and when the equity has value — or "vests" — are typically handled in a separate contract, as further described in the next section.

The following shareholders agreement is typical for a start-up with multiple owners. You will notice that it is relatively short, less than one-third the length of a typical post-venture capital investment shareholders agreement. We have inserted comments throughout explaining various provisions, and at the end of the document we have notes and questions designed to highlight the tensions in negotiating a contract like this among co-founders.

SHAREHOLDERS AGREEMENT
Minty, Inc.

THIS SHAREHOLDERS AGREEMENT (this "Agreement") is entered into as of September 12, 2020, by and among the individuals set forth on the signature pages hereto (the "Shareholders") and Minty, Inc., an Illinois corporation (the "Company").

> *The opening paragraph names the parties to the contract. It is typical to have the subject company also sign the contract, and it is necessary to have the company be a party if — as in this contract in Article 3 — the company makes covenants in the contract.*

The parties hereby agree as follows:

1.   Definitions.

1.01. "Fair Market Value" shall mean the fair market value of the Shares being valued, as determined in good faith by the Board of Directors of the Company.

> *See section 3.05, in which the purchase of shares after a shareholder's death is to be made at Fair Market Value. Notice that, in this definition of Fair Market Value, the Board of Directors makes the determination "in good faith."*

1.02. "Required Shareholders" shall mean Shareholders holding not less than two-thirds of the Shares held by all Shareholders.

> *This shareholders agreement uses the defined term "Required Shareholders" in places where shareholder approval is necessary for certain actions to take place. This corporation has two equal shareholders who expect to add additional shareholders who will own about 25 percent of the company. By setting the threshold at "not less than two-thirds of the Shares," the attorney has ensured that both founders' approval is required for any major actions by the company, even after the planned additional shares are sold.*

1.03. "Shareholder" shall mean any holder of Shares.

1.04. "Shares" shall mean any shares now outstanding or hereafter issued of the Company's Common Stock; any shares hereafter issued or issuable in substitution for such shares; and any other voting security of the Company.

2.   Election of Directors and Officers.

2.01. Each Shareholder shall vote all shares owned or controlled by such Shareholder (including any Shares hereafter acquired), at any regular special meetings of Shareholders of the Company, shall take all action by written consent in lieu of any such meeting of Shareholders, and shall take all other actions necessary to ensure that the Board of Directors shall consist of two persons or such other number of directors as may be approved by the Required Shareholders. The directors shall be Barry P. Peterson and Amy Warren, or such individuals who shall be elected as directors from time to time by the Required Shareholders.

> *In this section, the shareholders contractually agree to vote in favor of certain directors — themselves — to govern the company. Notice that they are not dispensing with the annual shareholder meeting to elect directors, they are merely agreeing that they will vote in a particular way when the meeting comes. If a shareholder votes differently than he has agreed to do in section 2.01, he will have breached the agreement but his (breaching) vote will stand unless a court orders otherwise.*

2.02. If a vacancy in the Board of Directors of the Company is caused by death, resignation, or disability of a Director or for any other reason, the Required Shareholders will elect a substitute Director.

2.03. A Director, without violating any provision in this Agreement, may resign at any time by giving written notice to the Company

3.   Management.

3.01. The Company's Board of Directors, in its sole discretion, shall determine from time to time whether dividends shall be declared and the amount thereof.

3.02. No sale, transfer, assignment, pledge, or other encumbrance or disposal (direct or indirect) of any Shares is permitted without the prior written approval of the Company's Board of Directors and the Required Shareholders. Prior to approving any such transfer, the transferee shall be required to execute a Statement of Acceptance in the form of Exhibit A [in which the transferee agrees to be bound by the terms of the Shareholders Agreement].

> *Section 3.02 prohibits the transfer of Company shares without the approval of the Required Shareholders and the board. Although this is a tough restriction on transfer, it ensures that the founders won't be stuck with different business co-owners unless they consent to that arrangement.*

3.03. Approved Sale. Subject to any provisions in the Articles of Incorporation of the Company and the Company's Bylaws, if the Required Shareholders approve a sale of all or substantially all of the Company's assets determined on a consolidated basis or a sale of all or substantially all of the Company's outstanding stock, whether by merger, recapitalization, consolidation, reorganization, combination or otherwise (collectively, an "Approved Sale"), each Shareholder hereby agrees to vote for, consent to, and raise no objections to such Approved Sale. If the Approved Sale is structured as (i) a merger or consolidation, each Shareholder will waive any dis-senter's rights, appraisal rights, or similar rights in connection with such merger or consolidation, or (ii) a sale of stock, each Shareholder will agree to sell all of his or its shares of stock of the Company and rights to acquire shares of stock on the terms and conditions approved by the Required Shareholders. Each Shareholder will take all necessary or desirable actions in connection with the consummation of the Approved Sale as requested by the Company and/or the Required Shareholders; provided, however, that any Shareholder compelled under this section to partic-ipate in an Approved Sale shall not be required to make any representations or warranties regarding the Company and shall have no indemnification obligation or other contractual liability for any representations or warranties regarding the Company beyond the consideration received by such Shareholder pursuant to such Approved Sale.

The Company will give each Shareholder notice of an Approved Sale not less than fifteen (15) days prior to consummation thereof (the "Approved Sale Notice").

3.04. Further Conditions Regarding Approved Sale. The obligations of the Shareholders with respect to the Approved Sale of the Company are subject to the satisfaction of the following conditions: (i) upon the consummation of the Approved Sale, each Shareholder will receive the same form of consideration and the same portion of the aggregate consideration that such Shareholder would have received if such aggregate consideration had been distributed by the Company in complete liquidation pursuant to the rights and preferences set forth in the Company's Articles of Incorporation as in effect immediately prior to such Approved Sale; and (ii) in the event and to the extent any Shareholder shall not be requested to partic-ipate in the Approved Sale, such Shareholder shall have the right to participate in the Approved Sale in accordance with the terms and conditions of this Agreement and shall exercise such right by delivering written notice to the Company within ten (10) days of receipt of the Approved Sale Notice.

> An "Approved Sale" is colloquially known as a "drag along." In the drag along provision, the shareholders agree that, if the requisite percentage of them agree to sell the company, all remaining shareholders will be "dragged along" with the sale — meaning they will go along with the sale and waive any right to object and waive all dissenters' rights. (See Chapter 11 for a description of dissenters' rights.)

3.05. In the event of the death of any Shareholder, the Company shall have the right, but not the obligation, to purchase the Shares from the decedent Shareholder's estate at a price equal to its Fair Market Value on the date of the Shareholder's death. The decision of whether to effect such purchase shall be made by the Board of Directors with the approval of the Required Shareholders. Prior to effectuating such a purchase, the Company must provide notice to dece-dent's estate of its intent to purchase the decedent Shareholder's interest within sixty (60) days of decedent's death. At the election of the Board, the Company may purchase the decedent Shareholder's interest by executing a promissory note, pay-able within five (5) years, with simple interest calculated at the rate of 5% interest per annum.

> *This section gives the Company the option to purchase a shareholder's shares when the shareholder dies. The Company must provide notice to the estate of its intent to make such a purchase within two months of the death.*

3.06. The Company shall not, without first obtaining the written approval of the Required Shareholders, take any action that:

(i) alters or changes the rights, preferences, powers, privileges, or restrictions of the Company's stock;

(ii) increases or decreases the authorized number of Company's stock;

(iii) results in the filing of a registration statement by the Company in connection with the IPO of the Company;

(iv) authorizes or issues (by reclassification or otherwise) any equity security having rights, preferences, powers, privileges, or restrictions senior to or on a parity with the currently outstanding Company stock with respect to voting, dividend, redemption, conversion, or liquidation or any other rights.

(v) results in the repurchase of any Company stock (except in connection with the termination of any employee or consultant of the Company or in accordance with Section 3.05);

(vi) effects a reclassification or recapitalization of the outstanding capital stock of the Company;

(vii) results in any Approved Sale, any merger or other corporate reorganization, any voluntary dissolution or liquidation or winding up, or any sale or exclusive license of all or substantially all of the Company's intellectual property;

(viii) results in the acquisition of stock or assets in connection with the acquisition of a business;

(ix) causes the aggregate amount of indebtedness for borrowed money of the Company or which the Company has guaranteed to exceed $10,000 or causes the Company to have pledged or granted a security interest in assets of the Company which have a book value in excess of $10,000;

(x) amends or waives any provision of the Company's Articles of Incorporation or Bylaws; or

(xi) results in a change of the form of entity of the Company from a subchapter S-corporation to another form.

> *With a few exceptions set forth in the corporations code (such as the decision to sell the company), the board of directors has authority to make all decisions for the Company. Section 3.06 limits the board's discretion on the specified matters, requiring shareholder approval to take those actions. These types of limitations are often called "Protective Provisions."*

4. Confidentiality.

4.01. Each Shareholder shall treat in confidence and not communicate, disclose, use to the detriment of the Company or for the benefit of any other person, or misuse in any way, any confidential information or trade secrets of the Company or any subsidiary or any other shareholder or its affiliates, including personnel information, secret processes, know-how, customer lists, or other technical data; provided, however, that this prohibition shall not apply to any information which

(1) such Shareholders can demonstrate is or becomes available to such Shareholder from a source other than the Company, or

(2) through no improper action of such shareholder, is or becomes publicly available or generally known in the industry, or

(3) is required to be disclosed under applicable law or judicial process, but only to the extent it must be disclosed, or

(4) is disclosed with the approval of the Board of Directors.

Each Shareholder acknowledges that any information or data such shareholder has acquired on any of these matters or items were received in confidence and as a fiduciary of the Company.

4.02. It is agreed among the parties that the Company would be irreparably damaged by reason of any such violation of the provisions of this Section, and that any remedy at law for a breach of such provisions would be inadequate. Therefore the Company shall be entitled to seek and obtain injunctive relief (including but not limited to a temporary restraining order, a temporary injunction, or a permanent injunction) against any Shareholder, such Shareholder's agents, assigns, or successors for a breach or threatened breach of such provisions, and without the necessity of proving actual monetary loss. It is expressly understood among the parties that this injunctive or equitable relief shall not be the Company's exclusive remedy for any breach of this section and the Company shall be entitled to seek any other relief or remedy that is available either by contract, statute, law, or otherwise for any breach hereof and it is agreed that the Company shall also be entitled to recover its attorneys' fees and expenses in any successful action or suit against any Shareholder relating to any such breach.

4.03. Notwithstanding the foregoing, the participation or involvement of any Shareholder in the Company shall not confer upon the Company or otherwise entitle the Company or any shareholder thereof to use or otherwise disclose in connection with the Company and its business and affairs the name of such Shareholder without such Shareholder's prior written consent.

> *This section of the shareholders agreement puts a confidentiality covenant on shareholders.*

5.   Representation and Warranties by Shareholders.

Each Shareholder hereby represents and warrants:

5.01. This Agreement has been duly executed and delivered by such Shareholder and constitutes the valid and binding obligation of such shareholder enforceable in accordance with its terms.

5.02. Such Shareholder understands that the Shares have not been registered under the Securities Act, and must be held indefinitely unless they are subsequently registered thereunder or an exemption from registration is available.

6.   Legend.

Each Certificate representing Shares shall be endorsed with a legend in substantially the following form:

"The transfer of the shares of stock represented by this Certificate is restricted under the terms of a Shareholders Agreement dated September 12, 2020, as it may be amended from time to time. A copy of the Agreement, with all amendments thereto, is on file at the principal office of the Company."

> *Article 6 of this agreement requires a legend to be placed on the stock certificates of the company. The purpose of the legend is to put potential transferees on notice that the shares cannot be freely transferred and have contractual obligations associated with them.*

7.   Specific Enforcement.

Because of the unique relationship of the Shareholders and the unique value of their interests in the Company, in addition to any other remedies which the Shareholders may have upon breach of the agreements contained herein, the obligations and rights contained in Paragraphs 2, 3, and 4 of this Agreement shall be specifically enforceable.

8.   Pre-emption.

The Articles of Incorporation and Bylaws of the Company shall at all times be, and be interpreted to be, consistent with the provisions of this Agreement, and the parties hereto shall not seek to enforce any provision of such Articles of Incorporation or Bylaws that is inconsistent with any provision of this Agreement.

9.   Illinois Law.

This Agreement shall be governed by the substantive law of the State of Illinois. Each party to this Agreement hereby submits to the jurisdiction of federal and state courts in the State of Illinois for all purposes including the enforcement of any arbitration award made pursuant to this Agreement.

10.   Miscellaneous.

10.01.   This Agreement constitutes the entire agreement of the parties with respect to the subject matter hereof, and supersedes all prior negotiations or agreements, whether written or oral. This Agreement shall be binding upon and inure to the benefit of the parties and their heirs, personal representatives, successors, and assigns.

10.02   This Agreement shall be construed to the maximum extent possible to comply with all of the terms and conditions required by law. If, notwithstanding the previous sentence, a court of competent jurisdiction concludes that any provision or wording of this Agreement is invalid or unenforceable under the applicable law, the invalidity or unenforceability of such provision or wording will not invalidate the entire Agreement. In such case, this Agreement will be construed so as to limit any term or provision so as to make it valid or enforceable within the requirements of applicable law and, in the event such term or provision cannot be so limited, this Agreement will be construed to omit such invalid or unenforceable provision or term.

10.03.   This Agreement may be amended by a writing signed by the Company and the Required Shareholders.

> *Although Article 10 of this agreement is referred to as "boilerplate" and might be ignored by clients, it contains important legal concepts. Section 10.03 says that an amendment does not need to be unanimous, which would be the default rule under contract drafting doctrine. Instead, it can be amended by the Required Shareholders.*

10.04.   Except as otherwise expressly provided herein, the rights and obligations of the parties pursuant to this Agreement may not be assigned without the express written consent of all other parties. Any assignment or attempted assignment made in violation of this Agreement shall be void.

IN WITNESS WHEREOF, the undersigned have executed this Shareholders Agreement as of the date first above written.

MINTY, INC.

By: _____
Name: _____
Title: _____

SHAREHOLDERS:

_____

Barry P. Peterson

_____

Amy Warren

Notes and Questions

1. Section 3.06 of this contract requires unanimity by the founders for many actions to take place. Would you counsel entrepreneurs to require unanimity on all decisions in the company? Only major decisions? Consider that one downside of requiring unanimity is that if the shareholders are deadlocked, the company cannot move forward. State law provides that a shareholder can apply to the court to dissolve the company in the event of a deadlock, but most entrepreneurs would prefer to avoid this draconian approach. How would you counsel entrepreneurs to resolve deadlocks? Would you add a provision to a shareholders agreement to handle this situation? Do you see any advantages to not addressing deadlocks in the written agreement and forcing entrepreneurs to either resolve their deadlocks or close down the new venture?

2. What advantages arise from requiring shareholder approval over certain decisions, as opposed to leaving those decisions to the board?

3. Section 3.02 prohibits all share transfers without the approval of the founders and the board. A less restrictive alternative is to grant existing shareholders — or even the company — a right of first refusal in the event of a proposed transfer.

A typical right of first refusal provision in a limited liability company operating agreement reads as follows:

> A Selling Member may sell or otherwise Transfer all or any part of its Membership Interests only in compliance with the provisions of this Section 6.1.
>
> (a) In the event that a Selling Member receives a bona fide unconditional third-party offer to purchase for cash all or any part of its Membership Interest, which the Selling Member has determined to accept, the Selling Member shall provide fourteen (14) days' prior written notice to the Manager and to each of the Members, of the proposed Transfer, the identity of the proposed purchaser, and the proposed cash purchase price (the "Asking Price") for the Membership Interest it is seeking to Transfer (the "Offered Interest"). Such notice shall constitute an irrevocable offer by the Selling Member to sell the Offered Interest to the Company and the Members for the Asking Price.
>
> (b) The Company, upon a determination by the Manager, and the Members (the "Exercising Members") shall have the right during such fourteen (14) day period to propose to acquire the Offered Interest for the Asking Price (or some portion of the Offered Interest for a pro rata portion of the Asking Price), payable entirely in cash. The closing of any sale pursuant to this Section 6.1 shall take place within fourteen (14) days following the end of such fourteen (14) day period (or such longer period as is reasonably required in order to satisfy and/or receive applicable governmental approvals).
>
> (c) If the Offered Interest is oversubscribed, first the Company shall have the right to acquire all or any portion of the Offered Interest. Thereafter, the Exercising Members shall have the right to acquire any remaining portion of the Offered Interest in proportion to their respective Proportionate Share of the then outstanding Common Membership Units.
>
> (d) If the Offered Interest is not proposed to be acquired by the Company or any of the Members by the end of the fourteen (14) day period specified in Section 6.1.1(b) then the Selling Member may Transfer the Offered Interest within an additional fourteen (14) days, at not less than the Asking Price, to the proposed third party purchaser.
>
> (e) If the Selling Member wishes to Transfer the Offered Interest to the proposed third party purchaser at a purchase price of less than the Asking Price, or after the fourteen (14) day period set for in (d) above, it must first follow the procedures set forth in subparagraphs (a)-(d) above with the new purchase price such Selling Member is seeking becoming the Asking Price.

What advantages and disadvantages are associated with a right of first refusal, as opposed to an outright prohibition on transfer? Which alternative do you think is more useful for a brand new entrepreneurial venture?

4. Another type of restriction on transfer is a so-called tag along or co-sale provision. Under this kind of provision, before an owner can sell its ownership interest, it must invite other owners to include a proportionate share of their ownership interest as part of the sale. A tag along provision might be drafted as follows (and would be placed immediately after the right of first refusal discussed in the prior note):

> (f) In the case of a proposed Transfer or Transfers in a single transaction or a series of related transactions by a Selling Member, if (x) the Company and Members do not exercise the right of first refusal pursuant to this Section 6.1.1, and (y) the Offered Interest is comprised of Membership Units exceeding twenty percent (20%) of the then outstanding Membership Units, then, as a further

condition to the Transfer by a Preferred Member or Common Member of the Offered Interest, such Member shall:

    (i) If a Preferred Interest is being sold, obtain for each other Preferred Member the right, but not the obligation, to sell the Offered Proportion of its Preferred Interest at the same purchase price and otherwise on the same terms and conditions. The "Offered Proportion" is the proportion of the aggregate Membership Interest of the class proposed to be sold held by the Selling Member prior to the proposed Transfer which is represented by the Offered Interest.

    (ii) If a Common Interest is being sold, obtain for each other Common Member the right, but not the obligation, to sell the Offered Proportion of its Common Interest at the same purchase price and otherwise on the same terms and conditions.

Who benefits most from a tag along? Do you think including this kind of provision is helpful to an entrepreneurial venture? Would you recommend this provision as company counsel? What if you were representing an individual shareholder?

5. Can you think of a good reason to include an outright prohibition on transfer without shareholder and board approval — as seen in this shareholders agreement — and also the lighter restrictions on transfer of a right of first refusal and a tag along?

6. What value does a "drag along" provision, like the one found in Section 3.03, add to an agreement among co-founders of a business? To what extent does the motivation for such a provision change if the entrepreneurial venture receives outside investment from investors who have voting shares and a seat on the board of directors?

7. What value, if any, is added by giving the company the right to buy a deceased shareholder's shares? Why is it important to have a time limit for the company's decision to exercise this right?

8. What advantages do you see in having the board of directors determine "Fair Market Value" for purposes of determining the price to be paid in connection with the repurchase of a deceased shareholder's shares? What other options for determining fair market value should founders of an entrepreneurial venture consider?

9. What is gained by including Section 5, the representations and warranties?

2. *Division of Equity Among Founders and Vesting*

One of the most difficult issues that arises among founders is the allocation of equity among the founding team. Ownership of a new business has economic and management consequences, in addition to the emotional need founders have to feel valued for their ideas, effort, and results. Moreover, at the founding of a new business it is impossible to know with certainty how much each founder will contribute (monetarily, conceptually, and in terms of effort), and it is similarly impossible to know whether all members of the founding team will remain with the venture. At the same time, someone needs to own the business, and adopting a "wait and see" attitude can often lead to significantly larger disagreements and more difficult conversations.

A very common resolution to this founder issue — and other issues identified in the reading below — is to divide equity and have the equity subject to various restrictions. The restrictions include limits on all economic and voting rights associated with the equity, and also typically give the company the right to repurchase the stock at a low price. Typically, the restrictions go away as to the shares on some predetermined schedule: for example, after a founder has been at the company one year, one-quarter of the shares may become unrestricted. In regard to founder equity, this removal of restrictions is referred to as "vesting," and equity that has had the restrictions removed is referred to as "vested equity."

For lawyers working with entrepreneurs, all of these intrafounder issues raise the kinds of sticky ethical issues discussed in Chapter 1: if the lawyer represents the new entity, and not the founders, how can the lawyer help to get these issues resolved? Oftentimes, the lawyer will just advise clients to get separate counsel (which the client may or may not do), and then offer to document whatever deal the clients reach.

In the following piece, a startup lawyer offers some answers to clients as to the need for, and ways to approach, allocation of founders' equity and vesting.

FOUNDER BASICS: FOUNDER'S STOCK, VESTING AND FOUNDER DEPARTURES

James Linfield, cooleygo.com (accessed July 2020)

WHAT IS FOUNDER'S STOCK?

"Founder's Stock" refers to the equity interest that is issued to Founders (and perhaps others — also check out my article Who is a "Founder"?) at or near the time the company is formed. It is often issued for a nominal cash payment (such as $0.0001 per share, which is the default value in the Cooley GO Docs Incorporation Package) and/or assignment of intellectual property. Often but not always the "Founder's Stock" is subject to a vesting schedule which gives the company the right to buy back unvested shares if a Founder leaves the company before the shares are fully vested.

Whether "Founder's Stock" has any rights different from other equity interests in a company depends on the agreements entered into between the Founder and the company, either at the time the stock is issued or later. . . .

WHY WOULD I WANT TO CONSIDER A VESTING SCHEDULE FOR MY FOUNDER'S STOCK?

Founder's Stock is often subject to a vesting schedule. Under a typical vesting schedule, the stock vests in monthly or quarterly increments over four years; if the Founder leaves the company before the stock is fully vested, the company has the right to buy back the unvested shares at the lower of cost or the then fair market value.

The vesting schedule may be agreed to at the time of the Founders Stock is first issued, or may be imposed later as a condition of investment by outside investors.

Why would a Founder agree to subject his or her shares to a vesting schedule at the outset of the company? Two possible reasons:

First, this may be part of the bargain among multiple founders. If a founder decides to leave, or is asked to leave, early in the company's existence, the vesting restriction protects the other founders from the "free rider" problem that would otherwise exist. While some founding teams stay together from beginning to end, it is fairly common for one or more Founders to leave the company in its early years. Absent a vesting restriction, the departed Founder gets a "free ride" on the efforts of those who remain to build the company.

Second, the restriction may be adopted in anticipation of future investment, as venture capital and angel investors generally seek some kind of vesting restrictions. Of course, one could wait until the time of investment to address the issue. However, if the Founders play "wait and see" they run the risk that the investors will propose something more onerous than the Founders might have come up with on their own. Conversely, if the Founders impose a reasonable vesting scheme, most investors will leave well enough alone, even if that scheme is not exactly what the investors might have preferred.

WHAT IS A "CLIFF"?

There is often a one year "cliff," meaning that the individual must be with the company for a year to vest the first increment. Often Founders are given some retroactive vesting credit for work done before the company was incorporated. While one year is common, you could use any time period.

Example: A company has three founders, one of whom has been working on the concept for a year and the others for three and six months, before the company is incorporated. The Founders might decide to subject their shares of Founders' Stock to a four-year vesting schedule, but give each of the Founders some retroactive credit reflecting their respective periods of work before incorporation.

However, vesting provisions often do include some protections for termination without cause following the sale of the company, as discussed below.

. . .

WHAT HAPPENS TO MY UNVESTED STOCK IF THE COMPANY IS SOLD OR I'M FIRED?

Vesting provisions on Founder's Stock may provide for acceleration of vesting following the sale of the company. There are two main variations:

- A "single trigger" provision accelerates the vesting of any unvested shares as of the time of the sale.
- A "double trigger" provision accelerates the vesting of any unvested shares if the company is sold and the employee is terminated without cause within some time period following the closing of the sale.

With a "single trigger" provision, the "golden handcuffs" are unlocked at the time of the sale, and it is up to the buyer to determine how to retain and motivate the team of the acquired company.

A "double trigger" provision keeps the "golden handcuffs" in place, but protects the employee from being terminated without cause by the buyer by accelerating the vesting of any unvested shares should that occur.

Sometimes acceleration of vesting can also occur if, following the sale of a company, the buyer significantly changes an employee's responsibilities or moves the place of work by more than, say, 50 miles. These "Good Reason" provisions accelerate vesting of unvested Founder's Stock if the employee elects to leave after a "Good Reason" event has occurred.

Founders often inquire about acceleration of vesting if the Founder is terminated without cause (not in connection with an acquisition of the Company). While this is not an unreasonable concern, be very careful about agreeing to vesting acceleration for a termination without cause. Vesting restrictions typically do not distinguish among the many reasons why a company and a Founder may part ways, although it is possible to provide that it applies only in the case of a termination without cause or voluntary termination. Most legal definitions of "cause" focus on bad behavior such as dishonesty, theft, or conviction of a felony. They typically don't reach more subjective assessments of effectiveness such as weak leadership or poor management skills. In an early stage company, an ineffective team member can jeopardize the entire enterprise. If that person is terminated and did not satisfy the cause definition, he or she may walk away with a significant portion of their stock in an unintended result.

. . .

Notes and Questions

1. A typical founder's vesting schedule would be "four years with a one-year cliff," meaning that the founder's equity is restricted for the first year. At the end of the first year, one-quarter of the equity vests. After that, the remaining three-quarters of the founder's equity typically vests in equal pieces every calendar quarter for the next three years, such that by the end of the fourth year, all equity is vested. What are the advantages and disadvantages to a company of this kind of vesting schedule? What are the advantages and disadvantages to founders who remain with the company for the full four years? What about founders who quit or are fired before their vesting is complete?

2. The Linfield piece mentions the challenges founders getting a "free ride" if their equity is not subject to vesting. Can a company protect itself against this same "free rider" problem as to fully-vested founders? For example, imagine a founder, who had been subject to a four-year vesting schedule, deciding to leave the company after four and a half years. Can the company anticipate the issue and do anything in the founders' agreement to handle that situation? Is there a reason the company should leave vested equity alone and allow founders to be free riders once they are fully vested?

3. When founders are granted equity that is subject to restrictions, they have two choices for how they pay tax on the equity they have received. They can either pay income tax on the fair value of the equity at the time it vests, or, if they prefer, they can make a so-called 83(b) election where they pre-pay the tax on all of the granted equity in advance of vesting at the fair market value at the time of grant. If founders pre-pay tax and then the equity fails to vest (for example, because they left the company), they cannot get the tax they paid back from the IRS. Why do well-advised founders typically choose to make 83(b) elections and pay all the tax up front?

PROBLEM

At a meeting with Andrew and Olivia, you asked the entrepreneurs some questions to help you recommend a specific legal form for their business. Your notes from the meeting are below.

— They have decided on the name "General Germ."
— Olivia has significant wealth and wants to make sure her personal assets are protected. Andrew does not have significant wealth.
— Olivia has a high income from her job and her other investments. Andrew is getting ready to quit his job to focus full time on their new venture.
— Clients imagine they will have to give equity as incentives when they recruit workers.
— Andrew has a friend who is a venture capitalist and Andrew believes the company will be able to secure VC financing within six months. He has not yet met formally with anyone from this VC firm.
— Olivia will contribute more capital to the business (including cash and her invention) than Andrew, and as such Olivia will have voting control. Andrew has agreed to this arrangement but wants veto power over significant decisions.
— Other than paying themselves modest salaries, clients expect to reinvest all profits back in the business for the first two years after launch.
— Clients expect to have an IPO within five years (remember to tell them later that it is unlikely in this market).
— They anticipate putting equal time into the business, and want their equity to vest on a "typical" schedule.
— They claim that filing fees associated with forming the business are irrelevant.

1. Review the information and determine which entity form you think would suit your clients best. What additional questions might you ask the client in a follow-up email to confirm your recommendation?

2. Once you have chosen an entity type, prepare the organizational document to be filed with the secretary of state of your state (Articles of Organization, Articles of Incorporation, Certificate of Limited Partnership, or other applicable document). Do not draft any complex provisions that might become applicable in the future (for example, if they receive venture capital funding) — just draft the basic document they will need to file today to get their company organized. Do not forget to check name availability.

3. Consider everything you have learned so far about your clients — from this chapter and the related problems at the end of the prior chapters. What are your best arguments for having Olivia and Andrew negotiate a shareholders agreement, operating agreement, or written partnership agreement (as applicable depending on the entity type they choose)? Prepare a list of issues for them to consider in discussing this document.

IV

INTELLECTUAL PROPERTY

For an entrepreneur launching a new venture, it is important to focus on intellectual property issues from the onset and from two perspectives. On the one hand, it is necessary to take adequate steps to sufficiently protect intellectual property rights in a timely manner. On the other hand, it is key to ensure that the new company does not infringe on intellectual property rights of others. In other words, it is important for the lawyer to help the entrepreneur develop both an offensive and a defensive strategy. From an offensive perspective, the entrepreneur wants to create strong intellectual property rights to stop others from infringing on those rights, and from a defensive perspective, she wants to minimize the risk of claims by third parties.

Quite often, some of the most valuable assets of a company are its intangible property. This is true not only for technology companies and software companies where the value of the intellectual property may be more obvious, but also for consumer goods companies where brand names, secret recipes, and specific processes are the backbone of continued success.

A. TRADEMARKS

A trademark is any word or phrase, name, symbol, sound, or device that identifies and distinguishes one company's products from those of others. Slogans, colors, shapes, sounds, and fragrances can even qualify as trademarks. For example, Owens-Corning has acquired trademark rights in the pink color of its fiberglass insulation product, and Harley Davidson has rights in the distinctive sound of its engine. Trademarks should uniquely identify a company's products and distinguish those products from ones made or sold by other companies. Service marks are a subset of trademarks, and they simply identify a service instead of a product.

The success of any business is largely dependent on its reputation and brand recognition. This important intangible asset is captured by the company's trademark rights in many of its marketing tools such as its brand name, slogans, logos, and packaging. If Company A sells high quality widgets and markets its widgets under a particular brand name and Company B was able to use a similar name that would lead consumers into purchasing widgets from Company B under the false belief that they were purchasing the widgets from Company A, then presumably both Company A and the consumers would be harmed. Trademark law helps protect both the trademark owner and the consumer from potential confusion that can result from companies using similar marks in related industries.

1. Trademark Protection

Trademark rights are of two types: rights arising under state common law (called "common law rights") and rights arising from federal registration with the United States Patent and Trademark Office or state registration with state officials.

Common law rights arise automatically from use of the mark in commerce — without any government filings. Since trademark law is intended to protect consumers against confusion as to the source of goods or services, common law rights generally protect only the geographic area in which the mark is being used. In addition, as with registered marks, common law marks only protect against marks that are "confusingly similar." (See the next section in this chapter for a discussion of the standards applied in trademark infringement analysis.) Although many entrepreneurs rely on common law marks to protect their ventures — especially in the early stages of the business — there is risk that the protection the entrepreneur receives will be too limited for a fast-growing venture. In particular, the geographic limitation on rights can be a significant challenge if the business grows. Imagine how difficult it may be to define the geographic scope of a business headquartered in Nashville, Tennessee that has a robust website offering to ship products nationally.

To register a mark, a venture files paperwork and pays a relatively modest fee with the USPTO or applicable state government. For a federal filing, the entrepreneur needs to show the mark is being used in commerce by including a "specimen" — which might be a photograph of the product and its label, a screen shot of a website offering a product for sale, a brochure offering a service for sale, or some other evidence. The USPTO checks the mark with other registered marks to determine whether there are other previously registered confusingly similar marks — and whether the mark is a "strong" mark suitable for protection or whether it is too "weak." If the mark passes the applicable standards and is not confusingly similar with another mark, the trademark is registered.

In the following case, the court explores the standards applied in securing common law trademark rights and also the process by which a company can register a mark with the USPTO. Following the Notes and Questions for this case, there is a selection from the United States Patent & Trademark Office Trademark Manual of Examining Procedure that describes the difference between "strong" and "weak" marks and a recent Supreme Court case examining a mark that the USPTO considered "generic" and not suitable for registration.

LUCENT INFORMATION MANAGEMENT, INC. v. LUCENT TECHNOLOGIES, INC.

United States Court of Appeals for the Third Circuit
186 F.3d 311 (1999)

GREENBERG, Circuit Judge.

I. INTRODUCTION

This trademark case involves the question of what constitutes "use" sufficient to establish common law trademark rights. Lucent Information Management, Inc. ("LIM") argues that it had common law rights in the mark "LUCENT" prior to Lucent Technologies, Inc. ("LTI"), based on its usage of that mark before LTI filed an intent to use ("ITU") application with the United States Patent and Trademark Office ("PTO"), indicating its intention to use the mark LUCENT in commerce. LIM further alleges that LTI did not act in good faith in adopting and using the mark. We find that LIM's limited use of the mark did not constitute prior use in commerce sufficient to establish rights in the mark, and that, as a result, LTI's adoption and use of the mark did not constitute trademark infringement, and was in good faith as a matter of law.

II. FACTUAL AND PROCEDURAL HISTORY

A. LIM's Adoption and Use of the Name and Mark LUCENT

. . .

In 1995 Norman Feinstein, Samuel Weinberg, Edward Eisen, and Cliff Armstrong formed LIM, a Pennsylvania corporation, to provide document imaging and management services, acting as a consultant on and re-seller of software and hardware. LIM selected the name LUCENT during the summer of 1995 after finding it in a dictionary. Since its formation, LIM has operated out of the Bala Cynwyd, Pennsylvania, office of Feinstein's other business, Corporate Consultants, Inc., an employee benefits company. The four principals are LIM's only employees and Feinstein's employees at Corporate Consultants perform LIM's clerical and bookkeeping work. In the fall of 1995, LIM began using contacts and referrals to inform individuals and companies of its services. On September 5, 1995, Feinstein sent a one-page letter on Corporate Consultants' letterhead to about 50 people to announce the services LIM would offer. On October 5, 1995, Armstrong installed a modem for the Israel Bonds Office in Philadelphia. While Armstrong, not LIM, received the payment of $323.50 for the installation, the purchaser's invoice shows LIM's name and address, and viewed favorably to LIM, this transaction was its first sale.

Through the end of 1995, LIM continued to seek clients from existing contacts and referrals. LIM did not do any public or paid advertising, relying instead on word of mouth and its solicitations of business from acquaintances of its principals.

In November 1995, LIM made sales presentations to acquaintances at NBC in New York, Aramark in Pennsylvania, and Nixon Uniform in Delaware, but these presentations did not result in sales. From December 1, 1995, to February 5, 1996, LIM made about 12 presentations and continued to promote the new business with people the principals met socially and in business. The date of February 5, 1996, is significant because on that [] date AT&T announced the creation of LTI to the public through a huge media campaign. On February 16, 1996, LIM made another sale, entering into a support agreement with a local bank. Finally, on April 29, 1996, LIM filed an application with the PTO to register LUCENT for computer and office-related services.

B.   LTI's Adoption and Use of the Name and Mark LUCENT

LTI is the telecommunication and technology business spun-off from AT&T in 1996. A consultant suggested LUCENT as a potential name for the new business. Frank L. Politano, a trademark attorney, coordinated the trademark clearance. In November 1995, AT&T obtained a trademark name search and two trademark search reports, all of which located companies using the mark LUCENT or variants of it. One of the three search results included a reference to LIM.

On November 30, 1995, LTI through its predecessor in interest filed an intent to use application ("ITU") with the PTO for the mark LUCENT for various telecommunications and computer-related goods and services.[3] When AT&T announced the spin-off on February 5, 1996, major newspapers and media covered the event. Many articles included LUCENT in the headline and LTI mailed out over 1.2 million announcements to potential customers. Like most of America, LIM learned about LTI in February 1996. On March 15, 1996, LIM's trademark counsel, John Caldwell, sent LTI a letter objecting to LTI's use of the name LUCENT, stating that LIM had adopted and used LUCENT on a "nationwide" basis. This cease-and-desist letter stated in part:

> In August and September, 1995, [LIM] began corresponding under the Lucent name. . . . This was a nationwide effort. . . . A copy of the letter sent at that time, with the addresses redacted, is enclosed. I also enclose a brochure available from [LIM] at that time. . . . I look forward to hearing from you with your assurance that a new name will be found for your company. . . .

Caldwell enclosed a copy of a promotional brochure and a letter to solicit clients on LIM letterhead dated September 5, 1995.[4]

---

3. The Trademark Law Revision Act of 1988 added provisions allowing for registration of a mark on a showing that the applicant has a "bona fide intention . . . to use a trademark in commerce." 15 U.S.C. § 1051(b). Filing such an "intent-to-use" application establishes priority as of the date of filing (except as against those already using the mark), but a statement of actual use must be filed within 6 months, which may be extended to 24 months. 15 U.S.C. § 1051(d). At the same time the law was revised to provide that " 'use in commerce' means the bona fide use of a mark in the ordinary course of trade, and not made merely to reserve a right in a mark." 15 U.S.C. § 1127.

4. Subsequently, LIM admitted that the letter had in fact been sent out on Corporate Consultants' letterhead. Significantly, the enclosed brochure did not in fact exist in September 1995, as LIM created it later.

On April 12, 1996, R.A. Ryan, AT&T's trademark counsel, responded to the March 15, 1996 letter, stating that she did not agree that LTI's use of the name "Lucent Technologies" created a likelihood of confusion, that the companies' markets did not overlap, and that their services and products are not confusingly similar. As we noted above, LIM thereafter filed an application to register the mark LUCENT. LIM's then-trademark counsel responded to the April 12, 1996 letter with a proposed agreement that each party would refrain from opposing the other parties' registration of the mark, and would use trade dress, advertising and marketing in a manner that would avoid likelihood of confusion. The parties, however, did not enter into that agreement. Shortly thereafter, LIM began this litigation.

. . .

IV. DISCUSSION

A. Trademark Infringement

Trademark law protects owners in the exclusive use of their marks when use by another is likely to cause confusion. Thus, to obtain relief a plaintiff in an infringement case must demonstrate its ownership of the mark. In considering who owns the mark LUCENT, the question before us is whether a reasonable trier of fact could find that LIM's activities prior to November 30, 1995, when LTI filed its ITU, established prior rights in the mark through use in commerce.

We consider events before November 30, 1995, because federal registration of a trademark is prima facie evidence of the mark's validity, the registrant's ownership of the mark, and its exclusive right to use the mark in commerce. Nevertheless, there are limitations on the right as section 7(c) of the Lanham Act states that "the filing of an application to register [a mark] shall . . . confer[] a right of priority, nationwide in effect, . . . against any other person except for a person . . . who, prior to such filing, has used the mark." Consequently, the parties agree that LIM must establish rights in the name and mark LUCENT by its prior "use [of the mark] in commerce" — "use" being defined as "the bona fide use of a mark in the ordinary course of trade. . . ."

It is a well-settled principle that a plaintiff must establish that it had prior rights or "priority" in the mark. Because LTI filed its ITU on November 30, 1995, LTI has priority over anyone using the mark after that date unless the person earlier used the mark. Accordingly, inasmuch as LIM does not assert prior registration, it can prevail only if it shows prior use of the mark "in a way sufficiently public to identify or distinguish the marked goods in an appropriate segment of the public mind as those of the adopter of the mark."

. . .

We measure "use" by the four-factor test of Natural Footwear Ltd. v. Hart, Schaffner & Marx, 760 F.2d 1383, 1398-99 (3d Cir. 1985). That case represented and is clearly applicable to the commonly recurring fact pattern of concurrent use of confusingly similar common-law trademarks in different regions. Here, we do not have geographic competition, with a senior user allegedly being established in an area, and a junior user moving in on that territory or trying to use the same mark in another region. From its outset LTI was willing and able to operate nationwide, and has undisputed national market penetration.

The facts before us vary from the classic geographic extent of use cases. However, we may assess the basic issue — market penetration based upon prior use of the mark — applying the Natural Footwear test, which, like similar tests in other circuits, measures the extent of a senior user's actual use and zone of expansion.

A party asserting trademark ownership in a trading area must show "clear entitlement" to protection of its trademark in a particular market. In other words, that party must introduce evidence to show its trademark "has achieved market penetration that is 'significant enough to pose the real likelihood of confusion among the consumers in that area.' " Natural Footwear adopted a four-factor test "to determine whether the market penetration of a trademark in an area is sufficient to warrant protection: (1) the volume of sales of the trademarked product; (2) the growth trends (both positive and negative) in the area; (3) the number of persons actually purchasing the product in relation to the potential number of customers; and (4) the amount of product advertising in the area."

Applying this test, we reach the same result as did the district court in granting LTI's motion for summary judgment. LIM's "volume of sales" in 1995 consisted of Armstrong's single sale for $323.50. This court has held that sales volume must be more than de minimis. "When sales activity does not exceed even a minimum threshold level, a court may properly conclude that market penetration . . . simply has not been demonstrated." Id. at 1400 (finding de minimis clothing sales of less than $5,000 and total of over 50 customers in at least two of the three years for which sales data were available). LIM asks us to consider *Blue Bell*, 508 F.2d at 1265, in which the Court of Appeals for the Fifth Circuit held that "even a single use in trade may sustain trademark rights if followed by continuous commercial utilization." Here, though, if we look for "continuous commercial utilization" beyond the first sale, as required under *Blue Bell*, we do not find that the continuous use — the further promotional efforts — "sufficiently public to identify or distinguish the marked goods in an appropriate segment of the public mind as those of the adopter of the mark."

Because LIM made only a single sale in the period before LTI filed its ITU, we cannot find and review "growth trends," the second factor in the *Natural Footwear* test. LIM has argued that it had the potential and intention to offer services to a nationwide market, but even considering the volume of potential clients in the Philadelphia area, we must conclude that the ratio of existing customers to potential customers is minute.

As for the fourth and final factor, advertising and promotion, LIM stresses that its efforts were not to reach the general public at first, but rather to cultivate its clientele from existing contacts. LIM does not assert that its advertising and promotion to the public were extensive in any region, let alone nationwide. We may take into account in this respect and more generally the nature of the market LIM has entered and the services it offers. LIM contends that as a start-up company with a limited budget, offering relatively expensive services which are not "sampled" easily by customers, it would be expected to take time for it to win over clients. Accordingly, it is understandable that it would try to establish the business through a small circle of existing business and personal contacts. LIM correctly notes that sales or presentations made to acquaintances or friends may be bona fide commercial uses.

But the fact remains that LIM existed for only about three months before LTI filed its ITU, had made but one sale in that period, had not invested any monies in public advertising or expanded beyond its initial set-up, and had made a relatively small number of sales presentations. LIM offers evidence of confusion generated by LTI's launch, such as phone calls intended for LTI coming to its office or people wondering whether it stole the mark from LTI. Nevertheless, LTI is correct when it stresses that LIM wants to protect its intention to create goodwill and a successful business, and not the goodwill and business itself. Certainly any new business will need time to get off the ground, but the courts cannot aid that effort by awarding trademark rights in an unregistered mark that the business hopes or anticipates will be used but has not been used. Thus, we agree with the district court that LTI has prior rights in LUCENT because it filed its ITU on November 30, 1995, and LIM has not shown prior use.

B. LTI's Good Faith Adoption and Use of the Mark lucent

LIM argues that LTI is liable for bad faith because it was aware of LIM's existence and/or use of the mark, but proceeded to adopt it anyway.[10] The issue is moot because LIM was not a senior user for the above reasons.

In any case, the only evidence LIM has raised as to whether there was bad faith is LTI's assertion of privilege during discovery as to what steps, if any, LTI took upon generating the trademark search which included the reference to LIM. In this context, we will not draw an adverse inference from the raising of privilege, as courts have found that reliance on the advice of counsel after conducting a trademark search is sufficient to defeat an inference of bad faith. Thus, while we have not decided whether a junior user's knowledge of the senior user's use of a mark is sufficient to attribute bad faith adoption of the mark, we see no reason to do so on this occasion.

V. CONCLUSION

For the foregoing reasons, we will affirm the district court's order of November 5, 1997, LIM's trademark infringement and related claims.

ACKERMAN, Senior District Court Judge, dissenting.

I respectfully dissent from the opinion of my learned colleagues. I agree that the majority has correctly identified the issue in this case, i.e., what constitutes "use" sufficient to establish a common law trademark. Because, however, I believe there are genuine issues of material fact which preclude entry of summary judgment on this record, I would reverse the summary judgment of the district court. I write also to clarify the process by which district courts should resolve common law trademark disputes.

. . .

10. [In evaluating the bad faith argument], we would consider whether LTI was "careless" in searching for uses of the mark. In *Fisons* we suggested, substituting the parties here for those in that case, that "the questions the district court should consider here are whether [LTI] conducted an adequate name search for other companies marketing similar goods under trademarks including the name LUCENT, and whether it followed through with its investigation when it found there were such companies. Did [LTI] consider the likelihood of confusion with other companies' marks and products (as opposed to considering the likelihood that someone would contest its new mark)? Did it attempt to contact companies using a similar mark, such as LIM? Was [LTI] careless in its evaluation of the likelihood of confusion?"

To establish a claim of common law trademark infringement, one must prove (1) it is the owner in the relevant area of a mark that is distinctive and protectable, and (2) that the defendant's actions cause a likelihood of confusion.

The primary issue in this appeal is whether LIM has used the "LUCENT" mark in a manner sufficient to confer ownership rights. In granting summary judgment to LTI in this case, the district court determined that no trier of fact could find that LIM had "used" the "LUCENT" mark to a degree sufficient to obtain common law trademark rights. In addressing that issue, the district court first looked to the standard of "use" traditionally applied to common law trademarks and then looked to the standards set forth in Natural Footwear Ltd. v. Hart, Schaffner & Marx, 760 F.2d 1383, 1398-99 (3d Cir. 1985). While I agree with the former approach, I do not agree with the latter. Thus, I also disagree with the majority's exclusive reliance on the test set forth in *Natural Footwear* to determine the threshold issue of use sufficient to obtain a common law trademark.

A. Standard of "Use" Under Common Law Trademark law

It is a well-established principle of trademark law that the exclusive right to a distinctive mark belongs to the party which first uses the mark in connection with its particular line of business. This first actual use in commerce, however, must be "deliberate and continuous, not sporadic, casual or transitory." Indeed, the right to use a mark exclusively is akin to a monopoly which derives from "its appropriation and subsequent use in the marketplace. The user who first appropriates the mark obtains an enforceable right to exclude others from using it, as long as the initial appropriation and use are accompanied by an intention to continue exploiting the mark commercially." It is axiomatic that if there is "no trade — no trademark."

The Lanham Act provides that "use" is "the bona fide use of a mark in the ordinary course of trade, and not made merely to reserve a mark . . . a mark shall be deemed to be in use in commerce . . . on services when it is used or displayed in the sale or advertising of services and the services are rendered in commerce." Although this standard of use applies to the amount of use required to achieve statutory trademark rights and may be lower than the "use" needed to obtain a common law trademark, that standard is instructive with respect to common law trademarks.

Traditionally, ownership of a trademark accrues when goods bearing the mark are "sold, displayed for sale or otherwise publicly distributed." Indeed, to establish prior use for a common law mark, distribution of the mark need not be wide-spread, but it must be of a public nature and more than de minimis. Actual sales are not necessary to establish prior use and extensive advertising alone may in some cases be sufficient to establish a common law trademark right.

The Sixth Circuit's recent decision in Allard Enterprises, Inc. v. Advanced Programming Resources, Inc., 146 F.3d 350 (6th Cir. 1998) is instructive on the application of the common law standard of "use." In *Allard*, the defendants began using the contested mark in 1989 in connection with its employee placement business. Defendants were not very successful and had no revenue prior to the relevant date, March 1994. Beginning in 1991, however, the defendants engaged in individualized attempts to place employees at large companies and contacted several large companies to inform them of its business. In 1993 and 1994, the defendants tried to place several employees with large companies with little success. In this regard, defendants sent a fax with two resumes to the company Lane Bryant. Defendants also sent a promotional mailing to 100 potential customers on March 30, 1994.

The Court of Appeals affirmed the district court's conclusion that defendants' conduct prior to March 1994, though not extensive or profitable, was sufficiently public to warrant common law trademark rights. The Sixth Circuit held that "as long as there is a genuine use of the mark in commerce, . . . ownership may be established even if the first uses are not extensive and do not result in deep market penetration or widespread recognition." Relying on the Fifth Circuit's opinion in *Blue Bell*, the court went on to hold that "such use need not have gained wide public recognition, and even a single use in trade may sustain trademark rights if followed by continuous commercial utilization."

Ultimately the Court of Appeals based its conclusion that the defendants had "used" the mark sufficiently on (a) defendants' attempt to complete genuine commercial transactions, (b) the commercial nature of their attempts which need not have "achieved wide public recognition" of the mark and (c) the consistent and continuous, though not high-volume, use of the mark. The court relied specifically upon the fact that the defendants had used the mark "on at least one fax, on at least one resume, and in numerous [oral] solicitations." The court further determined that although defendant's word-of-mouth advertisement campaign might not be preferred "it is not so atypical that no reasonable person could view it as 'commercial.' " The Sixth Circuit remanded the case for a finding of the area in which the defendants had continuously used their mark prior to plaintiff's registration.

Given the aforementioned standard of "use" applicable to a common law trademark, as exemplified in *Allard*, there are on this record genuine issues of material fact which preclude entry of judgment in favor of LTI. Here, a trier of fact may conclude that LIM had used the "LUCENT" mark sufficiently to obtain common law trademark rights. Specifically, LIM had not lain dormant prior to November 30, 1995. Rather, in August and September of 1995, soon after its inception, LIM began its marketing efforts. At that time, LIM hired a graphic designer to develop a logo, letterhead, business cards and other assorted documents such as messages, message pads, labels and brochures. LIM's marketing materials included a folder holding documents from manufacturers and software producers containing labels which identified LIM as the source of the products.

On September 5, 1995, Mr. Feinstein, one of LIM's principals, wrote a letter on the letterhead of another of his companies, Corporate Consultants, which introduced LIM, by name, and the services it provided. The letter was sent to between approximately 25-50 people: clients of Corporate Consultants and other contacts Mr. Feinstein viewed as potential customers. That letter referred to the services LIM was providing and specifically associated the "LUCENT" mark with those services[:] "The name Lucent was selected after extensive study and with various database searches. It is a derivation of translucent and well describes our mission of providing light, clarity, and guidance in a new and exciting field."

Beginning in October 1995, LIM entered into several distributorship agreements with hardware and software companies which authorized it to resell those companies' products. For example, in October 1995 LIM entered into a contract permitting LIM to resell File Magic software, as well as a contract with Tech Data. LIM's principals also attended an exposition in October 1995, sponsored by Imaging World Magazine, at which LIM was registered by its name and the attending LIM principals wore badges that bore the company name.

In November 1995, LIM received its business cards and letterhead from the printers and LIM's principals began distributing extensively their business cards, bearing the "LUCENT" mark, as a means of advertisement. In the Fall of 1995, LIM also directed its marketing efforts at prospects through personal solicitations via mail, phone and personal meetings. LIM, however, did not engage in any public or paid advertising but its employees discussed business with virtually everyone they came in contact with.

Ultimately, LIM made sales presentations to three companies prior to November 30, 1995, the date on which LTI filed its Intent to Use the "LUCENT" mark. The present records establish that on November 3, 1995 LIM made a presentation to ARAMARK in Philadelphia, on November 17, 1995 LIM made a presentation to NBC in New York, on November 21, 1995 LIM made its first of several presentations to Nixon Uniform in Delaware. Although LIM's initial contact with Nixon Uniform was through a personal friend, the solicitation letter and LIM's presentation was made to another Nixon Uniform employee with whom LIM had no prior connection.

Although LIM used various marketing techniques, it made only two sales prior to December 1, 1995. Specifically, on October 5, 1995 for $323.50 LIM installed a modem for the Israel Bonds Office in Philadelphia and provided related training. LIM's contact at the Israel Bonds Office was a friend of one of LIM's principals. LIM provided the Israel Bonds Office with an invoice on a pre-printed LIM form though payment was directed to Mr. Armstrong, one of LIM's principals. In addition to LIM's sale to the Israel Bonds Office, on October 17, 1995 LIM took an order from Corporate Consultants, Mr. Feinstein's company with whom LIM shared office space. The services rendered to Corporate Consultants included: network servers, network fax software, SCSI cards, scanners, and other peripherals as well as consultation services on the design of their document imaging system beginning on November 12, 1995.

Here, the court's grant of summary judgment to LTI grants LTI a monopoly to use the "LUCENT" mark without proof that it is clearly entitled to it. LIM's conduct prior to November 30, 1995 provides a basis upon which a trier of fact may determine that LIM had "used" the "LUCENT" mark to the degree necessary to show priority of use and ownership. Only a trier of fact making credibility determinations upon a fuller record can ultimately determine whether LIM's intentional and continuous marketing strategy, three sales presentations, participation in a trade show, distributorship contracts and sales were sufficient to establish a common law trademark right.

. . .

B. The Natural Footwear test

With respect to the district court's secondary reliance on the four-factor test announced in *Natural Footwear* to determine "use" and the majority's exclusive reliance on that test, I also dissent. Although the *Natural Footwear* test is useful at the remedy stage of a proceeding to determine the territorial limits of an injunction to delineate trademark rights between two remote users of a confusingly similar mark, that test is inapplicable to the threshold question of ownership. While I am mindful of the precedential value of *Natural Footwear*, I am also mindful that *Natural Footwear* does not stand alone as the governing principle of trademark law, and in this case, stands apart from the requisite threshold inquiry for a common law trademark.

. . .

There is no indication in the history or subsequent application of that [the *Natural Footwear*] four-factor test that it was intended to be used to discern the status of a prior user as an initial matter. Rather, the history and later reliance on the *Natural Footwear* test supports the conclusion that this test is a tool of equity designed to determine the appropriate remedy in a geographical dispute between two good faith users of a mark. In fact, one must remember that the *Natural Footwear* test is an exception to the well-established rule of law that a senior user is deemed the exclusive owner of the trademark.

It is plain from a review of these cases that the *Natural Footwear* test is an exception which grew out of the need to balance the equities between two remote users of the same mark where the remedy imposed is a permanent injunction. This test was not meant to be dispositive of the ownership of a mark between two concurrent users and stands in stark contrast to the standard relied upon by Judge Friendly in La Societe Anonyme des Parfums le Galion v. Jean Patou, Inc., 495 F.2d 1265, that "there must be a trade in the goods sold under the mark or at least an active and public attempt to establish such a trade."

In practice, this higher standard of use would deprive local start-up concerns in this circuit from obtaining common law trademark rights based upon their deliberate and continuous use of a mark. Indeed, such a test might make it "impossible, with respect to a valuable and desirable article or product of manufacture, designated by a particular brand or in a particular manner, ever to establish a trade." Simply, a company's attempts to establish a business with the aid of a trademark could be stifled by a competitor before that company's sales and "market penetration" ever reach the standard set forth in *Natural Footwear*. I do not believe this is what was intended under trademark law or under the Lanham Act. . . .

Putting aside for a moment the impact the majority's rule of use may have for start-up companies which are slow to achieve market penetration, one can easily foresee how this new rule may also present problems to long-established companies. The rule adopted by the majority means that trademark users which have engaged in continuous use of their mark albeit over a diffuse area will no longer have any trademark rights. By refusing all common law trademark rights to a long-standing, non-concentrated and moderately successful company under the *Natural Footwear* test, a junior user can enjoin that company from using a mark altogether. Such a result runs counter to trademark law.

In this global economy where goods are often sold over a wide area rather than in a neighborhood store, the majority's rule of use penalizes small companies which take advantage of the national market. It is ironic that the majority sets forth such a high standard of use in this day and age when there is a technological revolution underway in which the internet permits small trademark users to sell their goods and services to broad geographic areas. The majority's standard of use places a legal straightjacket on those companies and deprives them of all common law trademark rights. In the end, this will exclude a whole class of trademark users from obtaining rights through "use" rather than registration and will tilt the level playing field which has always been an indispensable ingredient in deciding trademark rights.

The sounder analysis, I respectfully suggest, is to determine first whether a company has engaged in sufficient use of a mark under common law trademark law and, if there is a finding of infringement by another company, the court should consider that first company's market penetration and other indicia of the equities involved in the case to fashion appropriate injunctive relief.

. . .

Notes and Questions

1. Are there measures LIM could have taken in the initial stages of its business development (prior to November 30, 1995) that would have established its rights in the mark "Lucent"? Keep in mind that the court stated LIM could only prevail if such actions showed use of the mark "in a way sufficiently public to identify or distinguish the marked goods in an appropriate segment of the public mind as those of the adopter of the mark."

2. Would the outcome of this case have been different if LIM had filed an application to register the mark "Lucent" with the USPTO prior to November 30, 1995? Based on the stated facts, is it likely that the USPTO would have accepted such application and registered the mark to LIM at that time?

3. How is the majority's definition of "use" different from the definition Judge Ackerman advocates in the dissent?

4. Imagine your client has developed an original brand name that is not confusingly similar to any currently outstanding marks. What advice would you give the client as to initial steps to take to ensure that the business is both creating — and documenting — its trademark rights?

5. As noted earlier, although a person or business may establish trademark rights simply by using the name in commerce (common law trademark rights), there are additional benefits and protections afforded when the trademark owners take the step of federally registering the mark on the Principal Register of the USPTO. Such benefits include constructive notice of ownership of the mark; evidence of ownership of the mark; possibility that, after five years, registration will become incontestable and constitute conclusive evidence of the right to use the mark; right to bar the importation of goods bearing infringing trademarks; right to institute trademark actions in federal court; and treble damages. Why do you think we have this complex central filing system at the USPTO and why do you think federally registered marks are entitled to greater protection under the law?

6. When a business wants to assert trademark or service mark rights in a good or service, it is common and advisable to "put the world on notice" by including the letters "TM" or "SM" following the mark. Once a mark is registered with the USPTO, the company can use the designation "®".

TRADEMARK MANUAL OF EXAMINING PROCEDURE
United States Patent & Trademark Office (October 2018)

1209.01 Distinctiveness/Descriptiveness Continuum

With regard to trademark significance, matter may be categorized along a continuum, ranging from marks that are highly distinctive to matter that is a generic name for the goods or services. The degree of distinctiveness — or, on the other hand, descriptiveness — of a designation can be determined only by considering it in relation to the specific goods or services.

At one extreme are marks that, when used in relation to the goods or services, are completely arbitrary or fanciful. Next on the continuum are suggestive marks, followed by merely descriptive matter. Finally, generic terms for the goods or services are at the opposite end of the continuum from arbitrary or fanciful marks. As stated in [a leading case on the subject], "[t]he generic name of a thing is in fact the ultimate in descriptiveness."

Fanciful, arbitrary, and suggestive marks, often referred to as "inherently distinctive" marks, are registrable on the Principal Register without proof of acquired distinctiveness.

Marks that are merely descriptive of the goods or services may not be registered on the Principal Register absent a showing of acquired distinctiveness. . . .

Matter that is generic for the goods or services is not registrable on either the Principal or the Supplemental Register under any circumstances. . . .

1209.01(a) Fanciful, Arbitrary, and Suggestive Marks

Fanciful marks comprise terms that have been invented for the sole purpose of functioning as a trademark or service mark. Such marks comprise words that are either unknown in the language (e.g., PEPSI, KODAK, and EXXON) or are completely out of common usage (e.g., FLIVVER).

Arbitrary marks comprise words that are in common linguistic use but, when used to identify particular goods or services, do not suggest or describe a significant ingredient, quality, or characteristic of the goods or services (e.g., APPLE for computers; OLD CROW for whiskey). See, e.g., Palm Bay Imports, Inc. v. Veuve Clicquot Ponsardin Maison Fondee En 1772, 396 F.3d 1369, 1372, 73 USPQ2d 1689, 1692 (Fed. Cir. 2005) (VEUVE — meaning WIDOW in English — held to be "an arbitrary term as applied to champagne and sparkling wine, and thus conceptually strong as a trademark"); Nautilus Group, Inc. v. Icon Health & Fitness, Inc., 372 F.3d 1330, 1340, 71 USPQ2d 1173, 1180 (Fed. Cir. 2004) (defining an arbitrary mark as "a known word used in an unexpected or uncommon way").

Suggestive marks are those that, when applied to the goods or services at issue, require imagination, thought, or perception to reach a conclusion as to the nature of those goods or services. Thus, a suggestive term differs from a descriptive term, which immediately tells something about the goods or services. See In re George Weston Ltd., 228 USPQ 57 (TTAB 1985) (SPEEDI BAKE for frozen dough found to fall within the category of suggestive marks because it only vaguely suggests a desirable characteristic of frozen dough, namely, that it quickly and easily may be baked into bread); In re The Noble Co., 225 USPQ 749 (TTAB 1985) (NOBURST for liquid antifreeze and rust inhibitor for hot-water-heating systems found to suggest a desired result of using the product rather than immediately informing the purchasing public of a characteristic, feature, function, or attribute); In re Pennwalt Corp., 173 USPQ 317 (TTAB 1972) (DRI-FOOT held suggestive of anti-perspirant deodorant for feet in part because, in the singular, it is not the usual or normal manner in which the purpose of an anti-perspirant and deodorant for the feet would be described).

Incongruity is a strong indication that a mark is suggestive rather than merely descriptive. In re Tennis in the Round Inc., 199 USPQ 496, 498 (TTAB

1978) (TENNIS IN THE ROUND held not merely descriptive for providing tennis facilities, the Board finding that the association of applicant's marks with the phrase "theater-in-the-round" created an incongruity because applicant's tennis facilities are not at all analogous to those used in a "theater-in-the-round"). The Board has described incongruity in a mark as "one of the accepted guideposts in the evolved set of legal principles for discriminating the suggestive from the descriptive mark," and has noted that the concept of mere descriptiveness "should not penalize coinage of hitherto unused and somewhat incongruous word combinations whose import would not be grasped without some measure of imagination and 'mental pause.'" In re Shutts, 217 USPQ 363, 365 (TTAB 1983) (SNO-RAKE held not merely descriptive of a snow-removal hand tool); see In re Vienna Sausage Mfg. Co., 156 USPQ 155, 156 (TTAB 1967) (FRANKWURST held not merely descriptive for wieners, the Board finding that although "frank" may be synonymous with "wiener," and "wurst" is synonymous with "sausage," the combination of the terms is incongruous and results in a mark that is no more than suggestive of the nature of the goods); In re John H. Breck, Inc., 150 USPQ 397, 398 (TTAB 1966) (TINT TONE held suggestive for hair coloring, the Board finding that the words overlap in significance and their combination is somewhat incongruous or redundant and does not immediately convey the nature of the product); cf. In re Getz Found., 227 USPQ 571, 572 (TTAB 1985) (MOUSE HOUSE held fanciful for museum services featuring mice figurines made up to appear as human beings, the Board finding that the only conceivable meaning of "mouse house," i.e., a building at a zoo in which live and/or stuffed mice are displayed, is incongruous).

Suggestive marks, like fanciful and arbitrary marks, are registrable on the Principal Register without proof of secondary meaning. Therefore, a designation does not have to be devoid of all meaning in relation to the goods/services to be registrable: . . .

1209.01(b) Merely Descriptive Marks

To be refused registration on the Principal Register under § 2(e)(1) of the Trademark Act, 15 U.S.C. § 1052(e)(1), a mark must be merely descriptive or deceptively misdescriptive of the goods or services to which it relates. A mark is considered merely descriptive if it describes an ingredient, quality, characteristic, function, feature, purpose, or use of the specified goods or services. See In re Gyulay, 820 F.2d 1216, 3 USPQ2d 1009 (Fed. Cir. 1987) (APPLE PIE held merely descriptive of potpourri); In re Bed & Breakfast Registry, 791 F.2d 157, 229 USPQ 818 (Fed. Cir. 1986) (BED & BREAKFAST REGISTRY held merely descriptive of lodging reservations services); In re MetPath Inc., 223 USPQ 88 (TTAB 1984) (MALE-P.A.P. TEST held merely descriptive of clinical pathological immunoassay testing services for detecting and monitoring prostatic cancer); In re Bright-Crest, Ltd., 204 USPQ 591 (TTAB 1979) (COASTER-CARDS held merely descriptive of a coaster suitable for direct mailing). Similarly, a mark is considered merely descriptive if it immediately conveys knowledge of a quality, feature, function, or characteristic of an applicant's goods or services.

     . . .

The determination of whether a mark is merely descriptive must be made in relation to the goods or services for which registration is sought, not in the abstract. This requires consideration of the context in which the mark is used or intended to be used in connection with those goods/services, and the possible significance that the mark would have to the average purchaser of the goods or services in the marketplace. Sources for considering the context in which the mark is or may be used include websites, publications, labels, packages, advertising material, and explanatory text on specimens for the goods and services.

It is not necessary that a term describe all of the purposes, functions, characteristics, or features of a product to be considered merely descriptive; it is enough if the term describes one significant function, attribute, or property.

. . .

The great variation in facts from case to case prevents the formulation of specific rules for specific fact situations. Each case must be decided on its own merits.

. . .

1209.01(c) Generic Terms

Generic terms are terms that the relevant purchasing public understands primarily as the common or class name for the goods or services. A generic term is "the ultimate in descriptiveness" under § 2(e)(1) and incapable of acquiring distinctiveness under § 2(f). A generic term also does not meet the statutory definition of a mark because it is incapable of denoting a unique source. In re Merrill Lynch, Pierce, Fenner, & Smith, Inc., 828 F.2d 1567, 1569 (Fed. Cir. 1987) ("Generic terms, by definition incapable of indicating source, are the antithesis of trademarks, and can never attain trademark status."). Thus, generic terms are not registrable on the Principal Register under § 2(f) or on the Supplemental Register.

Generic terms are refused registration on the Principal Register . . .

UNITED STATES PTO v. BOOKING.COM B.V.

Supreme Court of the United States
140 S. Ct. 2298 (2020)

Justice GINSBURG delivered the opinion of the Court.

This case concerns eligibility for federal trademark registration. Respondent Booking.com, an enterprise that maintains a travel-reservation website by the same name, sought to register the mark "Booking.com." Concluding that "Booking.com" is a generic name for online hotel-reservation services, the U. S. Patent and Trademark Office (PTO) refused registration.

A generic name — the name of a class of products or services — is ineligible for federal trademark registration. The word "booking," the parties do not dispute, is generic for hotel-reservation services. "Booking.com" must also be generic, the PTO maintains, under an encompassing rule the PTO currently urges us to adopt: The combination of a generic word and ".com" is generic.

In accord with the first- and second-instance judgments in this case, we reject the PTO's sweeping rule. A term styled "generic.com" is a generic name for a class of goods or services only if the term has that meaning to consumers. Consumers, according to lower court determinations uncontested here by the PTO, do not perceive the term "Booking.com" to signify online hotel-reservation services as a class. In circumstances like those this case presents, a "generic.com" term is not generic and can be eligible for federal trademark registration.

I

A

A trademark distinguishes one producer's goods or services from another's. Guarding a trademark against use by others, this Court has explained, "secure[s] to the owner of the mark the goodwill" of her business and "protect[s] the ability of consumers to distinguish among competing producers." Trademark protection has roots in common law and equity. Today, the Lanham Act, enacted in 1946, provides federal statutory protection for trademarks. We have recognized that federal trademark protection, supplementing state law, "supports the free flow of commerce" and "foster[s] competition."

The Lanham Act not only arms trademark owners with federal claims for relief; importantly, it establishes a system of federal trademark registration. The owner of a mark on the principal register enjoys "valuable benefits," including a presumption that the mark is valid. The supplemental register contains other product and service designations, some of which could one day gain eligibility for the principal register. The supplemental register accords more modest benefits; notably, a listing on that register announces one's use of the designation to others considering a similar mark. . . .

Prime among the conditions for registration, the mark must be one "by which the goods of the applicant may be distinguished from the goods of others." Distinctiveness is often expressed on an increasing scale: Word marks "may be (1) generic; (2) descriptive; (3) suggestive; (4) arbitrary; or (5) fanciful."

The more distinctive the mark, the more readily it qualifies for the principal register. . . .

At the lowest end of the distinctiveness scale is "the generic name for the goods or services." The name of the good itself (e.g., "wine") is incapable of "distinguish[ing] [one producer's goods] from the goods of others" and is therefore ineligible for registration. Indeed, generic terms are ordinarily ineligible for protection as trademarks at all.

B

Booking.com is a digital travel company that provides hotel reservations and other services under the brand "Booking.com," which is also the domain name of its website. Booking.com filed applications to register four marks in connection with travel-related services, each with different visual features but all containing the term "Booking.com."

Both a PTO examining attorney and the PTO's Trademark Trial and Appeal Board concluded that the term "Booking.com" is generic for the services at issue and is therefore unregistrable. "Booking," the Board observed, means making travel reservations, and ".com" signifies a commercial website. The Board then ruled that "customers would understand the term BOOKING.COM primarily to refer to an online reservation service for travel, tours, and lodgings." Alternatively, the Board held that even if "Booking.com" is descriptive, not generic, it is unregistrable because it lacks secondary meaning.

Booking.com sought review in the U. S. District Court for the Eastern District of Virginia. . . . [T]he District Court concluded that "Booking.com" — unlike "booking" — is not generic. The "consuming public," the court found, "primarily understands that BOOKING.COM does not refer to a genus, rather it is descriptive of services involving 'booking' available at that domain name." . . .

The PTO appealed only the District Court's determination that "Booking.com" is not generic. Finding no error in the District Court's assessment of how consumers perceive the term "Booking.com," the Court of Appeals for the Fourth Circuit affirmed the court of first instance's judgment. In so ruling, the appeals court rejected the PTO's contention that the combination of ".com" with a generic term like "booking" "is necessarily generic." . . .

We granted certiorari, and now affirm the Fourth Circuit's decision.

II

Although the parties here disagree about the circumstances in which terms like "Booking.com" rank as generic, several guiding principles are common ground. First, a "generic" term names a "class" of goods or services, rather than any particular feature or exemplification of the class. Second, for a compound term, the distinctiveness inquiry trains on the term's meaning as a whole, not its parts in isolation. Third, the relevant meaning of a term is its meaning to consumers. Eligibility for registration, all agree, turns on the mark's capacity to "distinguis[h]" goods "in commerce." Evidencing the Lanham Act's focus on consumer perception, the section governing cancellation of registration provides that "[t]he primary significance of the registered mark to the relevant public . . . shall be the test for determining whether the registered mark has become the generic name of goods or services."

Under these principles, whether "Booking.com" is generic turns on whether that term, taken as a whole, signifies to consumers the class of online hotel-reservation services. Thus, if "Booking.com" were generic, we might expect consumers to understand Travelocity — another such service — to be a "Booking.com." We might similarly expect that a consumer, searching for a trusted source of online hotel-reservation services, could ask a frequent traveler to name her favorite "Booking.com" provider.

Consumers do not in fact perceive the term "Booking.com" that way, the courts below determined. The PTO no longer disputes that determination. That should resolve this case: Because "Booking.com" is not a generic name to consumers, it is not generic.

III

Opposing that conclusion, the PTO urges a nearly per se rule that would render "Booking.com" ineligible for registration regardless of specific evidence of consumer perception. In the PTO's view, which the dissent embraces, when a generic term is combined with a generic top-level domain like ".com," the resulting combination is generic. In other words, every "generic.com" term is generic according to the PTO, absent exceptional circumstances.

The PTO's own past practice appears to reflect no such comprehensive rule. See, e.g., Trademark Registration No. 3,601,346 ("ART.COM" on principal register for, inter alia, "[o]nline retail store services" offering "art prints, original art, [and] art reproductions"); Trademark Registration No. 2,580,467 ("DATING.

COM" [***13] on supplemental register for "dating services"). Existing registrations inconsistent with the rule the PTO now advances would be at risk of cancellation if the PTO's current view were to prevail. We decline to adopt a rule essentially excluding registration of "generic.com" marks. As explained below, we discern no support for the PTO's current view in trademark law or policy.

A

The PTO urges that the exclusionary rule it advocates follows from a common-law principle, applied in Goodyear's India Rubber Glove Mfg. Co. v. Goodyear Rubber Co., 128 U. S. 598, 9 S. Ct. 166, 32 L. Ed. 535, 1889 Dec. Comm'r Pat. 257 (1888), that a generic corporate designation added to a generic term does not confer trademark eligibility. In *Goodyear*, a decision predating the Lanham Act, this Court held that "Goodyear Rubber Company" was not "capable of exclusive appropriation." Standing alone, the term "Goodyear Rubber" could not serve as a trademark because it referred, in those days, to "well-known classes of goods produced by the process known as Goodyear's invention." "[A]ddition of the word 'Company'" supplied no protectable meaning, the Court concluded, because adding "Company" "only indicates that parties have formed an association or partnership to deal in such goods." Permitting exclusive rights in "Goodyear [***14] Rubber Company" (or "Wine Company, Cotton Company, or Grain Company"), the Court explained, would tread on the right of all persons "to deal in such articles, and to publish the fact to the world."

"Generic.com," the PTO maintains, is like "Generic Company" and is therefore ineligible for trademark protection, let alone federal registration. According to the PTO, adding ".com" to a generic term — like adding "Company" — "conveys no additional meaning that would distinguish [one provider's] services from those of other providers." The dissent endorses that proposition: "Generic.com" conveys that the generic good or service is offered online "and nothing more."

That premise is faulty. A "generic.com" term might also convey to consumers a source-identifying characteristic: an association with a particular website. As the PTO and the dissent elsewhere acknowledge, only one entity can occupy a particular Internet domain name at a time, so "[a] consumer who is familiar with that aspect of the domain-name system can infer that BOOKING.COM refers to some specific entity." Thus, consumers could understand a given "generic.com" term to describe the corresponding website or to identify the website's proprietor. We therefore resist the PTO's position that "generic.com" terms are capable of signifying only an entire class of online goods or services and, hence, are categorically incapable of identifying a source.

. . .

While we reject the rule proffered by the PTO that "generic.com" terms are generic names, we do not embrace a rule automatically classifying such terms as nongeneric. Whether any given "generic.com" term is generic, we hold, depends on whether consumers in fact perceive that term as the name of a class or, instead, as a term capable of distinguishing among members of the class.

B

The PTO, echoed by the dissent, objects that protecting "generic.com" terms as trademarks would disserve trademark law's animating policies. We disagree.

The PTO's principal concern is that trademark protection for a term like "Booking.com" would hinder competitors. But the PTO does not assert that others seeking to offer online hotel-reservation services need to call their services "Booking. com." Rather, the PTO fears that trademark protection for "Booking.com" could exclude or inhibit competitors from using the term "booking" or adopting domain names like "ebooking.com" or "hotel-booking.com." The PTO's objection, therefore, is not to exclusive use of "Booking.com" as a mark, but to undue control over similar language, i.e., "booking," that others should remain free to use.

That concern attends any descriptive mark. Responsive to it, trademark law hems in the scope of such marks short of denying trademark protection altogether. Notably, a competitor's use does not infringe a mark unless it is likely to confuse consumers. In assessing the likelihood of confusion, courts consider the mark's distinctiveness: "The weaker a mark, the fewer are the junior uses that will trigger a likelihood of consumer confusion." When a mark incorporates generic or highly descriptive components, consumers are less likely to think that other uses of the common element emanate from the mark's owner. Similarly, "[i]n a 'crowded' field of look-alike marks" (e.g., hotel names including the word "grand"), consumers "may have learned to carefully pick out" one mark from another. And even where some consumer confusion exists, the doctrine known as classic fair use protects from liability anyone who uses a descriptive term, "fairly and in good faith" and "otherwise than as a mark," merely to describe her own goods.

These doctrines guard against the anticompetitive effects the PTO identifies, ensuring that registration of "Booking.com" would not yield its holder a monopoly on the term "booking." Booking.com concedes that "Booking.com" would be a "weak" mark. The mark is descriptive, Booking.com recognizes, making it "harder . . . to show a likelihood of confusion." Furthermore, because its mark is one of many "similarly worded marks," Booking.com accepts that close variations are unlikely to infringe. And Booking.com acknowledges that federal registration of "Booking.com" would not prevent competitors from using the word "booking" to describe their services.

The PTO also doubts that owners of "generic.com" brands need trademark protection in addition to existing competitive advantages. Booking.com, the PTO argues, has already seized a domain name that no other website can use and is easy for consumers to find. Consumers might enter "the word 'booking' in a search engine," the PTO observes, or "proceed directly to 'booking.com' in the expectation that [online hotel-booking] services will be offered at that address." Those competitive advantages, however, do not inevitably disqualify a mark from federal registration. All descriptive marks are intuitively linked to the product or service and thus might be easy for consumers to find using a search engine or telephone directory. The Lanham Act permits registration nonetheless. And the PTO fails to explain how the exclusive connection between a domain name and its owner makes the domain name a generic term all should be free to use. That connection makes trademark protection more appropriate, not less.

. . .

The PTO challenges the judgment below on a sole ground: It urges that, as a rule, combining a generic term with ".com" yields a generic composite. For the above-stated reasons, we decline a rule of that order, one that would largely disallow registration of "generic.com" terms and open the door to cancellation of scores of currently registered marks. Accordingly, the judgment of the Court of Appeals for the Fourth Circuit regarding eligibility for trademark registration is

Affirmed.

Justice BREYER, dissenting.

What is Booking.com? To answer this question, one need only consult the term itself. Respondent provides an online booking service. The company's name informs the consumer of the basic nature of its business and nothing more. Therein lies the root of my disagreement with the majority.

Trademark law does not protect generic terms, meaning terms that do no more than name the product or service itself. This principle preserves the linguistic commons by preventing one producer from appropriating to its own exclusive use a term needed by others to describe their goods or services. Today, the Court holds that the addition of ".com" to an otherwise generic term, such as "booking," can yield a protectable trademark. Because I believe this result is inconsistent with trademark principles and sound trademark policy, I respectfully dissent.

. . .

This case requires us to apply [trademark distinctiveness] principles in the novel context of internet domain names. Respondent seeks to register a term, "Booking.com," that consists of a generic term, "booking" (known as the second-level domain) plus ".com" (known as the top-level domain). The question at issue here is whether a term that takes the form "generic.com" is generic in the ordinary course. In my view, appending ".com" to a generic term ordinarily yields no meaning beyond that of its constituent parts. Because the term "Booking.com" is just such an ordinary "generic.com" term, in my view, it is not eligible for trademark registration.

Like the corporate designations at issue in Goodyear, a top-level domain such as ".com" has no capacity to identify and distinguish the source of goods or services. It is merely a necessary component of any web address. When combined with the generic name of a class of goods or services, ".com" conveys only that the owner operates a website related to such items. Just as "Wine Company" expresses the generic concept of a company that deals in wine, "wine.com" connotes only a website that does the same. The same is true of "Booking.com." The combination of "booking" and ".com" does not serve to "identify a particular characteristic or quality of some thing; it connotes the basic nature of that thing" — the hallmark of a generic term.

When a website uses an inherently distinctive second-level domain, it is obvious that adding ".com" merely denotes a website associated with that term. Any reasonably well-informed consumer would understand that "post-it.com" is the website associated with Post-its. Likewise, "plannedparenthood.com" is obviously just the website of Planned Parenthood. Recognizing this feature of domain names, courts generally ignore the top-level domain when analyzing likelihood of confusion.

Generic second-level domains are no different. The meaning conveyed by "Booking.com" is no more and no less than a website associated with its generic second-level domain, "booking." This will ordinarily be true of any generic term plus ".com" combination. The term as a whole is just as generic as its constituent parts.

. . .

In addition to the doctrinal concerns discussed above, granting trademark protection to "generic.com" marks threatens serious anticompetitive consequences in the online marketplace.

The owners of short, generic domain names enjoy all the advantages of doing business under a generic name. These advantages exist irrespective of the trademark laws. Generic names are easy to remember. Because they immediately convey the nature of the business, the owner needs to expend less effort and expense educating consumers. And a generic business name may create the impression that it is the most authoritative and trustworthy source of the particular good or service. These advantages make it harder for distinctively named businesses to compete.

Owners of generic domain names enjoy additional competitive advantages unique to the internet — again, regardless of trademark protection. Most importantly, domain name ownership confers automatic exclusivity. Multiple brick-and-mortar companies could style themselves "The Wine Company," but there can be only one "wine.com." And unlike the trademark system, that exclusivity is world-wide.

Generic domains are also easier for consumers to find. A consumer who wants to buy wine online may perform a keyword search and be directed to "wine.com." Or he may simply type "wine.com" into his browser's address bar, expecting to find a website selling wine. The owner of a generic domain name enjoys these benefits not because of the quality of her products or the goodwill of her business, but because she was fortunate (or savvy) enough to be the first to appropriate a particularly valuable piece of online real estate.

Granting trademark protection to "generic.com" marks confers additional competitive benefits on their owners by allowing them to exclude others from using similar domain names. Federal registration would allow respondent to threaten trademark lawsuits against competitors using domains such as "Bookings.com," "eBooking.com," "Booker.com," or "Bookit.com." Respondent says that it would not do so. But other firms may prove less restrained.

Indeed, why would a firm want to register its domain name as a trademark unless it wished to extend its area of exclusivity beyond the domain name itself? The domain name system, after all, already ensures that competitors cannot appropriate a business's actual domain name. And unfair-competition law will often separately protect businesses from passing off and false advertising.

Under the majority's reasoning, many businesses could obtain a trademark by adding ".com" to the generic name of their product (e.g., pizza.com, flowers.com, and so forth). As the internet grows larger, as more and more firms use it to sell their products, the risk of anticompetitive consequences grows. Those consequences can nudge the economy in an anticompetitive direction. At the extreme, that direction points towards one firm per product, the opposite of the competitive multifirm marketplace that our basic economic laws seek to achieve.

. . .

In sum, the term "Booking.com" refers to an internet booking service, which is the generic product that respondent and its competitors sell. No more and no less. The same is true of "generic.com" terms more generally. By making such terms eligible for trademark protection, I fear that today's decision will lead to a proliferation of "generic.com" marks, granting their owners a monopoly over a zone of useful, easy-to-remember domains. This result would tend to inhibit, rather than to promote, free competition in online commerce. I respectfully dissent.

Notes and Questions

1. What are some factors an entrepreneur should consider when initially creating a trademark that will be used by the business to promote her products? Would a mark that accurately describes the products be ideal because it would efficiently communicate to the target consumer group the purpose of the product? What

benefits might an entrepreneurial venture get from a descriptive mark that would be unavailable with a fanciful mark?

2. Decisions at the USPTO are made by trademark examiners, who are generally well-trained attorneys expert in this area. Do the standards set forth in the TMEP seem sufficiently objective that a consistent outcome is guaranteed?

3. Consider the Booking.com case. Why do you imagine generic words "are ineligible for protection as trademarks at all"?

4. The current Trademark Manual of Examining Procedure states that

> to establish that a proposed mark is generic, the examining attorney must show that the relevant public would understand the mark as a whole to have generic significance. See 1800Mattress.com, 586 F.3d at 1363, 92 USPQ2d at 1684 (affirming Board's conclusion that MATTRESS.COM was generic for "online retail store services in the field of mattresses, beds, and bedding," where the Board considered each of the constituent words, "mattress" and ".com" and determined that they were both generic, then considered the mark as a whole and determined that the combination added no new meaning, relying on the prevalence of the term "mattress.com" in the website addresses of several online mattress retailers who provide the same services as the applicant); In re Hotels.com, L.P., 573 F.3d 1300, 91 USPQ2d 1532 (Fed. Cir. 2009) (HOTELS.COM is generic for "providing information for others about temporary lodging; [and] travel agency services, namely, making reservations and bookings for temporary lodging for others by means of telephone and the global computer network," based on various definitions of "hotel," printouts from hotel reservation search websites showing "hotels" as the equivalent of or included within "temporary lodging," as well as evidence from applicant's website); In re DNI Holdings Ltd., 77 USPQ2d 1435 (TTAB 2005) (SPORTSBETTING.COM held generic for "provision of casino games on and through a global computer network wherein there are no actual monetary wagers; provision of contests and sweepstakes on and through a global computer network; providing a website on and through a global computer network featuring information in the fields of gaming, athletic competition and entertainment . . . ," where the record included multiple examples of use of the terms "sports betting" as well as the joined terms "sportsbetting" by both applicant and its competitors to refer to both sports wagering and providing information about sports wagering, and there was no indication of a realistic alternative connotation of the compound term . . .)

Is this instruction to examiners consistent with the *Booking.com* case? If you have a client with a so-called generic.com name, what will you advise about the potential for registering the mark?

4. Does Justice Breyer disagree with the majority about the standard used to determine whether a trademark is generic? Do you find the dissent's analysis persuasive?

5. Given the concerns with descriptive marks that are identified by the court, why do you imagine these marks are allowed to be registered? Why might a start-up choose a descriptive mark when they can get greater protection from a suggestive, arbitrary, or fanciful mark?

6. Although the USPTO makes decisions about whether or not to register a mark, registered marks can still be challenged in court on the ground that they should not have been registered (for example, because they are confusingly similar to other registered marks or because they are merely descriptive). Given this

fact and the other things you have learned so far about trademark law, what advice would you give to a client who receives a denial of registration from the USPTO? How about a client who has had a trademark approved for registration?

2. *Trademark Infringement*

As noted in the *Lucent* case, trademark law protects owners of a mark when use of that mark or a similar mark is likely to cause confusion. Trademark law also attempts to protect consumers from purchasing inferior (or simply unexpected) goods or services based on confusion over the source of such goods or services. In order to prove trademark infringement, the trademark owner must establish a likelihood that the allegedly infringing mark could confuse potential consumers. Courts will take many factors into consideration when determining whether trademark infringement has occurred. Surveys of potential consumers as to whether they actually found the marks confusing may be used as evidence. In the following case, the court discusses the elements of trademark infringement in the context of the sale of a business, including its primary trademark.

OSGOOD HEATING & AIR CONDITIONING, INC. v. OSGOOD

United States District Court for the Western District of Texas
75 U.S.P.Q.2d 1432 (2004)

. . .

I. BACKGROUND

Since 1968, Osgood Heating & Air Conditioning, Inc. ("Osgood") has operated in Austin, Texas, performing heating, air conditioning, and electrical services. On August 25, 1998, Plaintiff American Residential Services, L.L.C. ("ARS") acquired Osgood by entering into an Agreement and Plan of Reorganization ("Agreement") with Osgood's shareholders John K. Osgood, Sr., Nancy W. Osgood, John K. Osgood, Jr., Charles Osgood, and Brenda Osgood Hogan (collectively the "Shareholders"). Pursuant to the Agreement and the ARS Standard for Business Combinations ("Business Combinations") which was incorporated into the Agreement, ARS purchased Osgood, including its customer base, assets, goodwill, and the good reputation associated with its mark and trade name (the "Osgood Mark").

According to Plaintiffs, Defendants have recently commenced a scheme to infringe upon the Osgood Mark for their own benefit and to the detriment of Plaintiffs. Following the sale of Osgood to ARS, Charles Osgood started the company Service Wizard, Inc. ("Service Wizard"). Like Osgood, Service Wizard is in the heating and air conditioning business, serving customers in Austin, Texas. Plaintiffs contend Defendants, without permission from Plaintiffs, adopted and continue to use the mark "4-Osgood" in advertisements to promote their services in the Austin area. These advertisements include a televised advertisement where

Charles Osgood provides potential customers with the telephone number of "4-O-S-G-O-O-D." In addition, Defendants sponsor a local weather forecast on Channel 8 stating the forecast was brought to you by "4-O-S-G-O-O-D" and instructs the viewer to call that number for heat and air conditioning service. Defendants have also advertised the "4-O-S-G-O-O-D" telephone number in other outlets including Internet advertisements and the Yellow Pages. Moreover, the "4-O-S-G-O-O-D" telephone number (467-4663) is strikingly similar to Plaintiff Osgood's telephone number (869-4663). Finally, Defendants maintain a website at www.4osgood.com to advertise and solicit clients for their heating and air conditioning services in Austin.

. . .

1. Trademark Infringement Claim

To prove trademark infringement, Plaintiffs must show Defendants' use of the "4-Osgood" mark is likely to cause confusion among consumers as to the source, affiliation, and sponsorship. A "likelihood of confusion" means confusion is not just possible, but probable. In assessing whether use of a mark creates a likelihood of confusion, the Court should consider: (1) the type of mark allegedly infringed; (2) the similarity between the two marks; (3) the similarity of the products or services; (4) the identity of retail outlets and purchasers; (5) the identity of the advertising media used; (6) the defendants' intent; and (7) any evidence of actual confusion. The factors are flexible and nonexhaustive. They do not apply mechanically to every case and can serve only as guides, not as an exact calculus. "No one factor is dispositive, and a finding of a likelihood of confusion does not even require a positive finding on a majority of these [factors]." Elvis Presley Enters., Inc. v. Capece, 141 F.3d 188, 194 (5th Cir. 1998).

a. Type of Mark Allegedly Infringed

Trademarks are protected on a sliding scale based on their distinctiveness. Because the Osgood Mark is unrelated to heating and air conditioning, it is an arbitrary mark. See Quantum Fitness Corp. v. Quantum LifeStyle Ctrs., 83 F. Supp. 2d 810, 817 (S.D. Tex. 1999) ("An arbitrary mark has a common meaning unrelated to the product for which it has been assigned, such as APPLE when applied to computers."). The Osgood Mark is "inherently distinctive, because [its] intrinsic nature serves to identify a particular source of a product;" thus, entitling it to a high degree of protection. In the alternative, to the extent the Osgood Mark could be perceived as a surname, it has acquired distinctiveness through Plaintiffs' long and extensive usage of the mark for over 30 years. 15 U.S.C. §§ 1052 (e)(4) and (f) (requiring five years of continuous and exclusive use for prima facie evidence of the development of secondary meaning).

b. Similarity Between the Two Marks

"The similarity of the marks in question is determined by comparing the marks' appearance, sound, and meaning." The dominant portion of the Osgood Mark is the name "Osgood" in Osgood Heating & Air Conditioning. It is distinctive and "Osgood" is the name that has been associated with Osgood Heating & Air Conditioning since the company was created. "4-Osgood" is the dominant mark for Defendants. As such, the two marks are nearly identical in their legally relevant dominant portions. It is the dominant feature of a name or mark that is most important in gauging the likelihood of confusion. Demonstrating a defendant has copied a dominant feature of a mark may be sufficient in itself to show infringement. In a similar case in which a defendant had adopted as the dominant part of its name a substantially identical term used by the plaintiff, summary judgment was granted for the plaintiff.

c. Similarity of the Products or Services

"The greater the similarity between the products and services, the greater the likelihood of confusion." "The real issue is whether the products or services of [Defendants] are sufficiently related to those of [Plaintiffs] that they are likely to be associated in some way with [Plaintiffs] if sold under a similar name." Here, Plaintiffs and Defendants are in direct competition. Not only is Service Wizard in the heating and air conditioning market, it is also directly competing with Plaintiffs in Austin. Plaintiffs' goodwill is likely impaired because consumers may believe "4-Osgood" is somehow connected, affiliated with, or sponsored by Osgood Heating & Air Conditioning. *Elvis Presley*, 141 F.3d at 202 ("The danger of affiliation or sponsorship confusion increases when the junior user's ["4-Osgood"] services are in a market that is one into which the senior user would naturally expand.").

d. Identity of the Advertising Media Used

Defendants advertise over the Internet, in print, on television, and on the radio. Plaintiffs advertise using the same media. Thus, both parties advertise using the same channels.

e. Defendants' Intent

Defendants were obviously familiar with Plaintiffs and their rights in the Osgood Mark when they selected the infringing mark "4-Osgood," as Charles Osgood was one of the original founders of Osgood Heating & Air Conditioning, and was personally involved in selling the business to Plaintiffs. Defendants' conduct strongly supports a likelihood of confusion in this case.

In sum, based on the record before the Court at this time, the Court finds Plaintiffs have demonstrated a probability of success on the merits on their trademark infringement claim.

2. *Trademark Dilution Claim*

To prove trademark dilution under Texas law, Plaintiffs must show: (1) they own a distinctive mark; and (2) there is a likelihood of (a) dilution due to blurring, diminution in uniqueness and individuality of their mark, or (b) tarnishment, injury resulting from Defendants' use of the "4-Osgood" mark in a manner that tarnishes or appropriates goodwill and reputation associated with Plaintiffs' mark.

a.   Distinctive Mark

In analyzing the distinctiveness of a mark under the Texas anti-dilution statute, courts consider: "(1) whether the mark is arbitrary; (2) the length of time a user has employed the mark; (3) the scope of the user's advertising and promotions; (4) the nature and extent of the first user's business; and (5) the scope of the first user's reputation." These criteria are similar to those considered in the "Type of Mark Allegedly Infringed" section above, and thus are satisfied here as well.

b.   Dilution Due to Blurring

Dilution by blurring occurs when Defendants' use of Plaintiffs' mark creates a "loss of distinctiveness" and "raises the possibility that the mark will lose its ability to serve as a unique identifier of the plaintiff's product." Plaintiffs have shown their ability to expand their recognition and goodwill through the use of their Osgood Mark has been harmed by Defendants' use of the "4-Osgood" mark and telephone number to identify Defendants' services. This harm will only increase as Defendants' use expands. Accordingly, on their trademark dilution claim, Plaintiffs have also shown a strong likelihood of success on the merits.

B.   Plaintiffs Have Shown Irreparable harm

The harm to Plaintiffs from Defendants' trademark infringement and dilution is difficult to quantify, and thus injunctive relief is appropriate. The harm in this case includes frustrated and potentially lost customers of Osgood Heating & Air Conditioning misdirected to Service Wizard by the various advertisements bearing the "4-Osgood" mark and telephone number. Additionally, Plaintiffs have no way of knowing whether Service Wizard may be further eroding the Osgood Mark by providing low quality work under the auspices of the Osgood Mark. Plaintiffs have satisfied their burden of demonstrating irreparable injury.

C.   No Harm to Defendants

Plaintiffs must show the threat of irreparable harm outweighs the potential injury Defendants face if a preliminary injunction is granted. Here, the harm to Plaintiffs from Defendants' infringement and dilution outweighs any inconvenience to Defendants if their use of the "4-Osgood" mark or the "4-O-S-G-O-O-D" telephone number is enjoined. Service Wizard is a new company that has seemingly not invested much in establishing its own distinctive mark, as evidenced by the company's apparent need to infringe upon the Osgood Mark. Since the name Service Wizard is not related to Osgood Heating & Air Conditioning, it could easily operate under that name without the assistance of the "4-Osgood" mark or the "4-O-S-G-O-O-D" telephone number. The threatened injuries to Plaintiffs outweigh any damage the injunction might cause Defendants. Accordingly, the balance of harms supports the granting of injunctive relief.

D.   The Public Interest Favors the Preliminary Injunction

Finally, Plaintiffs must show the public interest is served by granting an injunction. "The public interest is always served by requiring compliance with Congressional statutes such as the Lanham Act and by enjoining the use of infringing marks." If a mark is entitled to protection, "it necessarily follows that the preliminary injunction serves the public interest." To protect the public from further confusion between Plaintiffs and Defendants, the Court will issue an injunction.

III.   CONCLUSION

In accordance with the foregoing:

IT IS ORDERED that Plaintiffs' Application for Preliminary Injunction is GRANTED.

. . .

Notes and Questions

1. Do you think the fact that defendants had sold their business (including the mark "Osgood") to plaintiffs affected the court's decision? In other words, if the facts remained the same except that the plaintiff and defendant had never met or transacted business together, would the outcome have been the same?

2. Would the outcome have been different if defendants had been using the mark "4-Osgood" in a window replacement business?

3. Refute defendants' potential argument that they are simply using their own last name to promote their new business. Can a surname be entitled to strong trademark protection?

4. When a client presents her attorney with a proposed new trademark, the attorney should help the client evaluate whether using the mark would pose a significant risk of trademark infringement claims by third parties. Prior to ordering a commercial search report, which can cost more than $1,000 for the report itself (even before taking into account attorney fees for reviewing the report), the attorney can conduct so-called knock-out searches on readily available databases to determine an initial risk assessment. As noted earlier, the test for trademark infringement is the likelihood of consumer confusion regarding the source of the products or services. The lawyer should search the United States Patent and Trademark Office database for registered and pending marks and also online search engines, such as Google, to find marks that have not been registered. In all searches, the lawyer should manipulate the search terms in an effort to find not only identical marks, but also potential similar marks being used in related industries. Although these searches are not comprehensive, they can provide an entrepreneur with sufficient information to decide whether to move forward with the proposed mark. If, based on these search results, the entrepreneur feels comfortable moving forward with the mark, the lawyer should suggest the option of a commercial search report, which may be more comprehensive. However, based on the cost, oftentimes entrepreneurs are comfortable relying on the preliminary searches and choose not to order a commercial search report.

3. Famous Marks

Federal law offers protection for a subcategory of trademarks that are classified as "famous." Famous marks, such as "Coca-Cola," are protected even if there is
no likelihood of confusion as long as the infringing mark in some way lessens the
capacity of the famous mark to identify goods and services. This harm to the famous
mark is called "dilution," and there is no need on the famous mark owner's part to
show that actual dilution has occurred — only that it is likely to occur. The net effect
of this law is that one cannot use a famous mark in any context, even if the industry
is completely different from the industry in which the famous mark is used. If an
entrepreneur wants to use a famous brand in a completely different way (for example, to make Nike brand power cables), steer them in another direction.

4. Loss of Trademark Rights

Once your client has been granted a trademark, it is important that the venture
continue to use the mark since "use in commerce" is what gives rise to trademark
rights. If a mark owner ceases to use the mark and has an intent not to continue
to use it, the mark is considered abandoned. Three consecutive years of nonuse is
considered prima facie evidence of abandonment. Once a mark is abandoned, any
other person can begin using the mark and develop rights in that mark.

In addition, a company can lose trademark rights if the mark becomes generic.
If consumers start to use a trademark to describe a category of goods or services, the
original trademark owner can no longer claim the exclusive right to use the mark.
Examples of trademarks that have become generic in the United States include
aspirin, escalator, laundromat, and zipper. All of these marks were formerly owned
by various companies that lost those rights due to consumer use as generic terms.

Notes and Questions

1. If an entrepreneur client purchases another business and advises you that it
intends to discontinue one of the brands contained in the purchased assets, what
advice would you give?

2. If you represented Johnson & Johnson or Google, is there any advice you
would give your clients on marketing strategies for Band-Aids and the Google
search engine?

B. COPYRIGHTS

Copyright is a form of protection provided to the authors of original works of
authorship, including literary, dramatic, musical, artistic, and certain other intellectual works. This protection is available to both published and unpublished works.
Copyright protection provides the exclusive right to the copyright owner (a) to copy
the work, (b) to develop derivative works, (c) to distribute or sell copies of the
work, (d) to perform the work in public, and (e) to display the work in public. The

copyright owner also has the right to exclude others from using or copying the work. Copyright protection does not give the copyright owner the right to prevent someone else from independently creating a similar or even identical work.

Copyright law protects the form or medium the author selects to communicate the idea, but does not protect the idea itself. When the idea itself and the way the idea is expressed cannot be separated, then they are considered to have merged and no copyright protection is available. Therefore, copyright protection is stronger when an idea can be expressed in many ways. For example, the woes and joys of two starry-eyed lovers, even if original, may not be removed from the public domain; however, the expression of this story in the form of a play script (such as William Shakespeare's Romeo & Juliet) can be protected by copyright law. On the other hand, creating a business directory by listing businesses and corresponding telephone numbers in alphabetical order cannot be protected by copyright law because in essence this is really the one way to construct a useful business directory. Copyright protection on this would ban all others from expressing the idea. The line between expression and idea can certainly be a difficult one to draw.

1. *Copyright Protection*

In order for a work to be eligible for copyright protection, it must meet the following three requirements. The work must be fixed in a tangible medium of expression. The work must also be original and not have been copied from another work. Finally, the work must show at least a minimum degree of creativity by the author. This is a fairly low standard and just must demonstrate some judgment by the author.

Copyright protection automatically arises when an original work that is creative is first fixed in a tangible medium of expression. That said, there are certainly methods to strengthen copyright protection and entrepreneurs should generally consider such options. Although not legally required, displaying a copyright notice on a work puts third parties on notice that the author is claiming copyright protection. Additionally, in order to file a copyright infringement action in the United States, the copyright owner must have registered it with the Register of Copyrights — and if such registration happens before infringement, the copyright owner is entitled to enhanced damages. Registering a work with the copyright office is relatively straightforward and can be done online at www.copyright.gov.

2. *Copyright Infringement*

KEPNER-TREGOE, INC. v. CARABIO
United States District Court for the Eastern District of Michigan
203 U.S.P.Q. 124 (1979)

This is an action for copyright infringement and breach of contract.

Plaintiff is a New Jersey corporation engaged in marketing and teaching management training programs. They are designed to strengthen a person's ability to define, analyze and solve problems which daily confront executives and supervisors. Defendants MICHAEL J. CARABIO and LAWRENCE E. PADLO are the principals of BUSINESS PROCESSES, INC. (BPI) which also markets and teaches management training programs and utilizes teaching materials similar to Plaintiff KEPNER-TREGOE's (K-T).

Padlo and Carabio are former employees of K-T. . . .

While employed by K-T, Padlo was principally engaged in marketing and teaching K-T's programs to industry and government groups. He did not write the texts and outlines used to teach the programs, but did prepare an outline for his personal use. Before he came to K-T, Padlo had little formal writing experience; however, while there he became familiar with K-T's materials. Carabio, on the other hand, did draft some K-T materials in preliminary form, primarily those used to teach K-T salesmen-instructors how to teach the programs. He also taught and prepared an outline for his own use.

BPI was formed by Padlo on July 18, three days after he left K-T. He had begun work on a set of program materials while he was still technically on K-T's payroll. As early as July 11 he sent worksheets to be used in the BPI programs to the printer. By the first of September Padlo had generated a set of teaching materials that were rough but complete enough to market. It was at this time he was joined by Carabio, who had tendered his resignation to K-T two weeks earlier. Carabio immediately performed a final revision and review of BPI's materials. On September 27 BPI obtained its first major customer, Chrysler Corporation, a former customer of K-T.

THE CREATION OF BPI'S MATERIALS

When Padlo left K-T, he surrendered all "formal documents" (copyrighted teaching materials). He retained his personal outline (prepared from K-T's works). In preparing BPI's materials, Padlo assembled all the information he could gather pertaining to the teaching of problem-solving programs. Much of this consisted of materials used by K-T's competitors. Padlo also used his personal K-T outline and drew upon his familiarity with K-T's materials. From this base of raw data, Padlo selected those ideas and approaches he felt were most effective. He tried to avoid direct copying.

Defendants admit similarity between BPI's materials and K-T's. They concede, even emphasize, similarity between BPI's materials and those of some of K-T's competitors. Defendants deny any direct copying of K-T's materials. Padlo kept no notes of his preparation.

THE CONTENTIONS OF THE PARTIES

K-T asserts there was substantial copying. It emphasizes that the BPI materials were prepared in a very short time by one with little formal writing experience on a low budget. (BPI operates out of Padlo's home and its capitalization is only $2,000.) Coupling this with numerous asserted similarities in format, outline and phrasing, and the fact that some of BPI's materials were prepared while Padlo was still on K-T's payroll, K-T contends a finding of copyright infringement is warranted. The case is sealed, K-T argues, by the marked-up K-T work sheets subpoenaed from the printer which, with only minor changes, were later marketed as part of BPI's material. Padlo admitted at trial that [where] BPI's materials used exactly the same phrasing to describe a concept or idea, the phrase was copied.

Defendants argue that although there are major similarities between BPI's material and K-T's, this is attributable to the limited ways the ideas taught by K-T can be expressed. In support of this, Defendants produced copies of the materials used by many of their competitors. I find a great deal of similarity among them. K-T, while arguing that Defendants' copying from others who, in turn, copied from K-T, is no defense, did not offer proof that any of the third-party materials had been copied from K-T.

   . . .

THE COPYRIGHTED MATERIALS

Much has been said of the copyrighted material at issue. My analysis builds on their singular nature, so I describe them in detail.

K-T teaches 5-day programs in what might be called applied reasoning and common sense in problem-solving techniques. Defendants teach a 3-day program. K-T has three levels of programs. . . . Each program has basically the same format and approach, keyed to what K-T apparently believes are the three major intellectual processes needed in corporate management. These are "problem-solving," "decision making" and "planning" techniques. (BPI teaches a fourth category called "concern analysis" which is an introductory analysis of the areas of inquiry that must "concern" anyone facing a management decision. Each of these three areas is presented to the student through four devices. First, an outline of the material; second, textual exposition, which essentially follows the outline; third, "cases" or problem examples in prose form; and, fourth, worksheets. . . . BPI's materials use the same basic approach, with the addition of concern analysis. . . .

The two companies' products are also similar in that they aim at the same markets. Except for the length of the programs, they are taught in the same manner[.] . . .

More specifically, the two program approaches teach the same kind of analysis. The problem-solving portion of both sets of materials proceeds by first stating the problem. BPI calls this the "problem statement," whereas K-T calls it the "Deviation Statement." Next, the inquiry is narrowed by describing the problem, i.e., by asking what the problem "is" and what it "is not," where it is and where it is not, and so forth. At this stage the analysis is characterized by the use of a litany "what-where-when-extent/magnitude" each followed by "is-is not" in both sets of materials. The other steps are, in order: Ask how is this problem different from other problems and from the absence of the problem; ask what changed when the problem first appeared (i.e. what are the possible causes); ask what are the possible causes (or, as others in the field have asked, what are the probable causes, potential causes, etc.); test for the most probable alternative; and, verify (document) the cause. I will not labor this further, suffic[e] it to say that the other sections of the problem-solving portion of K-T's materials track the outline, and that the other general topics (i.e., decision making and planning) follow the same sort of approach.

Plaintiff alleges infringements in each of four sections of BPI's work (outline-text, teaching outline, worksheets and cases). . . . Before commenting on the factual comparison basis for the infringement, I will discuss how the law applies.

I. K-T'S MATERIALS ARE COPYRIGHTABLE

In BPI's post-trial memorandum it asserts K-T's materials are not copyrightable, arguing the ideas presented are inextricable from their straightforward explanation. To protect K-T's material would protect the idea. Although I reject this argument's applicability, Defendants are on the right track, and have presented the key to this dispute.

The originality an author must contribute to a subject for his work to be copyrightable is extremely small. K-T's concepts admit sufficient variety of expression that their materials are copyrightable.

II. UNITY OF IDEA AND EXPRESSION

The insight that if an idea and its expression are of necessity close, the expression is not copyrightable, received its furthest extension in Morrissey v. Proctor & Gamble Co., 379 F.2d 675, 154 USPQ 193 (1st Cir. 1967). There the court held a contest rule uncopyrightable on the rationale that the rule's concept could be expressed in only a limited number of ways. The court wrote:

> "... When the uncopyrightable subject matter is very narrow, so that 'the topic necessarily requires,' if not only one form of expression, at best only a limited number, to permit copyrighting would mean that a party or parties, by copyrighting a mere handful of forms, could exhaust all possibilities of future use of the substance. In such circumstances it does not seem accurate to say that any particular form of expression comes from the subject matter. However, it is necessary to say that the subject matter would be appropriated by permitting the copyrighting of its expression. We cannot recognize copyright as a game of chess in which the public can be checkmated."

. . .

III. WHAT DOES COPYRIGHT COVER?

The first question is to determine exactly what K-T's copyright protects. In Nichols v. Universal Pictures Corp., 45 F.2d 119, 7 USPW 84 (2d Cir. 1930), Judge Learned Hand observed:

> "Upon any work . . . a great number of patterns of increasing generality will fit equally well, as more and more of the incident is left out. The last may perhaps be no more than a general statement of what the play is about, . . . but there is a point in this series of abstractions where they are no longer protected, since otherwise the playwright could prevent the use of his 'ideas,' to which, apart from their expression, his property is never extended . . . . Nobody has ever been able to fix that boundary, and nobody ever can . . . ."

The task is to determine in K-T's materials where the idea leaves off and its expression begins. In works of fiction this occurs at a fairly high level of abstraction. There are infinite themes, plots and characters that many be expressed in such variety that they may be given wide berth with no stifling effect by those who wish to express similar ideas. As to such works, a judge's instinctive impressions serve as well as any indicator whether there has been an infringement. But, such cases lead to pat formulations as the following from Miller Brewing Co. v. Carling O'Keefe Breweries, 452 F. Supp. 429, 439, 199 USPQ 470, 479 (W.D.N.Y. 1978):

> ". . . a copyright does not protect the holder from another's use of themes or plots, but rather the gist of copyright infringement is the pirating of particular expressions of thematic concepts by use of similar details, scenes, events and characterization."

In cases like this one, more penetrating analysis is called for. Instinct alone will not serve. Unthinking application of the "substantial similarity" test may produce the wrong result. A plaintiff can claim no protection for a more abstract level than he created. If the only original aspect of a work is its literal expression, only a nearly identical copy will infringe.

K-T enjoys no protection for its "approach" to problem-solving, namely, the analysis summarized in its outlines. K-T has no monopoly over the handling of a problem by stating it, then narrowing the inquiry by the "is-is not" technique, and so forth.

The most useful analysis of this problem, which has not been much improved through the years, is set forth in Baker v. Selden, 101 U.S. 99 (1880). The Court considered a system of ruling books in which accounts were kept which consisted of an introductory essay explaining the system and a series of ruled forms with headings. The Court noted, "The truths of a science . . . are the common property of the whole world [and] any author has the right to express the one, or explain and use the other, in his own way." The hard question in the case was presented because "[in] describing the art, the illustrations and diagrams employed happen to correspond more closely than usual with the actual working performed by the operator who uses the art."

Likewise, K-T has no exclusive right to package its problem-solving techniques and market them as a seminar to business and industry. Nor may K-T lay claim to solving problems or making decisions using the logical sequence outlined earlier. K-T has no monopoly on any pedagogical technique, such as the "outline-text-worksheets-cases" approach it uses, and it had no exclusive right to present any of its material in an outline or text format.

. . .

IV. THE EXTENT OF COPYRIGHT'S PROTECTION

Having expressed what K-T's copyright does not protect, I now take up its extent. I conclude K-T has what might be called a "thin" shell of protection around its materials.

This concept may be illustrated by the following quotation from Herbert Rosenthal Jewelry Corp. v. Kalpakian:

> What is basically at stake is the extent of the copyright owner's monopoly — from how large an area of activity did Congress intend to allow the copyright owner to exclude others?

. . .

Another crucial observation is that the "substantial similarity" test for infringement is much too simplistic. . . .

The usual statement of the rule is: to prove infringement the plaintiff must show copying of his work, and that it resulted in a work "substantially similar" to plaintiff's. Substantial similarity, it is said, should be judged by "whether an average lay observer [i.e., one within the audience at which the work is addressed] would recognize the alleged copy as having been appropriated from the copyrighted work." This is useful shorthand, but should not substitute for reasoned analysis. In practice the test is much modified; its contours depend on the subject matter of the copyright and a number of other factors.

The first of these is the already noted distinction between literary works and those which teach or explain a useful art or scientific process. This factor modifies the "substantial similarity" test. In a literary work, plot, theme, character and, as said in *Sid & Marty Krofft*, supra, at 1167, 196 USPQ at 104-105, "The total concept and feel" of the work, are important. This is because in literature, these things are wholly the creature of the writer. There is an unlimited variety which may be invented. Authors are not confined. In addition, there is no societal interest in many variants on a single theme or plot, nor is there the likelihood that by extending broad protection, entry to the market for literary works will be foreclosed. But with respect to the useful arts, there is a societal interest in having many offer the art in the marketplace. Our economy functions best under competition. And, if many can present variants on the copyrighted material, we hope that advances in its teaching will result. As a consequence, more similarity between two works of a commercial and useful character is required to find infringement than between two literary works. Two useful works might bear resemblance that would show infringement if literary, but which is not because they are technical. The "substantial similarity" test is modified.

The problem can be approached from another angle. Many cases say an idea and its expression may be closely related. It is the strong policy of copyright not to protect ideas. Free interchange of thought is paramount. To avoid protecting ideas, courts have limited the concept of substantial similarity. . . .

In yet another vein, the simpler the thing described, the more alike two explanations will be. To cite an extreme, how many ways may one describe how to draw a circle with a compass? To be sure, many outlandish methods using eccentric styles could be conceived. But there is no societal value in that. For better it is to narrow the protection to the first writer, in the interest of competition.

K-T has tried to deny that its material describes something simple. But the problem-solving K-T exalts is nothing more than what everyone with common sense does automatically. By describing it and elaborating on it, K-T cannot expropriate it.

The best example of this is K-T's explanation of the Problem Statement. A problem statement is a statement of the problem; a definition of the undesired state of things, and so forth. There are only so many ways it can be said, and they all sound alike. . . .

K-T's copyrights rest on an unstable foundation; barely copyrightable material.

In addition to these reasons for K-T's "thin" copyright, other factors weigh heavily. K-T dominates the market as to the programs it teaches. Defendants freely admit that a major selling point of their programs is that they are similar to K-T's. To succeed in this market, one must imitate K-T. K-T is a known quantity and industry's expectations have been molded in its direction. This is a tribute to K-T, but it does not give them a monopoly. Thus, a certain similarity may be expected.

. . .

One final point is, the amount of protection enjoyed depends upon the amount of protectible originality in the original work. K-T's material contains some originality that is not protectible. The only protectible aspect of K-T's materials is that measure by which it goes beyond the unprotectible underlying ideas. K-T can protect only the expression of that it has added to our store of knowledge on problem solving. . . .

In our case, K-T has contributed to its field. But much of its effort is not protectible. It consists of ideas in the public domain. K-T's outlines are the bare bones of the ideas. Any exposition of the ideas will be similar to the outlines, which are nearly uncopyrightable because so close to the ideas.

V. INFRINGEMENT

The ultimate question remains. I find that although K-T has what I have called a "thin" copyright, BPI has infringed it in certain minor respects.

1. Worksheets

I find no violation with respect to the worksheets. They are similar to K-T's due to defendants having drawn ideas from K-T. . . . The worksheets contain so little expression and there is so much difficulty separating the expression from the idea; the protection they enjoy extends little beyond actual xerographic reproduction. . . .

2. The Cases

The cases are the opposite end of the scale from the worksheets. In them I find the greatest room for "literary" creativity and divergence of expression from idea. The principles outlined in this opinion apply with least force to the cases.

(a) Handmixers v. Auto Heaters — Infringement

BPI's case is an obvious copy. The differences are trivial and only point out the similarity. . . .

(b) Dairyland Corp. v. Tamworth Petrochemical Corp. — Infringement

Once again BPI's case is an ingenious theft of K-T's. Both products are flat and square, are similarly distributed, suffer from an unknown reaction to electromagnetic radiation, and engender nearly identical customer problems. There are an infinite number of defective-product cases that could be written to illustrate exactly the same concepts.

(c) Poor Morale v. The Transfer — No Infringement

Both cases deal with a low-level female supervisor who causes morale problems through her officiousness and arbitrariness, especially among older employees. These facts make the problems similar but K-T's is presented through dialog; BPI's unconventional prose. BPI's case is much less specific than K-T's, focusing more on the shifts in company policy leading to the problem; K-T's seems to concentrate on personality-oriented causes (i.e., Joyce's father died).

(d) Spark-O-Matic v. Glade Manufacturing Co. — No Infringement

Both sets of filing-in worksheets list four potential candidates for approximately the same level of job opening and both set forth the same type of scoring and weighting-of-factor analysis, but the similarity does not extend beyond that. It seems all companies desiring to promote someone or hire someone into a position must consider the same factors, e.g., desired salary, health, willingness to relocate, experience, etc.

(e) Southwest City Branch Assistant Manager v. Branch Manager — No Infringement

This problem/case involves a promotion. There are several candidates, and in each case one is a woman. Again, except for the fact that in deciding whom to promote all companies must consider the same things, these problems are dissimilar. The BPI problem focuses on resumes and evaluative notes prepared by superiors while the K-T problem emphasizes recommendations and evaluative forms prepared by superiors. This difference gives the BPI case a different focus and, from a pedagogical standpoint, would seem to change the classroom dynamics which result. The BPI case is only nine pages; the K-T is thirty-three.

(f) Move of Northwest Branch v. Move of My Function — No Infringement

Aside from the fact that both cases involve operational moves, one struggles to find any similarity.

3. The Outlines and the Text (Sec. 1 of Ex. 11)

Analyzing these sections of the two sets of materials is the most difficult. On the one hand, K-T has no monopoly on its ideas or on the sequence in which they are presented. K-T has no exclusive property in the outline format. More important, K-T has no monopoly on the use of common words to carry its meaning. It has no proprietary interest in such words as "is" or "is not." The same holds true for "what, where, when and extent." . . .

However, BPI has infringed the copyright of K-T as to the text and outline in Ex. 11. My conclusion stems mainly from the numerous obvious paraphrases which appear throughout this section. . . .

4. Overall Outlines — No Infringement

If one is to teach this course, he must have some established procedures. They must track the course's development day to day.

. . .

VII. CONCLUSION

No statement rings more true than Judge Hand's in Peter Pan Fabrics, Inc. v. Martin Weiner Corp., 274 F.2d 487, 489, 124 USPQ 154, 155-156 (2d Cir. 1960):

> Obviously, no principle can be stated as to when an imitator has gone beyond copying the "idea" and has borrowed its "expression." Decisions must therefore inevitably be ad hoc.

In the end, my judgment must prevail. But there is nothing in the law that precludes one author from saving time and effort through the labors of others. . . . I have been guided in this case by the observation that one work does not infringe another if their similarity results from the limits on expression I have described. And of paramount importance, I think, is the public interest in the advancement of art, science and industry. Sometimes this must be placed ahead of the copyright holder's interest in the maximum profit from his creation. This fundamental distinction underlies the difference between patent and copyright. K-T's real concern in this case is that BPI has stolen its ideas and is profiting from them. Copyright simply does not remedy this.

. . .

Notes and Questions

1. The court states that "K-T has what might be called a 'thin' shell of protection around its materials," although the court had earlier cited the proposition that the "originality an author must contribute to a subject for his work to be copyrightable is extremely small." Reconcile these two statements and consider why you think the court viewed K-T's copyright protection in its materials as "thin."

2. The court distinguishes between worksheets and cases in its copyright infringement analysis. What lessons can you draw from this type of distinction, and what advice might you give, if your entrepreneur-client is a tutoring company? A company that produces videos explaining how to tackle common "do it yourself" home repair tasks? A company that publishes an advertiser-supported online directory of local businesses?

3. There are three basic categories for copyright infringement: direct, vicarious, and contributory. Direct copyright infringement occurs when someone violates one

of the exclusive rights of the copyright owner without such owner's permission and outside of the exception for fair use. Vicarious copyright infringement occurs when someone has the right and ability to supervise the infringing action of another and the supervisor has a financial interest in or incentive related to the infringement. Contributory copyright infringement is when a person with knowledge of the infringing activity, induces, causes, or materially contributes to the directly infringing activity or conduct of another. Discuss examples of each type of infringement and consider which type of infringing activity you think may have been at play in the above case.

4. Even when a work is entitled to copyright protection, others may make limited use of such work under the doctrine of fair use. This doctrine allows others to make limited use of copyrighted material without requiring permission from the copyright's holder. Examples of fair use include commentary, criticism, parody, news reporting, research, teaching, library archiving, and scholarship. It allows for the use of copyrighted material in another author's work. Under the copyright statute, a four-factor test is used in determining whether a use should be considered a fair use: (1) the purpose and character of the use, (2) the nature of the copyrighted work, (3) the amount and the substantiality of the portion of the work used, and (4) the effect of the use on the copyrighted work. Why do you think the law provides this exception and in what types of circumstances do you think this exception prevails? Can you think of businesses you know that take advantage of the fair use doctrine in producing goods or services?

5. A company is considered to be the "author" and therefore the owner of copyright in a work created by its employees or independent contractors when the copyrighted work meets the definition of "work made for hire" under the United States Copyright Act of 1976, § 101, which says in part:

> A "work made for hire" is —
>
> (1) a work prepared by an employee within the scope of his or her employment; or
>
> (2) a work specially ordered or commissioned for use as a contribution to a collective work, as a part of a motion picture or other audiovisual work, as a translation, as a supplementary work, as a compilation, as an instructional text, as a test, as answer material for a test, or as an atlas, if the parties expressly agree in a written instrument signed by them that the work shall be considered a work made for hire.

For an employee working within the scope of employment, an entrepreneur can be confident that — as to copyrightable works — the employee's work product is owned by the employer. The story is different, however, for independent contractors. Given that the work for hire doctrine only applies to independent contractors if there has been a written instrument agreeing that the work is a work made for hire, lawyers representing entrepreneurs must ensure this provision appears in contracts with independent contractors hired by the venture. Since the above statutory definition specifies that a limited set of categories of works by independent contractors can be considered works for hire, the lawyer must also include a provision assigning to the company all copyrightable works that are created for the venture but are not works for hire. A typical provision would read as follows:

> The Independent Contractor hereby agrees that all Work Product produced hereunder is deemed a "work made for hire" as defined in 17 U.S.C. § 101 for the Company. If, for any reason, any of the Work Product does not constitute a "work

made for hire," the Independent Contractor hereby irrevocably assigns to the Company, in each case without additional consideration, all right, title, and interest throughout the world in and to the Work Product, including all intellectual property rights therein.

3. *Digital Millennium Copyright Act*

Congress enacted the Digital Millennium Copyright Act (DMCA) in 1998, which implements two 1996 treaties of the World Intellectual Property Organization (WIPO). The DMCA amended certain provisions of the United States Copyright Act of 1976, Title 17 of the United States Code. It makes it a crime to use technology, devices, or services intended to circumvent measures designed to control access to copyrighted works. It also criminalizes the manufacture, distribution, or sale of technology and devices that would allow consumers to circumvent such access controls, whether or not there is actual infringement of copyright itself.

The DMCA also creates safe harbors that limit the liability of the providers of online services for copyright infringement by their users if certain conditions are met. Several of the safe harbors that provide this coveted limited liability for the providers of online services require affirmative actions to qualify. One such requirement is conditioned on proper compliance with the notice and takedown provisions of § 512 of the Copyright Act. The notice and takedown provisions permit a copyright owner to submit a notice of allegedly infringing material on its system to the provider's designated agent (who must be registered with the Copyright office). Once the provider acquires knowledge of the infringing material, it must take affirmative steps to remove or block the material. However, the person who posted the allegedly infringing material may serve a counter notification, including a sworn statement that he or she believes in good faith that the material was removed or disabled from the system as a result of mistake or misidentification. If a counter notification is served, the provider must provide the notification to the copyright owner, who then has ten business days to file a copyright infringement action. If the copyright owner does not seek judicial relief, the online service provider is required to restore the allegedly infringing material on its system within ten to 14 business days after receiving the counter notification. If the provider makes a good faith attempt to comply with the notice and takedown provisions, it is immune from any claims brought by the person whose material was taken down.

VIACOM INTERNATIONAL, INC. v. YOUTUBE, INC.
United States District Court for the Southern District of New York
718 F. Supp. 2d 514 (2010)

Defendants move for summary judgment that they are entitled to the Digital Millennium Copyright Act's ("DMCA"), 17 U.S.C. § 512(c), "safe harbor" protection against all of plaintiffs' direct and secondary infringement claims, including claims for "inducement" contributory liability, because they had insufficient notice, under the DMCA, of the particular infringements in suit.

Plaintiffs cross-move for partial summary judgment that defendants are not protected by the statutory "safe harbor" provision, but "are liable for the intentional infringement of thousands of Viacom's copyrighted works, . . . for the vicarious infringement of those works, and for the direct infringement of those works . . . because: (1) Defendants had 'actual knowledge' and were 'aware of facts and circumstances from which infringing activity [was] apparent,' but failed to 'act[] expeditiously' to stop it; (2) Defendants 'receive[d] a financial benefit directly attributable to the infringing activity' and 'had the right and ability to control such activity;' and (3) Defendants' infringement does not result solely from providing 'storage at the direction of a user' or any other Internet function specified in section 512."

Resolution of the key legal issue presented on the parties' cross-motions requires examination of the DMCA's "safe harbor" provisions, 17 U.S.C. § 512(c), (m) and (n) which state:

(c) Information residing on systems or networks at direction of users. —

(1) In general. — A service provider shall not be liable for monetary relief, or, except as provided in subsection (j), for injunctive or other equitable relief, for infringement of copyright by reason of the storage at the direction of a user of material that resides on a system or network controlled or operated by or for the service provider, if the service provider —

(A)(i) does not have actual knowledge that the material or an activity using the material on the system or network is infringing;

(ii) in the absence of such actual knowledge, is not aware of facts or circumstances from which infringing activity is apparent; or

(iii) upon obtaining such knowledge or awareness, acts expeditiously to remove, or disable access to, the material;

(B) does not receive a financial benefit directly attributable to the infringing activity, in a case in which the service provider has the right and ability to control such activity; and

(C) upon notification of claimed infringement as described in paragraph (3), responds expeditiously to remove, or disable access to, the material that is claimed to be infringing or to be the subject of infringing activity.

(2) Designated agent. — The limitations on liability established in this subsection apply to a service provider only if the service provider has designated an agent to receive notifications of claimed infringement described in paragraph (3), by making available through its service, including on its website in a location accessible to the public, and by providing to the Copyright Office, substantially the following information:

(A) the name, address, phone number, and electronic mail address of the agent.

(B) Other contact information which the Register of Copyrights may deem appropriate.

The Register of Copyrights shall maintain a current directory of agents available to the public for inspection, including through the Internet, in both electronic and hard copy formats, and may require payment of a fee by service providers to cover the costs of maintaining the directory.

(3) Elements of notification. —

(A) To be effective under this subsection, a notification of claimed infringement must be a written communication provided to the designated agent of a service provider that includes substantially the following:

(i) A physical or electronic signature of a person authorized to act on behalf of the owner of an exclusive right that is allegedly infringed.

(ii) Identification of the copyrighted work claimed to have been infringed, or, if multiple copyrighted works at a single online site are covered by a single notification, a representative list of such works at that site.

(iii) Identification of the material that is claimed to be infringing or to be the subject of infringing activity and that is to be removed or access to which is to be disabled, and information reasonably sufficient to permit the service provider to locate the material.

(iv) Information reasonably sufficient to permit the service provider to contact the complaining party, such as an address, telephone number, and, if available, an electronic mail address at which the complaining party may be contacted.

(v) A statement that the complaining party has a good faith belief that use of the material in the manner complained of is not authorized by the copyright owner, its agent, or the law.

(vi) A statement that the information in the notification is accurate, and under penalty of perjury, that the complaining party is authorized to act on behalf of the owner of an exclusive right that is allegedly infringed.

(B)(i) Subject to clause (ii), a notification from a copyright owner or from a person authorized to act on behalf of the copyright owner that fails to comply substantially with the provisions of subparagraph (A) shall not be considered under paragraph (1)(A) in determining whether a service provider has actual knowledge or is aware of facts or circumstances from which infringing activity is apparent.

(ii) In a case in which the notification that is provided to the service provider's designated agent fails to comply substantially with all the provisions of subparagraph (A) but substantially complies with clauses (ii), (iii), and (iv) of subparagraph (A), clause (i) of this subparagraph applies only if the service provider promptly attempts to contact the person making the notification or takes other reasonable steps to assist in the receipt of notification that substantially complies with all the provisions of subparagraph (A).

. . .

(m) Protection of privacy. — Nothing in this section shall be construed to condition the applicability of subsections (a) through (d) on —

(1) a service provider monitoring its service or affirmatively seeking facts indicating infringing activity, except to the extent consistent with a standard technical measure complying with the provisions of subsection (i); or

(2) a service provider gaining access to, removing, or disabling access to material in cases in which such conduct is prohibited by law.

(n) Construction. — Subsections (a), (b), (c), and (d) describe separate and distinct functions for purposes of applying this section. Whether a service provider qualifies for the limitation on liability in any one of those subsections shall be based solely on the criteria in that subsection, and shall not affect a determination of whether that service provider qualifies for the limitations on liability under any other such subsection.

Defendant YouTube, owned by defendant Google, operates a website at http://www.youtube.com onto which users may upload video files free of charge. Uploaded files are copied and formatted by YouTube's computer systems, and then made available for viewing on YouTube. Presently, over 24 hours of new video-viewing time is uploaded to the YouTube website every minute. As a "provider of online services or network access, or the operator of facilities therefor" as defined in 17 U.S.C. § 512(k)(1)(B), YouTube is a service provider for purposes of § 512(c).

From plaintiffs' submissions on the motions, a jury could find that the defendants not only were generally aware of, but welcomed, copyright-infringing material being placed on their website. Such material was attractive to users, whose increased usage enhanced defendants' income from advertisements displayed on certain pages of the website, with no discrimination between infringing and non-infringing content.

Plaintiffs claim that "tens of thousands of videos on YouTube, resulting in hundreds of millions of views, were taken unlawfully from Viacom's copyrighted works without authorization," and that "Defendants had 'actual knowledge' and were 'aware of facts or circumstances from which infringing activity [was] apparent,' but failed to do anything about it."

However, defendants designated an agent, and when they received specific notice that a particular item infringed a copyright, they swiftly removed it. It is uncontroverted that all the clips in suit are off the YouTube website, most having been removed in response to DMCA takedown notices.

Thus, the critical question is whether the statutory phrases "actual knowledge that the material or an activity using the material on the system or network is infringing," and "facts or circumstances from which infringing activity is apparent" in § 512(c)(1)(A)(i) and (ii) mean a general awareness that there are infringements (here, claimed to be widespread and common), or rather mean actual or constructive knowledge of specific and identifiable infringements of individual items.

1. LEGISLATIVE HISTORY

The Senate Committee on the Judiciary Report, S. Rep. No. 105-190 (1998), gives the background at page 8:

> Due to the ease with which digital works can be copied and distributed worldwide virtually instantaneously, copyright owners will hesitate to make their works readily available on the Internet without reasonable assurance that they will be protected against massive piracy. Legislation implementing the treaties provides this protection and creates the legal platform for launching the global digital online marketplace for copyrighted works. It will facilitate making available quickly and conveniently via the Internet the movies, music, software, and literary works that are the fruit of American creative genius. It will also encourage the continued growth of the existing off-line global marketplace for copyrighted works in digital format by setting strong international copyright standards.
>
> At the same time, without clarification of their liability, service providers may hesitate to make the necessary investment in the expansion of the speed and

capacity of the Internet. In the ordinary course of their operations service providers must engage in all kinds of acts that expose them to potential copyright infringement liability. For example, service providers must make innumerable electronic copies by simply transmitting information over the Internet. Certain electronic copies are made in order to host World Wide Web sites. Many service providers engage in directing users to sites in response to inquiries by users or they volunteer sites that users may find attractive. Some of these sites might contain infringing material. In short, by limiting the liability of service providers, the DMCA ensures that the efficiency of the Internet will continue to improve and that the variety and quality of services on the Internet will continue to expand.

. . .

When discussing section 512(d) of the DMCA which deals with information location tools, the Committee Reports contain an instructive explanation of the need for specificity:

> Like the information storage safe harbor in section 512(c), a service provider would qualify for this safe harbor if, among other requirements, it "does not have actual knowledge that the material or activity is infringing" or, in the absence of such actual knowledge, it is "not aware of facts or circumstances from which infringing activity is apparent." Under this standard, a service provider would have no obligation to seek out copyright infringement, but it would not qualify for the safe harbor if it had turned a blind eye to "red flags" of obvious infringement.
>
> . . .
>
> The important intended objective of this standard is to exclude sophisticated "pirate" directories — which refer Internet users to other selected Internet sites where pirate software, books, movies, and music can be downloaded or transmitted — from the safe harbor. . . .

The tenor of the foregoing provisions is that the phrases "actual knowledge that the material or an activity" is infringing, and "facts or circumstances" indicating infringing activity, describe knowledge of specific and identifiable infringements of particular individual items. Mere knowledge of prevalence of such activity in general is not enough. . . . As stated in Perfect 10, Inc. v. CCBill LLC, 488 F.3d 1102, 1113 (9th Cir. 2007):

> The DMCA notification procedures place the burden of policing copyright infringement — identifying the potentially infringing material and adequately documenting infringement — squarely on the owners of the copyright. We decline to shift a substantial burden from the copyright owner to the provider . . . .

That makes sense, as the infringing works in suit may be a small fraction of millions of works posted by others on the service's platform, whose provider cannot by inspection determine whether the use has been licensed by the owner, or whether its posting is a "fair use" of the material, or even whether its copyright owner or licensee objects to its posting. The DMCA is explicit: it shall not be construed to condition "safe harbor" protection on "a service provider monitoring its service or affirmatively seeking facts indicating infringing activity . . . ."

Indeed, the present case shows that the DMCA notification regime works efficiently: when Viacom over a period of months accumulated some 100,000 videos and then sent one mass take-down notice on February 2, 2007, by the next business day YouTube had removed virtually all of them.

2. CASE LAW

In *CCBill LLC,* supra, the defendants provided web hosting and other services to various websites. The plaintiff argued that defendants had received notice of apparent infringement from circumstances that raised "red flags": websites were named "illegal.net" and "stolencelebritypics.com," and others involved "password-hacking." As to each ground, the Ninth Circuit disagreed, stating "We do not place the burden of determining whether photographs are actually illegal on a service provider"; and "There is simply no way for a service provider to conclude that the passwords enabled infringement without trying the passwords, and verifying that they enabled illegal access to copyrighted material. We impose no such investigative duties on service providers."

. . .

[A] decision of the Second Circuit involved analogous claims of trademark infringement (and therefore did not involve the DMCA) by sales of counterfeit Tiffany merchandise on eBay, Inc.'s website. In Tiffany (NJ) Inc. v. eBay Inc., 600 F.3d 93 (2d Cir. April 1, 2010) the Court of Appeals affirmed the dismissal of trademark infringement and dilution claims against eBay's advertising and listing practices. The sellers on eBay offered Tiffany sterling silver jewelry of which a significant portion (perhaps up to 75%) were counterfeit, although a substantial number of Tiffany goods sold on eBay were authentic. The particular issue was "whether eBay is liable for contributory trademark infringement — i.e., for culpably facilitating the infringing conduct of the counterfeiting vendors" because "eBay continued to supply its services to the sellers of counterfeit Tiffany goods while knowing or having reason to know that such sellers were infringing Tiffany's mark." Tiffany alleged that eBay knew, or had reason to know, that counterfeit Tiffany goods were being sold "ubiquitously" on eBay, and the District Court had found that eBay indeed "had generalized notice that some portion of the Tiffany goods sold on its website might be counterfeit." Nevertheless, the District Court (Sullivan, J.) dismissed, holding that such generalized knowledge was insufficient to impose upon eBay an affirmative duty to remedy the problem. It held that "for Tiffany to establish eBay's contributory liability, Tiffany would have to show that eBay 'knew or had reason to know of specific instances of actual infringement' beyond those that it addressed upon learning of them."

The Court of Appeals held:

> We agree with the district court. For contributory trademark infringement liability to lie, a service provider must have more than a general knowledge or reason to know that its service is being used to sell counterfeit goods. Some contemporary knowledge of which particular listings are infringing or will infringe in the future is necessary.

. . .

Although by a different technique, the DMCA applies the same principle, and its establishment of a safe harbor is clear and practical: if a service provider knows (from notice from the owner, or a "red flag") of specific instances of infringement, the provider must promptly remove the infringing material. If not, the burden is on the owner to identify the infringement. General knowledge that infringement is "ubiquitous" does not impose a duty on the service provider to monitor or search its service for infringements.

. . .

4. CONCLUSION

Defendants are granted summary judgment that they qualify for the protection of 17 U.S.C. § 512(c), as expounded above, against all of plaintiffs' claims for direct and secondary copyright infringement. Plaintiffs' motions for judgment are denied.

. . .

Notes and Questions

1. This case represents a landmark decision for entrepreneurs and start-up companies that have built their business models around user-generated content. The district court granted summary judgment in YouTube's favor, finding that YouTube removed all the clips in the suit from its website in response to DMCA takedown notices and thus had the benefit of the DMCA's safe harbor provision. Why do you think the DMCA affords this protection and does not require online service providers to actively monitor content? If online service providers had such an affirmative obligation, how do you think this would affect the types of companies and business models that exist today?

2. What advice would you give an entrepreneur seeking to start an online retail site that would feature customer reviews of its products? What would your reaction be if the client said she expects to edit consumer posts for grammar and bad language?

C. TRADE SECRETS

Businesses may also protect certain confidential information through trade secret law. Trade secrets are governed by both Federal and state law, and therefore the definition of what constitutes a trade secret can vary somewhat based on the applicable statute. The general principles contained in the various state laws are very similar and are set forth in the Uniform Trade Secrets Act. This Act defines trade secret as information, including a formula, pattern, compilation, program, device, method, technique, or process that:

> (i) derives independent economic value, actual or potential, from not being generally known to, and not being readily ascertainable by proper means by, other persons who can obtain economic value from its disclosure or use, and
> (ii) is the subject of efforts that are reasonable under the circumstances to maintain its secrecy.

From a federal perspective, the Defend Trade Secrets Act at 18 U.S.C. § 1836 aligns closely with the Uniform Act, and gives plaintiffs a federal claim if trade secrets are misappropriated. The federal law defines trade secret as "all forms and types of financial, business, scientific, technical, economic, or engineering information, including patterns, plans, compilations, program devices, formulas, designs, prototypes, methods, techniques, processes, procedures, programs, or codes, whether tangible or intangible, and whether or how stored, compiled, or

memorialized physically, electronically, graphically, photographically, or in writing
if —

> (A) the owner thereof has taken reasonable measures to keep such informa-
> tion secret; and
> (B) the information derives independent economic value, actual or potential,
> from not being generally known to, and not being readily ascertainable through
> proper means by, another person who can obtain economic value from the disclo-
> sure or use of the information."

Trade secret protection may provide a useful (and much less expensive) alternative to patent protection, particularly for entrepreneurs working in fast-moving
industries or for inventions that can be monetized without being disclosed to the
public. In computer technology, for example, patents are quickly rendered worthless
because the underlying inventions are rapidly rendered obsolete by new products.
Many technologies would be obsolete before the patent application has proceeded
to issuance. By contrast, trade secret protection attaches immediately to ideas and
inventions that are kept confidential, and furthermore does not impose exacting
eligibility requirements for protection. In addition, unlike patent's 20-year term for
protection, trade secrets may last indefinitely so long as they remain confidential.
Trade secret statutes protects secrets against misappropriation; however, no protection is accorded against reverse engineering or independent discovery of the secret
material. It is important to keep trade secrets in mind as a possible alternate route
for entrepreneurs in certain industries and circumstances.

AMERICAN FAMILY MUTUAL INSURANCE COMPANY v. ROTH
United States Court of Appeals for the Seventh Circuit
485 F.3d 930 (2007)

POSNER, Circuit Judge:

The defendants — insurance agents who sold a variety of insurance products
on behalf of the plaintiff, their principal — appeal from the grant, after an evidentiary hearing conducted by a magistrate judge, of a preliminary injunction. After
being terminated by the plaintiff, the defendants had begun soliciting its customers,
precipitating this suit, which charges the defendants with breaking their agency
contract and stealing trade secrets. The appeal challenges so much of the injunction as bars the defendants "from using for any reason any information downloaded
from [the plaintiff's] database, including the names contained in Exhibit 34," and
"from servicing [the plaintiff's] customers." The issues presented by the appeal are
governed by Wisconsin law.

An addendum to the agency contract required the agent "to submit all new
business and changes through the system as directed by the Company." By "system"
the company meant its digitized database of customer information. The addendum
provided "that software and database provided contains confidential, proprietary
and trade secret information and that the agent and its employees will not use
nor disclose to third parties such information unless in the ordinary course of the
agent's business with the Company." The agent had access only to the information

in the database that concerned the customers whom he served. It might be customer information originated by the agent or information furnished to it by the company when another agent resigned and his customers had therefore to be reassigned. Some 2,000 policies were reassigned to the defendants in the course of their agency relationship with the plaintiff.

Exhibit 34 was a customer list that the defendants maintained separately from the plaintiff's database and used as a source of names for customer solicitations that they conducted after being terminated by the plaintiff. The list contained 1,847 names, of which the vast majority were also in the plaintiff's database. It is highly likely, though not certain, that most of those were names of customers in the group of 2,000 customers that the plaintiff had assigned to the defendants. The plaintiff points out that the contract forbade the defendants to use any name in the database, whatever the source of the name.

The contract can't really mean that agents are forbidden to solicit anyone whose name happens to appear in the database. They are not forbidden to solicit customers of the company's other agents, for having no access to the names of customers in the company's database they would not be free riding on the company's resources by soliciting such customers without having learned their names, or other information about them, from the database. It would be sheer coincidence if they happened to solicit a customer whose name was in the database.

But once agents enter customer information in the database, the information becomes the exclusive property of the plaintiff, or at least exclusive as against the agent. The information, insofar as it had been developed by the agent rather than supplied to him by the plaintiff, would be his trade secret initially — but only until he uploaded the information into the plaintiff's database, at which point it would become the plaintiff's trade secret. (This provision of the contract is a "grant-back" clause, common in patent and other intellectual-property settings.) Trade secrets can be sold, and once sold (rather than just licensed) can no longer be used by the seller.

There is nothing unconscionable, or even one-sided, about the arrangement that we've just sketched. The agents benefited from being able to use the plaintiff's database, as well as from receiving customers (the 2,000) from the plaintiff; in exchange they gave the plaintiff the right to keep, after termination of the agency relationship, any customer information that they'd acquired in the course of the relationship. Apparently they had, or at least think they had, some legal protection against termination designed to appropriate the customer information that they uploaded into the database, for they have sued the plaintiff for wrongful termination in a separate action pending in the district court.

But we have merely assumed up to now that any customer information in the plaintiff's database is a trade secret (originally the defendants' except for the names of customers furnished to them by the plaintiff). It would not be if it "was known outside the [employer's] business and the list could be readily reproduced [and] the information was available to all the employees of the firm, and much of the information that was available was far more pertinent to [the business] than the skeletal customer list." But does it matter whether there was a trade secret? The addendum to the agency contract forbids the defendants to use the information "unless in the ordinary course of [their] business with the [plaintiff]," and a contract forbidding disclosure of customer information is enforceable — but only if the contractual prohibition is reasonable in time and scope and, specifically, only if its duration is limited. Because such a prohibition limits competition, courts view it with some suspicion. Treating customer information as a trade secret limits competition as well, but such information is given enhanced legal protection as a trade secret only if there is some indication that the information has value apart from its value in limiting competition — that it represents an investment on the part of the firm seeking to protect it.

The nondisclosure provision contains no limitation of time; although it says it will continue in force only until the agency is terminated, the defendants do not argue that it terminates then, and it would not be a good argument; the agency contract is terminable by either party at will, and the plaintiff would hardly have agreed that the defendants could terminate it whenever they wanted to walk off with the confidential information in the plaintiff's database. But the omission of a limitation on the duration of the nondisclosure provision is not fatal to the plaintiff's claim. The customer information in the plaintiff's database is a trade secret, defined in the Uniform Trade Secrets Act, in force in Wisconsin, as information that both "derives independent economic value, actual or potential, from not being generally known to, and not being readily ascertainable by proper means by, other persons who can obtain economic value from its disclosure or use" and "is the subject of efforts to maintain its secrecy that are reasonable under the circumstances." Both conditions are satisfied. The names in the plaintiff's database are filtered for their suitability to buy insurance, resulting, as the magistrate judge remarked, in "a defined, manageable and economically viable universe of uniquely receptive potential customers."

. . .

So the plaintiff is entitled to an injunction. But there are problems with the wording of the injunction that the district court entered. The first provision we quoted, forbidding the use by the defendants of any information "downloaded" from the plaintiff's database, contains a potential loophole. "Downloading" could be thought to refer only to an electronic operation, such as transferring documents from electronic database to a computer's hard drive. So defined, it would exclude hand-copying information from a computer screen. We cannot order the district court to close the loophole, however, as the plaintiff has not filed a cross-appeal, asking that the injunction be modified.

Another problem with the first quoted provision — this one, however, properly raised in this court, by the defendants' appeal — is the inclusion in the prohibition against downloading of "the names contained in Exhibit 34." While most of the names are in the database, some are not, and there isn't any basis for forbidding the defendants to use those names.

The plaintiff itself acknowledges that the second provision we quoted, enjoining the defendants from "servicing" the plaintiff's customers, is overbroad as well as vague (what does "servicing" a customer for insurance mean?). It would forbid the defendants to solicit a person who became a customer of the plaintiff after the defendants were terminated and whom the defendants had solicited without any assist from information in the plaintiff's database, or who was an existing customer of the plaintiff but sought out the defendants rather than being solicited by them. Probably this provision should simply be stricken. But rather than try to work out the details of a proper injunction, we shall remand the case to the district court for the entry of a better-drafted injunction, while affirming so much of that court's decision as determines that the plaintiff is indeed entitled to a preliminary injunction.

AFFIRMED IN PART, VACATED IN PART, AND REMANDED WITH DIRECTIONS.

Notes and Questions

1. The court states that once the agents entered customer information in the database, it became the plaintiff's trade secrets. Do you think that all customer lists are trade secrets? What factors do you think a court would consider in determining when a customer list constitutes a trade secret? When a hair stylist leaves a salon, can he or she contact former clients to invite them to the new place of business or would the list of clients be a trade secret owned by the former employer?

2. What is the difference between a trade secret protected by the statute, and information that does not qualify as a trade secret but is still protected contractually in a confidentiality agreement? Imagine an entrepreneur who does not want to require employees to sign any contracts about confidentiality and says he'll just "stick with trade secret law." What questions would you ask the entrepreneur to determine how hard to push the confidentiality agreement issue?

3. What lessons can transactional lawyers draw from the court's discussion of the "downloading" loophole in the contract?

4. Why do you imagine Congress created a federal law concerning trade secrets? What do you make of the fact that the federal law is parallel to, and does not preempt or particularly enhance, state trade secret statutes?

D. PATENTS

Although patent law is a specialty, and a person must have a degree in a technology field to be admitted to the patent bar, lawyers representing entrepreneurs must understand the basics of patent law when advising clients on how to protect intellectual property. Patents may be used to protect inventions, new products, and new processes. A patent is essentially a set of exclusive rights granted by the federal government to an inventor for a specific period of time in exchange for a public disclosure of an invention by the inventor. Unlike copyrights and trademarks, patents allow the protection of functional features of inventions and products and provide the right to exclude others from making, using, or selling products that embody the protected functionality. The patent application must describe the invention in detail such that another person who is proficient in that field would be able to create and use the invention.

Patents are generally divided into two main categories: design patents and utility patents. There is also a third type of patent called a plant patent, which is used to protect certain new types of plants (like new varieties of roses, for example). The scope of protection provided by the patent is set forth in numbered sections called "claims."

Obtaining a patent can be a fairly complicated and expensive process. There are, of course, several requirements that must be met before a patent may be obtained. The invention must be within a class of patentable subject matter, it must be useful, it must be novel, and it cannot be an obvious extension of previously existing technology. In addition, drafting claims is a complicated business: they must be worded broadly enough to cover as much as possible, but narrowly enough to satisfy the United States Patent and Trademark Office, which only wants to offer the limited protection necessary to protect the invention. At the outset, however, it is important to determine the inventor (for patent ownership purposes) of the invention at issue.

1. Who Is an "Inventor"?

An inventor of a patent is the person (or persons) who conceived the underlying invention as it is to be applied in practice. The Federal Circuit Court — which is the federal appellate court with jurisdiction over all patent matters — considers conception complete when the idea is so clearly defined in the inventor's mind that only ordinary skill would be necessary to reduce the invention to practice. Since the inventor is the owner of the patent absent a written agreement to the contrary, entrepreneurs must understand this issue from two perspectives: first, they want to ensure they (and not their employers) own the inventions they intend to use in their new business (see Chapter 2); and second, they need to ensure the new venture owns all inventions conceived by its employees and independent contractors.

A single patent may have multiple inventors, and each inventor must be listed on the patent. By default, each inventor is a co-owner of the patent rights and may independently license or sue to enforce her interest. The Federal Circuit has explained that each co-inventor presumptively owns a pro rata undivided interest in the entire patent, no matter what their respective contributions. Ownership attaches to patents as a whole rather than to specific sub-parts of the patent that may have been invented by a particular individual. Thus, a co-inventor of only one part of an invention may gain entitlement to ownership of a much broader patent without some express agreement to the contrary. Therefore, it is important for inventors who cooperate in the inventive process to consider entering into a contract in advance setting forth the desired ownership structure.

2. Employee-Inventors

Inventors may assign away their rights by contract. An entrepreneur who conceives of an invention while in the employ of another company may have assigned away her rights, either by express contract or the implied terms of the employment relationship. Even if the employee retains ownership of the patent, she may also be required to license it to her former employer at no charge, as described below.

If an employee is hired to solve a technical issue or "hired to invent," then even in the absence of a contract, the employer will retain title to any patentable invention. When an employee who was not hired specifically to invent does end up inventing, ownership is generally determined by two factors: whether the invention relates to the employee's job duties and whether it was made using the facilities, tools, personnel, or other resources of the employer. When this type of employee invents something closely related to the employee's duties or using firm resources, the employee retains title. However, the invention is subject to an implied-in-law royalty-free license in favor of the employer. This license is called a "shop right."

Inventions unrelated to a job or made away from the office using employee resources often belong exclusively to the employee unless an employment contract states otherwise. However, legislation in several states regulates employment contracts so that despite employment contract terms to the contrary, employees may still own unrelated inventions made off-site. California's statute, which is typical for states with such legislation, renders unenforceable contracts assigning rights in inventions that an employee "developed entirely on his own time without using the employer's equipment, supplies, facilities, or trade secret information." The California statute, like most of these statutes, provides employers an exception for (1) inventions that "[r]elate . . . to the employer's business, or actual or demonstrably anticipated research or development," and (2) inventions that "[r]esult from any work performed by the employee for the employer." Therefore, it is very important to check state law in this area. Entrepreneurs need to understand what they've given (intentionally or inadvertently) to their employer, and also need to understand what they can — and can't — expect to own of the new venture's workers' creations.

3. Patent Requirements

As noted above, for an invention to be patented it must be within a class of patentable subject matter, it must be useful, it must be novel, and it cannot be an obvious extension of previously existing technology.

a. Patentable Subject Matter

Determining whether an invention is within a patentable subject matter is a difficult task. The federal statute says that patents can cover a "process, machine, manufacture, or composition of matter." While some inventions seem to fit squarely within our understanding of patents — such as a new type of robot for painting cars — others seem less of a slam dunk — such as a business method patent for a business that issues coupons on a social networking model. The United States Patent and Trademark Office has issued guidance on business method patents in response to recent Supreme Court action, saying:

> The factors below should be considered when analyzing the claim as a whole to evaluate whether a method claim is directed to an abstract idea:
> . . .
> Factors Weighing Toward Eligibility:
>
> — Recitation of a machine or transformation (either express or inherent). . . .
> — The claim is directed toward applying a law of nature. . . .
> — The claim is more than a mere statement of a concept. . . .
>
> Factors Weighing Against Eligibility:
>
> — No recitation of a machine or transformation (either express or inherent). . . .
> — Insufficient recitation of a machine or transformation. . . .
> — The claim is not directed to an application of a law of nature.
> — The claim is a mere statement of a general concept.
>
> . . .

b. Utility

It is rare for a patent to be challenged on the basis that it is not useful. The USPTO notes that "[t]he term 'useful' . . . refers to the condition that the subject matter has a useful purpose and also includes operativeness, that is, a machine which will not operate to perform the intended purpose would not be called useful, and therefore would not be granted a patent."

c. Novelty

As noted earlier in this section, in order to be eligible for patent protection, an invention must be within a class of patentable subject matter, it must be useful, it must be novel, and it cannot be an obvious extension of previously existing technology. Once an entrepreneur has determined that her invention is within a class of patentable subject matter and is useful (which it probably is or she would not be spending time working on patent protection), she must consider whether the invention is novel.

An invention will not be considered novel if (a) the invention is already known or used by others in the United States, or patented or described in a printed publication in the United States or a foreign country; or (b) the invention was patented or described in a printed publication in the United States or a foreign country or in public use or on sale in the United States, more than one year prior to the date of the application. The novelty of an invention is determined relative to the state of the art in the particular field of the invention at the time the invention was made.

d. Non-Obviousness

In addition to being novel, an invention must be "non-obvious" to be patentable. On this subject, the USPTO offers helpful guidance:

> The subject matter sought to be patented must be sufficiently different from what has been used or described before that it may be said to be nonobvious to a person having ordinary skill in the area of technology related to the invention. For example, the substitution of one color for another, or changes in size, are ordinarily not patentable.

4. Statutory Bar

To preserve her right to obtain a patent, the entrepreneur must be careful not to disclose her invention to the public. An inventor will be precluded from obtaining a patent if she has disclosed the invention more than one year before the filing date. The term "disclosed" generally means that the invention at issue has been publicly used or sold in the United States or was described in a printed publication in the United States or in any other country. The Federal Circuit has even held that slideshow presentations to an interested audience can constitute a disclosure in a printed publication under the statute. Accordingly, an entrepreneur making a pre-filing presentation to an interested audience, such as at an academic conference, trade show, or meeting of investors, should take precautionary measures to avoid the printed-publication bar.

The entrepreneur must also avoid selling the invention or offering it for sale before the critical date. Any offer to sell the invention prior to filing the patent application may jeopardize future patentability.

Disclosure of the invention before filing a patent application also introduces another risk: since the United States grants patents to the first inventor to file a patent application (see next section below), an inventor who discloses the invention might inadvertently encourage other inventors to race to the patent office to gain priority in the same invention.

It is also important for entrepreneurs to consider the fact that other countries, unlike the United States, do not have this one-year grace period. Therefore, throughout the world, any publication prior to filing a patent application may jeopardize the patentability of the invention.

In short, the prudent entrepreneur should apply for patent protection in the United States prior to public disclosure of the invention or any sales. If the entrepreneur lacks time or resources for a full application, the entrepreneur can consider — again, with the help of a trademark specialist — filing a provisional application before publicly presenting her invention and seeking funding.

The entrepreneur should also carefully document her inventive process, in order to corroborate her claims of inventorship.

5. Patent Priority

Since March 2013, the United States has granted priority for a patent using a "first to file" system. Under this system, the first inventor to file an application with the USPTO is granted the patent, regardless of the date of invention. Thus, entrepreneurs should apply for patents as early as possible, to avoid the possibility that another inventor files first.

6. Term of Patent

Utility patents last for 20 years from the date the patent application is filed. Design patents have a term of 14 years from the date of issue.

Notes and Questions

1. Patent law is highly complex, and numerous detailed requirements apply in determining the patentability of an invention. If an entrepreneur has developed an invention that she wants to protect, when would it be preferable to avoid filing a patent and instead protect the invention through trade secret law? Compare and contrast these options and specifically counter some of the advantages and disadvantages of each.

2. Assume you have a client who has called to tell you that she has come up with a fabulous new invention and wants you to start working on a patent application. She is very excited about the invention and tells you that she is even presenting the

idea to a few extremely interested investors first thing in the morning. She is also scheduled to present her invention at a prestigious conference next week where the "who's who" of the industry will be in attendance. What advice would you give your client and why?

3. Consider the assignment of inventions agreement included in the problem at the end of Chapter 2. In Chapter 2, such an agreement was a challenge to the entrepreneur. How might such an agreement be used to an entrepreneur's advantage once she has started her own business?

PROBLEM

At a meeting with you, Andrew and Olivia advise you that they have been discussing names for their new invention and that they think they have made some final decisions. They intend to name their invention the "Magic Wand" and they think a catchy slogan would be "Eat Fresh!" For some reason, they both think that the slogan has a familiar feel.

They also tell you that they think it would be great marketing to include information with their product on how to best keep food fresh (i.e., clever ways to wrap food, ideal storage temperatures, and typical freshness durations for common foods). They have put together a great one-page list of "tips" and recommendations that they intend to include in the package, along with a recipe from Olivia's grandmother for delicious cookies that stay fresh longer.

Andrew is particularly excited because he just found a file he thought he had lost with information and documents he had collected while at his last job. Among the found items is a list of manufacturing plants that he thinks could be helpful in manufacturing the Magic Wand, as well as a list of his best corporate customers to which he previously sold consumer health care items when he was in sales for a large consumer goods company. He thinks these companies might be very interested in carrying the Magic Wand.

Finally, your clients express some concern about someone "stealing" their idea. They are afraid that once the product is on the market, imitations will become a real problem. They never want anyone to be able to copy their invention.

1. You warn your clients that they should make an effort to avoid claims of trademark infringement or unfair competition from another member of the industry. Conduct searches on readily available databases (such as Google and the USPTO) and advise your clients if the proposed product name and slogan would likely expose the new company to risks of claims by third parties. Also, let them know whether you think the new company would have strong trademark rights in the proposed product name and slogan. Your clients are obviously not yet ready to market or sell their new product. What steps if any should they take to protect their branding ideas pending the formation of the business?

2. Do you think your clients can protect the "tips" sheet that they would like to include in the packaging? What advice would you give them? What about the recipe?

3. Is Andrew free to use the documents he found from his old job? What questions might you ask Andrew to better determine whether he is free to contact the manufacturers and customers?

4. Is your clients' fear of imitation Magic Wands valid? What advice can you give them that they might find comforting? Are there ways to eliminate copycat products?

V

FINANCING

There are two main ways entrepreneurs get the cash necessary to start their business: they either sell an ownership interest in the business, or they cause the business to borrow the necessary funds. Under the first approach, called an "equity financing," the business sells shares (if the venture is organized as a corporation), or membership interests/membership units (if the venture is organized as a limited liability company), or partnership interests (if the venture is organized as a partnership) to the founder or a third party. While founders will share upside with all equity investors if the venture is successful, they also share the risk of loss if the venture fails. Under the second approach, called a "debt financing," the business borrows money from the founder or a third party (oftentimes a bank), sometimes "secured" by collateral that a lender can foreclose on if the loan is not repaid. A hybrid approach involves borrowing or otherwise receiving money from an investor, with the intent that the amount borrowed or received will convert to equity securities at a future point in time. A client's goals for the business, and the availability and pricing of financing in the market, will dictate the most advisable way for the entrepreneur to raise capital and the most advisable type of investor or lender for the entrepreneur to seek. Throughout its life cycle, a business will generally take on both investors and debt. Fortunate businesses will also be able to engage in non-dilutive, non-debt financing, such as from foundation or government grants, by pre-selling products through kickstarter or Indiegogo, or even — ideally — through the sale of products or services in the ordinary course of business.

Most entrepreneurs will expect their attorneys to be conversant in the myriad financing options available, and will often turn to a lawyer for advice on how to best raise funds for a new venture, and perhaps even to provide introductions and contacts in the financial industry. In this chapter, we explore and compare the various methods entrepreneur clients use to finance their enterprises. We also discuss some of the important legal issues implicit in equity and debt financing, and the contract terms that typically dominate negotiations when entrepreneurs seek cash to start and operate their business.

A. INTRODUCTION AND OVERVIEW

Many companies go through a similar trajectory in financing a new business and raising additional cash to continue operating and expanding the business. Typically, when entrepreneurs first conceive of a business and need cash to get started, they look to their own personal assets. This approach is commonly known as "bootstrapping." Entrepreneurs are often willing to use their own savings, borrow on credit cards, and even mortgage their homes to get their business off the ground. It is very important to keep in mind that founders may structure their cash infusion as either debt or equity.

The obvious benefits of bootstrapping, among others, are the immediate availability of money without going to third parties, not having the pressure of potentially losing other people's money, not owing fiduciary duties to anyone else, avoidance of securities laws, and the flexibility of unilaterally setting a desired valuation. Additionally, those who are willing to commit not only their time, but also their own savings, send a strong signal to future investors. This is key down the road because future investors may be more interested in businesses in which founders have invested their own money, as this demonstrates both confidence and commitment.

As important as having so-called skin in the game may be for many reasons, entrepreneurs should also be counseled on the accompanying risks and costs. Many entrepreneurs have already quit their job to start their new venture and therefore have given up regular pay, health care benefits, and other financial security. Risking additional savings may put the entrepreneur in a precarious financial position that could cause undue stress on the entrepreneur, as well as tension in family relationships — neither of which is good for business and may affect the entrepreneur's ability to have a clear and focused mindset to make important business decisions. Additionally, businesses that are completely funded by founders miss out on having the expertise and contacts outside investors bring as well as the possibility for follow-on investments. Entrepreneurs who are limited to their own funds (depending, of course, on their personal wealth) may preclude quick growth.

Although this is a generalization, entrepreneurs tend to invest in their own businesses initially, quickly look to friends and family to help, move on to a seed round involving angel investors or venture capitalists and then, if the stars are aligned and the business has established a certain level of success, the next step is often identifying an appropriate venture capital firm or even identifying an exit opportunity (as discussed in Chapter 10). At the same time as the new company is identifying potential investors, it may also assess the possibility of a bank loan or a loan from some other third party. Most banks will not loan money to a business unless it has sufficient assets to secure the loan. Therefore, bank loans are often not an option for a new venture until it has grown sufficiently and acquired tangible value.

It is quite apparent that there are many factors for entrepreneurs and their lawyers to consider in evaluating financing options, especially as their businesses grow and require more and more (and more) cash. The following sections discuss in greater detail many of the attributes of both debt and equity financing arrangements, as well as the steps and options entrepreneurs face when raising money.

IMPROVING THE EFFICIENCY OF THE ANGEL FINANCE MARKET: A PROPOSAL TO EXPAND THE INTERMEDIARY ROLE OF FINDERS IN THE PRIVATE CAPITAL RAISING SETTING

John L. Orcutt, 37 Ariz. St. L.J. 861, 869-70 (2005)

When seeking external funding, new companies may look to raise debt capital or equity capital. With respect to rapid-growth start-ups, material debt financing is not widely available until they are highly mature companies. Debt financing involves borrowing money from a lender in exchange for a promise to repay the debt. Such repayment will involve repayment of the principal (i.e., the amount borrowed) and will also require interest payments that are meant to compensate the lender for its cost of lending the money. For small businesses generally, debt financing from commercial banks is a very important financing tool, with loans guaranteed by the Small Business Administration serving as a substantial source of small business capital. Because of the way that rapid-growth start-ups are structured, they are generally not eligible for such commercial bank loans. To begin with, rapid-growth start-ups are built for growth and will generally sacrifice near-term profitability for this growth. As a result, these companies typically face several years of negative earnings and, therefore, lack the necessary excess cash flow to make the required principal and interest payments. As well, rapid-growth start-ups generally do not have meaningful securable assets, which is a fundamental requirement for most loans to high-risk borrowers. The primary assets for a rapid-growth start-up are likely to be intellectual property assets, which are very difficult to collateralize.

Most rapid-growth start-ups, therefore, are left with equity financing as the only viable option to finance their company.

. . .

STARTING FROM SCRATCH: A LAWYER'S GUIDE TO REPRESENTING A START-UP COMPANY

Richard A. Mann, Michael O'Sullivan, Larry Robbins & Barry S. Roberts
56 Ark. L. Rev. 773, 817-29 (2004)

The first place many entrepreneurs get money from is themselves. Entrepreneurs must be personally and financially committed to the business. Many entrepreneurs mortgage their homes, raid retirement funds, and use credit cards to finance the initial operations of the business. Access to these sources of capital may be critical to a start-up business, but they come at a high emotional and financial cost.

After entrepreneurs have exhausted their personal financial resources, they usually turn to their friends and family for financing assistance. It should be noted, however, that institutional investors are hesitant to fund companies owned by a large number of individual investors or companies controlled by family members. In addition, a company having been funded by family and friends that ultimately fails can be financially catastrophic for the family and friends. The entrepreneur must disclose that the business may fail, and if it does (and the probability of that is high), the friends and family will lose their money invested. Failure invariably strains relationships. By adding multiple investors, an entrepreneur adds complexity, such as holding management meetings and potentially losing control of the business. Often the founders, together with family and friends, become the only investors in the "seed round" of financing. The proceeds of a seed round may be used for the company's preliminary research and development and marketing efforts. Even with significant seed funding, successful companies normally require several additional rounds of financing.

"Angels" provide entrepreneurs with another (or frequently a second) financing option. Angels are typically successful business people with a high net worth that invest in and often advise start-up companies. Angels frequently provide access to capital as well as sound business advice. Angels, as their nomenclature indicates, have been saviors to start-ups, historically investing as much as $50-100 billion annually. The amount of capital invested and the depth of involvement in the company vary significantly based upon the individual circumstances of the angel.

Following early stage financings, entrepreneurs often need additional growth capital. Creating a solid business plan is a key to attracting venture capitalists (VCs) to fund a company's growth. "Venture capital is a substantial equity investment in a non-public enterprise that does not involve active control of the firm." Virtually all venture capitalists focus intensely on the experience and maturity of the management team of an entrepreneurial company. Individual partners within a venture capital firm frequently specialize in a targeted business market, such as biotech or software. Similar to their prominent role in computer technology start-ups, VCs are arguably the "single most important form of financing" in the biotech industry as well. Attracting a VC with a reputation for success in many cases facilitates the operation and growth of a business. It is the reputation and contacts of the VC that impact customer decisions, supplier relationships, banking, legal and accounting relationships, as well as the recruitment of key employees.

VCs differ from angels in that they typically invest other investors' capital in start-ups. Generally, VCs are organized as limited partnerships. Investment risk is reduced for institutional investors by investing in multiple funds, in which money is pooled from wealthy individuals and institutions and then invested in various promising, young start-ups. VCs invest to make significant returns for their limited partners. . . . Company managers live in a constant pressure cooker, always evaluating any viable "exit strategy" in order to provide liquidity to a VC for taking the investment risk. During the 1980s VCs enjoyed an average long-term return on investment (ROI) of twenty-two percent per year while the ROI for the Standard & Poor's index of public companies was fourteen percent. In the boom days of 2000, some funds returned an amazing seventy-five to ninety percent. While many of the boom time start-ups will fail, VCs balance this certainty with other companies in the portfolio that become "Wild Ones."

. . .

Despite [unfavorable changes in the return on investment delivered by venture capitalists since their heyday in the late 1990s], VCs continue to make substantial investments in start-up companies. For founders, relinquishing more ownership is inevitable as VCs value start-ups in a manner that mirrors the downturn in public markets. Investors receive preferred stock that converts into a larger percentage of the company. If the investment is made after poor performance, the preferred stock may represent virtually all of the equity of the company. Even during the boom investment years, a typical start-up required several financing rounds before a successful exit. As a result, founders' percentage of ownership will almost always decline significantly by the time of exit.

    . . .

B. EQUITY FINANCING

As outlined in the introductory sections of this chapter, entrepreneurs tend to follow similar patterns when selling equity in their new business. Typically, the founding entrepreneurs are the first equityholders in the venture. From there, they seek "seed funding" from outsiders. Sometimes this money comes from their friends and family in what is usually called a "friends and family" round of financing, but it may equally come from wealthy individuals or groups of wealthy individuals who are called "angels" (or, if organized into a formal or informal group, "angel networks"). Some start-ups even secure seed funding from Venture Capital firms — a strategy by VC firms to get an early foot in the door on a hot startup. For those ventures lucky enough to get to the point of being ready for large infusions of cash, the next step may be a large investment from a venture capitalist.

At all levels of equity funding (and in particular in early rounds), founders and investors will likely have a great degree of uncertainty about the company's valuation. Whereas traditionally companies raise money by selling shares with varying economic and management rights at a negotiated price per share (called a "priced round"), in recent years a host of new options have arisen that allow founders to delay the valuation negotiation until there is greater certainty. After an initial period of bootstrapping, entrepreneurs often move to sell "convertible securities" that convert to equity in a future priced round, converting at the price per share negotiated by investors in that future round (often with a discount or other adjustment benefitting the early stage investor).

Convertible securities such as Convertible Notes and the Simple Agreement for Future Equity (or "SAFE") afford entrepreneurs the opportunity to raise money quickly, without definitively committing to any particular value of their company. From there, a priced round involving "Series Seed" equity, the sale of Preferred Stock, or even equity crowdfunding are options for the new venture.

In addition to selling equity to investors, entrepreneurs may have other equity issuances to consider. Accelerator programs that support new businesses often insist on equity as a condition to participating in their program. Employees often expect equity as part of their compensation arrangements. That said, entrepreneurs need to resist the temptation to reward all of their valuable advisors and supporters with equity. Many entrepreneurs feel so appreciative toward mentors that they wind up with numerous small equityholders, making the capitalization table of the business messy. Future sophisticated investors generally frown upon excessive investors owning fractional percentages, due in part to the administrative and management challenges of such a large group.

In this section, we move through these categories of equity investments, focusing on operative documents actually used in transactions of this type. As you read, notice the extent to which the deal terms vary in the different documents — presenting entrepreneurs and their counsel with a full toolkit from which to choose the best fundraising method in the circumstances at hand.

1. *Founder Investment/Bootstrapping*

To the distress of attorneys who want to ensure that the corporate veil is not pierced, founders often view their new venture as an extension of themselves. Accordingly, they happily bootstrap their new business out of their own pocket, from their own credit cards, or by taking personal loans. They deposit revenue to, and pay bills from, their personal bank account. One way to encourage discipline and adherence to formalities at an early stage is to have entrepreneurs go through the simple mechanics of purchasing their ownership of the business by making a cash deposit in a new business bank account and signing a simple document assigning their intellectual property to the new entity. In exchange for the cash and property, the business will issue equity securities to the founder, as in the example below. Clients must understand that if they decide to infuse more of their personal cash or assets in the business, they should do so in a similar manner, to be sure they keep a formal separation between themselves and the new venture.

RESOLUTIONS OF THE BOARD OF DIRECTORS OF EV, INC., AN ILLINOIS CORPORATION
Adopted at the Initial Meeting of the Board of Directors

The undersigned, being the directors of EV, Inc., an Illinois corporation (the "Corporation"), take the following action by their written consent without a meeting, in accordance with the provisions of the Illinois General Corporation Law and the bylaws of the Corporation:

[Common initial actions of the Board include Approval and Adoption of Bylaws, Election of Officers, Payment of Incorporation Expenses, Location of Principal Executive Offices, and Establishment of Bank Accounts.]

<u>Issuance of Shares</u>

RESOLVED: That the offer of Ian Gorton to purchase 250 shares of the Corporation's common stock, and of Betty Paul to purchase 250 shares of the Corporation's common stock, each in exchange for $5,000 cash plus the consideration set forth on the Assignment Agreement attached hereto as Exhibit A be, and they hereby are, accepted, and such shares of the Corporation's common stock, upon the execution and delivery of such Assignment Agreement and the delivery of the consideration set forth therein, shall be duly and validly issued, fully paid and non-assessable; and

RESOLVED FURTHER: That any officer of the Corporation be, and he or she hereby is, authorized and directed to take such other actions and execute such other documents as such officer may determine necessary or appropriate to consummate the transactions contemplated in the foregoing resolutions.

The Secretary of the Corporation is hereby directed to file this written consent with the minutes of the proceedings of the Board of Directors.

DATED: July 1, 2020

_____   _____
Ian Gorton   Betty Paul

<u>Exhibit A: Assignment Agreement</u>

ASSIGNMENT AGREEMENT

This Assignment Agreement dated as of July 1, 2020 is made by Ian Gorton and Betty Paul (each an "Assignor," collectively referred to as the "Assignors").

WHEREAS the Assignors are co-owners of EV, a business that creates and operates internet business concepts, including an online community for graphic designers (the "EV Business");

WHEREAS the Assignors own certain intellectual property and other assets related to the EV Business, including without limitation intellectual property (collectively the "EV Business Assets");

WHEREAS EV, Inc., an Illinois corporation (the "Corporation") was formed on the date hereof;

NOW THEREFORE, for good and valuable consideration, each Assignor hereby assigns all EV Business Assets owned by such Assignor to the Corporation and agrees to sign any necessary documents and otherwise assist the Corporation in registering and protecting its rights in EV Business Assets.

In witness of the above, the parties to this Assignment Agreement hereby have caused it to be executed as of the date first listed above.

[Signature blocks of Founders]

Notes and Questions

1. Why do you imagine it is typical for founders to purchase equity in their new business entities, rather than make a loan to the entity with a promise of repayment and a guaranteed interest rate?

2. Why should founders go to the trouble of documenting their initial purchase of equity in the formal manner shown above?

3. Prior to the execution of the Assignment Agreement above, who owns the business plan, prototypes, and other intellectual property of the new business? What consequences might you imagine an entrepreneurial venture would face if it did not make some provision for the acquisition of the intellectual property at the base of the business?

4. Key benefits of founder funding are that the venture (and founder) are not beholden to any outside investors and do not need to share economic growth in the business with other owners. What are some disadvantages of a self-funded financing approach?

2. Non-Founder Investors: Friends and Family, Angel Investors, and Venture Capitalists

With bootstrapping, founders own all of the equity in their business, and therefore bear all the risks and reap all the rewards of the business. Startup founders will almost always look to outsiders for investment in their business, which gives them access to outside money and allows them to spread the risk — albeit at the cost of giving away some upside if the business goes well. In subsequent sections, we will explore the ways in which founders accept equity investments, but first, it is useful to identify the different kinds of investors growth stage businesses may have.

A "friends and family" round of financing refers to investment by close friends and relatives of the founders. Typically, the friends and family are making the investment out of affection for the entrepreneur, rather than because they expect a significant return. Accordingly, they do little negotiation and will often be willing to take nonvoting equity in small percentages. That said, the money is not "free," especially when you take into account the emotional impact of taking an investment from friends and family. The entrepreneur needs to realize that every family event from the investment point forward will involve discussions of the business, including annoying questions from family members who may hold very small stakes in the business. Family members may make pointed comments about the entrepreneur's life outside the business as well — such as criticizing personal expenses or time spent away from the business. In addition, if things go badly, the entrepreneur and her friends and family will need to deal with the fact that the invested funds are all gone with no prospect of returning — or that family members have been diluted to even smaller ownership stakes by subsequent investors. In addition, personal matters within a family like death and divorce, not to mention estate planning, become more complicated when the people involved are also shareholders in the new venture.

"Angel investors," who also invest at the seed stage of a new business, typically have more cash available to invest than friends and family, and they negotiate for better economic rights (in the form of a larger percentage of the business or preferred returns on their investment) and better management rights (in the form of a large voting percentage or special approval rights over certain major company events). Angel investors come in a wide variety of shapes and sizes. Some are just wealthy individuals without industry or entrepreneurial experience, while others may have started, built, and exited hugely successful ventures in similar spaces to the entrepreneur's business. This latter type of angel is contributing not only much-needed cash but also mentorship, personal contacts, and industry expertise. These contributions can sometimes be even more valuable and instrumental than money in achieving ultimate success for the new company. In addition, there seems to be a growing trend toward angels forming groups or networks to evaluate and sometimes invest in companies together. Angels commonly invest using a so-called convertible note or SAFE, examples of which appear in the next section of this chapter. Alternatively, deal documents for angel investors can be similar to a friends and family round, with a purchase agreement evidencing the transaction, but the business terms of the equity being purchased will vary significantly depending on the type of angel making the investment.

Startups will also seek investment — increasingly, even at the seed stage — from investors known as "venture capitalists." Venture capital firms typically raise money from wealthy individuals for particular venture capital "funds," and then invest the money from those funds into growth stage businesses. Venture capitalists are sophisticated investors, with access to significantly larger amounts of capital than angels or friends and family. Venture capitalists also bring expertise and a wide professional network, which can accelerate a business's growth and lead to success. Receiving VC funding is also a badge of honor for a startup, particularly if the investor is renowned in the startup's industry or generally well-known with a top-notch reputation.

When venture capitalists invest at the seed stage, they will often use convertible securities of the type described later in this chapter. At the later stage, however, venture capitalists invest in "priced rounds," where they negotiate with founders over the amount of control they can exert over the business (commonly called "management rights"), the access they will have to information about the business ("information rights"), and the valuation of the business and the return they will receive on their investment if all goes well, or even if all goes poorly ("economic rights"). The article below outlines aspects of typical venture capital financings in priced rounds, and some of the risks to entrepreneurs of the way venture capital funds are organized.

ENGINEERING A VENTURE CAPITAL MARKET: LESSONS FROM THE AMERICAN EXPERIENCE
Ronald J. Gilson, 55 Stan. L. Rev. 1067, 1071-72 (2003)

The venture capital fund's equity investments in portfolio companies typically take the form of convertible preferred stock. While not required by the formal legal documents, the fund is also expected to make important noncash contributions to the portfolio company. These contributions consist of management assistance, corresponding to that provided by management consultants; intensive monitoring of the portfolio company's performance which provides an objective view to the entrepreneur; and the use of the fund's reputation to give the portfolio company credibility with potential customers, suppliers, and employees. While each investment will have a "lead" investor who plays the primary role in monitoring and advising the portfolio company, commonly the overall investment is syndicated with other venture capital funds that invest in the portfolio company at the same time and on the same terms.

The initial venture capital investment usually will be insufficient to fund the portfolio company's entire business plan. Accordingly, investment will be "staged." A particular investment round will provide only the capital the business plan projects as necessary to achieve specified milestones set out in the business plan. While first round investors expect to participate in subsequent investment rounds, often they are not contractually obligated to do so even if the business plan's milestones are met; the terms of later rounds of investment are negotiated at the time the milestones are met and the prior investment exhausted. Like the provision of non-capital contributions, an implicit, not explicit, contract typically governs the venture capital fund's right and obligation to provide additional rounds of financing if the portfolio company performs as expected. The venture capital fund's implicit right to participate in subsequent rounds — by contrast to its implicit obligation to participate — is protected by an explicit right of first refusal.

A critical feature of the governance structure created by the venture capital fund's investment in the portfolio company is the disproportionate allocation of control to the fund. [T]he governance structure of a venture capital-backed early stage, high technology company allocates to the venture capital investors disproportionately greater control than equity. It is common for venture capital investors to have the right to name a majority of a portfolio company's directors even though their stock represents less than a majority of the portfolio company's voting power. Additionally, the portfolio company will have the benefit of a series of contractual negative covenants that require the venture capital investors' approval before the portfolio company can make important business decisions, such as acquisition or disposition of significant amounts of assets, or a material deviation from the business plan. The extent of these negative covenants is related to whether the venture capital investors have control of the board of directors; board control acts as a partial substitute for covenant restrictions.

These formal levers of control are complemented by the informal control elements that result from the staged financing structure. Because a financing round will not provide funds sufficient to complete the portfolio company's business plan, staged financing in effect delegates to the investors, in the form of the decision whether to provide additional financing, the decision whether to continue the company's project.

Two final characteristics of investments in portfolio companies concern their terms and their expected performance. While these are not short-term investments, neither are they expected to be long-term. Because venture capital limited partnerships have limited, usually ten-year terms, GP's have a strong incentive to cause the fund's portfolio company investments to become liquid as quickly as possible. Assuming that the GP has invested most of a fund's capital by the midpoint of the fund's life, the GP then must seek to raise additional capital for a new fund in order to remain in the venture capital business. Because the performance of a GP's prior funds will be an important determinant of its ability to raise capital for a new fund, early harvesting of a fund's investments will be beneficial. Venture capital funds exit successful investments by two general methods: taking the portfolio company public through an initial public offering of its stock (an "IPO"); or selling the portfolio company to another firm. The likelihood of exit by an IPO or a sale has differed over different periods. . . . It is also common for the terms of a venture capital preferred stock investment to give the venture capital fund the right to require the portfolio company to redeem its stock. However, redemption does not operate as a viable exit mechanism because portfolio companies lack the funds to effect the redemption. Such put rights are better understood as a control device that can force the portfolio company to accommodate the fund's desire to exit by way of IPO or sale.

The fact that portfolio company investments are of limited duration rather than long term is critical to the operation of the venture capital market. The noncash contributions made by the venture capital fund to the portfolio company — management assistance, monitoring, and service as a reputational intermediary — share a significant economy of scope with its provision of capital. The portfolio company must evaluate the quality of the fund's proffered management assistance and monitoring, just as potential employees, suppliers, and customers must evaluate the fund's representations concerning the portfolio company's quality. Combining financial and nonfinancial contributions enhances the credibility of the information the venture capital fund proposes to provide the portfolio company and third parties. Put simply, the venture capital fund bonds the accuracy of its information with its investment.

The importance of the portfolio company investment's limited duration reflects the fact that the venture capital fund's noncash contributions have special value to early stage companies. As the portfolio company gains its own experience and develops its own reputation, the value of the venture capital fund's provision of those elements declines. By the time a portfolio company succeeds and the venture capital fund's exit from the investment is possible, the fund's noncash contributions can be more profitably invested in a new round of early stage companies.

But because of the economies of scope between cash and noncash contributions, recycling the venture capital fund's noncash contributions also requires recycling its cash contributions. Exit from a fund's investments in successful portfolio companies thus serves to recycle its cash and, therefore, its associated noncash contributions from successful companies to early stage companies.

The risk associated with portfolio company investments is reflected in the variability of returns. While some investments return many multiples of the original investment, a survey of the performance of venture capital-backed companies, not limited to early stage technology companies and therefore presenting less uncertainty than the category of investments that concern us here, reports wide variation in returns. In the sample studied, fifty percent of the total return was provided by only 6.8% of the investments. Over a third of the investments resulted in partial or total loss.

. . .

Notes and Questions

1. Friends and family rounds of financing are occasionally referred to as "Triple F" (referring to "Friends, Family, and Fools"), and equity investments by friends and family are often called "dumb money." What are these clearly derogatory terms describing friends and family trying to convey about these financing transactions, or perhaps about early-stage entrepreneurial ventures in general?

2. What do angel investors bring to an entrepreneurial venture that friends and family typically do not? What advantages and disadvantages will a founder encounter in the process of finding, wooing, and ultimately accepting financing from an angel or angel syndicate?

3. Gilson describes the goals that guide a venture capitalist in making investment decisions. In what ways are these goals likely different from friends and family in early seed rounds of a start-up? In what ways are they similar?

4. What do venture capitalists likely bring to the table that angel investors do not or cannot? How might this affect the price they pay for the equity they receive from an entrepreneurial venture?

5. What types of entrepreneurs would be best suited for venture capital funding, taking into account business strategies, personal goals, and professional goals?

3. Convertible Securities

Selling equity in a new company is a complicated affair. In addition to the aspects of raising money that one would always expect — finding potential investors, getting meetings with investors, creating a pitch deck that makes the case that investors should put money into the company's business, and so on — when selling shares of stock, one must deal with negotiating and documenting a valuation of the entrepreneurial venture and the specific terms of the stock to be sold.

Consider the following: when a company decides to sell shares of stock to an investor, the company and the investor need to agree on a price for the shares the investor is buying, and the percentage ownership stake the investor will get in the company. The amount being invested, combined with the ownership percentage being sold, then indicate the value of the entire company (the company's "valuation"). As a simple example, imagine a company in which the founders own 1,000,000 shares. Imagine the company sells 500,000 shares to an outside investor. After the transaction, the investor will own 1/3 of the company, since 500,000 is 1/3 of the 1,500,000 shares that will be outstanding after the transaction. If they sell those 500,000 new shares for an investment of $1,000,000, then that means the company is valued at $3,000,000 (since the investor paid one million dollars for one-third of the company). Investors want valuations to be low, so they can buy a larger piece of the company for their investment. Entrepreneurs generally want valuations to be high, but not too high, lest the next round of financing comes in at a lower valuation (a "down round"), which makes it looks as though the business is not doing well. Further complicating matters is the fact that in a new business with no real track record (and, in some cases, no product or service that is yet ready for the market), it is very difficult to find any subjective or objective measures of enterprise value.

In addition to the issue of needing to decide on a valuation, other business terms will be negotiated. As discussed further below in the section on "priced rounds," many business terms need to be negotiated before a sale of shares can occur. In addition to all of the negotiation, the agreed-upon terms need to be memorialized in a complex set of written documents.

For early stage entrepreneurs, these challenges make selling shares of stock incredibly difficult. Two solutions that have arisen — the Convertible Note and the Simple Agreement for Future Equity (or "SAFE") — allow entrepreneurs to defer valuation discussions until their businesses have more time to develop. The following articles describe these two investment options, and following that reading, you will study an example Convertible Note and a SAFE.

ESSAY: THE SAFE, THE KISS, AND THE NOTE: A SURVEY OF STARTUP SEED FINANCING CONTRACTS
John F. Coyle & Joseph M. Green, 103 Minn. L. Rev. Headnotes 42 (2018)

. . .

I.   THE "NEW" SEED FINANCING CONTRACTS

In the 1980s and 1990s, investors who wished to fund a technology startup typically chose from three basic options when it came time to structure that investment. First, they might choose to invest alongside the founders in exchange for plain-vanilla common stock. This investment structure was typically used in friends-and-family or angel rounds where the investors were personally known to the founders. Second, they might choose to invest in exchange for convertible preferred stock that was senior to the founders' shares of common stock and came with a panoply of additional rights and privileges. This investment structure was typically used when the investors were institutional venture capital funds making a more significant, post-seed-stage capital contribution in the startup. Third, and finally, they might choose to invest in exchange for a convertible note. This investment structure was typically used when the investors were making a bridge loan to a later-stage startup to keep it afloat until the next round of venture financing could be raised or an exit event (such as a sale or initial public offering) could be achieved.

As the costs of launching a startup plummeted in the mid-2000s, this contractual infrastructure began to evolve. The convertible note, in particular, was increasingly used to provide seed financing to technology companies at the earliest stages of their development. This shift was driven partly by cost considerations. The legal fees associated with a convertible note were substantially lower than the fees associated with convertible preferred stock (which required much longer, more complex contracts and filings with state authorities) and yet still allowed noteholders to eventually receive many of the benefits that they would have foregone had they instead purchased common stock. The shift was also driven by a desire to "punt" the delicate issue of valuation to a later date. By deferring the valuation discussion, the company gained time to reach developmental milestones that would allow for a higher valuation down the road that would be less dilutive for the founders.

The convertible note was also perceived to be a useful instrument in this space because it offered investors downside protection if the company failed and upside potential if the venture succeeded. While the note was technically debt — and hence entitled to priority over equityholders in the event of a liquidation — the investor could convert it into convertible preferred stock if the company were ever to raise additional capital. As an additional inducement, most notes provided that they would convert to convertible preferred stock at a "discount" to the price paid by the new investor, thereby rewarding the investor for her far-sightedness and compensating her for the additional risk that she took by investing earlier than the new equity investor. As time passed, it also became common for the note to set a ceiling on the price at which it would convert into equity — a valuation cap — that similarly incentivized investors to fund early-stage companies using this instrument.

Although the convertible note came to play a major role in the market for seed funding in the years after 2005, it contained several undesirable features from the perspective of the company. First, the notes accrued interest while they were outstanding. Though the interest rate was generally set low, and interest was not typically paid in cash (but rather tacked onto the principal and converted into equity), the need to keep track of exactly how much interest had accrued and the fact that it effectively increased the conversion discount was viewed as an unnecessary giveaway to investors and, perhaps even worse, a distraction adding unnecessary complexity at the time of conversion. Second, the fact that the notes had a maturity date upon which the investors could ask the company to repay the principal worried many founders. While neither the investor nor the company expected the note to be repaid — they assumed the note would convert into stock if the company proved to be successful — the existence of a maturity date gave the investor leverage to extract favorable concessions from the company in some cases. In response to these perceived problems with the convertible note, lawyers in Silicon Valley set about devising solutions. One such solution was the Simple Agreement for Future Equity (SAFE). . . .

A. THE SIMPLE AGREEMENT FOR FUTURE EQUITY

The SAFE was developed by Carolynn Levy, an attorney and partner at Y Combinator, and was first released in 2013. In many respects, the SAFE resembles the classic convertible note. Like the note, the SAFE will (1) convert into convertible preferred stock when the company issues such stock in a priced equity round, (2) typically contain a valuation cap that sets the highest valuation that can be used to determine the conversion price, and (3) convert into stock at a discount to the price paid by the new venture capitalist. Unlike the note, however, the SAFE lacks a maturity date and does not accrue interest. In essence, the SAFE is a convertible note that has had its debt-like features stripped away.

This unique combination of attributes means that it is difficult to classify the SAFE as either debt or equity. It lacks two of the key hallmarks of a debt instrument: an interest provision and a maturity date. It also does not appear to be equity because it does not give the investor the rights that are typically associated with holding equity, such as the rights to receive dividends or to vote on matters relating to the governance of the corporation. The SAFE is best conceptualized as an equity derivative contract by which the investor commits capital to the company today in exchange for the right to receive stock in the company in a future financing if certain contractual conditions are met. If this future financing never occurs, then the SAFE will likely be worthless. If this future financing comes to pass, however, then the SAFE will convert into the securities issued by the company pursuant to this financing — typically convertible preferred stock — at a discount to the price that the new investor is paying for that same stock.

Shortly after the SAFE was finalized in 2013, Y Combinator approached the institutional investors who frequently invest in Y Combinator companies to suggest that they use the SAFE to invest in the next batch of these companies. All of these investors agreed to use SAFEs to invest in the companies accepted into Y Combinator's 2014 winter program. With the rise of retail crowdfunding, the SAFE has gained a measure of additional notoriety — several crowdfunding websites offer versions of the SAFE to companies seeking to raise capital from retail investors via the internet.

. . .

THE EVOLUTION OF ENTREPRENEURIAL FINANCE: A NEW TYPOLOGY
J. Brad Bernthal, 2018 B.Y.U.L. Rev. 775 (2018)

. . .

5.   CONVERTIBLE DEBT

Convertible debt structures a high-risk capital investment in the form of a loan (aka, a "note") that anticipates a subsequent round of equity financing. In short, unlike a venture debt lender, a convertible debt investor does not seek her return through loan repayment. Rather, an investor parks capital with a company, in hopes that the investment will convert into ownership upon a subsequent preferred stock financing led by a sophisticated — often an institutional — investor.

Investors used convertible debt prior to 2005; however, earlier uses were primarily for growth and emerging stage company's "bridge" rounds. Beginning around 2005, convertible debt increasingly became used as a stand-alone financing round. For example, consider a Boulder-based startup from that time, Justin's Nut Butter. Justin Gold loved long bike rides. To power his bicycling passion, Justin made nut butter from original recipes, which provided an ideal high-protein snack during rides. In 2004, he produced jars of an eponymous product — Justin's Nut Butter — while working another full-time job. By 2006, with his product gaining popularity, Justin recognized a new market opportunity: an on-the-go squeeze pack to compete with sports gel packs and energy shots. To help fund this effort, Justin's Nut Butter raised outside capital from angel investors through an emerging startup investment instrument: convertible debt.

Convertible debt generally lowers direct, ex ante transaction costs relative to preferred stock issuances. Convertible debt does not require extended negotiations between a company and investors. Further, once an investment is complete, changes to a startup's charter and associated documents are typically unnecessary. Convertible debt's direct legal costs, as a result, are typically lower than traditional and light preferred equity.

Convertible debt has three key economic features. One, parties create a period of temporary debt during which the note holder is a creditor to the firm. Interest accrues on the note; however, no payment is required by the startup to a noteholder prior to maturity. Convertible debt does not require that a startup and its investors agree upon a company valuation. Convertible debt postpones the valuation decision, at least in theory, until a later time when more information about the company is available and the enterprise value can be more readily determined. Two, convertible debt prescribes that a subsequent qualified financing, defined as an equity issuance over a prescribed amount (which may range from $ 250,000 to $ 1 million), triggers automatic conversion of the outstanding balance of the note into equity. Upon conversion, the noteholder becomes an equity shareholder that holds the same class of preferred stock as the later investor takes. Three, the note may include mechanisms that provide a price benefit to an early investor upon conversion. For example, a valuation cap prescribes a ceiling on the price at which a convertible note converts. A conversion "discount," commonly prescribed in the note at 10-30%, rewards the noteholder for her early investment into a company. A noteholder typically may elect the benefit of the discount or a valuation cap, but not both.

From a control perspective, a holder of convertible debt has priority over shareholders in the event of company liquidation. Further, a most-favored-nations clause guarantees a convertible note investor that, if the company subsequently issues more debt on more favorable terms, then the investor has the option to adopt the terms. [F]ounders and managers are not required to personally guarantee the convertible debt loan. Upon maturity of a convertible note, the investor often has the option to either require repayment of a note or, alternatively, to convert into preferred stock.

From a time perspective, convertible note investors . . . are unlikely to see a financial return for a relatively long period of time, likely in the range of five to eight years required for the average startup to reach a liquidity event. . . . With respect to regulatory categories, as a matter of securities law, a convertible debt instrument is a security. Further, a convertible debt holder is not a shareholder entitled to fiduciary duties or other state law shareholder rights under corporate law. Finally, tax deductions on convertible debt interest payments may be available to a startup, so long as the debt is not viewed as a de facto equity position.

6. SIMPLE AGREEMENT FOR FUTURE EQUITY (SAFE) AND SIMILAR VARIANTS

The Simple Agreement for Future Equity (Safe) retains most aspects of convertible debt — except for the debt part. The Safe is an instrument popularized on the West Coast that is closely associated with accelerator programs. For example, MadKudu participated in the 2015 Techstars Boulder investment accelerator. MadKudu created a product, based upon big data tools and analytics, that small and mid-size companies use to identify useful patterns in customer behavior. Once the Techstars Boulder problem concluded, the startup's founders relocated to Mountain View, California. There they rejoined their families and worked to grow their company. To fuel operations, in November 2015 MadKudu raised a $ 1.4 million seed round from a French investment fund and several angel investors in the form of a Safe.

A Safe retains much of the structure of convertible debt; however, it eliminates an investor's right to loan repayment. For a startup like MadKudu, the Safe presents the same attraction as convertible debt: (1) lower direct transaction costs and (2) an instrument that sidesteps formal valuation. But since a Safe removes the loan feature, it is most accurately viewed as a type of contractual derivative – that is, an instrument with value derived from the value of another asset, in this case the startup's stock.

Economic aspects of the Safe closely resemble convertible debt. The Safe anticipates conversion of investment into future ownership upon issuance of preferred stock. Upon conversion, the Safe holder becomes an equity shareholder that holds the same class of preferred stock that the later investor takes. A valuation cap and a discount may be included.

In control aspects, however, the Safe differs considerably from convertible debt. The Safe diminishes the control an investor may exercise over a company. By removing the debt feature in the Safe, deal architects address two perceived problems with convertible debt. One, startups are often cash poor, which spurred concerns that use of debt may pull a startup into insolvency. Two, after a note matures, debt may be "called" by an investor. Pulling this control lever to demand payment after the note is due — so goes the argument — is inappropriately harsh in an entrepreneurial environment. The Safe removes this possibility for an early investor to "call" a note and potentially drag a company into insolvency. Indeed, if a company does not issue preferred stock, then a Safe holder lacks a mechanism to force conversion or repayment, which may leave an investment stranded in indefinite limbo.

From a time perspective, Safe investors are unlikely to see a financial return for the five-to-eight-year range that the average startup takes to reach a liquidity event. With respect to regulatory categories, as a matter of securities law, a Safe instrument is a security. Further, a Safe holder is not a shareholder entitled to fiduciary duties or other state law shareholder rights under corporate law.

Variants of the Safe exist, including the lesser-known Keep It Simple Security ("KISS"). The deferred ownership feature of these instruments, notably, is also attractive for regulatory reasons to effectuate investment into startups domesticated in certain foreign jurisdictions. For example, the international version of a Safe-type agreement used by Techstars, entitled the "Fixed Percentage Convertible Equity Agreement," avoids certain countries' prohibitions on foreign ownership of companies. By deferring ownership until some future time, the Safe-variant investment provides Techstars a future interest in a company while maintaining formal compliance with foreign ownership laws in countries that ban non-domestic shareholders.

CONVERTIBLE PROMISSORY NOTE FOR FRUIT TREE, LLC

NEITHER THIS CONVERTIBLE PROMISSORY NOTE NOR ANY OF THE SECURITIES ISSUABLE HEREUNDER HAVE BEEN REGISTERED UNDER THE SECURITIES ACT OF 1933, AS AMENDED (THE "ACT") OR ANY STATE SECURITIES LAWS, AND MAY NOT BE OFFERED, SOLD OR OTHERWISE TRANSFERRED, PLEDGED OR HYPOTHECATED IN THE ABSENCE OF A REGISTRATION STATEMENT IN EFFECT WITH RESPECT TO THE SECURITIES, OR DELIVERY TO THE COMPANY OF AN OPINION OF COUNSEL IN FORM AND SUBSTANCE SATISFACTORY TO THE COMPANY THAT SUCH OFFER, SALE OR TRANSFER, PLEDGE OR HYPOTHECATION IS IN COMPLIANCE WITH THE ACT OR UNLESS SOLD IN FULL COMPLIANCE WITH RULE 144 UNDER THE ACT.

> *[The above "legend" typically appears on stock certificates, promissory notes and other securities issued by privately held companies. The legend protects the issuer by putting investors on notice that the securities are not registered — and also is necessary to meet certain requirements of the securities laws (broadly discussed in the Securities Regulation section below).]*

CONVERTIBLE PROMISSORY NOTE

$ _____   **Date of Issuance:** _____

                                          [City],   [State]

    1. **Principal and Interest.** For value received, the undersigned, Fruit Tree, LLC, an Illinois limited liability company (the "Company"), hereby promises to pay to the order of _____ (the "Lender") the principal sum of $_____ plus interest on the principal amount hereof, at the rate of six percent (6%) simple interest per annum, and if such rate is determined to be usurious, then the rate shall be reduced to the highest legally permissible rate.

    2. **Maturity.** 24 months after the Date of Issuance (the "Maturity Date"), the Lender, in its sole discretion, shall choose to either be repaid the principal and accrued interest in full or convert the Note into equity as provided in Section 3.

    3. **Conversion.**

    (a) **Automatic Conversion in a Qualified Financing.** Upon the closing of the first sale or series of sales of equity securities by the Company after the date hereof which results in proceeds to the Company (not including the aggregate principal and accrued interest due on this Note) in the aggregate amount of at least $1,000,000 (a "Qualified Financing"), the outstanding principal balance of this Note together with accrued interest shall automatically convert on the date of the closing of such Qualified Financing, into the same securities issued in the Qualified Financing on the same terms and conditions applicable to the other investors participating in the Qualified Financing, except that the price per membership unit or other equity security paid by the Lender shall be adjusted as set forth below.

> *[This section provides for conversion of outstanding principal on the Note if the Company is able to meet fundraising goals agreed upon between the Lender and the Company. Note that the Lender will receive a discount on units acquired in the conversion.]*

(i) The following pricing shall apply if the Qualified Financing assumes a Pre-money Valuation (as defined below) of less than $4,000,000: (1) if the Qualified Financing is consummated within 6 months of the Date of Issuance, the price per membership unit or other equity security paid by Lender shall be the product of 0.9 and the price per membership unit or other equity security paid by the other investors participating in the Qualified Financing; and (2) if the Qualified Financing is consummated 6 months or more after the Date of Issuance, the price per membership unit or other equity security paid by Lender shall be the product of 0.8 and the price per membership unit or other equity security paid by the other investors participating in the Qualified Financing.

(ii) The following pricing shall apply if the Qualified Financing assumes a Pre-money Valuation of at least $4,000,000: the price per membership unit or other equity security shall be calculated based on a $4,000,000 Pre-money Valuation.

(iii) "Pre-money Valuation" means the valuation of the Company immediately prior to the receipt of the Qualified Financing.

(b) **Conversion on a Change of Control.** In the event of a Change of Control (as defined below) prior to repayment in full of the Note, immediately prior to such Change of Control, the outstanding principal and any accrued but unpaid interest this Note shall convert into membership units or other equity securities at a price per membership unit or other equity security equal to five dollars ($5.00), rounded down to the nearest whole membership unit or other equity security.

> *[In this section, the Lender is forced to convert on a sale of the Company.]*

The term "Change of Control" shall mean the sale, conveyance or other disposition of all or substantially all of the Company's property or business, or the Company's merger with or into or consolidation with any other corporation, limited liability company or other entity (other than a wholly owned subsidiary of the Company); provided that the term "Change of Control" shall not include (a) a merger of the Company effected exclusively for the purpose of changing the domicile of the Company, (b) an equity financing in which the Company is the surviving corporation, or (c) a transaction in which the equity holders of the Company immediately prior to the transaction own fifty percent (50%) or more of the voting power of the surviving corporation following the transaction.

(c) **Optional Conversion in Event of Default.** In an Event of Default (as defined below) prior to repayment in full of the Note, the Lender, in its sole discretion, shall choose to either be repaid the principal and accrued interest in full or convert the Note into equity. If the Lender chooses to convert the Note, the outstanding principal and any accrued but unpaid interest this Note shall convert into membership units or other equity securities at a price per membership unit or other equity security equal to five dollars ($5.00), rounded down to the nearest whole membership unit or other equity security.

[If the Company defaults, the Lender can choose either to be paid in cash or to convert to equity.]

An Event of Default will have occurred, if any of the following events occurs (each, an " Event of Default"): (i) The Company defaults in the payment of this Note, interest or principal, when due; (ii) The Company: (1) commences any proceeding or any other action relating to it in bankruptcy or seek reorganization, arrangement, readjustment of its debts, dissolution, liquidation, winding-up, composition or any other relief under the United States Bankruptcy Act, as amended, or under any other insolvency, reorganization, liquidation, dissolution, arrangement, composition, readjustment of debt or any other similar act or law, of any jurisdiction, domestic or foreign, now or hereafter existing; (2) admits its inability to pay its debts as they mature in any petition or pleading in connection with any such proceeding; (3) applies for, or consents to or acquiesces in, an appointment of a receiver, conservator, trustee or similar officer for it or for all or substantially all of its assets and properties; (4) makes a general assignment for the benefit of creditors; or (5) admits in writing its inability to pay its debts as they mature; (iii) any proceeding is commenced or any other action is taken against the Company in bankruptcy or seeking reorganization, arrangement, readjustment of its debts, dissolution, liquidation, winding-up, composition or any other relief under the United States Bankruptcy Act, as amended, or under any other insolvency, reorganization, liquidation, dissolution, arrangement, composition, readjustment of debt or any other similar act or law, of any jurisdiction, domestic or foreign, now or hereafter existing; or a receiver, conservator, trustee or similar officer for the Company or for all or substantially all of its assets and properties is appointed; and in each such case, such event continues for ninety (90) days undismissed, unbonded and non-discharged; or (iv) the Company materially breaches any agreement which the Company has entered with the Holder.

(d) **Optional Conversion into Equity on Maturity.** If no Qualified Financing, Change of Control or Event of Default occurs by the Maturity Date, then the Lender, in its sole discretion, shall choose to either be repaid the principal and accrued interest in full or convert the Note into equity. If the Lender chooses to convert the Note, the Note shall convert immediately prior to the Maturity Date into the right to receive a number of membership units or other equity securities at a price per membership unit or other equity security equal to five dollars ($5.00), rounded down to the nearest whole membership unit or other equity security.

> *[On maturity of the Note, the Lender can choose to be paid back in cash or to convert to equity.]*

4. **Mechanics of Conversion.** As soon as practicable after conversion of this Note pursuant to Section 3 hereof, the holder of this Note agrees to surrender this Note for conversion at the principal office of the Company at the time of such closing and agrees to execute all appropriate documentation necessary to effect such conversion, including, without limitation, the applicable equity purchase agreement. The Company, at its expense, will cause to be issued in the name of and delivered to the holder of this Note, a certificate or certificates for the number of membership units or other equity securities to which that holder shall be entitled on such conversion (bearing such legends as may be required by applicable state and federal securities laws in the opinion of legal counsel for the Company), together with any other securities and property to which the holder is entitled on such conversion under the terms of this Note. Such conversion shall be deemed to have been made immediately prior to the close of business on the applicable date set forth in Section 2 above, regardless of whether the Note has been surrendered on such date, provided that the Company shall not be required to issue a certificate for membership units or other equity securities to any Lender who has not surrendered such Lender's Note. No fractional membership units or other equity securities will be issued on conversion of this Note. If upon any conversion of this Note a fraction of a membership unit or other equity security results, the Company will round down to the next whole membership unit or other equity security.

5. **Payment.** All payments hereunder shall be made in lawful money of the United States of America directly to the Lender at the address of Lender set forth in Section 7(e), or at such other place or to such account as the Lender from time to time shall designate in a written notice to the Company.

The Company may not prepay the outstanding amount hereof in whole or in part at any time.

Whenever any payment hereunder shall be stated to be due, or any other date specified hereunder would otherwise occur, on a day other than a Business Day (as defined below), then, except as otherwise provided herein, such payment shall be made, and such payment date or other date shall occur, on the next succeeding Business Day. As used herein, "Business Day" means a day (i) other than Saturday or Sunday, and (ii) on which commercial banks are open for business in Chicago, Illinois.

[At the end of the Convertible Note, Lender makes representations and warranties about its ability to enter into the contract and its status as an "accredited investor" (see the Securities Regulation section below), and there are standard miscellaneous clauses and signature blocks.]

SAFE POST-MONEY VALUATION CAP WITH DISCOUNT
Y Combinator Management, LLC (2018)

THIS INSTRUMENT AND ANY SECURITIES ISSUABLE PURSUANT HERETO HAVE NOT BEEN REGISTERED UNDER THE SECURITIES ACT OF 1933, AS

AMENDED (THE "**SECURITIES ACT**"), OR UNDER THE SECURITIES LAWS OF CERTAIN STATES. THESE SECURITIES MAY NOT BE OFFERED, SOLD OR OTHERWISE TRANSFERRED, PLEDGED OR HYPOTHECATED EXCEPT AS PERMITTED IN THIS SAFE AND UNDER THE ACT AND APPLICABLE STATE SECURITIES LAWS PURSUANT TO AN EFFECTIVE REGISTRATION STATEMENT OR AN EXEMPTION THEREFROM.

[COMPANY NAME]

SAFE

(Simple Agreement for Future Equity)

THIS CERTIFIES THAT in exchange for the payment by [Investor Name] (the "Investor") of $[_____] (the "Purchase Amount") on or about [Date of Safe], [Company Name], a [State of Incorporation] corporation (the "Company"), issues to the Investor the right to certain shares of the Company's Capital Stock, subject to the terms described below.

This Safe is one of the forms available at http://ycombinator.com/documents and the Company and the Investor agree that neither one has modified the form, except to fill in blanks and bracketed terms.

The "Post-Money Valuation Cap" is $[_____].

> *[Although the SAFE does not have a valuation of the business, there is a maximum cap put on the valuation for purposes of the subsequent conversion. The idea is that investors can calculate the minimum percentage they will own of the company immediately post-conversion by dividing the Purchase Amount by the cap.]*

The "Discount Rate" is [100 minus the discount]%.

> *[The Discount Rate means that when the SAFE investment is converted to equity, the Investor will get a discount of a specified percentage off of the price being paid by the incoming investors in the equity round of financing.]*

See Section 2 for certain additional defined terms.

1. Events *[This section specifies the times that the SAFE converts or entitles the Investor to a cash payment as if conversion had occurred.]*

(a) Equity Financing. If there is an Equity Financing before the termination of this Safe, on the initial closing of such Equity Financing, this Safe will automatically convert into the number of shares of Safe Preferred Stock equal to the Purchase Amount divided by the Conversion Price.

In connection with the automatic conversion of this Safe into shares of Safe Preferred Stock, the Investor will execute and deliver to the Company all of the transaction documents related to the Equity Financing; provided, that such documents are the same documents to be entered into with the purchasers of Standard Preferred Stock, with appropriate variations for the Safe Preferred Stock if applicable, and provided further, that such documents have customary exceptions to any drag-along applicable to the Investor, including, without limitation, limited representations and warranties and limited liability and indemnification obligations on the part of the Investor.

(b) Liquidity Event. If there is a Liquidity Event before the termination of this Safe, this Safe will automatically be entitled to receive a portion of Proceeds, due and payable to the Investor immediately prior to, or concurrent with, the consummation of such Liquidity Event, equal to the greater of (i) the Purchase Amount (the "Cash-Out Amount") or (ii) the amount payable on the number of shares of Common Stock equal to the Purchase Amount divided by the Liquidity Price (the "Conversion Amount"). If any of the Company's securityholders are given a choice as to the form and amount of Proceeds to be received in a Liquidity Event, the Investor will be given the same choice, provided that the Investor may not choose to receive a form of consideration that the Investor would be ineligible to receive as a result of the Investor's failure to satisfy any requirement or limitation generally applicable to the Company's securityholders, or under any applicable laws.

Notwithstanding the foregoing, in connection with a Change of Control intended to qualify as a tax-free reorganization, the Company may reduce the cash portion of Proceeds payable to the Investor by the amount determined by its board of directors in good faith for such Change of Control to qualify as a tax-free reorganization for U.S. federal income tax purposes, provided that such reduction (A) does not reduce the total Proceeds payable to such Investor and (B) is applied in the same manner and on a pro rata basis to all securityholders who have equal priority to the Investor under Section 1(d).

(c) Dissolution Event. If there is a Dissolution Event before the termination of this Safe, the Investor will automatically be entitled to receive a portion of Proceeds equal to the Cash-Out Amount, due and payable to the Investor immediately prior to the consummation of the Dissolution Event.

(d) Liquidation Priority. In a Liquidity Event or Dissolution Event, this Safe is intended to operate like standard non-participating Preferred Stock. The Investor's right to receive its Cash-Out Amount is:

(i) Junior to payment of outstanding indebtedness and creditor claims, including contractual claims for payment and convertible promissory notes (to the extent such convertible promissory notes are not actually or notionally converted into Capital Stock);

(ii) On par with payments for other Safes and/or Preferred Stock, and if the applicable Proceeds are insufficient to permit full payments to the Investor and such other Safes and/or Preferred Stock, the applicable Proceeds will be distributed pro rata to the Investor and such other Safes and/or Preferred Stock in proportion to the full payments that would otherwise be due; and

(iii) Senior to payments for Common Stock.

The Investor's right to receive its Conversion Amount is (A) on par with payments for Common Stock and other Safes and/or Preferred Stock who are also receiving Conversion Amounts or Proceeds on a similar as-converted to Common Stock basis, and (B) junior to payments described in clauses (i) and (ii) above (in the latter case, to the extent such payments are Cash-Out Amounts or similar liquidation preferences).

(e) Termination. This Safe will automatically terminate (without relieving the Company of any obligations arising from a prior breach of or non-compliance with this Safe) immediately following the earliest to occur of: (i) the issuance of Capital Stock to the Investor pursuant to the automatic conversion of this Safe under Section 1(a); or (ii) the payment, or setting aside for payment, of amounts due the Investor pursuant to Section 1(b) or Section 1(c).

2. Definitions

"Capital Stock" means the capital stock of the Company, including, without limitation, the "Common Stock" and the "Preferred Stock."

"Change of Control" means (i) a transaction or series of related transactions in which any "person" or "group" (within the meaning of Section 13(d) and 14(d) of the Securities Exchange Act of 1934, as amended), becomes the "beneficial owner" (as defined in Rule 13d-3 under the Securities Exchange Act of 1934, as amended), directly or indirectly, of more than 50% of the outstanding voting securities of the Company having the right to vote for the election of members of the Company's board of directors, (ii) any reorganization, merger or consolidation of the Company, other than a transaction or series of related transactions in which the holders of the voting securities of the Company outstanding immediately prior to such transaction or series of related transactions retain, immediately after such transaction or series of related transactions, at least a majority of the total voting power represented by the outstanding voting securities of the Company or such other surviving or resulting entity or (iii) a sale, lease or other disposition of all or substantially all of the assets of the Company.

"Company Capitalization" is calculated as of immediately prior to the Equity Financing and (without double-counting):

- Includes all shares of Capital Stock issued and outstanding;
- Includes all Converting Securities;
- Includes all (i) issued and outstanding Options and (ii) Promised Options;
- Includes the Unissued Option Pool; and
- Excludes, notwithstanding the foregoing, any increases to the Unissued Option Pool (except to the extent necessary to cover Promised Options that exceed the Unissued Option Pool) in connection with the Equity Financing.

"Conversion Price" means the either: (1) the Safe Price or (2) the Discount Price, whichever calculation results in a greater number of shares of Safe Preferred Stock.

"Converting Securities" includes this Safe and other convertible securities issued by the Company, including but not limited to: (i) other Safes; (ii) convertible promissory notes and other convertible debt instruments; and (iii) convertible securities that have the right to convert into shares of Capital Stock.

"Discount Price" means the price per share of the Standard Preferred Stock sold in the Equity Financing multiplied by the Discount Rate.

"Dissolution Event" means (i) a voluntary termination of operations, (ii) a general assignment for the benefit of the Company's creditors or (iii) any other liquidation, dissolution or winding up of the Company (excluding a Liquidity Event), whether voluntary or involuntary.

"Dividend Amount" means, with respect to any date on which the Company pays a dividend on its outstanding Common Stock, the amount of such dividend that is paid per share of Common Stock multiplied by (x) the Purchase Amount divided by (y) the Liquidity Price (treating the dividend date as a Liquidity Event solely for purposes of calculating such Liquidity Price).

"Equity Financing" means a bona fide transaction or series of transactions with the principal purpose of raising capital, pursuant to which the Company issues and sells Preferred Stock at a fixed valuation, including but not limited to, a pre-money or post-money valuation.

"Initial Public Offering" means the closing of the Company's first firm commitment underwritten initial public offering of Common Stock pursuant to a registration statement filed under the Securities Act.

"Liquidity Capitalization" is calculated as of immediately prior to the Liquidity Event, and (without double- counting):

- Includes all shares of Capital Stock issued and outstanding;
- Includes all (i) issued and outstanding Options and (ii) to the extent receiving Proceeds, Promised Options;
- Includes all Converting Securities, other than any Safes and other convertible securities (including without limitation shares of Preferred Stock) where the holders of such securities are receiving Cash-Out Amounts or similar liquidation preference payments in lieu of Conversion Amounts or similar "as-converted" payments; and
- Excludes the Unissued Option Pool.

"Liquidity Event" means a Change of Control or an Initial Public Offering.

"Liquidity Price" means the price per share equal to the Post-Money Valuation Cap divided by the Liquidity Capitalization.

"Options" includes options, restricted stock awards or purchases, RSUs, SARs, warrants or similar securities, vested or unvested.

"Proceeds" means cash and other assets (including without limitation stock consideration) that are proceeds from the Liquidity Event or the Dissolution Event, as applicable, and legally available for distribution.

"Promised Options" means promised but ungranted Options that are the greater of those (i) promised pursuant to agreements or understandings made prior to the execution of, or in connection with, the term sheet for the Equity Financing (or the initial closing of the Equity Financing, if there is no term sheet), or (ii) treated as outstanding Options in the calculation of the Standard Preferred Stock's price per share.

"Safe" means an instrument containing a future right to shares of Capital Stock, similar in form and content to this instrument, purchased by investors for the purpose of funding the Company's business operations. References to "this Safe" mean this specific instrument.

"Safe Preferred Stock" means the shares of the series of Preferred Stock issued to the Investor in an Equity Financing, having the identical rights, privileges, preferences and restrictions as the shares of Standard Preferred Stock, other than with respect to: (i) the per share liquidation preference and the initial conversion price for purposes of price-based anti-dilution protection, which will equal the Conversion Price; and (ii) the basis for any dividend rights, which will be based on the Conversion Price.

"Safe Price" means the price per share equal to the Post-Money Valuation Cap divided by the Company Capitalization.

"Standard Preferred Stock" means the shares of the series of Preferred Stock issued to the investors investing new money in the Company in connection with the initial closing of the Equity Financing.

"Unissued Option Pool" means all shares of Capital Stock that are reserved, available for future grant and not subject to any outstanding Options or Promised Options (but in the case of a Liquidity Event, only to the extent Proceeds are payable on such Promised Options) under any equity incentive or similar Company plan.

3. Company Representations *[Both the Company and the Investor make very simple representations about their business and enforceability of the SAFE.]*

(a) The Company is a corporation duly organized, validly existing and in good standing under the laws of its state of incorporation, and has the power and authority to own, lease and operate its properties and carry on its business as now conducted.

(b) The execution, delivery and performance by the Company of this Safe is within the power of the Company and has been duly authorized by all necessary actions on the part of the Company (subject to section 3(d)). This Safe constitutes a legal, valid and binding obligation of the Company, enforceable against the Company in accordance with its terms, except as limited by bankruptcy, insolvency or other laws of general application relating to or affecting the enforcement of creditors' rights generally and general principles of equity. To its knowledge, the Company is not in violation of (i) its current certificate of incorporation or bylaws, (ii) any material statute, rule or regulation applicable to the Company or (iii) any material debt or contract to which the Company is a party or by which it is bound, where, in each case, such violation or default, individually, or together with all such violations or defaults, could reasonably be expected to have a material adverse effect on the Company.

(c) The performance and consummation of the transactions contemplated by this Safe do not and will not: (i) violate any material judgment, statute, rule or regulation applicable to the Company; (ii) result in the acceleration of any material debt or contract to which the Company is a party or by which it is bound; or (iii) result in the creation or imposition of any lien on any property, asset or revenue of the Company or the suspension, forfeiture, or nonrenewal of any material permit, license or authorization applicable to the Company, its business or operations.

(d) No consents or approvals are required in connection with the performance of this Safe, other than: (i) the Company's corporate approvals; (ii) any qualifications or filings under applicable securities laws; and (iii) necessary corporate approvals for the authorization of Capital Stock issuable pursuant to Section 1.

(e) To its knowledge, the Company owns or possesses (or can obtain on commercially reasonable terms) sufficient legal rights to all patents, trademarks, service marks, trade names, copyrights, trade secrets, licenses, information,

processes and other intellectual property rights necessary for its business as
now conducted and as currently proposed to be conducted, without any conflict with, or infringement of the rights of, others.

4. Investor Representations

(a) The Investor has full legal capacity, power and authority to execute and
deliver this Safe and to perform its obligations hereunder. This Safe constitutes
valid and binding obligation of the Investor, enforceable in accordance with
its terms, except as limited by bankruptcy, insolvency or other laws of general
application relating to or affecting the enforcement of creditors' rights generally and general principles of equity.

(b) The Investor is an accredited investor as such term is defined in Rule 501
of Regulation D under the Securities Act, and acknowledges and agrees that if
not an accredited investor at the time of an Equity Financing, the Company may
void this Safe and return the Purchase Amount. The Investor has been advised
that this Safe and the underlying securities have not been registered under the
Securities Act, or any state securities laws and, therefore, cannot be resold unless
they are registered under the Securities Act and applicable state securities laws
or unless an exemption from such registration requirements is available. The
Investor is purchasing this Safe and the securities to be acquired by the Investor
hereunder for its own account for investment, not as a nominee or agent, and
not with a view to, or for resale in connection with, the distribution thereof, and
the Investor has no present intention of selling, granting any participation in, or
otherwise distributing the same. The Investor has such knowledge and experience in financial and business matters that the Investor is capable of evaluating
the merits and risks of such investment, is able to incur a complete loss of such
investment without impairing the Investor's financial condition and is able to
bear the economic risk of such investment for an indefinite period of time.

5. Miscellaneous

(a) Any provision of this Safe may be amended, waived or modified by
written consent of the Company and either (i) the Investor or (ii) the majority-
in-interest of all then-outstanding Safes with the same "Post-Money Valuation
Cap" and "Discount Rate" as this Safe (and Safes lacking one or both of such
terms will be considered to be the same with respect to such term(s)), provided
that with respect to clause (ii): (A) the Purchase Amount may not be amended,
waived or modified in this manner, (B) the consent of the Investor and each
holder of such Safes must be solicited (even if not obtained), and (C) such
amendment, waiver or modification treats all such holders in the same manner. "Majority-in-interest" refers to the holders of the applicable group of
Safes whose Safes have a total Purchase Amount greater than 50% of the total
Purchase Amount of all of such applicable group of Safes. *[The amendment provision allows majority SAFE Investors to make changes applicable to all similarly-situated
SAFE Investors.]*

(b) Any notice required or permitted by this Safe will be deemed sufficient
when delivered personally or by overnight courier or sent by email to the relevant address listed on the signature page, or 48 hours after being deposited in
the U.S. mail as certified or registered mail with postage prepaid, addressed to
the party to be notified at such party's address listed on the signature page, as
subsequently modified by written notice.

(c) The Investor is not entitled, as a holder of this Safe, to vote or be deemed a holder of Capital Stock for any purpose other than tax purposes, nor will anything in this Safe be construed to confer on the Investor, as such, any rights of a Company stockholder or rights to vote for the election of directors or on any matter submitted to Company stockholders, or to give or withhold consent to any corporate action or to receive notice of meetings, until shares have been issued on the terms described in Section 1. However, if the Company pays a dividend on outstanding shares of Common Stock (that is not payable in shares of Common Stock) while this Safe is outstanding, the Company will pay the Dividend Amount to the Investor at the same time.

(d) Neither this Safe nor the rights in this Safe are transferable or assignable, by operation of law or otherwise, by either party without the prior written consent of the other; provided, however, that this Safe and/or its rights may be assigned without the Company's consent by the Investor to any other entity who directly or indirectly, controls, is controlled by or is under common control with the Investor, including, without limitation, any general partner, managing member, officer or director of the Investor, or any venture capital fund now or hereafter existing which is controlled by one or more general partners or managing members of, or shares the same management company with, the Investor; and provided, further, that the Company may assign this Safe in whole, without the consent of the Investor, in connection with a reincorporation to change the Company's domicile.

(e) In the event any one or more of the provisions of this Safe is for any reason held to be invalid, illegal or unenforceable, in whole or in part or in any respect, or in the event that any one or more of the provisions of this Safe operate or would prospectively operate to invalidate this Safe, then and in any such event, such provision(s) only will be deemed null and void and will not affect any other provision of this Safe and the remaining provisions of this Safe will remain operative and in full force and effect and will not be affected, prejudiced, or disturbed thereby.

(f) All rights and obligations hereunder will be governed by the laws of the State of [Governing Law Jurisdiction], without regard to the conflicts of law provisions of such jurisdiction.

(g) The parties acknowledge and agree that for United States federal and state income tax purposes this Safe is, and at all times has been, intended to be characterized as stock, and more particularly as common stock for purposes of Sections 304, 305, 306, 354, 368, 1036 and 1202 of the Internal Revenue Code of 1986, as amended. Accordingly, the parties agree to treat this Safe consistent with the foregoing intent for all United States federal and state income tax purposes (including, without limitation, on their respective tax returns or other informational statements).

[Signature Blocks]

Notes and Questions

1. The "pre-money" valuation of a company is the value of a company prior to the investment in a given financing round. The "post-money" valuation is the value of the company calculated immediately after the financing round. For example, if a company has a pre-money valuation of $3 million and an investor puts $1 million into the company, the post-money valuation is $4 million.

The original Y-Combinator SAFE was drafted with a valuation cap that was calculated on a pre-money basis. In 2018, they revised the SAFE so that now the valuation cap is calculated on a post-money basis. What do you imagine prompted the change, and why does it matter to founders?

2. Imagine your client has been approached by several angels who are interested in investing in the new venture. What factors would you encourage the client to consider in comparing the various angels?

3. Why might a client choose a convertible note over a straight sale of securities? Why might an angel or other investor prefer this mechanism to invest in a company?

4. Why is it customary for purchasers of convertible notes or equity interests to make representations about their status as "accredited investors"?

4.   *Priced Rounds*

In a priced round, the investor and the company agree on a valuation and the investor purchases an equity stake in the business — commonly shares of a corporation, or a membership interest in a limited liability company. By the time a company is ready for a priced round, the business has typically progressed to the point where it is ready for a larger cash infusion and there is at least some better sense of the company's potential.

In this section, we will first read a piece that explains when a company is ready for a priced round, including the so-called Series A round. From there, you will delve into two model term sheets for a priced financing rounds. A term sheet is typically used by business people to negotiate the key terms of a transaction. It is commonly written by business people, sometimes with the help of lawyers. The term sheet is not supposed to cover every legal contingency and nicety that would be covered in a so-called definitive agreement; rather, it is designed to highlight the key terms and present them in a practical format that is workable in a negotiation among business people. The two term sheets we have included are for a priced seed round of financing — designed for the standardized seed financing documents that are commonly used in practice – and a term sheet for a priced venture capital round — also for use with standardized documents that are prevalent in the real world. As you read the term sheets, notice the ways in which the theoretical business priorities mentioned in the article translate into practical language. Also note the ways the Series Seed term sheet is significantly different from the term sheet put out by the National Venture Capital Association. We have added annotations to the term sheets to help explain some of the various deal points.

WHAT IS THE DIFFERENCE BETWEEN "FRIENDS AND FAMILY", SEED AND SERIES A FINANCINGS?
Miguel Vega, www.cooleygo.com (accessed June 2020)

"Friends and family" financings: tapping your personal network

Entrepreneurs often need only modest amounts of capital in the early stages to cover expenses incidental to the business. Sometimes entrepreneurs cover the company's early expenses through personal savings or even credit card debt. However, in many cases they turn to people in their personal network, or "friends and family," for early capital needs. At this stage, the company may represent little more than a business plan laid out in a PowerPoint presentation and more "formal" sources of capital are invariably not yet available to the entrepreneur.

Friends and family financings can vary in size and structure, but are usually small investments structured as equity subscriptions, unsecured loans or sometimes convertible loan notes (for more information about convertible loan notes, see our Primer on Convertible Debt). However, it is not unusual to see the money invested without any documentation or due diligence whatsoever. While the convenience, low cost and speed of this approach is tempting, and many friends and family investors don't seem initially concerned about their investment, it is important to properly document the terms of the transaction to avoid misunderstandings about equity ownership to ensure that these investors understand the high risk nature of their investment, and to avoid frightening off later stage investors.

Seed financings: the first round from experienced, startup investors

The definition of a seed investment will vary somewhat depending on whom you ask. It would not be unusual for someone to refer to a larger friends and family financing as a seed financing. However, the term seed financing usually denotes a company's first round of financing from third party investors who regularly invest in startup companies. These investors are typically individual angel investors, formal angel organizations or even venture capital funds. Seed investments are usually made through a mix of equity and loans, or sometimes convertible loan notes (often with a cap on the conversion value — see also The (Troublesome) Convertible Note Cap), simplified (short form) "series seed" financing documents or (often if led by a VC) "full" Series A style investment documents (see below). The structure selected for the investment will depend on investor preference and the availability of tax incentives, and will be influenced by the amount raised. As a general matter it is fair to say that the larger the amount raised, the more likely that the investors will use more formal and detailed investment documents.

Subject to the caveats above, investment amounts under USD/EUR 1,000,000 or so will often use convertible notes or Series Seed investment documentation. Series Seed investment documents tend to be less extensive than Series A documentation and impose fewer restrictions on the company/management. They typically provide for simple, nonparticipating liquidation preferences (reimbursing the investor first), limited investor protective provisions, as well as participation rights and information rights, among other matters. Larger seed financings often use full Series A style investment documents.

In such cases, it is not unusual to still refer to the securities issued as "Series Seed Preferred Stock/Shares" simply because the company and/or the investor want to preserve the lettered rounds (e.g. Series A, Series B, etc.) for subsequent financings to signal that the company still is in its early stages of development. A common goal of a seed financing is to delay the need for the Series A financing until such time as the company can attain a significantly higher valuation.

Series A financings: the new beginning

Typically, the money raised in a Series A financing is used for "scaling up" as opposed to "starting up" and the investment amounts are larger than in seed financings. The larger investment amounts result in higher investor ownership levels. Series A investors, usually venture capital funds, often end up with 20% to 40% ownership of the

company post-financing. More importantly, it can be a time for significant governance changes — a revamped board of directors with professional venture capital
investors serving alongside founders and industry experts and, in some cases, less
founder representation. The process for raising a Series A financing from initial
contact to closing may take considerably longer than raising a friends and family
or seed financing and will require more polished presentations from the management team, more detailed legal, financial and commercial due diligence, and more
involvement from legal representation (on all sides).

The Series A financing documents are generally considerably more extensive
and contain many protective provisions that will impose significant restrictions on
company actions outside normal, day to day operations. The Series A terms may
also contain more onerous versions of the terms included in Series Seed investment
documents and will often introduce new concepts, such as anti-dilution protection
(i.e. not already introduced), and perhaps even accruing dividends, among other
matters. The National Venture Capital Association (US) and British Venture Capital
Association have developed sample documents that are often used as a baseline for
Series A investments, but the use of such model documentation is far from universal
and most law firms and indeed the majority of venture capital funds prefer to use
their own forms. The Series A terms must be negotiated with care as the terms can
prove difficult to change in subsequent financing rounds.

MODEL SERIES SEED TERM SHEET VERSION 3.2

Ted Wang, www.seriesseed.com (February 2014)

TERMS FOR PRIVATE PLACEMENT OF SERIES SEED PREFERRED
STOCK OF [*Insert Company Name*], INC.
[Date]

The following is a summary of the principal terms with respect to the proposed
Series Seed Preferred Stock financing of [_____], Inc., a [Delaware] corporation (the "*Company*"). Except for the section entitled "Binding Terms," this summary of terms does not constitute a legally binding obligation. The parties intend to
enter into a legally binding obligation only pursuant to definitive agreements to be
negotiated and executed by the parties.

Offering Terms

Securities to Issue:	Shares of Series Seed Preferred Stock of the Company (the "*Series Seed*").
Aggregate Proceeds:	$[_____] in aggregate.
Purchasers:	[Accredited investors approved by the Company] (the "*Purchasers*").
Price Per Share:	Price per share (the "*Original Issue Price*"), based on a pre-money valuation of $[____], including an available option pool of [___]%.

| Liquidation Preference: | One times the Original Issue Price plus declared but unpaid dividends on each share of Series Seed, balance of proceeds paid to Common. A merger, reorganization or similar transaction will be treated as a liquidation. |

The liquidation preference is the amount of money that a Purchaser will receive if there is a sale of the business or any similar transaction. It is called a "preference" because it is paid to the Purchasers prior to any distribution of proceeds of the sale to holders of Common Stock.

| Conversion: | Convertible into one share of Common (subject to proportional adjustments for stock splits, stock dividends and the like) at any time at the option of the holder. |

Preferred shares are typically convertible into common shares. The main reason a preferred holder would convert is because there was some economic or voting benefit associated with the conversion — for example, the investor would get more cash as a common holder because of some cap on the preferred or participating return, or to dominate a common class vote.

| Voting Rights: | Votes together with the Common Stock on all matters on an asconverted basis. Approval of a majority of the Preferred Stock required to (i) adversely change rights of the Preferred Stock; (ii) change the authorized number of shares; (iii) authorize a new series of Preferred Stock having rights senior to or on parity with the Preferred Stock; (iv) redeem or repurchase any shares (other than pursuant to employee or consultant agreements); (v) declare or pay any dividend; (vi) change the number of directors; or (vii) liquidate or dissolve, including any change of control. |

| Documentation: | Documents will be identical to the Series Seed Preferred Stock documents published at www.seriesseed.com, except for the modifications set forth in this Term Sheet. |

| Financial Information: | Purchasers who have invested at least [$_____] ("*Major Purchasers*") will receive standard information and inspection rights and management rights letter. |

| Participation Right: | Major Purchasers will have the right to participate on a pro rata basis in subsequent issuances of equity securities. |

| Board of Directors: | [___] directors elected by holders of a majority of common stock, [___] elected by holders of a majority of Series Seed and [___] elected by mutual consent. |

Purchasers will typically negotiate for some presence on the Company's board of directors.

| Expenses: | Company to reimburse counsel to Purchasers for a flat fee of $10,000. |

Legal fees in priced rounds can vary significantly, and are typically significantly higher than $10,000. The reason this amount is included in this term sheet and is reasonable for this kind of financing is that the Series Seed documents, like the SAFE, are intended to be standard and are not the subject of significant negotiation or legal attention.

Future Rights: The Series Seed will be given the same rights as the next series of Preferred Stock (with appropriate adjustments for economic terms).

Key Holder Matters   Each Key Holder shall have four years vesting beginning [_____]. Full acceleration upon "Double Trigger." Each Key Holder shall have assigned all relevant IP to the Company before closing.

Binding Terms: For a period of thirty days, the Company shall not solicit offers from other parties for any financing. Without the consent of Purchasers, the Company shall not disclose these terms to anyone other than officers, directors, key service providers, and other potential Purchasers in this financing.

[SIGNATURE BLOCKS]

MODEL VENTURE CAPITAL TERM SHEET

National Venture Capital Association
www.nvca.org (January 2019)

TERM SHEET
FOR SERIES A PREFERRED STOCK FINANCING OF
[INSERT COMPANY NAME], INC.
[_____ __, 20__]
This Term Sheet summarizes the principal terms of the Series A Preferred Stock Financing of [_____], Inc., a [Delaware] corporation (the "Company"). In consideration of the time and expense devoted and to be devoted by the Investors with respect to this investment, the No Shop/Confidentiality [and Counsel and Expenses] provisions of this Term Sheet shall be binding obligations of the Company whether or not the financing is consummated. No other legally binding obligations will be created until definitive agreements are executed and delivered by all parties. This Term Sheet is not a commitment to invest, and is conditioned on the completion of due diligence, legal review and documentation that is satisfactory to the Investors. This Term Sheet shall be governed in all respects by the laws of [_____the].

Offering Terms

Closing Date: As soon as practicable following the Company's acceptance of this Term Sheet and satisfaction of the Conditions to Closing (the "**Closing**"). [*provide for multiple closings if applicable*]

Investors: Investor No. 1: [_____] shares ([__]%), $[_____]
Investor No. 2: [_____] shares ([__]%), $[_____]
[as well other investors mutually agreed upon by Investors and the Company]

Amount Raised: $[_____], [including $[_____] from the conversion of principal [and interest] on bridge notes].

Price Per Share:	$[_____] per share (based on the capitalization of the Company set forth below) (the "**Original Purchase Price**").
Pre-Money Valuation:	The Original Purchase Price is based upon a fully-diluted pre-money valuation of $[_____] and a fullydiluted post-money valuation of $[_____] (including an employee pool representing [__]% of the fullydiluted post-money capitalization).
Capitalization:	The Company's capital structure before and after the Closing is set forth on Exhibit A.

> *The introductory section sets forth the main points of the deal — namely, how much the Investors are investing, and how much of the Company they get in return.*

CHARTER

> *All corporations have shares of common stock, which is the basic form of equity interest. Venture capitalists will generally not buy common stock when making their investment. Instead, they will purchase "preferred stock," which is another category of shares, created by filing an amendment to the Company's articles of incorporation. Preferred stock has whatever economic and management rights are set forth in the articles of incorporation, or "Charter."*

Dividends:	[*Alternative 1:* Dividends will be paid on the Series A Preferred on an asconverted basis when, as, and if paid on the Common Stock.]
	[*Alternative 2:* The Series A Preferred will carry an annual [__]% cumulative dividend [payable upon a liquidation or redemption]. For any other dividends or distributions, participation with Common Stock on an as-converted basis.]
	[*Alternative 3:* Non-cumulative dividends will be paid on the Series A Preferred in an amount equal to $[_____] per share of Series A Preferred when and if declared by the Board.]

> *A "when, as, and if" dividend basically means that the preferred only gets dividends if the common receive them, and if so, in the same proportionate amount as the common. A "cumulative" dividend accrues at a pre-set rate and is typically paid on a "liquidation event" (see below for description of liquidation event). A "when and if" or "noncumulative" dividend is paid in a pre-set amount, but only if the board says so (which means that it is just a guideline for a future potential dividend).*

Liquidation
Preference:
In the event of any liquidation, dissolution or winding up of the Company, the proceeds shall be paid as follows:

[*Alternative 1 (non-participating Preferred Stock)*: First pay [one] times the Original Purchase Price [plus accrued dividends] [plus declared and unpaid dividends] on each share of Series A Preferred. The balance of any proceeds shall be distributed pro rata to holders of Common Stock.]

[*Alternative 2 (full participating Preferred Stock)*: First pay [one] times the Original Purchase Price [plus accrued dividends] [plus declared and unpaid dividends] on each share of Series A Preferred. Thereafter, the Series A Preferred participates with the Common Stock pro rata on an as-converted basis.]

[*Alternative 3 (cap on Preferred Stock participation rights)*: First pay [one] times the Original Purchase Price [plus accrued dividends] [plus declared and unpaid dividends] on each share of Series A Preferred. Thereafter, Series A Preferred participates with Common Stock pro rata on an as-converted basis until the holders of Series A Preferred receive an aggregate of [_____] times the Original Purchase Price (including the amount paid pursuant to the preceding sentence).]

As with the series seed, the liquidation preference is the key economic benefit of the preferred stock. In Alternative 1 above, the holder of preferred gets a so-called preferred return on a liquidation of the business, which is basically her money back plus something extra (usually a multiple of the money invested). In Alternative 2, the investor gets the same preferred return on a liquidation, and then is "participating," which means that after she is paid the preferred return, she is paid a proportion of the remaining Company assets as if she owned common instead of preferred shares. Alternative 3 is the same as Alternative 2 except that the investor's share of the "common" round is capped.

A merger or consolidation (other than one in which stockholders of the Company own a majority by voting power of the outstanding shares of the surviving or acquiring corporation) and a sale, lease, transfer, exclusive license or other disposition of all or substantially all of the assets of the Company will be treated as a liquidation event (a **"Deemed Liquidation Event"**), thereby triggering payment of the liquidation preferences described above [unless the holders of [___]% of the Series A Preferred elect otherwise]. [The Investors' entitlement to their liquidation preference shall not be abrogated or diminished in the event part of the consideration is subject to escrow in connection with a Deemed Liquidation Event.]

> *By including mergers and sales of the business as "liquidation events" for purposes of the preferred return, the venture capitalist ensures she gets to cash out of the business whenever any major "exit" event occurs. In other words, the business doesn't actually have to shut down and liquidate for the VC to get a return on her investment — she can exit on any major Company transition.*

Voting Rights:

The Series A Preferred shall vote together with the Common Stock on an as-converted basis, and not as a separate class, except (i) [so long as [insert fixed number, or %, or "any"] shares of Series A Preferred are outstanding,] the Series A Preferred as a class shall be entitled to elect [_____] [(_)] members of the Board (the "Series A Directors"), and (ii) as required by law. . . .

> *The Voting Rights above and Protective Provisions below are the main ways in which the VC will exercise management rights over the Company. The positions on the Board are key to this dynamic and are present in virtually every VC deal of any magnitude. Notice that, in addition to having a say at the Board level, the Series A can block outright any major change in the Company.*

Protective Provisions:

[So long as [insert fixed number, or %, or "any"] shares of Series A Preferred are outstanding,] in addition to any other vote or approval required under the Company's Charter or Bylaws, the Company will not, without the written consent of the holders of at least [__]% of the Company's Series A Preferred, either directly or by amendment, merger, consolidation, or otherwise:

(i) liquidate, dissolve or windup the affairs of the Company, or effect any merger or consolidation or any other Deemed Liquidation Event; (ii) amend, alter, or repeal any provision of the Certificate of Incorporation or Bylaws [in a manner adverse to the Series A Preferred]; (iii) create or authorize the creation of or issue any other security convertible into or exercisable for any equity security, having rights, preferences or privileges senior to or on parity with the Series A Preferred, or increase the authorized number of shares of Series A Preferred; (iv) purchase or redeem or pay any dividend on any capital stock prior to the Series A Preferred, [other than stock repurchased from former employees or consultants in connection with the cessation of their employment/services, at the lower of fair market value or cost;] [other than as approved by the Board, including the approval of [_____] Series A Director(s)]; or (v) create or authorize the creation of any debt security [if the Company's aggregate indebtedness would exceed $[____] [other than equipment leases or bank lines of credit] [unless such debt security has received the prior approval of the Board of Directors, including the approval of [_____] Series A Director(s)]; (vi) create or hold capital stock in any subsidiary that is not a wholly-owned subsidiary or dispose of any subsidiary stock or all or substantially all of any subsidiary assets; [or (vii) increase or decrease the size of the Board of Directors].

Optional Conversion: The Series A Preferred initially converts 1:1 to Common Stock at any time at option of holder, subject to adjustments for stock dividends, splits, combinations and similar events and as described below under "Anti-dilution Provisions."

Like with Series Seed, the Preferred in a VC transaction will typically be convertible. Preferred shares will usually convert one-to-one, unless some subsequent financing uses a lower valuation of the Company — in which case the preferred investors are entitled to an adjustment to make their investment worth more. Sometimes the adjustment treats them as if they had invested in the later round at the lower valuation, which is called "full ratchet," or another adjustment representing a mathematical compromise, which is called "weighted average."

Anti-dilution Provisions: In the event that the Company issues additional securities at a purchase price less than the current Series A Preferred conversion price, such conversion price shall be adjusted in accordance with the following formula:

[*Alternative 1:* "Typical" weighted average:

$$CP_2 = CP_1 * (A+B) / (A+C)$$

CP_2 = Series A Conversion Price in effect immediately after new issue

CP_1 = Series A Conversion Price in effect immediately prior to new issue

A = Number of shares of Common Stock deemed to be outstanding immediately prior to new issue (includes all shares of outstanding common stock, all shares of outstanding preferred stock on an as-converted basis, and all outstanding options on an as-exercised basis; and does not include any convertible securities converting into this round of financing)

B = Aggregate consideration received by the Corporation with respect to the new issue divided by CP_1

C = Number of shares of stock issued in the subject transaction]

[*Alternative 2*: Full-ratchet — the conversion price will be reduced to the price at which the new shares are issued.]

[*Alternative 3*: No price-based anti-dilution protection.]

. . .

[Pay-to-Play: [Unless the holders of [__]% of the Series A elect otherwise,] on any subsequent [down] round all [Major] Investors are required to purchase their pro rata share of the securities set aside by the Board for purchase by the [Major] Investors. All shares of Series A Preferred of any [Major] Investor failing to do so will automatically [lose anti-dilution rights] [lose right to participate in future rounds] [convert to Common Stock and lose the right to a Board seat if applicable].]

A pay-to-play is a method of forcing investors to stick together and keep up with future capital needs of the business. If an investor doesn't put forth cash when it is required, there can be various financial and management punishments.

Redemption Rights: Unless prohibited by Delaware law governing distributions to stockholders, the Series A Preferred shall be redeemable from funds legally available for distribution at the option of holders of at least [__]% of the Series A Preferred commencing any time after [_____] at a price equal to the Original Purchase Price [plus all accrued but unpaid dividends]. Redemption shall occur in three equal annual portions. Upon a redemption request from the holders of the required percentage of the Series A Preferred, all Series A Preferred shares shall be redeemed [(except for any Series A holders who affirmatively opt-out)].

. . .

INVESTORS' RIGHTS AGREEMENT

Registration Rights:

Registration rights give the Investors the ability to force the Company to register the Investors' securities for sale to the public with the Securities and Exchange Commission. They are rarely actually used, but they give the Investors negotiating power if they feel the Company is avoiding registering securities to the Investors' detriment.

Registrable Securities: All shares of Common Stock issuable upon conversion of the Series A Preferred [and any other Common Stock held by the Investors] will be deemed "**Registrable Securities.**"

Demand Registration: Upon earliest of (i) [three-five] years after the Closing; or (ii) [six] months[18] following an initial public offering ("**IPO**"), persons holding [___]% of the Registrable Securities may request [one] [two] (consummated) registrations by the Company of their shares. The aggregate offering price for such registration may not be less than $[5-15] million. A registration will count for this purpose only if (i) all Registrable Securities requested to be registered are registered and (ii) it is closed, or withdrawn at the request of the Investors (other than as a result of a material adverse change to the Company).

Management and Information Rights: A Management Rights letter from the Company, in a form reasonably acceptable to the Investors, will be delivered prior to Closing to each Investor that requests one.

Any [Major] Investor [(who is not a competitor)] will be granted access to Company facilities and personnel during normal business hours and with reasonable advance notification. The Company will deliver to such Major Investor (i) annual, quarterly, [and monthly] financial statements, and other information as determined by the Board; (ii) thirty days prior to the end of each fiscal year, a comprehensive operating budget forecasting the Company's revenues, expenses, and cash position on a month-to-month basis for the upcoming fiscal year; and (iii) promptly following the end of each quarter an up-to-date capitalization table. A "Major Investor" means any Investor who purchases at least $[_____] of Series A Preferred.

Right to Participate Pro Rata in Future Rounds: All [Major] Investors shall have a pro rata right, based on their percentage equity ownership in the Company (assuming the conversion of all outstanding Preferred Stock into Common Stock and the exercise of all options outstanding under the Company's stock plans), to participate in subsequent issuances of equity securities of the Company (excluding those issuances listed at the end of the "Anti-dilution Provisions" section of this Term Sheet. In addition, should any [Major] Investor choose not to purchase its full pro rata share, the remaining [Major] Investors shall have the right to purchase the remaining pro rata shares.

---

18. The Company will want the percentage to be high enough so that a significant portion of the investor base is behind the demand. Companies will typically resist allowing a single investor to cause a registration. Experienced investors will want to ensure that less experienced investors do not have the right to cause a demand registration. In some cases, different series of Preferred Stock may request the right for that series to initiate a certain number of demand registrations. Companies will typically resist this due to the cost and diversion of management resources when multiple constituencies have this right.

Matters Requiring
Investor Director
Approval:

[So long as the holders of Series A Preferred are entitled to elect a Series A Director, the Company will not, without Board approval, which approval must include the affirmative vote of [one/both] of the Series A Director(s):

(i) make any loan or advance to, or own any stock or other securities of, any subsidiary or other corporation, partnership, or other entity unless it is wholly owned by the Company; (ii) make any loan or advance to any person, including, any employee or director, except advances and similar expenditures in the ordinary course of business or under the terms of a employee stock or option plan approved by the Board of Directors; (iii) guarantee, any indebtedness except for trade accounts of the Company or any subsidiary arising in the ordinary course of business; (iv) make any investment inconsistent with any investment policy approved by the Board; (v) incur any aggregate indebtedness in excess of $[_____] that is not already included in a Board-approved budget, other than trade credit incurred in the ordinary course of business; (vi) enter into or be a party to any transaction with any director, officer or employee of the Company or any "associate" (as defined in Rule 12b-2 promulgated under the Exchange Act) of any such person [except transactions resulting in payments to or by the Company in an amount less than $[60,000] per year], [or transactions made in the ordinary course of business and pursuant to reasonable requirements of the Company's business and upon fair and reasonable terms that are approved by a majority of the Board of Directors]; (vii) hire, fire, or change the compensation of the executive officers, including approving any option grants; (viii) change the principal business of the Company, enter new lines of business, or exit the current line of business; (ix) sell, assign, license, pledge or encumber material technology or intellectual property, other than licenses granted in the ordinary course of business; or (x) enter into any corporate strategic relationship involving the payment contribution or assignment by the Company or to the Company of assets greater than [$100,000.00].

Investors have a veto right over major things that could happen with the Company.

Non-Competition
and Non-Solicitation
Agreements:

Each Founder and key employee will enter into a [one] year non-competition and non-solicitation agreement in a form reasonably acceptable to the Investors.

RIGHT OF FIRST REFUSAL/CO-SALE AGREEMENT

Right of First
Refusal/Right of
Co-Sale
(Take-me-Along):

Company first and Investors second (to the extent assigned by the Board of Directors), will have a right of first refusal with respect to any shares of capital stock of the Company proposed to be transferred by Founders [and future employees holding greater than [1]% of Company Common Stock (assuming conversion of Preferred Stock and whether then held or subject to the exercise of options)], with a right of oversubscription for Investors of shares unsubscribed by the other Investors. Before any such person may sell Common Stock, he will give the Investors an opportunity to participate in such sale on a basis proportionate to the amount of securities held by the seller and those held by the participating Investors.

VOTING AGREEMENT

Board of Directors:

At the initial Closing, the Board shall consist of [_____] members comprised of (i) [*Name*] as the representative designated by [____], as the lead Investor, (ii) [*Name*] as the representative designated by the remaining Investors, (iii) [*Name*] as the representative designated by the Founders, (iv) the person then serving as the Chief Executive Officer of the Company, and (v) [___] person(s) who are not employed by the Company and who are mutually acceptable [to the Founders and Investors] [to the other directors].

> *Although under state law the Company can't take away a voting shareholder's right to vote for who will be on the Board, the Investors can (and do) require the voting shareholders to agree in advance to vote in favor of their designates on the Board.*

Drag Along:

Holders of Preferred Stock and the Founders [and all future holders of greater than [1]% of Common Stock (assuming conversion of Preferred Stock and whether then held or subject to the exercise of options)] shall be required to enter into an agreement with the Investors that provides that such stockholders will vote their shares in favor of a Deemed Liquidation Event or transaction in which 50% or more of the voting power of the Company is transferred and which is approved by [the Board of Directors] [and the holders of ____% of the outstanding shares of Preferred Stock, on an as-converted basis (the "**Electing Holders**")], so long as the liability of each stockholder in such transaction is several (and not joint) and does not exceed the stockholder's pro rata portion of any claim and the consideration to be paid to the stockholders in such transaction will be allocated as if the consideration were the proceeds to be distributed to the Company's stockholders in a liquidation under the Company's then-current Certificate of Incorporation.]

. . .

No Shop/   The Company agrees to work in good faith expeditiously
Confidentiality: towards a closing. The Company and the Founders agree
                    that they will not, for a period of [_____] weeks from the
                    date these terms are accepted, take any action to solicit,
                    initiate, encourage or assist the submission of any proposal,
                    negotiation or offer from any person or entity other than the
                    Investors relating to the sale or issuance, of any of the capital
                    stock of the Company [or the acquisition, sale, lease, license or
                    other disposition of the Company or any material part of the
                    stock or assets of the Company] and shall notify the Investors
                    promptly of any inquiries by any third parties in regards to
                    the foregoing. [In the event that the Company breaches
                    this no-shop obligation and, prior to [_____], closes any
                    of the above-referenced transactions [without providing the
                    Investors the opportunity to invest on the same terms as the
                    other parties to such transaction], then the Company shall
                    pay to the Investors $[_____] upon the closing of any such
                    transaction as liquidated damages.] The Company will not
                    disclose the terms of this Term Sheet to any person other
                    than officers, members of the Board of Directors and the
                    Company's accountants and attorneys and other potential
                    Investors acceptable to [_____], as lead Investor, without
                    the written consent of the Investors.

Expiration: This Term Sheet expires on [_____ __, 20__] if not accepted
                    by the Company by that date.

[SIGNATURE BLOCKS]

Notes and Questions

1. One key economic term that gives clients considerable anxiety and is the source of considerable discussion is the valuation of the venture. To determine the amount of the company the venture capitalist will receive in exchange for his investment, one must know how much the company is worth before the investment (the so-called pre-money valuation). As a simple illustration of the problem, suppose an investor is going to put $5 million into a business. If the business has a pre-money valuation of $10 million, the investor will own one-third of the business after the money has been invested (they will own $5 million of the $15 million the business is worth after the investment). On the other hand, if the pre-money valuation is $20 million, the investor will only own one-fifth of the business after the money has been invested (they will own $5 million of the $25 million the business is worth after the investment).

The lawyer is typically not expected to calculate a pre-money valuation for the business, and indeed valuation is typically a heavily negotiated business point that ultimately has more to do with negotiating power and perceived value than any particular actual valuation method. That said, lawyers should be aware of a couple of general valuation approaches. Under one method, experts find comparable businesses and extrapolate a value for the entrepreneurial venture. Under another type of model, experts will look at the financial statements of the business and extrapolate a value for the entrepreneurial venture by making the kinds of judgments described in Chapter 8. Sometimes they will multiply earnings numbers by some "multiple" that leads to implied company value. Of course, in a new venture without earnings, there is more guesswork to be done — there, investors may be left with trying to apply a discounted multiple to projections of cash flow. Valuations can also be adjusted for non-financial factors, such as a guaranteed seat on the board of directors or management rights, registration rights, and drag-along rights.

2. Why don't investors always seek the lowest pre-money valuation possible?

3. The two model term sheets you reviewed are quite different from one another. What are the key differences, and how do you explain the reasons behind them?

4. The NVCA model term sheet gives a few different variations on the type of equity the venture capitalist might purchase. Which of these seems most advantageous to a founder? How do you think venture capitalists and founders decide among these and the many other possible equity structures available?

5. What is the point of a right of first refusal? How is it different from a co-sale right? Who is the likely beneficiary of each of these rights as they are drafted in the model term sheet?

6. What is a drag along?

7. Does a "pay to play" provision (as described in the model term sheet) favor an investor, a founding entrepreneur, or both? When might your entrepreneur client hope to get a pay to play included as part of a deal?

8. Imagine a founder who is desperate for funding and an investor who therefore has significant bargaining power. Why might the investor choose not to impose the most aggressively investor-friendly terms when investing in the business?

9. Imagine your client has a surprise meeting scheduled with a venture capitalist but does not know anything about venture capital financings. What coaching would you do in advance of the meeting if you only had one hour to meet with the client? What are the most important business points for a client to understand before the meeting?

10. A capitalization table, or "cap table," is a chart that shows the equityholders in the venture and how much they each own. As a simple example, consider the following:

CAPITALIZATION TABLE FOR VENTURE ENTERPRISES, INC.

Holder	Common	Options for Common	Series A Preferred	Percentage of Issued and Outstanding	Percentage of Fully Diluted
Jim Founder	50,000			56.8%	50.0%
Employee Option Pool		12,000			12.0%
Sally Angel			38,000	43.2%	38.0%
TOTAL	50,000	12,000	38,000	100.0%	100.0%

In this capitalization table, we see how much of the company the founder owns, how much has been allocated to employee options, and how much has been sold to the angel investor. The percentages shown under the heading "Percentage of Issued and Outstanding" represent how much of the currently outstanding shares are held by the holders. Since the employee option pool has been set aside but no options have been issued and exercised from the pool, those shares are not included as "issued" or "outstanding" shares. When the percentages are calculated on a "fully diluted" basis, any shares that might ever be issued under existing contracts or other arrangements are assumed to be issued and outstanding, and thus the option pool shares are included. If you represent the founder, what do you notice about the founder's influence and ultimate ownership on an "issued and outstanding" basis? How does that change after assuming all employee options are issued and exercised? Depending on the business deal with Sally Angel, why might this change be a concern? Why might it be irrelevant?

5. Securities Regulation

While most people have at least a vague sense that "public companies" traded on the stock markets like the New York Stock Exchange are subject to regulation because they sell equity to the general public, entrepreneurs and their lawyers can easily forget that federal and state securities laws apply to all companies, regardless of size. A law school Securities Regulation course will spend a good amount of time on the definition of "security," but the key point to appreciate is that any equity ownership interest, or potential equity ownership interest, is a security. Thus, when an entrepreneurial venture issues stock to the founder, or grants an option to a worker in exchange for services, or sells preferred units to a venture capitalist, the venture has engaged in a transaction involving securities and is subject to regulation under the securities laws.

In the United States, there are two primary federal statutes, and associated regulations, that govern the sale of securities and are designed to protect investors in businesses. The Securities Act of 1933, known as the "Securities Act" or the " '33 Act," is built on a philosophy of disclosure — the idea that issuers of securities must disclose a tremendous amount of information about the business to potential investors before they invest directly in a company. The Securities Exchange Act of 1934, known as the "Exchange Act" or the " '34 Act," regulates trading of previously issued securities in the so-called secondary market. The Exchange Act requires issuers of securities to make regular reports to the market to inform investors, and also contains important anti-fraud provisions governing securities transactions.

Given that the securities laws cover all issuances of securities, lawyers must ensure their clients are compliant with applicable statutes and regulations from the outset. The key securities issue that should concern counsel to an entrepreneurial venture is based in the Securities Act. The mechanism the Securities Act uses to achieve its goal of full disclosure for investors is to require all securities to be registered with the Securities and Exchange Commission before they are offered for sale. The first time a company registers its securities and offers them for sale is referred to as an Initial Public Offering, or "IPO" (discussed in Chapter 10). Although entrepreneurs may dream of having an IPO when their companies are wildly successful, for the entrepreneurial venture, the registration requirements of the Securities Act are onerous and too expensive to be a practical option.

Accordingly, most entrepreneurs look for — and are often able to take advantage of — exemptions from registration under the Securities Act and its associated regulations. There are two primary ways entrepreneurs do this: the most common is to use the so-called "private placement" exemption from registration as set forth in Regulation D under the Securities Act. Entrepreneurs can also use Regulation Crowdfunding, a way of having many small investors putting in small amounts of money rather than a small number of investors investing larger amounts.

a. Private Placements under Regulation D

The primary exemption is contained in Section 4(2) of the statute, which exempts "transactions by an issuer not involving any public offering" from registration. This so-called private placement exemption is broad and a little vague. To clarify matters, the SEC has promulgated Regulation D, which provides "safe harbors" for issuers trying to fit within the 4(2) exemption from registration. The safe harbors try to establish that the people participating in the offering are limited in number, or at least able to protect themselves.

Investors are considered to be able to protect themselves under Regulation D if they are "accredited investors." The educational site investor.gov, which is maintained by the SEC, explains that accredited investors this way:

An *accredited investor*, in the context of a *natural person*, includes anyone who:

- earned income that exceeded $200,000 (or $300,000 together with a spouse) in each of the prior two years, and reasonably expects the same for the current year, OR
- has a net worth over $1 million, either alone or together with a spouse (excluding the value of the person's primary residence).

In addition to wealthy people, Rule 501 of the SEC's Regulation D tells us that term accredited investor also includes people who are sophisticated or have special knowledge of the issuer. For example the definition includes "Any director, executive officer, or general partner of the issuer of the securities being offered or sold, or any director, executive officer, or general partner of a general partner of that issuer." The SEC also considers "Any natural person holding in good standing one or more professional certifications or designations or credentials from an accredited educational institution that the Commission has designated as qualifying an individual for accredited investor status." So-called "family offices" with assets of at least $5 million are also included. In short, insiders, people with education the SEC considers relevant, wealthy people, and certain types of business organizations, are all considered to be able to protect themselves.

One safe harbor in Regulation D is found in Rule 504. This rule exempts up to $5,000,000 of securities in any 12-month period from registration, so long as the company sells in a state that requires disclosures to investors under its "blue sky" laws (see Note 3 below) or only sells to accredited investors while following a state law exemption from registration. Since most entrepreneurs are trying to avoid extensive disclosure obligations, the Rule 504 safe harbor is less popular for entrepreneurial ventures except in situations where they are only selling to accredited investors.

Rule 506, which is relied on by most ventures attracting large amounts of capital, permits an unlimited amount of money to be raised in any 12-month period, with these limitations:

- The issuer may only sell to up to 35 non-accredited investors who must be sophisticated, meaning they have sufficient knowledge on their own or with a representative such that they can evaluate the merits and risks of the investment (plus an unlimited number of accredited investors);
- The issuer must provide disclosure approximately equivalent to the disclosure provided on a registration statement to non-accredited investors, plus any disclosure provided to accredited investors (which is not subject to specific disclosure requirements);
- The issuer can't use general solicitation or advertising to sell the securities, unless the investors are all accredited investors, and the company takes reasonable steps to verify the accredited status of the investors.

In all Regulation D safe harbors, the company issuing the securities is required to electronically file a Form D with the SEC. Form D asks relatively straightforward questions about the company and the offering, and has no filing fee.

b. Regulation Crowdfunding

The word "crowdfunding" has several meanings. Entrepreneurs will often take advantage of sites like Kickstarter and Indiegogo, which give the public an opportunity to make a cash contribution to a company in exchange for some kind of tangible or intangible reward — such as a sticker, a product (if it is ever produced), or some kind of public acknowledgement. When companies use this kind of crowdfunding, the equity owners of the business continue to own the entire business, as they have not sold any ownership stake in the business — they've just received made some money.

The other type of crowdfunding is called "equity crowdfunding," which is when a company sells equity to a large number of investors who each invest a relatively small amount of money. Companies can avoid the registration requirements of the Securities Act if they engage in so-called Regulation Crowdfunding following the rules set by the SEC.

There are many reasons lawyers do not recommend equity crowdfunding as a fundraising measure, all centered around the idea that it is risky and complicated. Small investors are often demanding (they frequently request information from the company and expecting access to founders), and hard to keep track of in large numbers. They have, and exercise, voting rights, and are often more independent (and less informed) than professional investors. For a business that anticipates future fundraising from sophisticated investors, a capitalization table with a lot of equityholders can be a barrier to fundraising, as large investors prefer not to have the complication of multiple stockholders. In addition, more stockholders means more potential plaintiffs in a shareholder lawsuit, and more people who may later accuse the company of securities fraud if the investment does not go as planned.

Regulation crowdfunding allows companies to sell their securities only if it is done through a licensed broker-dealer or an SEC-approved online funding portal. Companies are limited in how much they raise through regulation crowdfunding — as of early 2020, they can only raise $1,070,000 in any 12-month period. In addition, investors are limited in how much they can invest in regulation crowdfunding — explained by the SEC on investor.gov as follows:

If either your annual income or your net worth is less than $107,000, then during any 12-month period, you can invest up to the greater of either $2,200 or 5% of the lesser of your annual income or net worth.

If both your annual income and your net worth are equal to or more than $107,000, then during any 12-month period, you can invest up to 10% of annual income or net worth, whichever is lesser, but not to exceed $107,000.

In addition, companies raising money using regulation crowdfunding must provide various disclosures about the business, all as set forth in the regulations. The disclosure obligations are significantly less burdensome than if the company were registering the securities for an initial public offering, but do require careful gathering of financial data and other facts about the business, include disclosure of risks. As with all disclosures made under the securities laws, entrepreneurs need to be very careful to ensure their disclosures are accurate and complete.

c.   Risk of Noncompliance with Securities Laws

Failure to comply with the Securities Act in this regard can have significant consequences for entrepreneurial ventures. Of particular concern is the right of investors to rescind transactions that did not comply. In the event the company is successful, it is unlikely an investor would take advantage of this kind of claim. It would be more likely to come up when a venture is not doing as well as anticipated, which would compound problems for the company as it would likely not have money to repay investors the amounts they initially invested. Additionally, replacement investments would likely be on worse terms, if they were available at all.

Additionally, entrepreneurs need to be careful to ensure they are complete and accurate in the disclosures they make to investors. If they do not, they run the risk of being accused of securities fraud.

Notes and Questions

1. Rule 506 of Regulation D allows issuances to an unlimited number of accredited investors. Regulation crowdfunding limits the amount unaccredited investors can put into a company. Why do you think the SEC is more protective of non-accredited investors than accredited investors?

2. Given your thoughts on why we have determined accredited investors don't need the same protections as the general public, do you think the definition of "accredited investor" accomplishes those intentions?

3. As described above, most entrepreneurs look for — and are often able to take advantage of — exemption from registration under one of the Regulation D safe harbors. An attorney's analysis does not stop at the federal regulations, however. Each state has a set of its own securities laws, called "blue sky laws." While some states are relatively straightforward in their approach and mirror federal regulations, other states, such as California, are more aggressive than the SEC in protecting investors and require that significant additional restrictions be met before a company sells its securities. Since securities regulations are intended to protect investors, the entrepreneur's lawyer must look at blue sky laws in all states where securities will be offered to potential investors.

4. In what situations can you imagine equity crowdfunding would be a good route for a new business seeking to raise capital?

5. What impact do you imagine securities regulation has on entrepreneurial ventures? Does this body of law make it easier or more difficult to raise capital? Consider both positive and negative effects in your thinking.

C. DEBT FINANCING

As discussed earlier in this chapter, entrepreneurs finance their businesses by selling equity, borrowing necessary funds, or (typically) a combination of both methods. As a business grows and expands and consequently requires additional capital, it is likely that the business will eventually seek a bank loan. It is important for the entrepreneur's attorney to understand the complex legal rules that govern this area as well as the relevant language and vocabulary in order to walk the client through what can otherwise be a daunting and overwhelming experience.

1. Loan Facilities

Depending on the specific reason for seeking a loan, the entrepreneurial venture may require either a term loan or a revolving loan. Revolving loans are generally used to finance the working capital needs of a business for a specific period of time. Under a revolving line of credit, the outstanding loan amount will fluctuate depending on the borrower's everyday cash needs. A borrower may reborrow amounts it has repaid under a revolving loan up to a specified limit. Term loans, on the other hand, are generally made for a specific business purpose such as an acquisition of another company, purchasing equipment, or funding real estate construction. Term loans are generally made in lump sums (or installments) and may not be reborrowed as amounts borrowed under the term loan are repaid.

2. Secured Lending

If a loan is unsecured, a lender who is not repaid is limited to suing the borrower based on a breach of contact claim for nonpayment and potentially stands in line with other unsecured creditors (if there are any) for payment. Accordingly, lenders generally require that business loans be secured by collateral owned by the borrower so that in the event of nonpayment of the loan, the lender may sell the assets and retain the proceeds up to the outstanding amount due under the loan.

Article 9 of the Uniform Commercial Code governs the mechanics of and rules for creation, perfection, priority, and enforcement of a security interest in most personal property and fixtures. Article 9 describes how to create an enforceable security interest in collateral and furthermore sets forth the rights of secured parties against one another. It also provides for a central system of filing security interests and notice to third parties of the existence of such interests.

SUMMARY OF REVISED UCC ARTICLE 9 (2000)
Edwin E. Smith (Bingham McCutchen LLP Legal Alert, January 28, 2001) reprinted with permission

. . .

SCOPE OF ARTICLE 9

Article 9 is entitled "Secured Transactions." It generally applies to any interest (regardless of its form) created by contract in personal property and fixtures and which secures payment or other performance of an obligation. That interest is referred to as a security interest, and the property subject to the security interest is referred to as collateral. Article 9 also generally applies to sales of accounts, chattel paper, promissory notes and payment intangibles (the definitions for these terms being discussed below). Moreover, Article 9 includes agricultural liens and all consignments, even true consignments, within its scope.

Parties.

Debtor and Obligor. Article 9 refers to the debtor as the person who has a property interest in the collateral other than a security interest or other lien. The term "debtor" also includes a seller of accounts, chattel paper, promissory notes or payment intangibles, a person who has a property interest in collateral subject to an agricultural lien, and a consignee. Article 9 refers to the person who owes the secured obligation as the obligor.

Secured Party. The person in whose favor a security interest is granted is referred to in Article 9 as the secured party. The term "secured party" also includes a buyer of accounts, chattel paper, promissory notes or payment intangibles, the person who holds an agricultural lien and a consignor. A secured party may be a "representative" for holders of secured obligations, such as an indenture trustee or collateral agent, where the security interest is granted to the secured party as representative.

Form of Transaction is Irrelevant. The form of the transaction or the label which the parties put on the transaction is irrelevant for purposes of determining whether Article 9 applies. Rather, the determination as to whether Article 9 applies is based on the economic reality of the transaction. For example, a transaction may be characterized by the parties as a sale or a lease of goods, but, if in economic reality a security interest is being created, Article 9 will nevertheless apply. It is also not required that the parties refer in their documents to a "security interest" being created under a "security agreement." Even if the parties use other terms, such as "assignment," "hypothecation," "conditional sale," "trust deed" or the like, Article 9 still applies whenever a security interest in personal property is being created. Similarly, it is generally irrelevant, for purposes of Article 9, whether title to the collateral is in the name of the debtor or the secured party.

Exclusions.

Generally. Although Article 9 covers most security interests in personal property and fixtures, certain interests in personal property collateral are outside of the scope of Article 9. These interests include common law bailments and true leases, the latter being governed by UCC Article 2A.

Specific Exclusions. In §§ 9-109(c) and (d), Article 9 expressly excludes certain transactions and types of personal property collateral from Article 9's scope. These specific exclusions encompass transactions preempted by federal law, landlords' liens, and certain of the following transactions or liens: statutory and common law liens, wage claims, security interests created by governments and governmental subdivisions and agencies, sales of accounts and chattel paper, insurance claims, judgment claims, rights of set-off, real estate interests, tort claims, and deposit accounts. . . .

Effect of Exclusion. Of course, even though a type of assignment or a type of property may be excluded from Article 9's scope, it is still often possible for a secured party to obtain a security interest in that type of property under other federal or state statutes or under common law.

ARTICLE 9 COLLATERAL CATEGORIES

Article 9 categorizes collateral into different types, primarily based upon the debtor's use of the collateral. It is important for the secured party to determine the type of collateral in which the secured party is taking a security interest, since that determination will in turn guide the secured party in, among other things, deciding how to perfect the security interest. Collateral types under Article 9 may be discussed broadly as comprising personal property consisting of goods, investment property, semi-intangible property, and other intangible property. . . .

ATTACHMENT

Article 9 uses the term attachment to describe the moment at which a security interest becomes enforceable against the debtor. For a security interest to attach, a number of events must have occurred: (1) value must have been given; (2) the debtor must have rights in the collateral; and (3) either (i) the collateral must be in possession of the secured party by agreement of the debtor or, if the collateral is investment property, a deposit account, electronic chattel paper or a letter-of-credit right, the secured party must have "control" of the collateral; or (ii) the debtor must have authenticated a security agreement that contains a description of the collateral. A security agreement is the agreement under which a security interest is granted or provided for. The following discussion provides a fuller description of these elements of attachment.

Value. In general, value is given for any consideration sufficient to support a simple contract. Some examples of value include a loan of money, a binding commitment to lend money, the issuance of a guarantee or acting as an accommodation party. Value also includes whole or partial satisfaction of a pre-existing claim.

Rights in the Collateral. As a general matter, the debtor can only grant a security interest in whatever ownership or other rights it has. Similarly, the secured party can generally enjoy no greater rights in the collateral than the debtor itself holds unless the UCC provides otherwise. Note, however, that a mere power of the debtor to transfer collateral is sufficient to satisfy the "rights in the collateral" requirement. Thus, a seller of accounts may have the power to transfer rights in the sold accounts where the interest of the buyer in the accounts is unperfected, and a consignee may have the power to transfer rights in consigned goods where the consignor's interest in the consigned goods is unperfected.

Possession of or Control by the Secured Party or Security Agreement. The secured party must either possess the collateral, or, in case of investment property, a deposit account, electronic chattel paper or a letter-of-credit right, the secured party must have "control" of the collateral; or the debtor must have authenticated a security agreement describing the collateral. The description of the collateral in the security agreement must be sufficient reasonably to identify the collateral. These requirements are further discussed below.

Possession. A secured party may satisfy the possession requirement by using a third party who possesses the collateral, if the collateral is in possession of the third party by agreement of the debtor and the third party acknowledges in a signed writing or other authenticated record that it holds for the secured party. If the collateral is a certificated security in registered form, there needs to be delivery to the secured party under § 8-301.

Control. The concept of "control" applies to investment property, deposit accounts, electronic chattel paper and letter-of-credit rights. The requirements for control are further discussed below under "Perfection."

Security Agreement. A security agreement must be "authenticated" by the debtor. The term authenticated includes a normal signature on a written document but it also encompasses an electronic transmission.

Reasonable Identification of the Collateral. The security agreement must reasonably identify the collateral. The concept of reasonable identification is a flexible one, permitting identification in a variety of ways: a specific listing, a reference to a category, collateral type or quantity, or use of a computational formula. However, an "all asset" description in a security agreement is insufficient. And a description by collateral type alone is insufficient if the collateral is a commercial tort claim or, in a consumer transaction, if the collateral is consumer goods, a security entitlement, a securities account or a commodity account. If the collateral is timber to be cut, a real estate description in the security agreement is required.

After-acquired Property. Article 9 permits a security agreement to contain an after-acquired property clause. But the secured party generally may not obtain a security interest in after-acquired consumer goods as original collateral unless the debtor acquires rights in the consumer goods within 10 days after the secured party gives value. Moreover, a security interest in a commercial tort claim will attach only to a tort claim existing at the time that the security agreement is signed or otherwise authenticated. The security interest will not attach as original collateral to an after-acquired commercial tort claim. . . .

PERFECTION

An attached security interest which will prevail over a creditor using judicial process to obtain a lien on the collateral, including a trustee in bankruptcy having the status of a lien creditor under . . . the Bankruptcy Code on the commencement of the debtor's bankruptcy, is a <u>perfected</u> security interest under Article 9. But it should be emphasized that only an attached security interest can become a perfected security interest. There are three primary ways in which an attached security interest may be perfected. First, the secured party may file a properly completed financing statement in the appropriate filing office. Second, the secured party may take possession of the collateral or, in the case of investment property, a deposit account, electronic chattel paper or a letter-of-credit right, may obtain control of the collateral. Third, in a few cases, the security interest may be perfected automatically upon attachment. Depending upon the category of collateral, there may be only one method of perfection or several.

Perfection by Filing. Generally, most types of security interests either may or must be perfected by filing a properly completed financing statement in the appropriate filing office.

Contents of Financing Statement. A financing statement, to be sufficient, must provide the debtor's name and the name of the secured party or its representative and indicate the collateral covered by the financing statement. Where the collateral is timber to be cut, as-extracted collateral or fixtures (in the case of a fixture filing), additional information is required for the financing statement to be sufficient. Moreover, while an "all-asset" collateral description is insufficient in a security agreement, it is sufficient in a financing statement. A financing statement may still be effective even though it contains errors, so long as the errors are minor and are not seriously misleading. A debtor's name on a financing statement that varies from the debtor's legal name is not seriously misleading if a search of the records of the filing office under the debtor's legal name would disclose the financing statement.

Authorization by the Debtor. In order to accommodate electronic filing, there is no requirement in Article 9 that a financing statement be signed by the debtor. But the secured party may not file a financing statement against the debtor unless the filing is authorized by the debtor. That authorization is automatic in the case of a filing describing the collateral no more broadly than the collateral description contained in a security agreement authenticated by the debtor. However, a secured party will need an authorization authenticated by the debtor to pre-file a financing statement in advance of a security agreement being authenticated by the debtor, or to file a financing statement with a collateral description broader than that contained in the debtor's authenticated security agreement. A secured party that files a financing statement without the debtor's authorization may be liable to the debtor for actual or statutory damages.

Office in Which Filing Should be Made. Article 9 contains choice of law rules to determine in which jurisdiction a filing must be made. These choice of law rules are discussed in further detail below. Once the jurisdiction in which the filing must be made is determined, the financing statement must be filed in the central filing office in that jurisdiction, typically the Secretary of State's office. However, rather than a filing in the central filing office, a local filing in the applicable real estate recording office is required for as-extracted collateral, timber to be cut or a fixture filing.

What Constitutes Filing. Communication of the financing statement to the filing office, together with payment of the correct filing fee, constitutes filing. Article 9 sets forth reasons for which a filing office may refuse to accept a financing statement for filing, thereby rendering the filing ineffective even if it is otherwise sufficient. These reasons include the communication of the financing statement by a means not authorized by the filing office and the failure to tender a payment at least equal to the filing fee. They also include the failure to provide in the financing statement other information, such as the debtor's mailing address, whether the debtor is an individual or an organization, and, if the debtor is an organization, the debtor's type and jurisdiction of organization and the debtor's state organizational identification number or a statement that the debtor has none. The reasons set forth in § 9-516(b) are the only grounds for filing office rejection. If there are such grounds for the filing office to reject the filing but the filing office nevertheless accepts the filing, the filing is still effective so long as the financing statement meets the requirements for sufficiency of the financing statement. . . .

. . .

Perfection by Possession. Certain types of collateral may or must be perfected by possession.

Money. A secured party's security interest in money must be perfected by possession by the secured party.

Instruments. A secured party may perfect a security interest in an instrument by either filing or possession.

Certificated Securities. A security interest in a certificated security may be perfected by filing, possession or control. A secured party's perfection of a security interest in a certificated security by possession is accomplished by the secured party taking delivery of the certificated security. . . . Delivery generally means that the secured party obtains possession of the security certificate even if a necessary indorsement is lacking.

Chattel Paper. As an alternative to perfection by filing, a security interest in tangible chattel paper may be perfected by the secured party's taking possession of the tangible chattel paper.

Other Collateral. A security interest in goods and negotiable documents may be perfected by filing or by the secured party's taking possession of the collateral.

Possession by Third Parties. Where the secured party wishes to perfect a security interest in collateral by possession but the collateral is in the possession of a third party "bailee," Article 9 requires the third party in possession of collateral, other than goods covered by a document of title, to authenticate a record acknowledging that it is holding the collateral for the secured party. For perfection by such possession and authentication to be effective, the third party may not be the debtor or a lessee in the ordinary course from the debtor. A secured party in possession of collateral does not relinquish possession if the secured party delivers the collateral to a possible purchaser of the collateral (other than the debtor or an ordinary course lessee of the collateral) for inspection and return.

Perfection by Control. The concept of control applies to perfection of a security interest in investment property, deposit accounts, electronic chattel paper and letter-of-credit rights.

Investment Property. A security interest in investment property may be perfected by control as well as by filing. The concept of control is the same under Article 9 as it is under UCC Article 8 and includes delivery, with indorsements, of certificated securities to the secured party, an agreement by the issuer of uncertificated securities that the issuer will honor instructions from the secured party without further consent of the debtor, and an agreement by a bank, broker or other securities intermediary holding a securities account, or by a commodity intermediary, that it will honor instructions from the secured party without further consent of the debtor. Control also includes registering the securities, the securities account or the commodity account in the name of the secured party. Where the secured party is the debtor's securities intermediary or commodity intermediary, the securities intermediary or commodity intermediary automatically has control.

Deposit Accounts. A security interest in a deposit account as original collateral may be perfected only by the secured party obtaining control over the deposit account. A secured party obtains control over a deposit account if it is the depositary bank or if the deposit account is in the secured party's name. A secured party also has control if the depositary bank enters into an agreement with the secured party that the depositary bank will comply with instructions from the secured party as to the funds in the deposit account, without further consent from the debtor.

Electronic Chattel Paper. A security interest in electronic chattel paper may be perfected by control or by filing. A secured party obtains control over electronic chattel paper if there is only one authoritative or identifiable copy of the electronic record of the chattel paper, the copy of the record identifies the secured party and its interest, the copy is communicated to and maintained by the secured party or its designated custodian, the copy is readily identifiable as the authoritative copy and any revision of the authoritative copy is readily identifiable as authorized or unauthorized.

Letter-of-Credit Rights. A security interest in a letter-of-credit right may be perfected by the secured party obtaining control over the letter-of-credit right. Control is the sole method of perfection of a security interest in a letter-of-credit right unless the security interest in the letter-of-credit right is perfected as a supporting obligation. A secured party has control over a letter-of-credit right if the issuer or nominated person has consented to an assignment of proceeds of the letter of credit. . . .

Automatic Perfection. In some situations, no additional steps beyond attachment are necessary to perfect a security interest.

Generally. The following security interests . . . are automatically perfected upon attachment: a purchase-money security interest in consumer goods, a sale of promissory notes or payment intangibles, an assignment of accounts or payment intangibles which does not alone or in conjunction with other assignments to the same assignee transfer a significant part of the outstanding accounts or payment intangibles of the assignor, a security interest arising under UCC Article 2, 2A or 4 or by delivery of a financial asset under 9-206(c), a security interest in investment property created by a securities intermediary or commodity intermediary, an assignment of a health-care-insurance receivable to the health-care provider, a security interest in favor of an issuer or nominated person in documents presented to the issuer or nominated person for draw under a letter of credit, an assignment for the benefit of creditors, and a security interest created by an assignment of a beneficial interest in a decedent's estate.

Supporting Obligations. In addition, Article 9 provides for automatic attachment of a security interest in a supporting obligation if the security interest in the supported collateral has attached and for automatic perfection of a security interest in a supporting obligation if the security interest in the supported collateral is perfected.

Temporary Automatic Perfection. A security interest in instruments, certificated securities and negotiable documents is temporarily perfected for a period of 20 days to the extent that it arises for new value given under an authenticated security agreement. A security interest in proceeds is temporarily perfected for a period of 20 days.

Other Methods of Perfection. Federal and state statutes may, of course, provide for methods of perfection of security interests in vessels, aircraft, intellectual property and titled goods (such as motor vehicles that are not inventory of a dealer). Compliance with these methods of perfection constitutes the equivalent of perfection by filing under Article 9. A security interest in titled goods that are inventory held for sale or lease by a person in the business of selling goods of that kind is perfected by filing, rather than by notation of the secured party's security interest on the certificates of title. A security interest in goods covered by a nonnegotiable document may be perfected by filing as to the goods, by issuance of the document in the name of the secured party or by notification to the bailee of the secured party's interest.

PRIORITY

Even though a security interest has attached and become perfected, it may not prevail over other creditors and other interested parties. The ranking of various interests in the same collateral among the secured party and other claimants raises the question of whether a secured party's security interest has <u>priority</u> over the interests of these other parties.

General Creditors. A secured party will prevail over unsecured creditors with respect to collateral in which the secured party has a perfected security interest. Even if the secured party fails to perfect its security interest, the secured party will still prevail over unsecured creditors with respect to collateral in which the secured party has an unperfected security interest, at least outside of the debtor's bankruptcy.

<u>Lien Creditors.</u>

Definition. A lien creditor is a creditor who has acquired a lien on the debtor's property by judicial process and includes a trustee in bankruptcy.

Secured Party vs. Lien Creditor Generally. A perfected secured party will prevail over a lien creditor holding a lien on the secured party's collateral so long as the secured party's security interest in the collateral is perfected at or before the time when the lien arises. Even if the security interest is not perfected, the secured party will prevail over the lien creditor so long as, before the lien arises, the secured party has filed a financing statement covering the collateral and . . . the debtor has authenticated a security agreement describing the collateral or the secured party has possession or control of the collateral.

Future Advances. Future advances by the secured party on collateral in which the secured party's security interest is superior to the lien of the lien creditor on the original advance will likewise be secured by the collateral in priority to the lien creditor's lien, so long as the future advances are made within the later of 45 days after the lien arose and the time that the secured party obtained knowledge of the lien or are made pursuant to a commitment incurred without knowledge of the lien.

Purchase-money Security Interests. A secured party taking a purchase-money security interest (see "Purchase-money Secured Parties" discussed below) will also have priority over a lien creditor holding a lien on the purchase-money collateral so long as the secured party perfected its security interest by filing before the expiration of a period of 20 days after the debtor received possession of the collateral.

Other Non-Purchase Secured Parties. Absent another Article 9 priority rule to the contrary, in cases in which there is more than one secured party claiming a security interest in the same collateral, the first secured party to file a financing statement or perfect its security interest has priority. This is the so-called "first-to-file-or-perfect" priority rule. It follows that a perfected security interest in collateral prevails over an unperfected security interest in the collateral. If both security interests are unperfected, the first security interest to attach has priority.

Purchase-money Secured Parties. A <u>purchase-money security interest</u> is a security interest in collateral which is either taken by a supplier of that collateral to finance its purchase price or a security interest given to a third party lender in the collateral purchased with the proceeds of the lender's loan. The purchase-money collateral must generally be goods. But it may also be software sold or licensed with goods which are themselves purchase-money collateral, if the software is acquired principally for use with the goods. A holder of a perfected purchase-money security interest, who has taken certain applicable steps, achieves super priority, i.e., its security interest in the purchase-money collateral will rank ahead of any security interest which would otherwise be entitled to priority under the first-to-file-or-perfect priority rule. To achieve super priority, the purchase-money secured party must take the following steps:

Inventory Collateral. If the collateral is inventory, the purchase-money secured party must perfect its security interest before the debtor receives possession of the inventory. In addition, the purchase-money secured party must notify existing holders of a security interest of record in the same type of inventory of the purchase-money lender's intention to take a purchase-money interest in the inventory in advance of the debtor receiving possession of the inventory. The notice is effective for a period of five years. Purchase-money inventory advances may be cross-collateralized so that the total of the purchase-money inventory advances from the same supplier or lender may be secured by successive shipments of the purchase-money inventory collateral from the same supplier or financed by the same lender.

Farm Products Livestock Collateral. Article 9 contains analogous purchase-money priority rules for purchase-money security interest in farm products livestock. The purchase-money priority also extends to products of the livestock in their unmanufactured state.

Other Collateral. If the security interest is in collateral other than inventory or farm products livestock, the purchase-money secured party must perfect its security interest before the expiration of a period of 20 days after the debtor obtains possession of the collateral.

If two secured parties, one being a supplier and the other being a lender, each claim purchase-money priority over the same collateral, the supplier's purchase-money security interest prevails over that of the lender. In addition, a purchase-money security interest in a commercial transaction does not lose its status as a purchase-money security interest merely because it also secures non-purchase-money obligations, the purchase-money obligations are also secured by non-purchase-money collateral, or the purchase-money obligations have been renewed or refinanced.

Consignors. Article 9 treats all consignments, . . . whether "true" consignments or security consignments, as purchase-money security interests and requires consignors to comply with Article 9 rules applicable to purchase-money secured parties in order to obtain priority.

Buyers, Lessees and Non-exclusive Licensees in Ordinary Course. Customers of the debtor who buy the debtor's goods in the debtor's ordinary course of business take free of the security interest of the debtor's secured party even if they know of the security interest. But only a customer of the debtor that takes possession of the goods or has a right to recover the goods from the debtor under UCC Article 2 may be an ordinary course buyer. A buyer of consumer goods has a right to recover the goods from the debtor under UCC Article 2 when the buyer acquires a special property in the goods. The acquisition by a buyer of a special property in goods generally occurs at the time that the goods are identified to the sales contract. In addition, a buyer of goods collateral from a debtor may not take free of the secured party's security interest as a buyer in the ordinary course if the secured party is in possession of the goods. . . .

Buyers and Other Transferees Not in the Ordinary Course. Generally, if the debtor sells or otherwise disposes of collateral outside of the ordinary course and the disposition is not authorized by the secured party holding a perfected security interest in that collateral, the security interest continues in the collateral and continues perfected notwithstanding its disposition. Future advances by the secured party will likewise be secured in priority to the interest of the buyer, so long as the future advance is made within the earlier of 45 days after the sale arose and the secured party's obtaining knowledge of the sale or the secured party makes the advance pursuant to a commitment entered into without knowledge of the lien and before the expiration of a period of 45 days after the buyer's purchase. If the security interest is unperfected, the buyer gives value and the buyer has no knowledge of the security interest, the buyer acquires its interest in the collateral free of the secured party's security interest.

Negotiable Documents. During the period that goods are in the possession of a bailee who has issued a negotiable document covering the goods, a security interest perfected in the negotiable document has priority over a security interest perfected in the goods during that period. In addition, where goods are evidenced by a negotiable document, a holder of the negotiable document to whom the negotiable document has been duly negotiated prevails over an earlier security interest in the goods to the extent provided in UCC Article 7.

Instruments. A security interest in an instrument perfected by filing is generally subordinate to the interest of another secured party or other purchaser if the other secured party or other purchaser takes possession of the instrument for value, in good faith and without knowledge that the purchase violates the rights of the secured party that perfected by filing. A holder in due course of a negotiable instrument has priority over an earlier secured party to the extent set forth in UCC Article 3.

Chattel Paper.

Generally. If a security interest in chattel paper is perfected only by filing, not by possession of tangible chattel paper or control of electronic chattel paper, an ordinary course new value purchaser of the chattel paper who takes possession of the tangible chattel paper or control of the electronic chattel paper in good faith has priority over the security interest so long as the purchaser is without knowledge that the purchase violates the secured party's rights. If the secured party's interest is legended on the chattel paper, the purchaser is viewed to have knowledge that the purchase will violate the secured party's rights.

"Merely as Proceeds." An ordinary course new value purchaser of chattel paper who takes possession of tangible chattel paper or control of electronic chattel paper in good faith will have priority over a security interest in the chattel paper claimed "merely as proceeds" by an existing secured party who has perfected its security interest by filing, even if the purchaser knows of the security interest, so long as the secured party's interest is not legended on the chattel paper.

"New Value." Article 9 defines "new value," with one exception, to require additional monetary or other specific consideration. The one exception is where an inventory secured party, by taking possession of tangible chattel paper or control of electronic chattel paper that is proceeds of its inventory collateral, would qualify for priority under . . . but for its failure to provide "new value." In that situation, the inventory secured party need not make an additional advance for value previously given by it to constitute "new value". . . .

Investment Property. A security interest in investment property perfected by control is superior to a security interest in the same investment property perfected by filing, even if control occurs after the time of filing. If competing security interests are each perfected by control, they rank in priority of the time of obtaining control. Even so, a security interest perfected by control in favor of the debtor's securities intermediary has priority over a security interest perfected by filing or other control. A secured party's possession by agreement of a security certificate in registered form, without any necessary indorsements, results in the secured party's security interest in the certificated security being superior to another secured party's security interest in the certificated security perfected by filing. Where investment property collateral is transferred to a person protected under UCC Article 8's adverse claim cutoff rules, the transferee remains protected under UCC Article 8.

Deposit Accounts. A security interest in a deposit account perfected by control is superior to a security interest in the deposit account perfected by another method (e.g., in the case where a security interest in original collateral, other than the deposit account, was perfected and the secured party holding that security interest has an automatically perfected security interest in the deposit account as proceeds of the original collateral). If competing security interests are each perfected by control, they rank in priority of the time of obtaining control. But a security interest perfected by control in favor of the debtor's depositary bank, and the depositary bank's right of recoupment or set-off, are superior to a security interest of a competing secured party perfected by control or another method unless the competing secured party obtained perfection by control by becoming the depositary bank's customer on the deposit account. A transferee of funds from a deposit account in which the secured party has a security interest takes free of the secured party's security interest unless the transferee acts in collusion with the debtor in violating the rights of the secured party.

Letter-of-Credit Rights. A security interest in a letter-of-credit right perfected by control is superior to a security interest in a letter-of-credit right perfected automatically as a supporting obligation. If competing security interests in the letter-of-credit right are each perfected by control, they rank in priority of the time of obtaining control. A security interest in a letter-of-credit right is subordinate to the rights of a transferee beneficiary or nominated person[.] . . .

Claimants as to Proceeds.

Definition. Proceeds are whatever is received upon the sale, exchange or other disposition or collection of collateral. Investment property distributions, partnership and limited liability company interest distributions, rentals for the lease of goods, and licensing royalties are all proceeds of the underlying collateral. Claims arising out of the loss, nonconformity or interference with the collateral are also proceeds.

Attachment. Upon the sale, exchange or other disposition or collection of collateral, a secured party's security interest continues in any "identifiable" proceeds. Common law tracing rules, such as, for example, the "lowest intermediate balance" test when cash proceeds are commingled with other funds in a deposit account, may be used to determine what proceeds are identifiable.

Perfection. The perfection of the secured party's security interest in proceeds continues for a period of 20 days. Unless the proceeds are identifiable cash proceeds, the secured party may be required to take additional steps during that 20-day period to continue the perfection of its security interest beyond the 20-day period.

Priority Generally. A secured party's priority as to its security interest in the proceeds will usually date from the time of the secured party's priority as to its security interest in the original collateral for the purposes of applying the first-to-file-or-perfect priority rule. But an inventory purchase-money secured party entitled to priority over an earlier filed secured party has a priority security interest in proceeds of the inventory sold or otherwise disposed of only in limited circumstances:

- if the proceeds are identifiable cash proceeds received by the debtor on or before delivery of the inventory to the buyer,
- if the proceeds are instruments, chattel paper or proceeds of the chattel paper to which the purchase-money secured party, typically by taking possession of the instrument or chattel paper, is entitled to priority under § 9-330, or
- if the purchase-money security interest is in farm products livestock. Moreover, a transferee of money will take free of the interest of a secured party claiming the money as proceeds unless the transferee has acted in collusion with the debtor in violating the rights of the secured party.

Priority Where Certain Original Collateral Has Priority under a Non-temporal Perfection Rule. As discussed above, a perfected possessory or control security interest in a deposit account, investment property, a letter-of-credit right, chattel paper, an instrument or a negotiable document may have priority over a security interest perfected by an earlier filing. In these cases, the secured party with priority as to the original collateral and who has a perfected security interest in the proceeds also has priority in the proceeds if the proceeds are cash proceeds or are of the same type as the original collateral, and, in the case of proceeds that are proceeds of proceeds, any intervening proceeds are cash proceeds, are of the same type as the original collateral, or are an account relating to the collateral. In addition, under certain circumstances, priority in the proceeds is based upon the first to file rather than under the "first-to-file-or-perfect" priority rule. Those circumstances arise where:

- each secured party has a perfected security interest in a deposit account, investment property, a letter-of-credit right, chattel paper, an instrument or a negotiable document perfected by a method other than filing, and
- the proceeds are not cash proceeds or a deposit account, investment property, a letter-of-credit right, chattel paper, an instrument or a negotiable document.

Otherwise, the "first-to-file-or-perfect" priority rule applies as to the proceeds.

Returned or Repossessed Goods. . . . Article 9 treats returned or repossessed goods as proceeds of the accounts, chattel paper or other payment rights created when the goods were sold. Moreover, if a chattel paper purchaser has priority over a secured party claiming a security interest in the debtor's inventory, the chattel paper purchaser has priority over the inventory secured party on returned or repossessed goods arising from the chattel paper.

Agricultural Lien Proceeds. Article 9 does not address proceeds of an agricultural lien. Article 9 leaves to other law, presumably the statute under which the agricultural lien is created, whether the agricultural lien extends to proceeds and, if so, whether the agricultural lien in proceeds is perfected and what priority it has over a competing claimant.

Statutory and Agricultural Liens. A possessory lien on goods for services and materials furnished in the ordinary course given by statute or common law has priority over a secured party's security interest in the goods unless the lien is given by statute and the statute provides otherwise. If the lien is an agricultural lien, the general Article 9 priority rules apply unless the agricultural lien is given by statute and the statute provides otherwise.

Unpaid Sellers. An unpaid seller that has not taken a perfected purchase-money security interest entitled to priority in goods sold to a debtor will not usually prevail over a secured party of the debtor holding a perfected security interest in the goods acquired by the debtor. This is the case even if the unpaid seller has a reclamation claim to the goods under UCC Article 2. But an unpaid seller that retains possession of the goods that it sells to the debtor will have priority over a secured party of the debtor holding a perfected security interest in goods acquired by the debtor.

Real Estate Claimants as to Fixtures. A security interest in fixtures may be perfected by a regular Article 9 filing as to the goods or by a fixture filing filed at the office in the jurisdiction where real estate mortgages are recorded, and which provides that it is being filed in the real estate records. . . .

Crops. A perfected security interest in crops has priority over the interest of an owner or mortgagee of the real estate on which the crops are grown if the debtor is the owner or is in possession of the real estate.

Accessions. Article 9 generally leaves to the other priority rules set forth in part 3 of Article 9 the resolution for determining the priority between competing secured parties holding security interests in goods which are accessions, including the priority dispute between a security party holding a security interest in an accession and a secured party holding a security interest in the whole of the goods. However, a security interest in an accession is junior to a security interest in the whole perfected by compliance with a certificate of title statute. For example, in the event that a debtor grants to a secured party a security interest in a motor vehicle perfected by notation of the secured party's interest on the motor vehicle's certificate of title and the debtor also grants to a seller of tires to the debtor a security interest in the tires perfected automatically or by filing, the motor vehicle secured party will prevail as to the tires if the tires become accessions to the motor vehicle.

Commingled Goods. If goods in which one secured party has a perfected security interest are commingled with other goods in which another secured party has a perfected security interest, if neither secured party otherwise has a prior security interest in the other's goods, and if the identity of each secured party's collateral is lost in a product or mass, then each security party's security interest attaches to the product or mass. Their priority then ranks equally in accordance with a formula by which each secured party is allocated the proportion of the product or mass which the value of that secured party's collateral bore to the sum of the values of both parties' collateral at the time that the collateral became commingled.

Filing Office Records. Although the filing of a financing statement that is improperly rejected by the filing office is effective under [the] "tender rule," nevertheless the security interest is subordinate to the interest of a subsequent secured party or other purchaser giving value in reliance upon the clean record in the filing office. In addition, a secured party may, inadvertently or otherwise, file a financing statement containing information . . . that is incorrect. For example, the secured party may incorrectly state in the financing statement the type of organization or mailing address of the debtor. In such a case, the secured party's security interest is subordinate to a later perfected secured party, and a purchaser, other than a secured party, of the collateral takes free of the earlier secured party's security interest, if the later secured party or other purchaser gives value in reliance upon the incorrect information.

Creditors Senior by Contractual Subordination. Any secured party may contractually subordinate its security interest to a secured party or other person whose interest would not otherwise have priority.

Production-Money Secured Parties (Optional). Article 9 contains an optional set of model provisions for those jurisdictions that wish to provide a priority security interest, referred to as a <u>production-money security interest</u>, for extenders of new credit enabling a debtor to produce crops if the proceeds of the credit are in fact used for the production of the crops. These provisions . . . are analogous to the purchase-money security interest provisions for inventory[.] . . .

ENFORCEMENT

Article 9 sets forth various rights and remedies of a secured party with respect to the collateral upon the debtor's default. Article 9 also requires that the secured party proceed to enforce its security interest in ways which give minimum protections to the debtor and certain other interested parties.

. . .

PERSONAL BANKRUPTCY IN THE 21ST CENTURY: EMERGING TRENDS AND NEW CHALLENGES: VELVET BANKRUPTCY
David Hahn, 7 Theoretical Inq. L. 523 (2006)

A. THE REAL WORLD: PERSONAL GUARANTEES

Limited liability is considered to be one of the cornerstones of corporate law. Personal liability is a key element that a potential entrepreneur takes into account before engaging in business, and thus, limited liability is perhaps the single most important reason for incorporating. Nonetheless, the real world's landscape of small-medium enterprises (SMEs) depicts a strikingly different picture. A common practice for SMEs is that in order to obtain financing, usually in the form of a bank loan, the primary shareholder (the entrepreneur) is required by the bank to undertake a personal guarantee of the corporation's obligations to the bank. Indeed, the prevalence of personal undertakings by primary owners of businesses is documented in the literature on SMEs. Ronald Mann posited that the wide use of personal guarantees as security for bank loans to small businesses explains the existence of unsecured credit in this sector. His findings support the commonly accepted perception that lenders insist on obtaining the personal guarantee of the business owner in all but rare cases. Berger and Udell examined financing of small firms in the form of lines of credit. Their data show that 53% of the firms examined collateralize assets as security for the financing obtained, and 41% secure the financing by personal guarantees. Similarly, Avery, Bostic, and Samolyk found that for small firms, relying heavily on loan financing, the personal obligations of the owners are crucial for obtaining the requisite financing. According to their data, personal guarantees are more prevalent than personal collateral, although the two serve as complementary measures. Personal guarantees serve as practical substitutes for the collateralizing of corporate assets. Thus, firms short of assets available for collateralization will tend to rely on personal commitments of the owners.

The undertaking of a personal guarantee by the entrepreneur is a contractual bypass of the legal principle of limited liability. The result of this contractual opt-out is that the entrepreneur is protected by virtue of limited liability against most of the corporate creditors other than the bank. In other words, the personal

guarantee lifts the limited liability shield selectively. The protection of limited liability is contractually waived in favor of the SME's principal creditor, the bank. The
lending bank usually holds a large percentage of the aggregate claims against the
SME. Thus, effectively, despite the de jure protection of limited liability, de facto
the entrepreneur is exposed to significant personal liability vis-à-vis the bank. The
theoretical premise of limited liability as an entrepreneur-friendly feature of incorporation is simply outdated.

B. THE NORMATIVE ROLE OF PERSONAL GUARANTEES

It has been shown that under contemporary corporate law, limited liability is a
baseline principle, from which SMEs invariably deviate selectively in favor of their
lending bank. This begs the question: What economic purpose is served by the
personal guarantee, and should this purpose be condoned by the law? One possible
purpose could simply be the desire of the bank to enhance its collection rights,
should the SME default on its loan. For those firms whose assets would prove insufficient to pay off the loan, a personal guarantee widens the pool of assets available
for payment to the lenders. In addition, to the extent that the lender is concerned
with its priority vis-à-vis the other corporate creditors, a personal guarantee allows
the lender to enjoy a private source of collection in which it does not share pro rata
with the other creditors.

However, interestingly enough, the use of personal guarantees is not correlated
with the owner's personal wealth. Even owners with very few collectible assets are
often required to sign a personal guarantee. In addition, such an explanation of
the personal guarantee arrangement is troubling. Of all the SME's creditors, only
banks, the most sophisticated and diversified creditors, are careful to enhance their
collection rights. Other creditors: trade creditors, the government, employees,
and tort creditors, do not enjoy such an economic benefit. Like insurance companies, because of the large number and diversification of their unrelated customers,
banks are the most efficient risk-bearers of the borrowers' defaults. Easterbrook and
Fischel explained the rationale of limited liability by relying on the banks' superior
risk-bearing capabilities. Why, then, would the most efficient risk-bearer contract
around limited liability while the other creditors remain to bear its legal consequences? If limited liability altogether is unsatisfactory and has gone bankrupt, then
it should be abolished and all creditors should be able to collect from the entrepreneur. But if the law still recognizes the virtue of limited liability, then the preferential
treatment of lending banks invites a different justification for personal guarantees.

A bank's demand of a personal guarantee from an SME's entrepreneur
serves as a bonding device that combats the perils of excessive risk-taking at the
corporate level. It was shown earlier that the economic cost of limited liability
is the risk of overinvestment by the entrepreneur. The effective way to reduce
this hazard is to take away some of the protection that the entrepreneur enjoys
and expose her to some personal liability. By tying the entrepreneur's personal
wealth to the results of the corporation's business performance, the controlling
person — the entrepreneur — is expected to manage the business with more
restraint and financial responsibility. As the controlling person, the entrepreneur is most likely the most efficient risk-avoider in the SME. By undertaking personal liability the entrepreneur internalizes the risks of the SME failure. Shifting
the risk of insolvency from the most efficient risk-bearer (the lending bank) to

the most-efficient risk-avoider (the entrepreneur) lowers the probability of its occurrence. This, in turn, reduces the lender's costs associated with dealing with the corporate entity, whose owners enjoy limited liability under corporate law. The selectivity of this shift, that is, that only the bank enjoys the personal liability of the entrepreneur while the other creditors continue to bear the SME's risk of failure, may be explained as a matter of agency. Among corporate creditors, the bank is best positioned to monitor effectively, and at the lowest cost, the actions of the SME and its controlling entrepreneur. The other creditors can enjoy these monitoring services of the bank. The personal guarantee may be explained as the legal device that effectuates the bank's monitoring. By allowing the bank to collect from the entrepreneur, should the SME default, the bank is provided with an enforceable legal measure to keep the entrepreneur at bay. The bank receives an exclusive guarantee in exchange for the benefit the SME's other creditors enjoy. Otherwise, the other creditors would likely free-ride and the bank's incentive to monitor would decrease.

C. THE COSTS OF PERSONAL GUARANTEES

In the context of SMEs, the pendulum has swung from full entrepreneur protection under limited liability to significant entrepreneur exposure by virtue of the practice of personal guarantees. While the personal guarantee mitigates the moral hazard of excessive risk-taking, it nonetheless comes with some costs of its own. First and foremost, personal guarantees are liable to be used excessively by the lending industry, thus creating unnecessary costs for borrowers. In addition, many entrepreneurs are risk-averse and thus would underinvest as a result of the guarantees. . . .

Notes and Questions

1. Article 9 of the UCC states that a security interest in goods may be perfected either by possession or by filing a UCC-1 Financing Statement in the appropriate office. In practice, secured parties generally perfect a security interest in goods by filing rather than by possession. Discuss why this is the case.

2. Why is it important for a potential lender to know whether the company seeking financing has existing secured debt when deciding whether to make a secured loan? Why is it not sufficient for the lender to simply require the debtor to disclose existing debt as opposed to the lender ordering its own UCC searches (which is what lenders do in practice prior to funding a loan)? If there were no system in place that allowed a lender to search existing liens, what effect would this have on the lending industry and the availability of debt financing for businesses?

3. What are some reasons a bank would require a founder of a business to sign a personal guarantee for a business loan? Are there any reasons a bank may require such a guarantee in the event the founder does not have significant personal assets? How does the founder's guarantee affect the limited liability protection afforded to the founder by organizing the business as a corporation or limited liability company?

4. Your client's friends have started a company, Cunningham's Candy Co. (the "Company"), selling a new type of candy. On September 1, 2006 your

client lends her friends $50,000. Without your help, your client drafts a simple promissory note evidencing the loan and showing the terms of repayment. On September 1, 2007, the Company obtains a loan from ABC Bank secured by the Company's assets. On November 15, 2007, ABC Bank files a UCC financing statement (with the correct office) listing all of the Company's assets as collateral. On November 1, 2007, the Company obtains a loan from Gold Brick Bank. Gold Brick pre-files its UCC financing statement (with the correct office) also listing all of the Company's assets as collateral. On March 15, 2008, the Company receives a default letter from ABC Bank and subsequently receives a default letter from Gold Brick Bank. Although the Company had a few big accounts, it was not able to keep up with the scheduled repayments from the banks. Sometime in April, the Company files for bankruptcy. The Company has approximately $15,000 worth of inventory and accounts receivables totaling $80,000. There is $43,000 still outstanding on your client's loan, over $200,000 owed to ABC Bank, and $100,000 owed to Gold Brick Bank. Your client feels somewhat relieved that there is enough money to pay back her loan. However, each bank argues that it is entitled to the entire $95,000. Your client thinks that is unfair since she made her loan first. Who wins? Why is this a fair result, and specifically what are the policy assumptions underlying the result?

5. Your client, Cape Cod Cranberry, LLC, has secured a new business loan and needs to determine how much it can borrow under the revolving facility. Your client has come to you for help. Assume your client has $1,000,000 of eligible accounts and $3,000,000 of eligible inventory. Also, assume the borrowing base formula is set forth below. What is your client's availability? Is there any other information you need to know?

> LOANS: Subject to the terms and conditions of this Agreement, so long as no Event of Default is then continuing, Bank shall advance an amount to Borrower up to the sum of the following sublimits (the "Loan Limit"):
>
> > a. Up to seventy percent (70%) of the face amount (less maximum discounts, credits, and allowances which may be taken or granted to Account Debtors in connection therewith in the ordinary course of such Borrower's business) of such Borrower's Eligible Accounts; plus
> >
> > b. Up to sixty percent (60%) of the lower of the cost or market value of such Borrower's Eligible Inventory (as determined by an appraiser acceptable to Bank during each calendar year); minus
> >
> > c. Such reserves as Bank elects, in its sole discretion, to establish from time to time; provided, that the Loan Limit for Borrower shall in no event exceed $2,000,000 (the "Maximum Loan Limit") provided, that Bank may, in its sole discretion, elect from time to time to make loans in excess of the Maximum Loan Limit.

PROBLEM

Assume Olivia and Andrew organized their business as a corporation called "General Germ, Inc." and have been operating for a year or so with some success. In a prior transaction (and without your help), they sold 5 percent of the outstanding common shares to friends and family for a total equity infusion of $500,000 (which assumes a $10 million post-money valuation of the company). They did not ask their friends and family to sign any kind of Shareholders Agreement. General

Germ also borrowed money from Olivia's Aunt Helen pursuant to the terms of this promissory note:

PROMISSORY NOTE

FOR VALUE RECEIVED, General Germ, Inc., an Illinois corporation (the "Company"), hereby promises to pay to the order of Helen Nathan ("Payee"), the principal amount of One Hundred Fifty Thousand Dollars ($150,000) (the "Principal Amount"), plus interest on the unpaid Principal Amount outstanding, in lawful money of the United States of America, which interest shall begin to accrue quarterly on the date hereof. From the date hereof through the Maturity Date, interest shall accrue quarterly at an annual rate equal to the rate of interest publicly announced from time to time by the Bank of America, N.A. as its reference rate or prime rate.

The Principal Amount and any interest accrued and unpaid on the unpaid Principal Amount shall be due and payable in full seven years from the date hereof (the "Maturity Date").

The Company, at any time and from time to time, without premium or penalty, may prepay the Principal Amount in whole or in part (provided that any partial prepayment shall be in an integral multiple of $1,000), together with all interest accrued and unpaid on the amount prepaid to the date of prepayment.

In the event that the Company (i) generally ceases to pay its debts as they become due, (ii) makes a general assignment for the benefit of creditors, (iii) files any petition under any bankruptcy or insolvency law or (iv) has filed against it any such petition or commenced against it any action for the appointment of a receiver or trustee and that filing or action is not stayed or dismissed within 60 days after the filing or commencement thereof, then the Principal Amount and all accrued and unpaid interest thereon immediately shall become due and payable in full. The Company shall pay all costs and expenses incurred by the Payee for the collection of all sums due hereunder after the occurrence and during the continuation of any event listed in the immediately preceding sentence, including reasonable attorneys' fees and expenses and court costs.

This Note shall be governed by and construed in accordance with the laws of the State of Illinois.

[General Germ Signature Block and Date]

Olivia and Andrew have planned a significant expansion, and have come to you with several questions regarding raising money.

1. General Germ, Inc. has been approached by Vulture Venture Capital LLC. VVC wants to acquire a new class of stock of General Germ: Series A Participating Preferred Stock. The Series A will have a liquidation preference of twice the amount invested, plus it will participate alongside the common stock after the preferred return has been paid. The Series A will represent 25 percent of the total post-money outstanding shares of General Germ. Another attribute of the Series A is that it will permit VVC to appoint two members of the six-member board of directors of

General Germ. VVC proposes to pay $3,000,000 for its 25 percent interest (which assumes a $12 million post-money valuation of the company).

(a) Olivia and Andrew ask whether they need the permission of (i) his friends and family investors, and (ii) Aunt Helen as a lender, to accept VVC's investment terms.

(b) Uncle John, who initially bought $100,000 of General Germ common stock, has discovered that VVC's proposed investment terms are more favorable than his. He demands comparable treatment for himself, as if he had invested his $100,000 in the Series A round.

(c) VVC has also expressed its strong desire to buy out the existing friends and family investors at the same price they paid for the equity plus a modest return on their investment. They think the investors should jump at this opportunity, since they are getting a premium over the price VVC is paying for the Series A Preferred. They have hinted that if they can't buy out the pesky friends and family, they may walk away from the investment entirely. What advice will you give your client?

2. Both VVC and General Germ are well aware that the $2 million equity infusion will not be sufficient to finance the planned expansion. Together they have approached Mezzo Soprano Lenders to try to concurrently obtain bank debt. Mezzo has proposed a $3 million loan secured by the assets of General Germ and a personal guarantee by Andrew and Olivia.

(a) Olivia knows that Aunt Helen was comfortable making her loan because she knew that General Germ has substantial assets and because Olivia is financially well off. She asks you how the Mezzo debt would affect Aunt Helen's ability to be repaid in the event General Germ fails and is forced to file for bankruptcy. She also asks for your advice on what she should communicate to Aunt Helen.

(b) Andrew asks you whether he should sign the personal guaranty, and what are the repercussions.

VI

EMPLOYMENT LAW

Many successful entrepreneurs have said that they would rather have a B idea and an A team to execute the idea than the reverse. The decision of whom to hire is one of the most important predictors of the ultimate success or failure of a business. Therefore, it is not a surprise that entrepreneurs will put a great deal of thought and energy into hiring a management team as well as other workers.

However, from the moment a new venture begins the process of hiring its first worker, the entrepreneur is hit with a barrage of legal considerations based on state and federal statutes, regulations, and common law rules. Without paying close attention to the law, a new venture can inadvertently create significant legal problems. It must determine the worker's correct classification as an employee or otherwise, provide required protections and benefits, manage expectations, and minimize liability. By ignoring the rules that govern this area, a new venture can face expensive litigation and incur substantial penalties.

Later, this chapter discusses many of the key federal employment statutes and laws. We primarily examine laws that prohibit discrimination and provide workplace benefits to employees. Although we focus on federal legislation, states often impose additional restrictions on employers and provide employees with broader rights and protections. Therefore, as is the case with every issue on which lawyers advise clients, it is crucial to consider applicable state law.

Many of the federal laws we review only apply to workers who fall into the category of "employees." Workers hired as "independent contractors" are not subject to these laws. In fact, many companies attempt to hire independent contractors instead of employees for this very reason. Said another way, such companies attempt to classify workers as independent contractors as opposed to employees, in order to avoid the application of employment laws and gain other benefits discussed below. However, there is a legal distinction between employees and independent contractors and the classification is not something the worker and company can agree to on their own. Courts (and the Internal Revenue Service) will apply myriad factors to determine if a worker was properly classified. Similarly, there are legal requirements that must be satisfied in order to properly classify someone as an unpaid intern. Even if a worker is willing and perhaps eager for an unpaid internship, this interest alone is not sufficient. Therefore, it is important to understand how to classify workers — and we begin this chapter by examining the distinction between an independent contractor and an employee.

A. WORKER CLASSIFICATION: INDEPENDENT CONTRACTORS VERSUS EMPLOYEES

When a company hires someone as an independent contractor as opposed to an employee, the company is not required to withhold income taxes, pay Social Security and Medicare taxes, or provide workers' compensation insurance or various other employee benefits. As noted above, the company is also not subject to many employment laws. It is easy to understand why companies (especially start-ups with limited cash) often try to classify workers as independent contractors. However, it is crucial to properly classify workers as either independent contractors or employees because misclassification yields significant penalties for the company and, in some cases, the company's individual managers. Additionally, in the absence of a written agreement, the distinction between an employee and an independent contractor affects ownership of work product created by a worker. The following case examines many of the factors used to properly differentiate employees from independent contractors under a "control" test and discusses the impact of such determination.

JUSTMED, INC. v. BYCE
United States Court of Appeals for the Ninth Circuit
600 F.3d 1118 (2010)

At the heart of this case is a dispute over whether a small technology start-up company owns the source code developed for its product. Its informal employment practices raise questions as to whether defendant-appellant Michael Byce was an employee when he developed the source code. After a bench trial, the district court entered judgment and ordered a permanent injunction against Byce, in favor of plaintiff-appellee JustMed, Inc., Byce's former employer. Among other things, the district court found that JustMed owns the software program used on its digital audio larynx device under the work-for-hire doctrine of the Federal Copyright Act, because Byce wrote the source code for the company as an employee, not as an independent contractor. The district court also found that Byce misappropriated the software under the Idaho Trade Secrets Act. Byce appeals both rulings. We . . . affirm in part and reverse in part.

I

Joel Just and Michael Byce are former brothers-in-law who together developed the idea of a digital audio larynx, a device to help laryngectomees — individuals whose larynxes have been surgically removed — produce clearer speech. Both have degrees in electrical engineering and experience working in the computer industry.

Initially, the two began discussing the idea in 1994 on a family vacation. Just and Byce brainstormed ideas for how to advance such devices — in particular how to produce a hands-free device, rather than one that required the user to hold the device against the throat — and, in 1995, they applied for a patent as co-inventors of a "system and method for monitoring the oral and nasal cavity," which was issued to them in 1998.

Byce worked on the project between 1995 and 1998, but no one did any further work on the device from 1999 — when Byce's wife, the sister of Just's wife Ann, unexpectedly died — until 2003. Then, in 2003, Joel and Ann Just formed JustMed, Inc., based in Beaverton, Oregon, to continue development of the product. Just recruited a former business associate, Jerome Liebler, to help work on the idea. He offered founders' options to Byce, and Byce ultimately invested $25,000 in return for 130,000 shares. Byce also accepted a position on JustMed's board of directors, serving with the Justs.

Just and Liebler worked full time developing a new hardware prototype and writing source code for the product. Liebler wrote a majority of the code, working at his home on his own computers. The code was never released outside of the company, and notices on the code stated that it was copyrighted by JustMed, although the code was not registered with the United States Copyright Office.

Since it was not yet producing a product, the company operated financially by selling shares to family members and by relying on loans from the Justs. Just and Liebler did not receive a cash salary and instead were compensated with shares of stock.

By the summer of 2004, JustMed had a marketable product called "JusTalk." Liebler, however, moved to Kentucky, making it difficult for him to continue his work on the product. At the same time, Byce expressed interest in becoming more involved with the company. Liebler was still drawing half of his salary, but agreed to have the whole package — at that point, $90,000 per year, paid as 15,000 shares per month, each share valued at 50 cents — transferred to Byce and to have Byce take over development of the source code.

At trial, Just testified that Byce was hired as an employee to replace Liebler, who was also an employee, and that Byce agreed to be paid a salary in shares of stock. Byce, on the other hand, testified that while he expected to be adequately compensated in shares upon transferring ownership of the source code, he never understood himself to be an employee and had no "explicit knowledge" that he was accruing shares as compensation.

JustMed and Byce had no written employment agreement. Byce never filled out an I-9 employment verification form or, until 2005, a W-4 tax withholding form. At most, Just documented Byce's salary and duties in a notebook that he kept, although the notation indicating when Byce started was not recorded until several months after Byce began working on the source code. Although Byce began full-time work on the source code in September 2004 and began accruing JustMed stock in October, he never received share certificates for the stock he received as compensation. Indeed, the company generally did not keep formal records other than a series of notebooks Just maintained to track conversations and events. While Byce worked for JustMed, the company did not issue Byce a W-2 wage statement form, withhold taxes, or pay workers' compensation or unemployment insurance. Nor did the company provide benefits for Byce or report his employment to the state. Just testified that he did not think much of this was necessary because he thought of Byce as a JustMed "executive," and because JustMed was modeled on prior startup technology businesses that

Just had been involved with, where employees were paid exclusively in stock and the stock was never reported as income because of its uncertain value.

Although Byce was carrying on Liebler's duties, Byce operated differently, because he did not live and work in Oregon as Liebler had. Instead, Byce worked from his home in Boise, Idaho, using his own computer. Just provided Byce with the original code created by Liebler and various materials necessary to Byce's development work, including JusTalk units, schematics, data sheets, batteries, chargers, assemblers, source code, and headsets. Byce set his own hours, often working late into the night, and Just did not tell him how to spend his days. As Byce developed new versions of the source code, he would e-mail the new version to Just, who would compile it and load it onto the JusTalk to evaluate its performance. Whereas Just had previously worked side-by-side with Liebler, Just and Byce often communicated by phone or e-mail, and occasionally would meet in Boise or Portland or somewhere in between. The two exchanged ideas and discussed the functionality of the code, as well as improvements that needed to be made. Just, admittedly a poor programmer, never made changes to the source code, and by the time this dispute arose, Byce had substantially rewritten the source code Liebler had developed. According to Byce, only 21 lines of code from the last version Liebler worked on remained, out of approximately 3500 to 4000 lines total.

While he was working on the source code, Byce was included in the company profile brochure and had a JustMed business card. He was alternatively referred to as the "Director of Research and Development" and the "Director of Engineering," the latter title supplied by Byce himself. Although he was primarily working on the source code, Byce also updated the company Web site and attended conferences, marketing meetings, and demonstrations on behalf of JustMed.

Because he was not earning money, Byce was living on credit, and by May 2005 he was worried about his financial situation. He told Just that he would soon need cash. In response, Just agreed to have JustMed pay Byce half in cash and half in shares. Byce filled out a W-4 form, and the company issued three checks for him as payment for May, June, and July 2005.

Byce, however, never cashed the checks. At this point, Byce became concerned that Just did not view him as an equal in the corporation. In order to protect what he perceived as his intellectual property, Byce changed the copyright statement on the software, so that it now read "Copyright (c) Mike Byce 2005" instead of copyright JustMed.

Then, while Byce was working in the Oregon office two days before Just was scheduled to meet with a potential merger or buy-out partner, Byce deleted all copies of the source code from JustMed's computers. Byce testified that he made the decision after seeing a spreadsheet showing a large disparity between the number of shares Byce owned and those shares that the Justs and Liebler owned. In its memorandum decision, the district court found that Byce deleted the code to gain leverage over Just in Byce's efforts to acquire a greater share of the company. The next day, Byce raised with Just the disparity in ownership between Byce and the other primary shareholders. The two talked for several hours, but Just declined to give additional shares to Byce. During this conversation, Byce did not mention that he had deleted the source code from JustMed's computers.

Just still had a recent version of the object code loaded on a JusTalk unit, but after flying to Chicago for his demonstration meeting, Just could not get the unit to work. Hoping this was a curable problem, Just tried to recompile the source code on his laptop and then load it onto the unit, only to discover that he no longer had a copy of the source code. Just called Byce about the missing code, but Byce claimed to have assumed "revision control," meaning that he had removed the source code to insure that no one else would make changes to it.

Only upon returning to Oregon did Just realize that Byce had deleted the source code from all of JustMed's computers. Just was able to recover some prior versions of the source code files, but not the most recent one. Byce later returned the latest version of the source code, with some of the programmer's notes removed, but only after JustMed filed suit against Byce and the Idaho state court issued a temporary restraining order. Because Just did not trust the code he received from Byce, JustMed has since worked from older versions of the code to develop the device.

JustMed filed suit in state court, and Byce removed the case to federal court, asserting that it required determination of ownership of the software under the Copyright Act. The district court denied JustMed's motion to remand after it decided that the case required application of federal copyright law, in particular, the work-for-hire doctrine. Byce later counterclaimed, seeking a judgment declaring that he is the sole author and owner of the software under the Copyright Act. JustMed asserted only state law claims, including misappropriation of a trade secret, conversion, breach of fiduciary duty, and intentional interference with a prospective economic advantage.

After a bench trial, the district court found in favor of JustMed and held that Byce was an employee when he wrote the software, so that JustMed owned the copyright to the software. The court also found Byce liable for misappropriation of a trade secret, conversion, and breach of his fiduciary duty. This timely appeal followed.

. . .

A

Under the Copyright Act of 1976, copyright ownership "vests initially in the author or authors of the work."[3] An exception exists, however, for "works made for hire," in which case "the employer or other person for whom the work was prepared is considered the author" and owns the copyright, unless there is a written agreement to the contrary. As it is relevant here, a "work made for hire" is "a work prepared by an employee within the scope of his or her employment." Thus, whether Byce owns the source code copyright turns on whether he was an employee of JustMed or an independent contractor.[4]

The Supreme Court has explained that absent any textual indications to the contrary, when Congress uses the terms "employee," "employer," or "scope of employment," it means to incorporate principles from the general common law of agency. Accordingly, "the hiring party's right to control the manner and means by which the product is accomplished" is the central inquiry here. Factors relevant to this inquiry include: the skill required for that occupation, the source of the instrumentalities and tools, the location of the work, the duration of the relationship between the parties, whether the hiring party has the right to assign additional projects to the hired party, the extent of the hired party's discretion over when and how long to work, the method of payment, the hired party's role in hiring and paying assistants, whether the work is part of the regular business of the hiring party,

---

3. Computer software, including the source and object codes, can be subject to copyright protection.

4. The parties do not appear to dispute that if Byce was an employee, he was acting within the scope of his employment when he wrote the source code.

whether the hiring party is in business, the provision of employee benefits, and the tax treatment of the hired party. Because "the common-law test contains no shorthand formula or magic phrase that can be applied to find the answer, all of the incidents of the relationship must be assessed and weighed with no one factor being decisive." Nationwide Mut. Ins. Co. v. Darden, 503 U.S. 318, 324, 112 S. Ct. 1344, 117 L. Ed. 2d 581 (1992); see also Aymes v. Bonelli, 980 F.2d 857, 861 (2d Cir. 1992) ("It does not necessarily follow that because no one factor is dispositive all factors are equally important, or indeed that all factors will have relevance in every case. The factors should not merely be tallied but should be weighed according to their significance in the case.").

Byce argues on appeal that the district court improperly weighed the factors and ignored crucial facts, especially JustMed's tax treatment of Byce, the failure to provide him with benefits, the failure to fill out appropriate employment forms, the lack of any written agreement regarding Byce's employment or salary, and the lack of stock certificates for shares Byce was accruing.

However, taking the various factors into account, we conclude that the district court did not err in finding that Byce was an employee. In particular, the contemplated duration of the relationship, the tasks Byce did for JustMed, the fact that Byce earned a salary from JustMed, and the nature of JustMed's business all support the finding that Byce was an employee. While no one factor is decisive, we draw some guidance in weighing the factors from JustMed's status as a technology start-up company. The evidence of the way JustMed operates gives support to the finding that Byce was an employee. Admittedly, some of the factors that Byce points to support his position, but mostly they are entitled to little weight when viewed in light of the way JustMed conducts its business.

JustMed hired Byce primarily to work on the JusTalk software, but he was not hired for a specific term or with a discretely defined end product in mind. JustMed continuously worked on the source code to improve its effectiveness and capability. Although Byce's work on the source code lasted only nine months, it was halted not because the code's development had reached a logical termination point but because of the parties' dispute. Thus, the fact that the parties contemplated a relationship of indefinite duration cuts in favor of finding Byce an employee.

Byce did other work for JustMed as well. He updated the company's Web site and demonstrated the JusTalk units at tradeshows. Byce had previously worked on the Web site when he acted only as a director and shareholder for the company, but his continued work on tasks besides programming indicates JustMed could have assigned additional projects to Byce. Moreover, his formal title indicates that he had broad duties within JustMed, as well as a relationship with the company that was intended to be permanent.

JustMed hired Byce to replace Liebler, an employee, and paid him the same salary that Liebler received.[5] At trial Byce disputed that there was any agreement as to

---

5. While an employer's designation of a person as an employee or independent contractor is not always relevant because employers often have an incentive to designate an individual as one or the other, see, e.g., Vizcaino v. Microsoft Corp., 97 F.3d 1187, 1189 (9th Cir. 1996) ("Large corporations have increasingly adopted the practice of hiring temporary employees or independent contractors as a means of avoiding payment of employee benefits, and thereby increasing their profits."), aff'd en banc, 120 F.3d 1006 (9th Cir. 1997), both Liebler and JustMed believed they had an employee-employer relationship. This fact cuts in favor of similarly finding Byce an employee, as he essentially stepped into Liebler's role. That Byce replaced Liebler also indicates that the JusTalk software was an ongoing concern for the company, not a discrete project that JustMed expected Byce to simply finish and be done with.

how he would be paid, and Byce continues to argue that the lack of a written agreement regarding salary and the lack of stock certificates undermine the salience of this factor. But the district court did not find credible Byce's inability to recall what he was being paid and how. Although independent contractors are often paid upon completion of a specific job, see *CCNV*, 490 U.S. at 753 (independent contractor was to be paid upon completion of sculpture), Byce was paid a regular monthly salary in the same way as other JustMed employees. This weighs heavily in favor of finding him an employee, even though much of the salary came in the form of stock.

Also militating in favor of JustMed is the fact that its primary business was the development and marketing of the JusTalk device. Byce's work was integral to JustMed's regular business, since the JusTalk cannot work without functioning software. Cf. *Aymes*, 980 F.2d at 863 (finding programming work for swimming pool company not part of the firm's regular business but stating that "work done by a computer programmer employed by a computer software firm would be done in the firm's regular business"). Indeed, there is evidence that JustMed tried to sell consumers on the JusTalk precisely by emphasizing that the software could constantly be updated. It seems highly unlikely that JustMed would leave such an important, continuous responsibility to an independent contractor who would terminate his relationship with the company upon completing a working version of the software.

While some factors initially seem to favor Byce, on closer examination they are insufficient to find him an independent contractor.[6]

It is true, for example, that Just did not exercise much control over the manner and means by which Byce created the source code. However, this is not as important to a technology start-up as it might be to an established company. Byce was an inventive computer programmer expected to work independently.[7] The business model and Byce's duties do not require that the project be completed in a particular manner or that Just continuously oversee Byce's work, so long as JustMed eventually found itself with a marketable product. Moreover, Just did have some input into Byce's work on the software, even if it was given by e-mail and phone. Cf. id. at 862 (input from client regarding computer program's functions "weighs heavily in favor of finding [programmer] . . . an employee"); but see *CCNV*, 490 U.S. at 752 ("[T]he extent of control the hiring party exercises over the details of the product is not dispositive.").

The nature of the business and the work similarly means that Byce's ability to set his own hours and the fact that he worked from home are not particularly relevant. As a programmer, Byce could, in essence, ply his craft at any time and from any place without significant impairment to its quality or his ability to meet JustMed's needs. So although physical separation between the hiring party and the worker is often relevant to determining employment status, it is less germane in light of the kind of work Byce was doing. Of course, computer programming is a skilled profession, which weighs in favor of finding Byce not an employee, but given the other factors and the fact that JustMed's regular business requires it to employ programmers, we find this far from conclusive.

Byce's strongest argument turns on JustMed's failure to pay benefits and fill out the appropriate employment forms, and JustMed's tax treatment of Byce. Some courts have relied heavily on these factors as "highly probative of the true nature of the employment relationship." There is a danger, however, in relying on them

---

6. Some of the factors also are inconclusive. For example, Byce was unlikely to need additional help, so it is not relevant who might pay for this hypothetical extra help.

7. In this regard, see Restatement (Second) of Agency § 220, comment e, which explains that "[t]he custom of the community as to the control ordinarily exercised in a particular occupation is of importance."

too heavily, because they do not bear directly on the substance of the employment relationship — the right to control. In this case, the factors do not decisively favor Byce, especially when one considers JustMed's business model.

We note Byce did eventually fill out a W-4 form and have taxes withheld once he started receiving paychecks from JustMed. The tax treatment here is therefore more ambiguous than in other copyright cases where courts have relied on the hiring party's treatment of the hired party as an independent contractor — for example, by not withholding taxes and by giving the hired party 1099 forms — and only later asserted that the individual was an employee. While an inherent unfairness exists in a company claiming a worker to be an independent contractor in one context but an employee in another, that is not the case here.

JustMed's treatment of Byce with regard to taxes, benefits, and employment forms is more likely attributable to the start-up nature of the business than to Byce's alleged status as an independent contractor. The indications are that other employees, for example Liebler, were treated similarly. Insofar as JustMed did not comply with federal and state employment or tax laws, we do not excuse its actions, but in this context the remedy for these failings lies not with denying the firm its intellectual property but with enforcing the relevant laws.

As a small start-up company, JustMed conducted its business more informally than an established enterprise might. This fact can make it more difficult to decide whether a hired party is an employee or an independent contractor, but it should not make the company more susceptible to losing control over software integral to its product. Weighing the common law factors in light of the circumstances and JustMed's business, we conclude that the district court did not err in holding that Byce was an employee and that the source code was a work made for hire.

. . .

CONCLUSION

For the foregoing reasons, we agree with the district court that Byce was an employee of JustMed at the time he wrote the JusTalk source code, and that JustMed owns the software. . . .

Notes and Questions

1. Why do you think it is the case that a worker and a business owner may not simply agree between themselves as to whether the worker will be considered an employee or an independent contractor? What public policy concerns are at play?

2. The court acknowledged that Byce worked from his own home, used his own computer, set his own hours, and was not told how to spend his days. He was not provided with benefits and JustMed failed to fill out appropriate employment forms. The court admitted that some of these factors that Byce pointed out did support his position that he was an independent contractor. However, the court stated that those factors were "entitled to little weight when viewed in light of the way JustMed conducts its business." What advice would you have given Byce at the onset of his relationship with JustMed if he had come to you as his attorney to help ensure he would be considered an independent contractor?

3. As you learned in Chapter 4, intellectual property created by workers may or may not automatically be owned by the company, depending on whether the worker

is an employee or an independent contractor. Since ownership of source code was a key issue for JustMed, what advice might you have given to JustMed in 2004 concerning the work Byce was doing?

4. If a person or business is hiring a worker and is not certain as to whether the worker should be classified as an employee or independent contractor, the Internal Revenue Service provides the option of completing the SS-8 form (Determination of Worker Status) and receiving a determination as to worker classification from the IRS. In making its determinations, the IRS looks at behavioral control (asking such questions as whether the company or the worker decides when and how the worker does her work), financial control (asking such questions as whether the worker provides their own supplies, how the worker is paid, and who bears financial risks associated with the worker's work) and the relationship of the parties (asking such questions as whether the company provides benefits to the worker, whether the worker has his own business, and whether the worker has signed a non-compete). Generally, the more independence and control the worker has over his work and profit, the more likely the worker will be found to be an independent contractor. What are some of the pros and cons of completing and submitting the SS-8 form that you would mention to a client who is a hiring a new worker and prefers to classify the worker as an independent contractor, but is not sure that is the proper choice?

Common law on the issue of worker classification and classification tests vary from state to state and sometimes even within states. The California Supreme Court's decision in Dynamex Operations West, Inc. v. Superior Court of Los Angeles reexamined the existing judicial standard in California for distinguishing independent contractors from employees in classifying workers for purposes of California wage orders and the "ABC" test.

> Under the ABC test, a worker is deemed to be an employee unless the employer shows:
> (A) that the worker is free from the control and direction of the hiring entity in connection with the performance of the work, both under the contract for the performance of the work and in fact;
> (B) that the worker performs work that is outside the usual course of the hiring entity's business; and
> (C) that the worker is customarily engaged in an independently established trade, occupation, or business of the same nature as the work performed.

DYNAMEX OPERATIONS WEST v. SUPERIOR COURT
Supreme Court of California (2018)
4 Cal. 5th 903

Under both California and federal law, the question whether an individual worker should properly be classified as an employee or, instead, as an independent contractor has considerable significance for workers, businesses, and the public generally. On the one hand, if a worker should properly be classified as an employee, the hiring business bears the responsibility of paying federal Social Security and payroll taxes, unemployment insurance taxes and state employment taxes, providing workers' compensation insurance, and, most relevant for the present case, complying with numerous state and federal statutes and regulations governing the wages, hours, and working conditions of employees. The worker then obtains the protection of the applicable labor laws and regulations. On the other hand, if a worker should properly be classified as an independent contractor, the business does not bear any of those costs or responsibilities, the worker obtains none of the numerous labor law benefits, and the public may be required under applicable laws to assume additional financial burdens with respect to such workers and their families.

Although in some circumstances classification as an independent contractor may be advantageous to workers as well as to businesses, the risk that workers who should be treated as employees may be improperly misclassified as independent contractors is significant in light of the potentially substantial economic incentives that a business may have in mischaracterizing some workers as independent contractors. Such incentives include the unfair competitive advantage the business may obtain over competitors that properly classify similar workers as employees and that thereby assume the fiscal and other responsibilities and burdens that an employer owes to its employees. In recent years, the relevant regulatory agencies of both the federal and state governments have declared that the misclassification of workers as independent contractors rather than employees is a very serious problem, depriving federal and state governments of billions of dollars in tax revenue and millions of workers of the labor law protections to which they are entitled.

The issue in this case relates to the resolution of the employee or independent contractor question in one specific context. Here we must decide what standard applies, under California law, in determining whether workers should be classified as employees or as independent contractors for purposes of California wage orders, which impose obligations relating to the minimum wages, maximum hours, and a limited number of very basic working conditions (such as minimally required meal and rest breaks) of California employees.

In the underlying lawsuit in this matter, two individual delivery drivers, suing on their own behalf and on behalf of a class of allegedly similarly situated drivers, filed a complaint against Dynamex Operations West, Inc. (Dynamex), a nationwide package and document delivery company, alleging that Dynamex had misclassified its delivery drivers as independent contractors rather than employees. The drivers claimed that Dynamex's alleged misclassification of its drivers as independent contractors led to Dynamex's violation of the provisions of Industrial Welfare Commission wage order No. 9, the applicable state wage order governing the transportation industry, as well as various sections of the Labor Code, and, as a result, that Dynamex had engaged in unfair and unlawful business practices under Business and Professions Code section 17200.

. . .

I. FACTS AND PROCEEDINGS BELOW

. . .

Dynamex is a nationwide same-day courier and delivery service that operates a number of business centers in California. Dynamex offers on-demand, same-day pickup and delivery services to the public generally and also has a number of large business customers — including Office Depot and Home Depot — for whom it delivers purchased goods and picks up returns on a regular basis. Prior to 2004,

Dynamex classified its California drivers as employees and compensated them pursuant to this state's wage and hour laws. In 2004, Dynamex converted all of its drivers to independent contractors after management concluded that such a conversion would generate economic savings for the company. Under the current policy, all drivers are treated as independent contractors and are required to provide their own vehicles and pay for all of their transportation expenses, including fuel, tolls, vehicle maintenance, and vehicle liability insurance, as well as all taxes and workers' compensation insurance.

Dynamex obtains its own customers and sets the rates to be charged to those customers for its delivery services. It also negotiates the amount to be paid to drivers on an individual basis. For drivers who are assigned to a dedicated fleet or scheduled route by Dynamex, drivers are paid either a flat fee or an amount based on a percentage of the delivery fee Dynamex receives from the customer. For those who deliver on-demand, drivers are generally paid either a percentage of the delivery fee paid by the customer on a per delivery basis or a flat fee basis per item delivered.

Drivers are generally free to set their own schedule but must notify Dynamex of the days they intend to work for Dynamex. Drivers performing on-demand work are required to obtain and pay for a Nextel cellular telephone through which the drivers maintain contact with Dynamex. On-demand drivers are assigned deliveries by Dynamex dispatchers at Dynamex's sole discretion; drivers have no guarantee of the number or type of deliveries they will be offered. Although drivers are not required to make all of the deliveries they are assigned, they must promptly notify Dynamex if they intend to reject an offered delivery so that Dynamex can quickly contact another driver; drivers are liable for any loss Dynamex incurs if they fail to do so. Drivers make pickups and deliveries using their own vehicles, but are generally expected to wear Dynamex shirts and badges when making deliveries for Dynamex, and, pursuant to Dynamex's agreement with some customers, drivers are sometimes required to attach Dynamex and/or the customer's decals to their vehicles when making deliveries for the customer. Drivers purchase Dynamex shirts and other Dynamex items with their own funds.

In the absence of any special arrangement between Dynamex and a customer, drivers are generally free to choose the sequence in which they will make deliveries and the routes they will take, but are required to complete all assigned deliveries on the day of assignment. If a customer requests, however, drivers must comply with a customer's requirements regarding delivery times and sequence of stops.

Drivers hired by Dynamex are permitted to hire other persons to make deliveries assigned by Dynamex. Further, when they are not making pickups or deliveries for Dynamex, drivers are permitted to make deliveries for another delivery company, including the driver's own personal delivery business. Drivers are prohibited, however, from diverting any delivery order received through or on behalf of Dynamex to a competitive delivery service.

Drivers are ordinarily hired for an indefinite period of time but Dynamex retains the authority to terminate its agreement with any driver without cause, on three days' notice. And, as noted, Dynamex reserves the right, throughout the contract period, to control the number and nature of deliveries that it offers to its on-demand drivers.

In January 2005, Charles Lee — the sole named plaintiff in the original complaint in the underlying action — entered into a written independent contractor agreement with Dynamex to provide delivery services for Dynamex. According to Dynamex, Lee performed on-demand delivery services for Dynamex for a total of 15 days and never performed delivery service for any company other than Dynamex. On April 15, 2005, three months after leaving his work at Dynamex, Lee filed this lawsuit on his own behalf and on behalf of similarly situated Dynamex drivers.

In essence, the underlying action rests on the claim that, since December 2004, Dynamex drivers have performed essentially the same tasks in the same manner as when its drivers were classified as employees, but Dynamex has improperly failed to comply with the requirements imposed by the Labor Code and wage orders for employees with respect to such drivers. The complaint alleges five causes of action arising from Dynamex's alleged misclassification of employees as independent contractors: two counts of unfair and unlawful business practices in violation of Business and Professions Code section 17200, and three counts of Labor Code violations based on Dynamex's failure to pay overtime compensation, to properly provide itemized wage statements, and to compensate the drivers for business expenses.

. . .

As already noted, Dynamex's petition for review challenged only the Court of Appeal's conclusion that the trial court properly determined that the wage order's definitions of "employ" and "employer" may be relied upon in determining whether a worker is an employee or an independent contractor for purposes of the obligations imposed by the wage order. We granted the petition for review to consider that question.

II. RELEVANT WAGE ORDER PROVISIONS

We begin with a brief review of the relevant provisions of the wage order that applies to the transportation industry.

In describing its scope, the transportation wage order initially provides in subdivision 1: "This order shall apply to all persons employed in the transportation industry whether paid on a time, piece rate, commission, or other basis," except for persons employed in administrative, executive, or professional capacities, who are exempt from most of the wage order's provisions.

Subdivision 2 of the order, which sets forth the definitions of terms as used in the order, contains the following relevant definitions:

> "(D) 'Employ' means to engage, suffer, or permit to work.
> "(E) 'Employee' means any person employed by an employer.
> "(F) 'Employer' means any person as defined in Section 18 of the Labor Code, who directly or indirectly, or through an agent or any other person, employs or exercises control over the wages, hours, or working conditions of any person."

Thereafter, the additional substantive provisions of the wage order that establish protections for workers or impose obligations on hiring entities relating to minimum wages, maximum hours, and specified basic working conditions (such as meal and rest breaks) are, by their terms, made applicable to "employees" or "employers."

Subdivision 2 of the wage order does not contain a definition of the term "independent contractor," and the wage order contains no other provision that otherwise specifically addresses the potential distinction between workers who are employees covered by the terms of the wage order and workers who are independent contractors who are not entitled to the protections afforded by the wage order.

III. BACKGROUND OF RELEVANT CALIFORNIA
JUDICIAL DECISIONS

We next summarize the most relevant California judicial decisions, providing a historical review of the treatment of the employee or independent contractor distinction under California law.

The difficulty that courts in all jurisdictions have experienced in devising an acceptable general test or standard that properly distinguishes employees from independent contractors is well documented. As the United States Supreme Court observed in Board v. Hearst Publications (1944) 322 U.S. 111, 121 [88 L. Ed. 1170, 64 S. Ct. 851]: "Few problems in the law have given greater variety of application and conflict in results than the cases arising in the borderland between what is clearly an employer-employee relationship and what is clearly one of independent, entrepreneurial dealing. This is true within the limited field of determining vicarious liability in tort. It becomes more so when the field is expanded to include all of the possible applications of the distinction."

As the above quotation suggests, at common law the problem of determining whether a worker should be classified as an employee or an independent contractor initially arose in the tort context — in deciding whether the hirer of the worker should be held vicariously liable for an injury that resulted from the worker's actions. In the vicarious liability context, the hirer's right to supervise and control the details of the worker's actions was reasonably viewed as crucial, because " '[t]he extent to which the employer had a right to control [the details of the service] activities was . . . highly relevant to the question whether the employer ought to be legally liable for them. . . .' " (Borello, supra, 48 Cal. 3d 341, 350.) For this reason, the question whether the hirer controlled the details of the worker's activities became the primary common law standard for determining whether a worker was considered to be an employee or an independent contractor.

. . .

At the outset, it is important to recognize that over the years and throughout the country, a number of standards or tests have been adopted in legislative enactments, administrative regulations, and court decisions as the means for distinguishing between those workers who should be considered employees and those who should be considered independent contractors. The suffer or permit to work standard was proposed and adopted in 1937 as part of the FLSA, the principal federal wage and hour legislation.

. . .

As already noted (ante, pp. 950–951, fn. 20), a number of jurisdictions have adopted a simpler, more structured test for distinguishing between employees and independent contractors — the so-called "ABC" test — that minimizes these disadvantages. The ABC test presumptively considers all workers to be employees, and permits workers to be classified as independent contractors only if the hiring business demonstrates that the worker in question satisfies each of three conditions: (a) that the worker is free from the control and direction of the hirer in connection with the performance of the work, both under the contract for the performance of the work and in fact; and (b) that the worker performs work that is outside the usual course of the hiring entity's business; and (c) that the worker is customarily engaged in an independently established trade, occupation, or business of the same nature as that involved in the work performed.

. . .

We find merit in the concerns noted above regarding the disadvantages, particularly in the wage and hour context, inherent in relying upon a multifactor, all the circumstances standard for distinguishing between employees and independent contractors. As a consequence, we conclude it is appropriate, and most consistent with the history and purpose of the suffer or permit to work standard in California's wage orders, to interpret that standard as: (1) placing the burden on the hiring entity to establish that the worker is an independent contractor who was not intended to be included within the wage order's coverage; and (2) requiring the hiring entity, in order to meet this burden, to establish each of the three factors embodied in the ABC test — namely (A) that the worker is free from the control and direction of the hiring entity in connection with the performance of the work, both under the contract for the performance of the work and in fact; and (B) that the worker performs work that is outside the usual course of the hiring entity's business; and (C) that the worker is customarily engaged in an independently established trade, occupation, or business of the same nature as the work performed.

. . .

We briefly discuss each part of the ABC test and its relationship to the suffer or permit to work definition.

1. Part A: Is the Worker Free from the Control and Direction of the Hiring Entity in the Performance of the Work, Both Under the Contract for the Performance of the Work and in Fact?

First, as our decision in *Martinez* makes clear (*Martinez*, supra, 49 Cal. 3d at p. 58), the suffer or permit to work definition was intended to be broader and more inclusive than the common law test, under which a worker's freedom from the control of the hiring entity in the performance of the work, both under the contract for the performance of the work and in fact, was the principal factor in establishing that a worker was an independent contractor rather than an employee. Accordingly, because a worker who is subject, either as a matter of contractual right or in actual practice, to the type and degree of control a business typically exercises over employees would be considered an employee under the common law test, such a worker would, a fortiori, also properly be treated as an employee for purposes of the suffer or permit to work standard. Further, as under *Borello*, supra, 48 Cal. 3d at pages 353-354, 356-357, depending on the nature of the work and overall arrangement between the parties, a business need not control the precise manner or details of the work in order to be found to have maintained the necessary control that an employer ordinarily possesses over its employees, but does not possess over a genuine independent contractor. The hiring entity must establish that the worker is free of such control to satisfy part A of the test.

2. Part B: Does the Worker Perform Work that is Outside the Usual Course of the Hiring Entity's Business?

Second, independent of the question of control, the child labor antecedents of the suffer or permit to work language demonstrate that one principal objective of the suffer or permit to work standard is to bring within the "employee" category all individuals who can reasonably be viewed as working "in [the hiring entity's] business" (see *Martinez*, supra, 49 Cal. 4th at p. 69, italics added), that is, all individuals who are reasonably viewed as providing services to the business in a role comparable to that of an employee, rather than in a role comparable to that of a traditional independent contractor. Workers whose roles are most clearly comparable to those of employees include individuals whose services are provided within the usual course of the business of the entity for which the work is performed and thus who would ordinarily be viewed by others as working in the hiring entity's business and not as working, instead, in the worker's own independent business.

Thus, on the one hand, when a retail store hires an outside plumber to repair a leak in a bathroom on its premises or hires an outside electrician to install a new electrical line, the services of the plumber or electrician are not part of the store's usual course of business and the store would not reasonably be seen as having suffered or permitted the plumber or electrician to provide services to it as an employee. On the other hand, when a clothing manufacturing company hires work-at-home seamstresses to make dresses from cloth and patterns supplied by the company that will thereafter be sold by the company, or when a bakery hires cake decorators to work on a regular basis on its custom-designed cakes, the workers are part of the hiring entity's usual business operation and the hiring business can reasonably be viewed as having suffered or permitted the workers to provide services as employees. In the latter settings, the workers' role within the hiring entity's usual business operations is more like that of an employee than that of an independent contractor.

Treating all workers whose services are provided within the usual course of the hiring entity's business as employees is important to ensure that those workers who need and want the fundamental protections afforded by the wage order do not lose those protections. If the wage order's obligations could be avoided for workers who provide services in a role comparable to employees but who are willing to forgo the wage order's protections, other workers who provide similar services and are intended to be protected under the suffer or permit to work standard would frequently find themselves displaced by those willing to decline such coverage. As the United States Supreme Court explained in a somewhat analogous context in *Alamo Foundation*, supra, 471 U.S. at page 302, with respect to the federal wage and hour law: "[T]he purposes of the [FLSA] require that it be applied even to those who would decline its protections."

. . .

Competing businesses that hire workers who perform the same or comparable duties within the entities' usual business operations should be treated similarly for purposes of the wage order.

Accordingly, a hiring entity must establish that the worker performs work that is outside the usual course of its business in order to satisfy part B of the ABC test.

3.   Part C: Is the Worker Customarily Engaged in an Independently Established Trade, Occupation, or Business of the Same Nature as the Work Performed for the Hiring Entity?

Third, as the situations that gave rise to the suffer or permit to work language disclose, the suffer or permit to work standard, by expansively defining who is an employer, is intended to preclude a business from evading the prohibitions or responsibilities embodied in the relevant wage orders directly or indirectly — through indifference, negligence, intentional subterfuge, or misclassification. It is well established, under all of the varied standards that have been utilized for distinguishing employees and independent contractors, that a business cannot unilaterally determine a worker's status simply by assigning the worker the label "independent contractor" or by requiring the worker, as a condition of hiring, to enter into a contract that designates the worker an independent contractor. This restriction on a hiring business's unilateral authority has particular force and effect under the wage orders' broad suffer or permit to work standard.

As a matter of common usage, the term "independent contractor," when applied to an individual worker, ordinarily has been understood to refer to an individual who independently has made the decision to go into business for himself or herself. Such an individual generally takes the usual steps to establish and promote his or her independent business — for example, through incorporation, licensure, advertisements, routine offerings to provide the services of the independent business to the public or to a number of potential customers, and the like. When a worker has not independently decided to engage in an independently established business but instead is simply designated an independent contractor by the unilateral action of a hiring entity, there is a substantial risk that the hiring business is attempting to evade the demands of an applicable wage order through misclassification. A company that labels as independent contractors a class of workers who are not engaged in an independently established business in order to enable the company to obtain the economic advantages that flow from avoiding financial obligations that a wage order imposes on employers unquestionably violates the fundamental purposes of the wage order. The fact that a company has not prohibited or prevented a worker from engaging in such a business is not sufficient to establish that the worker has independently made the decision to go into business for himself or herself.

Accordingly, in order to satisfy part C of the ABC test, the hiring entity must prove that the worker is customarily engaged in an independently established trade, occupation, or business.

It bears emphasis that in order to establish that a worker is an independent contractor under the ABC standard, the hiring entity is required to establish the existence of each of the three parts of the ABC standard. Furthermore, inasmuch as a hiring entity's failure to satisfy any one of the three parts itself establishes that the worker should be treated as an employee for purposes of the wage order, a court is free to consider the separate parts of the ABC standard in whatever order it chooses. Because in many cases it may be easier and clearer for a court to determine whether or not part B or part C of the ABC standard has been satisfied than for the court to resolve questions regarding the nature or degree of a worker's freedom from the hiring entity's control for purposes of part A of the standard, the significant advantages of the ABC standard — in terms of increased clarity and consistency — will often be best served by first considering one or both of the latter two parts of the standard in resolving the employee or independent contractor question.

4.   Conclusion Regarding Suffer or Permit to Work Definition

In sum, we conclude that unless the hiring entity establishes (A) that the worker is free from the control and direction of the hiring entity in connection with the performance of the work, both under the contract for the performance of the work and in fact, (B) that the worker performs work that is outside the usual course of the hiring entity's business, and (C) that the worker is customarily engaged in an independently established trade, occupation, or business, the worker should be considered an employee and the hiring business an employer under the suffer or permit to work standard in wage orders. The hiring entity's failure to prove any one of these three prerequisites will be sufficient in itself to establish that the worker is an included employee, rather than an excluded independent contractor, for purposes of the wage order.

. . .

V. CONCLUSION

For the reasons discussed above, the judgment of the Court of Appeal is affirmed.

Notes and Questions

1. This case represents a significant change in California law. How do you think it will impact companies in the gig economy space like Uber, Grubhub, and others in hiring decisions?

2. Do you think the standard set forth in this case benefits workers or companies more?

B. WORKER CLASSIFICATION: UNPAID INTERNS

Many businesses have unpaid interns. In fact, sometimes entrepreneurs may think they have a great idea to save money by hiring unpaid interns. Internships are not only valuable to the entrepreneurial venture, they also provide a great opportunity to the interns to learn about an industry, gain experience, develop new skills, and meet potential mentors. Internships can be the key to finding long-term employment in the future. However, similar to the distinction between employees and independent contractors, valid internship programs must meet certain legal criteria. Although businesses that have unpaid interns are required to adhere to certain legal standards, many businesses either knowingly or unknowingly violate the law by having unpaid interns work in ways that are not in compliance with the law in this area.

The Fair Labor Standards Act requires "for-profit" employers to pay employees for their work. Interns, however, may not be "employees" under the FLSA — in which case the FLSA does not require compensation for their work. If an intern is considered an employee, then the intern is subject to the FLSA and must receive at least minimum wage and time-and-a-half overtime compensation. If an intern is not considered an employee, the intern is not subject to the FLSA and is not entitled to minimum wage and overtime compensation. Said another way, interns who are actually employees must be paid and interns who are not employees may be unpaid.

In April 2010, the Wage and Hours Division of the Department of Labor issued a list of six criteria that must be met in order for a person to qualify as a legal unpaid intern at a for-profit organization. The six criteria are:

1. The internship, even though it includes actual operation of the facilities of the employer, is similar to training that would be given in an educational environment;
2. The internship experience is for the benefit of the intern;
3. The intern does not displace regular employees, but works under close supervision of existing staff;
4. The employer that provides the training derives no immediate advantage from the activities of the intern;
5. The intern is not necessarily entitled to a job at the conclusion of the internship; and
6. The employer and the intern understand that the intern is not entitled to wages for the time spent in the internship.

Only if an intern satisfied all six factors would it be permissible for the intern to be unpaid. This rigid test led to significant lawsuits challenging employer classification of unpaid interns and resulted in many companies canceling their internship programs for fear of liability.

It is obvious how difficult it would have been for companies to meet all of these criteria. There are quite a few examples of companies that were sued by former interns for lost wages and backpay alleging they were unfairly classified as interns when they should have been classified as employees. Many companies lost in court or settled and then cancelled their internship programs. Although it is understandable why companies cancelled their internship programs, most people agree that internships can be very beneficial to the intern and see value in companies offering these programs, provided they are not designed to take advantage of workers who should be paid employees.

In 2018, the Department of Labor replaced the six-factor test with the "primary beneficiary" test. This test requires a determination of whether the employer or the intern is the primary beneficiary of the relationship. If the employer is the primary beneficiary, the intern must be paid, but if the intern is the primary beneficiary, the intern may be unpaid.

Seven factors are relevant:

1. The extent to which the intern and the employer clearly understand there is no expectation of compensation. (Any promise of compensation suggests the intern is an employee.)
2. The extent to which the internship provides training that would be similar to that which would be given in an educational environment, including the clinical and other hands-on training provided by educational institutions.
3. The extent to which the internship is tied to the intern's formal education program by integrated coursework or the receipt of academic credit.
4. The extent to which the internship accommodates the intern's academic commitments by corresponding to the academic calendar.
5. The extent to which the internship's duration is limited to the period in which the internship provides the intern with beneficial learning.

6. The extent to which the intern's work complements, rather than displaces, the work of paid employees while providing significant educational benefits to the intern.
7. The extent to which the intern and the employer understand that the internship is conducted without entitlement to a paid job at the conclusion of the internship.

The primary beneficiary test is much more reasonable and more flexible than the previous six-factor test. One very important difference is that with the primary beneficiary test, no single factor is dispositive. Instead, we can evaluate an internship in light of whether the intern is the primary beneficiary even if not every factor on the list is met. It is important to note that this test applies only to interns of for-profit employers. Interns at non-profits are considered volunteers and may be unpaid, provided that the intern volunteers without any expectation of compensation.

Notes and Questions

1. Why do you think a worker and a business owner may not simply agree between themselves that the worker will be considered an intern? What public policy concerns are at play? What advice would you give a start-up client that wants to start an internship program?

2. Why do you think the Department of Labor moved to the primary beneficiary test for interns? How do you think this change will impact internship programs?

C. EMPLOYMENT STATUTES AND CASE LAW

Once a business begins hiring employees, it is crucial to understand and consider the many employment laws and regulations that must be followed. Below we identify the major federal employment legislation that lawyers representing entrepreneurs should understand, but it is far from a comprehensive list of all employment laws. Additionally, many states have their own versions of employment laws that may provide broader protection than that afforded by federal laws, so lawyers must acquaint themselves with state statutes. Employment law is another area where counsel to an entrepreneur must know enough to understand the basic layout of applicable laws and regulations while recognizing that an expert's advice is frequently advisable.

1. Fair Labor Standards Act

The Fair Labor Standards Act establishes a national minimum wage, guarantees overtime pay in certain jobs, and restricts child labor. Under the FLSA, all non-exempt employees must be paid a minimum hourly wage, which was increased to $7.25 per hour effective July 24, 2009, and the employer must pay for hours worked in excess of 40 hours in one week at an increased rate of one and one-half times the regular rate. Certain employees are exempt from the wage requirements of the FLSA.

However, exemptions tend to be narrowly construed. In general, exempt employees are higher paid, work with less supervision, and meet other statutory criteria.

2. Workers' Compensation

Workers' compensation statutes require employers to provide a form of insurance that covers income replacement and medical benefits for employees who are injured in the course of employment. The workers are entitled to receive these benefits regardless of the level of care that the employer took to prevent such accidents. It is, in essence, a "no-fault" system. However, the damages available to injured employees are capped and often lower than in typical lawsuits based on torts.

3. Occupational Safety and Health Act

The federal Occupational Safety and Health Act requires workplaces to be "free from recognized hazards" that could cause serious injury or death. The Act attempts to ensure that employees work in a safe and healthy workplace. All businesses engaged in interstate commerce are subject to the Act other than state and federal governments.

The Act also created the Occupational Safety and Health Administration to oversee and evaluate compliance with health and safety standards. OSHA promulgates health and safety rules regarding a variety of workplace issues. This agency investigates employer health and safety compliance and requires detailed records of health and safety incidents. The agency may bring administrative enforcement actions against employers who are not in compliance with its health and safety standards.

4. Title VII of the Civil Rights Act

Title VII of the Civil Rights Act of 1964 prohibits employment discrimination based on race, color, religion, sex, or national origin, and was later amended to expand the coverage of sex discrimination to include discrimination based on pregnancy, childbirth or related medical conditions, and marriage status for women. The United States Supreme Court ruled that the definition of "sex" includes sexual orientation and gender identity. All businesses with 15 or more employees are subject to this legislation.

There are three categories of discrimination claims under Title VII: disparate treatment, disparate impact, and harassment.

Title VII disparate treatment claims are based on alleged intentional discrimination by an employer and consist of a three-pronged analysis. The first part requires that the employee establish a prima facie case by showing (1) she is a member of the protected class and (2) she was denied an employment benefit for which she was qualified. Once a prima facie case has been made by the employee, the employer must show evidence of a nondiscriminatory reason for the employment decision at issue. The employee then must show that the reason offered is a mere pretext for the discriminatory action.

An employee does not need to prove intentional discrimination in a claim based on disparate impact. The employee must identify and prove that a particular employment practice, which might appear neutral on its face, had a disparate impact on the basis of race, color, religion, sex, national origin, or other protected class. Disparate impact claims often use statistical evidence to show discrimination.

Employees can also bring claims under Title VII alleging harassment. The most common type of harassment claim and the type that often makes the headlines is sexual harassment. Quid pro quo sexual harassment refers to retaliation against an employee in the form of a denial of an employment benefit for refusal to submit to sexual advances by a supervisor. An employee can also establish harassment under Title VII by showing that a hostile work environment existed. A hostile work environment claim must show that an employee was subject to unwelcome comments or conduct based on being a member of a protected class and that such comments or conduct were pervasive and unreasonably interfered with such employee's ability to work effectively and created an intimidating, hostile, or offensive work environment.

Title VII does provide an affirmative defense to otherwise prohibited discriminatory actions. An employer may make an employment decision based on religion, sex, or national origin if one of those classes is a bona fide occupational qualification reasonably necessary for the normal operation of that particular business or organization. A "bfoq" can be a defense to intentional discrimination, but the burden is on the employer to prove that there is a reasonable basis for determining that people from an otherwise protected class would be unable to perform a particular job. The bfoq defense is never an option for discrimination based on race or color.

5. Americans with Disabilities Act

The Americans with Disabilities Act prohibits discrimination on the basis of a disability and requires employers to make reasonable accommodations so that employees with disabilities may perform job responsibilities. The ADA does not require employers to make accommodations that would constitute an undue hardship on the employer. The ADA covers employers with 15 or more employees who work at least 20 or more weeks in a year.

6. Age Discrimination in Employment Act

The Age Discrimination in Employment Act prohibits discrimination on the basis of age and covers workers age 40 and older. The ADEA applies to all companies and organizations that are involved in interstate commerce and have at least 20 employees.

EQUAL EMPLOYMENT OPPORTUNITY COMMISSION v. GO DADDY SOFTWARE, INC.
United States Court of Appeals for the Ninth Circuit
581 F.3d 951 (2009)

Youssef Bouamama was terminated from his job at Go Daddy Software, Inc. ("Go Daddy"). The Equal Employment Opportunity Commission ("EEOC") brought suit against Go Daddy on Bouamama's behalf in federal district court. A jury returned a verdict in favor of the EEOC on the claim that Bouamama had been unlawfully terminated in retaliation for engaging in protected activity.

Go Daddy moved in the district court for a judgment as a matter of law under Federal Rule of Civil Procedure 50(b), arguing that there was insufficient evidence that Bouamama engaged in protected activity; or, if he did engage in protected activity, that there was insufficient evidence that there was a causal connection between that activity and his termination. In the alternative, Go Daddy moved for a new trial under Federal Rule of Civil Procedure 59(a). The district court denied both motions. We affirm.

I.   BACKGROUND

Go Daddy is a for-profit corporation that assists individuals and companies in registering domain names on the Internet. Go Daddy operates a call center from which employees provide sales and technical support to customers over the telephone. Go Daddy also has a Tech Support/Web Board department that responds to customer requests over email.

In September 2001, Bouamama, a Muslim of Moroccan national origin, interviewed for a job at Go Daddy. Brett Villeneuve, a supervisor in the call center, participated in the interview. Go Daddy hired Bouamama on a temporary basis as a Technical Support Representative in the Tech Support/Web Board department. Bouamama began working on September 20, 2001, for $12 per hour.

Shortly after Bouamama was hired, Villeneuve became the operations manager of the call center, which meant that he was in charge of the employees in both the call center and in the Tech Support/Web Board department. Villeneuve testified that although Bouamama was assigned to the Web Board, he occasionally answered calls for the call center. Some customers complained about Bouamama's manner on the phone. Nevertheless, on December 13, 2001, Villeneuve converted Bouamama to a full-time, regular employee, raising his wage to $14 per hour, and providing him with medical, dental, and disability benefits, and paid vacations and holidays. At trial, Villeneuve described Bouamama as "a good rep. . . . [T]echnically knowledgeable. His typing skills were good. He put out good, solid answers."

Between December 2001 and February 2002, Villeneuve overheard Bouamama speaking to a customer in French. Bouamama testified that "after I finished with the customer [Villeneuve] was asking me about . . . where I'm from and what language I was speaking and what, you know, religion I was practicing." Bouamama testified that he told Villeneuve that he was a Muslim from Morocco who spoke Arabic. He also testified that he "really didn't feel that it was appropriate to ask me this kind of questions but in the meantime, you know, I want a job, we were at war, so I just let it go."

Villeneuve remembered the conversation differently. He testified that overhearing the phone call with the customer was "pretty cool. . . . [W]hen the phone conversation ended, I asked him — I verified that it was French. I thanked him for . . . helping out the customer. I asked him if there were any other languages that he spoke." Bouamama responded that, in addition to English and French, he spoke Arabic. Villeneuve testified that it was a "huge help" to have a representative who spoke other languages. When asked whether Bouamama seemed upset by the question about what languages he spoke, Villeneuve testified, "No, not particularly. . . . [H]e was kind of smiling like he was proud of the fact [that] . . . he's trilingual. That's neat."

In 2002, Villeneuve created "Team Lead" positions. In addition to handling sales and support inquiries from customers, each Team Lead supervised a crew of sales representatives. Bouamama applied to be a Team Lead, but, according to Villeneuve's testimony, he was initially denied the position because of "his abruptness with people, his demeanor, his abrasiveness." Villeneuve testified that Bouamama complained, and that Villeneuve reversed his position, promoting Bouamama to Team Lead on February 25, 2002. Bouamama's wage was increased to $16 per hour.

Shortly after Bouamama was promoted to Team Lead, the position of Inbound Sales Manager became available. Four or five people, including Bouamama, applied for the position, and Villeneuve gave the position to Bouamama. The promotion took effect on July 11, 2002. In this new position, Bouamama was responsible for preparing reports and for tracking phone calls, sales by individual employees and teams of employees, and sales of different Go Daddy products. Bouamama's compensation was increased to $46,000 per year plus bonus. Bouamama testified that he often worked weekends, without being asked and without being paid overtime or requesting to be paid overtime, so that he could keep up with the demands of the new position.

Bouamama testified that after his promotion to Inbound Sales Manager he complained to Heather Slezak, who worked in Go Daddy's Human Resources Department, about his conversation with Villeneuve that had occurred about six months earlier when Villeneuve overheard Bouamama speaking to a customer in French. Bouamama testified that he could not recall if Slezak promised to speak to Villeneuve about this, or if she said something like Villeneuve "is the way how [he] is, don't worry about him, he don't really mean stuff." According to Bouamama, neither he nor Slezak followed up on this. According to Slezak, Bouamama never complained to her about Villeneuve.

Bouamama testified that, in addition to his comments made following Bouamama's conversation in French, Villeneuve made at least one other discriminatory comment in his presence, saying, "The Muslims need to die. The bastard Muslims need to die." Villeneuve was talking to other employees in the hallway near Bouamama's cubicle when he made this comment. Bouamama testified that he did not respond to Villeneuve or complain about him because "[w]e were at war. . . . After September 11 things changed, people are hurt, you know, I was hurt . . . and, you know, you try to be compassionate. I understand maybe the anger that some people are expressing. . . ." Bouamama testified further that he did not complain because "[t]here's a culture in Go Daddy. You complain you get fired."

On April 1, 2003, Go Daddy hired Craig Franklin from an outside company to be Director of Call Center Operations. Franklin had 20 years of experience in call centers and had supervised 1,500 employees in his prior job. Villeneuve, who had previously managed the call center, was demoted. He was no longer a member of Go Daddy's Executive Staff, and he lost the authority to hire and fire workers without approval. Villeneuve reported to Franklin.

On his second day on the job, Franklin reorganized Go Daddy's call center. He testified that in planning the reorganization, he did not solicit advice from Villeneuve or Slezak. Franklin decided to eliminate thirteen Team Lead positions, the Weekend Sales Manager position, and the Inbound Sales Manager position held by Bouamama. Franklin testified that he did not examine the competencies of any of the individuals holding the positions before he decided to eliminate them. Franklin created four new Sales Supervisor positions that employees, including those whose positions had been eliminated, could apply for.

On April 4, 2003, Franklin, Villeneuve, and Slezak met with Bouamama and informed him that his position was being eliminated. According to Bouamama, he was told that he could apply for one of the new Sales Supervisor positions or "walk away." When asked what he understood the phrase "walk away" to mean, Bouamama testified, "Well, somebody repeat that five times to you it means quit on your own. That's what it means." During cross-examination, Bouamama was asked again if he had been told what would happen if he "didn't apply for the [new] position or if [he] didn't get the position." Bouamama responded:

A: Yes, sir.
Q: You were told you could take a position back on the floor, answering the phones, or you could accept a severance package.
A: Accept a severance package?
Q: Isn't that what they told you?
A: No. They told me that, you know, you can apply for this position and — you know, or you can walk away.

This testimony by Bouamama about his options conflicts with the testimony of others. Villeneuve testified that employees who applied unsuccessfully for the Sales Supervisor positions "had two options. If you didn't get the position, you could go back to the phones, with a — we changed your pay rate so they weren't starting out at base all over again. We increased their pay based on tenure. . . . If you chose not to go back to the phones, you could leave the company, and we had a severance package for everybody." Franklin testified similarly, stating that "we encouraged" applicants who did not get the Sales Supervisor position "to go back to the phones."

During the morning of April 7, 2003, Franklin stopped by Bouamama's cubicle. Bouamama testified as follows:

A: I was working on my cubicle, Mr. Craig Franklin show up around like 8:30, nine o'clock in the morning and he came around me and he saw some pictures in my cubicle and trouble with the conversation started with where are these pictures from, and I said Morocco, and he said, "Are you from Morocco?" I said, "Yes." He said, "Are you Muslim?" I said, "Yes." And by the time I was going to engage the conversation with him I kind of like look at him in the face why he's asking me these questions and he looked at me and he said, "You know, you're lucky that I like you," and he walked away to his desk.
Q: So you didn't say anything in response?
A: I didn't get a chance to talk to him.
Q: Did you have any statistical information in your cubicle that Mr. Franklin was there to obtain?
A: Mr. Franklin, you know, he's the new director of the Call Center. He has access [t]o any information he wants to without really asking me. As a matter of fact, I volunteered to give him an update about the department. He cancelled three times the meeting.
Q: So he could have obtained statistical information from other locations, is that right?
A: That's correct.

Franklin recalled the conversation differently. He testified that he saw the pictures and remarked that they were beautiful and asked where they were from. Bouamama told him that they were from Morocco. Franklin testified that he did not ask Bouamama where he was from or what religion he practiced. He further testified that Bouamama did not volunteer that he was a Muslim and that he, Franklin, had not said, "You know, you're lucky that I like you."

Bouamama testified that during the afternoon of April 7, after the exchange with Franklin, he complained to Slezak in the Human Resources department of Go Daddy:

Q: What did you tell her?

A: I told her that this is the second time that people are concerned and taking interest about, you know, where I'm from, my religion. You know, I can understand that it was happening with [Villeneuve] but this guy here [Franklin], I don't know him and two days ago he came and telling me that he doesn't care about my history and he wanted to eliminate my position. The next day he's taking interest for who I am and where I'm from. So I wanted her to look into it. She said that she will look into it.

Q: So you told — you told her this was the second time that somebody had complained — had made comments about you?

A: That was, I would say, the second or third time that I spoke to her about some matters like that.

Q: So you had gone to Miss Slezak to complain about comments about your national origin and religion before?

A: That's correct.

Slezak denied that Bouamama ever complained to her.

On April 9, 2003, Franklin, Villeneuve, and Slezak interviewed Bouamama for one of the Sales Supervisor positions. The panel interviewed thirteen other candidates during that day and the next. The panelists unanimously agreed to hire six of the candidates, two more than Franklin originally planned. Bouamama was not among those hired. According to Villeneuve's testimony, Bouamama ranked "[l]ower, towards the bottom of the frame" compared to other candidates. Villeneuve also testified that neither religion nor national origin played any role in the panel's decisions.

Slezak testified that the panel met with Bouamama on April 14 and told him that he did not get a Sales Supervisor position. According to Slezak, "We thanked him for his time, encouraged him to stay with the organization because there would be opportunity in the future, and presented him the same options to retain a position . . . or take a severance package and leave the company." This is consistent with the testimony of Villeneuve and Franklin that Bouamama, like other unsuccessful candidates, had the option to "go back to the phones." According to Slezak, "all of the unsuccessful candidates, aside from Mr. Bouamama, selected right then and there to retain a position with the company as an inbound Sales Representative." According to Franklin, Bouamama said "I'm not going back to the phones." Slezak testified that the panel gave Bouamama two days to make a final decision.

Bouamama testified that the purported meeting with the panel on April 14 never took place. He testified that he learned that he did not get the Sales Supervisor position directly from Bob Parsons, Go Daddy's CEO, on April 14. According to Bouamama, Parsons called him into his office, told him that he did not get the

Sales Supervisor position, and told him that he would be doing "sales statistics" for
the company. Bouamama testified that Parsons said, "I don't want you [to] worry
about what's going on in the sales department[,] and I want you to be my ears and
my eyes for the company." According to Bouamama, "[m]y understanding was that
[I would] wait two weeks for the transitions and help [Franklin] and all the others
as to . . . what they need[ed] to do on the department and then I will be moving to
another department doing statistics, sales or statistics analysis."

Parsons' testimony was inconsistent with Bouamama's. Parsons testified that
Bouamama called him to express his disappointment at not getting the Sales
Supervisor position. Parsons testified that he promised Bouamama that he "would
see what I could do." He further testified that he explained to other executives
that he thought Bouamama "was a good employee" and that "because of — of his
personality issues, with his abrasiveness, particularly with female employees, that
maybe a supervisor position for now was not a good idea for him, but maybe there
was something else in the company." He testified that another executive, Barbara
Rechterman, mentioned that she was planning to create a marketing analyst position, and she and Parsons agreed that Bouamama, who had a background in math-
ematics, might be a good fit for it.

Bouamama testified that at the end of the day on April 14, he passed Franklin's
office on the way to the parking lot, and "the first thing that [Franklin] said is come
here, the F word. You know, I look at him like, 'What?' And he said, 'Come here.'"
According to Bouamama, Villeneuve and Slezak were in the room. Bouamama testified that he responded, "Hey, you know, I just spoke to Mr. Bob Parsons" and that
he then went home.

Bouamama testified that on the morning of April 15, 2003, he met with
Rechterman to discuss the marketing analyst position, and that she asked him to
write a report "related to sales product and cost" and to deliver it to her by noon.
He further testified that he emailed her a "preliminary report" around 11:30 and
asked if it was satisfactory. Rechterman did not respond. Bouamama sent her a final
report around 2:30, and again she did not respond. Bouamama testified that he
went to Rechterman's office at about 3:00 to inquire about the report, and that
the first thing she said was "I don't know [why] they send you to my department.
You need to go ask Mr. Craig Franklin why you didn't get the Sales Supervisor position." Bouamama testified that he went to speak to Franklin, whose first words were,
"Oh, I thought I took care of you." He testified that Franklin said he had to talk to
Rechterman. Bouamama testified that he had been at work for ten hours at that
point, and that he responded, "I'm tired of all this, I'm going home."

Rechterman recalled her interaction with Bouamama differently. She testified
that she gave Bouamama a project involving "conversion rates," which were the
"basis of the analysis in [her] department," and that she explained the project to
him twice, initially and when Bouamama came back to her with questions. She testified that she did not give him a deadline and that it was "not a difficult project
at all." She further testified that Bouamama's final product was "inaccurate" and
"wrong" and that she told him that she "didn't think it was going to work out for
him in an analytical role."

On the morning of April 17, 2003, Bouamama called in sick and went to the
EEOC. Bouamama testified that he "was there to find out what are my rights. . . . I
went to EEOC to find out there is something that is going on to me, do you think
that this company is doing something wrong or not?" On a questionnaire asking
him to describe the harm for which he was filing a complaint, Bouamama wrote, "in

process of being demoted or choice to walk away. [B]een asked so many time[s] [w] here I am from and [w]hat religion I practice." After completing the questionnaire, Bouamama had a two-hour interview with an EEOC investigator.

Bouamama testified that he went to work on the afternoon on April 17, 2003, in response to a telephone call from Slezak, who said "there is something urgent that we need to talk about." He met with Slezak and Franklin. According to Bouamama, Slezak said, "You did not get the Sales Supervisor position and you're not going to go back to the floor." He testified that she continued, "This is how it is . . . effective today immediately. You are no longer with the company." He testified that Slezak offered him the severance package. When asked whether Slezak or Franklin offered him the sales representative position — i.e., a return to the phones — Bouamama testified, "No. They never did." When asked if he would have taken such a position if it had been offered to him, Bouamama testified, "I will. I'm not a quitter. I will go back to the floor and I will prove myself again and I will pro[ve] them wrong." When asked if he left his job voluntarily, he testified, "No, I did not."

On or before April 29, 2003, Bouamama signed an EEOC "Charge of Discrimination" form. He stated on the form, inter alia, that "[o]n April 7, 2003, I was again asked where I was from, my religion and what languages I spoke. I was told that if I was not selected for a supervisory position I could 'go back to the beginning' (meaning I could demote to my original sales position), or I had a choice to 'walk away.' " When asked at trial about the EEOC questionnaire he filled out on April 17 and the Charge of Discrimination form he filled out on April 29, Bouamama stated, "I told [the EEOC investigator] that on my initial . . . first meeting with [Slezak], [Villeneuve] as when they called me they going to eliminate my position I have a choice to apply for it . . . or walk away or go back to the floor." Both the questionnaire and Charge of Discrimination form were introduced into evidence.

The EEOC brought suit against Go Daddy in federal district court on Bouamama's behalf, making essentially two claims — a discrimination claim and a retaliation claim. First, it claimed that religion and/or national origin was a motivating factor in Go Daddy's decision not to promote Bouamama to Sales Supervisor and in its later decision to terminate him. Second, it claimed that Go Daddy failed to promote Bouamama to the position of Sales Supervisor and later terminated his employment in retaliation for engaging in protected activities.

After closing arguments, outside the presence of the jury, Go Daddy made an oral motion under Rule 50(a) for judgment as a matter of law. In its entirety, the motion was:

> With regard to the Commission's discrimination claims, Go Daddy believes there's no legally sufficient evidence for a reasonable jury to find for the Commission. There's insufficient evidence that any of the panelists commented on or considered Mr. Bouamama's religion or national origin during the selection process for the Sales Supervisor position.
>
> With regard to a separation, there's insufficient evidence that any of the panelists commented on or considered Mr. Bouamama's national origin when they offered him a choice between Sales Representative — going back to the Sales Representative position or offering him a severance agreement.
>
> There's also insufficient evidence that the panel considered his religion, Muslim.
>
> With regard to the comparators [sic], there's insufficient evidence that Go Daddy treated Mr. Bouamama differently than the employees outside his protected

class. There's been no evidence at trial regarding the national origin or religion of the successful candidates, the unsuccessful candidates, or the decision-makers in this case.

With regard to the Commission's retaliation claim, there hasn't been any evidence that Miss Slezak told any other panel members regarding the alleged reports made to her by Mr. Bouamama. Mr. Franklin and Mr. Villeneuve both testified that, in fact, Miss Slezak had not reported any protected activity to them, and without this knowledge, knowledge by one of the three panel members is insufficient for the jury to return a verdict on retaliation.

. . .

The jury returned a verdict in favor of the EEOC on the retaliation claim. The jury otherwise returned a verdict in favor of Go Daddy. The jury awarded Bouamama $5,000 for mental and emotional pain and suffering and $135,000 for lost earnings. The jury also awarded $250,000 in punitive damages.

Following the verdict, Go Daddy filed a renewed motion for judgment as a matter of law under Federal Rule of Civil Procedure 50(b). . . .

The district court denied Go Daddy's Rule 50(b) and Rule 59(a) motions. . . .

Go Daddy appeals the district court's denial of its Rule 50(b) motion for judgment as a matter of law and its Rule 59(a) motion for a new trial. For the reasons that follow, we affirm the district court.

. . .

III.   DISCUSSION

We divide our discussion into two parts. First, we address Go Daddy's appeal of the district court's denial of its motion under Rule 50(b) for judgment as a matter of law. Second, we address Go Daddy's appeal of the district court's denial of its motion under Rule 59(a) for a new trial.

A.   Rule 50(b) Motion for Judgment as a Matter of Law

. . .

Go Daddy's first argument in its Rule 50(b) motion is that there was insufficient evidence at trial to show Bouamama engaged in protected activity. . . .

Go Daddy's second argument in its Rule 50(b) motion is that even if there were sufficient evidence that Bouamama engaged in protected activity, there was insufficient evidence that Go Daddy terminated him because of this activity. . . .

1.   Protected Activity

Under Title VII of the Civil Rights Act, an employer cannot "discharge any individual, or otherwise . . . discriminate against any individual with respect to his compensation, terms, conditions, or privileges of employment, because of such individual's . . . religion . . . or national origin." An employer cannot retaliate against an employee for "oppos[ing] any practice made an unlawful employment practice by this subchapter." Under the latter provision, a complaint by an employee that a supervisor has violated Title VII may constitute protected activity for which the employer cannot lawfully retaliate.

In its brief to us, Go Daddy makes two specific arguments in support of its argument that there is insufficient evidence that Bouamama engaged in protected activity.

First, Go Daddy argues that the jury should not have believed that Bouamama complained to Slezak about what he claimed to perceive as discrimination. In his testimony, quoted above, Bouamama stated that he complained to Slezak either two or three times about what he perceived as discriminatory comments. Slezak testified that he never complained to her. Under the substantial evidence standard, we hold that Bouamama's testimony is adequate to support the jury's conclusion that Bouamama was more credible on this point, even though it might have been "possible to draw a contrary conclusion."

Second, Go Daddy argues that even if Bouamama did complain to Slezak, this was not protected activity under the Supreme Court's decision in Clark County School District v. Breeden, 532 U.S. 268, 121 S. Ct. 1508, 149 L. Ed. 2d 509 (2001). In *Breeden*, the Court held that "offhand comments, and isolated incidents (unless extremely serious)" do not amount to discrimination. If a person has been subjected to only an isolated incident, a complaint about that incident does not constitute protected activity unless a reasonable person would believe that the isolated incident violated Title VII. This reasonable person determination requires "[l]ooking at all the circumstances, including the frequency of the discriminatory conduct [] [and] its severity[.]"

Go Daddy insists in its brief that Bouamama's complaint to Slezak on April 7 about his exchange with Franklin earlier in the day was, at most, a complaint about an "offhand comment" or an "isolated incident." It writes, "Even assuming the jury completely bought Bouamama's testimony about his alleged single complaint to Slezak on April 7, 2003[,] about an incident that occurred earlier that same day, that conduct fails to reach the bar set [by] the United States Supreme Court in [*Breeden*]."

Go Daddy's argument ignores Bouamama's actual testimony. As recounted above, Bouamama testified that he complained to Slezak two or three times about comments that had been made about his national origin and religion. His complaint on April 7 about Franklin's comments was only the latest of these. In his testimony, he specifically re-counted that he had previously complained to Slezak about a conversation in which Villeneuve, his supervisor, asked about the languages he spoke (French and Arabic) and about his religion (Muslim).

Bouamama also testified that Villeneuve later made a comment near his cubicle, "The Muslims need to die. The bastard Muslims need to die." However, he testified that he did not complain on that occasion because "[t]here's a culture in Go Daddy. You complain you get fired." The fact that Bouamama did not report these comments does not make them irrelevant to the inquiry concerning the reasonableness of his belief that a violation of Title VII had occurred.

"Looking at all the circumstances" requires us to take note not only of all comments of which Bouamama complained but also of the context in which they were made. Franklin's comments on April 7 were not "isolated" from the terms and conditions of Bouamama's employment. At the time of those comments, Bouamama had just received word that his position had been eliminated and that his only option to avoid demotion involved an application process to be headed by Franklin. There is, thus, a strong nexus between Franklin's comments and the terms of Bouamama's continued employment, as noted by Bouamama himself in his final report to Slezak.

Further, if a person has been subjected to more than one comment, and if those comments, taken together, would be considered by a reasonable person to violate Title VII, that person need not complain specifically about all of the comments to which he or she has been subjected. Unreported comments, in other words, are relevant to the inquiry concerning the reasonableness of the belief that a violation has occurred. In such circumstances, a complaint about one or more of these comments is protected behavior. We do not read *Breeden* to require more.

There is, therefore, evidence to support a reasonable person's conclusion that the conduct to which Bouamama had been subjected at Go Daddy went beyond mere "offhand comments" and "isolated incidents," and that Bouamama's two, and possibly three, complaints to Slezak were therefore protected activity. We hold that this testimony satisfies the "any evidence" standard applicable to a faulty Rule 50(b) motion.

2. Causation

We evaluate separately each of Go Daddy's two specific arguments in support of its argument that there was insufficient evidence to support a conclusion that Bouamama's complaints to Slezak motivated Go Daddy's decision to terminate him.

a. Evidence That Slezak Told Franklin About Bouamama's Complaints

Bouamama testified that he complained about Franklin to Slezak on April 7, 2003. Slezak testified that on April 9 and 10, 2003, she and Franklin, along with Villeneuve, interviewed 14 candidates for the Sales Supervisor positions. After the interviews were complete, she testified that "the three of us, [Franklin], [Villeneuve], and myself . . . started to talk about the candidates." She further testified that on April 11 and 14, 2003, she, Franklin, and Villeneuve met with all 14 of the candidates individually to tell them whether they were selected. Franklin corroborated this testimony. Bouamama testified that on April 14, 2003, when he passed Franklin's office and Franklin said "come here, the F word," Slezak was in Franklin's office.

The district court found, "Mr. Bouamama testified that he was terminated by Mr. Franklin and Ms. Slezak. He also testified that he complained to Ms. Slezak about discriminatory conduct by Mr. Franklin only days before his termination. . . . [T]he Court concludes that the jury reasonably could have found that both Mr. Franklin and Ms. Slezak were aware of the protected activity and that their termination of Mr. Bouamama was in response to that activity."

We agree with the district court. A reasonable jury hearing the testimony just recounted could have concluded that Slezak had ample opportunities to inform Franklin of Bouamama's complaint and had, in fact, done so. We therefore hold, under the substantial evidence standard, applicable to a properly made Rule 50(b) motion, that there was sufficient evidence to support the jury's conclusion.

b. Evidence That Go Daddy Decided on April 4 to Terminate Bouamama

Nothing in the record supports a conclusion that Go Daddy decided on April 4 to terminate Bouamama. Bouamama testified specifically to the contrary, as did Villeneuve, Franklin, and Slezak.

Bouamama testified that he was told during his meeting with Slezak, Franklin, and Villeneuve on April 4 that his position was being eliminated and that he could apply for one of the new Sales Supervisor positions, or that he could "walk away." Later, in response to a separate question about the April 4 meeting, Bouamama testified, "They told me that, you know, you can apply for this position and — you know, or you can walk away." As Bouamama understood the phrase, being told that he could "walk away" did not mean that he was fired. Rather, as recounted above, Bouamama specifically testified that "walk away" meant that he could "quit on his own."

Bouamama also testified that he had been given the option to apply for one of the new Sales Supervisor positions "or walk away or go back to the floor." This statement is consistent with what Bouamama wrote on the EEOC questionnaire that he filled out on the morning of April 17, before he was terminated. He wrote that he was "in process of being demoted or choice to walk away." It is also consistent with his statement on the EEOC Charge of Discrimination form: "I was told that if I was not selected for a supervisory position I could 'go back to the beginning' (meaning I could demote to my original sales position), or I had a choice to 'walk away.' "

Villeneuve testified that unsuccessful applicants for the Sales Supervisor positions "could go back to the phones." Franklin testified that "we encouraged" applicants who did not get the Sales Supervisor position "to go back to the phones." Slezak testified that on April 14, 2003, after telling Bouamama that he did not get the Sales Supervisor position, "We thanked him for his time, encouraged him to stay with the organization because there would be opportunity in the future, and presented him the same options to retain a position . . . or take a severance package and leave the company."

Based on this testimony, the jury could reasonably conclude that at the time of his meeting with the panel on April 14, 2003, Bouamama had the option of returning to his original sales position at Go Daddy.

Bouamama's and Rechterman's testimony about the additional project assigned to Bouamama are also inconsistent with an April 4 decision to terminate. A jury could very reasonably conclude that the assignment of a new project on April 15 contradicts the assertion Go Daddy now makes. Indeed, the very fact that Bouamama was still at work at Go Daddy on April 15 (and apparently still employed on April 17 when he called in sick) belies a decision to terminate on April 4. By April 14, Go Daddy had eliminated Bouamama's position and determined that he would not receive one of the Sales Supervisor assignments. Yet he continued to show up at work and to complete assignments, even new ones.

To understate the matter, there is evidence that Go Daddy's decision to terminate Bouamama was not made on April 4, but rather was made sometime between April 14, when he was told he could return to his original sales position, and April 17, when he was told that he was terminated. We hold that this evidence satisfies the "any evidence" standard applicable to a faulty Rule 50(b) motion.

B. Motion for New Trial

In support of its Rule 59(a) motion for a new trial, Go Daddy essentially repeats the same arguments that we have examined and rejected above. Because the record contains "evidence in support of the verdict," and because Go Daddy has failed to show that the district court "made a mistake of law," the district court did not abuse its discretion in denying Go Daddy's motion for a new trial.

CONCLUSION

For the foregoing reasons, we affirm the district court's denial of Go Daddy's motion for judgment as a matter of law under Rule 50(a), and we affirm the district court's denial of Go Daddy's motion for a new trial under Rule 59(a).

. . .

Notes and Questions

1. The court seemed to focus a great deal on the date of termination. The court specifically stated that there was evidence that Go Daddy's decision to terminate Bouamama was not made on April 4, but rather was made sometime between April 14 and April 17. Why is this fact important and why did the court focus on it?

2. Suppose you represent a growing internet start-up with an inexperienced management team. The CEO tells you she is thinking of firing their ad sales manager, who is a tall white male in his 20s. She confides in you that she thinks advertisers would prefer to hear a female voice making sales by phone, and that on sales calls customers seem intimidated by the ad sales manager's height. Given what you have learned from the Go Daddy case, what advice do you have for the CEO?

3. Oftentimes when employees are terminated, they are asked to sign a severance agreement that states that the employee waives his or her right to sue the employer in exchange for a severance payment. A waiver in a severance agreement generally is valid when an employee knowingly and voluntarily consents to the waiver. What are the types of factors a court would likely consider in determining whether such a waiver should be enforced and whether the employee knowingly and voluntarily consented to the waiver? If the court determines that the waiver is not enforceable and permits the former employee to bring a discrimination suit against the former employer, do you think the severance payment should be returned?

4. Consider whether the following employment practices/actions of your client, ABC Moving Company, would likely be in violation of one of the federal statutes barring various forms of employment-related discrimination. Consider also whether there is additional information you need from your client.

   a. ABC Moving Company requires that all applicants seeking employment as movers pass an English language test.

   b. ABC Moving Company also requires that all applicants seeking employment as receptionists pass an English language test.

   c. ABC Moving Company requires that all of its movers weigh more than 150 pounds and be taller than 5'6".

   d. ABC Moving Company only hires movers under the age of 40 because in its experience the required heavy lifting is too much for older people.

D.   EMPLOYMENT AGREEMENTS

A common theme that comes up time and time again in the advice a lawyer should be giving a client starting a new venture is "put it in writing!" For certain key employees, it is crucial to document the terms of an employment relationship in a written contract setting forth the agreed upon arrangement. It is very difficult to resolve disputes in the future if there is not an enforceable contract setting forth the intentions and agreements of the parties at the onset of the relationship, and with an important employee the stakes are too high to leave the arrangement to chance. After all, absent a written employment agreement, employees are considered to be "at will," meaning they can be fired or — possibly more concerning to an entrepreneurial venture — quit at any time.

These terms of an employment agreement should include the duties or services to be provided, the work schedule, and the compensation and benefits to be received by the employee. The agreement should also set forth the duration of the employment, how the employment may be terminated, and any severance arrangements. Even if the venture does not want to address those issues and wants to keep the employee in an "at will" status, an employment agreement or confidentiality agreement should state that the employee is required to keep proprietary information confidential. Employers also typically require employees to assign all rights and title to works created and inventions developed to the company, either in their employment agreement or in a separate "assignment of inventions" agreement. Chapters 2 and 4 describe these provisions and the various limitations on such provisions in more detail. The parties should also consider whether the agreement should contain non-competition provisions and non-solicitation provisions. As noted in Chapter 2, the enforceability of such provisions post-employment (and in the absence of a sale of the business) varies from state to state.

If the venture wants to deliver something to a job candidate in writing but does not want to take on specific obligations as to pay, severance, or other matters, the lawyer can help the client draft an "offer letter." An offer letter is basically a marketing piece that offers at will employment at a particular starting salary. While it typically does not guarantee any term of employment or severance to the employee, it can be useful as a recruitment tool. When used in connection with a confidentiality and assignment of inventions agreement, an offer letter provides flexibility and security to the entrepreneurial venture while simultaneously giving comfort to the employee.

E. EQUITY COMPENSATION

New companies are often short on cash and at the same time need to build a strong management team. As noted earlier in this chapter, the strength of the management team is one of the most important ingredients of a successful venture. Many investors rely as much on the track record of the founders and management team as the business idea itself. New ventures need to be creative in recruitment strategies in order to attract and retain top talent while reserving as much cash as possible to build and grow the business. Therefore, offering equity compensation is an attractive way of supplementing leaner salaries. Compensating with equity in addition to a salary has the added benefit of closely aligning the incentives of the employees with those of the founders and other initial investors. Everyone makes more money if the company is successful because its shares or membership units are worth more.

Although it is not the only method, many equity incentive packages come in the form of stock options. A stock option is a right to purchase shares of stock of the company in the future at today's price. If the price of the stock rises, then the worker can pay a lower price for something that is worth more. Stock options typically are "granted" (given) to the worker but cannot be exercised right away. Instead, they "vest" (become exercisable) over time or upon the achievement of certain goals — encouraging employees to stay with the company for longer periods of time or perform better to meet the vesting goals. Options are typically governed by two documents: a "plan" and a "grant agreement." The plan document sets forth rules that govern all options granted by the company and may cover such issues as whether options are exercisable after an employee is terminated, whether shares issued on the exercise of options are subject to any restrictions on transfer, whether the company has the right to repurchase the shares in certain circumstances and at what price, and so forth. The grant agreement tends to be a shorter document personalized to each employee receiving a grant of options, and sets forth the number of options being granted, the exercise price and the applicable vesting schedule.

There are two types of stock options, which are classified for tax purposes either as nonqualified stock options (NQSOs) or statutory stock options. The tax treatment of stock options depends on the classification of the option. NQSOs are typically used to compensate corporate officers and other employees. However, they are not restricted to employees of the company. Therefore, anyone providing services to the company may receive NQSOs. This can include directors and independent contractors. The tax treatment for NQSOs is generally not as favorable to the holder as statutory stock options. Stock options meeting the requirements for statutory stock options may, under certain circumstances, receive tax-favorable treatment. Statutory stock options include incentive stock options (ISOs) and options granted under employee stock purchase plans. It is important to note that there are a number of additional restrictions on the issuance of ISOs as compared to NQSOs (e.g., type of recipient, number that may be granted and exercised in a given year, etc.), so it is often the case that early-stage companies will opt for NQSOs for simplicity. Under the tax rules imposed by § 409(a) of the Internal Revenue Code, the pricing of stock options for both ISOs and NQSOs has become a more important issue. As a general rule, companies will need to ensure that the exercise price for the options is set at fair market value as of the date of grant, which often makes it worthwhile to spend the money on an outside "409(a) valuation" in connection with any grants.

PROBLEM

Olivia and Andrew have advised you that they are considering hiring Brad Jacobs to help with both sales and marketing. Brad worked in sales for several years after graduating from business school. From their initial conversations with Brad, Olivia and Andrew have told you Brad would work from his own home; use his own computer, phone, and car; there would be no set hours that he would be required to work; and he would be paid a commission of 12 percent on all orders he receives. They would like Brad to show the same company spirit they show by wearing a Germ Genie polo shirt or dress shirt when he is on sales calls. They were particularly impressed by Brad because he had great ideas for marketing and sales materials and strategies that he planned to create to market the product. Olivia and Andrew expect they will hire other sales reps in the future and they could use the materials and strategies Brad develops to train new hires.

Olivia and Andrew have a host of other concerns they express to you regarding their anticipated relationship with Brad. They like Brad, but are a little nervous about cash flow and want to make sure they don't have to pay Brad his commission on any order until the company actually receives payment from the customer. They also explain to you that although they think either party should be able to terminate the relationship with reasonable notice, they want to ensure they have help for the annual health technology expo in Las Vegas that takes place each June. They do not want Brad to be able to terminate the relationship within six weeks of the show. They are also concerned that Brad may decide to represent competing products while he is promoting Magic Wand. They are not sure this is necessarily a problem, but ask for your thoughts. Finally, they think it is important to maintain the integrity of their brand and want approval rights over any orders Brad obtains.

Olivia and Andrew tell you they have heard from friends that it is better to classify workers as independent contractors rather than employees. They are not sure why this is the case and would like you to briefly explain the differences. They would also like advice on how to classify Brad, hopefully as an independent contractor.

Draft an email to Olivia and Andrew of client-appropriate length with concrete advice on how they can best structure the relationship between the company and Brad, and any steps they should take to achieve their objective. In addition, using your law firm's form document below and any other forms or information you find in your research, draft an independent contractor agreement and explain any unusual or important clauses in your email.

INDEPENDENT CONTRACTOR AGREEMENT

This Independent Contractor Agreement (this "Agreement") is entered into as of the date set forth below between [COMPANY], an Illinois limited liability company (the "Company"), and the person, firm, or organization whose name is set forth below (the "Contractor," and, together with the Company, the "Parties").

RECITALS

The Contractor represents that he or she has compiled with all Federal, State, and local laws regarding business permits, licenses, reporting requirements, tax withholding requirements, and other legal requirements of any kind that may be required to carry out said business and the Scope of Work which is to be performed as an independent contractor pursuant to this Agreement.

The Company desires to engage and contract for the services of the Contractor to perform certain tasks as set forth below. The Contractor desires to enter into this Agreement and perform as an independent contractor for the company and is willing to do so on the terms and conditions set forth below.

NOW, THEREFORE, in consideration of the above recitals and the mutual promises and conditions contained in this Agreement, the Parties agree as follows:

Status as Independent Contractor

1. The Contractor is not an employee of the Company, and nothing in this Agreement shall be construed to create an employment relationship between the two Parties. The Contractor shall not participate in any employee benefit plan or program. The Contractor shall have exclusive control of the method of performance of his or her duties and shall independently manage and control its activities subject only to the terms

of this Agreement.

Scope of Work

2. The Contractor shall devote as much time, attention, and energy as necessary to complete the project(s) or achieve the objective(s) set forth in the Scope of Work document attached hereto (the "Scope of Work").

3. The Contractor shall be responsible to the management of the Company, but the Contractor shall supply all necessary equipment, materials, and supplies. The Contractor will not rely on the equipment or offices of the Company for completion of tasks and duties set forth pursuant to this Agreement. Any advice given to the Contractor regarding the Scope of Work shall be considered a suggestion only, not an instruction. The Company retains the right to inspect, stop, or alter the work of the Contractor to assure its conformity with this Agreement.

Compensation and Reimbursement

4. Contractor will be paid on an hourly, a daily, or a total project basis, as set forth in the Scope of Work document.

5. In addition to the compensation provided for in Paragraph 4, the Contractor will be reimbursed for reasonable and necessary expenses incurred in performing the Scope of Work outlined in this Agreement, subject to the prior written approval of the Company.

Withholding of Taxes

6. All income paid to the Contractor under this Agreement shall constitute income from self-employment and the Contractor shall be required to pay self-employment taxes on his or her own. Because of the Contractor's status as an independent contractor, the Company shall have no obligation or liability whatsoever to the Contractor for workers' compensation, federal and state payroll taxes, unemployment compensation, minimum wages, Social Security assessments, foreign taxes, or similar charges applicable to an employment relationship.

Confidentiality

7. Information and materials supplied to the Contractor by the Company or by a client of the Company shall be treated as confidential and shall not be disclosed or used in any way not connected with the assignment for which the Contractor has been engaged without the Company's written authorization.

Non-Solicitation

8. At no time during the term of this Agreement, and for a period of 180 days following the completion of an engagement, shall the Contractor provide services to any of the Company's clients except in the Contractor's capacity as an independent contractor engaged by the Company.

Return of Property

9. On the request of the Company or upon the termination of this Agreement, the Contractor will immediately return to the Company all tools, sketches, technical drawings, and other materials containing information related in any way to the Company or our business or client(s),

including all records created or obtained by the Contractor in connection with this Agreement.

Intellectual Property

10. Any intellectual property pertaining to the business of the Company including, but not limited to, inventions, discoveries, graphic designs, trademarks, copyrights, and innovations, written or composed by the Contractor shall be the property of the Company. On request and without additional compensation, the Contractor will execute whatever copyright applications, assignments, or other documents are required to confirm the Company's ownership of such materials.

Insurance

11. The Contractor will carry liability insurance relative to the Scope of Work that he, she, or it forms for the Company.

Termination

12. This Agreement and the engagement hereunder may be terminated either (i) by mutual agreement of the Parties or (ii) by either Party at any time upon 30-days written notice to the other Party. Upon termination of this Agreement and the engagement hereunder, the Company shall be obligated to pay the Contractor all fees or other compensation for services rendered prior to termination, and to reimburse related costs incurred, in accordance with the terms of this Agreement, except that the Company may reduce or otherwise offset such payments by the amount of damages incurred in the event that termination is based upon the breach of the Contractor's obligations.

Dispute Resolution

13. Any dispute between the Parties to this Agreement involving the construction or application of any of the terms, provisions, or conditions of this Agreement, shall on written request of either party served on the other, be submitted first to mediation and then if still unresolved to binding arbitration before a single arbitrator in Chicago, Illinois, U.S.A. Said mediation or binding arbitration shall comply with and be governed by the provisions of the American Arbitration Association for Commercial Disputes.

Indemnification

14. The Contractor shall defend, indemnify, hold harmless, and insure the Company from any and all damages, expenses, or liability resulting from or arising out of, any negligence or misconduct on the Contractor's part, or from any breach or default of this Agreement which is caused or occasioned by the acts of the Contractor. The Contractor shall insure that its employees and affiliates take all actions necessary to comply with the terms and conditions set forth in this Agreement. The Contractor shall name Company as an additional insured on all related insurance policies including workers' compensation, and general liability.

Notices

15. Any and all notices, demands, or other communications required or desired to be given hereunder by any party shall be in writing and shall be validly given or made to another party if personally served, or if deposited

in the United States mail, certified or registered, postage prepaid, return receipt requested. If such notice or demand is served personally, notice shall be deemed constructively made at the time of such personal service. If such notice, demand, or other communication is given by mail, such notice shall be conclusively deemed given five days after deposit thereof in the United States mail addressed to the party to whom such notice, demand, or other communication is to be given as follows:

If to the Contractor: To the person and address set forth below

If to the Company: [COMPANY ADDRESS AND CONTACT NAME]

Any party hereto may change its address for purposes of this paragraph by written notice given in the manner provided above.

Governing Law

16. The laws of the State of Illinois shall govern the validity of this Agreement, the construction of its terms, and the interpretation of the rights and duties of the Parties. Jurisdiction and venue for all purposes shall be in the County of Cook, State of Illinois.

IN WITNESS WHEREOF the undersigned have executed this Agreement as of _____, 20__. The Parties agree that facsimile signatures shall be as effective as if originals.

[COMPANY]

By: _____
Name: _____
Title: _____

Agreed and accepted:

_____
Print Contractor's Name

By: _____
Name: _____
Title: _____

_____
Street Address

_____
City, State, and Zip Code

_____
EIN or Social Security Number

VII

OPERATIONAL CONTRACTS

In the dense and often abstract world of a first-year Contracts course, it is easy to forget that businesses — including entrepreneurial ventures — rely on contracts. Whether the business is a service provider, a retail store, or an online community, it enters into contracts with customers, suppliers, community members, workers, and owners. For the attorney representing an entrepreneur, it is important to recognize what contracts exist, to be sure, but the subsequent art is in choosing the right type of contract for a particular relationship and then drafting the contract in a manner that best serves the client. While transactional lawyers are sometimes derided as scriveners trained in the art of "find-and-replace," the task of assembling a contract is actually much more complex than just finding a good form. Lawyers need good example contracts where they are available, to be sure, but even more so they must understand the underlying substantive legal areas, including contract enforceability and interpretation and also the particular doctrine applicable to the subject matter of the contract, be it intellectual property law, employment law, warranty law, securities law, real estate law, import/export laws, or any other area. Since substantive rules often vary by state, the practitioner must also understand state-specific complexities and conventions.

In this chapter, we start with a sketch of the basic substantive sections of commercial contracts and a discussion of various contract drafting styles. From there, we move to some specific thoughts on the pitfalls and opportunities of drafting contracts for an entrepreneurial venture. Since contract drafting is best learned in practice, you will notice that we have few notes following the readings in this chapter. Instead, we encourage you to consider the problem at the end of the chapter, which asks you to draft a contract based on business terms we provide.

While all businesses should be diligent about documenting deals and having enforceable contracts in place setting forth agreed-upon terms, oftentimes new ventures and entrepreneurs are less likely to take this important step. There are several reasons why this is the case. Entrepreneurs are especially anxious to get started on building and growing their new business and may view the exercise of getting a contract signed as an impediment to moving forward. Also, entrepreneurs likely have very limited cash, so the thought of spending precious capital to pay lawyers to create contracts may seem to be wasteful at best. Entrepreneurs often have business relationships with friends, family members, or former classmates, and it may seem awkward or even insulting to request to have a contract signed. Entrepreneurs may also feel that they have little leverage initially and are so happy to get a new client or customer that they are afraid to scare off business by insisting on the formalities of a contract.

Excitement, passion, a sense of inadequacy or awkwardness, and frugality are all understandable sentiments of a new entrepreneur, but they should not stand in the way of getting a contract in place and ensuring that parties have agreed upon specific terms and conditions. Many new businesses have failed because contracts were not signed when a deal was made and future faulty memories or perhaps greed have caused those once good deals to head south. For example, after a company purchases inventory that it expects to be delivered prior to the holidays, the distributor may recall that time was not of the essence. Lawyers representing entrepreneurs need to be ready to counsel clients on the importance of contracts generally and then be willing to work with those clients to create contracts that may feel more appropriate or comfortable to entrepreneurs as opposed to large established businesses.

Finally, we note that while this chapter will not provide a review of your first-year Contracts course, we will from time to time refresh you on concepts you encountered in that course so you can see the practical application of the theory you learned earlier in your law school career.

A. ANATOMY OF A CONTRACT

Contracts come in a variety of shapes and sizes. Sometimes, like with the example in this section, contracts are long, formal documents with titles, opening paragraphs, long wordy explanations and definitions sections, and multiple cross-references. Other times, contracts are short, seemingly innocuous documents — like a letter that asks the other party to sign at the bottom, or an email sent to a customer asking the customer to reply if she agrees. For the lawyer, choosing the right format can be as important as some of the drafting in the contract itself. Lawyers working with entrepreneurs for the first time often draft long and comprehensive documents that actually hinder the client in trying to get her business off the ground. As an example, take an entrepreneur who asks the lawyer to draft a customer contract for a new consulting business. If the lawyer drafts an overly complex agreement, the entrepreneur may find the contract is met with resistance on sales calls ("sorry, I can't sign now, I need to send this to the legal department"), whereas a simple letter agreement or one-page proposal might be signed on the spot. Of course, lawyers need to balance the expedience of a short and easy contract with the need to protect the client. Part of the art of contract drafting is making these trade-offs, and discussing them with the client.

If a lawyer uses the traditional transactional document, it will contain roughly the following sections, in some order or another and only if applicable: a title, an opening paragraph, recitals, definitions, main operative paragraphs documenting the business deal, representations and warranties, covenants, conditions to closing, closing mechanics, term and termination provisions, indemnification, boilerplate, and signature blocks. The best way to understand what these terms mean is to see them in a contract, like the one below. The comments are our explanations as to the various sections of the contract. Note that not every contract needs to follow this format — we are merely seeking to explain the anatomy of a typical contract. Indeed, in the contract below you will not find closing matters addressed since there is no formal "closing" of the contemplated deal. For some contracts with hefty closing mechanics, see Chapter 10.

MANUFACTURING AGREEMENT

> *TITLE: The title of the contract is typically centered and in bold, and often — though not always — gives a sense of the subject matter of the contract.*

This Manufacturing Agreement, made effective as of January 1, 2020, by and between Schott's Shots, Inc. ("Buyer"), and Builders Ltd. ("Seller").

> *OPENING PARGRAPH: The first paragraph of the document typically lays out the name of the contract, the date of the contract, and the parties to the contract. When a capitalized word appears in quotation marks between parentheses it means that, for purposes of this contract, the capitalized word will have the legal definition that immediately precedes it. In the example above, every time the contract uses the word "Buyer" it is to be understood that the contract is referring to Schott's Shots, Inc.*

WITNESSETH:

WHEREAS, Buyer is in the business of designing, manufacturing, and marketing electronic novelty items;

WHEREAS, Seller owns and operates a factory which has the capability of manufacturing products of the type Buyer designs, manufactures and markets;

WHEREAS, Buyer and Seller now wish to enter into this Agreement to arrange for the manufacture by Seller and the purchase by Buyer of certain Products;

> *RECITALS: The recitals, which in a very traditional contract appear beneath the word "witnesseth" but in more modern forms appear under the word "recitals" or "background," are typically nonbinding sentences that tell the story of how the parties came to decide to enter into the contract together.*

NOW, THEREFORE, in consideration of the foregoing, the mutual covenants and agreements contained herein and for other good and valuable consideration, the receipt and sufficiency of which are hereby acknowledged, the parties hereto hereby agree as follows:

> *The "now therefore" paragraph may be thought of as part of the opening paragraph, and basically just says the parties agree to the terms of the contract. Thinking back on your Contracts course, notice the way in which drafters often try to get over the issue of whether there is consideration for the deal.*

Section 1. Definitions. As used in this Agreement, the following terms shall have the following respective meanings (such meanings being equally applicable to both the singular and plural forms of the terms defined):

> *DEFINITIONS: In formal contracts, defined terms are typically grouped together unless they appear in the opening paragraph or in only one place in the contract. Different lawyers have different levels of attention to this detail, but there is no denying the convenience of knowing to turn to section 1 whenever the reader is unsure how to interpret a capitalized word.*

"Affiliates" means any Person or entity (i) which directly or indirectly Controls, or is Controlled by, or is under common Control with a party hereto or (ii) twenty-five percent (25%) or more of the voting securities of which is directly or indirectly beneficially owned or held by a party hereto.

"Agreement" means this Manufacturing Agreement, including all amendments, modifications and supplements hereto and any exhibits or schedules to any of the following.

"Build Requirement" shall have the meaning ascribed thereto in Section 2.1.

"Business" shall mean the business of designing, manufacturing, and marketing electronic novelty items.

"Buyer Competitors" means any Person, other than the Buyer, engaged in the Business in any manner.

"Buyer Customers" means any Person who purchases any item from Buyer, including but not limited to Products under this Agreement and items which contain Products as a component thereof, and any Person to whom it is foreseeable Buyer may attempt to sell any Products or items which contain Products in the future.

"Causing Party" shall have the meaning ascribed thereto in Section 4.2.

"Completion Date" shall have the meaning ascribed thereto in Section 2.2.

"Confidential Information" shall have the meaning ascribed thereto in Section 9.1.

> *Notice in the preceding definitions that a definition explained later in the contract is not included here, merely incorporated by cross-reference. A lawyer will use this approach where, in the lawyer's judgment, defining the term in the applicable operative paragraph makes the contract easier to understand.*

"Control" means the possession, directly or indirectly, of the power to direct or cause the direction of the management and policies of a person or entity, whether through the ownership of voting securities, by contract or otherwise.

"Developments" shall have the meaning ascribed thereto in Section 8.

"Failure Analysis Program" shall have the meaning ascribed thereto in Section 6.4.

"Forecast" shall have the meaning ascribed thereto in Section 2.1.

"Intellectual Property" means all rights held by Buyer, including, but not limited to, Buyer's patents, copyrights, author's rights, trademarks, trade names, service marks, mask works, "know-how" and trade secrets, irrespective of whether such rights arise under U.S. or international intellectual property, unfair competition, or trade secret laws.

"Master Schedule" shall have the meaning ascribed thereto in Section 2.1.

"Maximum Defect Level" shall have the meaning ascribed thereto in Section 7.4.

"On Time" shall have the meaning ascribed thereto in Section 5.2.

"Person" means an individual or a corporation, limited liability company, partnership, trust, incorporated or unincorporated association, joint venture, joint stock company, governmental authority or other person of any kind.

> *While it may seem unnecessary to define certain terms (such as "Person" above), lawyers desire precision in their documents so that they will be interpreted exactly as the parties intend should an issue ever arise. Shorter contracts often use fewer defined terms and rely on common usage where the attorney perceives the risk of misinterpretation to be low.*

"Prevailing Party" shall have the meaning ascribed thereto in Section 16.3.

"Price" means the price paid by Buyer for Products manufactured by Seller under this Agreement, and refers to both the unit price and extended price of such Products; such price is determined according to Section 5.3.

"Product" is defined as the items set forth in Schedule 1 and manufactured by Seller in compliance with the requirements of this Agreement and the applicable Purchase Orders. Products includes all prototype units, pre-production units and production units. Products may be added to or deleted from Schedule 1 by mutual written consent of the parties. Any such addition or deletion shall be set forth in an amendment to this Agreement signed by the parties and containing a revised Schedule 1 reflecting the addition or deletion.

"Purchase Order" means the purchase order of the Seller, substantially in the form attached hereto as Exhibit A, or such form as may be completed in accordance with the terms of this Agreement.

"Terminating Party" shall have the meaning ascribed thereto in Section 4.2.

"Works In Progress" shall have the meaning ascribed thereto in Section 4.3.

Section 2.   Order and Purchase of Products.

> *MAIN OPERATIVE PARAGRAPHS: In this contract and most formal agreements, the key business deal is laid out early on in the contract. Here, the deal is that Buyer is buying Products from Seller.*

2.1 Master Schedule. Each week throughout the term of this Agreement, Buyer shall provide Seller with a schedule for the purchase of Products (the "Master Schedule"). Each Master Schedule will include (a) a three-month build requirement for the three months beginning with the date the Master Schedule is delivered to Seller, which shall specify the quantity and type of Products the Buyer desires to purchase and time(s) by which Buyer requires such Products (the "Build Requirement"); and (b) a three-month forecast for the three months following the period in (a), which shall estimate the quantity and type of Products the Buyer may desire to purchase and the time(s) for delivery of such Products (the "Forecast"). The Forecast is provided for Seller's convenience only, and does not constitute an order or commitment of any kind by Buyer.

2.2 Completion Date; Purchase Orders. Within three business days of receipt of the Master Schedule, Seller shall notify Buyer of the date(s) by which it can deliver the products described in the Build Requirement (the "Completion Date"). The Completion Date shall not be more than four (4) weeks from the date specified in the Build Requirement. Once Seller has notified Buyer of the Completion Date, if such date is satisfactory to Buyer, Buyer shall issue a Purchase Order for the quantity specified in the Build Requirement at the Price. Once the Purchase Order has been issued, Buyer shall be obligated to Buy, and Seller shall be obligated to sell, the specified quantity of Products, at the Price, to be delivered On Time.

2.3 Changes to Purchase Orders. Once a Purchase Order has been issued by Buyer under this Agreement, the terms of the Purchase Order can only be amended through a written instrument signed by Buyer. Any proposed alterations to a Purchase Order shall be negotiated in good faith by both parties, but if the Purchase Order is not amended, it shall continue to bind both parties.

2.4 Inability of Seller to Follow the Master Schedule. Seller has three business days after receipt of the Master Schedule to notify Buyer if Seller will not be able to meet any new or revised delivery requirements specified in the Build Requirement or any new or revised forecasted delivery requirements specified in the Forecast. Such notification shall not relieve Seller of its obligations under this Agreement.

Notice the ways in which the lawyers are trying to dictate how certain foreseeable failures can be handled. One key job of the entrepreneur's lawyer is to protect the entrepreneur if it cannot fulfill the terms of a contract, and also if the other party cannot meet its obligations.

Section 3.   Term. The term of this Agreement commences on the date stated above and continues until terminated in accordance with Section 4.

Section 4.   Termination.

4.1 Termination for Convenience. Either party may terminate this Agreement for any reason, with or without cause, upon ninety (90) days' written notice to the other party.

4.2 Termination for Cause. This Agreement may be terminated by one party (the "Terminating Party") for cause immediately by written notice to the other party (the "Causing Party") upon the occurrence of any of the following events:

(a) the Causing Party ceases to do business, or otherwise terminates its business operations;

(b) the Causing Party shall petition or apply to any tribunal for the appointment of a trustee or receiver of the Causing Party, or of all or substantially all of its assets, or shall commence any proceeding relating to the Causing Party under any bankruptcy, reorganization, arrangement, insolvency, re-adjustment of debt, dissolution or liquidation law of any jurisdiction, whether now or hereafter in effect or shall make an assignment for the benefit of creditors or shall admit in writing its inability to pay its debts generally as they become due; or any petition or application referred to in this Section 4.2(b) shall have been filed, or any such proceedings shall have been commenced, against the Causing Party and (i) the Causing Party shall have consented thereto, or (ii) an order shall have been entered (A) adjudicating the Causing Party a bankrupt or insolvent, or (B) appointing any such trustee or receiver, or (C) approving the petition in any such proceedings, and any such order shall not have been vacated, stayed or reversed within ninety days after the entry thereof;

(c) Seller fails to make On Time delivery three times;

(d) Seller reaches or exceeds the Maximum Defect Level; or

(e) the Causing Party fails to comply with any provision of this Agreement and such failure is not corrected by the Causing Party within 10 days after receipt of written notice from the Terminating Party specifying in reasonable detail such failure.

4.3 Rights Upon Termination. Upon termination in accordance with this Section 4, Buyer's sole and exclusive liability to Seller shall be to pay for Products already completed and delivered.

TERM AND TERMINATION: Contracts will almost always have some provision detailing the length of time the entire contract will be binding (the term) and the conditions under which it can come to an end (a termination). The contract will also explain what happens if it is terminated, which can range from immediate cessation of the relationship to some provision for ongoing completion of particular obligations. Oftentimes, outcomes are different depending on why a contract is terminated.

Section 5.   Packing, Delivery, Shipping, Pricing, Payment.

5.1 Packing. All items must be suitably packed and marked as designated by Buyer, or, in the absence of a designation, in accordance with the requirements of common carriers in a manner to secure lowest transportation cost and industry-standard, safe transport for the Products. Buyer's Purchase Order number must be clearly marked on all invoices, packages, bills of lading and shipping orders. There will be no additional charges to Buyer for packing.

5.2 Delivery and Shipping. All deliveries of Products shall be F.O.B. Port of Long Beach. Goods shall be considered "On Time" when they are at the dock in the port no earlier than five days prior to the Completion Date and no later than the Completion Date. If Seller-responsible actions necessitate the use of premium transportation to ensure On Time delivery, Seller shall, in addition to other remedies permitted Buyer by this Agreement or by law, be solely responsible for the expense of such premium transportation. Title and risk of loss or damage to Products shall pass to Buyer upon On Time delivery to the carrier at the port dock, subject to Buyer's right to reject non-conforming Products. Buyer will arrange for forwarding services from the port dock to Buyer's facility.

5.3 Pricing.

> *In this contract, the obligation to pay is discussed in section 2.1 and the amount to be paid appears later. Remember that this contract is just an example and that details like this term might appear in any number of places, depending on the contract's author.*

(a) Initial Price. Buyer and Seller shall agree on an initial price for Products. In the negotiation over Price, the parties shall take into account component prices, anticipated purchase volume as indicated in the Master Schedule, current market prices for similar products manufactured by other manufacturers, taxes that may be assessed on Buyer and other factors reasonably impacting the costs of manufacturing the products.

(b) Quarterly Review of Price. The Price is to be formally reviewed by the parties at the start of each calendar quarter and, after a good faith negotiation, the Price will be adjusted by mutual agreement in writing including an effective date of the adjusted Price. The prevailing Price will remain in effect until the parties agree in writing to modify the Price. Price adjustments shall take into account market fluctuations in component prices, Product purchase volume increases or decreases, cost-saving measures taken by Seller and other factors reasonably impacting the costs of manufacturing the Products.

(c) Price Reduction and Buyer's Obligations. Buyer's continued purchases under this Agreement will be subject to Seller's ability to deliver Products at prices and of a quantity competitive in the then-current marketplace. Seller shall use its best efforts to reduce prices to Buyer at all times through any and all methods, including but not limited to, manufacturing, processing and packaging improvements.

(d) Taxes. Buyer shall pay any sales, use, excise or similar tax attributable to purchase of the Products. All taxes must be stated separately on Seller's invoices.

5.4 Payment. Seller may submit invoices for Products to Buyer upon On Time delivery of such Product. Each invoice shall specify Buyer's Purchase Order number, description, date of shipment, quantity shipped, unit price, extended price, taxes assessed and such other information as may be reasonably requested by Buyer from time to time. Payment terms will be (a) net thirty (30) calendar days after receipt by Buyer of the invoice, or (b) net sixty (60) calendar days after receipt by Buyer of the invoice with a one percent (1%) carrying charge assessed. Buyer shall have no obligation to pay for any Product that is rejected or as to which acceptance is revoked.

Section 6.   Inspection and Acceptance.

6.1 Inspection by Seller. Seller will inspect and test all Products prior to shipment to Buyer. Each delivered Product must include complete test results for each test the parties may mutually agree in good faith are necessary for the particular category of Products. Test data may be kept on file at Seller's manufacturing facility and must be immediately available to Buyer upon request.

6.2 Source Inspection by Buyer. Seller will afford the officers, employees, agents and other representatives of Buyer full and free access to the plants, properties, books and records of Seller and its affiliates, and will permit them to make extracts from and copies of such books and records. Such inspection and any related testing may take place prior to the shipment of Buyer's Products. From time to time, Seller will furnish Buyer with such additional financial and operating data and other information as to the financial condition, results of operations, businesses, properties, assets, liabilities or future prospects of Seller and its affiliates as Buyer may request.

6.3 Inspection and Acceptance by Buyer. Notwithstanding any prior payment or inspection by Buyer, all products are subject to final inspection and acceptance by Buyer at Buyer's facility, or in accordance with quality control standards to be agreed upon by Buyer and Seller. If Buyer rejects any portion for failure to conform with the requirements of a Purchase Order, Buyer will notify Seller of the rejection in writing, giving reasons for the rejection. Seller then has the option to repair or replace the nonconforming Products within thirty (30) days at Buyer's or Seller's facility. Rejected items will be returned to Seller at Seller's expense. If Seller fails to act to correct any nonconforming Product within thirty (30) days after written notice by Buyer, then Buyer may, at Seller's risk and expense, return any nonconforming Products to Seller.

6.4 Buyer's Failure Analysis Program. As part of its inspection procedure under this Section 6, Buyer will design and implement a program to determine the cause of failures in the field or at audit (the "Failure Analysis Program"). Under the Failure Analysis Program, Product failures will be categorized as either design defects or workmanship defects. Design defects will be the responsibility of Buyer, and shall not contribute to the Maximum Defect Level as defined below in Section 7.4. In the case of workmanship defects, Seller shall, at Seller's sole expense, promptly (i) diagnose the source of the failures of the Product; (ii) correct all defects or non-conformities in the manufacture and/or testing of the Product which are the source of such failures; (iii) provide Buyer with a summary of such diagnostic and correction activities; and (iv) repair or replace all failed units of the Product with fully conforming products and reimburse Buyer for all direct freight costs incurred by Buyer in connection with such failure.

Section 7.   Warranties.

> *Since this contract is for the manufacture of goods, the warranties referred to in these paragraphs are product warranties. Do not confuse this kind of warranty with the "representations and warranties" appearing in section 12.*

7.1 Generally. Seller warrants to Buyer that all Products delivered under this Agreement shall (i) be free from defects in workmanship and material; (ii) contain all new materials; (iii) conform to the applicable descriptions, specifications and drawings, if any, that appear on Schedule 1 hereto; (iv) conform to the requirements of the relevant Purchase Order including, but not limited to, the applicable descriptions, specifications and drawings that have been agreed to by the parties; (v) to the extent that the Products are not manufactured pursuant to detailed designs furnished by Buyer, all items will be free from defects in design and suitable for the intended purposes; and (vi) are merchantable and fit for the purpose intended.

7.2 Repair and Replacement of Defective Products. Defective Products returned shall be repaired or replaced by Seller at its sole expense within thirty (30) days after Seller's receipt of such defective Products. Buyer will prepay shipping charges for Products returned to Seller under this section. Seller will promptly reimburse Buyer for prepaid freight charges and will ship repaired or replacement Products to Buyer at Seller's expense. Any Product which is repaired or replaced by Seller shall be warranted as provided in this section.

7.3 Defective Products Not Repaired or Replaced. If any Products are returned by Buyer and the returned goods are not (i) repaired or replaced by Seller, and (ii) delivered to Buyer, then Seller will refund to Buyer any money, notes, or property paid or given for the Products, or Seller will credit the account of Buyer in a like amount.

> *Again, as you read these paragraphs, note the way the lawyers drafting the contract have tried to cover many different potential performance failures.*

7.4 Maximum Defect Level. "Maximum Defect Level" means the point at which (i) the number of defective units of the Product delivered in at least two shipments equals or exceeds five-hundredths of one percent (0.05%) of the total number of units of the Product that were received by Buyer in such shipments; or (ii) any other defect found to exist within any lot that may (a) seriously endanger the marketability of the affected Product or (b) seriously degrade the reputation of Buyer if the defect is not timely corrected and customer complaints shall have been received by Buyer relating to the defect. Units that are determined by the Failure Analysis Program to be defective by reason of design defects will not be counted as defective for the purposes of this Section 7.4. Buyer may terminate this Agreement pursuant to Section 4 when it has identified failures exceeding the Maximum Defect Level in addition to any other remedies it may have.

> COVENANTS: *In simple terms, a "covenant" is just a promise to do something. (A "negative covenant" is a promise not to do something.) In that sense, the entire contract is filled with covenants. However, in particular kinds of contracts the word "covenant" may have different meanings. The "covenants" in a loan agreement include promises as to the financial status of a borrower in the future. The "covenant" in a non-compete agreement is an agreement not to compete with a business. Here, we might loosely call sections 8 and 9 covenants, since they are promises that enhance, but do not constitute, the main bargain.*

Section 8. Intellectual Property. The Intellectual Property rights in and to the Products are owned by the Buyer and are protected by the United States and international copyright and patents laws and treaty provisions. This Agreement does not constitute a sale or license agreement and does not transfer to the Seller any title or ownership interest in or to the Products or any patent, copyright, trade secret, trade name, trademark, or other proprietary or Intellectual Property rights related to the Products. Except for rights expressly granted herein, the Buyer retains all of its right, title and interest to the Products and to any modifications, improvements, reports, designs, inventions, specifications or other materials developed in connection with the Seller's manufacture of the Products, whether developed by Buyer or Seller, and all Intellectual Property rights therein (collectively, "Developments").

Section 9.   Confidentiality; Publicity.

9.1 Restrictions on Disclosure and Use. Except as required for performance under this Agreement or as otherwise provided herein or as required by law, all documentation and technical and business information and intellectual property in whatever form recorded that a party provides to the other party orally or in writing ("Confidential Information") shall remain the property of the furnishing party and may be used by the receiving party only as provided in this section. "Confidential Information" shall include, without limitation, Intellectual Property, Buyer technology, Buyer specifications, Buyer Developments, Buyer memoranda, Buyer bulletins, Buyer drawings, quantities or prices specified when Purchase Orders are placed or forecasts are made, the Master Schedule, billing matters including invoicing and amounts past due, and defect levels in Product manufacture.

Confidential Information (i) shall not be reproduced or copied, in whole or in part, except for use as expressly authorized in this Agreement; (ii) shall, together with any full or partial copies thereof, be returned or destroyed when no longer needed or upon any termination of this Agreement; and (iii) shall be disclosed only to employees or agents of a party with a need to know. Moreover, such Confidential Information shall be used by the receiving party only for the purposes contemplated under this Agreement or in the exercise of the rights it may receive expressly under the provisions of this Agreement. Unless the furnishing party consents in this Agreement or otherwise in writing, such Confidential Information shall be kept in strict confidence by the receiving party. The receiving party shall treat such Confidential Information as proprietary using the same degree of care that it would normally use in protecting its own proprietary information, but in no event less than reasonable care.

These restrictions on the use or disclosure of Confidential Information shall survive this Agreement for a period of five (5) years from the date of termination. These restrictions on the use or disclosure of Confidential Information shall not apply to any Confidential Information (i) which can be proven to be or have been independently developed by the receiving party or lawfully received free of restriction from another source having the right to so furnish such Confidential Information; (ii) after it has become generally available to the public without breach of this Agreement by the receiving party or any of its Affiliates; (iii) which at the time of disclosure to the receiving party was known to such party free of restriction and clearly evidenced by documentation in such party's possession; or (iv) which the furnishing party agrees in writing is free of such restrictions.

Each of the parties recognizes that the unauthorized use or disclosure of the Confidential Information would cause irreparable injury to the furnishing party for which it would have no adequate remedy at law, and that an actual or contemplated breach of this Section shall entitle the disclosing party to obtain immediate injunctive relief prohibiting such breach, in addition to any other rights and remedies available to it.

9.2 Additional Seller Covenants.

(a) Publicity. Seller shall not issue any news release, advertisement, publicity, or promotional material regarding this Agreement or Buyer's relationship with Seller or Buyer's relationship with its customers without Buyer's prior written consent.

(b) Manufacturing Facilities. Seller acknowledges that its manufacturing facilities may also provide services to Buyer's Customers. If and when a facility is used for such purposes, Seller shall use its best efforts to ensure that no Confidential Information is transmitted to Buyer's Customers. Such efforts shall include, but not be limited to, (i) restricting access to areas of the facility where Buyer's products are manufactured to Seller employees; and (ii) ensuring that no Seller employees who work on projects for Buyer be staffed on projects for Buyer's Customers.

(c) Notice. Seller will immediately notify Buyer in writing in the event that (i) there is any breach of this Section 9; or (ii) there is any attempt made by a Person not party to this Agreement to gain access to any Confidential Information.

Section 10.   Indemnification. Seller shall indemnify, defend and hold harmless Buyer and its affiliates, promptly upon demand at any time and from time to time, against any and all losses, liabilities, claims, actions, damages and expenses, including, without limitation, reasonable attorney's fees and disbursements, arising out of or in connection with any of the following: (a) any misrepresentation or breach of any warranty made by Seller; (b) any breach or nonfulfillment of any covenant or agreement made by Seller; (c) any defects in Products manufactured by Seller; and (d) the manufacturing of Products by Seller.

> *INDEMNIFICATION: Indemnification, which is discussed in greater detail in Chapter 109, is a risk management strategy in which one party agrees to cover the other party's losses in connection with the deal. If the parties have equal bargaining power, it is common to see a "mutual indemnification" clause in which both parties indemnify the other.*

Section 11.   Remedies. The remedies reserved in this Agreement are cumulative and in addition to any other remedies provided in law or equity.

Section 12.   Representations and Warranties.

> *REPRESENTATIONS AND WARRANTIES: A representation is a statement of facts as of the time the representation is made. For example, in the representation in 12.1(a) below, each party is stating, as of the signing of the document, that it has the right to sign the Agreement. A warranty is a promise that the representation is accurate. In the warranty of 12.1(a) below, each party is promising that its statement that it had the right to sign the Agreement was true.*

> *Lawyers have added warranties to representations to give plaintiffs an additional cause of action if a representation turns out to have been untrue ("not only did you make an untrue representation, you also breached your promise that it was true"). In practice, representations are always coupled with warranties.*

> *The kinds of representations and warranties you will see in a contract vary significantly depending on the subject matter of the contract. In the sale of business contracts in Chapter 1110, for example, there are extensive representations and warranties about the state of the business being sold, as opposed to the relatively slim representations and warranties in this contract.*

12.1 Generally. Each of the parties hereto severally, as to itself only, and not jointly, hereby represents and warrants to the other party to this Agreement that:

(a) such party has the full right, power and authority to execute, deliver and perform this Agreement and to bind all persons or entities, if any, for which it is acting pursuant to this Agreement;

(b) this Agreement has been duly executed and delivered by or on behalf of such party and constitutes a legal, valid and binding obligation of such party and all persons or entities, if any, for which such party is acting, enforceable against such party, and all such persons or entities, if any, for which it is acting, in accordance with its terms, except as such enforceability may be limited by bankruptcy, insolvency or other similar laws affecting the rights of creditors generally or by the application of general equity principles;

(c) no consent, approval, authorization or order of any other Person is required for the execution, delivery or performance of this Agreement by such party or any such persons or entities, if any, for which it is acting; and

(d) neither the execution, delivery nor performance of this Agreement by such party or any such persons or entities, if any, for which it is acting will (i) conflict with, or result in a breach of, or constitute a default under, or result in a violation of, any agreement or instrument to which such party or any such persons or entities, if any, for which it is acting is a party or by which such party or any such persons or entities, if any, for which it is acting or its or their property is bound, or (ii) result in the violation of any law or order, judgment, writ, injunction, decree or award or any governmental authority applicable to such party.

Section 13. Compliance With Laws.

13.1 Generally. In performing under this Agreement, all applicable governmental laws, regulation, orders, and other rules of duly constituted authorities will be followed and complied with in all respects by both parties.

> BOILERPLATE: *The pejorative term "boilerplate" suggests that provisions toward the end of the contract, which are common in many formal agreements, are "standard" and have little significance. While the remaining provisions in this contract are probably all considered boilerplate, as you read them think about what they are trying to cover and the risks associated with not including them.*

Section 14. Relationship of Parties.

14.1 Generally. The relationship of the Buyer and Seller is that of independent contractors and this Agreement does not create a general agency, joint venture, partnership, employment relationship, or franchise between the parties. Neither party is authorized to or has the power to obligate or bind the other party in any manner whatsoever. Furthermore, each party assumes full responsibility for its employees, agents or other personnel assigned by it to perform work pursuant to this Agreement, regardless of their place of work, and shall be solely responsible for payment of salary, including withholding of any income taxes, social security, workers' compensation and the like.

14.2 Exclusivity. Seller covenants not to provide manufacturing services for any Buyer Competitors unless Buyer consents in writing, such consent to be given or withheld at Buyer's sole discretion. Notwithstanding this or any other provisions of this

Agreement, Buyer may procure Products from other sources, including negotiating
and entering into manufacturing agreements with manufacturers other than Seller.

Section 15. Force Majeure. The failure of Seller to perform any of its obligations under this Agreement shall not be excused, nor shall Buyer be restricted in
exercising any of its remedies, because such failure was due to any act of God, fire,
casualty, flood, war, strike, lockout, labor slowdowns, epidemic, quarantine restrictions, destruction of production facilities, failure to obtain export licenses, riot,
insurrection, civil unrest, act of government, a substantial worldwide shortage of
parts and materials, or any other cause beyond the control of Seller.

Section 16. Governing Law; Dispute Resolution.

16.1 Governing Law. This Agreement and the rights and obligations of the parties hereunder shall be governed by, and construed and interpreted in accordance
with, the laws of the State of New York without giving effect to the choice of law
principles thereof.

16.2 Consent to Jurisdiction. Each party hereto hereby irrevocably consents to
the jurisdiction of the federal and state courts of New York in any action or proceeding arising out of or relating to this Agreement, and agrees that all claims in respect
of such action or proceeding shall be heard and determined in such courts.

16.3 Attorneys' Fees. In the event of any legal proceeding to enforce or con-
strue any of the provisions of this Agreement or any obligations of either party in
connection herewith, the prevailing party shall be entitled to its reasonable attorneys' fees and costs incurred in connection therewith.

Section 17. Miscellaneous.

17.1 Assignment. No assignment by Seller of any rights, including rights to
moneys due or to become due under this Agreement, or delegation of any duties
under this Agreement or under any Purchase Orders subject to this Agreement, is
permitted or binding on Buyer until Buyer's written consent has first been obtained.
If Seller undergoes any change such that it is Controlled by either a different Person
or an additional Person, or if Seller sells or transfers more than 25% of its assets or
business, or is merged or consolidated into or with any other Person, such change
or transaction shall be considered an assignment under this Section. Buyer may
assign any rights under this Agreement and may delegate any duties under this
Agreement or under any Purchase Orders subject to this Agreement with or without notice to Seller, and such assignment of rights or delegation of duties shall be
permitted and binding on Seller, but no such assignment or delegation shall relieve
Buyer of its obligations hereunder.

17.2 Entire Agreement; Amendment; Waiver. This Agreement: (a) contains
the entire agreement among the parties hereto with respect to the subject matter hereof, (b) supersedes all prior written agreements and negotiations and oral
understandings, if any, with respect thereto, and (c) may not be amended or sup-
plemented or waived except by an instrument or counterparts thereof in writing
signed by the party to be charged. The waiver by any party of a breach of any term
or provision of this Agreement shall not be construed as a waiver of any subsequent
breach.

17.3 Invalidity of Provision; Severability. If any provision of this Agreement is
held to be illegal, invalid or unenforceable in any jurisdiction under present or
future laws effective during the term hereof, such provisions shall be fully sever-
able and this Agreement shall be construed and enforced as if such illegal, invalid
or unenforceable provision had never comprised a part hereof with the remaining provisions remaining in full force and effect and not affected by the illegal,

invalid or unenforceable provision or by severance herefrom. In lieu of such illegal, invalid or unenforceable provision there shall be added automatically as part of this Agreement a provision as similar in terms to such illegal, invalid, or unenforceable provision as may be possible and still be legal, valid and enforceable. Furthermore, the illegality, invalidity, or unenforceability of any provision of this Agreement in any jurisdiction shall not affect the validity or enforceability of this Agreement, including that provision, in any other jurisdiction.

17.4 Headings; Execution in Counterparts. The headings and captions contained herein are for convenience of reference only and shall not control or affect the meaning or construction of any provision hereof. This Agreement may be executed in any number of counterparts, each of which shall be deemed to be an original and all of which together shall constitute one and the same instrument.

17.5 Notice. All notices and other communications provided for herein shall be dated and in writing and shall be deemed to have been duly given (i) on the date of delivery, if delivered personally or by telecopier, receipt confirmed, or (ii) on the second following business day, if delivered by a recognized overnight courier service, in either case, to the party to whom it is directed at the address set forth below (or at such other address as any party hereto shall hereafter specify by notice in writing to the other parties hereto).

(a) If to Buyer: Schott's Shots, Inc.
                        Attn: Vice President, Manufacturing
                        222 8th Street
                        New York, NY 10027
                        Telecopier: (646) 646-6460

(b) If to Seller: Builders Ltd.
                        Attn: President
                        491 Main Street
                        South Palms, CA 35303
                        Telecopier: (310) 310-3100

SIGNATURE BLOCKS: Parties sign a contract to indicate the mutual assent necessary to form a legal contract. The signature blocks at the bottom of a formal contract typically follow the format below. The agent of the business signs on the line marked "By," and that person's name and title is printed or typed on the corresponding lines below. The signature blocks are generally preceded by the "In witness whereof" line.

IN WITNESS WHEREOF, the parties hereto have executed this Agreement as of the date first above written.

SCHOTT'S SHOTS, INC.   BUILDERS LTD.
By: _____   By: _____
Name: Name:
Title: Title:

Notes and Questions

1. What circumstances can you imagine in which the "boilerplate" in this contract might be important? Assuming you represent Schott's Shots, are there any issues covered by the boilerplate that are sufficiently important that you would discuss them with your client before the contract is signed?

2. Assume you represent Schott's Shots, and your client has asked you to simplify the contract significantly. What sections would you delete entirely, what sections would you simplify, and what sections would you leave exactly as they are?

3. Assume you represent Builders, and your client has been providing electronic novelty items for Schott's Shots for years without a written manufacturing agreement on a "purchase order" basis (meaning orders were placed but no long-form contract like the agreement above was attached). Out of the blue, Schott's Shots asks your client to review and sign a long-form manufacturing agreement. What advice would you give your client concerning Schott's Shots' possible motivations, and what would you advise your client upon being presented with the contract above?

4. Look at Section 17.3, which is a so-called blue pencil provision. Under this section, if it turns out that any provision of the contract is unenforceable, it is struck from the contract and replaced with an enforceable provision covering the same concept as much as can be enforced. Assuming a court would follow 17.3, why wouldn't all contract drafters include aggressive, potentially unenforceable provisions and rely on blue pencil provisions? Your answer may depend on the state: when considering blue pencil provisions as applied to non-compete covenants, courts in New York have often respected these clauses and rewritten non-competes to make them enforceable (see, e.g., BDO Seidman v. Hirshberg, 93 N.Y.2d 382 (N.Y. 1999)), whereas the Indiana Supreme Court recently declared that "Indiana courts employ the 'blue pencil doctrine' to revise unreasonable noncompetition agreements. This doctrine, though, is really an eraser." (Heraeus Med., LLC v. Zimmer, Inc., 135 N.E.3d 150 (Ind. 2019)).

B.   DRAFTING OPERATIONAL CONTRACTS

There are several matters that are typically handled before the attorney ever sets pen to paper in preparing a business contract. At the outset, it is important that the client fully understand the business deal. Lawyers can help clients in this regard by preparing a simple "term sheet." A term sheet is a short document, typically with organized bullet points or short sentences, outlining the key negotiated terms of the deal. The term sheets you saw in Chapter 5 are typical in terms of format (although the NVCA term sheet is, given the complexity of a typical venture capital transaction, a bit long).

Once the client and the other side agree on the basic terms in the term sheet, the lawyer must begin drafting. Rather than draft "cold" without the benefit of any sample documents, lawyers almost always start with what they call a "form." A form contract is not like an online form, where there are a few blank lines to complete and the job is done. Rather, a form contract is a sample agreement for a similar transaction that the lawyer can use as a starting point. For lawyers practicing in law firms, it is typical for a firm (or group of lawyers within the firm) to have a preferred form and format for various types of contracts. For sole practitioners, it might be that the lawyer finds forms online. While there are myriad legal forms available on the internet, lawyers generally agree that using forms from legal research services like Lexis, Westlaw, and Practical Law Company yield better results — in large part because the forms available from those sources are edited by experts. Once the lawyer has identified several possible forms, he needs to choose among them and use them effectively, which is the subject of the next two articles. In drafting a contract from a form, the lawyer must take a critical eye to every provision since every client, every adversary, and every deal is different.

As discussed in the introduction to Section A above, the form of the contract (long-form, short-form, letter agreement, or some other approach) is key to meeting the client's goals. Lawyers should also ask themselves what type of language and approach will best serve the client. While leading legal writing scholars often advocate a "plain language" approach, some clients — notably large corporations and entrepreneurs from the corporate world — prefer a more traditional drafting approach. As a general rule and for their own job security, junior lawyers should follow senior lawyers' leads in drafting style. By the same token, when representing an entrepreneur, more straightforward language may be best to minimize confusion. In the third piece below, the author gives suggestions on how to avoid ambiguity in drafting, which is a key lesson when drafting a contract.

DRAFTING EFFECTIVE CONTRACTS:
HOW TO REVISE, EDIT AND USE FORM AGREEMENTS*

Susan M. Chesler, American Bar Association, Business Law Today
(November/December 2009)

. . .

1. *Think through the life of the contract under various fact patterns.* First, hypothesize performance. What will happen, moment by moment, if the parties comply with all of the terms in a timely manner? Does the contract contain all of the necessary "rules" and details to assist the parties in knowing how to perform their duties? Most form contracts do not adequately set forth the steps necessary for the parties to understand what needs to be done to carry out their contractual obligations. Every contract should clearly answer these six questions: (1) who is obligated to perform; (2) what is the obligation; (3) by when must the obligation be performed; (4) where will the performance take place; (5) how is the obligation to be performed; and (6) if performance involves money or goods, how much?

Second, envision nonperformance and default. Ask yourself what if one or both parties fail to perform all or part of the contract — are the consequences of failure to perform stated in the agreement and closely linked to the performance required? [G]et into the habit of resolving these issues at the drafting stage, rather than waiting for the parties to have a dispute. The contract should protect your client by stating a remedy for the potential default of each obligation. Default provisions contained in most form contracts are rarely adequate and they generally do not comply with the parties' intentions; the remedy of the default provision is usually termination of the contract and for many breaches, the nondefaulting party still does not desire to terminate the contractual relationship.

Finally, consider the worst case scenario. Assume that the parties become hostile toward each other, seeking to undermine the other party at every opportunity. Will the contract provide sufficient guidance to govern the relationship? Will it provide sufficient guidance to a court interpreting the contract or imposing remedies, if necessary?

2. *Clearly and consistently set forth the parties' rights and obligations.* In its most basic sense, a contract sets forth the private law governing the parties' relationship. Therefore, it is vital that it clearly and precisely sets forth the parties' contractual obligations and rights. It is also very important that these duties and rights are consistently drafted throughout the contract. While there are several acceptable choices of language to use when drafting, the key is to be consistent throughout the agreement. [W]henever a party has a mandatory contractual obligation, state that obligation with the word *shall* and never use the word *shall* to have any other meaning. Thus, you should be able to substitute "has the duty to" whenever you use the word *shall*. Since a mandatory contractual obligation is synonymous with a legal duty, a party's failure to perform that duty rises to the level of a breach and may result in an award of damages.

On the other hand, whenever a party does not undertake a legal obligation, but is entitled to exercise a right or privilege under the contract, state the authorization with the word *may*; you should be able to substitute "is authorized to" or "is entitled to" whenever you use the word *may*. The contract must clearly distinguish between a party's mandatory legal duty subject to breach, and his or her privilege to perform.

Finally, state conditions with the word *must*; you should be able to substitute "has to do X before Y will happen" whenever you use the word *must*. The key distinction between a mandatory duty and one that is conditional is that in the latter, the party's legal obligation to perform does not become mandatory unless and until the condition is met. In other words, the party's failure to perform that obligation results in a breach only if and when the condition has been met.

3. *Understand every provision of the contract.* One of the problems with using a form contract is that you were not the drafter of the document; thus, you may not understand every provision of the agreement, and not every provision in the form is relevant to the transaction at hand. I offer this guidance to my students: when using a form agreement, never leave in a provision because you do not understand its purpose (do not assume it must be important or relevant), and never take out a provision simply because you do not understand its purpose. You must review each provision until you understand it completely. Only then can you decide whether to include, omit, or modify that provision.

4. *Use recitals and definitions to reflect the parties' specific transaction.* Although not part of the operative terms of the contract, recitals can effectively be used to state the parties' intentions or to provide relevant background information. Since the contract may eventually require interpretation by a court, it should include within its four corners all of the information that may be useful to explain the parties' contractual relationship, any past history, and the parties' intentions that may not be clear from the operative terms of the contract itself. For example, while courts are becoming increasingly hostile to contracts in which parties surrender fundamental

rights, such as access to the court system, if the parties truly wish to waive their rights to a jury trial, they may do so. In these contracts, the waiver should be drafted so that it is clear and conspicuous, and the recitals should include some language regarding the parties' intent to waive their legal rights to a jury trial. However, drafters must be careful not to include any representations in the recitals that may have legal significance because the recitals are not part of the body of the agreement and, therefore, there may not be any legal remedies if the representations are, in fact, false.

Additionally, the use of definitions enables the drafter to tailor the meanings of certain terms used in the contract to the subject transaction, and also can prevent inadvertent changes of language. Generally, if the word or phrase as used in the contract is intended to vary in any way from the standard dictionary definition of that word or phrase, or if the word or phrase does not have a standard dictionary definition, it should be defined within the contract. There are three basic types of definitions: (1) precise definitions, drafted using the word *means*; (2) enlarging definitions, drafted using the phrase "including but not limited to" after the definition, followed by illustrative examples; and (3) limiting definitions, drafted using the phrase "but does not include" after the definition, followed by the limitations of the definition. An example of each type of definition follows: (1) "Land" means the property located at 123 Smith Lane; (2) "Land" means the property located at 123 Smith Lane, including but not limited to the residential house, separate garage, and vacant barn; or (3) "Land" means the property located at 123 Smith Lane, but does not include the vacant barn.

Throughout the semester, I remind my students numerous times of the golden rule of contract drafting: never change your language unless you wish to change your meaning, and always change your language if you wish to change your meaning. In an effort to teach them to draft contracts with the goal of avoiding litigation, ambiguity is not tolerated.

5. *Use plain language.* Contracts should be drafted with clarity and should be easy to read and understand by legal and lay audiences alike. Thus, omit legal jargon and unnecessary words, and eliminate wordy phrases from form contracts. I tell my students to think like an attorney, but to try not to sound like one. Since the words of the document will govern the parties' relationship, rights, and legal duties, they should clearly communicate their meaning to the parties themselves, and not only to their counsel. As most practicing lawyers are aware, a majority of available form contracts fail to adhere to this advice. They are strewn with "whereas," "witnesseth," and "to wit" — all of which detract from the readability and comprehension of the contract. It is also important to check to see if your jurisdiction has a plain language law, mandating contracts to be written in a clear and coherent manner using words with common meanings; in fact, in some states, plain language laws dictate the number of syllables in the words and the number of words in each paragraph of the contract. Failure to follow the application of plain language laws may impact the enforceability of the contract.

6. Use proper grammar, a clear writing style, and logical organization. Contracts generally describe events that will take place in the future, but it is a continually speaking document and should be drafted in the present tense. Draft using the active voice. Ask who is obligated to do something or to refrain from doing something, and make the subject do the action. When drafters use the active voice, the identity of the actor is clear. This is vital so that the contract clearly and unequivocally expresses the parties' legal duties.

In addition, draft useful headings and organize the terms around those headings. Even if your form contract contains a boilerplate provision stating that the headings should not have any operative meaning, the fact is that those headings are read by the parties, their counsel, and possibly a court; therefore, make them work. Keep sentences short, where possible, or use tabulation for clarity. Be sure to connect modifying words to what they modify, i.e., in "the new house and car" phrase, is the car new too? Finally, use proper punctuation to avoid costly misinterpretation of the contract. For example, one legal dispute resulted in a finding that the contract could be terminated at any time with proper notice, contrary to one party's understanding that the contract had an initial five-year term. This ruling was based solely on the (mis)placement of a single comma, and saved the other party to the agreement an estimated $1 million by enabling it to terminate the contract within the first five years of the contract term.

. . .

USING FORMS FOR DRAFTING HELP — TIPS FOR YOUNG LAWYERS

G. Wogan Bernard, American Bar Association, Probate and Property (January/February 2011)

In today's legal environment, clients and attorneys want things done quickly, efficiently, and cost-effectively. The wheel should not be reinvented but simply improved, and advancements in technology have made it easier on lawyers to produce solid work product in an efficient and timely manner.

All lawyers have been in the situation in which someone wants something drafted quickly and have found themselves scrambling to determine where to begin. In situations like these, lawyers — young and old — turn to the nearest sample or form as a template to begin their work product. Forms are excellent tools and should be used in practice. But before sending that certain lease, purchase agreement, will, power of attorney, or court filing off to the client or court, here are a few thoughts and tips that should be considered.

KNOW YOUR SOURCE

Where did the form come from? Did you get it from a periodical, a treatise, or even Google? Did you pull the form from your firm's document management database or from an e-mail from a law school friend? Do you know who the author is? Was the author even a lawyer? And the law constantly changes. A good form used yesterday can become outdated tomorrow. An old mortgage that contains outdated material, references repealed state statutes, or that fails to contain a necessary provision can simply become a waste of time. An old sample will might have been a great source a few years ago, but that old will might be just that — old and outdated.

REMEMBER YOUR CLIENT

When working off another's work or samples, keep in mind the party you represent. You might be asked to quickly draft a lease for a commercial landlord, and your mentoring partner gives you a sample lease to use or work from: "Use this lease;

I have used it a bunch in the past." You review the lease, and it appears to have all the bells and whistles that a lease should contain. The catch? The supervising attorney forgot to mention that the form lease he gave you was drafted in favor of a commercial tenant, not a landlord. Always keep in mind the party you are representing and the specific needs and goals in the document you are preparing on its behalf.

SWEAT THE SMALL STUFF

Some forms found in periodicals or treatises are prepared for a national audience and may not contain state-specific language or nuances required or needed for your particular state. Some samples might be so issue-specific that they fail to contain the important boilerplate choice of law, waivers, indemnities, and so on. On the flip side, some forms might contain too much boilerplate and not the specific issue you face. In choosing and working from a form, keep in mind the little nuances and aspects important to your issue.

PROOFREAD

Proofread, proofread, proofread! Even basic forms can contain glaring, embarrassing errors. Many forms have blanks to be filled in that, depending on what is filled in, can affect other parts of the document. Check all capitalized terms because something might be capitalized or defined in the form but not in your draft. And spell-check is not enough. Proofread!

NO PERFECT FORM

Using a form is only the beginning. Look through as many samples as possible. Comparing your final work to the initial sample you worked from or other similar documents is a great way to see what you might have missed and catch the little mistakes. Even a form you have created is likely not perfect, and lawyers should always look for ways to improve.

Forms are great resources to assist young lawyers in drafting documents and educating themselves on foreign and unfamiliar issues. Almost every lawyer remembers the time he or she did something for the first time (both the good and the bad), and using forms to begin the drafting process is a great tool to ease the anxiety and move efficiently toward the final product.

AMBIGUOUS DRAFTING AND THE 12-POUND CAT
Jeffrey S. Ammon
This article originally appeared in the Plain Language Column of
The Michigan Bar Journal (July 2011)

A recent Michigan Court of Appeals decision can teach us how to avoid ambiguous drafting. To appreciate the ambiguity that the decision addressed, imagine this sign at your local kennel: *We accept only cats and dogs weighing less than 10 pounds.* Now ask yourself: will the kennel accept your 12-pound cat? That is, does the 10-pound limit apply only to dogs, or also to cats?

Experienced contract drafters will recognize this as a "trailing modifier" problem. When a modifying phrase follows a string of two or more items, does the phrase modify just the last item, or every item in the string?

The Court of Appeals faced this ambiguity in *Lafarge Midwest, Inc. v. City of Detroit*. In that case, a taxpayer claimed that its property, located in a Michigan renaissance zone, was exempt from school-bond millage under MCL 211.7ff:

> (1) For taxes levied after 1996, except as otherwise provided in subsection [ ]
> (2) . . . real property in a renaissance zone and personal property located in a renaissance zone is exempt from taxes collected under this act. . . .
>
> (2) Real and personal property in a renaissance zone is not exempt from collection of the following:
>
> (a) A special assessment levied by the local tax collecting unit in which the property is located.
>
> (b) Ad valorem property taxes specifically levied for the payment of principal and interest of obligations approved by the electors or *obligations pledging the unlimited taxing power of the local governmental unit.* [Emphasis added.]

The taxpayer and the City of Detroit agreed that subsection 2(b) describes two kinds of obligations: those approved by electors and those pledging a local-governmental unit's unlimited taxing power. Since the school bonds did not pledge unlimited taxing power, the remaining question was whether the bonds had been approved by the electors.

But which group of electors needed to approve the bonds so that taxes could be imposed? The bonds had been approved by a vote of only school-district electors, not electors of the entire city.

Does the trailing-modifier phrase *of the local governmental unit* modify the word *electors*? The taxpayer argued it did, and the court agreed: the phrase modified both kinds of obligations. Therefore, subsection 2(b) did not apply. The school-bond millage could not be imposed on the taxpayer.

The court's analysis attached tremendous significance to the word *the*:

> Next, we consider whether the phrase "of the local governmental unit" applies to "obligations approved by the electors," as held by the Tax Tribunal. Guidance is gleaned from the statutory language. The Legislature used the word "the" with respect to "electors." "The" is a definite article which, when used especially before a noun — like "electors" — has a specifying or particularizing effect. . . . If the provision had simply said "electors," it may have referred to electors generally, as the dissent opines. However, because the phrase "of the local governmental unit" is within the same statutory provision, we conclude that "the electors" must be the electors of the local governmental unit. This interpretation recognizes that the legislature is presumed to be familiar with the rules of statutory construction, as well as the rules of grammar. This construction is also in compliance with the mandate to "give effect to every word, phrase, and clause in a statute and avoid an interpretation that would render any part of the statute surplusage or nugatory."

The court says it must give effect to every word. But its analysis does the opposite. Look at the way subsection 2(b) repeats the word *obligations*. Doesn't that signal that what follows the second *obligations* refers only as far back as that word? The drafter seemed to carefully start over again with that word. But the court's analysis makes that second reference to obligations meaningless, contradicting the court's desire to give every word significance.

In addition, *the* electors might well refer to *the* electors who had to vote on that particular bond issue. That would give effect to the word *the*. The court does not even address this alternate and equally plausible reference for *the*.

More sensibly, the court demonstrated little patience for the rather arbitrary rule of the last antecedent. That rule provides that a modifier following a list of two or more items generally modifies only the last item in the string. (Thus, the *10-pound* phrase in my example would apply only to dogs, not to cats.) But now the court is picking and choosing among the rules of statutory construction.

Context can sometimes help resolve ambiguity. What if the kennel in my example were named *Cats and Their Small Friends*? That context would support a customer's conclusion that the weight limit applies only to dogs.

And looking beyond the text itself could have helped the court effectuate the legislative intent in this case. School districts and cities had been routinely collecting school-bond millage from renaissance-zone taxpayers since 1996 when these zones were created. This decision surprised school districts so much that legislation was promptly enacted to reverse the court's interpretation. If the court's opinion could have acknowledged that longstanding statewide practice and the reading it took for granted, the court might have reached a different result.

This case also teaches us that the court has a high tolerance for ambiguous drafting. As amazing as it seems, the court in this case concluded that subsection (b) was not ambiguous. But it took two sets of lawyers, a trial and trial-court opinion, and four pages of Court of Appeals analysis to determine what this subsection means. If that doesn't signal ambiguity, what does?

At any rate, it's best not to tolerate that much potential ambiguity in your drafting. After all, plain drafting could have avoided this entire dispute. The drafters could have used a vertical list, for example. Depending on which interpretation the drafter intended, subsection (b) would be rewritten in one of the following two ways:

> (a) obligations of a local governmental unit that
> > (i) are approved by its electors; or
> > (ii) pledge its unlimited taxing power.

Or this:

> (b) obligations that
> > (i) are approved by electors; or
> > (ii) pledge a local governmental unit's unlimited taxing power.

Vertical lists are not the only way to avoid ambiguity with trailing modifiers. If the phrase modifies both items, you could rewrite subsection (b) to read:

> obligations of a local governmental unit that are approved by its electors or that pledge its unlimited taxing power.

Or use a dash:

> obligations approved by electors — or obligations pledging the unlimited taxing power — of the local governmental unit.

Mid-sentence dashes are used for just this purpose in the restyled Federal Rules of Civil Procedure and Federal Rules of Evidence. For example, FR Civ P 4(b) states: "A summons — or a copy of a summons that is addressed to multiple defendants — must be issued for each defendant to be served."

Another way to avoid ambiguity if the phrase modifies only the second of the two items: list that item and the phrase first. Thus, the City in this case would have accepted the following:

> obligations that pledge the local governmental unit's unlimited taxing power or obligations that are approved by electors.

And do not think that you can always solve this trailing-modifier ambiguity simply by placing the modifying phrase before a string instead of after it. For example, what if I had titled this article *Avoiding Ambiguity and the 12-Pound Cat?* Would you have expected to learn not just how to improve your writing but also how to elude large felines?

So handle trailing modifiers with care. And even if the kennel accepts your 12-pound cat, put it on a diet.

FAUX CONTRACTS
Cathy Hwang, Virginia Law Review (2019)

In contexts ranging from the mundane to the momentous, parties turn to documents that look like enforceable formal contracts, but that fall short of being legally binding — and also seem unmoored from formal or informal enforcement. In business transactions, this is particularly odd: parties have the means and sophistication to use binding, formal contracts, but appear to elect not to use them. Why do parties go through the trouble of drafting formal-looking agreements that they do not enforce? And if there is no formal or informal enforcement, what motivates parties to abide by contractual terms?

This Article shows how these "faux contracts" — formal-looking documents that explicitly exclude enforcement of any kind — add value in ways that real contracts cannot. Non-binding term sheets in mergers and acquisitions ("M&A") are the driving example, but non-binding documents like term sheets are found in many complex business transactions. These faux contracts allow parties to harness the organizational and clarification benefits of creating a contract, while excluding most consequences of breach. . . .

Non-binding or unenforceable agreements can be found in many contexts. Non-competition clauses in California employment agreements are good examples. These agreements restrict an employee's ability to work for a competitor for some time after leaving the original employer. Non-competition clauses are valid and enforceable legal contracts in most states. In 2008, however, the California Supreme Court reaffirmed, in a splashy and well-publicized case, the state's long-standing position that non-competition clauses are unenforceable. Nonetheless, California employers and employees continued to sign them — even though an employer cannot take the issue to court if an employee breaches the clause. Surrogacy contracts where they are outlawed, contracts for illegal activity, Internet click-wrap agreements with unconscionable terms, and certain prenuptial agreement provisions offer just a few more examples of parties entering into non-binding or unenforceable agreements.

Non-binding or unenforceable agreements in these situations, however, are unsurprising. In these contexts, unequal bargaining power between the parties, lack of knowledge about the contract's unenforceable nature, or lack of viable binding alternatives can often explain why parties turn to non-binding agreements.

. . .

While term sheets have many formal-looking bells and whistles — they are written in legal language, often with the advice of counsel, and signed by parties — parties agree that the "business terms" are legally non-binding and unenforceable. In other words, parties can breach those business terms — terms about price, what is sold, and how — without being taken to court. Why do sophisticated parties enter into non-binding agreements? And if enforcement is off the table, what accounts for the fact that once a term sheet is signed, parties proceed to act as though they have signed a binding document, usually later entering into a definitive formal document on terms that closely resemble the term sheet's?

Much of contract law assumes that enforcement is an important way to motivate behavior. This assumption also underlies much of legal scholarship and theory: jail time for committing crimes, fines imposed for infringing intellectual property rights, and sanctions for violating regulations and treaties are all examples of formal enforcement mechanisms that are believed to motivate behavior.

Where formal enforcement is unavailable, inadequate, or not preferred, informal enforcement, such as reputational sanctions, can fill the gap or provide support for formal enforcement. The importance of informal enforcement is especially well-documented in tightly knit communities, such as those of rural ranchers, whalers, high-seas pirates, and diamond merchants, among others. In these communities, individuals are repeat players, so poor behavior in one transaction will sully their future transactions — a result that many individuals wish to avoid. Robust relational contracting relationships also exist in a variety of businesses on the West Coast, in the Midwest, and in Hollywood filmmaking. Because M&A parties can be one-off players in the M&A market (and therefore do not have the same reputational concerns as a repeat player in a tightly knit community), the non-binding and unenforceable nature of these business terms is particularly surprising. Moreover, like the formal contracting scholarship, the relational contracting scholarship also relies on enforcement (although of the extralegal variety) as an important motivator.

This Article takes a different route. Existing literature largely focuses on enforcement — the back end of contracting — but some contracts have no "back end." For one thing, contracting parties often simply abide by the terms to which they agreed. For another, even when disputes arise, many contracts are not formally enforced through litigation — parties simply renegotiate or settle. In modern contracts between corporate and commercial parties, formal enforcement is perhaps even rarer, as parties have become leerier of high litigation costs and the disclosure of sensitive information during the discovery process. Even the cheaper, faster, and more private arbitration processes have become very expensive. Without dispute, there is no documented enforcement, no opinion, and no evidence that a scholar can examine to draw conclusions about contracting, breach, or enforcement — so studying contract law from the back end necessarily gives insight into only a small sliver of contracting practice.

Because studying ex post enforcement paints an incomplete picture, studying ex ante contract design has become an important way to understand some of the basic questions of contract law and theory: How do parties enter into contracts? . . . [T]his Article takes a close look at a particularly odd type of contract — the formal-looking but non-binding and unenforced "faux contract" — and asks why sophisticated business parties willingly choose to enter into them and adhere to them.

. . .

I. WHY USE A CONTRACT?: THE CONVENTIONAL UNDERSTANDING

Across many areas of the law, enforcement (or the threat of it) is understood as a way to motivate behavior. Fear of imprisonment, for instance, may deter crime. The imposition of damages for faulty product design may motivate product designers to create better products.

In contract law, the same conventional wisdom holds: formal enforcement, such as reliance and expectation damages imposed by a court, is understood to deter parties from breaching a contract unless there is a case for efficient breach. Modern contract law scholarship has also shown that informal — that is, non-judicial or arbitral — enforcement can also do important work in motivating parties to adhere to contracts when formal enforcement falls short. In fact, contracting parties sometimes so prefer informal enforcement over formal enforcement that they select informal enforcement, even when formal enforcement is available.

. . .

A. The Limits of Formal Enforcement

Formal contracting — and formal enforcement — is most easily understood as the traditional type of contracting that law students learn in their first year of law school. . . .

Scholars have noted that formal enforcement has many benefits, the most obvious of which is that courts (or arbitrators) can "unpack[] complex behavior and assess[] responsibility." In their roles as fact-finders, formal enforcers can also serve as impartial verifiers of information that parties provide. At the end of the adjudication, formal enforcers — especially courts backed by the government — can also enforce their sanctions. Another benefit of formal enforcement is that it allows parties to make credible promises. As Alan Schwartz and Bob Scott have noted, parties want the power to make contracts legally enforceable because "enforcement . . . permits parties to make believable promises to each other when reputational or self-enforcement sanctions will not avail." Thus, they note that formal enforcement does not just protect the party who suffers from a broken promise — it also benefits the party who wants to make the promise.

Relying on formal enforcement, however, has its own problems. Others have noted, for instance, that "the court's power to compel disclosure is limited," which means that even a court cannot always verify information, accurately gauge wrongdoing, or impose an efficient level of sanction. This is especially true when courts are structured as an adversarial system: if neither party brings forth or seeks relevant factual information, the court may simply be unable to access that information.

Formal enforcement is also expensive — and perhaps no enforcement is more expensive than modern formal enforcement of complex corporate and commercial contracts in public courts. In corporate contexts, parties also worry about more than the astronomical cost of hiring experienced lawyers, months of motion practice, and potentially high payouts. They also worry that commercial litigation will distract management and lead to an invasive discovery process that airs corporate dirty laundry or exposes corporate secrets.

Modern contracting parties — especially sophisticated commercial parties — have developed some new strategies to deal with the high costs of formal enforcement. Opting into binding arbitration is a common and well-documented strategy that still relies on formal enforcement. Parties rely on arbitrators to have specialized expertise that reduces the court's learning time and reduces mistakes in the outcome, or to have expedited discovery rules that limit cost and time spent on the dispute. Arbitration awards are also often confidential, which protects the parties' privacy.

. . .

B. The Limits of Informal Enforcement

In contrast to formal enforcement, which relies on courts and arbitrators to determine right from wrong, informal enforcement relies on parties themselves to enforce the contract and to levy appropriate sanctions. Other scholars have documented the ways in which parties use informal enforcement to curb bad behavior. While informal enforcement offers an alternative (or, by some accounts, a complement) to formal enforcement, it too relies on the threat of ex post sanction to curb ex ante opportunism.

. . .

As compared to formal enforcement, informal enforcement has some benefits. For instance, parties in close-knit communities can often observe breaches better and at a lower cost than a court or outside observer. . . .

But, as others have noticed, there are pitfalls. One of the biggest is that parties might over-enforce. For example, consider a supplier who breaches a contract by failing to deliver the correct breed of chicken to a buyer. That supplier is otherwise a good supplier — one who completes her orders on time, who sells at fair prices, and who regularly contributes to the chicken-trading community in other socially beneficial ways. When the supplier delivers the wrong breed of chicken, a slap on the wrist may be most appropriate. For example, a court could award damages to the buyer. If the same contract was enforced informally, however, the community of chicken traders might over-enforce: they might spread the word that the supplier's chickens were rubbish, that she was untrustworthy, and that nobody should do business with her. As a result of this word-of-mouth informal enforcement, the chicken supplier is driven out of business, when she might otherwise have continued to be a trustworthy, contributing, reliable member of the chicken-trading community.

For informal enforcement to be effective, the party whose reputation is harmed must also care about the harm to his or her reputation, which is not always the case. For example, where trading relationships are one-off, one might easily imagine a party behaving opportunistically without fear of tarnishing their reputation.

. . .

II.   OPTING OUT OF ENFORCEMENT

. . .

Non-binding or unenforceable agreements are commonplace: illegal contracts, such as those governing the production of adult films, surrogacy contracts, and contracts with minors, are easy examples. But these examples are also unsurprising. In these and other contexts, non-binding agreements are a second-best solution: parties might prefer formal contracts, but something stands in the way of their ability to form them.

Moreover, in many of these contexts, there is another overlay: the non-binding agreements are made in situations where informal enforcement is strong. And sufficient informal enforcement can create the right kind of environment for a non-binding agreement to work, even where parties are sophisticated. In his 2015 study of Hollywood contracting, for instance, Jonathan Barnett found that major Hollywood films are often produced only on the basis of non-binding term sheets. In Hollywood contracting, like in M&A deals, parties are sophisticated and presumably have the means and knowledge to enter into real contracts. Nonetheless, they appear to choose to use non-binding agreements, even though their deals are high-stakes and one party's reneging can cause serious and unrecoupable damage to the other. In Hollywood, however, personal networks can be thick, and Barnett describes Hollywood contracting as being enforced by "significant but limited reputational pressures." He further notes that, where reputational sanctions might be weak in Hollywood deals, more formalization sometimes fills the gap.

. . .

A.   M&A Term Sheets

It is useful to take a brief pause to describe the paradigmatic faux contract, and the primary motivating example of this Article — the M&A term sheet. In private M&A deals — that is, deals where parties do not file securities disclosures about the deal terms — parties often enter into a non-binding preliminary agreement before entering into a binding acquisition agreement. These preliminary agreements are variously called term sheets, letters of intent ("LOIs"), or memoranda of understanding, but for ease, this Article generally calls them term sheets. While term sheets exist in a variety of business contexts — venture financing, bank financing, joint ventures, and the like — there are industry norms, regulatory overlays, and other factors that make those term sheets somewhat different than M&A term sheets. . . .

Term sheets vary in how they look, but generally come in three varieties. Some are simple, unsigned documents that list material business terms: a document that simply "lays out terms." Others look more like contracts: they have formal language and signatures. These often also include a combination of binding and non-binding provisions, and contain an additional provision noting which provisions are binding and which ones are not. Still another type of term sheet tries to create some physical separation between the binding and non-binding parts, but note that the two are related. . . .

Term sheets often have additional features that make them look like formal, legally binding, and enforceable contracts: they are often written in legal language, made to look serious and formal, and contain space for parties to sign their names.

Parties spend time negotiating them. While it is hard to get a precise estimate of how many term sheets lead to real contracts, M&A lawyers report that once term sheets are signed, parties tend to sign acquisition agreements, and on similar terms to those in the term sheet. But despite their formal bells and whistles, and the fact that parties adhere to their terms, the term sheets' business terms are not binding and enforceable.

. . .

B. Separation of Contracting and Enforcement

. . . An easy way to think about [contract] enforcement is with the old analogy of sticks and carrots. Formal enforcement acts like a stick: parties who behave poorly will be punished in court, usually by being liable for some kind of damage payment to the wronged counterparty. Informal enforcement is a bit like a stick, but also like a carrot. When a party misbehaves, their reputation might be damaged, causing them to lose future business or social capital within their community — the stick. When a party behaves well, however, their reputation might be enhanced, and they might gain more business or social capital. In that way, informal enforcement is a carrot.

In the contract theory literature, informal enforcement is useful as a motivator in two ways. Sometimes, it fills the gap when a formal enforcer is absent. In fact, others have observed that parties will design arrangements specifically to exclude formal enforcers. Lisa Bernstein, for instance, describes Midwestern manufacturers' supply contracts, which are "long and detailed," as "designed to keep the law — in the sense of legal enforcement of contractual obligations — largely out of their relationship with their suppliers." Other times, informal enforcement works in concert with formal enforcement by adding a little more "stick" atop the one that formal enforcement provides. Whether parties rely on formal or informal enforcement, however, the conventional wisdom is clear: a stick or a carrot motivates behavior.

In particular, sticks and carrots are understood to mitigate certain transaction costs that arise during deal making, such as search and information costs, bargaining costs, and enforcement costs. In a transaction, parties inevitably have different information and incentives. In any sort of buy-sell transaction, for instance, the seller has the best information about the asset being sold, including the asset's shortcomings. At the same time, the seller wants to obtain the highest price, while the buyer wants the lowest. Together, information asymmetries and misaligned incentives motivate a seller to withhold negative information about the asset in order to obtain the highest price. A contract allows parties to introduce provisions, along with related enforcement mechanisms, that are understood to bridge some of the information and incentive gaps of contracting. In acquisition agreements, for example, earnout, indemnification, and representation and warranty provisions create obligations for sellers to disclose negative information about the asset, and pair those obligations with threats of enforcement and liability when sellers fail to do so. In a house or car sale, agreements might include similar disclosures and warranties that attempt to mitigate misaligned incentives and close information gaps.

Faux contracts begin with a different premise. As a first step, the front-and back-ends of a faux contract appear to be decoupled. Deal lawyers, for instance, uniformly reported that M&A term sheets, while formal-looking, are almost never binding or formally enforceable . . .

. . .

Notes and Questions

1. Do form contracts become irrelevant if your client tells you she wants you to draft something short and simple?

2. Ammon argues against ambiguity. Can you imagine circumstances where your client might be served well by an ambiguous contract?

3. Hwang makes the point that some contracts are unenforceable by their nature (for example, if the subject matter is illegal) and other are unenforceable by their explicit terms (for example, non-binding term sheets). Why would any business choose to use unenforceable contracts, and why would any lawyer agree to draft a "faux contract"?

4. Entrepreneurs often enter into contracts knowing that they lack the resources to enforce them with legal action. Does this state of affairs suggest entrepreneurs should not use contracts? Are there benefits to be realized from unenforced contracts?

PROBLEM

Olivia and Andrew have decided they need to establish a presence on the internet as they further develop their business. Through LinkedIn, they found Kim Samuels, a crackerjack computer science grad student with prior web design experience, to develop their website for them. They have emailed you the following business terms for the deal with Kim:

— We will pay Kim $8,000 for the whole project as follows:
  — When she creates and we approve the initial wireframe, we will pay her $2,000.
  — When she delivers a beta of the site, we will pay her an additional $4,000.
  — When she finishes all the revisions on the site after the beta, we will pay her the last $4,000.
— She thinks she can get the whole thing done in two months.
— We are responsible for writing all the copy for the site.
— She will design the site so we can easily add e-commerce functionality, but she will not program any e-commerce stuff for us — it will just be an informational site with some ability for people who use the product to post reviews and advice.

Draft a website design and development agreement for General Germ, Inc., to use with Kim. You will need to find a good form and draft the contract according to the terms your client has outlined. Remember that some forms will be drafted in a manner that advantages the web developer, and some will be drafted in a manner that advantages the client. If you can, you should use a client-friendly form. If there are provisions you think are advisable that your client did not mention, be sure to include them (understanding that you will need to explain the whole document, including new concepts, to your client when you deliver your work product).

VIII

CONDUCTING BUSINESS ONLINE

It's difficult to imagine an entrepreneurial venture — even a brick and mortar business — that does not have an online presence. Start-up companies' websites and apps can run the gamut from advertising or providing basic information to complex portals on which customers can place orders for products, services can be delivered, and money can change hands. While there are certain legal issues that only arise online — federal regulations that focus on online privacy, for example — it is important to remind clients that the other legal aspects of running a business apply equally to online activities. Clients may think that reserving a particular URL for a website is equivalent to trademark protection, not realizing that the "use in commerce" and consumer confusion standards discussed in Chapter 4 continue to apply and that registration of a trademark (which may also be the domain name) with the United States Patent and Trademark Office is still advisable. Similarly, clients may want to post a notice on their website looking for investors, not realizing that the securities laws discussed in Chapter 5 will impact any online strategy for raising capital. Clients may see other sites flagrantly infringing copyrights and conclude that the copyright laws do not apply in the same way online, when of course we know from Chapter 4 that they do. Online user agreements may seem like boilerplate and clients may be used to clicking through them, but they are actually contracts subject to the same underlying law — and drafting mechanics — as written contracts covered in Chapter 7 that are designed to be signed by hand. And in a potential violation of both copyright and contract law, many companies copy privacy policies from competitors to save on legal expenses without understanding the terms contained in the "borrowed" language, only to inadvertently breach the agreement and face litigation.

In this chapter, we focus on two issues that are especially relevant in the online world: online privacy, and e-commerce issues like online customer contracts and terms of sale.

A.   CUSTOMER PRIVACY

Most entrepreneurs understand from personal experience or from watching current events that internet privacy is an issue businesses face. For the lawyer, the challenge is not so much in convincing the client that she might need an online privacy policy, but rather getting the client to focus on what substantive terms to include in such a policy and the impact those terms may have on the client's business. For example, a privacy policy that prohibits sharing customer information with third parties may sound great to an entrepreneur who wants the venture to be perceived by customers as decent and good and most importantly safe, but if that same entrepreneur has financial projections that include revenue from selling customer email addresses, there is a disconnect the lawyer must address. A client also may not plan to "sell" customer email addresses, but may be surprised that trading its list with another company may be the same under the law even when no cash changes hands.

It is also important to realize that there is no "one size fits all" privacy policy. For example, a complex social networking-based business will have different privacy concerns than an online store collecting financial information, and an "online brochure" type website that collects no personal information may not need a privacy policy at all.

Online privacy is a complex area of the law, in large part because there are multiple federal and state statutes and regulations that govern the area. Moreover, Europe has become influential on American companies and policymakers, and there are notable attempts to put forth a federal privacy regime that covers all personally identifiable information collected, not just in the limited areas currently regulated under federal law. In the next few paragraphs, we will outline key provisions in the more prominent privacy statutes, all of which have — to one extent or another — developed into separate legal specialties where advice of an expert is recommended.

1.   Federal Trade Commission Act

The Federal Trade Commission is a consumer protection agency with broad responsibility. It enforces the Federal Trade Commission Act, which prohibits unfair or deceptive acts or practices by businesses. Consistent with this prohibition, the FTC requires companies to follow any stated privacy policies they have, and to take reasonable and appropriate measures to protect consumer information. The FTC has been fairly active in enforcing the FTC Act in these areas, and the related area of being transparent with consumers when making changes to privacy policies.

It is important to note that the FTC Act does not currently require companies to have online privacy policies — although such policies are required by other regulatory regimes described below. The FTC does, however, promulgate a set of best practices for online privacy and security of information. Historically, the agency recommended the so-called notice and choice model of privacy protection. Under this approach, consumers are made aware of the company's practices regarding consumer information and then are given the option of either "opting in" or "opting out" of the proposed use of data.

More recently, the FTC has been exploring other recommended best practices to address the changing online world. In the notes that follow the privacy policies below, you will read about the directions in which the FTC is heading when making recommendations about online privacy. While FTC-promulgated best practices are not binding, lawyers representing entrepreneurs must take them into account, as they shine light on areas where the FTC may bring enforcement actions in the future.

2.   Children's Online Privacy Protection Act (COPPA)

The Children's Online Privacy Protection Act, or COPPA, governs websites that are directed at children, or where operators have actual knowledge that their websites are collecting information from children under 13. It requires a clearly written, understandable privacy policy that is linked in a clear and prominent manner. The privacy policy must state:

- The name and contact information of website operators;
- The kinds of personal information collected from children, and how it is collected;
- How the personal information is used;
- Whether the information is disclosed to third parties and the purposes for which the information will be used;
- That the parent has the option to agree to collection and use of the information but may opt out of the disclosure to third parties;
- That the operator will not require more disclosure than reasonably necessary;
- That parents can review their children's personal information and have it deleted or refuse to allow it to be used.

In addition, site operators are required to make a direct notice to parents that includes the information above plus notifies the parent that it wishes to collect the information and that the parent's consent is required for the collection and use of the information. The site operator must then obtain verifiable parental consent.

The FTC has enforcement authority over COPPA.

3.   Complex Privacy Statutes

Given the changing world of online privacy, it is difficult for a lawyer focused on representing entrepreneurs to be an expert in all applicable statutes, particularly when the statutes themselves are complex and require specialized knowledge. That said, a lawyer must be able to recognize a client who may face these difficult regulatory regimes and know to call in an expert attorney. The Gramm-Leach-Bliley Act, which regulates financial institutions, and the Health Insurance Portability and Accountability Act, which regulates health information, are two such statutes.

The Gramm-Leach-Bliley Act applies to financial institutions, such as banks, securities firms, insurance companies, credit card companies, and non-bank mortgage lenders or brokers. The GLB Act regulates non-public personal information, and requires financial institutions to have clear, conspicuous, and accurate privacy notices. In addition, consumers are entitled to certain opt-out rights under the GLB Act.

The Health Insurance Portability and Accountability Act governs individually identifiable health information and applies to health care providers, pharmacies, health plans, and other companies that come into contact with health information. HIPAA sets forth specific standards for the privacy, security, and transmission of health data.

4. State Statutes

Some states regulate online privacy in a similar way to the federal statutes described above. States may have statutes that enhance the consumer protections in the FTC Act, and others add protections to health information or financial information along the lines of HIPAA and the GLB Act. In light of recent data security breach scandals, most states (led by California) have adopted security breach notification statutes. California has also become a national leader with the California Consumer Privacy Act, adopted in 2018. The CCPA covers any business that collects personally identifiable information of a California resident and meets certain additional criteria. Under the CCPA, consumers have a right to know what information about them has been collected, what it's being used for, and if it's being sold, who is buying it. Consumers also have the right to opt out of having their information sold and cannot be commercially penalized for it (or, if they are under 16, they need to opt in to having their information sold). They also have the right to have their information deleted. The Attorney General of California enforces the CCPA, but consumers also have a private right of action that can be exercised individually or by class action.

5. The European Union's General Data Protection Regulation

BINDING EFFECTS OF THE EUROPEAN GENERAL DATA PROTECTION REGULATION (GDPR) ON U.S. COMPANIES
Dr. Manuel Klar, 11 Hastings Sci. & Tech. L.J. 101 (2020)

I. INTRODUCTION

The territorial scope of the European General Data Protection Regulation (GDPR), which has been in force since May 25, 2018, extends well beyond the European borders. In the past, European data protection law had already applied for companies which had an establishment in the European Union (EU). Now under the GDPR, the territorial scope has expanded through the introduction of a "marketplace rule" or "destination approach." As a result, the new provisions of European data protection law also apply for the first time to companies worldwide which are not domiciled in the European Union, but offer goods or services to data subjects in the European Union or monitor their behavior. [T]he hurdles for the geographic applicability of the GDPR are by no means high. As a matter of fact, a great many companies outside of the EU have to comply with European data protection law. This affects not only large international corporate groups, but also small and medium-sized companies in particular . . .

   . . .

V.   CONSEQUENCES FOR U.S. COMPANIES WHICH ARE SUBJECT TO THE GDPR

If a U.S. company falls under the GDPR, it must comply with the provisions therein to the same extent as an EU company which is bound to the stipulations of the GDPR. There is no "layered approach" in this regard. If the company offers goods or services to persons in the European Union or monitors their behavior, it must appoint a representative in the European Union (see A.). With regard to the other duties which are to be fulfilled, a distinction must be made as to whether the U.S. company is acting as a controller or as a processor within the meaning of the GDPR. Independent of that, the U.S. company will then have to comply with a great many other duties, breaches of which are subject to fines (see B.). However, it must be pointed out that at present it is still completely unclear whether, and if so how, a breach of these duties by U.S. companies would be prosecuted by European supervisory authorities.

A.   Appointment of a Representative in the EU

In the cases set out in Article 3(2) GDPR, i.e., if U.S. companies offer goods or services in the EU or monitor their behavior, the controller or processor must designate a representative in the European Union in writing. However, this does not apply for processing which is occasional, does not include, on a large scale, processing of special categories of data as referred to in Article 9(1) GDPR or processing of personal data relating to criminal convictions and offences referred to in Article 10 GDPR, and is unlikely to result in a risk to the rights and freedoms of natural persons, taking into account the nature, context, scope and purposes of the processing.

The representative must be established in one of the Member States where the data subjects are whose personal data are being processed in relation to the offering of goods or services to them, or whose behavior is being monitored.

   . . .

B.   Further Duties

In order to determine what further duties a U.S. company must comply with under the GDPR, a distinction must be made as to whether the U.S. company is acting as a "controller" or a "processor" within the meaning of the GDPR.

A legal definition of the term "controller" is provided in Article 4 No. 7 GDPR. It covers any natural or legal person, public authority, agency or other body which, alone or jointly with others, determines the purposes and means of the processing. If individual natural persons are acting, it must be asked who the actions is to be attributed to — the acting person him- or herself (who in that case would be the controller) or the organization for which that person works (which would then be the controller). Any economic links or de facto influence which may exist would not play any role in identifying the controller. The approach that needs to be taken in this regard is not an economic, but rather a legal one. Accordingly, legally independent companies are each their own controller, even if they are affiliated with each other in a group. It follows from the definition of "controller" that the possibility of a joint controllership exists . . .

Another important actor within the framework of the GDPR is the processor. Pursuant to Article 4 No. 8 GDPR, a processor is any natural or legal person, public authority, agency or other body which processes personal data on behalf of the controller. Typical cases of processing are, for example, file destruction, support by computer centers, offers of Software as a Service (SaaS), cloud services, etc. Processing is not carried out in the case of, for example, the engagement of attorneys or the preparation of tax declarations by tax advisors. The processor must render services for the controller on the basis of a contract pursuant to Article 28 GDPR. In relation to the controller, the processor more or less functions as . . . a "puppet". If the processor steps out of the framework prescribed for it, however, then it will be deemed to be a controller pursuant to Article 28(10) GDPR — with the consequence that it will be subject to all of the duties incumbent on controllers.

. . .

1.   Ascertaining the Lawfulness of the Processing

If the U.S. company is to be considered a controller, it will first and foremost be held responsible for the lawfulness of the processing. The central rule in European data protection law in this sense would then be that the processing of personal data is generally prohibited. It may occur only if either the data subjects consent to it or another statutory criterion for permissibility applies, in particular from the definitive list in the general clauses of Articles 6 and 9 GDPR, but also under national law insofar as the GDPR explicitly grants this possibility through the various opening clauses.

This "prohibition with reservation of permission," which every controller has to comply with, specifies the statutory reservation on the national level for the public sphere as a general principle of EU law, which must always be complied with in cases of interference with fundamental rights. Conversely, in the non-public sphere, this prohibition with reservation of permission restricts the fundamental rights of the controller. Each individual phase of the data processing requires legitimation, and thus a data subject's consent which merely covers the collection and storage is not sufficient for the transfer of data. It must therefore always be carefully examined whether each intended use of personal data in every phase can be supported by a criterion for permissibility. If this is not possible, then it will be necessary to refrain from processing the personal data involved. Moreover, the overarching necessity principle applies along with the prohibition with reservation of permission, as is made particularly clear with the criteria for permissibility set out in [the GDPR], under which the processing of personal data is permissible only if this is necessary within the scope of the respective criterion for permissibility, i.e. if no sensible or reasonable alternative exists to the manner of data processing that is being contemplated in order to achieve the desired objective.

2. *Information Requirements*

Furthermore, the GDPR provides for comprehensive information require-ments for controllers. In the view of the legislature, in order for data subjects to be able to avail themselves of possible options for action, it is necessary that they know in the first place that the controller is processing personal data relating to them. Proceeding from this transparency concept which is enshrined in the transparency principle of Article 5(1)(a) GDPR, the regulators have created comprehensive information requirements for the controller.

With regard to the information to be provided to the data subjects, a distinc-tion must be made as to whether the data are collected from the data subject, and thus they themselves are functioning as direct data sources (in which case Article 13 GDPR is to be applied), or if the data are collected not from the data subjects themselves, but from, for example, third parties or publicly accessible sources (in which case Article 14 GDPR applies). As a rule, the controller is obligated to provide the data subject with information such as its identity and contact details, the contact details of a data protection officer, where applicable, the purposes of the processing for which the personal data are intended, the legal basis for the processing, and the recipients or categories of recipients of the personal data. Generally, this infor-mation must also state the period for which the data will be stored and explain the rights to oppose the processing to which the data subject is entitled.

How the controller fulfills this duty in practice will depend on the situation at hand. If data processing on websites is involved, the data subjects will normally be informed by way of a privacy policy. If contracts are concluded, the information may be conveyed in a separate data protection information if appropriate.

3. *Other Obligations vis-à-vis Data Subjects*

Articles 15 et seq. of the GDPR set out additional specific data protection rights benefitting data subjects which U.S. companies must comply with if they are subject to the GDPR as controllers.

For example, in the view of the European lawmakers it is of essential importance for data subjects to be able to learn by obtaining access to information whether the controller is processing any personal data concerning them, and if so, what personal data is involved. . . . The data subject has the right to obtain information in partic-ular on whether personal data are being processed by the controller and if that is the case, information on the purposes of the processing, the categories of personal data which are being processed and the recipients or categories of recipients of the data. In fact, the data subject must be provided with a copy of his or her personal data, provided that this does not adversely affect the rights of any third parties. In practice, fulfilling this right to information can result in a great expenditure of time and money. . . .

[The GDPR] provides the data subject with the right to obtain from the con-troller the rectification of inaccurate personal data concerning him or her. Taking into account the purposes of the processing, the data subject also has the right to have incomplete personal data completed. . . .

Pursuant to Article 17(1) GDPR, subject to certain conditions, the data subject additionally has the right to obtain from the controller the erasure of personal data concerning him or her without undue delay. . . .

Subject to certain conditions, a data subject has the right under Article 18 GDPR to demand that the controller restrict the processing of personal data concerning him or her. What is meant here is the blocking of personal data. . . .

Article 20 GDPR grants the data subject a right against the controller to data portability upon request. This right, which provides data subjects with a comprehensive power to dispose of "their" data, was newly created in the GDPR. . . . The right to data portability — like the right to information — is meant to ensure that the data subject can further strengthen the control over his or her own data. At the same time, it should be possible and as uncomplicated as possible for a data subject to switch from one controller to a different one, which may provide more data protection-friendly systems. . . .

Pursuant to Article 21 GDPR, in certain situations the data subject has the right to object to the processing of personal data affecting him or her by a controller, thus ensuring that the controller will no longer be allowed to process the data involved. . . .

4.   Designation of a Data Protection Officer

. . . U.S. companies within the scope of the GDPR will have to designate a data protection officer if their core activities, i.e., the most important work processes which are necessary to achieve their objectives, consist of processing operations which, by virtue of their nature, their scope and/or their purposes, require regular and systematic monitoring of data subjects on a large scale or their core activities consist of processing on a large scale of special categories of data (concerning health, genetic data, etc.).

. . .

5.   Documentation Duties

[T]he controller is not only responsible for the lawfulness of the data processing, but must consistently be able to demonstrate it (accountability). In practice, this can only be achieved by way of complete documentation.

. . .

6.   Notification Duties

Controllers are additionally obliged to notify data protection breaches to the competent supervisory authority without undue delay. . . .

In the event of a personal data breach, the controller must not only inform the supervisory authority, but also, under certain circumstances, the data subjects as well. This is necessary if the breach is likely to result in a high risk to the rights and freedoms of natural persons. The system involved is the reverse of that for the duty to notify the supervisory authority: the communication is not necessary as a rule, but only in exceptional cases if the breach is likely to result in a high risk to the rights and freedoms of natural persons. However, the communication will not be required if, for example, the relevant data are protected by technical and organizational protection measures (such as effective encryption), due to countermeasures taken by the controller, the high risk to the rights and freedoms of data subjects is no longer likely to materialize or the communication would involve disproportionate effort to carry out. In the latter case, individual communications would be replaced by a public communication or similar measure in a form which will make it possible for the data subjects to obtain knowledge of the breach. . . .

7. Data Protection Impact Assessment

Under Article 35 GDPR, it is mandatory for certain processing operations that the controller carry out a data protection impact assessment.

. . .

As you read the following privacy policies, consider the covenants being made by the site, any burdens or options being given to users, and the language being used to explain these concepts.

CRAIGSLIST PRIVACY POLICY
July 2015 (accessed July 2020)

This policy details how data about you is used when you access our websites and services (together, "CL") or interact with us. If we update it, we will revise the date, place notices on CL if changes are material, and/or obtain your consent as required by law.

1. Protecting your privacy

- We take precautions to prevent unauthorized access to or misuse of data about you.
- We do not run ads, other than the classifieds posted by our users.
- We do not share your data with third parties for marketing purposes.
- We do not engage in cross-marketing or link-referral programs.
- We do not employ tracking devices for marketing purposes.
- We do not send you unsolicited communications for marketing purposes.
- We do not engage in affiliate marketing (and prohibit it on CL).
- We do provide email proxy & relay services to reduce unwanted email.
- Please review privacy policies of any third party sites linked to from CL.

2. Data we use to provide/improve our services and/or combat fraud/abuse:

- data you post on or send via CL, and/or send us directly or via other sites.
- credit card data, which is transmitted to payment processors via a security protocol (e.g. SSL).
- data you submit or provide (e.g. name, address, email, phone, fax, photos, tax ID).
- web log data (e.g. web pages viewed, access times, IP address, HTTP headers).

- data collected via cookies (e.g. search data and "favorites" lists).
- data about your device(s) (e.g. screen size, DOM local storage, plugins).
- data from 3rd parties (e.g. phone type, geo-location via IP address).

3. Data we store

- We retain data as needed for our business purposes and/or as required by law.
- We make good faith efforts to store data securely, but can make no guarantees.
- You may access and update certain data about you via your account login.

4. Circumstances in which we may disclose user data:

- to vendors and service providers (e.g. payment processors) working on our behalf.
- to respond to subpoenas, search warrants, court orders, or other legal process.
- to protect our rights, property, or safety, or that of users of CL or the general public.
- with your consent (e.g. if you authorize us to share data with other users).
- in connection with a merger, bankruptcy, or sale/transfer of assets.
- in aggregate/summary form, where it cannot reasonably be used to identify you.

International Users — By accessing CL or providing us data, you agree we may use and disclose data we collect as described here or as communicated to you, transmit it outside your resident jurisdiction, and store it on servers in the United States. For more information please contact our privacy officer at privacy@craigslist.org.

CNN PRIVACY STATEMENT
July 2020

Thank you for visiting a WarnerMedia News & Sports property. This Privacy Policy explains our online information practices and the choices you can make about information collected through our websites, applications ("apps"), services, connected devices (e.g., connected TVs), and other offerings (each a "Site" or collectively, the "Sites"). This Privacy Policy applies to any Site that links directly to this policy. For certain offerings on our Sites, there may be additional notices about our information practices and choices. Please read those additional privacy disclosures to understand how they apply to you. Our Privacy Policy is designed to provide transparency into our privacy practices and principles. You can learn about our WarnerMedia and AT&T affiliates by visiting the affiliates' page.

TABLE OF CONTENTS

- INFORMATION WE COLLECT
- HOW WE USE THE INFORMATION
- INFORMATION SHARING AND DISCLOSURE

- YOUR CHOICES AND CONTROLS
- COOKIES AND OTHER TECHNICAL INFORMATION
- INFORMATION SECURITY
- HOW YOU CAN ACCESS OR CORRECT INFORMATION
- ADDITIONAL INFORMATION REGARDING CHILDREN'S PRIVACY
- INTERNATIONAL TRANSFER
- NOTIFICATION REGARDING PRIVACY POLICY UPDATES
- HOW TO CONTACT US
- CALIFORNIA AND CCPA PRIVACY RIGHTS AND DISCLOSURES
- AFFILIATES (Please visit the affiliates' page to review our list of affiliates)

INFORMATION WE COLLECT

We may collect different types of information during your interactions with our Sites and through our advertising and media across the Internet and mobile apps. This information may include personal information (e.g., name, phone number, postal address, email address, and certain payment information), technical information (e.g., device identifier, IP address, browser type, operating system) and usage information (e.g., how you use and navigate to and from our Sites, and information about content or advertisements you have been shown or have clicked on). We may combine these types of information together, and collectively refer to all of this information in this Privacy Policy as "Information." Information may be collected as described below and through the use of cookies, web beacons, pixels, and other similar technologies by us or by other companies on our behalf. Below we describe the types of Information we may collect:

Registration, account, and sign-up information. We may collect Information in the course of your use of, or registration with, our Sites. For example, when you create an account, register for or download an app, or sign-up for a product or service, you may provide us with certain personal information. This type of personal information may include name, phone number, postal address, fax number, email address, or certain payment information (e.g., credit card and billing information). We may also collect Information about your interest in and use of various products, programs, services, and content available on or through our Sites.

Other information you provide. When you interact with our Sites, you may share other information about yourself by, for example, publishing and sharing the information with the Site's website or in the Site's community, creating a or profile, or filing out a survey or application. Sometimes you may also choose to provide more sensitive forms of personal information to us, such as information regarding your physical or mental health, biometric data, race or ethnicity, religious or philosophical beliefs, sex life, sexual orientation, political opinions, or trade union membership. For example, we may collect this type of sensitive information if you participate in surveys, focus groups, or opportunities to test new products, programs, or services. We collect this sensitive information with your consent, if required by law, and we take steps to protect and limit any use of it to the purposes for which it is provided.

Information from others; inviting friends. On some of our Sites we may collect Information other people submit about you. For example, a friend might submit Information to invite you to participate in an offering, make recommendations, or share content. By processing these requests, we may receive your Information, including a recipient's name, postal address, email address, telephone number, or information about your interest in and use of various products, programs, services, and content. Some of our Sites also allow users to invite friends to participate in activities by providing their friends' contact details or importing contacts from your address book or from other sites.

Information from other sources. We may combine Information we receive online with other information, including usage information from our other Sites and our online advertising and media. We may also supplement or combine Information with information from a variety of other sources or outside records, such as demographic, transaction history, or personal information, and we may use that combined information in accordance with this Privacy Policy.

Information you provide through social media. You can engage with some of our content and offerings, such as videos, games, apps, and other offerings on or through third party communities, forums, and social media sites, platforms, services, plug-ins, and applications ("Social Media Sites"). When you link to or interact with our Sites, content, or offerings through Social Media Sites, you may allow us to receive certain Information from your social media account (e.g., name, user ID, email address, profile photo, photos and videos, gender, birthday, location, your list of friends and their contact details, people you follow and/or who follow you, the posts or the 'likes' you make). We may also receive Information from your interaction with our content (e.g., content viewed, game performance, high scores, and information about advertisements you have been shown or have clicked on). By providing this Information or otherwise interacting with our Sites through Social Media Sites, you consent to our use of Information from the Social Media Sites in accordance with this Privacy Policy. For information about how you can customize your privacy settings on Social Media Sites, and how those Social Media Sites handle your personal information and content, please refer to their privacy help guides, privacy policies, and terms of use.

Information you provide through public forums. If you post or share Information or content, such as photos, letters, videos, or comments, while participating in online forums on our Sites, or when you interact with our Sites through Social Media Sites, depending on your privacy settings, this Information or content and your username may become public on the Internet or within a community of users. We cannot prevent further use of this Information once you share it in a publicly available forum. For information about how you can customize your privacy settings on Social Media Sites, and how those Social Media Sites handle your personal information and content, please refer to their privacy help guides, privacy policies, and terms of use.

Location information. We may have access to certain Information about your location, such as your country or address, when you provide it either directly or via device information. If you access our Sites on your mobile device, we may collect Information about your device's precise location. We also may derive a general location from device information (such as an IP address).

Information you provide through camera access. For some Sites, we will ask for permission to access your device's camera. If you grant permission, you may be able to take pictures or video within the app experience or to access certain augmented reality ("AR") features. Some of these features may rely on camera systems to track movements of your eyes and other facial features or your immediate surroundings to apply AR effects. Information gathered from some facial scanning technology (e.g. TrueDepth API), is only used to make these services and features available to you and is only persistent on the device during use of the AR features. Other facial scanning technology may be used for research, analytics, and enhancing consumer experiences.

Video and streaming information. For some Sites, we collect information about the films, TV shows, and videos that you view. For example, if you stream video content using our Sites, we may collect information about your interaction with that content or service, such as the title and genre, watchlists you compile, and searches you conduct, duration and number of streams and downloads and system information related to streaming and download quality.

Technical and usage information. We also collect certain technical and usage information when you use our Sites, such as the type of device, browser, and operating system you are using, your Internet service provider or mobile carrier, unique device identifier, IDFA or IDFV, MAC address, IP address, device and browser settings, the webpages and apps you use, advertisements you see and interact with, and certain Site usage information. See our Cookies and Other Technical Information section for more information on how we may use these technologies to collect this Information.

HOW WE USE THE INFORMATION

We use Information for the purposes described in this policy or disclosed at the time of collection or with your consent.

Providing and marketing products and services. We may use the Information we collect about you through our Sites to fulfill your requests for, and otherwise provide or analyze your use of our products, programs, services and content, to facilitate sharing and other interactions with Social Media Sites, and to provide, develop, maintain, personalize, protect, and improve your experience and our offerings. For example, we use Information we collect to enable you to do things like (i) watch trailers, movies, programs, and video clips, (ii) get entertainment news and updates, (iii) get information about our products, programs, services, and content, (iv) locate and access personalized information or functionality based on your interests or location (e.g., find stores, theaters, or show times), (v) buy digital content, movie tickets, or other purchases (vi) play games, (vii) engage with interactive features, activities, and Social Media Sites, (viii) read and post comments, content, and reviews, (ix) fill out surveys or provide feedback, or (x) enter promotions, contests, and sweepstakes. We may also use Information to offer, market, and advertise products, programs, and services from us and our affiliates, business partners, and select third parties that we believe may be of interest to you.

Communicating with you and others. We may use Information about you to communicate with you, such as (i) to notify you when you win one of our contests or sweepstakes or when we make changes to our policies or user agreements, (ii) to respond to your inquiries and provide you with customer service, (iii) to communicate with you about your purchases or transactions, (iv) to contact you about your account, or (v) to send you information about promotions, offerings, and Site features. You may also choose to receive push notifications from us on your mobile device. If you choose to submit content for publication online or in other forums, we may publish your screen name or username and other Information you have provided to us on our Sites, the Internet, or elsewhere. We use Information that you provide about others to enable us to send them invitations, promotions, or other content on your behalf or through our Sites. From time to time, we also may use this Information to offer, market, or advertise products, programs, or services to them from us and our affiliates, and business partners.

Use of technical and usage information. We may use technical and usage information to improve the design, functionality and content of our Sites and to enable us to personalize your experience with our Sites and offerings. For example, we may use this Information (i) to provide, develop, maintain, personalize, protect, and improve our Sites, products, programs, and services and to operate our business, (ii) to perform analytics, including to analyze and report on usage and performance of our Sites, (iii) to protect against, identify, and prevent fraud and other unlawful activity, (iv) to create aggregate data about groups or categories of our users, and (iv) for us and our affiliates, business partners, and select third parties to target, offer, market, or advertise products, programs, or services.

Compliance. We may use Information we collect to detect, investigate, and prevent activities on our Sites that may violate our terms of use, could be fraudulent, violate copyright, or other rules or that may be otherwise illegal, to comply with legal requirements, and to protect our rights and the rights and safety of our users and others.

INFORMATION SHARING AND DISCLOSURE

We may share and disclose Information in the following ways or for any other purpose disclosed at the time of collection:

With your consent. We may disclose Information when you provide us with your consent to do so.

Legal and law enforcement purposes. We may disclose Information in response to legal process, for example in response to a court order or a subpoena, or in response to a law enforcement agency's request. We also may disclose such Information to third parties: (i) in connection with fraud prevention activities, (ii) where we believe it is necessary to investigate, prevent, or take action regarding illegal activities, (iii) in situations that may involve violations of our terms of use or other rules, (iv) to protect our rights and the rights and safety of others, and (v) as otherwise required by law.

Change of control. We may transfer Information in the event of a business transaction, such as if we or one of our business units or our relevant assets are acquired by, sold to, or merged with another company or as part of a bankruptcy proceeding or a business reorganization.

Service providers. Organizations that perform services for us may have access to Information to help carry out the services they are performing for us, such as, but not limited to, creation, maintenance, hosting, and delivery of our Sites, products, and services, conduct marketing, handle payments, email and order fulfillment, administer contests, conduct research and analytics, or customer service.

Affiliates. We may disclose Information to affiliates. For example, we may share Information we collect with our affiliates to provide, improve, offer, market, and otherwise communicate with you about their own products and services. Our products and services may be developed, managed, marketed and sold by a variety of our affiliates. We share Information that may identify you internally among affiliates publicly recognized as a WarnerMedia affiliate, such as Xandr and the AT&T family of companies. Public recognition may derive from, for example, use of common branding elements, advertising, press, social media reports or other public form of notice. We require the affiliate to protect the Information consistent with this Policy. We may also combine Information that identifies you personally with data that comes from an affiliate that has a different privacy policy. When we do that, our Policy applies to the combined data set. You can learn about our WarnerMedia and AT&T affiliates by visiting the WarnerMedia affiliates' page.

Business partners and third parties. We may also share Information with business partners and third parties (e.g., other companies, retailers, research organizations, advertisers, ad agencies, advertising networks and platforms, participatory databases, publishers, and non-profit organizations) that may want to market products or services to you. If we share personal information with such unaffiliated third parties for their own marketing purposes, we provide you with an opportunity to opt out of such uses either at the point of collection or through the choice mechanisms set forth in this Privacy Policy. To learn more about your choices, please see our Your Choices and Controls section below.

Linked sites. Some of our Sites contain links to other sites, including Social Media Sites, whose information practices may be different from ours. Information you submit to other sites will be governed by the other sites' privacy policies and terms.

Sponsors and co-promotions. We may sometimes offer content or programs (e.g., contests, sweepstakes, promotions, games, applications or Social Media Site integrations) that are sponsored by or co-branded with identified third parties. By virtue of these relationships, the sponsoring or co-branding parties may collect or obtain Information from visitors that participate in the activity. We have no control over these sponsoring or co-branding parties' use of this Information. We encourage you to visit the privacy policy of any such sponsoring or co-branding party to learn about their data practices prior to providing Information through sponsored or co-branded content or programs.

Advertising networks. We may share certain information with parties to provide advertising to you based on your interests. For more information, please see our Ad Choices section below.

YOUR CHOICES AND CONTROLS

Marketing communications and sharing with third parties. We provide you with an opportunity to express your preferences with respect to receiving certain marketing communications from us, and our sharing of personal information with unaffiliated third parties for their direct marketing purposes. If you ever decide in the future that you would like to update these preferences, you may (i) log in to an account you have created with us at one of our Sites to adjust your settings, or (ii) send us an email at wmprivacy@warnermediagroup.com. To opt out of receiving our email marketing communications, you can also follow the "unsubscribe" instructions provided in any marketing email you receive from us. If you previously chose to receive push notifications on your mobile device from us, but no longer wish to receive them, you can manage your preferences through your device or app settings, depending on the type of device. If you have signed up to receive text messages from us and no longer wish to receive such messages, you may follow the instructions to stop the delivery of such messages, which may include by replying "STOP" to the received text message.

For California residents, please see below for additional information on the choices we provide to you.

Ad Choices. On our own or working with affiliates or third parties, we may present advertisements and engage in data collection, reporting, ad delivery and response measurement, and site analytics on our Sites and on third party websites across the Internet and applications over time. We, our affiliates, or third parties may use cookies, web beacons, pixels, software development kits ("SDKs") or similar technologies to collect information across websites, services, and apps over time to perform this activity. We, our affiliates, or third parties may use and transfer this information in order to help serve advertising that may be more relevant to your interests on and off our Sites and across your devices and browsers. This type of advertising is known as interest-based advertising. We, our affiliates, or third parties may also use this information to associate your different browsers and devices together for interest-based advertising and for other purposes like research, analytics, internal operations, fraud prevention, and enhancing consumer experiences.

For more information about interest-based advertising on your desktop or mobile browser, and to opt out of this type of advertising by third parties that participate in self-regulatory programs, please visit the Network Advertising Initiative website and/or the Digital Advertising Alliance ("DAA") Self-Regulatory Program for Online Behavioral Advertising website. To learn more about interest-based advertising in mobile apps and to opt out of this type of advertising by third parties that participate in the DAA's AppChoices tool, please use this link to download the version of AppChoices for your device. Please note that any opt-out choice you exercise through these programs will apply to interest-based advertising by the third parties you select, but will still allow the collection of data for other purposes, including research, analytics, and internal operations. You may continue to receive advertising, but that advertising may be less relevant to your interests.

To opt out of our own collection, use, and transfer of data as described above for interest-based advertising, please visit our Privacy Center to opt-out. Please note that if you opt out, we will continue to collect data for other purposes, including research, analytics, and internal operations. You may continue to receive advertising on our Sites based on your activities on our Sites.

You may have more options depending on your mobile device and operating system. For example, most device operating systems (e.g., iOS for Apple phones, Android for Android devices, and Windows for Microsoft devices) provide their own instructions on how to limit or prevent the delivery of tailored in-application advertisements. You may review the support materials and/or the privacy settings for the respective operating systems to learn more about these features and how they apply to tailored in-app advertisements.

Precise location information. To disable the collection of precise location information from your mobile device through our mobile apps, you can access your mobile device settings and choose to limit that collection.

See also our Cookies and Other Technical Information section for more choices about managing other technical and usage information.

COOKIES AND OTHER TECHNICAL INFORMATION

Cookies and other technologies. We, and our affiliates, vendors, and business partners may send "cookies" to your computer or use similar technologies to understand and enhance your online experience at our Sites and through our advertising and media across the Internet and mobile apps.

Cookies are small text files placed in your browser. We may also use pixels or "web beacons" that monitor your use of our Sites. Web beacons are small strings of code that provide a method for delivering a graphic image on a webpage for the purpose of transferring data, such as the IP address of the computer that down-loaded the page on which the web beacon appears, the URL of the page on which the web beacon appears, the time the page containing the web beacon was viewed, the type of browser that fetched the web beacon, and the identification number of any cookie on the computer previously placed by that server. We may also integrate SDKs into our applications to perform similar functions as cookies and web beacons. For example, SDKs may collect technical and usage information such as mobile device identifiers and your interactions with the Site and other mobile apps.

We may use cookies and other technologies to help recognize your browser or device, maintain your preferences, provide certain Site features, and collect Information about interactions with our Sites, our content, and our communications. For example, when corresponding with you via HTML capable email, web beacons and other technologies let us know about your activity, including whether you received and opened our email, clicked through a link, or otherwise interacted with our content, and this information may be associated with Information previously collected.

We may also use cookies and other technologies (i) to provide, develop, maintain, personalize, protect, and improve our Sites, products, programs, and services and to operate our business, (ii) to perform analytics, including to analyze and report on usage and performance of our Sites and marketing materials, (iii) to protect against, identify, and prevent fraud and other unlawful activity, (iv) to create aggregate data about groups or categories of our users, (v) to synchronize users across devices, affiliates, business partners, and select third parties, and (vi) for us and our affiliates, business partners, and select third parties to target, offer, market, or advertise products, programs, or services. Cookies and other technologies also facilitate, manage, and measure the performance of advertisements displayed on or delivered by or through us and/or other networks or sites. By visiting the Site, whether as a registered user or otherwise, you acknowledge, and agree that you are giving us your consent to track your activities and your use of the Site through the technologies described above, as well as similar technologies developed in the future, and that we may use such tracking technologies in the emails we send to you.

Managing cookies and other technologies. Cookies can either be persistent (i.e., they remain on your computer until you delete them) or temporary (i.e., they last only until you close your browser). Check your browser settings to learn how to delete cookies.

You may adjust your browser to reject cookies from us or from any other website. Controlling cookies via browser controls may not limit our use of other technologies. Please consult your browser's settings for more information. However, blocking cookies or similar technology might prevent you from accessing some of our content or Site features.

Some of our Sites may use locally stored objects ("LSOs") to provide certain content, such as video on demand, video clips, or animation, and a better user experience. Adobe's Flash player and similar applications use this technology to remember settings, preferences, and usage similar to browser cookies. Flash cookies are not managed through your web browser, but you can access your Flash management tools by visiting Adobe's web site. Your browser may also offer other tools to delete or reject other LSOs; please check your browser's settings or help menu for more information.

Some of our sites may use Google Analytics to analyze traffic. You can find out more information about Google Analytics cookies by visiting the following location provided: https://developers.google.com/analytics/devguides/collection/analyt-icsjs/cookie-usage. To opt out of Google Analytics relating to your use of our Sites, you can download and install the Browser Plugin available by visiting the following location provided: https://tools.google.com/dlpage/gaoptout?hl=en.

Some Sites may feature Nielsen proprietary measurement software, which will allow users to contribute to market research, such as Nielsen TV Ratings. To learn more about the information that Nielsen software may collect and your choices, please see the Nielsen Digital Measurement Privacy Policy by visiting the follow-ing location provided: https://www.nielsen.com/us/en/legal/privacy-statement/digital-measurement/

We do not currently take actions to respond to Do Not Track signals because a uniform technological standard has not yet been developed. We continue to review new technologies and may adopt a standard once one is created.

See the Your Choices and Controls section to learn how to control data collec-tion for certain purposes.

INFORMATION SECURITY

We have put in place reasonable controls designed to help safeguard the per-sonal information we collect via the Sites. However, no security measures are per-fect, and we cannot assure you that personal information that we collect will never be accessed or used in an unauthorized way.

HOW YOU CAN ACCESS OR CORRECT INFORMATION

To access personal information that we have collected about you online from Sites on which this Privacy Policy is posted, or to update your user profile, please log into your account if you have created one with us, or send an email to wmprivacy@warnermediagroup.com. For California residents, please see below for additional information on accessing information about you.

ADDITIONAL INFORMATION REGARDING CHILDREN'S PRIVACY

On most Sites, we do not knowingly collect information from children. On some Sites, we may ask the user to provide us with the user's age information. If the person indicates that he or she is under 13 years old, as permitted by law, we will (i) collect no or limited personal information (e.g., persistent identifier and/or email address only) from that individual, (ii) inform the child that a parent's verifi-able consent is required, and/or (iii) collect the email address of the user's parent in addition to the user's email address. We may use the parent's email address to seek the parent's verifiable consent or notify the parent of his/her child's online activities and enable the parent to unsubscribe his/her child from a newsletter or other similar activity. Once a parent provides consent, we may use any information collected from a child consistent with the rest of this Privacy Policy and/or the terms of the consent provided by the parent. If a user is under 13, we will not condition his/her participation in an online activity on the disclosure of more personal information than is reasonably necessary to participate in the activity. If you would like to review any personal information that we have collected online from your child, have this personal information deleted from our active servers, and/or request that there be no further collection or use of your child's personal information, or if you have questions about these information practices, you may contact us at wmprivacy@warnermediagroup.com, or at WarnerMedia Privacy Office, 4000 Warner Blvd., Bldg. 160, Burbank, CA 91522.

INTERNATIONAL TRANSFER

We operate internationally, and many of our computer systems are currently based in the United States, which means Information we collect will be processed by us in the U.S. where data protection and privacy regulations may not offer the same level of protection as in other parts of the world, such as the European Union. If you use or visit our Sites from outside the United States, you consent to the collection and/or processing in the United States of Information we collect from you.

NOTIFICATION REGARDING PRIVACY POLICY UPDATES

From time to time, we may update this Privacy Policy. We will notify you about material changes to this Privacy Policy by placing a notice on our Sites. We encourage you to periodically check back and review this policy so that you always know our current privacy practices.

HOW TO CONTACT US

If you have any questions about this Privacy Policy you may contact us at: wmprivacy@warnermediagroup.com or at WarnerMedia Privacy Office, 4000 Warner Blvd., Bldg. 160, Burbank, CA 91522 or contact us toll free at 833-WM-PRVCY (833-967-7829) or TTY: 833-PRVCY-TT (833-778-2988).

CALIFORNIA AND CCPA PRIVACY RIGHTS AND DISCLOSURES

This California and CCPA Privacy Rights and Disclosure section was last updated July 1, 2020 and addresses legal obligations and rights laid out in the California Consumer Privacy Act ("CCPA") and other laws that apply only to California residents. These obligations and rights apply to businesses doing business in California and to California residents and information that identifies, relates to, describes, is reasonably capable of being associated with, or could reasonably be linked, directly or indirectly, with California consumers or households ("California Information"). It does not apply to information that has been de-identified or aggregated as provided by CCPA.

CALIFORNIA INFORMATION WE COLLECTED AND SHARED

This section provides the information California residents need to exercise their rights over their California Information. Here is information about the California Information we have collected from and shared about consumers in the year before this section was last updated.

California Information We Collected

In the year before this section was last updated, we may have collected the following categories of California Information:

- Address and other identifiers — such as name, phone number, postal address, zip code, email address, account name or number, date of birth, driver's license number, payment card numbers, or other similar identifiers
- Characteristics of protected classifications — such as race, ethnicity, or sexual orientation
- Unique and other online identifiers — such as IP address, device IDs, or other similar identifiers that relate to your device and its operating system
- Commercial information — such as products or services purchased, obtained, or considered, or other purchasing or consuming histories or tendencies
- Internet or other electronic network activity information — such as browsing history, search history, and information regarding your interactions with our Sites, and content such as videos, ads, websites, and devices such as smart TVs, streaming media, browsers and apps
- Professional information or educational Information — such as your current occupation
- Biometric information
- Audio, visual, or similar information — such as photos, videos, video footage (CCTV) or recordings you choose to post to our Sites or provide by granting us access to your camera while using Sites or services
- Location information — such as your device's precise location in connection with certain Sites
- Inferences or audience segmentation — such as individual profiles, preferences, characteristics, and behaviors
- In-Game or online viewing activities — such videos, content, and pages viewed

We may have collected or sold these categories of California Information for the following business or commercial purposes:

- Performing services on behalf of the business — such as customer service, processing or fulfilling orders, providing content recommendations, and processing payments
- Auditing customer transactions
- Fraud and crime prevention
- Debugging errors in systems
- Marketing and advertising
- Internal research, analytics and development — e.g., user-preference analytics
- Developing, maintaining, provisioning or upgrading networks, products, services, or devices

We may have obtained California Information from a variety of sources, including:

- Directly from you — such as technical and usage information when you use our Sites
- Linked sites — such as Social Media Sites and third-party platforms
- Our affiliates
- Our joint ventures and promotional and strategic partners
- Information suppliers
- Distributors and other vendors
- Marketing mailing lists
- Other users submitting information about you — such as to invite you to participate in an offering, make recommendations, or share content
- Publicly available sources

Disclosures of California Information:

In the year before this section was last updated, we may have disclosed the following categories of California Information to third parties:

- Address and other identifiers — such as name, phone number, postal address, zip code, email address, account name or number, date of birth, driver's license number, payment card numbers, or other similar identifiers
- Characteristics of protected classifications — such as race, ethnicity, or sexual orientation
- Unique and other online identifiers — such as IP address, device IDs, or other similar identifiers that relate to your device and its operating system
- Commercial information — such as products or services purchased, obtained, or considered, or other purchasing or consuming histories or tendencies
- Internet or other electronic network activity information — such as browsing history, search history, and information regarding your interactions with our Sites, and content such as videos, ads, websites, and devices such as smart TVs, streaming media, browsers and apps
- Professional information or educational Information — such as your current occupation
- Biometric information
- Audio, visual, or similar information — such as photos, videos, video footage (CCTV) or recordings you choose to post to our Sites or provide by granting us access to your camera while using Sites or services
- Location information — such as your device's precise location in connection with certain Sites
- Inferences or audience segmentation — such as individual profiles, preferences, characteristics, and behaviors
- In-Game or online viewing activities — such videos, content, and pages viewed

We may have disclosed each of these categories of California Information to the following categories of third parties:

- Affiliates — These entities are associated with us through common ownership. For a list of affiliates, please visit the affiliates' page.

- Service Providers — These entities process information on our behalf for business purposes, helping us provide products or services to you
- Social Media Platforms — These entities maintain networks connecting individuals and organizations – such as Facebook, LinkedIn, or Twitter
- Advertising Partners — These entities help us advertise our products or services, as well as connect us with others who want to place advertisements on some of our products or services
- Analytics Partners — These entities help us collect data on how our products or services are used, so that we can improve them and better understand our consumers
- Promotional Partners — We partner with these entities to jointly promote our products, for example by running contests or other promotional campaigns
- Government Entities — These entities include law enforcement authorities, regulatory agencies, and courts

Categories of California Information sold to third parties

The CCPA defines "sale" very broadly. It includes the sharing of California Information in exchange for anything of value. According to this broad definition, in the year before this section was last updated, we may have sold the following categories of California Information to third parties:

- Address and other identifiers — such as name, phone number, postal address, zip code, email address, account name or number, date of birth, driver's license number, payment card numbers, or other similar identifiers
- Characteristics of protected classifications — such as race, ethnicity, or sexual orientation
- Unique and other online identifiers — such as IP address, device IDs, or other similar identifiers that relate to your device and its operating system
- Commercial information — such as products or services purchased, obtained, or considered, or other purchasing or consuming histories or tendencies
- Internet or other electronic network activity information — such as browsing history, search history, and information regarding your interactions with our Sites, and content such as videos, ads, websites, and devices such as smart TVs, streaming media, browsers and apps
- Professional information or educational Information — such as your current occupation
- Biometric information
- Audio, visual, or similar information — such as photos, videos, video footage (CCTV) or recordings you choose to post to our Sites or provide by granting us access to your camera while using Sites or services
- Location information — such as your device's precise location in connection with certain Sites
- Inferences or audience segmentation — such as individual profiles, preferences, characteristics, and behaviors
- In-Game or online viewing activities — such videos, content, and pages viewed

We may have sold each of these categories of California Information to the following categories of third parties:

- Affiliates — These entities are associated with us through common ownership. For a list of affiliates, please visit the affiliates' page.

- Social Media Platforms — These entities maintain networks connecting individuals and organizations — such as Facebook, LinkedIn, or Twitter
- Advertising Partners — These entities help us advertise our products or services, as well as connect us with others who want to place advertisements on some of our products or services
- Analytics Partners — These entities help us collect data on how our products or services are used, so that we can improve them and better understand our consumers
- Promotional Partners — We partner with these entities to jointly promote our products, for example by running contests or other promotional campaigns

YOUR CALIFORNIA PRIVACY RIGHTS TO REQUEST DISCLOSURE OF INFORMATION WE COLLECT AND SHARE ABOUT YOU

If you are a California resident, California Civil Code Section 1798.83 permits you to request information about our practices related to the disclosure of your personal information by certain members of the WarnerMedia family of companies to certain third parties for their direct marketing purposes. You may be able to opt out of our sharing of your personal information with unaffiliated third parties for the third parties' direct marketing purposes in certain circumstances. Please send your request (along with your full name, email address, postal address, and the subject line labeled "Your California Privacy Rights") by email at wmprivacy@warnermediagroup.com.

In addition, if you are a California resident, the CCPA grants you the right to request certain information about our practices with respect to California Information. In particular, you can request the following:

- The categories and specific pieces of your California Information that we've collected
- The categories of sources from which we collected California Information
- The business or commercial purposes for which we collected or sold California Information
- The categories of third parties with which we shared California Information

You can submit a request to us for the following additional information:

- The categories of third parties to whom we've sold California Information, and the category or categories of California Information sold to each
- The categories of third parties to whom we've disclosed California Information, and the category or categories of California Information disclosed to each

YOUR RIGHT TO REQUEST THE DELETION OF CALIFORNIA INFORMATION

Upon your request, we will delete the California Information we have collected about you, except for situations when that information is necessary for us to: provide you with a product or service that you requested; perform a contract we entered into with you; maintain the functionality or security of our systems; comply with or exercise rights provided by the law; or use the information internally in ways that are compatible with the context in which you provided the information to us, or that are reasonably aligned with your expectations based on your relationship with us.

YOUR RIGHT TO ASK US NOT TO SELL YOUR CALIFORNIA INFORMATION

You can always tell us not to sell your California Information by visiting our Privacy Center.

HOW TO EXERCISE YOUR CALIFORNIA RIGHTS

You may exercise your rights to request access to your California Information, deletion of your California Information, or to request we not sell your California Information by visiting our Privacy Center. You can also contact us toll free at 833-WM-PRVCY (833-967-7829) or TTY: 833-PRVCY-TT (833-778-2988) and an agent will assist you with submitting a request. These requests are generally free. When you submit a request, we will usually ask you to provide an email address which we will contact to confirm the request was not fraudulently submitted.

In addition, for access and deletion requests, we will use a third-party verification service to confirm that you are who you say you are. Our verification service does this by matching information you provide against information held about you in its records, or, if necessary, by allowing you to submit documents proving your identity.

If you are the parent of a child under 13 years of age, you may also submit a request on behalf of your child. In that event, we will ask you to provide your child's email address, to verify your identity, and to submit a signed form authorizing us to proceed with the request regarding your child's California Information.

You may also designate an authorized agent to submit a request on your behalf. To do so, we will require either (1) a valid power of attorney, or (2) signed written permission from you. In the event your authorized agent is relying on signed written permission, we may also need to verify your identity and/or contact you directly to confirm permission to proceed with the request.

Your authorized agent can make a request by contacting us toll free at 833-WM-PRVCY (833-967-7829) or TTY: 833-PRVCY-TT (833-778-2988).

OUR SUPPORT FOR THE EXERCISE YOUR DATA RIGHTS

You have the right not to receive discriminatory treatment if you exercise any of the rights explained in this section of the Privacy Policy. We are committed to providing you control over your California Information, we will not disadvantage you if you choose to exercise your rights.

CALIFORNIA CONSUMERS UNDER 16 YEARS OLD

CCPA has specific rules regarding the use of California Information from consumers under 16 years of age. In particular, consistent with the CCPA, if we knowingly collect the California Information of a consumer under the age of 16, we will not sell the information unless we receive affirmative permission to do so. If the consumer is between the ages of 13 and 16 years of age, the consumer may provide that permission; if the consumer is under the age of 13, the consumer's parent or guardian must provide the permission. As of the Effective Date of this Privacy Policy, we do not have actual knowledge that we sell California Information of consumers under 16 years of age.

If you would like further information on how we handle California Information from consumers under the age of 16 years of age, or if you have questions about these information practices, you may contact us at wmprivacy@warnermediagroup.com, or at WarnerMedia Privacy Office, 4000 Warner Blvd., Bldg. 160, Burbank, CA 91522.

CALIFORNIA CONSUMERS UNDER 18 YEARS OLD

California consumers who are registered users of the Sites and under 18 years of age may request removal of content or information they posted on the Sites. We will remove such content or information when we are required to do so by law. To request removal of content or information you posted on the Sites, you may contact us at wmprivacy@warnermediagroup.com, or at WarnerMedia Privacy Office, 4000 Warner Blvd., Bldg. 160, Burbank, CA 91522.

However, even if we remove the content or information that you posted, we cannot completely prevent further use or disclosure of that content or information by others once you have shared it in a publicly available forum.

Notes and Questions

1. Given the ubiquity of privacy policies online, attorneys and entrepreneurs alike are often surprised at how few companies are actually required by statute to have privacy policies. That said, most companies feel it is good practice to have privacy policies, both to give themselves guidance as to how to treat personal information, and to establish a trusting relationship with customers from the outset. In addition, some companies may be required by contracts with third parties to keep certain information private and to have a privacy policy. For example, Google's contract with sites hosting adwords requires hosts to have a privacy policy, and credit card processors require sites that use their services to post and follow privacy policies even when not required by law.

2. Some sites display certification to help users feel secure using the site and comfortable sharing information. Certifications are obviously not required by law, but given their increasing prevalence, it seems they do help users feel they can trust the website. As counsel to a start-up, would you recommend having your client display a certification seal, or do you think it could increase potential liability?

3. Consider the businesses of Craigslist and CNN, and the proportion of user-generated content on each site. Both sites operate nationwide and are also available internationally. How do you explain the differences in length, complexity, and content of the privacy policies of these two companies? Do you find it surprising?

4. In an edited portion at the end of his article, Klar notes that "In the US, the strong influence exerted by California's comparatively high data protection standards on the other states is known as the 'California effect.' With regard to the

GDPR, it is becoming apparent that the extraterritorial approach of European data protection is leading to a 'Brussels effect' worldwide." What strategies might you use when representing entrepreneurs to help them navigate the numerous and occasionally baffling sets of application (or potentially applicable) privacy regulations?

5. Note the manner in which craigslist and CNN handle changes to their privacy policies. What do you think is the best practice for an entrepreneurial venture? Does your answer change if the business is, say, an online retail store selling clothing versus a new social networking venture?

B.   E-COMMERCE AND ONLINE CONTRACTS

At its base, e-commerce is really just "commerce." If an entrepreneur opens a store in downtown Minneapolis and starts selling smartphone accessories, many of the basic issues in the sales transaction are the same as if the same entrepreneur launched a website offering smartphone accessories. In particular, at a minimum, the entrepreneur needs to be able to collect payment in exchange for delivering a product, set forth any return policies, and charge sales tax where appropriate. Students who have taken a Sales course or studied Article 2 of the Uniform Commercial Code in a first-year Contracts course will know that the same rules apply online as in-person for most transactions.

Understanding that the basic retailer-customer relationship is the same, the online nature of an e-commerce transaction and nation- and world-wide availability of websites introduces complexity, particularly in the area of sales tax. In addition, websites that offer services in exchange for a fee or a willingness to be exposed to advertising will often ask consumers to enter into contracts governing the relationship. It is in these two areas — sales tax and online contracts — that the lawyer representing an online entrepreneur will need competence.

1.   Sales Tax

Your client may believe that retailers are only required to charge sales tax in states where they have a physical presence such as a retail store, office, or warehouse. Until recently, your client would have been right: a required "physical presence" for state sales tax has been both the rule and the practice until recently. In the 2018 case South Dakota v. Wayfair, Inc., the United States Supreme Court considered a law passed by South Dakota that required sellers of "tangible personal property" that lacked a physical presence in South Dakota to remit sales tax in the same manner used by sellers that had a physical presence. In a 5 - 4 decision, the Court held that states can charge sales and use taxes on purchases made from out-of-state sellers, even if those sellers do not have a physical presence in the state.

2.   Online Contracts

The fundamentals of contract law — offer and acceptance, consideration, and so on — apply in online transactions just as they do in person. In addition, statutory and common law rules about whether a consumer contract is unconscionable and therefore unenforceable apply online. On the simpler issue of contract formation, however, the advice to the entrepreneur is straightforward and easy to follow. To ensure a meeting of the minds sufficient to make a contract, entrepreneurs should make online user agreements comprehensible and conspicuous on their sites. In addition, customers should be required to take an affirmative step to show they agree with the contract, such as clicking an "I agree" button or checking a checkbox. Some ventures go farther, requiring the customer to scroll to the end of the contract or click a pop-up before proceeding with a transaction. Courts have generally found contracts that require this kind of affirmative step (referred to as "clickwrap" agreements) to be enforceable. Contracts that do not require an affirmative "acceptance" step by the customer (referred to as "browse-wrap" agreements) are of more questionable enforceability; some courts will enforce them if there is evidence of actual or prominent constructive notice of the terms, and others will not.

IN RE ZAPPOS.COM, INC., CUSTOMER DATA SECURITY BREACH LITIGATION
United States District Court for the District of Nevada
893 F. Supp. 2d 1058 (2012)

. . .

I. RELEVANT FACTUAL BACKGROUND

Zappos is an online retailer of apparel, shoes, handbags, home furnishing, beauty products, and accessories. Plaintiffs are Zappos customers who gave personal information to Zappos in order to purchase goods via Zappos.com and/or 6PM.com. In mid-January 2012, a computer hacker attacked Zappos.com and attempted to download files containing customer information such as names and addresses from a Zappos server (the "Security Breach"). Plaintiffs allege that on January 16, 2012, Zappos notified Plaintiffs via email that their personal customer account information had been compromised by hackers. Plaintiffs have filed complaints in federal district courts across the country seeking relief pursuant to state and federal statutory and common law for damages resulting from the Security Breach.

II. PROCEDURAL BACKGROUND

On June 14, 2012, the United States Judicial Panel on Multidistrict Litigation (the "MDL Panel") transferred nine pending actions to the District of Nevada for coordinated or consolidated pretrial proceedings. On July 16, 2012, the MDL Panel transferred an additional case into this action. . . .

Also on June 14, 2012, Defendants' Motion to Compel Arbitration and Stay Action was filed in this Court. [Subsequently, plaintiffs filed an opposition to the motion to compel arbitration.] . . .

III. LEGAL STANDARD

The Federal Arbitration Act ("FAA") provides that contractual arbitration agreements "shall be valid, irrevocable, and enforceable, save upon such grounds as exist at law or in equity for the revocation of any contract." 9 U.S.C. § 2. Arbitration agreements are enforced under sections 3 and 4 of the FAA, which provide "two parallel devices for enforcing an arbitration agreement." Moses H. Cone Mem'l Hosp. v. Mercury Constr. Corp., 460 U.S. 1, 22, 103 S. Ct. 927, 74 L. Ed. 2d 765 (1983). Section 3 gives courts the power to provide "a stay of litigation in any case raising a dispute referable to arbitration," while section 4 empowers courts to provide "an affirmative order to engage in arbitration."

The FAA "is a congressional declaration of a liberal federal policy favoring arbitration agreements, notwithstanding any state substantive or procedural policies to the contrary." Moses H. Cone Mem'l Hosp., 460 U.S. at 24[.]

Despite this strong federal policy in favor of arbitration, arbitration is a "matter of contract," and no party may be required to submit to arbitration "any dispute which he has not agreed so to submit." Howsam v. Dean Witter Reynolds, Inc., 537 U.S. 79, 79, 123 S. Ct. 588, 154 L. Ed. 2d 491 (2002)[.] A court's discretion for compelling arbitration is thus limited to a two-step process of "determining (1) whether a valid agreement to arbitrate exists, and if it does; (2) whether the agreement encompasses the dispute at issue." Chiron Corp. v. Ortho Diagnostics Sys., Inc., 207 F.3d 1126, 1130 (9th Cir. 2000). A party cannot be ordered to arbitration unless there is "an express, unequivocal agreement to that effect." Samson v. NAMA Holdings, LLC, 637 F.3d 915, 923 (9th Cir. 2010).

With regard to the determination of whether there is a valid agreement to arbitrate between the parties, "the liberal federal policy regarding the scope of arbitrable issues is inapposite." Comer v. Micor, Inc., 436 F.3d 1098, 1104 n.11 (9th Cir. 2006). Instead, federal courts "should apply ordinary state-law principles that govern the formation of contracts." First Options of Chicago, Inc. v. Kaplan, 514 U.S. 938, 944, 115 S. Ct. 1920, 131 L. Ed. 2d 985 (1995). Under Nevada law, "[b]asic contract principles require, for an enforceable contract, an offer and acceptance, meeting of the minds, and consideration." May v. Anderson, 121 Nev. 668, 119 P.3d 1254, 1257 (Nev. 2005)[.] Put differently, an enforceable contract "requires a manifestation of mutual assent in the form of an offer by one party and acceptance thereof by the other . . . [and] agreement or meeting of the minds of the parties as to all essential elements." (Keddie, 580 P.2d at 957).

IV. DISCUSSION

The arbitration agreement at issue, founds in the Disputes section of the Terms of Use of the Zappos.com website, provides as follows:

> Any dispute relating in any way to your visit to the Site or to the products you purchase through the Site shall be submitted to confidential arbitration in Las Vegas, Nevada, except that to the extent you have in any manner violated or threatened to violate our intellectual property rights, we may seek injunctive or other appropriate relief in any state or federal court in the State of Nevada. You hereby consent to, and waive all defense of lack of personal jurisdiction and forum non conveniens with respect to venue and jurisdiction in the state and federal courts of Nevada. Arbitration under these Terms of Use shall be conducted pursuant to

the Commercial Arbitration Rules then prevailing at the American Arbitration Association. The arbitrator's award shall be final and binding and may be entered as a judgment in any court of competent jurisdiction. To the fullest extent permitted by applicable law, no arbitration under this Agreement shall be joined to an arbitration involving any other party subject to this Agreement, whether through class action proceedings or otherwise. You agree that regardless of any statute or law to the contrary, any claim or cause of action arising out of, related to or connected with the use of the Site or this Agreement must be filed within one (1) year after such claim or cause of action arose or be forever banned.

Additionally, the first paragraph of the Terms of Use provides in relevant part: "We reserve the right to change this Site and these terms and conditions at any time. ACCESSING, BROWSING OR OTHERWISE USING THE SITE INDICATES YOUR AGREEMENT TO ALL THE TERMS AND CONDITIONS IN THIS AGREEMENT, SO PLEASE READ THIS AGREEMENT CAREFULLY BEFORE PROCEEDING." (Id. (emphasis in original).)

A.   Plaintiffs Did Not Agree to the Terms of Use

The Court's first step when presented with a motion to compel arbitration is to determine whether a valid agreement to arbitrate exists.

It is undisputed that Zappos' Terms of Use constitutes what federal courts have deigned a "browsewrap" agreement. With a browsewrap agreement, a website owner seeks to bind website users to terms and conditions by posting the terms somewhere on the website, usually accessible through a hyperlink located somewhere on the website; in contrast, a "clickwrap" agreement requires users to expressly manifest assent to the terms by, for example, clicking an "I accept" button. "Because no affirmative action is required by the website user to agree to the terms of a contract other than his or her use of the website, the determination of the validity of a browsewrap contract depends on whether the user has actual or constructive knowledge of a website's terms and conditions." Van Tassell v. United Mktg. Grp., 795 F. Supp. 2d 770, 790 (N.D. Ill. 2011)[;] see also Mark A. Lemley, Terms of Use, 90 Minn. L. Rev. 459, 477 (2006) ("Court may be willing to overlook the utter absence of assent only when there are reasons to believe that the [website user] is aware of the [website owner's] terms."); Note, Ticketmaster Corp. v. Tickers.com, Inc.: Preserving Minimum Requirements of Contract on the Internet, 19 Berkeley Tech. L.J. 495, 507 (2004) ("[S]o far courts have held browsewrap agreements enforceable if the website provides sufficient notice of the license."). Where, as here, there is no evidence that plaintiffs had actual knowledge of the agreement, "the validity of a browsewrap contract hinges on whether the website provides reasonable notice of the terms of the contract." Van Tassell, 795 F. Supp. 2d at 791 (citing Specht, 306 F.3d at 32).

Here, the Terms of Use hyperlink can be found on every Zappos webpage, between the middle and bottom of each page, visible if a user scrolls down. For example, when the Zappos.com homepage is printed to hard copy, the link appears on page 3 of 4. The link is the same size, font, and color as most other non-significant links. The website does not direct a user to the Terms of Use when creating an account, logging in to an existing account, or making a purchase. Without direct evidence that Plaintiffs click on the Terms of Use, we cannot conclude that Plaintiffs ever viewed, let alone manifested assent to, the Terms of Use. The Terms of Use is inconspicuous, buried in the middle to bottom of every Zappos.com webpage among many other links, and the website never directs a user to the Terms of Use. No reasonable user would have reason to click on the Terms of Use, even those users who have alleged that they clicked and relied on statements found in adjacent links, such as the site's "Privacy Policy." This case is therefore factually similar to cases that have decline to enforce arbitration clauses, such as Hines v. Overstock.com, wherein the Court refused to enforce an arbitration provision because the plaintiff "lacked notice of the Terms and Conditions because the website did not prompt her to review the Terms and Conditions and because the link to the Terms and Conditions was not prominently displayed so as to provide reasonable notice of the Terms and Conditions." 668 F. Supp. 2d 362, 367 (E.D.N.Y. 2009) aff'd 380 F. App'x 22 (2d Cir. 2010); see also *Specht*, 306 F.3d at 32 ("[A] reference to the existence of license terms on a submerged screen is not sufficient to place consumers on inquiry or constructive notice of those terms."); *Van Tassell*, 795 F. Supp. 2d at 792 (declining to enforce arbitration provision where "a user only encounters the Conditions of Use after scrolling to the bottom of the home page and clicking the 'Customer Service' link, and then scrolling to the bottom of the Customer Service page or clicking the 'conditions of Use, Notices & Disclaimers' link located near the end of a list of links on the page."); Koch Indus., Inc. v. Does, No. 2:10CV1275DAK, 2011 U.S. Dist. LEXIS 49529, 2011 WL 1775765, at *24-25 (D. Utah May 9, 2011) (finding there was no manifested assent where the "Terms of Use . . . were available only through a hyperlink at the bottom of the page, and there was no prominent notice that a user would be bound by those terms."); Cvent, Inc. v. Eventbrite, Inc., 739 F. Supp. 2d 927, 936-37 (E.D. Va. 2010) (declining to enforce "Terms of Use" where "link only appears on Cvent's website via a link buried at the bottom of the first page" and "users of Cvent's website are not required to click on that link, nor are they required to read or assent to the Terms of Use in order to use the website or access any of its content."). We therefore agree with the *Hines* court: "Very little is required to form a contract nowadays — but this alone does not suffice." 668 F. Supp. 2d 362, 367. Where, as here, there is no acceptance by Plaintiffs, no meeting of the minds, and no manifestation of assent, there is no contract pursuant to Nevada law.

B.   The Terms of Use Constitutes an Illusory Contract

The [Plaintiffs] argue that because the Terms of Use grants Zappos the unilateral right to revise the Arbitration Clause, the contract is illusory and therefore unenforceable. In other words, Plaintiffs argue that the Arbitration Clause is illusory because Zappos can avoid the promise to arbitrate simply by amending the provision, while Zappos.com users are simultaneously bound to arbitration.

Most federal courts that have considered this issue have held that if a party retains the unilateral, unrestricted right to terminate the arbitration agreement, it is illusory and unenforceable, especially where there is no obligation to receive consent from, or even notify, the other parties to the contract.

Here, the Terms of Use gives Zappos the right to change the Terms of Use, including the Arbitration Clause, at any time without notice to the consumer. On one side, the Terms of Use purportedly binds any user of the Zappos.com website to mandatory arbitration. However, if a consumer sought to invoke arbitration pursuant to the Terms of Use, nothing would prevent Zappos from unilaterally changing the Terms and making those changes applicable to that pending dispute if it determined that arbitration was no longer in its interest. In effect, the agreement allows

Zappos to hold its customers and users to the promise to arbitrate while reserving its own escape hatch. By the terms of the Terms of Use, Zappos is free at any time to require a consumer to arbitrate and/or litigate anywhere it sees fit, while consumers are required to submit to arbitration in Las Vegas, Nevada. Because the Terms of Use binds consumers to arbitration while leaving Zappos free to litigate or arbitrate wherever it sees fit, there exists no mutuality of obligation. We join those other federal courts that find such arbitration agreements illusory and therefore unenforceable.

C. Equitable Estoppel

"The equitable estoppel doctrine prevents a plaintiff signatory to a contract that contains an arbitration provision from avoiding the agreement to arbitrate if the plaintiff's claims rely on the contract as the basis for relief." Ahlers v. Ryland Homes Nev., LLC, No. 52511, 2010 WL 3276221, at *2 (Nev. 2010)[.]

Defendants argue that Plaintiffs cannot assert breach of contract actions against Zappos.com while seeking to avoid the arbitration provision of the Terms of Use. However, Plaintiffs' breach of contract claims do not rely upon the contract they seek to avoid, the Terms of Use, which they never viewed, but on other statements and guarantees found on the website. Furthermore, this issue is more appropriate for individual litigation in each of the member cases of the [present] actions as it depends on the allegations found in each complaint. We therefore decline to apply the doctrine of equitable estoppel here.

V. CONCLUSION

A court cannot compel a party to arbitrate where that party has not previously agreed to arbitrate. The arbitration provision found in the Zappos.com Terms of Use purportedly binds all users of the website by virtue of their browsing. However, the advent of the Internet has not changed the basic requirements of a contract, and there is no agreement where there is no acceptance, no meeting of the minds, and no manifestation of assent. A party cannot assent to terms of which it has no knowledge or constructive notice, and a highly inconspicuous hyperlink buried among a sea of links does not provide such notice. Because Plaintiffs did not assent to the terms, no contract exists, and they cannot be compelled to arbitrate. In any event, even if Plaintiffs could be said to have consented to the terms, the Terms of Use constitutes an illusory contract because it allows Zappos to avoid arbitration by unilaterally changing the Terms at any time, while binding any consumer to mandatory arbitration in Las Vegas, Nevada. We therefore decline to enforce the arbitration provision on two grounds: there is no contract, and even if there was, it would be illusory and therefore unenforceable.

Notes and Questions

1. In January 2012, Zappos had a massive security breach affecting 24 million customers. As you know from reading the case, a class action suit ensued, and Zappos moved to compel arbitration based on the site's Terms of Use. In reaching

its decision, the court stated, "[W]e cannot conclude that Plaintiffs ever viewed, let alone manifested assent to, the Terms of Use. The Terms of Use is inconspicuous, buried in the middle to bottom of every Zappos.com webpage among many other links, and the website never directs a user to the Terms of Use. No reasonable user would have reason to click on the Terms of Use. . . . [T]he advent of the Internet has not changed the basic requirements of a contract, and there is no agreement where there is no acceptance, no meeting of the minds, and no manifestation of assent. A party cannot assent to terms of which it has no knowledge or constructive notice, and a highly inconspicuous hyperlink buried among a sea of links does not provide such notice. Because Plaintiffs did not assent to the terms, no contract exists, and they cannot be compelled to arbitrate."

Given what you have learned from this case, what advice would you give a start-up client with respect to drafting its Terms of Use?

2. The court also focused on the fact that Zappos reserved the unilateral right to change the Terms of Use at any time. Why did the court find this problematic and what advice would you give a client regarding its ability to make changes to online policies?

As you read the following online user agreement, consider the steps the drafters have taken to make the contract more likely to be enforced, and areas where you think they could have improved.

IMGUR TERMS OF SERVICE
Effective: April 24, 2019

THE ESSENTIALS

Using our app to do anything other than access the links to this "Terms" page or accessing any page of our website other than our home page and this "Terms" page constitutes your consent to these terms of use and to our Privacy Policy. If you do not consent, do not use our website.

Your use of our website to do anything beyond simply accessing/viewing it (that is, uploading, downloading, commenting, etc.), constitutes not merely your consent, but also your electronic signature, meaning that you are contractually bound by these terms and by our Privacy Policy.

OUR COMMUNITY RULES

These Terms of Use are our contract with you. We also have community rules, developed thanks to input from the Imgurian community, that serve as rules for using Imgur publicly.

STUFF NOT TO DO

If someone else might own the copyright to it, don't upload it. Don't upload gore, "hate speech" (i.e., demeaning race, gender, age, religious or sexual orientation, etc.), or material that is threatening, harassing, defamatory, or that encourages violence or crime. Don't upload illegal content such as child porn or nonconsensual ("revenge") porn. Don't hotlink to adult content or to file-sharing, gambling, torrent, warez, or Imgur rip-off sites. Don't impersonate someone else. Also, don't use Imgur to host image libraries you link to from elsewhere, content for your website, advertising, avatars, or anything else that turns us into your content delivery network. If you do — and we will be the judge — or if you do anything illegal, in addition to any other legal rights we may have, we will ban you along with the site you're hotlinking from, delete all your images, report you to the authorities if necessary, and prevent you from viewing any images hosted on Imgur.com. We mean it.

STUFF TO DO, PLEASE

Please have tons of fun! That's what Imgur is all about. If something isn't fun — if you see anything on our site that shouldn't be there because it violates our policies, is illegal (e.g. revenge porn or child porn), or for some other reason, please let us know by emailing us at abuse@imgur.com.

ABOUT IMAGES YOU UPLOAD

You can upload images anonymously and share them online with only the people you choose to share them with. If you make them publicly available, they may be featured in the gallery. If you share an image publicly with Facebook, Twitter, Digg, Reddit, etc., then it may end up in the gallery.

THE DETAILS
Version 3.404/24/2019

INTELLECTUAL PROPERTY

By uploading a file or other content or by making a comment, you represent and warrant to us that (1) doing so does not violate or infringe anyone else's rights; and (2) you created the file or other content you are uploading, or otherwise have sufficient intellectual property rights to upload the material consistent with these terms. With regard to any file or content you upload to the public portions of our site, you grant Imgur a non-exclusive, royalty-free, perpetual, irrevocable worldwide license (with sublicense and assignment rights) to use, to display online and in any present or future media, to create derivative works of, to allow downloads of, and/or distribute any such file or content. To the extent that you delete any such file or content from the public portions of our site, the license you grant to Imgur pursuant to the preceding sentence will automatically terminate, but will not be revoked with respect to any file or content Imgur has already copied and sublicensed or designated for sublicense. Also, of course, anything you post to a public portion of our site may be used by the public pursuant to the following paragraph even after you delete it.

USE OF IMGUR CONTENT

By downloading an image or copying other user-generated content (UGC) from Imgur, you agree that you do not claim any rights to it. The following conditions apply:

- You may use UGC for personal, non-commercial purposes.
- You may use UGC for anything that qualifies as fair use under copyright law, for example journalism (news, comment, criticism, etc.), but please include an attribute ("Imgur" or "courtesy of Imgur") next to where it is displayed.
- You may not use UGC for non-journalistic commercial purposes.
- Your use of UGC is at your own risk. IMGUR MAKES NO WARRANTIES OF NON-INFRINGEMENT, and you will indemnify and hold Imgur harmless from any copyright infringement claims arising out of your use of the UGC. (See our general disclaimers below.)

You may not copy or use any portions of our site that are not UGC except within the limits of fair use.

NOTICES OF CLAIMED COPYRIGHT INFRINGEMENT (OR OTHER TYPES OF INFRINGEMENT)

If you see anything on our site that you believe infringes your copyright rights, you may notify our Digital Millennium Copyright Act ("DMCA") agent by sending the following information:

- Identification of the copyrighted work or works claimed to have been infringed. IMPORTANT: please include your copyright registration number. If your work is not yet registered, please include a copy of the application to register the work that you filed with the Copyright Office. A copyright infringement claim based on a U.S. work can only be filed if the work has been registered (http://www.copyright.gov/eco/). Registration currently takes about seven months.
- Identification of the material on our servers that is claimed to be infringing and that is to be removed, including the URL or other information to enable us to locate the material.
- A statement that you have a good faith belief that use of the material in the manner complained of is not authorized by you as copyright owner, or by your agent, or by law.
- A statement that the information in your notice is accurate, and under penalty of perjury, that you are the owner (or authorized to act on behalf of the owner) of the exclusive copyright right that is allegedly being infringed.
- Your physical or electronic signature, or of someone authorized to act on your behalf.
- Instructions on how we may contact you: preferably email, but also address and phone.

Because a high percentage of DMCA takedown notices are not valid, Imgur reserves the right to ignore DMCA notifications based on unregistered works.

Our agent to receive such notifications of claimed infringement is Alan Schaaf.

Email: abuse@imgur.com
Mailing Address:
Imgur Inc.
600 California Street, 11th floor
San Francisco, CA 94108

Use the same procedure for any claimed trademark violations or other infringe-ments. If we receive a DMCA takedown demand for material you posted that we believe constitutes fair use, we will attempt to notify you if we have your contact info; otherwise we are under no obligation to notify you regarding the removal. We reserve the right to refuse to remove any material that in our view constitutes fair use. If we identify you as a "repeat infringer," we will block or remove your images and terminate any accounts you have with us. (If we notify you of a DMCA removal and you respond with a legitimate counter-notice, that won't count toward being a repeat infringer.) Keep in mind that we reserve the right to remove any content at any time whether or not it infringes or violates any of our policies.

USE OF TRADEMARK

Any uses of our name, trademarks, and logos must follow our Trademark Use Policy.

DISCLAIMER OF WARRANTIES, LIMITATIONS
OF REMEDIES, INDEMNITY

Although of course we strive to make Imgur as dependable as possible, Imgur's services are provided on an AS IS — WITH ALL FAULTS basis. Your use of our service is entirely at your own risk. We do not guarantee the availability of our service at any given time, or the reliability of our service when it is running. We do not guar-antee the integrity of, or the continued availability of, files on our servers. Whether we make backups, and if so, whether restoration of those backups will be available to you, is at our discretion. IMGUR DISCLAIMS ALL WARRANTIES, EXPRESS AND IMPLIED, INCLUDING WITHOUT LIMITATION IMPLIED WARRANTIES OF FITNESS AND MERCHANTABILITY. NOTWITHSTANDING ANYTHING ELSE STATED IN THESE TERMS, AND IRRESPECTIVE OF WHETHER IMGUR TAKES OR DOES NOT TAKE MEASURES TO REMOVE INAPPROPRIATE OR HARMFUL CONTENT FROM ITS SITE, IMGUR HAS NO DUTY TO MONITOR ANY CONTENT ON ITS SITE. IMGUR DOES NOT ASSUME RESPONSIBILITY FOR THE ACCURACY, APPROPRIATENESS, OR HARMLESSNESS OF ANY CONTENT APPEARING ON IMGUR.COM THAT IS NOT PRODUCED BY IMGUR, INCLUDING BUT NOT LIMITED TO USER CONTENT, ADVERTISING CONTENT, OR OTHERWISE.

Your sole remedy for the loss of any services and/or of any images or other data you may have stored on Imgur's service is to discontinue your use of our service. IMGUR WILL NOT BE LIABLE FOR ANY DIRECT, INDIRECT, INCIDENTAL, SPECIAL, CONSEQUENTIAL, OR PUNITIVE DAMAGES ARISING OUT OF

YOUR USE OF, OR INABILITY TO USE, IMGUR'S SERVICES, EVEN IF IMGUR HAS BEEN ADVISED OF OR REASONABLY SHOULD HAVE KNOWN OF THE POSSIBILITY OF SUCH DAMAGES. NO CAUSE OF ACTION ARISING OUT OF YOUR USE OF IMGUR'S SERVICES MAY BE BROUGHT MORE THAN ONE YEAR AFTER IT OCCURS.

YOU WILL INDEMNIFY AND HOLD IMGUR AND ALL OF ITS PERSONNEL HARMLESS FROM ALL LOSS, LIABILITY, CLAIMS, DAMAGES AND EXPENSES, INCLUDING REASONABLE ATTORNEY FEES, ARISING OUT OF OR RELATED TO YOUR VIOLATION OF THESE TERMS, YOUR INFRINGEMENT OF ANY THIRD PARTY'S RIGHTS, AND ANY HARM CAUSED TO ANY THIRD PARTY AS A RESULT OF YOUR UPLOADING OF FILES, COMMENTS, OR ANYTHING ELSE TO OUR SERVERS.

MISCELLANEOUS

"Imgur" or "we" refers to Imgur, Inc., a Delaware corporation, and its successors and assigns. "You" refers to any person who has consented to these terms or has become contractually bound to them, whether such person is identified or not at the time. These terms are governed by California law, excluding its conflicts of law principles, and if there is a lawsuit between you and Imgur, jurisdiction and venue will lie exclusively in the State where the defendant is located, if within the United States, or in Santa Clara County, California otherwise. If any part of these terms is invalid, the remaining provisions will be unaffected. These Terms of Use constitute the entire agreement among the parties relating to this subject matter, and they will continue to govern any issues that arise out of your use of Imgur's services even after you discontinue using them. We may revise these terms from time to time without notice. Whenever we do so, we will so indicate by changing the version date at the top. Any changes apply as of the time they are posted. Imgur is not meant for use by children under age 13; if your child is younger than 13 please allow him or her to use it only under your supervision.

Parental control protections (such as computer hardware, software, or filtering services) are commercially available that may assist you in limiting access to material that is harmful to minors. See e.g., www.toptenreviews.com/software/security/best-internet-filter-software.

Notes and Questions

1. To what extent do you find the writing style employed by counsel to Imgur to be different from what you saw in the privacy policies you read in Section A of this chapter? Do you think one writing style or another may lead a court to find a particular policy to be more or less enforceable against site users?

2. What do you make of the section of the policy called "Stuff to Do"? Is it pure marketing or is there a substantive need for, or benefit from, this section?

3. Imgur is a site on which people host and share images. What additional sections do you imagine might be added to the terms and conditions if it were an e-commerce site selling physical products? What if it were a dating app? A streaming service? What sections (if any) of the existing terms do you imagine would be eliminated or abridged in any of those cases?

4. Who owns the intellectual property associated with the content on the Imgur website? How might you advise a client about ownership of IP where the site encourages users to upload text, photos, videos, or other protectable content?

5. Thinking back to Chapter 4 and armed with your understanding of online user agreements, what is the purpose of the "NOTICES OF CLAIMED COPYRIGHT INFRINGEMENT" section of the contract?

6. When a user registers for an account with Imgur, the registration page includes the language "By creating a user account, you agree to be bound by our terms of service, privacy policy, and ccpa, and you also agree that our community rules apply." In addition, there is a link to the terms and the privacy policy at the bottom of the main Imgur page. If you were Imgur's lawyer, would you suggest any changes to this approach for notifying users of the online contract they are making? Do you see any potential downsides to an approach that is conservative from a legal standpoint? Where do you imagine there might there have been friction between Imgur's management and its counsel?

7. At the top of the user agreement, it says "Using our app to do anything other than access the links to this 'Terms' page or accessing any page of our website other than our home page and this 'Terms' page constitutes your consent to these terms of use and to our Privacy Policy. . . . Your use of our website to do anything beyond simply accessing/viewing it (that is, uploading, downloading, commenting, etc.), constitutes not merely your consent, but also your electronic signature, meaning that you are contractually bound by these terms and by our Privacy Policy." At the end of the user agreement, it says "Any changes apply as of the time they are posted." Courts have held that this type of consent and amendment provision, where users are not given notice of changes but rather need to uncover them on their own, are unenforceable on the grounds that there has been no acceptance of the amended contract by the user. Similarly, retroactive changes to online policies have been found to be unenforceable on the grounds that there is no consideration for the past changes. Other courts have found prospective changes to terms of use, even those that affect prior activity on a site, to be enforceable on the grounds that permitting the user to continue to access the site constitutes consideration.

(a) Which of these approaches seems more correct to you, in light of what you learned in first-year Contracts?
(b) What advice would you give to a client on this subject as to (i) what she should include in her online user agreement, and (ii) what her actual procedure should be when she makes changes to her terms of use? Note that your answers to (i) and (ii) might be different from each other.

8. Some terms of use will include a reference to the Controlling the Assault of Non-Solicited Pornography and Marketing Act of 2003 (popularly known as "CAN-SPAM"). CAN-SPAM covers emails whose primary purpose is "the commercial advertisement or promotion of a commercial product or service." CAN-SPAM does not apply if the message is primarily transactional or based on an ongoing business relationship, such as an email sent to facilitate a transaction already agreed upon by the recipient, or an email with warranty or recall information, or an email that delivers goods or services already agreed to by the recipient. For emails that do not meet this exception, CAN-SPAM requires a few straightforward things that most entrepreneurs will find easy to follow: (i) the email cannot use false or misleading header information, (ii) the email cannot use deceptive subject lines, (iii) the

message must be identified somehow as an advertisement, (iv) the email must inform recipients where the sender is located, (v) the email must tell recipients how to opt out of future messages, (vi) the sender must honor opt-out requests promptly, and (vii) the sender must monitor what other people are doing with commercial emails on the sender's behalf. CAN-SPAM also requires emails that contain sexually explicit material to include "SEXUALLY-EXPLICIT" at the beginning of the subject line and meet certain additional requirements. Violators of CAN-SPAM can be subject to injunctions and civil liability, and also civil penalties of up to $16,000 for each email that violates CAN-SPAM.

PROBLEM

Without consulting you in advance, Olivia and Andrew hired a designer to build the website at www.generalgerm.com. They have yet to make any sales through the site, but it has had a few visitors. They have asked you to audit the site from a legal perspective.

Review the site, and draft an email of appropriate length to your clients identifying any issues you find. Include in your email any suggestions or changes to the site that you propose your clients make. Although you should be sure to consider the issues addressed in this chapter, do not neglect the issues you learned in other chapters in conducting your analysis.

IX

RISK MANAGEMENT

Entrepreneurial ventures often share two complementary and unfortunate characteristics: they are high-risk, and they are resource-poor. Take, for example, a hypothetical start-up corporation that is developing a medical device. Imagine that the founders are medical students who noticed that surgeons could use a new type of scalpel when conducting hand surgery. The students design an innovative scalpel, and using the last of their personal savings, they arrange for the product to be manufactured overseas. The scalpel is very good, and is free of defects in design and manufacture. Now imagine a patient loses function in his hand after a surgery that used the new scalpel, and further assume it was due to a post-surgery infection that had nothing to do with the scalpel. The patient sues the doctor, the hospital, and all associated medical device companies including the start-up corporation. Assuming the students were careful in setting up and maintaining their entity, they are free from personal liability. The business, however, is brand new and has limited available cash. One possibility is that the business cannot afford to hire effective counsel or mount an effective defense in the litigation. In that case, the company likely loses and is forced to go out of business. Another equally troubling possibility is that the business hires counsel and prevails in the litigation, but the expense of the litigation is so great that the company is still forced to go out of business. Another possibility is that the entity is insured, but that the insurance is inadequate to cover the losses — or perhaps the time the entrepreneurs need to spend on the lawsuit distracts them from continuing to sustain and grow the business. No matter how you slice it, the entrepreneurs lose.

Too often, lawyers representing entrepreneurs focus on the strength of their clients' positions from the perspective of the legal doctrine — in the example above, a lawyer might have told the start-up, "Don't worry, if you're sued you will prevail on the merits since your product is free from defect." The focus on the client's legal position ignores the fact that even meritless lawsuits are expensive and can destroy the new venture, regardless of whether the start-up has a good legal position. Success on the merits is only the beginning of counseling a client on risk management; the lawyer must also advise the client on how to avoid litigation as much as possible.

The other chapters of this casebook focus on legal doctrine as it affects entrepreneurs, and will help lawyers to prepare their clients for success on the merits.
This chapter focuses on the risks faced by a new business, and explores ways in which
lawyers can help their clients avoid or at least minimize costly disputes that — right
or wrong — can destroy a new business before it has had a chance to succeed.

A.   RISK MANAGEMENT GENERALLY

Risk management is the process of identifying, analyzing, and controlling
threats to a company's assets and earnings. Lawyers working with entrepreneurs
are particularly well suited to identifying and analyzing risks, and the best lawyers
are able to work with clients to anticipate future risks, and then take steps to reduce
risk and lessen the impact of risks that can't be avoided. When counseling clients
on this point, it is important to focus on practical approaches to potential threats,
while not alarming the client. As always, understanding your client's personality is
essential: some clients will dismiss and ignore risk, and others will become overly
focused on it. Approaching your client with the right tone and content — along
with strategies for handling the risks you identify — is likely to yield the best results
for the business going forward.

MITIGATING FINANCIAL RISK FOR SMALL BUSINESS ENTREPRENEURS

Michelle M. Harner, 6 Ohio St. Entrepreneurial
Bus. L.J. 469 (2011)

I.   INTRODUCTION

Small businesses make up approximately 99.7% of all U.S. employer firms and
frequently are cited as engines of economic growth. Yet, the odds of building a successful small business are stacked against entrepreneurs. An estimated seven out of
ten new small businesses survive their first two years of existence but only five out of
ten remain in operation past the five-year mark. These statistics are not surprising
given the regulatory burdens imposed on small businesses and the multiple (and
often unaccounted for) operational, legal, financial and other risks facing small
business entrepreneurs.

This essay re-examines the risks encountered by small business entrepreneurs
and the potential value of enterprise risk management (ERM) in helping entrepreneurs identify and manage those risks. ERM is a holistic approach to firm risk management that considers and reconciles firm-wide risks in a single process. Although
typically viewed as a method of helping large, complex firms understand how risks
across their various divisions interact, ERM also can assist smaller firms in understanding their risks and developing a proactive plan to mitigate overall risk exposure. In this context, ERM can help small business entrepreneurs turn potential
liquidation into a "successful failure."

The successful failure concept recognizes the inherent risk in new ventures and encourages entrepreneurs to embrace this risk. By taking inventory of potential risks (or barriers to success), entrepreneurs can better utilize available tools, such as the U.S. Bankruptcy Code, to address their operational or financial challenges or recreate themselves altogether. Business owners have a tendency to ignore problems or evaluate their ventures through rose-colored glasses, thereby postponing remedial actions that could save or strengthen their operations. Policymakers and investors can help entrepreneurs take a more proactive approach and facilitate successful failures by incorporating ERM tools into small business regulations.

. . .

III. AN OVERVIEW OF ERM

ERM commonly is defined as:

> a process, effected by an entity's board of directors, management and other personnel, applied in strategy setting and across the enterprise, designed to identify potential events that may affect the entity, and manage risk to be within its risk appetite, to provide reasonable assurance regarding the achievement of entity objectives.

Traditional risk management tends to view risks in particular areas or silos of operation, such as tax, foreign currency or human resources. In contrast, ERM analyzes risks throughout the subject firm to gauge the firm's overall risk exposure.

Notably, ERM is not a process designed or even intended to eliminate all risks associated with a firm's operations. First, such a result likely is not feasible. Second, such a result generally is not desirable. Risk is inherent in business operations, and some level of risk typically is necessary to facilitate profits and productivity. ERM thus is designed to help firms determine their risk appetite-i.e., the level of risk that is acceptable to the firm's management and that does not threaten the firm's long-term viability. In this vein, ERM is not counterproductive for small business entrepreneurs.

A. *Origins of ERM*

Risk management is not a novel concept. Individuals have long worked to explain risk and uncertainty and to develop processes to identify and manage them. Most such processes focus on quantifiable risk, but commentators have increasingly discussed the need also to evaluate uncertainty. Modern corporate scandals and the Great Recession have underscored the importance of uncertainty in the risk management equation.

The Committee of Sponsoring Organizations of the Treadway Commission (COSO) initially developed ERM to help businesses respond to increasing regulation of internal and external controls and risk management matters generally. In so doing, COSO created a framework that encourages firms to create a risk-aware culture that permeates from the top of the organizational structure. Although risk managers have a role to play, ERM requires the active participation of boards of directors and senior executives in the process. It also focuses on communication at all levels of the organization and meaningful risk dialogue.

ERM does not limit itself to quantifiable risks; rather, the spirit and breadth of the process offer opportunities for firms to evaluate uncertainties (or ambiguity) as well. This aspect of ERM garnered much attention following the Great Recession, as risk discourse turned to notions of unknown risks, "black swans" and the failure of risk modeling. This aspect and the general flexibility of ERM also make it potentially both viable and highly valuable in the small business context.

. . .

IV.   THE POTENTIAL VALUE OF ERM FOR SMALL BUSINESSES

Admittedly, risk and failure are part of the business lifecycle. Not every firm regardless of size can or should be saved. But businesses offering necessary or desirable concepts, products or services should be given a fighting chance. ERM could be a very effective tool for small business entrepreneurs in that fight.

. . .

A.   Small Business Failure and ERM

As discussed above, many factors may contribute to a small business's failure. Among these factors are inexperience, inadequate financing, poor planning, mismanagement, unexpected growth, unanticipated litigation and cognitive biases. Several of these factors go hand in hand and may accelerate a firm's demise. For example, an entrepreneur who is over-optimistic may make bad decisions or fail to plan appropriately. She also may be inexperienced or a seasoned entrepreneur who failed to learn from prior experiences. The most common reasons for failure are lack of adequate funding and experience.

Although the literature is continuing to proliferate and evolve, several studies suggest a causal connection between over-optimism and negative firm performance, as well as a significant (though unsurprising) link between a lack of planning and firm failure, in the small business context. These studies align with anecdotal evidence and common sense. For example, the over-optimism study supports the notion that "there needs to be a balance between optimism and realism between goals and forecasting." Nevertheless, changing behaviors and improving business planning strategies do not naturally flow from such studies. They do, however, flow from ERM.

A tailored ERM process may help small business entrepreneurs ask hard questions and better plan for potential risks and uncertainty. Given the potential personal attributes and biases of many entrepreneurs, standardized questions and some objective review processes likely are necessary components of any effective ERM process. Notwithstanding differences in concepts, products or services offered, many small businesses face similar barriers to success factors such as experience, financing, planning and litigation exposure. Asking entrepreneurs about each of these potential categories of risk or uncertainty is a first step in improving business planning strategies. Encouraging entrepreneurs to provide meaningful responses to those questions and accordingly, develop appropriate business plans certainly, would be more difficult. Outside assistance likely would be necessary here either from consultants, investors or policymakers.

. . .

C.   Gambling with ERM to Produce Successful Failures

ERM has an important role to play in small business planning; a role that could foster more wins on the entrepreneur's scorecard. One final challenge in this process, however, will be educating entrepreneurs about the function of ERM in the context of business planning. ERM for small businesses must be used to help entrepreneurs identify and increase their chances of overcoming potential risks and uncertainty. It should not be used to try to filter out business concepts, products or services before they have been tested in the market. Such an approach likely would stifle innovation and the entrepreneurial spirit.

Any ERM process — whether developed by the entrepreneur or through a standardized questionnaire — should be directly tied to fostering small businesses' success stories. Those stories may include successful failures by allowing the entrepreneur to identify potentially fatal risks or uncertainty in sufficient time to change course, secure alternative financing, alter marketing or production schedules, or even successfully utilize the federal bankruptcy process or other insolvency laws. As COSO explains, "[ERM] enables management to effectively deal with uncertainty and associated risk and opportunity, enhancing the capacity to build value."

Notes and Questions

1. The concept of Enterprise Risk Management seems appealing in helping startups to succeed. At what stage of development of a new venture would it be useful?

2. Suppose your client has told you that they don't want "any unnecessary billing — just do what's necessary to get the business in shape." How might you suggest to the client that they consider spending time and money on a risk management process?

B.   LITIGATION AND LITIGATION ALTERNATIVES

The readings in this section first introduce the challenge and cost of litigation, and the difficulty of assessing risks and outcomes in the litigation context. Of course, understanding the problem is only the beginning of the challenge for the lawyer representing an entrepreneur — and so the readings quickly move to ways of handling disputes before or after they arise. The most simple and effective approach discussed below is avoiding disputes to begin with, but this strategy may fit in the "easier said than done" category for particular businesses or personality types. A second strategy — settling disputes early in the litigation process — may be cost-effective but unappealing to entrepreneurs who are convinced they are "right." Establishing alternative dispute resolution mechanisms at the outset in a business deal, which is a third approach explored in this section, can enhance any risk management strategy if it is applied intelligently and in combination with other risk management strategies.

In all of these approaches, entrepreneurs must consider the personality and motivations of the potential or actual plaintiff. Employees (former and current), customers, and vendors constitute the bulk of potential litigants. In some cases, kind words and a nominal gesture such as a free replacement product can placate a potential litigant. In others, an open line of communication where grievances are taken seriously goes a long way to identifying issues early and diffusing potentially explosive situations. Lawyers should counsel their clients that creativity, kindness, and courtesy can go a long way in avoiding expensive litigation.

IS IT POSSIBLE TO TRY A $100,000 BUSINESS CASE TO A JURY WITHOUT BANKRUPTING YOURSELF AND YOUR CLIENT?

Joseph M. Matthews
71 Fla. B. J. 65 (1997)

One hundred thousand dollars sounds like a lot of money. To almost any small business, it is probably more than an entire year's profit and easily could be the difference between solvency and insolvency for the business. Even if the business is capable of surviving a $100,000 hit, or at least carrying it for a couple of years until a dispute can be resolved through legal process, the end result of the journey through the dispute resolution system must be able to produce an economically reasonable outcome, not just an outcome that meets some judicial notions of fair play.[1]

The civil justice system must provide dispute resolution that meets acceptable standards of due process and equal protection. However, it also must do so at a reasonable cost. If it too often fails to provide all three — due process, equal protection, and cost effectiveness — public confidence in the system will diminish. While the civil justice system cannot be expected to provide due process, equal protection, and cost effectiveness all the time, it must provide them most of the time. Most important, it must be capable of providing all three most of the time.

In most major cities, the civil justice system (particularly trial by jury) is in danger of failing to meet its obligation to provide due process and equal protection for the resolution of small business disputes in a reasonably cost-efficient manner most of the time. The reasons are varied and come from all three segments of the system: 1) the lawyers; 2) the court; and 3) the litigants.

The math is simple but the economics are devastating. A review of the time and expense of litigating a simple business case resembles this:

1) Initial client interview and correspondence regarding fee agreement: 3-5 hrs
2) Preliminary research and draft complaint: 5-10 hrs
3) Draft preliminary discovery requests: 3-5 hrs
4) Interview friendly witnesses and review documents: 5 hrs
5) Motion to dismiss (research, draft, and attend hearing): 5-15 hrs
6) Review answer/counterclaim; research, and prepare reply to affirmative defenses: 1-3 hrs
7) Prepare for and conduct 10 depositions (5 hrs each): 50 hrs

---

1. Much like the family of a dead patient does not want to hear a surgeon say that the operation was a success, most business litigants do not want to hear that they won the case if it cost more than the amount in controversy.

8) Motion for summary judgment: 10-20 hrs
9) Trial preparation: 10-20 hrs
10) Trial (3 days × 10 hrs per day): 30 hrs

If costs are held to $5,000, the total is just over $40,000, or 40 percent of the $100,000 in controversy. . . . If opposing counsel does not concede the case and files the inevitable counterclaim, or if the demands of a trial practice require some other lawyer in the firm to be available in the case of a problem or to help with the trial, the numbers will quickly double. If an expert is involved, the costs are often uncontrollable. These fees and costs will be incurred monthly during the life of the lawsuit, which probably will average about two years, from initial client interview to termination of the case.

In most medium to large cities, it has become economically impossible to handle a $100,000 commercial lawsuit, whether between individuals, small businesses, or large business enterprises. In many communities, even small businesses have begun to hire lawyers to serve as in-house counsel to handle as much legal work as possible, including many small to medium size lawsuits. Alternative dispute resolution methods, including mandatory and binding arbitration, have become essential components of many business strategies for survival. . . .

A MARKET IN LITIGATION RISK
Jonathan T. Molot
76 U. Chi. L. Rev. 367 (2009)

If, as Oliver Wendell Holmes observed, the "law" is "nothing more" than "prophesies of what the courts will do in fact," then the practice of law is essentially a predictive enterprise. The lawyer's job is to examine the facts of his client's situation and the relevant legal materials and to predict how a court will apply the law to the facts. When law schools educate students "to think like lawyers," they are in important respects teaching their students to think like judges and anticipate judicial decisions. And, given this emphasis on predicting judicial decisions, it is no surprise that the bench, the bar, and the academy place a great premium on rendering judicial decisions more predictable and accessible to lawyers and their clients.

But no matter how much judges may strive for clarity and predictability, law practice will always be laden with uncertainty. It is a lawyer's responsibility not only to internalize the judicial perspective and predict judicial reactions, but also to manage legal risk when the law is unclear and judicial rulings are difficult to predict. The transactional lawyer rarely says "yes" or "no" to a transaction and more often helps clients structure conduct so as to manage legal risks in the face of uncertainty. The litigator likewise tends less often to give black or white answers — about winning or losing a lawsuit — and more often to advise clients on how to handle litigation, when to settle, and for how much. Lawyers are risk managers whose specialized training gives them a unique understanding of a particular category of risk.

Indeed, in important respects law practice is simply another branch of risk management. The very same clients who rely on lawyers to manage legal risk often rely on other experts to manage a variety of other risks. One expert may evaluate the risk of natural disasters, such as hurricanes or earthquakes. Another expert may focus on market risks, perhaps looking at broad threats to the global economy or perhaps specializing in narrower risks affecting particular industry sectors (for example, home building or computer software) or particular commodities (for example, oil or corn). Although the process of predicting the reactions of courts, markets, and natural forces may differ dramatically, there is also a strong similarity among these various endeavors. Professionals in each field may rely on different tools and different skill sets to make predictions and weigh odds, but they all are in a fundamental sense engaged in managing risk in the face of uncertainty.

There remains, however, an important difference between litigation-risk management and risk management in these other fields — a difference which reflects a serious shortcoming of law practice today. Unlike lawyers, professionals in these other fields not only advise on the nature and extent of risk, but also can relieve risk bearers of risk — enabling them to hedge or offload it through market transactions. An airline concerned that its annual profits may turn on fluctuations in oil prices will hire an expert not only to evaluate the risk of a spike in oil prices but also to employ hedge contracts or trade in the futures markets to dispose of that risk. Indeed, corporate risk managers routinely take advantage of a variety of hedge contracts and insurance policies to protect against all sorts of market risks and natural and manmade disasters. Nor are these risk-transfer mechanisms available only to large corporations. The family farmer may be as well equipped as the multinational corporation to offload risk via the futures markets and to make sure that his annual income does not turn on fluctuations in crop prices. And individual homeowners carry property and liability insurance just like big corporations. The insurance business, the futures markets, and a burgeoning risk-management industry with an ever-expanding array of hedge offerings can relieve risk bearers of potentially devastating risks and pool those risks over broader groups of capital providers better able to bear them. As a result, risk managers in various fields are well equipped not only to advise on risks but also to dispose of them.

Risk-transfer mechanisms have developed in these other fields in large part because experts in these fields have not confined themselves to the singular role of advising risk-bearing clients. To be sure, some risk managers perform a function analogous to that of lawyers — helping clients to structure conduct so as to minimize risk. But this is not the only way that a risk expert can put his skills to work. Instead of advising the airline or farmer worried about commodity prices or storm damage, an expert may advise an investment bank, hedge fund, or insurance company that is contemplating relieving the airline or farmer of risk. This latter group of risk experts looks at risk as a profit opportunity rather than an evil to be avoided. Moreover, upon viewing risk as a profit opportunity, many of these risk experts begin to trade in risk as principals, rather than as agents. Many, if not most, are compensated based on their performance — that is the way investment banks pay their traders and hedge fund investors pay hedge fund managers — and some amass sufficient capital to trade in risk for their own accounts, rather than those of employers or investors.

When it comes to legal risks, in contrast, the risk-transfer mechanisms available to risk bearers are not nearly as well developed, in large part because lawyers cling to their traditional role as agents for risk-bearing clients. Although the legal profession has come to recognize just how important risk management is to law practice, and lawyers have taken increasingly sophisticated approaches to managing risk for their clients, the legal profession has not yet taken the important step that other risk managers have taken toward viewing risk not only as an evil that a particular client may wish to avoid but also as a profit opportunity that some other market participant may wish to embrace. With few exceptions, lawyers confine themselves to advising their clients on legal risks — on how best to handle a contract dispute, a regulatory challenge, or a lawsuit — and do not offer clients a way to hedge against legal risk while the relevant problems are still pending. . . .

This absence of a well-developed risk-transfer mechanism for litigation risk in particular may help explain why litigation risk is so daunting for American businesses and why lawyers and litigation are so unpopular. To get a sense of the costs associated with this shortcoming of legal risk management, consider the plight of a company that finds itself defending a relatively large lawsuit — not the sort of run-of-the-mill, low-stakes lawsuit that the company's lawyers routinely handle without involving senior management, but rather a high-stakes suit that could substantially affect the company's financial condition. The company may ask its lawyers at the outset how much the lawsuit will cost (in legal fees and payments to the plaintiff), but the lawyers will only be able to make predictions, and very likely there will be more than one trajectory that the lawsuit may follow. At best, the defendant might hope for a quick, inexpensive disposition in the form of a reasonable settlement or perhaps even a victory in motion practice. At worst, the company might have to suffer through protracted, expensive litigation and face the possibility of a devastating judgment. For as long as a lawsuit is pending, then, the defendant remains exposed to a broad range of potential liability that it does not consider to be part of its core business and that it does not want to affect its financial condition. Indeed, how much the company ultimately will pay for the lawsuit will depend only in part on the company's pre-lawsuit conduct and the merits of the lawsuit. The resulting settlement or judgment will also depend upon the performance of its own lawyers and those of the plaintiff, on the views of the presiding judge and/or jury, and on a host of procedural rulings that may be only tangentially related to the merits. Some of these factors — such as the judge, the jury, and opposing counsel — are completely beyond the party's control. Other factors may be within its control — for example, hiring a good general counsel and an effective, yet cost-conscious, law firm may reduce total litigation payouts — but even those factors are not within the company's core business mission. The company will want its profits to turn on the quality of its products or services, the effectiveness of its marketing, and the care with which it manages its operating costs. It simply will not want its bottom line to depend upon how well it handles litigation. The risk of paying more or less for a given lawsuit is not the sort of core business risk that the company is ideally suited to bear.

That a company's financial condition may depend upon the outcome of a pending lawsuit can be of concern not just to the company's management and owners but also to third parties whose perception of the company may be vitally important to its success. When the company decides to borrow money to finance its operations — either in a private placement or through a public bond offering — its ability to do so and its cost of financing will depend upon how these third parties view its future earnings and cash flow. When a company seeks an equity investment or is the potential subject of a private sale or public offering, the due diligence into the company's future prospects will be even more intense. To the extent that future earnings will depend upon the company's core business abilities — factors like production prowess, marketing skill, cost control, and management experience — potential lenders or investors are reasonably well equipped to assess the company's future earnings. That is, after all, what public and private capital markets are all about — bringing capital to productive enterprises based on predictions about how that capital is best employed. But when a company's future prospects depend upon high-stakes litigation, potential lenders and equity investors are even less likely than the company's own management to be able to assess the relevant risks. In some instances, potential investors or lenders may consider large, pending litigation a deal breaker. If the suit is potentially big enough relative to the size of the company, the investor or lender may simply be unable or unwilling to spend the time to become comfortable enough with the risk. Or, if the capital supplier is willing to proceed despite the risk, it will likely do so on much less favorable terms for the company — compensating itself for the risk by reducing its valuation of the company (in the case of an equity investment) or increasing the interest rate it will charge (in the case of debt). The true costs of high-stakes litigation to a corporate defendant can thus far exceed the time and money it actually devotes to the litigation process.

. . .

Notes and Questions

1. Transactional business lawyers often believe that they should leave dispute resolution to litigators and just focus on making deals and helping clients move forward with their business. To what extent do you agree with this type of thinking, and to what extent do you think this view might hurt a transactional client? Thinking back on the competence rule you studied in Chapter 1, do you think there are ethical ramifications to the typical transactional lawyer's way of thinking?

2. Molot's article is primarily focused on litigation risks faced by large companies. In what ways are these risks more significant for entrepreneurial ventures? In what ways are the risks less significant?

3. Molot explains how the conception of "risk management" for lawyers is unique among risk management specialists. Is he right? What ways might lawyers address the need of clients to hedge against litigation risks?

4. When a client faces a potential problem — even what might seem to be a disaster — the first call is often to the lawyer. How can the attorney use this situation as an opportunity to build the relationship?

5. The excerpt from the Matthews piece paints a painful picture of litigation costs. What are some possible ways you might try to convey the importance of risk management to an ambitious and optimistic entrepreneur who is unconcerned with the possible downside of her actions?

SKIP THE AGGRAVATION OF A COURT BATTLE
Dondi P. Gaston
Entrepreneur Philippines Magazine (May 2007)

Anyone who's been through litigation knows how messy, expensive, time-consuming, and stressful it can be. Thus, it is a wise entrepreneur who avoids getting sidetracked into a legal battle.

After all, there's no guarantee that one can win in a litigious contest. Each of the three points-of-view in the case — those of the two contending parties and that of the judge — bears weight on the final result, with the business owner having control over only one.

It is therefore advisable for the entrepreneur to adopt a prudent risk management policy that evaluates and measures potential litigation risks and develops strategies to address them. One such strategy can very well be avoiding litigation altogether.

AVOIDANCE

To avoid litigation, an entrepreneur should be conscious of the business areas where the highest potential for liability exists. For example, companies that rely heavily on a huge labor force would be at greater risk of facing labor cases; they should therefore be meticulous in setting an employment policy. Appliance retailers for their part would have more potential litigation risk arising from defective goods, so they should be keenly aware of manufacturers' warranties on the products they are selling. And for obvious reasons, those who manage daycare centers should always keep a tight focus on safety.

In businesses heavily regulated by law, to have a working knowledge of the pertinent laws would be a good first step to avoiding the risk of violating them. In the case of a drugstore, for instance, the owner should know all the laws that pertain to the sale and distribution of regulated drugs.

Ordinarily, however, disagreements that give rise to litigation often result from daily transactions and dealings. There is therefore hardly a better advice for interacting with people than to follow the ethic of reciprocity or more popularly known as the Golden Rule: "Treat others as you would like to be treated." Stated otherwise, "Don't treat others in a way that you don't want to be treated." This applies equally well to business — to your customers, clients, suppliers, and service contractors — as to interpersonal relationships. Just putting this rule to practice can greatly reduce the risks of litigation.

It is also a good habit to put in writing all business agreements and understandings even if they only involve simple transactions. It is when such dealings are not properly documented that disagreements usually arise. People have a peculiar way of recollecting past events that tilts things in their favor when the time of reckoning comes, and rare is the contending party that agrees with the other's interpretation of events.

Also, when drafting a document, the goal should be to make it as clear as possible to avoid any misunderstanding. If goods are being ordered, it should be stated in the clearest possible terms: the kind, the specific brand; the model; the number, weight, volume, and description; and the exact address where the goods are to be delivered and at what time. The parties are well advised to also stipulate the consequences of delay or non-delivery. Will there be a reduction in price, an increase in volume, a credit for future orders, or a cancellation?

In some cases, the parties may also opt to include an arbitration or mediation clause in their contracts. This will provide a less expensive and faster procedure for settlement of potential disputes.

When in doubt, however, it may be advisable to consult a lawyer. A lawyer can help answer questions that pertain to business operations such as employment matters, tax filings, and the like, and may also be helpful in drafting major contracts. Spending a little money now for professional legal advice can spare the entrepreneur from a major litigation expense later.

SETTLEMENT

The purpose of litigation is to provide relief under the law, be it for protection, collection of some money claim, or some other form of redress. From the entrepreneur's standpoint, however, litigation is best used only to protect his or her business interests and not as a venue for proving a point. The best option is therefore to settle disputes as early as possible so the business can go on as usual.

When a dispute starts to reveal its colors, it is always a good policy to address the situation right away to minimize further misunderstandings. In almost all cases, ignoring the problem or simply being inattentive and unconcerned about it will make the offended party angrier. For instance, imagine getting the silent treatment from a dealer when you complain about a brand-new car that spends more time in the repair shop than on the road. The next thought that obviously will come to mind is to look for a lawyer from among your numerous relatives.

At any rate, when faced with such situations, it might be a good idea to arrange a meeting for negotiating a settlement. During such meetings, it is wise to write down what has been agreed upon. Even a simple statement on what the real issue is often already clarifies the matter for both parties, thus minimizing the possibility of the situation giving birth to other issues.

In such situations, of course, one should be in the right frame of mind to be able to address the situation effectively. If those attending a settlement meeting are both on the warpath, it would be obvious what the outcome will be: the next meeting will most likely be in front of a judge.

It is therefore helpful to consider the following when in the middle of negotiations:

- Leave emotions and pride in check. While it may not be possible to completely keep emotions and pride out of the way in an electrically charged situation, they should not be allowed to take center stage when making important decisions. When emotions and pride run wild, so will the chances of arriving at a settlement.
- Be clear about all the facts. A cursory understanding of the situation will not do, and neither will a vague feeling of what seems right. A full appreciation of all the relevant facts is a must.
- Don't be too stubborn to compromise. The alternative is litigation, which may involve a mountain of legal fees and years of court appearances. In the end, the judgment could be adverse, and by that time a compromise would be too late.
- Don't be greedy. A potentially litigious situation does not necessarily give one the right to claim unreasonable demands. When one becomes greedy, it almost always drives the other party against the wall, giving him or her no choice other than to seek the intervention of the courts. Keep in mind that profits should come from the operations of the business and not from conflict.
- Communicate. The chances of resolving issues are greatly increased when both parties are able to comprehend and appreciate where each is coming from. This obviously takes an open mind and an open ear.

A COURT CASE

There may be times, however, when a business owner is constrained by the circumstances to protect and defend his or her interests in court. This usually happens when negotiations for a settlement break down or when rights are brazenly violated. This is what the courts are for.

In these situations, a lawyer will more than likely be involved. During the initial consultations with the lawyer, it is best to ask questions that will lead to a better understanding of what lies ahead: the costs, the time frame, and the chances of a favorable judgment. This information will help the business owner get a clear assessment of what is involved in proceeding with the case as against opting for a settlement.

ADR: A USER'S GUIDE
Ruth D. Raisfeld
31 Westchester Bus. J. 71 (2004)

In a broad sense, "alternative dispute resolution" refers to a range of options for resolving conflict, typically with the intervention of a trained third party professional whom both sides to the conflict view as a neutral. Alternative dispute resolution methods have been institutionalized in various government programs throughout the world and increasingly in the United States. In the legal world, alternative dispute resolution ("ADR") is used to resolve threatened and/or pending litigation involving domestic relations, commercial matters, employment relations, construction, energy, securities, environment, as well as community disputes involving neighbors, small businesses, landlord-tenant, etc.

This article provides a primer for commercial lawyers about ADR processes and how they can use these procedures to serve the interests of their clients. As the lower courts and government agencies continue to grapple with burgeoning civil dockets, ADR procedures — special masters, arbitration, mediation, fact-finding — are being adopted on a widespread basis. Nearly every court has some form of dispute resolution procedure. More federal and state agencies have mechanisms by which cases are referred to ADR. Finally, arbitration agreements, often with mediation as a pre-requisite, appear in numerous construction, consumer, franchise, security, employment and health-care related agreements. See J. Spencer, "Signing Away Your Right To Sue," The Wall Street Journal (October 1, 2003), at D1 ("In an effort to fend off lawsuits, a growing number of companies . . . are asking consumers to agree to 'mandatory arbitration' and waive their right to sue the company if a dispute arises.").

II.   TYPES OF ADR PROCEDURES

A.   Negotiation

1. "Unassisted negotiation involves only the people (at least two but often many) enmeshed in a dispute. Through negotiation, they communicate with each other in an effort to reach agreement." L. Singer, Settling Disputes, 2d ed. (1994) at 16.

There are two kinds of unassisted negotiation: "competitive," in which negotiators seek to maximize their own gains, usually at the expense of other parties, and "collaborative," which is more of a problem-solving approach, commonly described as "win-win." Id.

2. "Assisted negotiation involves outsiders to a dispute, who bring the parties together and, most of the time, help them to resolve their own disagreements. They may also attempt to predict the likely outcome if the dispute were adjudicated. All decisions remain in the hands of the parties themselves." Id. at 19. There are various forms of assisted negotiation:

a. "fact-finding" — a trained neutral third party investigates the circumstances leading to the dispute and issues a report containing "findings of fact." "Fact-finding" is often used in labor-management agreements as an intermediate step in a grievance-arbitration procedure.

b. "neutral evaluation" — sometimes coupled with fact-finding, a trained neutral third party assesses the facts and the applicable law and provides an opinion as to the strengths and weaknesses of each party's position in a litigation and the likelihood of success on the merits. "Early neutral evaluation" programs, in which attorneys with special expertise in a given subject area serve as neutrals, were developed by the federal courts to lead parties to settlement of pending cases.

B. "Mediation"

A trained third party neutral is selected by the parties (or appointed by a tribunal) to assist the parties in resolving their dispute. Often they are members of a panel or are associated with a dispute resolution organization and they serve pursuant to written mediation agreements.

The hallmark of mediation is that the mediator meets with both sides, in joint or separate caucuses, and guides the parties through exchange of information and exploration of interests and positions in a confidential setting with the goal of enabling the parties to reach agreement themselves. The mediator has no power to render a binding opinion or impose a settlement.[3] Generally, discussions that take place during the mediation are deemed to be confidential in accordance with the parties' mediation agreement or are treated as "settlement discussions" under state and federal evidentiary rules. . . .

A Uniform Mediation Act has been drafted by the National Conference of Commissioners on Uniform State Laws, February 4, 2002. ("UMA"). The UMA establishes an evidentiary and discovery privilege that defines the parameters of mediation confidentiality in legal proceedings. While some states have enacted the UMA, it has been controversial [elsewhere.] . . .

C. Adjudication

Adjudication "involves binding decision-making by courts, administrative agencies or private arbitrators." Singer at 27.

1. "Arbitration" — a creature of written contract, arbitration is a private dispute resolution forum, in which one or more arbitrators hears testimony and receives documentary evidence from both parties. Arbitrators issue written decisions which the parties have agreed are final and binding. Such decisions are generally subject

---

3. In some circumstances, the parties to mediation may authorize the mediator to "arbitrate" the dispute and render a binding opinion. This is known as "med-arb."

to very narrow grounds of judicial review. . . . Arbitration has long been a part of the American judicial system and is a favored form of alternative dispute resolution. Critics, however, argue that arbitration has become overly formal, expensive, and can be as protracted and complicated as traditional civil litigation.

Litigation over the enforceability and scope of arbitration agreements has intensified as parties attempt to address more and more procedural and substantive issues in their arbitration agreements: e.g., discovery, depositions, remedies, punitive damages, statutory rights, arbitral expenses and fees. Courts continue to struggle "to reconcile deference to arbitration with competing policy interests and individual rights." . . .

2. Litigation — "is the traditional and most formal method of dispute resolution. The advantages of formal discovery and binding decisions supported by reasoned opinions provided by trials and appeals, with or without a jury, must be balanced against the expense and time required to resolve the dispute by trial." Brown Rudnick Berlack Israels LLP, "Alternative Dispute Resolution Practice Description" (2002).

Although litigation remains the most typical dispute resolution mechanism used in the United States today, the delays, expense, and unpredictability of litigation are compelling more attorneys and their clients to look at alternatives. As more disputes are being mediated, attorneys must learn a new brand of advocacy that is more appropriate to the mediation forum.

. . .

SELECTION FROM CONDITIONS OF USE
Amazon.com (2018)

DISPUTES

Any dispute or claim relating in any way to your use of any Amazon Service, or to any products or services sold or distributed by Amazon or through Amazon.com will be resolved by binding arbitration, rather than in court, except that you may assert claims in small claims court if your claims qualify. The Federal Arbitration Act and federal arbitration law apply to this agreement.

There is no judge or jury in arbitration, and court review of an arbitration award is limited. However, an arbitrator can award on an individual basis the same damages and relief as a court (including injunctive and declaratory relief or statutory damages), and must follow the terms of these Conditions of Use as a court would.

To begin an arbitration proceeding, you must send a letter requesting arbitration and describing your claim to our registered agent Corporation Service Company, 300 Deschutes Way SW, Suite 304, Tumwater, WA 98501. The arbitration will be conducted by the American Arbitration Association (AAA) under its rules, including the AAA's Supplementary Procedures for Consumer-Related Disputes. The AAA's rules are available at www.adr.org or by calling 1-800-778-7879. Payment of all filing, administration and arbitrator fees will be governed by the AAA's rules. We will reimburse those fees for claims totaling less than $10,000 unless the arbitrator determines the claims are frivolous. Likewise, Amazon will not seek attorneys' fees and costs in arbitration unless the arbitrator determines the claims are frivolous. You may choose to have the arbitration conducted by telephone, based on written submissions, or in person in the county where you live or at another mutually agreed location.

We each agree that any dispute resolution proceedings will be conducted only on an individual basis and not in a class, consolidated or representative action. If for any reason a claim proceeds in court rather than in arbitration **we each waive any right to a jury trial**. We also both agree that you or we may bring suit in court to enjoin infringement or other misuse of intellectual property rights.

APPLICABLE LAW

By using any Amazon Service, you agree that the Federal Arbitration Act, applicable federal law, and the laws of the state of Washington, without regard to principles of conflict of laws, will govern these Conditions of Use and any dispute of any sort that might arise between you and Amazon.

SELECTION FROM TERMS OF USE
Instagram (2018)

HOW WE WILL HANDLE DISPUTES.

- Except as provided below, you and we agree that any cause of action, legal claim, or dispute between you and us arising out of or related to these Terms or Instagram ("claim(s)") must be resolved by arbitration on an individual basis. Class actions and class arbitrations are not permitted; you and we may bring a claim only on your own behalf and cannot seek relief that would affect other Instagram users. If there is a final judicial determination that any particular claim (or a request for particular relief) cannot be arbitrated in accordance with this provision's limitations, then only that claim (or only that request for relief) may be brought in court. All other claims (or requests for relief) remain subject to this provision.
- Instead of using arbitration, you or we can bring claims in your local "small claims" court, if the rules of that court will allow it. If you don't bring your claims in small claims court (or if you or we appeal a small claims court judgment to a court of general jurisdiction), then the claims must be resolved by binding, individual arbitration. The American Arbitration Association will administer all arbitrations under its Consumer Arbitration Rules. You and we expressly waive a trial by jury.

    The following claims don't have to be arbitrated and may be brought in court: disputes related to intellectual property (like copyrights and trademarks), violations of our Platform Policy, or efforts to interfere with the Service or engage with the Service in unauthorized ways (for example, automated ways). In addition, issues relating to the scope and enforceability of the arbitration provision are for a court to decide.

    This arbitration provision is governed by the Federal Arbitration Act.

You can opt out of this provision within 30 days of the date that you agreed to these Terms. To opt out, you must send your name, residence address, username, email address or phone number you use for your Instagram account, and a clear statement that you want to opt out of this arbitration agreement, and you must send them here: Facebook, Inc. ATTN: Instagram Arbitration Opt-out, 1601 Willow Rd., Menlo Park, CA 94025.

- Before you commence arbitration of a claim, you must provide us with a written Notice of Dispute that includes your name, residence address, username, email address or phone number you use for your Instagram account, a detailed description of the dispute, and the relief you seek. Any Notice of Dispute you send to us should be mailed to Facebook, Inc., ATTN: Instagram Arbitration Filing, 1601 Willow Rd. Menlo Park, CA 94025. Before we commence arbitration, we will send you a Notice of Dispute to the email address you use with your Instagram account, or other appropriate means. If we are unable to resolve a dispute within thirty (30) days after the Notice of Dispute is received, you or we may commence arbitration.

- We will pay all arbitration filing fees, administration and hearing costs, and arbitrator fees for any arbitration we bring or if your claims seek less than $75,000 and you timely provided us with a Notice of Dispute. For all other claims, the costs and fees of arbitration shall be allocated in accordance with the arbitration provider's rules, including rules regarding frivolous or improper claims.

- For any claim that is not arbitrated or resolved in small claims court, you agree that it will be resolved exclusively in the U.S. District Court for the Northern District of California or a state court located in San Mateo County. You also agree to submit to the personal jurisdiction of either of these courts for the purpose of litigating any such claim.

- The laws of the State of California, to the extent not preempted by or inconsistent with federal law, will govern these Terms and any claim, without regard to conflict of law provisions.

SELECTION FROM TERMS OF USE
Wikimedia Foundation (2014)

[This whole section of the Wikimedia Terms of Use is highlighted in yellow on the Wikimedia website.]

13. DISPUTES AND JURISDICTION

We hope that no serious disagreements arise involving you, but, in the event there is a dispute, we encourage you to seek resolution through the dispute resolution procedures or mechanisms provided by the Projects or Project editions and the Wikimedia Foundation. If you seek to file a legal claim against us, you agree to file and resolve it exclusively in a state or federal court located in San Francisco County, California. You also agree that the laws of the State of California and, to the extent applicable, the laws of the United States of America will govern these Terms

of Use, as well as any legal claim that might arise between you and us (without reference to conflict of laws principles). You agree to submit to the personal jurisdiction
of, and agree that venue is proper in, the courts located in San Francisco County,
California, in any legal action or proceeding relating to us or these Terms of Use.

To ensure that disputes are dealt with soon after they arise, you agree that
regardless of any statute or law to the contrary, any claim or cause of action you
might have arising out of or related to use of our services or these Terms of Use
must be filed within the applicable statute of limitations or, if earlier, one (1) year
after the pertinent facts underlying such claim or cause of action could have been
discovered with reasonable diligence (or be forever barred).

Notes and Questions

1. Of the many alternatives to litigating, which do you think are most appealing
to entrepreneurial clients? Why? To what extent do your perceptions of a typical
"entrepreneur personality" play into your analysis?

2. To what extent is an understanding of the variety of litigation alternatives important in drafting the following types of transactional contracts: (a) customer contracts,
(b) vendor contracts, (c) sale of business contracts, (d) employee contracts? Assuming
you represent an entrepreneurial venture, do any of the types of contracts in (a) through
(d) seem particularly appropriate for some flavor of alternative dispute resolution? Are
there any where the entrepreneurial venture might prefer to "go to court"?

3. If it is true that entrepreneurs are passionate, optimistic, and personally connect with their businesses in a way that many workers at larger companies do not,
are there any particular challenges you might face in counseling an entrepreneur
on dispute resolution alternatives that might not be relevant if you were counseling
inside counsel at a major corporation?

4. Consider the excerpts from the customer contracts for Amazon, Instagram,
and Wikimedia, the publisher of Wikipedia.

(a) Why do you think each company chose the policy it has? Are there differences in the companies (for example, in their business models, customer base,
or history) that might explain the different policies?

(b) What would you have recommended as a dispute resolution mechanism
for each company, and why? Are there factors at play that might lead you to
make a different recommendation if the companies were at the start-up phase,
rather than more mature businesses?

C. INDEMNIFICATION AND INSURANCE

Sections A and B of this chapter make the case that businesses are well advised
to spot risks in advance, avoid disputes as much as possible, and to handle those
disputes that do arise as efficiently as possible. In Section C, we explore two related
strategies businesses deploy to manage risk: by seeking indemnification from the
parties with whom they contract, and by purchasing insurance.

1. *Introduction to Indemnification and Insurance*

LIMIT TRANSACTION RISKS BY USING INDEMNITY AGREEMENTS, INSURANCE
Brett Schouest
San Antonio Bus. J. (Sept. 3, 2007)

When entering into a business relationship and/or a transaction, whether it is a construction project or oilfield services agreement, the specter of third-party claims is a reality of business. Therefore, it is important to consider indemnity and insurance options to protect yourself from such claims.

Indemnity. An indemnity agreement is a contract provision in which one party will reimburse the other party for losses incurred because of third-party claims. An example would be a contractor indemnifying a landowner for a claim by one of the contractor's employees injured while performing services on the landowner's property. Generally, indemnity agreements can range from broad-form indemnity, indemnifying for all liability that may arise from the transaction — including liability for the indemnitee's own fault or negligence — to limited-form indemnity, indemnifying to the extent of the indemnitor's own fault.

Supporting indemnity agreements with insurance. It has often been said that indemnity obligations are "only worth the paper they are written on." This is especially true when the indemnitor is a small company (such as the contractor mentioned above) with limited financial status to back the obligations placed upon it. In order to provide the indemnitee (the previously mentioned landowner) with assurance that the obligation is meaningful, the parties should consider supporting the contractual indemnification obligation with insurance. Typically, liability insurance policies do not provide coverage for an insured's contractual obligations. However, policies usually contain exceptions for "insured contracts," which are typically defined to cover a contractually assumed indemnification obligation related to the business of the indemnitor (the contractor, for example). As such, typical general liability policies may provide some coverage to support contractual indemnity obligations. If not, endorsements can be added to insurance policies to provide the indemnification obligation coverage.

Additional insured coverage. An additional way to ensure that the indemnitee (the landowner) is not merely relying upon the financial wherewithal of the indemnitor (the contractor) is to require that the indemnitee be named as an additional insured on the liability policies of the indemnitor. Additional insured status makes the indemnitee an insured under the indemnitor's own insurance policies, albeit subject to all of the policy terms and restrictions (including policy limits, deductibles, exclusions, claims notice provisions, etc.)

Typically, the additional insured endorsements will relegate coverage to liability arising from the indemnitor's ongoing activities, but optional additional insured endorsements can expand coverage to completed operations following cessation of the indemnitor's operations.

Who and what is covered/certificates of insurance. It is important to specify in the contract requiring additional insured status what specific coverages are required, as well as to ensure that the policy under which the party is added contains those coverages. For instance, in a transaction involving chemical manufacturing or transport, an additional insured would not want the policy to contain a pollution exclusion which would effectively eliminate coverage in event of a spill or emission. It is also important to ensure that the policy has been properly endorsed to include the indemnitee as an additional insured, whether by automatic broad form — blanket additional endorsements or specific named and scheduled additional insured endorsements.

Reliance is often too heavily placed upon certificates of insurance for additional insureds to confirm their status. The certificate of insurance is issued by the indemnitors and itself does not create coverage or additional insured status; rather, such coverage or status is created only by the terms of the insurance policy/endorsement and/or the contract between the parties requiring additional insured status. . . . Therefore, a party requiring additional insured status should require that, prior to commencement of the transaction, it be provided with not only the certificate of insurance, but also the policy and applicable endorsements itself for review. Bottom line — the best practice is to go directly to the policy and endorsements up front to ensure that the needed coverages and additional insured status have been provided.

Keep your documents handy. Also too often, after receiving contracts with indemnification and additional insured provisions, along with the related insurance policies and certificates of insurance, once the transaction commences, parties place such documents in a file not to be seen again. These documents can, however, be very valuable for invoking any indemnity and additional insured rights for problems and claims that arise in connection with the transaction. Therefore, special consideration should be given to maintaining the contracts, policies and certificates in an active transaction file. This can be particularly important to ensure timely notice of a claim is made to avoid losing coverage for the claim.

Indemnification, properly supported by insurance, and additional insured status, properly confirmed, can be powerful allies for a party in a transaction which may involve litigation at some point. Taking the proper steps to ensure indemnification and additional insured rights are enforceable and remain in place is the key.

2. *Indemnification Provisions*

As discussed in the Schouest piece above, indemnification is a contractual promise by one party to reimburse the other party for losses related to the transaction at hand. On one extreme, an indemnification provision may be drafted so broadly as to cover any losses related to the transaction whether or not the indemnifying party is responsible for the loss. On the other extreme, the provision may be so narrow as to only cover one particular circumstance. Between those extremes, however, is the typical indemnification provision in which the indemnifying party will reimburse losses that the indemnifying party was in some way responsible for — because it failed to perform as promised, for example, or because it made representations that were not true. The amount of covered losses may be capped in an indemnification provision — for example, it may be capped at the total amount received by the indemnifying party in the transaction — or it may be unlimited. Notice how, in the following sample indemnification provisions, the indemnified party seeks to protect itself as much as possible.

SELECTION FROM INTERNATIONAL
MANUFACTURING AGREEMENT
(2005)

. . .

INDEMNIFICATION

Seller shall indemnify, defend and hold harmless Buyer and its affiliates, promptly upon demand at any time and from time to time, against any and all losses, liabilities, claims, actions, damages and expenses, including, without limitation, reasonable attorney's fees and disbursements, arising out of or in connection with any of the following: any misrepresentation or breach of any warranty made by Seller; any breach or nonfulfillment of any covenant or agreement made by Seller; any defects in Products manufactured by Seller; and the manufacturing of Products by Seller.

. . .

SELECTION FROM USER AGREEMENT
eBay.com (2020)

. . .

17. INDEMNITY

You will indemnify and hold us (including our affiliates and subsidiaries, as well as our and their respective officers, directors, employees, agents) harmless from any claim or demand, including reasonable legal fees, made by any third party due to or arising out of your breach of this User Agreement, your improper use of our Services or your breach of any law or the rights of a third party.

. . .

SELECTION FROM JOINT VENTURE AGREEMENT
FOR ENTERTAINMENT INDUSTRY START-UP
(2005)

. . .

"Affiliate" shall mean with respect to a specified Person, any other Person directly or indirectly controlled by, controlling, or under common control with the specified Person.

. . .

"Person" shall mean an individual, corporation, partnership, limited liability company, estate, trust, joint venture, association, government (and any branch, division, agency or instrumentality thereof), governmental entity or other entity.

. . .

10.1. Developer Indemnity. Developer shall indemnify, defend, and hold harmless Producer and its Affiliates and their respective direct and indirect, past, present and future officers, directors, managers, members, partners, owners, employees, licensees, successors, and assigns (collectively, the "Producer Indemnitees") from and against all actions, causes of action, suits, debts, obligations, losses, damages, amounts paid in settlement, liabilities, costs, and expenses whatsoever, including reasonable attorneys' fees (collectively, "Losses"), whether arising out of a claim involving a third party or between the parties to this Agreement, resulting to, imposed upon, asserted against, or incurred by any of Producer Indemnitees in connection with, or arising out of or relating to (a) any breach or misrepresentation by Developer under this Agreement, and (b) any claim that the exploitation of any of the rights granted under this Agreement or that any Developer Mark infringes any mark of any Person or any intellectual property, privacy or other right of any Person.

10.2. Producer Indemnity. Producer shall indemnify and hold harmless Developer and its direct and indirect, past, present and future officers, directors, managers, members, partners, owners, employees, licensees, successors, and assigns (collectively, the "Developer Indemnitees") from and against any and all Losses resulting to, imposed upon, asserted against, or incurred by any of the Developer Indemnitees in connection with, arising out of or relating to any breach or misrepresentation by Producer under this Agreement.

10.3. Third Party Claims. If any claim, demand, action or proceeding is made or commenced by any third party (a "Third Party Claim") against any party that is entitled to be indemnified with respect thereto under this Section 10 (the "Indemnified Party"), the Indemnified Party shall give the party obligated to provide the indemnity (the "Indemnifying Party") prompt notice thereof; the failure to give such notice shall not affect the liability of the Indemnifying Party under this Agreement except to the extent the failure materially and adversely affects the ability of the Indemnifying Party to defend the Third Party Claim. The Indemnifying Party shall have the right to assume the defense and resolution of the Third Party Claim provided it uses counsel of national reputation reasonably satisfactory to the Indemnified Party and provided that (a) the Indemnified Party shall have the right to participate in the defense of the Third Party Claim at its own expense through counsel of its choice (control of the defense will remain with the Indemnifying Party if properly assumed hereunder), (b) the Indemnifying Party shall not consent to the entry of any judgment or enter into any settlement that would require any act or forbearance on the part of the Indemnified Party or which does not unconditionally release the Indemnified Party from all liability in respect of the Third Party Claim without the prior written consent of the Indemnified Party, which consent shall not be unreasonably withheld, conditioned or delayed, and (c) the Indemnified Party may undertake the defense of the Third Party Claim, at the Indemnifying Party's expense, if the Indemnifying Party fails promptly to assume and diligently to prosecute the defense in accordance with the terms hereof.

10.4. Limitations of Liability. No claim may be made by any party hereunder against any other party hereto or any Affiliate, director, member, manager, officer, employee, attorney or agent thereof for any special, indirect, consequential, incidental or punitive damages in respect of any claim for breach of contract or any other theory of liability arising out of or related to the transactions or relationships contemplated by this Agreement or any other transaction, relationship, act, omission, or event arising or occurring in connection therewith. Each party waives, releases and agrees not to sue upon any claim for any such damages, whether or not accrued and whether or not known or suspected to exist in its favor; provided, however, that this provision shall not limit the liability of any party to indemnify another party under this Section 10 for all Losses it may suffer as a result of any Third Party Claims.

Notes and Questions

1. If a party breaches a contract, the non-breaching party can sue for damages. What does an indemnification clause add that isn't otherwise covered by the general law of contracts?

2. Compare the indemnification provisions above. Which party in each contract do you imagine had greater negotiating power? How do you explain the difference in complexity among the provisions?

3. Imagine your client has designed a consumer product and is hiring another start-up to manufacture the product. Your client is comforted by the fact that the other start-up is willing to provide unlimited contractual indemnification for all manufacturing defects. Do you have any cautionary advice for your client?

3. Insurance

Entrepreneurs should meet with competent insurance brokers to determine appropriate coverage. The attorney should be able to refer her client to credible brokers and should understand the coverage that is ultimately purchased. If an issue ever arises that might implicate insurance coverage, the lawyer will likely be asked to be involved in — or even manage — the process. The following brief readings introduce insurance vocabulary and some key principles the lawyer should understand.

GET BUSINESS INSURANCE
sba.gov (2020)

SIX COMMON TYPES OF BUSINESS INSURANCE

After you purchase insurance that's required by law, you can find insurance to cover any other business risk. As a general rule, you should insure against things you wouldn't be able to pay for on your own.

Speak to insurance agents to find out what kinds of coverage makes sense for your business, and compare terms and prices to find the best deal for you. Here are six common kinds of business insurance to look for.

Insurance type	Who it's for	What it does
General liability insurance	Any business.	This coverage protects against financial loss as the result of bodily injury, property damage, medical expenses, libel, slander, defending lawsuits, and settlement bonds or judgments.
Product liability insurance	Businesses that manufacture, wholesale, distribute, and retail a product.	This coverage protects against financial loss as a result of a defective product that causes injury or bodily harm.
Professional liability insurance	Businesses that provide services to customers.	This coverage protects against financial loss as a result of malpractice, errors, and negligence.
Commercial property insurance	Businesses with a significant amount of property and physical assets.	This coverage protects your business against loss and damage of company property due to a wide variety of events such as fire, smoke, wind and hail storms, civil disobedience and vandalism.
Home-based business insurance	Businesses that are run out of the owner's personal home.	Coverage that's added to homeowner's insurance as a rider can offer protection for a small amount of business equipment and liability coverage for third-party injuries.
Business owner's policy	Most small business owners, but especially home-based business owners.	A business owner's policy is an insurance package that combines all of the typical coverage options into one bundle. They simplify the insurance buying process and can save you money.

LIABILITY INSURANCE 101 FOR BUSINESS LITIGATORS
Christine Spinella Davis, American Bar Association, The Young Lawyer (April 2009)

. . .

INSURANCE POLICIES AS CONTRACTS

Insurance policies are contracts between policyholders and carriers. They are interpreted generally based on standard contract principles, and the parties look to the policy's language to determine obligations. The important difference between the interpretation of general contracts and insurance policies is the doctrine of contra proferentum ("against the author or proffer"), which courts follow in coverage disputes: If policy language is ambiguous and could reasonably be interpreted in favor of either party, it will be applied in favor of policyholders.

COMMON TERMS AND CONCEPTS

Insurance terminology is quite easy to grasp. For example, insurance is either "first-party" or "third-party." First-party insurance, such as health and disability insurance, protects the insured from its own loss. Third-party insurance is liability insurance, protecting the insured from loss arising from liability to a third party. Common examples of third-party insurance are homeowners policies, which provide liability coverage to the insured for accidents to visitors on the premises (and even conduct off the premises), and automobile policies, which provide liability coverage to the insured for claims brought by the injured driver of the other vehicle in the case of a traffic accident.

To activate or "trigger" an insurance policy, an event specified in the policy must take place during the policy period. It could be property damage, bodily injury, or the filing of a lawsuit. Usually, an event that triggers insurance policies is either the occurrence that leads to the lawsuit (occurrence-based policy) or the filing of a lawsuit (claims-made policy), which is particularly important for third-party insurance claims. Under the former, the policy is triggered if the underlying harm takes place during the policy period, regardless of when the third party filed the lawsuit. Under the latter, the policy is triggered if the third party makes the claim during the defined policy period.

Policyholders often purchase multiple, vertical layers of insurance. The first level of insurance and the first policy to be triggered is called the "primary policy." All layers above the primary policy are called "excess policies."

Excess policies protect a policyholder from a catastrophic loss. An excess policy typically "follows form" to the primary policy, which means that it adopts most of the primary policy's terms and conditions. A policyholder might, for a given period, have one liability policy that provides $10 million in coverage, then a policy above that provides coverage from $10 million to $30 million, and then another policy providing coverage between $30 million and $50 million. When defending a client, particularly a corporate client, inquire into its insurance coverage. Sometimes a policyholder may not even be aware of its right to, and amount of, coverage for particular allegations.

CARRIER AND POLICYHOLDER DUTIES

Insurance carriers and policyholders have duties under an insurance policy. A liability carrier has a duty to "indemnify" an insured party for liability to a third party if the liability falls within the terms of coverage. This determination requires analysis of all policy language. Liability policies also often obligate carriers to defend policyholders against third-party claims. This obligation can be either a duty to defend the insured or a duty to reimburse the insured for defense costs. The defense obligation is much broader than the duty to indemnify. A carrier must defend a policyholder if there is a "potential" for coverage based on a complaint.

Courts generally interpret "potential for coverage" liberally to the policyholder's advantage. A carrier generally is then responsible under the policy for all reasonable defense costs incurred by the policyholder.

In addition to paying premiums, a policyholder has a duty to provide notice of a claim to its carrier "as soon as practicable," i.e., in a reasonable time. In some states, failure to provide notice in a timely manner may be a complete bar to coverage, or at least a bar to expenses incurred prior to the notice. In most states, failure to provide timely notice prevents coverage only if the late notice prejudiced the carrier. Either way, if the policyholder believes there is coverage, the policyholder should put the carrier on notice of the claim as soon as possible to protect recovery rights. If you are inexperienced in such disputes, raise the notice issue with the client or partner with whom you work to ensure preservation of the client's insurance rights. You may even want to offer to assist the client with the formal notice.

A policyholder also has a duty to cooperate with the carrier defending a claim on its behalf. The policyholder must keep the insurer informed of all major case developments, respond to the carrier's reasonable inquiries, notify the carrier, and attempt to obtain its consent before settling an underlying lawsuit. Failure to do any of these could result, in extreme cases, in the loss of the policyholder's rights. As counsel, you should work with the client to keep the carrier in the loop and provide it with requested information; you also should consider and address with the client any potential waiver implications by such disclosures.

. . .

Notes and Questions

1. Entrepreneurial ventures typically delay the purchase of insurance during the start-up phase, and wait until they launch their product or service before investigating insurance options. How does this strategy strike you, as counsel to a start-up?

2. Would you feel comfortable recommending a business insurance broker to your client? Would you feel comfortable attending the initial meeting? Regardless of your comfort level, are either of these good ideas, and why or why not?

PROBLEM

Andrew and Olivia have started a "soft launch" of the Magic Wand by having "Tupperware Party"-style events in peoples' homes at which they will demonstrate the product and offer it for sale. At a typical party, Andrew or Olivia will arrive with several Magic Wands, some promotional materials, and trays of appetizers. Once they arrive, they sanitize the kitchen counter and lay out the appetizers. Then, they instruct the partygoers on how to use the Magic Wand and have them test the product. Andrew and Olivia always bring one tray of appetizers that they have previously laced with relatively harmless bacteria so that the partygoers are able to detect bacteria on at least one item. Typically, the demonstrations involve laughs, free-flowing wine (not for Andrew and Olivia, of course), and snacking on the "safe" appetizers.

Understanding that intentionally bringing bacteria into someone's home is risky, Andrew and Olivia took steps, without your prior knowledge, to minimize their liability. In addition to instructing guests not to eat any appetizers until they have been tested, Andrew and Olivia provide very clear instruction on how to use the product. In addition, they have the host of every Magic Wand event sign the following waiver, which they wrote themselves:

GENERAL GERM/MAGIC WAND

I have agreed to allow General Germ, Inc. to conduct a demonstration of its Magic Wand product in my home. I agree that I will:

— Provide a clean, tidy, and safe kitchen environment in which to conduct the demonstration; and
— Be responsible for my guests' behavior during the demonstration.

I also agree that General Germ, Inc. is not responsible for any accidents that happen during the demonstration or any illnesses that may occur as a result of my guests or me failing to follow the rules of the demonstration.

Date: _____

Host signature: _____

Print name: _____

Olivia and Andrew believe the demonstration model will help them build good word of mouth before officially launching their product for sale.

1. The clients have given you a copy of the document they ask event hosts to sign. They say they like the modest length and the easy-to-understand writing style, and they just wants to make sure "it's all legal, but please no legalese."

(a) Are there any sections of the waiver that you would recommend they revise?

(b) What additional legal concepts would you suggest they add to the contract?

(c) They typically bring the contract to each demonstration and ask the event host to sign it upon their arrival. Would you suggest a different implementation?

2. The clients have taken great comfort in the corporation structure of the business, because they know it can shield their personal assets in the event General Germ, Inc. has financial problems.

(a) Are there other steps, beyond the waiver discussed in Question 1, that they should consider to further reduce their individual risk?

(b) Are there other steps, beyond the waiver discussed in Question 1, that they should consider to further reduce risk for the business?

If it is helpful when thinking about this Question 2, consider the following unfortunate possibilities:

(i) a guest gets food poisoning because the host had previously put raw poultry on the kitchen counter, and Andrew's attempt to sanitize the counter before the demonstration was unsuccessful;

(ii) a guest pokes herself in the eye with the probe end of the Magic Wand while Olivia has turned her back;

(iii) a guest has too much to drink during the demonstration, drives himself home, and causes a car accident;

(iv) a guest eats the bacteria-laced appetizers before they have been tested;

(v) a guest eats the bacteria-laced appetizers after another guest tested them incorrectly and pronounced them safe.

———————

X

———————

EXIT STRATEGIES

Some entrepreneurs found a business with two closely related goals in mind: build the business fast, and sell it for a lot of money. Other entrepreneurs hope their business will give them a healthy income during their lifetime, and then expect to pass the business on to the next generation. Still other entrepreneurs don't know what they want long term, whether from their business, from their lawyer, or from anyone else. In counseling these categories of clients, and clients with a myriad of other endgames in mind, lawyers must understand the variety of exit strategies available to entrepreneurial ventures. Even before the formal organization of the business, a lawyer must understand the client's goals and motivations and structure the business in the manner most likely to optimize the client's ultimate exit strategy. The lawyer must also understand that a client's goals are also a work in progress and will likely change and develop as the business grows. Therefore, the lawyer needs to appreciate that some degree of flexibility and room for "surprise" is essential.

In this chapter, we focus on exit strategies where founders wind up owning little to none of the continuing business — as opposed to private placement-type transactions that were discussed in Chapter 5, where the entrepreneur may well still own a significant piece of the business after the transaction is concluded. The first type of transaction we consider — the outright sale of the business to a third party or parties — is the most common exit strategy for an entrepreneurial venture. The second type of transaction — the initial public offering, or IPO — is less common but captures the imagination of many ambitious entrepreneurs.

A. SELLING THE ENTREPRENEURIAL VENTURE — MERGERS AND ACQUISITIONS

When an entrepreneur client decides to sell her business, the lawyer must immediately begin to draw from at least five specialized areas: state corporate law,

383

state and federal tax law, antitrust law, federal securities law, and accounting standards. Other areas of law, such as contract law, employment law, and intellectual property law, also come into play and can take on an important role. While a lawyer in today's world will rarely be an expert in all of these areas, the entrepreneur's counsel needs to be at least conversant in them in order to develop a legal strategy for the change of control transaction.

One key area for lawyers to understand is the fiduciary duty implications of selling a venture. These issues are typically covered in a Business Associations or Corporations course, or a stand-alone Mergers and Acquisitions course. The following case reviews and discusses these issues — particularly duty of loyalty issues — in the context of an exit transaction. In particular, the case highlights the problems that can occur in venture-backed companies where the holders of preferred stock, who control the board, have different economic interests than the holders of common stock. As you read, notice the different exit paths the board considered before settling on the sale of a business through a merger.

IN RE TRADOS INCORPORATED SHAREHOLDER LITIGATION
Court of Chancery of Delaware
73 A.3d 17 (2013)

TRADOS Inc. ("Trados" or the "Company") obtained venture capital in 2000 to support a growth strategy that could lead to an initial public offering. The VC firms received preferred stock and placed representatives on the Trados board of directors (the "Board"). Afterwards, Trados increased revenue year-over-year but failed to satisfy its VC backers. In 2004, the VC directors began looking to exit. As part of that process, the Board adopted a management incentive plan (the "MIP") that compensated management for achieving a sale even if the transaction yielded nothing for the common stock.

In July 2005, SDL plc acquired Trados for $60 million in cash and stock (the "Merger"). Under Trados's certificate of incorporation, the Merger constituted a liquidation that entitled the preferred stockholders to a liquidation preference of $57.9 million. Without the MIP, the common stockholders would have received $2.1 million. The MIP took the first $7.8 million of the Merger consideration. The preferred stockholders received $52.2 million. The common stockholders received nothing.

. . .

The plaintiff contended that instead of selling to SDL, the Board had a fiduciary duty to continue operating Trados independently in an effort to generate value for the common stock. Despite the directors' failure to follow a fair process and their creation of a trial record replete with contradictions and less-than-credible testimony, the defendants carried their burden of proof on this issue. Under Trados's business plan, the common stock had no economic value before the Merger, making it fair for its holders to receive in the Merger the substantial equivalent of what they had before. . . .

I. FACTUAL BACKGROUND

. . .

A. Trados's Early Days

Defendant Jochen Hummel and Iko Knyphausen founded Trados in 1984. Hummel became Chief Technology Officer and served on the Board. . . .

By the late 1990s, Trados enjoyed a dominant position in the desktop [document] translation market. To expand, Trados sought to penetrate the enterprise market. . . .

At the turn of the third millennium of the Common Era, Trados sought VC funding to spur its growth and help position itself for an IPO. At the time, Trados differed significantly from the stereotypical dot-com startup. Trados had been around for sixteen years and sold a successful desktop product. . . .

B. Wachovia Invests in Trados

In early 2000, Trados came to the attention of First Union Capital Partners, the predecessor to Wachovia Capital Partners, LLC ("Wachovia"). . . . Around March 2000, after conducting due diligence, Wachovia invested $5 million. . . .

As part of the investment, Wachovia obtained the right to designate a director. Wachovia designated [Wachovia Partner David] Scanlan.

C. Hg Invests in Trados

Around the same time, Trados came to the attention of Mercury Capital, the predecessor to Hg Capital LLP ("Hg"). For simplicity, this decision refers only to Hg. In April 2000, Hg invested $10.25 million. . . .

In August 2000, Hg invested an additional $2 million. . . . In September 2000, Hg [invested another] $2.3 million.

Like Wachovia, Hg obtained the right to designate a director. The relevant director for this case is defendant Lisa Stone, a partner at Hg[.]

D. Trados Builds Its Business

By February 2001, Trados was attracting new, large corporate clients. In May, Trados released the latest version of its desktop software, Trados 5.

In September 2001, Wachovia and Hg made [an aggregate of $3 million in] follow-on investments. . . .

At the end of 2001, Trados released the MultiTerm Client Server, an enterprise product that provided a web interface for customer databases. Revenue for the year reached $15.9 million, a 14% increase over 2000, even after the negative effects of the 9/11 terrorist attacks.

E. Trados Acquires Uniscape

Although Trados was growing and making progress in the enterprise market, management felt the Company could accelerate its growth with an acquisition. Trados focused on Uniscape, Inc., a software company with a superior enterprise product. . . .

Like Trados, Uniscape had received several rounds of VC funding. Uniscape's principal backer was Sequoia Capital ("Sequoia"), a prominent Silicon Valley VC firm. Through various funds, Sequoia had invested $13 million in Uniscape. Defendant Sameer Gandhi, the Sequoia partner who sponsored the Uniscape investment, served on its board.

Another member of the Uniscape board was defendant Joseph Prang, the CEO of Conformia Software, Inc. Prang and a business partner used Mentor Capital Group LLC ("Mentor") as their investment vehicle. Through Mentor, Prang had invested approximately $700,000-750,000 of his own money in Uniscape.

In May 2002, Trados and Uniscape merged in a stock-for-stock transaction that valued Trados at $30 million, Uniscape at $11 million, and the post-transaction entity at $41 million. . . .

. . .

In the transaction, Sequoia gained the ability to designate two Trados directors. Sequoia designated Gandhi and Prang.

F. Invision Invests in Trados

In August 2002, Trados raised $2 million from Invision AG, a Swiss private equity firm. . . .

Invision received the ability to designate a director and named defendant Klaus-Dieter Laidig in December 2002. Unlike Scanlan, Stone, and Gandhi, Laidig was not the Invision partner who sponsored the Trados investment. Laidig was a technology consultant who previously worked as an executive at Hewlett-Packard for over thirty years. Laidig had a part-time consulting relationship with Invision that paid him a nominal amount for handling various projects. Laidig served on the boards of two other Invision portfolio companies and advised one of Invision's funds.

G. Trados Continues to Grow Slowly

The Board hoped that the Uniscape transaction would transform Trados. The transaction sought to unite the strengths of Trados's desktop software and Uniscape's enterprise platform, but integration difficulties plagued the combined company. . . .

In August 2003, Invision invested another $2 million. . . .

. . .

By the end of 2003, Trados generated $24.8 million in revenue, achieving 25% year-over-year growth and making budget. Enterprise product revenue reached $3.0 million, representing more than 200% growth year-over-year. On the downside, the Company remained unprofitable, and its cash balance declined. . . .

In early 2004, with Trados coming off a record revenue year, Gandhi asked the head of software investment banking for JMP Securities ("JMP"), Kevin McClelland, to approach Trados's then-CEO, Dev Ganesan. McClelland's mission was to reach out to Ganesan and begin setting the table for a sale by discussing "opportunities for Trados in the public equities and M&A markets." . . .

H.   The Board Replaces Ganesan

. . .

During the April 20 meeting, the Board terminated Ganesan. The directors appointed Hummel as Acting President, but instructed him to consult with Scanlan and Gandhi "before taking any material action on behalf of the Corporation." . . . The Board also decided to explore whether the Company could be sold in the near-term. The Board sent Hummel to meet with Trados's principal commercial relationships — Microsoft, Bowne Global Solutions ("Bowne"), and Documentum, Inc. — to explore their interest in the Company. They also decided to have JMP "test the waters" for a potential sale with a broader set of acquirers.

Hummel struck out. In June 2004, he met with Microsoft, historically a large user of Trados's desktop product. In April 2000, to solidify the relationship, Microsoft had purchased 6,927,660 shares of Trados common stock. Microsoft listened appreciatively to Hummel's report on recent developments but made clear they had no interest in acquiring Trados. Hummel's efforts with Bowne and Documentum were similarly unsuccessful.

Gandhi took the lead on the broader market canvass. On June 24, 2004, David Silver of Santa Fe Capital Group contacted Gandhi about one of his clients, SDL, who was "prepared to make an offer" for Trados. Gandhi quickly signed a nondisclosure agreement with Silver. At the same time, Gandhi and [Trados CFO James] Budge negotiated the terms of Trados's engagement of JMP. On June 30, Trados formally retained JMP to "advise [Trados] concerning opportunities for maximizing shareholder value, which may include a sale or merger of the Company." . . .

Meanwhile, Scanlan worked with an executive search firm to identify candidates for the CEO position. His efforts ultimately led to defendant Joseph Campbell, the former COO of iManage, Inc., a company in the enterprise content management space. Campbell oversaw a highly successful sale of iManage to Interwoven in 2003. . . .

I.   The Board Decides to Hire Campbell and
Passes on a Distressed Sale

On July 7, 2004, the Board approved hiring Campbell, and Scanlan suggested that the Board consider adopting a plan to incentivize senior executives to pursue a sale, which later became the MIP. The Board agreed, recognizing that otherwise the management team "may not have sufficient incentives to remain in the Company's service and to pursue a potential acquisition of the Company, due to the high liquidation preference of the Company's preferred stock."

At the same meeting, McClelland reviewed the prospects for a sale. . . . JMP's full valuation range was quite broad, extending from $20.4 million to $169.8 million.

JMP's materials identified twenty-eight potential acquirers. . . . Only SDL seemed serious.

...On July 26, [SDL CEO Mark] Lancaster called McClelland and offered $40 million for the Company, consisting of $10 million in cash and $30 million in stock.

Given the low value that SDL put on the Company, the directors rejected the offer. ...

[The court then details the ways in which the new CEO, Campbell, was able to improve the company's results, which led to increased interest from SDL.]

L.   Exit Discussions Intensify

On January 10, 2005, Lancaster emailed Campbell and stated "there is sufficient potential that exists for an SDL-Trados combination" such that the two should "continue a more detailed dialogue." On January 17, Campbell reported to Scanlan that Lancaster was "very serious about taking next steps" and asked to meet with Stone and Scanlan before his next meeting with Lancaster. Campbell also mentioned that he was "having another conversation" with Bowne, a major customer, and Golden Gate Capital, a private equity firm.

On January 19, 2005, Campbell met with Scanlan and Stone and reviewed a presentation he had prepared entitled "Confidential M&A Discussions." Campbell outlined three "Hypothes[e]s for Trados Exit," labeled (i) Merge-Up, (ii) Harvest, and (iii) Merge-Up Adjacent. The Merge-Up option entailed a merger with SDL, Bowne, or Lionbridge. This option was "low risk," could be achieved within six months, and yielded valuation expectations of 1.3-1.6 times revenue based on median trading multiples of comparable companies. The Harvest option contemplated a private equity firm like Golden Gate Capital acquiring both Trados and Bowne. This option was "higher risk," could be achieved within nine months, and yielded valuation expectations "greater" than 2.0 times revenue. The highest risk option was Merge-Up Adjacent, which contemplated repositioning Trados as an enterprise content management provider and then achieving a merger in that space. The anticipated timeline for this option was twelve to eighteen months, and valuation expectations were less clear. The presentation did not include a stand-alone alternative.

On January 20, 2005, Campbell followed up with Scanlan, asking point blank: "What is an acceptable offer for Trados?" Scanlan responded that "it really depends on the nature of the opportunity and the cash/stock dynamic" but promised to "give the dollar figure some thought." Shortly thereafter, Scanlan asked Campbell to prepare "a proceeds waterfall analysis by class of stock and shareholder that reflects the current ownership of the company and the management incentive plan," and "run three sensitivities at $50 million, $60 million and $70 million." Scanlan said that looking at the numbers "may move along people's view[s] on our alternatives."

On January 21, 2005, Campbell updated Scanlan, Gandhi, and Stone about his discussions with Lancaster, reporting that they had a "very open and candid conversation" about "potentially putting our companies together." ...

M.   SDL and Trados Agree on Price and Structure

On February 2, 2005, the Board met for an update on Trados's financial performance and to consider prospects for a transaction. Campbell trumpeted the Company's [good] fourth quarter results[. . .].

Campbell then presented his stand-alone business plan for 2005-2007. [The plan included strategies for increasing growth.] Campbell testified that discussion of the business plan lasted "fifteen minutes." During depositions, the VC directors and Prang could not recall considering it. There was zero interest in funding it.

Campbell then updated the Board on the M&A efforts: (i) SDL had made "an updated working offer in January," (ii) a merger with Bowne would "have to wait 6-9 months," and (iii) a merger with Lionbridge would be "possible later in the year but not likely at as high a valuation as SDL." The Board authorized Campbell to contact Lancaster and "put a bar out there to say, look, we're not going to agree on this, . . . unless you are thinking in terms of a 60-plus number. . . ."

On February 11, 2005, Campbell and Lancaster met, and Campbell conveyed the $60 million price. After balking initially, Lancaster agreed. The consideration would be $50 million in cash and $10 million in SDL stock. To make the price more palatable for his board, Lancaster asked that Trados pay its legal expenses and JMP's fee out of the sale proceeds. The two executives roughed out a letter of intent (the "LOI").

Campbell shared the news with the Board. Stone sent a positive report to her partners at Hg. . . .

On March 29, 2005, Campbell updated the Board on the M&A process and reported that Bowne was "in play" with Lionbridge as the likely acquirer. This combination would remove two of the three most likely purchasers of Trados under Campbell's low risk Merge-Up strategy. It also took away the other component (Bowne) of the Harvest strategy. From an operational perspective, it meant that one of Trados's major customers (Bowne) would be owned by a company that had been seeking aggressively to compete with Trados (Lionbridge). The deal posed a competitive threat to SDL as well, but to the extent SDL felt compelled to respond with an acquisition of its own, Trados was not its only potential target. In short, the Bowne-Lionbridge development made SDL look like the only opportunity for a near-term exit, with going it alone and the less certain Merge-Up Adjacent strategy as fallbacks.

On April 5, 2005, SDL finally responded with comments to the LOI. The purchase price and structure remained substantially the same. Campbell called a special meeting of the Board to consider the LOI. On April 8, the Board gathered via conference call, reviewed the terms of the deal, and approved it. On April 11, Campbell and Lancaster executed the LOI.

. . .

O. The Merger is Approved and Closes

On June 9, 2005, Trados's compensation committee (consisting of Gandhi, Scanlan, and Stone) approved a $250,000 bonus for Campbell and a $150,000 bonus for Budge. The bonuses were given for exemplary performance, including "[y]ear over year revenue growth exceeding market growth," "forecast profitability" for the second quarter of 2005, and "[c]reation of three viable exit strategies for the Company."

On June 15, 2005, the Board met to approve the Merger. Under the MIP, the first 13% of the $60 million proceeds ($7.8 million) went to Campbell, Hummel, Budge, and other employees. Campbell's share of the MIP was 30% ($2.34 million). During the Merger negotiations, SDL insisted that Campbell enter into a non-competition agreement, but SDL would not dig any further into its pockets to compensate him for it. To preserve the deal, Campbell agreed to the non-compete. . . .

At the time of the Merger, the total liquidation preference on the preferred stock was $57.9 million, including accumulated dividends. The proceeds remaining after the MIP payments — approximately $52.2 million — went to satisfy the liquidation preference. Each of the preferred stockholders received less than their full liquidation preference but more than their initial investment.

. . .

At the June 15, 2005 meeting, the Board determined that the Merger was "advisable and in the best interests of the Company and its stockholders" and formally "authorized, adopted and approved" it. The Board also approved and recommended to stockholders an amendment to the Company's certificate of incorporation that reset the liquidation preferences of the preferred stock at the specific amounts they would receive in the Merger.

All that remained were the necessary stockholder approvals, one by the preferred and one by the common. . . .

On June 17, 2005, Trados's stockholders approved the Merger. Microsoft abstained, advising Campbell that "the economic result from the perspective of our equity interest is not such that we are prepared to actively vote in favor. . . . "

P.   The Plaintiff Sues

Plaintiff Marc Christen owned about 5% of Trados's common stock. . . . On July 3, 2008 . . . Christen filed [a] lawsuit, individually and on behalf of a class of Trados's common stockholders, alleging that the former Trados directors breached their duty of loyalty by approving the Merger.

. . .

II.   LEGAL ANALYSIS

. . .

A.   The Breach Of Fiduciary Duty Claim

. . .

1.   *The Standard of Conduct*

Delaware corporate law starts from the bedrock principle that "[t]he business and affairs of every corporation . . . shall be managed by or under the direction of a board of directors." 8 Del. C. § 141(a). When exercising their statutory responsibility, the standard of conduct requires that directors seek "to promote the value of the corporation for the benefit of its stockholders."

. . .

The duty to act for the ultimate benefit of stockholders does not require that directors fulfill the wishes of a particular subset of the stockholder base. . . . Stockholders may have idiosyncratic reasons for preferring decisions that misallocate capital. Directors must exercise their independent fiduciary judgment; they need not cater to stockholder whim.

More pertinent to the current case, a particular class or series of stock may hold contractual rights against the corporation and desire outcomes that maximize the value of those rights. Unless a corporation's certificate of incorporation provides otherwise, each share of stock is common stock. If the certificate of incorporation grants a particular class or series of stock special "voting powers, . . . designations, preferences and relative, participating, optional or other special rights" superior to the common stock, then the class or series holding the rights is known as preferred stock. If the certificate of incorporation is silent on a particular issue, then as to that issue the preferred stock and the common stock have the same rights. Consequently, as a general matter, "the rights and preferences of preferred stock are contractual in nature." A board does not owe fiduciary duties to preferred stockholders when considering whether or not to take corporate action that might trigger or circumvent the preferred stockholders' contractual rights. Preferred stockholders are owed fiduciary duties only when they do not invoke their special contractual rights and rely on a right shared equally with the common stock. Under those circumstances, "the existence of such right and the correlative duty may be measured by equitable as well as legal standards." Thus, for example, just as common stockholders can challenge a disproportionate allocation of merger consideration, so too can preferred stockholders who do not possess and are not limited by a contractual entitlement. Under those circumstances, the decision to allocate different consideration is a discretionary, fiduciary determination that must pass muster under the appropriate standard of review, and the degree to which directors own different classes or series of stock may affect the standard of review.

To reiterate, the standard of conduct for directors requires that they strive in good faith and on an informed basis to maximize the value of the corporation for the benefit of its residual claimants, the ultimate beneficiaries of the firm's value, not for the benefit of its contractual claimants. In light of this obligation, "it is the duty of directors to pursue the best interests of the corporation and its common stockholders, if that can be done faithfully with the contractual promises owed to the preferred." Put differently, "generally it will be the duty of the board, where discretionary judgment is to be exercised, to prefer the interests of the common stock — as the good faith judgment of the board sees them to be — to the interests created by the special rights, preferences, etc. . . . . of preferred stock." . . .

In this case, the directors made the discretionary decision to sell Trados in a transaction that triggered the preferred stockholders' contractual liquidation preference, a right that the preferred stockholders otherwise could not have exercised. The plaintiff contends that the Board should not have agreed to the Merger and had a duty to continue operating Trados on a stand-alone basis, because that alternative had the potential to maximize the value of the corporation for the ultimate benefit of the common stock. The Trados directors, of course, contend that they complied with their fiduciary duties.

2. The Standards of Review

To determine whether directors have met their fiduciary obligations, Delaware courts evaluate the challenged decision through the lens of a standard of review. In this case, the Board lacked a majority of disinterested and independent directors, making entire fairness the applicable standard.

"Delaware has three tiers of review for evaluating director decision-making: the business judgment rule, enhanced scrutiny, and entire fairness." Delaware's default standard of review is the business judgment rule. The rule presumes that "in making a business decision the directors of a corporation acted on an informed basis, in good faith and in the honest belief that the action taken was in the best interests of the company." . . .

Enhanced scrutiny is Delaware's intermediate standard of review. Framed generally, it requires that the defendant fiduciaries "bear the burden of persuasion to show that their motivations were proper and not selfish" and that "their actions were reasonable in relation to their legitimate objective." . . .

In *Revlon*, the Delaware Supreme Court extended the new intermediate standard to the sale of a corporation. Here too, enhanced scrutiny applies because of the potential conflicts of interest that fiduciaries must confront. . . .

Entire fairness, Delaware's most onerous standard, applies when the board labors under actual conflicts of interest. Once entire fairness applies, the defendants must establish "to the court's satisfaction that the transaction was the product of both fair dealing *and* fair price." "Not even an honest belief that the transaction was entirely fair will be sufficient to establish entire fairness. Rather, the transaction itself must be objectively fair, independent of the board's beliefs."

To obtain review under the entire fairness test, the stockholder plaintiff must prove that there were not enough independent and disinterested individuals among the directors making the challenged decision to comprise a board majority. . . .

In this case, the plaintiff proved at trial that six of the seven Trados directors were not disinterested and independent, making entire fairness the operative standard. This finding does not mean that the six directors necessarily breached their fiduciary duties, only that entire fairness is the lens through which the court evaluates their actions.

a.   The Management Directors: Campbell and Hummel

Two of the directors — Campbell and Hummel — received personal benefits in the Merger. The plaintiff proved that the benefits were material to them [including payments under the MIP, board fees, and post-transaction compensation], rendering Campbell and Hummel interested in the decision to approve the Merger.
. . .

b.   The VC Directors: Gandhi, Scanlan, And Stone

Three of the directors — Gandhi, Scanlan, and Stone — were fiduciaries for VC funds that received disparate consideration in the Merger in the form of a liquidation preference. Each faced the dual fiduciary problem identified in Weinberger v. UOP, Inc., 457 A.2d 701, 710 (Del. 1983), where the Delaware Supreme Court held that there was "no dilution" of the duty of loyalty when a director "holds dual or multiple" fiduciary obligations. . . . "There is no 'safe harbor' for such divided loyalties in Delaware." The plaintiff proved at trial that Gandhi, Scanlan, and Stone faced a conflict of interest as dual fiduciaries.
. . .

i.   Economic Incentives

VCs invest through preferred stock with highly standardized features, although individual details vary. VC preferred stock typically carries a preference upon liquidation, defined to include a sale of the company, that entitles the holders to receive specified value before the common stock receives anything. It usually earns a cumulative dividend which, if unpaid, steadily increases the liquidation preference. It also entitles the preferred holder to convert into common stock at a specified ratio in lieu of receiving the liquidation preference. The preferred stock in this case carried each of these features.

There is nothing inherently pernicious about the standard features of VC preferred stock. The sophisticated contract rights, the use of staged financing, and the gradual acquisition of board control over the course of multiple financing rounds help VCs reduce the risk of entrepreneur opportunism and management agency costs. . . .

The cash flow rights of typical VC preferred stock cause the economic incentives of its holders to diverge from those of the common stockholders. . . . "Because of the preferred shareholders' liquidation preferences, they sometimes gain less from increases in firm value than they lose from decreases in firm value. This effect may cause a board dominated by preferred shareholders to choose lower-risk, lower-value investment strategies over higher-risk, higher-value investment strategies." The different cash flow rights of preferred stockholders are particularly likely to affect the choice between (i) selling or dissolving the company and (ii) maintaining the company as an independent private business. "In particular, preferred dominated boards may favor immediate 'liquidity events' (such as dissolution or sale of the business) even if operating the firm as a stand-alone going concern would generate more value for shareholders." In these situations, "[l]iquidity events promise a certain payout, much [or all] of which the preferred shareholders can capture through their liquidation preferences. Continuing to operate the firm as an independent company may expose the preferred-owning VCs to risk without sufficient opportunity for gain."

The distorting effects "are most likely to arise when, as is often the case, the firm is neither a complete failure nor a stunning success." . . .

ii. Personal Incentives

. . .

Three forms of exit are common [in VC backed companies]. An IPO is the gold standard and most lucrative; liquidation via sale to a larger company (a trade sale) is a second-best solution; and a write-off is the least attractive."[V]enture capitalists will sometimes liquidate an otherwise viable firm, if its expected returns are not what they (or their investors) expected, or not worth pursuing further, given limited resources and the need to manage other portfolio firms." This may seem irrational, but "it makes perfect economic sense when viewed from the venture capitalist's need to allocate [his] time and resources among various ventures." "Although the individual company may be economically viable, the return on time and capital to the individual venture capitalist is less than the opportunity cost." VC firms strive to avoid a so-called "sideways situation," also known as a "zombie company" or "the living dead," in which the entity is profitable and requires ongoing VC monitoring, but where the growth opportunities and prospects for exit are not high enough to generate an attractive internal rate of return. These companies "are routinely liquidated," usually via trade sales, "by venture capitalists hoping to turn to more promising ventures."

iii. The Evidence That the VC Directors Faced a Conflict in This Case

. . . At trial, the plaintiff had the burden to prove on the facts of this case, by a preponderance of evidence, that (i) the interests of the VC firms in receiving their liquidation preference as holders of preferred stock diverged from the interests of the common stock and (ii) the VC directors faced a conflict of interest because of their competing duties. The plaintiff carried his burden.

. . .

[T]he evidence at trial established that Gandhi faced a conflict and acted consistent with Sequoia's interest in exiting from Trados and moving on. As Gandhi explained at trial, when Sequoia invests, it hopes for "really fast" growth and "very large outsized returns." Within six months after the Uniscape merger, Gandhi had concluded that Trados would not deliver outsized returns and that Sequoia's "real opportunity" was only "to recover a fraction" of its $13 million investment in Uniscape. By the end of 2002, Gandhi had decided not to put significant time into Trados beyond Board meetings and only to attend by phone unless meetings were held locally. From his perspective, this was simply a matter of prioritizing his time based on how Trados would perform for Sequoia relative to other opportunities with "a lot of upside." He later elaborated: "[M]y most, you know, limited resource is just where I'm putting my time. And it's just better to work on something brand-new that has a chance. . . . Is [the next Sequoia investment] going to be Google?"

. . .

The evidence at trial established that Scanlan had similar incentives. . . . Wachovia was the earliest VC investor in Trados and bought in before the technology bubble popped. . . . Despite rebuffing SDL's initial low-ball offer, Scanlan testified that the Board "never let SDL go. We knew they were the only party, and we had to figure out a way." Scanlan also recommended and designed the MIP to incentivize top management to favor a sale even at valuations where the common stock would receive zero.

. . .

. . . Stone was the least aggressive in seeking an exit. The evidence at trial nevertheless established that Stone had the same desire to exit and faced the same conflict of interest as Gandhi and Scanlan, although she was more open to considering a sale in 12-18 months rather than pushing for a near-term outcome. Stone candidly admitted that "[a]ll private equity firms, ourselves included, are always, from the moment we buy [] a business, looking for an exit." . . .

Based on this evidence and other materials on which the plaintiff relied, the plaintiff carried his burden to show that Gandhi, Scanlan, and Stone were not independent with respect to the Merger. They wanted to exit, consistent with the interests of the VC firms they represented.

c.   The Outside Directors: Laidig And Prang

Two of the directors — Laidig and Prang — were neither members of management nor dual fiduciaries. The plaintiff did not challenge Laidig's disinterestedness and independence. By contrast, the plaintiff contended that (i) Prang was not independent because of his close business relationship with Gandhi and Sequoia, and (ii) he was not disinterested because he beneficially owned preferred stock through Mentor, his investment vehicle, and received a liquidation preference for his shares.

Because of the web of interrelationships that characterizes the Silicon Valley startup community, scholars have argued that "so-called 'independent directors'" on VC-backed startup boards "are often not truly independent of the VCs." "Many of these directors are chosen by the VCs, who tend to have much larger professional networks than the entrepreneurs or other common shareholders." If there is a "conflict of interest" between the VCs and common stockholders, the "independent directors" have incentives to side with the VCs.

. . .

At trial, the plaintiff could not rely on general characterizations of the VC eco-system. The plaintiff had to prove by a preponderance of evidence that Prang was not disinterested or independent in this case. The plaintiff carried his burden.

Prang had a long history with Sequoia, dating back to Sequoia's investment in Aspect Development, where Prang was President and COO. After Aspect Development, Sequoia asked Prang to work with them on other companies, and Gandhi recalled "a number where we worked very collaboratively. . . . " One was Uniscape. The relationship led to Prang investing about $300,000 in three Sequoia funds, including Sequoia X, which owned Trados preferred stock. At the time of the Merger, Prang was also the CEO of Conformia Software, a company backed by Sequoia where Gandhi served on the board. When Sequoia obtained the right to designate two members of Trados's Board, Sequoia designated Gandhi and Prang. Having considered these facts as a whole and evaluated Prang's demeanor, I find that Prang's current and past relationships with Gandhi and Sequoia resulted in a sense of "owingness" that compromised his independence for purposes of deter-mining the applicable standard of review.

The plaintiff also introduced sufficient evidence at trial to establish that the $220,633 that Prang received in the Merger (through Mentor) was material to him . . .

3. Entire Fairness

A reviewing court deploys the entire fairness test to determine whether the members of a conflicted board of directors complied with their fiduciary duties. . . .

"The concept of fairness has two basic aspects: fair dealing and fair price." Fair dealing "embraces questions of when the transaction was timed, how it was initi-ated, structured, negotiated, disclosed to the directors, and how the approvals of the directors and the stockholders were obtained." Fair price "relates to the eco-nomic and financial considerations of the proposed merger, including all relevant factors: assets, market value, earnings, future prospects, and any other elements that affect the intrinsic or inherent value of a company's stock." Although the two aspects may be examined separately, "the test for fairness is not a bifurcated one as between fair dealing and price. All aspects of the issue must be examined as a whole since the question is one of entire fairness." But "perfection is not possible, or expected. . . . "

a. Fair Dealing

The evidence pertinent to fair dealing weighed decidedly in favor of the plain-tiff. Indeed, there was no contemporaneous evidence suggesting that the directors set out to deal with the common stockholders in a procedurally fair manner. . . .

i. Transaction Initiation

Fair dealing encompasses an evaluation of how the transaction was initiated. In this case, the VC directors pursued the Merger because Trados did not offer sufficient risk-adjusted upside to warrant either the continuing investment of their time and energy or their funds' ongoing exposure to the possibility of capital loss. An exit addressed these risks by enabling the VCs to devote personal resources to other, more promising investments and by returning their funds' invested capital plus a modest return. The VC directors did not make this decision after evaluating Trados from the perspective of the common stockholders, but rather as holders of preferred stock with contractual cash flow rights that diverged materially from those of the common stock and who sought to generate returns consistent with their VC funds' business model.

. . .

ii.   Transaction Negotiation And Structure

Fair dealing encompasses questions of how the transaction was negotiated and structured. To analyze these aspects of the Merger requires an understanding of the MIP.

VC-backed portfolio companies commonly adopt plans similar to the MIP to incent management to favor exits. Debate has raged for decades over whether similar severance arrangements at public companies advance stockholder interests. From a judicial perspective, the answer depends on the facts. Here, the structure and operation of the MIP provide evidence of unfair dealing towards the common stock.

. . .

The MIP paid a percentage of the total consideration achieved in any sale to senior management, before any amounts went to the preferred or the common. The percentage payout increased as the value of the deal increased. . . .

. . .

As a practical matter, at deal prices below the preferred stockholders' liquidation preference, the preferred bore the entire cost of the MIP because the common would not be entitled to any proceeds. Nothing about that is procedurally or substantively unfair. Once the deal price exceeded the liquidation preference, however, the MIP took value away from the common. . . . [At the price of the transaction as it occurred,] the common stockholders contributed 100% of their ex-MIP proceeds while the preferred stockholders only contributed 10% ($5.7 million / $57.9 million).

There is no evidence in the record that the Board ever considered how to allocate fairly any incremental dollars above the liquidation preference. Until the Merger proceeds cleared the preference, each dollar was allocated between management and the preferred stockholders, with management receiving its assigned percentage and the preferred taking the rest. But once the consideration topped the preference, thereby implicating the rights of the common, the additional dollars were not fairly allocated. All of the additional dollars went to management and the preferred. The common would not receive anything until the deal price exceeded the preference by more than the MIP payout.

. . .

Without the MIP, in a transaction that valued Trados at $60 million, Campbell, Budge, and Hummel would have received nothing for their options, and Hummel would have received approximately $0.5 million for his common stock (excluding any participation by the Series A and BB). In confronting that reality, their personal financial interests would have been aligned with the interests of the common stockholders as a whole, giving them strong reasons to evaluate critically whether the Board should pass on the Merger and continue to operate Trados as a stand-alone entity with the prospect of a higher-valued exit in the future. Perhaps the Board would have reached the same decision, but the process would have been different.

The MIP changed matters dramatically. In a transaction at $60 million, the MIP allocated $7.8 million to senior management, with Campbell, Budge, and Hummel collectively receiving $4.2 million. Instead of $0.5 million, Hummel's share was $1.092 million . . . On top of that, the MIP's cutback feature ensured that to the extent any MIP participants might receive consideration at higher deal values in their capacity as equity holders, their MIP payout would be reduced by the amount of the consideration received. The combination eliminated any financial incentive for senior management to push for a price at which the common stock would receive value or to favor remaining independent with the prospect of a higher valued sale at a later date.

The MIP converted the management team from holders of equity interests aligned with the common stock to claimants whose return profile and incentives closely resembled those of the preferred. Campbell and Hummel in fact acted and voted in a manner that served the preferred stockholders' desire for a near-term sale. Given its design and effect, the MIP is evidence that the Board dealt unfairly with the common when negotiating and structuring the Merger.

iii.   Director Approval

Fair dealing encompasses questions of how director approval was obtained. Except for Laidig, all of the directors were financially interested in the Merger or faced a conflict of interest because they owed fiduciary duties to entities whose interests diverged from those of the common stockholders. The MIP played a role here as well, because it gave Campbell and Hummel a direct and powerful incentive to vote in favor of the deal.

The element of Board approval also encompasses how the directors reached their decision. A director's failure to understand the nature of his duties can be evidence of unfairness. Directors who cannot perceive a conflict or who deny its existence cannot meaningfully address it. The defendants in this case did not understand that their job was to maximize the value of the corporation for the benefit of the common stockholders, and they refused to recognize the conflicts they faced.

During his deposition, Laidig volunteered that the Trados directors never considered the common stockholders:

Q:	. . . Was it the best thing for the common stockholders to sell the company?
Laidig:	To tell you the truth, between common and preferred was only a topic which really popped up through this court case. I didn't even remember this thing as being a debate or discussion on the board. . . .
Q:	You don't recall any discussion at the board level as between the interests of the common stockholders[?]
Laidig:	No. . . . It only once came up, you know, in conjunction with the stock option plan, you know, when we reduced the value. That's what I have a vague memory of.

. . .

iv.   Stockholder Approval

Finally, fair dealing encompasses questions of how stockholder approval was obtained. The defendants never considered conditioning the Merger on the vote of a majority of disinterested common stockholders. The vote on the Merger was delivered by the preferred, who controlled a majority of the Company's voting power on an as-converted basis, and other "[l]arge [f]riendlies," such as Hummel. . . .

"Stockholders in Delaware corporations have a right to control and vote their shares in their own interest." "They are limited only by any fiduciary duty owed to other stockholders. It is not objectionable that their motives may be for personal profit, or determined by whim or caprice, so long as they violate no duty owed [to] other shareholders." The fact that the preferred stockholders voted in their own interest is therefore not evidence of unfair dealing. The failure to condition the deal on a vote of the disinterested common stockholders is likewise not evidence of unfairness; it simply deprives the defendants of otherwise helpful affirmative evidence of fairness. The effect of the MIP on Hummel's voting preferences, however, provides some additional evidence of unfairness.

b. Evidence Pertinent to Fair Price

In contrast to the evidence on fair dealing, which decidedly favored the plaintiff, the evidence on fair price was mixed. Consistent with the amount of consideration that the common stockholders received in the Merger, the defendants strived at trial to demonstrate that the common stock had no value. As with their trial testimony on issues relevant to fair dealing, the defendants adopted aggressive positions that were contrary to the contemporaneous documents and their earlier testimony. But as will be seen in the unitary fairness determination, their evidence on price fairness was ultimately persuasive.

[The court explores the defendants' views as to the financial condition of Trados (which were that it was a failing entity), the plaintiffs' views that the common stock had value because the directors had set an option price of ten cents per share, a valuation performed by JMP, and valuations performed by experts hired by both plaintiff and defendants.]

c. The Unitary Determination Of Fairness

Although the defendant directors did not adopt any protective provisions, failed to consider the common stockholders, and sought to exit without recognizing the conflicts of interest presented by the Merger, they nevertheless proved that the transaction was fair. The Delaware Supreme Court has characterized the proper "test of fairness" as whether "the minority stockholder shall receive the substantial equivalent in value of what he had before." If Trados's common stock had no economic value before the Merger, then the common stockholders received the substantial equivalent in value of what they had before, and the Merger satisfies the test of fairness.

Despite the directors' often problematic testimony, they proved that Trados did not have a reasonable prospect of generating value for the common stock. Trados's ability to do so depended on financing its business plan with internally generated cash and the remaining venture debt. To the extent Trados needed outside funds, the Company could not raise them. None of the VC firms would put more money into Trados, and they had no obligation to. Trados also could not return to the venture debt market. . . .

If Trados could not self-fund its business plan, then the Company could not execute it. Even if it could self-fund, Trados had to build value at a rate exceeding the 8% cumulative dividend earned by the preferred to generate a return for the common. Having considered the directors' trial testimony, the documentary record, and Jarrell's DCF analysis, I believe that Trados would not be able to grow at a rate that would yield value for the common. Trados likely could self-fund, avoid bankruptcy, and continue operating, but it did not have a realistic chance of generating a sufficient return to escape the gravitational pull of the large liquidation preference and cumulative dividend.

. . .

In light of this reality, the directors breached no duty to the common stock by agreeing to a Merger in which the common stock received nothing. The common stock had no economic value before the Merger, and the common stockholders received in the Merger the substantial equivalent in value of what they had before.

Under the circumstances of this case, the fact that the directors did not follow a fair process does not constitute a separate breach of duty. As the Delaware Supreme Court has recognized, an unfair process can infect the price, result in a finding of breach, and warrant a potential remedy. On these facts, such a finding is not warranted. The defendants' failure to deploy a procedural device such as a special committee resulted in their being forced to prove at trial that the Merger was entirely fair. Having done so, they have demonstrated that they did not commit a fiduciary breach.

. . .

Notes and Questions

1. A majority of the preferred shares of Trados were held by investors who had significant control over the Trados board. Who do you imagine held the common stock?

2. Where did the Trados board go wrong?

3. What exit strategies did the Trados board consider? Why did they choose the sale to SDL over other strategies?

4. What were the specific conflicts of interest faced by each director?

5. Can we learn from this opinion that shareholders should not be given the right to designate directors of a venture — or at least that a company will be in a better position if any such designees do not participate in votes concerning exit strategies?

6. Is it ever appropriate for a board to vote in favor of a sale of the company in a situation where there is no consideration available for common stockholders?

7. What do you make of the fact that the court determines that the Trados directors breached their fiduciary duties and failed to conduct the exit in a procedurally fair way, and yet ultimately determines that the transaction was fair?

8. If you were counsel to the Trados board members who were designated by owners of preferred stock, what advice would you give them to avoid the fiduciary duty problems in the case?

There are three main structures for so-called M&A transactions: stock sales, asset sales, and mergers. In the following sections, we explore state laws applicable to the transactions, agreements made by parties to the transactions, and broadly discuss other legal issues an entrepreneur's counsel should understand in preparing a client for any of these major legal events.

1.   Stock Sales

A stock sale is when one company, often called the "buyer" or "acquirer," purchases the stock of another company, often called the "target," from the target's shareholders. In that way, the buyer owns the target, and the target's shareholders receive the bargained-for consideration. These transactions are typically documented in stock purchase agreements like the document below, in which Wild Oats Markets, Inc. acquires Kathy's Natural Food Ranch Market-West, Inc.

Stock sales are, in some ways, the most straightforward of the M&A structures: one company decides to buy another company directly from its owners. A simple diagram for the steps in a stock purchase transaction where the acquirer acquires all outstanding shares in the target company follows:

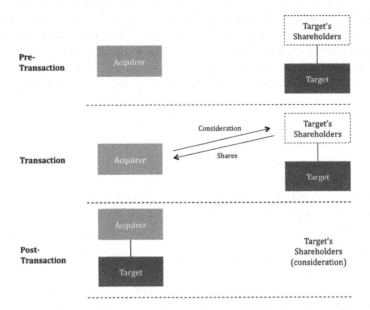

As you read the admittedly dense Share Purchase Agreement below, keep in mind that all that is happening is that one company is buying another from its owners. We have added comments throughout the document with explanations or thoughts on various key provisions.

EXHIBIT 2.3 TO WILD OATS MARKETS, INC. FORM S-1 REGISTRATION STATEMENT UNDER THE SECURITIES ACT OF 1933
Filing Date: August 30, 1996

SHARE PURCHASE AGREEMENT

This SHARE AND PURCHASE AGREEMENT (the "Agreement") is made as of July 14, 1994, by and among WILD OATS MARKETS, Inc., a Delaware corporation with its principal office at 1668 Valtec Lane, Boulder, Co. 80301 ("Buyer"), and the holders of the

Common Stock of KATHY'S NATURAL FOOD RANCH MARKET, INC. and KATHY'S NATURAL FOOD RANCH MARKET-WEST, INC. (Nevada corporations referred to collectively herein as the "Corporations"); (The holders of the Common Stock of the Corporations are referred to collectively as the "Selling Stockholders"); KATHY MELBY, an individual; and RICH ARCARIS, an individual. Certain other individual employees of the Corporations listed on Exhibit A attached hereto (the "Key Employees"), and also listed on Exhibit A, holders of options on the Selling Stockholder's stock ("Option-holders") are also signatories to this agreement for the limited purpose of relinquishing their claim to stock, if any, and receipt of consideration therefor.

RECITALS

A. Selling Stockholders own, in aggregate, all of the issued and outstanding shares of capital stock of the Corporations (the "Shares"), and the Selling Stockholders desire to sell all such Shares to Buyer for cash and other consideration.

B. The parties previously entered into the Option Agreement dated July 14, 1994 (the "Option Agreement") in which the parties agreed to enter into this Agreement upon the satisfaction of certain conditions, and a Management Agreement dated July 14, 1994 (the "Management Agreement") pursuant to which the Buyer is operating the Stores.

C. This Agreement has been approved by the Boards of Directors of the Corporations and is hereby approved by the Selling Stockholders, who constitute all the shareholders of Corporations.

AGREEMENT

NOW, THEREFORE, in consideration of their mutual covenants, promises, and obligations set forth in this Agreement, the parties agree as follows:

1. DESCRIPTION OF TRANSACTION

1.1 Purchase Price. The Purchase Price of the Shares is as follows:

(a) Two Million Four Hundred Thousand Dollars ($2,400,000) cash or certified funds, paid upon execution of the Option Agreement and held in escrow until the Closing, as defined below, plus One Hundred Thousand Dollars ($100,000) plus accumulated interest, which Buyers paid to Selling Stockholders as earnest money; all to be distributed, one-half to the Option-holders and one-half to the Selling Stockholders, at closing;

(b) Four Hundred Eighty Thousand Dollars ($480,000) in cash/common stock of Buyer, to be paid or distributed to the Key Employees . . . ;

(c) One Million Five Hundred Thousand Dollars ($1,500,000), one-half to be paid to the Selling Stockholders and one-half to the Option-holders in cash or certified funds on or before April 14, 1995 . . . ;

(d) One Million Six Hundred Thousand Dollars ($1,600,000), one-half to be paid to the Selling Stockholders and one-half to the Option-holders in cash or certified funds on or before October 14, 1995;

(e) The amount, if any, in cash or certified funds to be paid on or before April 14, 1995, by which the Wholesale Value (as defined herein) of the Inventory (as defined herein) of the Corporations' retail stores exceed the sum of Seven Hundred Thousand Dollars ($700,000). . . . Said amount is to be paid one-half to Selling Stockholders and one-half to Option-holders;

(f) Assumption of certain long-term debts . . . ;

(g) Cash or certified funds at Closing, to be paid one-half to Selling Stockholders and one-half to Option-holders, in the amount of any lease deposits for the Stores, utility deposits, sales tax deposits, pro-rated insurance premiums and other deposits of like nature. . . .

> *Some of the consideration being paid is in cash, and some can be paid in stock of the Buyer. Sometimes sellers will want to own an ongoing interest in the business and will ask for this type of consideration, and sometimes buyers will insist on it to lower their cash outlay.*

. . .

> *The "mechanics" of the closing are set forth in these next sections — basically, these are the concrete steps to be taken to consummate the sale.*

1.2 Closing. The closing of the purchase and sale of the Stock hereunder shall take place at a closing ("Closing"), which shall be held at the offices of Thomas KLC, 4625 South 2300 East, Salt Lake City. The Closing shall take place at 10:00 A.M. or such time and place as the Buyer and Seller may agree.

1.3 Assets of the Corporations. The primary assets of the Corporations include two retail natural foods stores in Las Vegas, Nevada, located at 3455 East Flamingo Road (the "East Store") and 6720 West Sahara Boulevard (the "West Store") (The East Store and the West Store are referred to collectively as the "Stores") and the fixtures, equipment, inventories and leases pertaining to the Stores. An equipment list is attached as Exhibit 1.3

1.4 Inventory. On July 13th and 14th, 1994, representatives of Buyer and the Corporations will be present at the West Store and East Store, respectively, and shall simultaneously and together perform an Inventory (as defined below) of the Stores for purposes of Section 1.1(e). . . .

1.5 Action by Selling Stockholders at Closing. At Closing, subject to the terms and conditions of this Agreement and pursuant to documents reasonably satisfactory in form and substance to Buyer and its counsel, Selling Stockholders shall deliver to Buyer:

(a) Certificates representing the Shares, duly endorsed or accompanied by stock powers duly executed in blank and otherwise in form acceptable for transfer on the books of the Corporations, with such stock certificates to be delivered to the escrow agent;

(b) The stock books, stock ledgers, minute books, and corporate seal, if any, of the Corporations and all other books and records of the Corporations being located at the corporate premises of the Corporations;

(c) Resignations of the Corporations' directors and officers, as identified on attached Exhibit 1.5(c);

(d) Copies of any books and records pertaining to the Stores' operations . . . ;

(e) Certified copies of all Board of Directors and Shareholders actions and approvals required for Selling Stockholders to consummate the transactions contemplated hereunder;

(f) A list setting forth the known accrued vacation and sick time of employees of the Corporations as of the Closing;

(g) Buyer may obtain, if desired, letters from Nevada Sales Tax authorities certifying that the Stores' sales tax accounts are current.

1.6 Action by Buyer at Closing. At Closing, subject to the terms and conditions of the Agreement and pursuant to documents reasonably satisfactory in form and substance to Selling Stockholders, Buyer shall:

(a) Pay the Two Million Five Hundred Thousand Dollars ($2,500,000) with interest accrued pursuant to the Option Agreement, which amount shall be deemed paid against the purchase price.

(b) Pay, in cash or certified funds, and distribute Buyer's common stock to the Key Employees . . . ;

(c) Deliver to the Selling Stockholders and Option-holders [a series of promissory notes for the various categories of consideration described in section 1.1.] . . .

(f) Pay to the Selling Stockholders and Option-holders, in cash or certified funds, the amount of any lease deposits for the Stores, utility deposits, sales tax deposits, pro-rated insurance premiums and other deposits of like nature . . . ;

(g) Grant to Selling Stockholders a subordinated security interest (in form satisfactory to Selling Stockholders) in all fixtures, equipment and assets of the Corporations in existence immediately prior to Closing, as additional security for Buyer's obligations. . . .

2. ESCROW OF SHARES

At Closing, Selling Stockholders and Buyer shall deliver to Zions First National Bank, as Escrow Agent ("Escrow Agent") a certificate representing 100% of the Shares (the "Escrow Shares") for the purpose of securing the payment of the Purchase Price. . . .

An escrow can serve an important purpose in a transaction like this — the shares will not be released unless and until the transaction works out exactly as planned.

---

3. TRANSITION OF BUSINESS

3.1 Trade Names, Trademarks, and Service Marks. The parties understand and agree that Buyer may use the name "Kathy's" (in any form or derivative) as a tradename, trademark or servicemark but only in the city of Las Vegas and all other rights to such name shall remain with some or all of the Selling Stockholders/Corporations. . . .

3.2 Store Operations. The parties entered into a Management Agreement dated July __, 1994, under which Buyer has operated the stores since, 1994. Until Closing, Buyer shall continue to operate the Stores in the ordinary and usual course of business. After Closing, Buyer shall be responsible for the operation of the Stores.

3.3 Employees. Selling Stockholders do not warrant or represent that any of the employees will agree to continue to work at the Stores or otherwise work for Buyer. Buyer agrees to pay sick and vacation pay, accrued as of Closing. Prior to Closing, Selling Stockholders will make available to Buyer all records concerning the Corporations' employee compensation and benefits.

3.4 Transition Assistance. From the execution of the Option Agreement, Arcaris and Melby each hereby agree to assist Buyer in the transition of the business to Buyer for which assistance Arcaris and Melby shall be paid [a set fee for a set list of services].

4. REPRESENTATIONS AND WARRANTIES OF THE SELLING STOCK-HOLDERS

Selling Stockholders, represent and warrant as follows:

> *In these sections, the Selling Stockholders make promises as to the state of the business. In places where you see language like "to the best of their knowledge," you can surmise that counsel to the sellers asked that her clients not be held responsible for problems of which they are not aware. This is a frequent point of negotiation.*

4.1 Organization, Good Standing, Enforceability. To the best of their knowledge, the Corporations are duly organized, validly existing, and in good standing under the laws of the State of Nevada and have full corporate power and authority to carry on business in the State of Nevada and to own or hold under lease or similar agreement the properties and assets they now own or hold; and have full corporate power and authority to carry out the transactions contemplated hereby. This Agreement has been duly executed and delivered by Selling Stockholders and is a valid, binding and legal obligation of Selling Stockholders enforceable against Selling Stockholders in accordance with its terms. Selling Stockholders have the power and authority to enter into and perform their obligations under this Agreement.

4.2 Capitalization and Subsidiaries. As of the date of this Agreement, the total authorized capital stock of Kathy's Natural Food Ranch Market, Inc. consists of 25,000 shares of stock, no par value per share. As of July 14, 1994, 6667 and 2/3 shares were issued and outstanding and 333 and 1/3 shares were held in the treasury.

As of the date of this Agreement, the authorized capital stock of Kathy's Natural Ranch Market-West, Inc. consists of 25,000 shares of stock, no par value per share. As of July 14, 1994, 100 shares were issued and outstanding and no shares were held in the treasury.

All issued and outstanding shares and other securities of the Corporations are duly authorized, validly issued, issued in compliance with federal and state laws, fully paid, nonassessable and free of preemptive rights. Except as set forth in this Agreement, there are no outstanding options, warrants, conversion privileges, contracts or other rights to purchase or acquire any shares of either Corporation.

Neither Corporation holds an interest in any subsidiary or affiliate corporation.

4.3 No Approvals or Notices Required; No Conflicts with Other Agreements or Orders. The execution and delivery of this Agreement do not, and the consummation of the transactions contemplated hereby will not, violate any provision of the Articles of Incorporation or Bylaws of the Corporations. [With limited exceptions,] the execution, performance and delivery of this Agreement do not and the consummation of the transactions contemplated hereby will not (a) require any consent, approval or authorization of any person or governmental authority, the failure to obtain which could have a material adverse effect upon the transactions contemplated hereby; (b) constitute a material violation of any provision of law applicable to Selling Stockholders; or (c) violate any provision of, or result in the acceleration of any obligation under, any material mortgage, lien, lease, agreement, instrument, order arbitration award, judgment or decree to which Selling Stockholders or the Corporations are a party or by which Selling Stockholders or the Corporations are bound.

4.4 Financial Statements. Selling Stockholders have delivered to Buyer financial statement information dated (1) as of December 31, 1990, 1991, 1992, and 1993 and (2) as of May 31, 1994 (collectively "Financial Statements"). The information from which the financial statements have been prepared are true and accurate. Such financials have not been prepared in accordance with generally accepted accounting principles.

4.5 Undisclosed Liabilities. To the best of Selling Stockholders' knowledge, except as disclosed to Buyer in writing, there are no undisclosed liabilities or obligations arising from contracts or otherwise with respect to the Selling Stockholders and the Corporations that are not covered by insurance.

4.6 Leaseholds. The Lease for the East Store (the "Store Lease") and the equipment lease rights and obligations (collectively the "Leaseholds") pertaining to the Stores are as set forth in the Store Lease and the equipment leases, true and complete copies of which are attached as Exhibit 4.6 and which have previously been provided to Buyer.

4.7 Equipment. To the best of their knowledge, the Corporations have good and marketable title to all equipment listed on attached Exhibit 1.3, free and clear of any liens, mortgages, pledges, encumbrances, claims and charges of any kind except those that have been disclosed to Buyer in writing.

5. REPRESENTATIONS AND WARRANTIES OF BUYER

Buyer hereby represents and warrants as follows:

5.1 Organization, Good Standing, Enforceability. Buyer is duly organized, validly existing, and in good standing under the laws of the State of Delaware and has, or will soon have, full corporate power and authority to carry on business in the State of Nevada and to own or hold under lease or similar agreement the properties and assets it will own or hold; and has full corporate power and authority to carry out the transactions contemplated hereby. This Agreement has been duly executed and delivered by Buyer and is a valid, binding and legal obligation of Buyer enforceable in accordance with its terms. Buyer has the power and authority to enter into and perform its obligations under this Agreement.

5.2 No Approvals or Notices Required; No Conflicts with Other Agreements or Orders. The execution and delivery of this Agreement do not, and the consummation of the transactions contemplated hereby will not, violate any provision of the Certificate of Incorporation or Bylaws of Buyer. The execution, performance and delivery of this Agreement do not and the consummation of the transactions contemplated hereby will not (a) require any consent, approval or authorization of any person or governmental authority, the failure to obtain which could have a material adverse effect upon the transactions contemplated hereby; (b) constitute a material violation of any provision of law applicable to Buyer; or (c) violate any provision of, or result in the acceleration of any obligation under, any material mortgage, lien, lease, agreement, instrument, order, arbitration award, judgment or decree to which Buyer is a party or by which Buyer is bound.

5.3 Brokers. Neither Buyer nor anyone acting on its behalf has retained any broker, finder, or agent, or agreed to pay any brokerage fees, finder's fees, or commissions with respect to the transactions contemplated by this agreement.

5.4 Financial Statements. Buyer acknowledges that Selling Stockholders are relying upon Buyer's financial statements provided to them as being a fair and accurate representation of the financial condition of Buyer. Selling Stockholders further rely on Buyer's business experience and expertise to ensure that the Agreement and the transactions related thereto strictly comply with any and all federal securities or state blue sky laws.

6. ACCESS AND INFORMATION

6.1 Access and Information. Selling Stockholders have provided and will give Buyer and its counsel, accountants, and other representatives reasonable access, during normal business hours throughout the period prior to Closing, to all of the Assets, and all books, contracts, commitments, and records of the Corporations and will furnish Buyer during such period with all information as Buyer may reasonably request. Buyer shall advise Sellers in writing prior to Closing of any information it has obtained as a result of its investigation which it believes has or may result in a breach of any representation or warranty of Sellers set forth in this Agreement or the Exhibits attached hereto.

6.2 Confidentiality; Return of Documents. Buyer and Selling Stockholders will hold in confidence all confidential information obtained by them from the other party under this Agreement. If the transaction contemplated by this Agreement is not consummated buyer and Selling Stockholders will continue to hold such information in confidence and will return all documents and records containing such information.

7. CONDUCT OF BUSINESS PRIOR TO CLOSING

The Buyer inserts this section to ensure that there is no funny business on the part of the Sellers between the time the deal is made and the time it is consummated.

7.1 Ordinary Course. Except with respect to the obligations which Buyer has expressly assumed pursuant to the Management Agreement, following the execution of this Agreement and prior to the Closing, Selling Stockholders will:

(a) Not commit to any employment agreements or employee benefit plans, or increase employee compensation;

(b) Not incur any indebtedness materially affecting the Corporations;

(c) Not solicit any offers or engage in any discussions with any third parties regarding any sale of any material portion of the assets of the Corporations or the sale of any of the Shares.

8. CONDITIONS PRECEDENT TO BUYER'S OBLIGATIONS

The obligations of Buyer under this Agreement are subject to the satisfaction (or waiver in writing by Buyer), prior to or at Closing, of each of the following conditions:

8.1 Correctness of Representations and Warranties. Buyer shall not have discovered any material error, misstatement, or omission in the representations and warranties made by Selling Stockholders in this Agreement or in any Schedules or Exhibits attached hereto. The representations and warranties of Selling Stockholders contained in this Agreement shall be deemed to have been made again at and as of the time of the Closing and shall be true and accurate in all material respects at such time, except as to such normal adjustments that may occur.

8.2 Compliance with Agreement. Selling Stockholders shall have performed and complied with all obligations and requirements of this Agreement to be performed or complied with by Selling Stockholders prior to or at Closing.

8.3 Authorization. Buyer shall have received copies of corporate resolutions authorizing Selling Stockholders to enter into this Agreement and perform the terms and conditions hereof.

9. CONDITIONS PRECEDENT TO OBLIGATIONS OF SELLING STOCK-HOLDERS

The obligations of Selling Stockholders under this Agreement are subject to the satisfaction (or waiver in writing by Sellers), prior to or at Closing, of each of the following conditions:

9.1 Correctness of Representations and Warranties. Selling Stockholders shall not have discovered any material error, misstatement, or omission in the representations and warranties made by Buyer in this Agreement. The representations and warranties of Buyer in this Agreement shall be deemed to have been made again at and as of the time of the Closing and shall be true and accurate in all material respects at such time.

9.2 Compliance with Agreement. Buyer shall have performed and complied with all obligations and requirements of this Agreement to be performed or complied with by Buyer prior to or at Closing.

9.3 Authorization. Selling Stockholders shall have received copies of corporate resolutions authorizing Buyer to enter into this Agreement and perform the terms and conditions hereof.

10. CONDITION PRECEDENT TO OBLIGATION OF BUYER

10.1 Discharge of Loans on West Store. The obligations of Buyer under this Agreement is subject to the satisfaction prior to or at the Closing of the condition that Selling Stockholders shall have good and marketable title to the premises from which the West Store operates. . . .

10.2 Buyer's Obligations Regarding Discharge of Loans on West Store. Buyers shall be responsible for [certain limited obligations] in connection with the discharge of the Corporation from liability under the Loans. . . .

10.3 Release of Escrow of Advance. Selling Stockholders and Option-Holders shall be entitled to receive the Two Million Five-Hundred Thousand Dollars ($2,500,000.00) deposited into escrow and given as earnest money upon closing, if not sooner.

11. REAL ESTATE

11.1 Real Estate Not to be Included as Asset. Buyer will not acquire the real property of the Corporations located at 6720 West Sahara Boulevard, which was recently acquired and improvements constructed thereon[.] . . .

11.2 Real Estate Lease for West Store Premises. On or before Closing, by Lease Agreement satisfactory to both Buyer and Selling Stockholders (attached as Exhibit 11.1), Buyer shall lease from Selling Stockholders the premises from which the West Store conducts its operations [on specified terms].

11.3 Landlord Consent. Buyer shall use its best efforts to obtain any necessary consents, including, but not limited to, the consent of the Landlord of the East Store (if required) and non-disturbance agreements from the Lenders who finance the West Store. . . .

12. DISCOUNTS FROM SUPPLIERS

12.1 Supplier Discounts. For a period of 5 years from the date of this Agreement, Buyer shall make full effort to enable Selling Stockholders related corporation, at their present Utah location, to receive the same product discounts that Buyer receives from suppliers which discounts are generally at least 15.5% off the book price. . . .

13. CLASSICS SOUTHWEST

13.1 Shelf Space. For a period of 5 years, Selling Stockholders' related company, Classics Southwest, Inc. (or other such entity as Selling Stockholders may designate) shall be given shelf space for the display and sale of its products in Buyer's stores. For the two Las Vegas Stores, such shelf space shall be a section of two and one-half linear feet, extending up and down (top to bottom) from those two and one-half linear feet. For Buyer's other stores, the shelf space shall be a section one and one-half linear feet, extending up and down (top to bottom) from this one and one-half linear feet. The shelf space contemplated herein shall be located in the stores in areas comparable to that which Classics Southwest currently displays its products in the existing Las Vegas Stores.

14. MISCELLANEOUS

14.1 Covenant Not to Compete. Each of the Selling Stockholders hereby agree that it will not at any time within the five year period immediately following Closing, directly or indirectly engage in, or have any interest in any person, firm, corporation, or business (whether as an employee, officer, director, agent, security holder, creditor, consultant, or otherwise) that engages in any activity which is the same as or competitive with activity engaged in by the Corporations within a twenty (20) mile radius of the Stores in Las Vegas, Nevada.

14.2 Arbitration; Litigation. Any controversy or claim arising out of or relating to this Agreement, or the breach thereof, shall be settled by arbitration. . . .

14.3 Survival of Representations and Warranties. All representations, covenants, and warranties set forth herein shall be deemed to be material and to have been relied upon by the Parties hereto and shall survive Closing.

14.4 Payment of Fees and Expenses. The Corporations shall pay for the reasonable legal, accounting and other expenses of Selling Stockholders related to this transaction and accrued as of Closing. Otherwise, each party shall pay and be responsible for all of the fees and expenses of its own counsel [and other advisors].

. . .

IN WITNESS WHEREOF, the parties have executed this Agreement as of the date first written above.

[Signatures of Selling Stockholders, Option-Holders, Buyer and Key Employees]

Notes and Questions

1. A deal diagram, like the diagram that appears at the beginning of this section of the chapter, maps the parties involved in a transaction, including the entities, shareholders, creditors, and the flow of assets, consideration, ownership, third-party interests, and other major factors in the transaction. For any professional trying to understand the way a deal is structured, a diagram like this provides a helpful analytical structure. Create a deal diagram for the Wild Oats deal.

2. In a stock sale, there is no change in the seller's corporate charter, and there is no separate transfer of the seller's rights and obligations in contracts, permits, or other documents. Only ownership of the target itself has transferred, and all contracts with the target would seemingly continue uninterrupted and unaffected. However, some contracts (commonly leases or permits) can specifically require the consent of the other party if there is a change in ownership of the target. Lawyers learn about these requirements by reviewing all contracts and other documents related to the target during the due diligence period (see Note 7). Did Wild Oats or the Sellers need the consent of any other parties to do the deal? How would the ability to gain these consents impact the deal?

3. State law will control certain elements of the stock purchase transaction. First, it will provide the legal authority for companies to make stock purchase deals. In Delaware, § 122 of the Delaware General Corporation Law lists general corporate powers, including the authority to do a stock purchase and sale transaction. All other states include similar provisions in their corporate statutes.

Next, state law will describe the required shareholder and board approval in order for the transaction to take place (note that the parties may decide, by contract or other agreement, to secure additional approvals). What approvals were necessary in the Wild Oats deal? In most stock purchase deals, only the acquirer's board must approve the transaction under state law. The target shareholders are not required to give formal approval because each shareholder has the option to sell — or not sell — its shares. In addition, since the target company is not involved in the transaction, the target board's approval is not needed. Some states have different rules that require, at least in some circumstances, the target's board to approve the sale, so the lawyers will need to consult the state laws that govern their client's approval process.

One reason that parties agree to a stock sale is that it generally does not require shareholder approval by either the acquirer's shareholders or the target's board. When would this be favorable or unfavorable? For many entrepreneurs who own their companies and have a limited number of shareholders, a stock sale can be an easy way to transfer interests. It transfers the entire entity to a new owner, and it can be relatively quick to complete. For targets that are owned by a large number of shareholders, this transaction can be more difficult to consummate because it may require bargaining with each of the shareholders, especially if any decide to hold out for more than their proportionate share of the consideration. An attorney who is planning ahead for an entrepreneurial client will often include a "drag along" provision in the shareholders agreement or operating agreement for her client (see Chapter 3). A drag along is a contractual agreement by the venture's owners that they will go along with any sale of the business — regardless of how it is structured — if the deal is approved by a specified percentage of the owners. In this way, company owners agree in advance that they will not "hold out" for more money in a deal that has received broad approval by the other owners.

4. Aside from state corporate rules, the details of a stock sale are governed by contract. The stock purchase agreement will contain the terms and conditions of the transaction itself, will govern the parties' behavior prior to the "closing" (the consummation) of the deal, and will specify the parties' rights and obligations to each other after the closing. Lawyers will play a critical role in negotiating the terms of their client's agreement, and they will have the most extensive knowledge about the contract provisions and what is beneficial for their client.

While each agreement is specifically tailored to the transaction it governs, most agreements contain the same overall structure and provisions. A typical stock purchase agreement contains the following provisions in this order: introductory matters, description of the deal structure, description of the consideration, representations and warranties, covenants, conditions to closing, closing transaction mechanics (e.g., where, when the closing will take place), post-closing agreements, miscellaneous provisions, and schedules and exhibits. Does the Wild Oats Agreement follow this structure? What additional provisions might parties want to include in building a contract for a stock sale transaction?

5. M&A deals will typically follow the steps in this timeline:

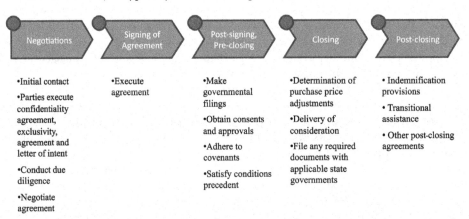

Some M&A deals can take weeks to complete, while others can take months, depending on the parties, their relationship, and the complexity of the deal.

Attorneys and other professionals are involved in every part of the process. Entrepreneurs who have not participated in M&A transactions before will often rely heavily on their lawyers to explain all parts of the transaction, and to draft documents that accurately reflect the business deal.

6. During the negotiation period, lawyers for the buyer will conduct extensive due diligence and lawyers for the seller will prepare and make available information about the target. Thinking about entrepreneurs, entrepreneurial ventures, and start-ups generally, what complications in due diligence do you imagine in an entrepreneurial company sale transaction?

7. Look at sections 4 and 5 of the Wild Oats Agreement. The representations and warranties section serves three main purposes. First, it is a method to obtain disclosure about the participating parties and the target, and provide assurance about the reliability of the information each party provides. Second, it is used as a basis for the conditions to close the transaction if there is a time lapse between the signing of an agreement and the closing. Third, it can be used as a basis for a party's right to indemnification if one party breaches one or more of its representations or warranties. In this contract, what is the substance of each party's representations and warranties? Which party makes more extensive disclosure, and why might that be?

8. Some of the representations and warranties in the Wild Oats Agreement contain the language "to the best of their knowledge" as opposed to an absolute statement of fact. What is the effect of the knowledge qualifiers used in sections 4 and 5?

9. Sections 12 and 13 of the Wild Oats Agreement are specific to this deal. Section 12 provides that the buyer will make a full effort to get supplier discounts for the sellers, and section 13 provides that the buyer will retain shelf space for products from the sellers' affiliate company. What is the purpose of these sections? Are they concessions for the buyer? Lawyers should remember that the agreement for the buyer and the seller can involve any aspect of the business that their client favors. In this case, the buyer may have agreed to these provisions, which are clearly in the seller's interest, in exchange for some other seller concession or simply as a gesture of goodwill.

2. Asset Sales

An asset sale is different from a stock purchase, even if the documents appear similar and the end result (one company purchases the business of another) is similar. In an asset sale transaction, an acquiring company purchases individual assets from the target company, rather than buying the entire company from its shareholders. As part of the deal, the acquirer will commonly assume some or all of the target's liabilities. The acquirer also typically pays consideration to the target. The Asset Purchase Agreement below documents the acquisition of the assets of restaurateur State Street Café and Pizzeria, Inc. by entertainment conglomerate Blue Moon Group, Inc.

In an asset sale, there is no change in the ownership structure of either company. Once the assets have been transferred and consideration paid to the target company, a common next step is that the target dissolves and liquidates and, after settling any remaining accounts, distributes the consideration to its shareholders.

The acquirer continues the business with the new assets. A simple asset sale transaction can be diagrammed as follows:

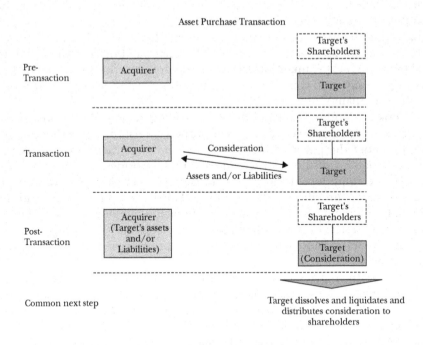

Asset Purchase Transaction

Target dissolves and liquidates and distributes consideration to shareholders

---

EXHIBIT 10.3 TO BLUE MOON GROUP, INC. REPORT ON FORM 10-QSB
Filing Date: November 24, 2004

ASSET ACQUISITION AGREEMENT

This Asset Acquisition Agreement (the "Agreement") is made as of the 1st day of September, 2004, by and among, BLUE MOON GROUP, INC., a Delaware corporation (hereafter, "Buyer"), and STATE STREET CAFE AND PIZZERIA, INC., an Illinois corporation (hereafter "Seller").

BACKGROUND

WHEREAS, the Seller is engaged in business as a restaurateur; and

WHEREAS, the Seller desires to sell substantially all of its assets and, under the terms and conditions set forth in this Agreement, the Buyer has agreed to purchase such assets and assume certain of the Seller's obligations; and

WHEREAS, the Buyer, is a Delaware corporation engaged in holding various entertainment properties and subsidiaries, that desires to purchase the assets of the Seller;

NOW, THEREFORE, in consideration of the foregoing and of the mutual promises, covenants, representations, warranties, and agreements contained herein, and intending to be legally bound, the Seller, the Buyer, and the Buyer agree as follows:

ARTICLE I
SALE AND PURCHASE OF ASSETS

Section 1.01 Purchased Assets. Subject to the terms and conditions of this Agreement, on the Closing Date (as defined in Section 2.01), Seller will sell to Buyer, and Buyer will purchase from Seller, the assets of Seller listed below (collectively, the "Purchased Assets"). The Purchased Assets will be purchased free and clear of all security interests, liens, restrictions, claims, encumbrances or charges of any kind ("Encumbrances"), except as provided herein. The Purchased Assets will include the following items:

> *If you represent the selling venture, you should watch to ensure the Buyer is getting everything that has been bargained for — which might include everything except personal effects if that is the deal. Specific exclusions are in section 1.03. The Buyer will want the purchase agreement to go into some detail in listing the assets to ensure it has everything it needs to run the business after the closing.*

(a) Intellectual Property. All trademarks and trademark applications, and all patents and patent applications, . . . all goodwill associated therewith, and all computer software developed by Seller, including all documentation thereof and all other Intellectual Property . . . of Seller, and all rights to use the name "State Street Cafe and Pizzeria, Inc.";

(b) Promotional Rights. All marketing or promotional designs, brochures, advertisements, concepts, literature, books, media rights, rights against any other Person in respect of any of the foregoing and all other promotional properties, in each case primarily used or useful or developed or acquired by the Seller for use in connection with the ownership and operation of the Purchased Assets;

(c) [other specified assets];

(d) Customer Lists and other Intangible Assets. All other intangible assets, including without limitation all customer lists, goodwill, "know-how," proprietary information and trade secrets relating to the Seller's business operations; and all manufacturers' warranties (including pending warranty claims) and manuals relating to the Purchased Assets;

(e) Seller's Deposits and Prepayments. All of the Seller's lease deposits on leases assumed by Buyer;

(f) Permits. All permits relating to the operation of Seller's business, to the extent such permits are transferable and whether or not all action necessary to effect such transfer has been taken prior to the Closing;

(g) Leases. All real property leases of Seller, to the extent such are assignable.

(h) Telephone and Facsimile Numbers. The right to use the telephone and facsimile machine numbers assigned to Seller's places of business in Illinois;

(i) Books and Records. Except as expressly set forth in Section 1.03, all papers, documents, computerized databases and records of Seller relating to the Purchased Assets and its business operations, including without limitation all software design documents, source code, employer records and workers' compensation records relating to employees hired by the Buyer, sales records, marketing records, accounting and financial records, and maintenance and production records; and

(j) Claims Relating to Purchased Assets. All claims, causes of action, rights of recovery and rights of setoff of every type and kind relating to the Purchased Assets and all claims, causes of action, rights of recovery and rights of setoff of every type and kind relating to the Assumed Obligations. . . .

Section 1.02 Assumed Obligations. In consideration of Buyer's purchase of the Purchased Assets, subject to the terms and conditions set forth herein, on the Closing Date the Seller shall assign to the Buyer and the Buyer shall assume and discharge in a timely fashion all of the liabilities and obligations of the Seller set forth on Schedule 1.02 (hereafter collectively referred to as the "Assumed Obligations").

> *In this section, the Seller is able to ensure the Buyer has taken all debts and other obligations. Buyers will typically want to exclude some listed obligations — all of which will, of course, be taken into account when initially negotiating the purchase price.*

Except as expressly set forth in this Section 1.02, the Buyer shall have no responsibility for any of the Seller's obligations . . . , and all such obligations shall remain with the Seller and are herein referred to as the "Excluded Obligations."

Section 1.03 Excluded Assets. The Purchased Assets shall not include any of the Seller's rights, privileges, title or interest in the following assets (hereafter referred to as the "Excluded Assets"):

(a) Books and Records. All of the Seller's minute books, stock books, tax returns and books and records directly relating to the Excluded Obligations and all of Seller's books and records except to the extent that such records relate to the intellectual property purchased hereunder;

(b) Rights Hereunder. All rights and claims of the Seller under this Agreement; and

(c) Contracts not Assigned. All rights of the Seller in, to and under those leases, purchase orders, contracts and other agreements not being assigned to the Buyer pursuant to Section 1.01.

(d) Tangible Personal Property. All of the tangible personal property leased to Seller pursuant to [the Agreement].

(e) Additional Cash. Seller's cash in excess of that specified in Section 1.01(c).

Section 1.04 Consideration. In addition to the assumption of the Assumed Obligations, at the Closing, Buyer shall deliver to Seller 625,000 shares of Buyer's restricted common stock.

Section 1.05 Allocation of Purchase Price. At or prior to the Closing, the Buyer and the Seller shall execute a written instrument . . . setting forth by asset category and amount the mutually agreed allocation of the consideration being paid by the Buyer for the Purchased Assets [for tax purposes].

Section 1.06 Tax Consequences. For federal income tax purposes, the transactions contemplated hereby are intended to constitute a "reorganization" within the meaning of Section 368 of the Code [see end of this chapter for further discussion of this concept]. . . .

ARTICLE II
CLOSING; DOCUMENTS OF CONVEYANCE

Section 2.01 Closing. Subject to the satisfaction of the conditions set forth in Articles VI and VII, the purchase and sale contemplated hereby shall be consummated at a closing (referred to herein as the "Closing") to be held at the offices of Buyer in Tampa, Florida, on September 1, 2004 (the "Closing Date"). The purchase and sale shall be deemed effective for all purposes as of the close of business on the Closing Date (the "Effective Time").

> *Notice the similarities and differences between these closing mechanics and the closing mechanics in the stock sale described earlier in this chapter.*

Section 2.02 Actions to be Taken at the Closing. At the Closing, the Parties will take the following actions and deliver the following documents:

(a) Seller will execute and deliver to Buyer a Bill of Sale and Assignment Agreement . . . together with such other instruments of conveyance and evidence of the transfer of title to the Purchased Assets from Seller to Buyer as Buyer may reasonably request.

(b) Buyer will deliver to Seller certificates representing 625,000 shares of Buyer's common stock in exchange for the Purchased Assets.

(c) Buyer will deliver to Seller in the Form in Exhibit an agreement that in the invent of insolvency of the Buyer at any point until through and including December 31, 2006 the Seller can return all common shares of the Buyer received by the Seller and receive all of the assets the Seller originally conveyed [plus other specified protections for Seller].

(d) Buyer will deliver to Seller an Assumption and Release Agreement. . . .

(e) Buyer and Seller will each deliver to the others (to the extent applicable), all consents and approvals (including, without limitation, resolutions and incumbency certificates of the directors and officers of each, and necessary minutes or resolutions of the stockholders of each) required for each party to enter into this Agreement and consummate the transactions described herein.

All instruments of conveyance shall be free of all Encumbrances except for any liens securing the Assumed Obligations and shall be in form and content reasonably acceptable to counsel for the Buyer and the Seller.

. . .

Section 2.04 Transfer of Possession. Simultaneously with the Effective Time, the Seller shall give the Buyer full possession and enjoyment of the Purchased Assets.

. . .

ARTICLE III

Intentionally left blank.

ARTICLE IV
REPRESENTATIONS AND WARRANTIES OF BUYER

The Buyer represents and warrants to the Seller and covenants with the Seller, as follows:

Section 4.01 Due Organization. Buyer is a corporation duly organized, validly existing and in good standing under the laws of Delaware and has all necessary power and authority to conduct its business in the manner in which its business is currently being conducted. Each subsidiary of Buyer is a corporation duly organized, validly existing and in good standing under the laws of its place of incorporation and has all necessary power and authority to conduct its business in the manner in which its business is currently being conducted.

Section 4.02 Capitalization, Etc. The capitalization of Buyer consists of 50,000,000 shares of voting common stock, of which at Closing, less than 25,000,000 will be issued and outstanding and 5,000,000 shares of preferred stock, of which none are issued and outstanding. The relative rights and preferences of any of the preferred stock have not been established. All of the outstanding shares of Buyer's common stock have been duly authorized and validly issued, and are fully paid and non-assessable, and none of such shares is subject to any repurchase option or restriction on transfer, except as provided in Schedule 4.02. All of such shares have been issued in compliance with applicable securities laws. . . .

Section 4.03 Financial Statements. Buyer has delivered to Seller [accurate and complete financial statements].

Section 4.04 Tax Matters. Except as set forth on Schedule 4.04, all Tax Returns required to be filed by or on behalf of Buyer or any of its subsidiaries with any Governmental Body [have been accurately filed].

Section 4.05 Insurance. Buyer and each of its subsidiaries has maintained, and will maintain insurance coverage against liability, loss or casualty with respect to its operations. A description of all such policies is hereto attached as Schedule 4.05.

Section 4.06 Legal Proceedings. Except as set forth on Schedule 4.06, there is no pending Legal Proceeding, and, to the best of the knowledge of Buyer, no Person has threatened to commence any Legal Proceeding: (i) that involves Buyer, any subsidiary of Buyer, or any of the assets owned or used by Buyer or its subsidiaries and which, if decided against Buyer or the subsidiaries, would have a Material Adverse Effect on the financial condition, business or properties of Buyer or the subsidiary; or (ii) that challenges, or that may have the effect of preventing, delaying, making illegal or otherwise interfering with any of the transactions contemplated by this Agreement.

Section 4.07 Assets. Buyer and its subsidiaries have good, valid and marketable title to all assets shown on the most recent Buyer Financial Statements, free and clear of any liens, except as disclosed on Schedule 4.07. . . .

Section 4.08 Intentionally left blank

Section 4.09 Compliance with Laws. To the best knowledge of Buyer, it and each of its subsidiaries has at all times conducted its business in compliance with all applicable laws. . . .

Section 4.10 Guarantees. Neither Buyer nor any of its subsidiaries has guaranteed or pledged any assets with respect to any obligation or indebtedness of any Person or Entity.

Section 4.11 Authority; Binding Nature of Agreement. Buyer has the absolute and unrestricted right, power and authority to enter into and to perform its obligations under this Agreement; the execution, delivery and performance by Buyer of this Agreement have been duly authorized by all necessary action on the part of Buyer and its board of directors; and the approval of Buyer's shareholders is not required. This Agreement constitutes the legal, valid and binding obligation of Buyer, enforceable against it in accordance with its terms. . . .

Section 4.12 Non-Contravention. Neither (i) the execution delivery or performance of this Agreement or any of the other agreements referred to in this

Agreement, nor (ii) the consummation of any of the transactions contemplated by this Agreement, will directly or indirectly (with or without notice or lapse of time) [contravene or conflict with any applicable law, contract, or other legal document or finding].

. . .

Section 4.13 Environmental Matters.

(a) Buyer and each of its subsidiaries has complied with and is in compliance with all [applicable environmental laws], except to the extent that noncompliance with any Environmental Law, either singly or in the aggregate, does not and would not have a Material Adverse Effect[.]

. . .

Section 4.14 Significant Customers; Material Contracts and Commitments. Schedule 4.14 hereto contains an accurate list of (i) all significant customers of Buyer . . . and (ii) all material contracts, commitments, and leases to which Buyer or any of its subsidiaries is a party or by which it or its properties are bound. . . . Except to the extent set forth on Schedule 4.14 hereto, (i) none of Buyer's significant customers have canceled or substantially reduced or, to the knowledge of Buyer are currently attempting or threatening to cancel or substantially reduce their purchases of goods or services, (ii) Buyer and its subsidiaries have complied with its material commitments and obligations and are not in default under any of the Buyer Material Contracts and no notice of default has been received with respect to any thereof and (iii) there are no Buyer Material Contracts that were not negotiated at arm's length with third parties not affiliated with Buyer or any officer, director or stockholder of Buyer or its subsidiaries. No employees of Buyer or any of its subsidiaries are represented by any labor union or covered by any collective bargaining agreement and, to the best of Buyer's knowledge, no campaign to establish such representation is in progress. Buyer considers its relationship with its employees to be good.

Section 4.15 Employee Benefit Plans. All employee benefit plans, programs and policies (whether formal or informal, and whether maintained for the benefit of a single individual or more than one individual) [of Buyer are listed on Schedule 4.15 and are in compliance with law].

Section 4.16 Intellectual Property.

(a) Buyer owns, free and clear of any Encumbrance, or has the valid right to use all Intellectual Property . . . used by it and its subsidiaries in their respective businesses as currently conducted. . . .

Section 4.17 Software Licenses. Buyer has all necessary licenses to use all material third-party software used in Buyer's business, and Buyer's use of third-party software does not infringe the rights of any Person.

Section 4.18 Full Disclosure. This Agreement, and all documents delivered by Buyer to Seller in connection with the transactions contemplated herein, do not (i) contain any representation, warranty or information that is false or misleading with respect to any material fact, or (ii) omit to state any material fact necessary in order to make the representations, warranties and information contained and to be contained herein and therein not false or misleading.

Section 4.19 Valid Issuance. The Buyer common stock to be issued and delivered pursuant to the transactions contemplated herein will, when issued in accordance with the provisions of this Agreement, be validly issued, fully paid and nonassessable. . . .

ARTICLE V
REPRESENTATIONS AND WARRANTIES OF SELLER

Seller represents and warrants, to and for the benefit of Buyer and Buyer as follows as of the date hereof and as of the Closing Date:

> *The Buyer will demand representations and warranties about the business and the Seller as a company even though it is buying assets to ensure enforceability of the contract and that the business can be run as a going concern.*

Section 5.01 Due Organization. Seller is a corporation duly organized, validly existing and in good standing under the laws of the State of Illinois and has all necessary power and authority to conduct its business in the manner in which its business is currently being conducted.

Section 5.02 Financial Statements. Seller has delivered to Buyer [accurate and complete financial statements].

Section 5.03 Tax Matters. Except as set forth on Schedule 5.03, all Tax Returns required to be filed by or on behalf of Seller with any Governmental Body [have been accurately filed and all taxes have been paid].

Section 5.04 Insurance. Seller has maintained, and will maintain through the Closing Date, insurance coverage against liability, loss or casualty with respect to the operations of Seller. A description of all such policies is hereto attached as Schedule 5.04.

Section 5.05 Legal Proceedings. Except as set forth on Schedule 5.05, there is no pending Legal Proceeding, and, to the best of the knowledge of Seller, no Person has threatened to commence any Legal Proceeding: (i) that involves Seller or any of the assets owned or used by Seller and which, if decided against Seller, would have a Material Adverse Effect on the financial condition, business or properties of Seller; or (ii) that challenges, or that may have the effect of preventing, delaying, making illegal or otherwise interfering with any of the transactions contemplated by this Agreement.

Section 5.06 Assets. Seller has, and will have at the Closing, good, valid and marketable title to all of the Purchased Assets, free and clear of any liens, except as disclosed on Schedule 5.06. Seller has not sold, transferred, assigned or conveyed any of its right, title and interest, or granted or entered into any option to purchase or acquire any of its right, title or interest, in and to any of the Purchased Assets or its business. No third party has any option or right to acquire Seller's business or any of the Purchased Assets.

Section 5.07 Real Property. Seller owns no real property. Schedule 5.07 includes a complete list of the real property leased by Seller ("Seller Leased Real Property"). Seller has a valid leasehold interest in the Seller Leased Real Property and will deliver to Buyer at Closing a certificate confirming that such leases are in full force and effect.

Section 5.08 Compliance with Laws. To the best knowledge of Seller, it has at all time conducted its business in compliance with all applicable laws . . . [.]

Section 5.09 Authority; Binding Nature of Agreement. Subject only to the approval of its shareholders, Seller has the absolute and unrestricted right, power and authority to enter into and to perform its obligations under this Agreement; and the execution, delivery and performance by Seller of this Agreement has been duly authorized by all necessary action on the part of Seller and its board of directors. Subject to the approval of Seller's shareholders, this Agreement constitutes the legal, valid and binding obligation of Seller, enforceable against Seller in accordance with its terms. . . .

Section 5.10 Non-Contravention. Neither (i) the execution, delivery or performance of this Agreement or any of the other agreements referred to in this Agreement, nor (ii) the consummation of any of the transactions contemplated by this Agreement, will directly or indirectly (with or without notice or lapse of time) [contravene or conflict with any applicable law, contract or other legal document or finding].

. . .

Section 5.11 Environmental Matters.

(a) Seller has complied with and is in compliance with all [applicable environmental laws], except to the extent that noncompliance with any Environmental Law, either singly or in the aggregate, does not and would not have a Material Adverse Effect[.]

. . .

Section 5.12 Significant Customers; Material Contracts and Commitments. Schedule 5.13 hereto contains an accurate list of all material contracts [of Seller]. . . . Except to the extent set forth on Schedule 5.13 hereto, (i) Seller has complied with its material commitments and obligations and is not in default under any of the Seller Material Contracts and no notice of default has been received with respect to any thereof and (ii) there are no Seller Material Contracts that were not negotiated at arm's length with third parties not affiliated with Seller or any officer, director or stockholder of Seller. Seller is not bound by or subject to (and none of its respective assets or properties is bound by or subject to) any arrangement with any labor union. No employees of Seller are represented by any labor union or covered by any collective bargaining agreement and, to the best of Seller's knowledge, no campaign to establish such representation is in progress. Seller considers its relationship with its employees to be good.

Section 5.13 Intellectual Property.

(a) Seller owns, free and clear of any Encumbrance, or has the valid right to use all Intellectual Property . . . used by it in its business as currently conducted. . . .

Section 5.14 Software Licenses. Seller has all necessary licenses to use all material third-party software used in Seller's business, and Seller's use of third-party software does not infringe the rights of any Person.

Section 5.15 Full Disclosure. This Agreement, and all documents delivered by Seller to Buyer and Buyer in connection with the transactions contemplated herein, do not (i) contain any representation, warranty or information that is false or misleading with respect to any material fact, or (ii) omit to state any material fact necessary in order to make the representations, warranties and information contained and to be contained herein and therein not false or misleading. Buyer and Buyer have completed their due diligence investigation of Seller.

ARTICLE VI
CONDITIONS PRECEDENT TO OBLIGATIONS OF
BUYER AND BUYER

The obligations of Buyer and Buyer to consummate the transactions contemplated by this Agreement are subject to the satisfaction, at or prior to the Closing, of each of the following conditions:

Section 6.01 Accuracy of Representations. Each of the representations and warranties made by Seller in this Agreement and in each of the other agreements and instruments delivered to Buyer and Buyer in connection with the transactions contemplated by this Agreement shall have been accurate in all respects as of the date of this Agreement, and shall be accurate in all respects as of the Closing Date as if made on the Closing Date.

Section 6.02 Performance of Covenants. Each covenant or obligation that Seller is required to comply with or to perform at or prior to the Closing shall have been complied with and performed in all respects.

Section 6.03 Consents. All Consents required to be obtained in connection with the transactions contemplated by this Agreement shall have been obtained and shall be in full force and effect.

Section 6.04 Agreements and Documents. Buyer shall have received a certificate executed by Seller containing the representation and warranty of Seller that each of the representations and warranties set forth in Article V is accurate in all material respects as of the Closing Date as if made on the Closing Date and that the conditions set forth in Article VI have been duly satisfied.

Section 6.05 Additional Loans. Intentionally left blank.

ARTICLE VII
CONDITIONS PRECEDENT TO OBLIGATIONS OF SELLER

The obligations of Seller to consummate the transactions contemplated by this Agreement are subject to the satisfaction, at or prior to the Closing, of the following conditions:

Section 7.01 Accuracy of Representations. Each of the representations and warranties made by Buyer and Buyer in this Agreement and in each of the other agreements and instruments delivered to Seller in connection with the transactions contemplated by this Agreement shall have been accurate in all respects as of the date of this Agreement, and shall be accurate in all respects as of the Closing Date as if made on the Closing Date.

Section 7.02 Performance of Covenants. All of the covenants and obligations that Buyer or Buyer is required to comply with or to perform at or prior to the Closing shall have been complied with and performed in all respects.

Section 7.03 Consents. All Consents required to be obtained in connection with the transactions contemplated by this Agreement shall have been obtained and shall be in full force and effect.

Section 7.04 Agreements and Documents. Seller shall have received a certificate executed by each of Buyer and Buyer, and containing the representation and warranty of each that each of the representations and warranties set forth in Articles III and IV are accurate in all material respects as of the Closing Date as if made on the Closing Date and that the conditions set forth in Article VII have been duly satisfied.

ARTICLE VIII
SURVIVAL OF REPRESENTATIONS AND WARRANTIES; INDEMNIFICATION

Section 8.01 Survival of Representations and Warranties. All of the representations and warranties of Buyer and Seller contained in this Agreement shall survive the Closing and shall continue for a period of one year following the Closing Date.

Section 8.02 Seller Indemnity. Subject to the provisions of Section 8.04 hereof, Seller shall defend, indemnify and hold harmless Buyer (and their respective directors, officers, employees, agents, affiliates, successors and assigns) from and against any and all [losses related to the transaction]. . . .

ARTICLE IX
CONDUCT OF THE PARTIES AFTER CLOSING

Section 9.01 Cooperation. The Buyer and the Seller will cooperate upon and after the Closing Date in effecting the orderly transfer of the Purchased Assets to the Buyer. . . .

Section 9.02 Access to Books and Records. As long as the Buyer retains any books and records of Seller's business acquired by the Buyer hereunder, it will provide the Seller with reasonable access during customary business hours to such books and records . . . [.]

Section 9.03 Use of Name. The Seller shall discontinue the use of its name or any derivation thereof effective upon the Closing Date. Promptly after the Closing Date, the Seller shall change its corporate name to a name other than "STATE STREET CAFE AND PIZZERIA, INC." or any derivation thereof.

> *Notice that, in connection with buying the business, the Buyer wants to ensure that the trademark is entirely its own.*

Section 9.04 Repayment of Obligations. The Seller agrees to pay all of the Seller's liabilities and obligations (other than the Assumed Obligations). . . .

ARTICLE X
MISCELLANEOUS

. . .

Section 10.09 Governing Law; Venue.

. . .

(b) Any legal action or other legal proceeding relating to this Agreement or the enforcement of any provision of this Agreement shall be brought in or otherwise commenced in any state or federal court located in Hillsborough County, Florida.

. . .

Section 10.15 Board Appointment. Intentionally left blank.

Section 10.16 Share Combination. Intentionally left blank.

The parties hereto have caused this Agreement to be executed and delivered as of the date first above written.

[Signatures of Buyer and Seller]

EXHIBIT A
CERTAIN DEFINITIONS

For purposes of the Agreement (including this Exhibit A):

. . .

MATERIAL ADVERSE EFFECT. A violation or other matter will be deemed to have a "Material Adverse Effect" on a Person if such violation or other matter (considered together with all other matters that would constitute exceptions to the representations and warranties set forth in the Agreement or in any Closing Certificate but for the presence of "Material Adverse Effect" or other materiality qualifications, or any similar qualifications, in such representations and warranties) would have a material adverse effect on such Person's business, condition, assets, liabilities, operations, financial performance or prospects.

. . .

Notes and Questions

1. State statutes grant authority to business organizations to engage in asset purchase transactions. In this case, Blue Moon Group will be controlled by and subject to Delaware law, and State Street Café by and to Illinois law.

Next, applicable state law will describe the required shareholder and board approval in order for the transaction to take place. In Delaware, the first part of § 271 of the General Corporation Law outlines the following procedural requirements:

> Every corporation may at any meeting of its board of directors or governing body sell, lease or exchange all or substantially all of its property and assets, including its goodwill and its corporate franchises, upon such terms and conditions and for such consideration, which may consist in whole or in part of money or other property, including shares of stock in, and/or other securities of, any other corporation or corporations, as its board of directors or governing body deems expedient and for the best interests of the corporation, when and as authorized by a resolution adopted by the holders of a majority of the outstanding stock of the corporation entitled to vote thereon or, if the corporation is a nonstock corporation, by a majority of the members having the right to vote for the election of the members of the governing body, at a meeting duly called upon at least 20 days' notice. The notice of the meeting shall state that such a resolution will be considered.

What approvals are needed for the target to consummate the deal in the Blue Moon transaction? Typically, on the buyer side, only board approval is required. As with stock sales, the parties may elect to secure additional approvals as part of the deal.

2. State laws differ in one important respect when it comes to asset sale transactions. Under some state codes, target shareholders who do not vote in favor of the asset sale transaction (those who do not vote, or who vote against the transaction) are given so-called appraisal rights or dissenters' rights, even if the transaction is approved by a majority of shareholders. Appraisal rights entitle the "dissenting shareholders" to receive cash equal to the fair market value of the shares that they hold. In that way, the statute protects shareholders from receiving non-cash consideration or a less-than-fair price in the asset sale transaction. In general, in order

to receive appraisal rights, dissenting shareholders must give notice to the target company that they oppose the transaction and are going to demand the fair market value of their shares. Sometimes the target and dissenting shareholders will be able to work out a compromise; otherwise, the shareholders can file a claim in court. The court will then appraise the company and order payment to the dissenting shareholders. While this remedy appears to favor shareholders, in practice it is costly, time consuming, and sometimes the court-ordered remedy may be less valuable than the consideration paid in the transaction because the fair market value excludes any potential value to be realized by the synergy.

Illinois law grants appraisal rights like these to shareholders of the target in an asset sale. Had State Street Café been organized in Delaware, there would be no appraisal rights for its stockholders, as Delaware does not grant appraisal rights for asset sales. If you represent an entrepreneur, is it better to organize the new business in a state that grants appraisal rights in asset sale transactions, or in a state that does not?

3. Like stock sales, asset sales are mainly a matter of contract. The parties to the transaction will execute an asset purchase agreement, similar to the one above, which will contain the details of the transaction. Asset purchase agreements are often more complicated than stock purchase agreements because the acquirer must outline all of the individual assets that it is purchasing. Anything left out will not be transferred. In addition, the parties must agree to an allocation of the liabilities. In the Blue Moon example above, the agreement contains both "Assets" and "Excluded Assets." Can you see the difficulty in trying to specify which assets fall into which category? What provisions could the seller and the acquirer use that would protect and further their respective interests?

4. One key benefit of an asset purchase transaction for acquirers is that they can specify which assets they will purchase and which liabilities they will assume. This will save the acquirer from spending money on assets that it does not value, and it will also limit unforeseen liabilities. What drawbacks do you imagine in this structure, both for the acquirer and for the target?

5. One complication with asset purchase transactions is that some of the target's assets may be subject to contracts, permits, or other restrictions, and the target or acquirer may need to get permission from third parties to transfer the assets. In addition, it is often the case that some of the value in the business being purchased is in the contractual arrangements the target has in place, and absent a provision specifically permitting the target to assign a contract, the contract is not assignable without the consent of the third party. Third parties may see an asset sale transaction as an opportunity to renegotiate a contract, particularly if they are not comfortable with the buyer as a new contracting party. If you represent an entrepreneur who sees an asset sale as a potential exit strategy, what steps can you take to prepare the client's contracts for this possible outcome?

6. The purchase price is often one of the most contested parts of any M&A transaction. When the seller is a private company and there is no ready market value for the company, negotiations over purchase price can be particularly difficult. The companies will hire experts to determine the selling company's value, and the buyer and seller will negotiate purchase price. Lawyers will also need to consider several other aspects of the payment, such as the timing of the payments, the type of consideration, the tax treatment, the security of receiving the payments, and the client's liquidity or any other individual concerns.

Compare the payment type and payment schedules in the two agreements above (found in section 1.1 of the Wild Oats Agreement, and sections 1.01 through 1.04 of the Blue Moon Agreement). How do they differ? Which types of guarantees are built in for the seller and/or acquirer related to the purchase price?

7. Parties can agree to any form of consideration. We typically think of cash and shares of stock as consideration in M&A transactions, but consideration can include promissory notes, the assumption of liabilities, in-kind assets, the performance of services, or any combination thereof. Lawyers will want to understand their clients' interests when they negotiate the type of consideration. They will also need to understand the implications of paying with one type of consideration versus another. For example, if the acquirer offers securities as part of the consideration, then there will be specific valuation issues and securities laws concerns, as described later in this chapter. In addition, using stock to pay for the transaction could qualify the deal as a "tax-free reorganization," also discussed later in this chapter.

8. Where are the covenants in this agreement? What purpose do they serve?

9. What is the purpose of Articles VI and VII, and which provisions in those articles seem to be the most important?

10. The accuracy of the representations and warranties at closing is an important aspect for closing. Usually, the parties will qualify this portion with language such as "in all material respects," which is found in sections 6.04 and 7.04 of this agreement. The purpose of these qualifiers is to ensure that the agreement will not fall apart if some less important breaches come to light. If the parties are concerned about specific matters, lawyers should draft those provisions and not rely on the "in all material respects" language to cover the matter.

Many agreements contain a separate provision that if there are material adverse events (outside the representations and warranties and covenants) that affect the target, then the acquirer will have the opportunity to terminate the deal. This provision shifts risk from the buyer to the seller during the time period between the signing of the agreement and the closing.

It is easy to understand why a buyer would require a target to make representations and warranties about its business: the buyer wants to know what it is buying. In this contract, the buyer makes significant representations and warranties about the buyer's business in addition to the representations and warranties made by target. Why might the target have required these representations and warranties by the buyer?

11. After the deal has closed and consideration has been exchanged, the parties may have ongoing obligations to one another. Parties can outline their conduct after closing and also provide for the survival of representations and warranties and related indemnification. What challenges do you imagine lawyers face when they try to manage the parties' conduct post closing? Post closing, the parties will have less incentive to deal cooperatively with each other, and the acquirer may even run into difficulty locating the proper authority for the seller to assert its claims. Therefore, it is generally the acquirer who will ask for certain conditions or arrangements from the seller in the event that problems with the target company arise (though sometimes sellers will ask for indemnification as well). One important element will be the time frame of the seller's obligation post closing. In the agreement above, the parties agreed that the sellers would indemnify the acquirer for any breaches of representations and warranties for a period of one year post closing. The time period can be shorter or longer, and some acquirers may seek an indefinite term of indemnification for unidentified liabilities. Additionally, the acquirer may want to obtain some security that it will receive payment. There are several ways an acquirer can do

this, whether it is holding back a portion of the purchase price, putting money into escrow, obtaining security interests in assets, or getting third-party guarantees. The seller will want to cap this exposure, so the seller will want to negotiate the amount of recovery. How were these aspects of the deal handled in the contract above?

12. Several sections in the document are marked "Intentionally Left Blank." Why would a lawyer intentionally leave a section of a document blank? If you represent a client and the attorneys for the other side give you a draft of a document with certain provisions that are "intentionally left blank," what might you conclude about the document you have been given?

3. Merger

A merger is a transaction in which the target, sometimes called the "merging company" or the "disappearing company," merges with and into the acquiring company, often called the "surviving company." The target ceases to exist as a separate company, and the shareholders of the target receive consideration in the transaction. The contract below (and associated press release, included to give you a sense of the transaction before you dig deeper into the complex agreement) documents the acquisition of PayPal, Inc. by eBay Inc.

Since mergers are consummated under the provisions of applicable state statutes, the kinds of mergers we discuss in this book are called "statutory mergers." A simple merger of the type we are describing is called a "direct" (or "forward") merger, and can be diagrammed as follows:

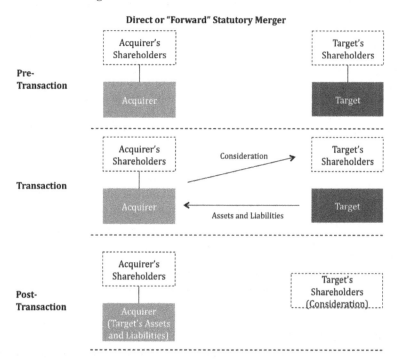

There are two other main types of statutory mergers, which are slightly more complicated than the simple direct merger described above. In a "forward triangular" merger, the target merges with and into a subsidiary of the acquirer, such that the target ceases to exist and the acquirer's subsidiary is the surviving company. In a "reverse triangular" merger, a subsidiary of the acquirer merges with and into the target, such that the subsidiary of the acquirer ceases to exist and the target is the surviving company. In both of these triangular structures, the result is that the business of the target (including all assets and liabilities) is in a wholly-owned subsidiary of the acquirer, and the owners of the target receive consideration.

EXHIBIT 99.3 TO EBAY INC. FORM 8-K
Filed July 8, 2002

San Jose and Mountain View, CA, July 8, 2002 — In a move that will help millions of Internet users buy and sell online, eBay Inc. (Nasdaq: EBAY; www.ebay.com), the world's online marketplace, today announced that it has agreed to acquire PayPal, Inc. (Nasdaq: PYPL; www.paypal.com), the global payments platform. The acquisition, which is subject to various stockholder, government and regulatory approvals, is expected to close around year-end 2002.

A natural extension of eBay's trading platform, the acquisition supports the company's mission to create an efficient global online marketplace. Payment is a vital function in trading on eBay and integrating PayPal's functionality into the eBay platform will fundamentally strengthen the user experience and allow buyers and sellers to trade with greater ease, speed and safety.

The agreement also should benefit eBay shareholders. The combination of the two networks should expand both platforms while minimizing shared operational costs. Strengthening the marketplace and realizing the efficiencies made possible by the acquisition will increase the value of both businesses.

eBay will acquire all of the outstanding shares of PayPal in a tax-free, stock-for-stock transaction using a fixed exchange ratio of 0.39 eBay shares for each PayPal share. Based on eBay's stock price on July 5, 2002, the acquisition is valued at $1.5 billion. According to preliminary estimates, the recognized purchase price is also expected to include approximately $18 million for acquisition-related costs. The calculation of the final purchase price may vary significantly from these estimates, and will depend upon a number of factors, including the length of time necessary to close the transaction, and the value of eBay stock at closing.

The transaction is expected to be immediately accretive to eBay's pro-forma earnings per share. On a GAAP basis the company will initially incur incremental charges for stock-based compensation and amortization of intangible assets of approximately $4 million and $9 million per quarter, respectively. Accordingly, eBay expects the transaction to be dilutive on a GAAP reported basis.

"eBay and PayPal have complementary missions. We both empower people to buy and sell online," said Meg Whitman, President and CEO of eBay. "Together we can improve the user experience and make online trading more compelling. We can also capture greater value from the e-commerce opportunities occurring both on and off our site."

"eBay and PayPal have built vibrant user networks on the Internet," said Peter Thiel, Founder and CEO of PayPal. "The beauty of this deal is that it will allow us to offer our communities new tools and added flexibility to do more business. Integrating our services is a win-win situation for millions of current and future online consumers."

PayPal, which will continue to operate as an independent brand, is a leading online payments solution. Approximately 60% of PayPal's business takes place on eBay, making it the most preferred electronic payment method among eBay users. The remaining 40% occurs primarily among small merchants who constitute a potential new audience for eBay. Likewise, eBay's community of 46 million users worldwide represents a growth opportunity for PayPal. eBay's current payment service, eBay Payments by Billpoint, will be phased out after the close of the transaction.

PayPal will continue to provide a variety of consumer services, including its popular Web Accept product, which makes it possible for independent online merchants to accept payment directly at their web sites. In view of the uncertain regulatory environment surrounding online gaming, eBay plans to phase out PayPal's gaming business after the transaction closes. Gaming providers who use PayPal will have ample opportunity to find alternative payment solutions.

. . .

ANNEX A TO EBAY INC. REGISTRATION STATEMENT ON FORM S-4/A
Filed August 28, 2002

AGREEMENT AND PLAN OF MERGER

AGREEMENT AND PLAN OF MERGER (hereinafter called this "Agreement"), dated as of July 7, 2002, among PAYPAL, INC., a Delaware corporation (the "Company"), EBAY INC., a Delaware corporation ("Parent"), and VAQUITA ACQUISITION CORP., a Delaware corporation and a wholly-owned subsidiary of Parent ("Merger Sub," with the Company and Merger Sub sometimes being hereinafter collectively referred to as the "Constituent Corporations").

RECITALS

WHEREAS, the respective boards of directors of each of Parent, Merger Sub and the Company have approved the merger of Merger Sub with and into the Company (the "Merger") and approved the Merger upon the terms and subject to the conditions set forth in this Agreement;

WHEREAS, the respective boards of directors of each of Parent and the Company have determined that the Merger is advisable and in the best interests of their respective companies and stockholders and accordingly have agreed to effect the Merger upon the terms and subject to the conditions set forth in this Agreement;

WHEREAS, it is intended that, for federal income tax purposes, the Merger shall qualify as a ["tax free"] reorganization [see discussion at the end of this chapter];

WHEREAS, in order to induce Parent and Merger Sub to enter into this Agreement, certain stockholders of the Company have each entered into a Stockholders Agreement with Parent with respect to the approval of the Merger and certain restrictions on the transfer of securities of the Company and Parent (collectively, the "Stockholders Agreements");

WHEREAS, in order to induce Parent and Merger Sub to enter into this Agreement, certain officers of the Company are simultaneously entering into employment, non-compete and non-solicitation agreements with Parent to become effective at the Effective Time (as defined below) (collectively, the "Employment Agreements"); and

WHEREAS, the Company, Parent and Merger Sub desire to make certain representations, warranties, covenants and agreements in connection with this Agreement.

NOW, THEREFORE, in consideration of the premises, and of the representations, warranties, covenants and agreements contained herein, the parties hereto agree as follows:

ARTICLE I
THE MERGER; CLOSING; EFFECTIVE TIME

> *Merger mechanics are typically more closely controlled by statute than stock sale or asset sale mechanics. The provisions in these sections are designed to comply with applicable state law while also providing a roadmap for completion of the transaction.*

1.1. The Merger. Upon the terms and subject to the conditions set forth in this Agreement, at the Effective Time (as defined in Section 1.3), Merger Sub shall be merged with and into the Company and the separate corporate existence of Merger Sub shall thereupon cease. The Company shall be the surviving corporation in the Merger (sometimes hereinafter referred to as the "Surviving Corporation"), and the separate corporate existence of the Company with all its rights, privileges, immunities, powers and franchises shall continue unaffected by the Merger, except as set forth in Article II. The Merger shall have the effects specified in the Delaware General Corporation Law, as amended (the "DGCL").

1.2. Closing. The closing of the Merger (the "Closing") shall take place (i) at the offices of Sullivan & Cromwell . . . as promptly as practicable . . . after the last to be fulfilled or waived of the conditions set forth in Article VII . . . or (ii) at such other place and time and/or on such other date as the Company and Parent may agree in writing (the "Closing Date").

1.3. Effective Time. As of the Closing Date, the Company and Parent will cause a Certificate of Merger (the "Delaware Certificate of Merger") to be executed, acknowledged and filed with the Secretary of State of Delaware as provided in Section 251 of the DGCL. The Merger shall become effective at the time when the Delaware Certificate of Merger has been duly filed with and accepted by the Secretary of State of Delaware (the "Effective Time").

ARTICLE II
CERTIFICATE OF INCORPORATION AND BY-LAWS OF
THE SURVIVING CORPORATION

2.1. The Certificate of Incorporation. The Amended and Restated Certificate of Incorporation of the Company as in effect immediately prior to the Effective

Time shall be the certificate of incorporation of the Surviving Corporation (the "Charter"), until duly amended as provided therein or by applicable law, except that Article IV of the Charter shall be amended to read in its entirety as follows: "The aggregate number of shares that the Corporation shall have the authority to issue is 1,000 shares of Common Stock, par value $1.00 per share."

2.2. The By-Laws. The by-laws of the Company in effect at the Effective Time shall be the by-laws of the Surviving Corporation (the "By-Laws"), until thereafter amended as provided therein or by applicable law.

ARTICLE III
OFFICERS AND DIRECTORS OF THE SURVIVING CORPORATION

> *When companies merge, it is important to explain who will be in charge when it is all over. This issue does not arise in the same way in an asset purchase or stock purchase, because it is assumed — absent some agreement to the contrary — that the buyer will be in charge. In this merger, there are two potential groups who could be in charge: the PayPal people and the eBay people. Based on the provisions below, can you conclude who is really the "buyer" here and who is the "seller"?*

3.1. Directors. The directors of Merger Sub at the Effective Time shall, from and after the Effective Time, be the directors of the Surviving Corporation until their successors have been duly elected or appointed and qualified or until their earlier death, resignation or removal in accordance with the Charter and the By-Laws.

3.2. Officers. The officers of the Company at the Effective Time shall, from and after the Effective Time, be the officers of the Surviving Corporation until their successors have been duly elected or appointed and qualified or until their earlier death, resignation or removal in accordance with the Charter and the By-Laws.

ARTICLE IV
EFFECT OF THE MERGER ON CAPITAL STOCK; EXCHANGE OF CERTIFICATES

4.1. Effect on Capital Stock. At the Effective Time, as a result of the Merger and without any action on the part of Parent, Merger Sub or the Company or their respective stockholders:

(a) Merger Consideration. Each share of the Common Stock, par value $0.001 per share, of the Company (a "Share" or, collectively, the "Shares") issued and outstanding immediately prior to the Effective Time (other than Shares owned by Parent, Merger Sub or any other direct or indirect subsidiary of Parent (collectively, the "Parent Companies") or Shares that are owned by the Company or any direct or indirect subsidiary of the Company and in each case not held on behalf of third parties (each, an "Excluded Share" and collectively, "Excluded Shares")) shall be converted into, and become exchangeable for 0.39 shares (the "Exchange Ratio"), of Common Stock, par value $0.001 per share, of Parent ("Parent Common Stock"). At the Effective Time, all Shares shall no longer be outstanding and shall be automatically cancelled and retired and shall cease to exist, and each certificate (a "Certificate") formerly representing any of such Shares (other than Excluded Shares) shall thereafter represent only the right to the merger consideration set forth in this Section 4.1(a) and the right, if any, to receive pursuant to Section 4.2(d) cash in lieu of fractional shares into which such Shares have been converted pursuant to this Section 4.1(a).

(b) Cancellation of Shares. Each Excluded Share shall, by virtue of the Merger and without any action on the part of the holder thereof, cease to be outstanding, shall be automatically cancelled and retired without payment of any consideration therefor and shall cease to exist.

(c) Merger Sub. At the Effective Time, each share of Common Stock, par value $0.001 per share, of Merger Sub issued and outstanding immediately prior to the Effective Time shall be converted into one share of Common Stock, par value $0.001 per share, of the Surviving Corporation.

4.2. Exchange of Certificates for Shares. [This section explains the procedural steps by which shareholders can exchange their shares of PayPal for shares of eBay in the transaction.]

4.3. Dissenters' Rights. In accordance with Section 262 of the DGCL[, which excepts publicly traded corporations from the dissenters' rights statute because the shares can be easily sold into the public market], no appraisal rights shall be available to holders of Shares in connection with the Merger.

. . .

ARTICLE V
REPRESENTATIONS AND WARRANTIES

5.1. Representations and Warranties of the Company. [Here, PayPal made a full set of representations and warranties as to its legal structure, its business and financial statements, its assets (including intellectual property), its liabilities and potential liabilities, and so on. The idea behind this language is the same as in the stock acquisition and asset acquisition agreements above: the buyer wants the seller to be legally responsible for the promises it is making as to the state of the business being sold.]

5.2. Representations and Warranties of Parent and Merger Sub. [Here, eBay and its newly created wholly-owned subsidiary make representations and warranties as to their ability to enter into the agreement and certain other aspects of their legal and business status. In deals where the consideration in the merger is all cash, the representations and warranties by the acquirer will be limited, since the selling shareholders mostly just care about the cash they will receive when the deal closes. In deals like this one, where the target shareholders receive stock of the acquirer, a more robust set of representations and warranties are appropriate since target shareholders want to be sure the consideration they are receiving is valuable.]

ARTICLE VI
COVENANTS

6.1. Interim Operations. The Company covenants and agrees as to itself and its Subsidiaries that, after the date hereof and prior to the Effective Time . . . :

(a) the business of it and its Subsidiaries shall be conducted in all material respects in the ordinary course consistent with past practice . . . ;

(b) it shall not (i) issue, sell, pledge, dispose of or encumber any capital stock owned by it in any of its Subsidiaries; (ii) amend its certificate of incorporation or by-laws; (iii) split, combine or reclassify its outstanding shares of capital stock; (iv) declare, set aside or pay any dividend payable in cash, stock or property in respect of any capital stock other than dividends from its direct or indirect wholly-owned Subsidiaries; or (v) repurchase, redeem or otherwise acquire, except (x) in connection with the Stock Plans and (y) for the repurchase of unvested Shares issued as restricted stock or issued upon the early exercise of options from departing employees at a repurchase price equal to the lower of the employees' purchase or exercise price or the fair market value of such Shares at the time of repurchase; or (vi) permit any of its Subsidiaries to purchase or otherwise acquire, any shares of its capital stock or any securities convertible into or exchangeable or exercisable for any shares of its capital stock;

(c) neither it nor any of its Subsidiaries shall (i) issue, sell, pledge, dispose of or encumber any shares of, or securities convertible into or exchangeable or exercisable for, or options, warrants, calls, commitments or rights of any kind to acquire, any shares of its capital stock of any class or any other property or assets (other than [specifically listed arrangements]); (ii) other than in the ordinary and usual course of business, transfer, lease, license, guarantee, sell, mortgage, pledge, dispose of or encumber any other property or assets or incur or modify any material indebtedness or other liability; (iii) make or authorize or commit for any capital expenditures other than as set forth on Schedule 6.1(c)(iii) hereto; (iv) make any acquisition of, or investment in, assets or stock of or other interest in, any other Person or entity; (v) enter into any Contract the terms of which contemplate material changes in the obligations, rights or responsibilities of any party thereto or any terms therein after giving effect to the Merger; (vi) enter into, modify, amend or terminate any Material Contract except in the ordinary course consistent with past practice or without the prior consent of Parent, which consent shall not be unreasonably withheld or delayed; (vii) enter into or amend any Contract for payment processing without the prior consent of Parent, which consent shall not be unreasonably withheld or delayed; (viii) enter into any non-competition Contracts or other Contracts that purport to limit in any respect either the type of business in which it (or, after giving effect to the Merger, the Parent or its Subsidiaries) may engage or the manner or locations in which any of them may so engage in any business; (ix) enter into any partnership, joint venture, strategic alliance, revenue or profit sharing agreement or similar arrangement with any Person; or (x) change or modify its line of business from the line of business in which it is engaged as of the date hereof or enter into any new line of business;

(d) neither it nor any of its Subsidiaries shall terminate, establish, adopt, enter into, make any new grants or awards under, amend or otherwise modify, any Benefit Plans, amend or modify the terms of any Company Option or increase the salary, wage, bonus or other compensation of any employees (except for (i) increases in salary, wages, bonuses or other compensation of non-executive employees made in the ordinary course of business consistent with past practice and (ii) subject to Section 6.1(c)(i), the grant of options to new employees of the Company pursuant to the Stock Plans);

(e) neither it nor any of its Subsidiaries shall (i) commence any litigation or arbitration proceeding or any regulatory or other governmental action or proceeding with or before any Governmental Entity other than ordinary contract and commercial litigation that the Company does not reasonably expect to result in total costs to the Company in excess of $300,000 and except for litigation to which the Parent consents, which consent shall not be unreasonably withheld or delayed, (ii) settle or compromise any material claims or litigation without the prior consent of Parent, which consent shall not be unreasonably withheld or delayed, or (iii) waive, release or assign any material rights or claims without the prior consent of Parent, which consent shall not be unreasonably withheld or delayed;

(f) neither it nor any of its Subsidiaries shall make any material Tax election or permit any material insurance policy naming it as a beneficiary or loss-payable payee to be cancelled or terminated except in the ordinary and usual course of business; and

(g) neither it nor any of its Subsidiaries will authorize or enter into an agreement to do any of the foregoing.

6.2. Acquisition Proposals. The Company agrees that neither it nor any of its Subsidiaries nor any of the officers and directors of it or its Subsidiaries shall, and that it shall not authorize or knowingly permit its and its Subsidiaries' employees, agents and representatives (including any investment banker, attorney or accountant retained by it or any of its Subsidiaries) to, directly or indirectly, initiate, solicit, knowingly encourage or facilitate any inquiries or the making of any proposal or offer with respect to a merger, reorganization, share exchange, consolidation or similar transaction involving, or any purchase of all or any material portion of the assets of, or 20% or more of the equity securities in, the Company or any of its Subsidiaries (any such proposal or offer being hereinafter referred to as an "Acquisition Proposal"). The Company further agrees that neither it nor any of its Subsidiaries nor any of the officers and directors of it or its Subsidiaries shall, and that it shall not authorize or knowingly permit its and its Subsidiaries' employees, agents and representatives (including any investment banker, attorney or accountant retained by it or any of its Subsidiaries) not to, directly or indirectly, engage in any negotiations concerning, or provide any confidential information or data to, or have any discussions with, any Person relating to an Acquisition Proposal, or otherwise entertain or knowingly facilitate any effort or attempt to make or implement an Acquisition Proposal; provided, however, that nothing contained in this Agreement shall prevent the Company or its Board of Directors or its officers, employees, agents or representatives from (A) complying with Rule 14e-2 promulgated under the Exchange Act with regard to an Acquisition Proposal or making any disclosure required by applicable law; (B) at any time prior, but not after, the Stockholders Meeting (as defined in Section 6.4) is convened, providing information in response to a request therefor by a Person who has made an unsolicited bona fide written Acquisition Proposal if the Board of Directors receives from the Person so requesting such information an executed confidentiality agreement on terms substantially similar to those contained in the Confidentiality Agreement (as defined in Section 9.7); (C) engaging in any negotiations or discussions with any Person who has made an unsolicited bona fide written Acquisition Proposal; or (D) recommending such an Acquisition Proposal to the stockholders of the Company, if and only to the extent that, in each such case referred to in clause (B), (C) or (D) above, the Board of Directors of the Company determines in good faith (after consultation with its outside legal counsel) that such action is necessary in order for its directors to comply with their respective fiduciary duties under applicable law and the Board of Directors determines in good faith (after consultation with its financial advisor) that such Acquisition Proposal is, or is reasonably likely to result in, a Superior Proposal. A "Superior Proposal" is an Acquisition Proposal that, if accepted, would be reasonably likely to be consummated (taking into account the legal, financial and regulatory aspects of the proposal) and would, if consummated, result in a transaction more favorable to the Company's stockholders from a financial point of view than the transaction contemplated by this Agreement. The Company agrees that it will immediately cease and cause to be terminated any existing activities, discussions or negotiations with any parties conducted heretofore with respect to any Acquisition Proposal. The Company agrees that it will take the necessary steps to promptly inform the individuals or entities referred to in the first sentence hereof of the obligations undertaken in this Section 6.2 and in the Confidentiality Agreement (as defined in Section 9.7). The Company agrees that it will notify Parent immediately if any such inquiries, proposals or offers are received by, any such information is requested from, or any such discussions or negotiations are sought to be initiated or continued with, any of its representatives indicating, in connection with such notice, the name of such Person and the material terms and conditions of any proposals or offers. The Company also agrees that it will promptly request each Person that has heretofore executed a confidentiality agreement in connection with its consideration of acquiring it or any of its Subsidiaries to return or destroy all confidential information heretofore furnished to such Person by or on behalf of it or any of its Subsidiaries.

6.3. Information Supplied. The Company and Parent each agrees, as to itself and its Subsidiaries, that none of the information expressly supplied or to be supplied by it or its Subsidiaries for inclusion or incorporation by reference in [the securities filings and shareholder mailings in connection with the Merger will contain any untrue statement of a material fact or omit to state any material fact required to be stated therein or necessary in order to make the statements therein, in light of the circumstances under which they were made, not misleading]. . . .

6.4. Stockholders Meeting. The Company will take, in accordance with applicable law and its certificate of incorporation and by-laws, all action necessary to call, hold and convene a meeting of holders of Shares (the "Stockholders Meeting") as promptly as reasonably practicable . . . to consider and vote upon the approval of this Agreement. Except on the determination of the occurrence of a Superior Proposal and during such time as there remains a Superior Proposal or as the Company's Board of Directors may determine in good faith (after consultation with its outside legal counsel) in order to comply with its fiduciary duties under applicable law, the Company's Board of Directors shall recommend such approval, the Company's Board of Directors shall not amend, modify, withdraw, condition or qualify such recommendation and shall take all lawful action to solicit such approval. . . .

6.5. Filings; Other Actions; Notification. (a) The Company and Parent shall promptly prepare and file with the SEC [all required filings.]

. . .

(d) The Company and Parent shall cooperate with each other and use (and shall cause their respective Subsidiaries to use) their respective commercially reasonable efforts to take or cause to be taken all actions, and do or cause to be done all things, necessary, proper or advisable on its part under this Agreement and applicable Laws to consummate and make effective the Merger and the other transactions contemplated by this Agreement as soon as practicable, including preparing and filing as promptly as practicable all documentation to effect all required notices, reports and other filings and to obtain as promptly as practicable all consents, registrations, approvals, permits and authorizations required to be obtained from any third party and/or any Governmental Entity in order to consummate the Merger or any of the other transactions contemplated by this Agreement; provided, however, that nothing in this Section 6.5 shall require, or be construed to require, Parent to proffer to, or agree to, sell or hold separate and agree to sell, before or after the Effective Time, any assets, businesses, or interest in any assets or businesses of Parent, the Company or any of their respective Affiliates (or to consent to any sale, or agreement to sell, by the Company of any of its assets or businesses) or to agree to any material changes or restriction in the operations of any such assets or businesses. Nothing in this Section shall require Parent or the Company to take any action which would be inconsistent with the fiduciary duties of its Board of Directors as such duties would exist under applicable law in the absence of this Section.

. . .

6.6. Taxation. Parent and Company intend the Merger to qualify as a ["tax-free"] reorganization. . . .

6.7. Access. Upon reasonable notice, and except as may otherwise be required by applicable law, the Company and Parent each shall (and shall cause its Subsidiaries to) afford the other's officers, employees, counsel, accountants and other authorized representatives ("Representatives") reasonable access, during normal business hours throughout the period prior to the Effective Time, to its properties, books, contracts and records and, during such period, each shall (and shall cause its Subsidiaries to) furnish promptly to the other all information concerning its business, properties and personnel as may reasonably be requested, provided that no investigation pursuant to this Section shall affect or be deemed to modify any representation or warranty made by the Company, Parent or Merger Sub, and provided, further, that the foregoing shall not require the Company or Parent to permit any inspection, or to disclose any information, that in the reasonable judgment of the Company or Parent, as the case may be, would result in the disclosure of any trade secrets of third parties or violate any of its obligations with respect to confidentiality if the Company or Parent, as the case may be, shall have used commercially reasonable efforts to obtain the consent of such third party to such inspection or disclosure. All requests for information made pursuant to this Section shall be directed to an executive officer of the Company or Parent, as the case may be, or such Person as may be designated by either of its officers, as the case may be. All such information shall be governed by the terms of the Confidentiality Agreement and applicable antitrust and trade regulation laws. Notwithstanding the generality of the foregoing, access to "Highly Confidential Information" (as defined in the Confidentiality Agreement) shall be restricted in accordance with the terms of such Confidentiality Agreement.

. . .

6.10. Publicity. The initial press release shall be a joint press release and thereafter the Company and Parent each shall consult with each other prior to issuing any press releases or otherwise making public announcements with respect to the Merger and the other transactions contemplated by this Agreement and prior to making any filings with any third party and/or any Governmental Entity with respect thereto, except as may be required by law or by obligations pursuant to any listing agreement with or rules of the Nasdaq National Market.

6.11. Benefits. [This section describes the consideration to be paid to holders of stock options and the ways in which other employee benefit plans will transition after the Merger.]

. . .

6.13. Indemnification; Directors' and Officers' Insurance. (a) From and after the Effective Time, Parent agrees that it shall indemnify and hold harmless each present and former director and officer of the Company, (when acting in such capacity) determined as of the Effective Time (the "Indemnified Parties"), against any costs or expenses (including reasonable attorneys' fees), judgments, fines, losses, claims, damages or liabilities (collectively, "Costs") incurred in connection with any claim, action, suit, proceeding or investigation, whether civil, criminal, administrative or investigative (collectively, "Claims"), arising out of matters existing or occurring at or prior to the Effective Time (including the transactions contemplated hereby), whether asserted or claimed prior to, at or after the Effective Time, to the fullest extent that the Company would have been permitted under Delaware law and any Claims arising from or related to the transactions contemplated hereby (and Parent shall also advance expenses as incurred to the fullest extent permitted under applicable law, provided the Person to whom expenses are advanced provides an undertaking to repay such advances if it is ultimately determined that such Person is not entitled to indemnification); and provided, further, that any determination required to be made with respect to whether an officer's or director's conduct complies with the standards set forth under Delaware law shall be made by independent counsel mutually selected by the Surviving Corporation and the Indemnified Party.

. . .

(c) Parent shall cause the Surviving Corporation to maintain the Company's existing officers' and directors' liability insurance ("D&O Insurance") for a period of six years after the Effective Time. . . .

(d) If the Surviving Corporation or any of its successors or assigns (i) shall consolidate with or merge into any other corporation or entity and shall not be the continuing or surviving corporation or entity of such consolidation or merger or (ii) shall transfer all or substantially all of its properties and assets to any individual, corporation or other entity, then, and in each such case, proper provisions shall be made so that the successors and assigns of the Surviving Corporation shall assume all of the obligations set forth in this Section.

. . .

6.15. Retention of Certain Employees. The Company and Parent shall work together in good faith using reasonable efforts to retain selected key employees of the Company and its Subsidiaries, including new employment terms as appropriate.

6.16. Conduct of Merger Sub. Parent will take all action necessary to cause Merger Sub to perform its obligations under this Agreement and to consummate the Merger on the terms and conditions set forth in this Agreement.

. . .

ARTICLE VII
CONDITIONS

7.1. Conditions to Each Party's Obligation to Effect the Merger. The respective obligation of each party to effect the Merger is subject to the satisfaction or waiver at or prior to the Effective Time of each of the following conditions:

(a) Stockholder Approval. This Agreement shall have been duly approved by holders of Shares constituting the Company Requisite Vote in accordance with applicable law and the certificate of incorporation and by-laws of the Company.

. . .

(c) Litigation. No court or Governmental Entity of competent jurisdiction shall have enacted, issued, promulgated, enforced or entered any statute, law, ordinance, rule, regulation, judgment, decree, injunction or other order (whether temporary, preliminary or permanent) that is in effect and restrains, enjoins or otherwise prohibits consummation of the Merger or the other transactions contemplated by this Agreement (collectively, an "Order"), and no Governmental Entity shall have instituted any proceeding seeking any such Order.

[All securities laws must have been complied with and all required federal and state filings made.]

7.2. Conditions to Obligations of Parent and Merger Sub. The obligations of Parent and Merger Sub to effect the Merger are also subject to the satisfaction or waiver by Parent at or prior to the Effective Time of the following conditions:

(a) Representations and Warranties. The representations and warranties of the Company set forth in this Agreement shall be true and correct as of the date of this Agreement (without regard to any materiality qualification contained in such representation or warranty) and as of the Closing Date (without regard to any materiality qualification contained in such representation or warranty) as though made on and as of the Closing Date (except to the extent any such representation or warranty expressly speaks as of an earlier date); provided, however, that notwithstanding anything herein to the contrary, this Section 7.2(a) shall be deemed to have been satisfied even if such representations or warranties are not so true and correct unless the failure of such representations or warranties to be so true and correct, individually or in the aggregate, has had, or is reasonably likely to have, a Company Material Adverse Effect. Parent shall have received a certificate signed on behalf of the Company by the President of the Company to such effect.

(b) Performance of Obligations of the Company. The Company shall have performed in all material respects all obligations required to be performed by it under this Agreement at or prior to the Closing Date, and Parent shall have received a certificate signed on behalf of the Company by the President of the Company to such effect.

(c) Absence of Certain Changes. Since the date hereof, there shall not have been any change in the financial condition, properties, prospects, business or results of operations of the Company and its Subsidiaries or any development or combination of developments that, individually or in the aggregate, has had or is reasonably likely to have, individually or in the aggregate, a Company Material Adverse Effect.

(d) Regulatory Consents. [All necessary approvals, waivers, and consents must have been obtained, except where the failure to do so would not have a Company Material Adverse Effect.]

(e) Tax Opinion. Parent shall have received the opinion of Sullivan & Cromwell, counsel to Parent, dated the Closing Date, to the effect that the Merger will be treated for Federal income tax purposes as a ["tax-free" reorganization.]

. . .

7.3. Conditions to Obligation of the Company. The obligation of the Company to effect the Merger is also subject to the satisfaction or waiver by the Company at or prior to the Effective Time of the following conditions:

(a) Representations and Warranties. The representations and warranties of Parent and Merger Sub set forth in this Agreement shall be true and correct as of the date of this Agreement (without regard to any materiality qualification contained in such representation or warranty) and as of the Closing Date (without regard to any materiality qualification contained in such representation or warranty) as though made on and as of the Closing Date, (except to the extent any such representation and warranty expressly speaks as of an earlier date); provided, however, that notwithstanding anything herein to the contrary, this Section 7.3(a) shall be deemed to have been satisfied even if such representations or warranties are not so true and correct unless the failure of such representations or warranties to be so true and correct, individually or in the aggregate, has had, or is reasonably likely to have, a Parent Material Adverse Effect. The Company shall have received a certificate signed on behalf of Parent by the President of Parent and the President of Merger Sub to such effect.

(b) Performance of Obligations of Parent and Merger Sub. Each of Parent and Merger Sub shall have performed in all material respects all obligations required to be performed by it under this Agreement at or prior to the Closing Date, and the Company shall have received a certificate signed on behalf of Parent and Merger Sub by the President of Parent to such effect.

(c) Absence of Certain Changes. Since the date hereof, there shall not have been any change in the financial condition, properties, prospects, business or results of operations of the Parent and its Significant Subsidiaries or any development or combination of developments that, individually or in the aggregate, has had or is reasonably likely to have, individually or in the aggregate, a Parent Material Adverse Effect.

(d) Regulatory Consents. [All necessary approvals, waivers, and consents must have been obtained, except where the failure to do so would not have a Parent Material Adverse Effect.]

(e) Tax Opinion. The Company shall have received the opinion of Kirkland & Ellis, counsel to the Company, dated the Closing Date, to the effect that the Merger will be treated for Federal income tax purposes as a ["tax-free" reorganization.]

(f) Nasdaq National Market Listing. The shares of Parent Common Stock issuable to the Company stockholders and the shares of Parent Common Stock issuable pursuant to the Company Options and Company Warrants assumed by Parent pursuant to this Agreement shall have been authorized for listing on the Nasdaq National Market upon official notice of issuance.

. . .

ARTICLE VIII
TERMINATION

> *See Note 5 following this contract for more discussion of termination. The termination fee in section 8.5 is sometimes referred to as a "breakup fee."*

8.1. Termination by Mutual Consent. This Agreement may be terminated and the Merger may be abandoned at any time prior to the Effective Time, whether before or after the approval by stockholders of the Company referred to in Section 7.1(a), by mutual written consent of the Company and Parent by action of their respective Boards of Directors.

8.2. Termination by Either Parent or the Company. This Agreement may be terminated and the Merger may be abandoned at any time prior to the Effective Time by action of the Board of Directors of either Parent or the Company if (i) the

Merger shall not have been consummated by December 31, 2002 . . . ; provided, however, that [the date can be extended in certain enumerated circumstances relating to the antitrust laws] (the "Termination Date"); . . . (ii) the approval of the Company's stockholders required by Section 7.1(a) shall not have been obtained at a meeting duly convened therefor or at any adjournment or postponement thereof; or (iii) any Order permanently restraining, enjoining or otherwise prohibiting consummation of the Merger shall become final and non-appealable. . . .

8.3. Termination by the Company. This Agreement may be terminated and the Merger may be abandoned at any time prior to the Effective Time, whether before or after the approval by stockholders of the Company referred to in Section 7.1(a), by action of the Board of Directors of the Company if there has been a breach of any representation, warranty, covenant or agreement made by Parent or Merger Sub in this Agreement, or any such representation and warranty shall have become untrue after the date of this Agreement, such that Section 7.3(a) or 7.3(b), as applicable, would not be satisfied and such breach or condition is not curable or, if curable, is not cured within 30 days after written notice thereof is given by the Company to Parent.

8.4. Termination by Parent. This Agreement may be terminated and the Merger may be abandoned at any time prior to the Effective Time by action of the Board of Directors of Parent if (i) the Board of Directors of the Company shall have withdrawn or adversely modified its approval or recommendation of this Agreement or (ii) there has been a breach of any representation, warranty, covenant or agreement made by the Company in this Agreement, or any such representation and warranty shall have become untrue after the date of this Agreement, such that Section 7.2(a) or 7.2(b), as applicable, would not be satisfied and such breach or condition is not curable or, if curable, is not cured within 30 days after written notice thereof is given by Parent to the Company.

8.5. Effect of Termination and Abandonment. (a) In the event of termination of this Agreement and the abandonment of the Merger pursuant to this Article VIII, this Agreement (other than as set forth in Section 9.1) shall become void and of no effect with no liability on the part of any party hereto . . . ; provided, however, except as otherwise provided herein, no such termination shall relieve any party hereto of any liability or damages resulting from any willful breach of this Agreement.

(b) If this Agreement is terminated by Parent pursuant to Section 8.4(i) in the case of a withdrawal or adverse notification of the Company's Board of Directors' approval or recommendation of this Agreement in the absence of an Acquisition Proposal, then the Company shall promptly, but in no event later than two days after the date of such termination, pay Parent a termination fee of $5,000,000 and shall promptly, but in no event later than two days after being notified of such by Parent, pay all of the charges and expenses, including those of the Exchange Agent, incurred by Parent or Merger Sub in connection with this Agreement and the transactions contemplated by this Agreement, in each case payable by wire transfer of same day funds.

(c) In the event that an Acquisition Proposal shall have been made to the Company or any of its Subsidiaries or any of its stockholders or any Person shall have publicly announced an intention (whether or not conditional) to make an Acquisition Proposal with respect to the Company or any of its Subsidiaries and thereafter this Agreement is terminated by either Parent or the Company . . . and thereafter the Company enters into any agreement to consummate a transaction or series of transactions which, had such agreement been proposed or negotiated during the term of this Agreement, would have constituted an Acquisition Proposal (each, a "Company Acquisition Agreement"), which is publicly announced within twelve (12) months after the termination of this Agreement and is consummated within eighteen (18) months after the termination of this Agreement . . . , then the Company shall, contemporaneously with such consummation, pay Parent a termination fee of $45,000,000 and shall promptly, but in no event later than two days after being notified of such by Parent, pay all of the charges and expenses, including those of the Exchange Agent, incurred by Parent or Merger Sub in connection with this Agreement and the transactions contemplated by this Agreement, in each case payable by wire transfer of same day funds.

. . .

ARTICLE IX
MISCELLANEOUS AND GENERAL

. . .

9.9. Obligations of Parent and of the Company. Whenever this Agreement requires a Subsidiary of Parent to take any action, such requirement shall be deemed to include an undertaking on the part of Parent to cause such Subsidiary to take such action. Whenever this Agreement requires a Subsidiary of the Company to take any action, such requirement shall be deemed to include an undertaking on the part of the Company to cause such Subsidiary to take such action and, after the Effective Time, on the part of the Surviving Corporation to cause such Subsidiary to take such action.

. . .

IN WITNESS WHEREOF, this Agreement has been duly executed and delivered by the duly authorized officers of the parties hereto as of the date first written above.

[Signatures of Company, Parent, and Merger Sub]

Notes and Questions

1. Although the transaction is billed as an "acquisition" of PayPal by eBay, eBay does not actually purchase shares of PayPal stock or PayPal assets, as was done in the Wild Oats and Blue Moon transactions. Rather, eBay acquires PayPal through a statutory merger. Which of the merger structures described in the introductory paragraphs to this section (A.3 Merger) of the chapter was used? Diagram the transaction.

2. The stock and asset purchase transactions we read about earlier in the chapter are authorized by state statute, and must be conducted in accordance with the statute, but the transactions are consummated through a contract among the parties. Mergers are also authorized by state statutes and must be conducted in accordance with the statute, but they are consummated through by operation of law upon the filing of a document with the applicable secretary of state.

3. In Delaware, mergers must be approved by the board of directors and a majority of the shareholders of both constituent companies. In light of these approval requirements, can you think of a strategic reason why the eBay-PayPal transaction was structured as a triangular merger, rather than a direct merger?

4. What is the difference between a "covenant" (Article VI) and a "condition" (Article VII)? Which of the covenants seem most important to the deal, or the most risky, from PayPal's perspective? Which conditions?

5. Article VIII explains when the merger transaction can be terminated prior to consummation, and outlines certain financial consequences when the deal is terminated in particular situations. What effect might these financial consequences have on PayPal if it is seeking a better offer from another buyer? Are there circumstances in which a better offer could or should be accepted by PayPal?

6. Under section 9.9, eBay and PayPal agree to cause their subsidiaries to do any actions those subsidiaries are required to do under the contract. What loophole were the drafting attorneys trying to close with this provision? Why would the eBay and PayPal lawyers draft the contract in this manner, rather than just having the subsidiaries become parties to the contract and agree themselves that they would take the required actions?

4. *Additional Considerations*

In addition to the contract and business entity law concerns discussed above, there are several other areas that are important to M&A deals. An entrepreneur's lawyer must be aware of fiduciary duties, tax law, and securities law, all of which come into play when advising clients on the deal.

a.   **Fiduciary Duties**

Many M&A and business law textbooks focus on the fiduciary duties of the contracting parties in an M&A deal. As a practical matter, and notwithstanding the Trados case that opened this chapter, very few private M&A deals wind up involving any kind of litigation at all, let alone disputes actually arising because of fiduciary duty violations. This pattern is especially true in entrepreneurial transactions where the seller usually controls the business and all important decision making. That said, attorneys must be aware of these issues to ensure that throughout the process the parties avoid flagrant fiduciary duty violations, as they are an easy basis on which an unusually dissatisfied party in a deal can bring a lawsuit.

As you have likely learned in Business Associations or another course, state law, mostly common law, governs the legal duties of fiduciaries. As discussed in Trados, the "business judgment rule," "enhanced scrutiny," and "entire fairness" are the standards of review typically applied to director actions. In M&A deals, the business judgment rule may not apply and the board's action may be subject to a higher level of scrutiny. In some states, the business judgment rule does not apply in an M&A deal where there is a change in control of the company, and enhanced scrutiny is the standard. Furthermore, the court imposes an obligation on the sellers to obtain the highest price available for shareholders in certain circumstances. Where directors face a conflict of interest in a transaction, as in Trados, the entire fairness standard can apply.

All of these matters are covered in law school M&A or other business law courses, but for the entrepreneur's lawyer it is important to understand that fiduciary duties are at play in M&A transactions, and boards must be appropriately counseled to ensure that they meet the applicable standards of conduct.

b.   Tax Impact

The tax impact is often the most important factor for the parties when they decide how to structure the deal. An M&A deal can be structured in one of four ways: a taxable stock purchase, a taxable sale of assets, a taxable merger, or a tax-deferred reorganization.

In a taxable stock purchase deal, the target's shareholders will pay tax on the difference between their basis in their stock (typically the purchase price they paid for the stock) and the consideration paid by the acquirer for their stock. Because the transaction is between the target's shareholders and the acquirer, the target company does not pay taxes on the transaction. The acquirer does not pay taxes on the transaction, and it will receive the target company's basis in its assets, unless it is eligible to make a special election under the Internal Revenue Code to receive the assets on a so-called step-up basis (which means the basis of the assets rises to the market value at the time of the purchase). This latter option is appealing to buyers because a higher basis in the assets means a lower tax paid on the eventual sale of those assets.

In a taxable asset purchase, the target company will pay taxes on the difference between the tax basis of the assets sold and the consideration that the target received, plus any liabilities assumed by the buyer. For the acquirer, the asset purchase is not a taxable event. The acquirer will receive the assets and the basis in the assets equal to the purchase price plus liabilities it has assumed. If the target company liquidates after the transaction is consummated, then the company's shareholders will receive the proceeds from the sale and be taxed on their share of the proceeds, calculated as the difference between the shareholders' basis in their stock (typically the purchase price they paid for the stock) and the value of the consideration received from the liquidation. Depending on the target company's circumstances, this double taxation may be unfavorable and result in a smaller gain after tax for the shareholders. In a taxable merger, the tax outcome is the same as an asset sale and then liquidation. Both the target company and the target shareholders are taxed, and the acquirer receives the target company at the basis of the purchase price plus liabilities.

The Internal Revenue Code also allows for so-called tax-free reorganizations, which provide for tax deferral if a transaction meets certain criteria. In essence, a transaction can be considered "tax-free" if the owners of the business being sold receive ownership in the purchaser as a substantial portion of the sale consideration. The effect of a tax-free reorganization is that the target shareholders do not recognize a gain or a loss on the transaction until they sell the acquirer's stock. Taxes are not avoided, but they are postponed. If the shareholders receive a combination of stock and other consideration, then the other consideration is taxed at the time of sale and the acquirer's stock is taxed when sold.

Given the complexity of the rules governing the tax treatment of these transactions, and the fact that every business deal is different, most attorneys for entrepreneurs enlist the help of an accountant or tax attorney (or often both) who can give detailed advice on this aspect of the deal.

c.   Federal and State Securities Laws

Federal and state securities laws may cover M&A transactions as well. The two most common ways in which the securities laws will impact a transaction are the following: First, if the consideration is an investment security, the securities laws will dictate rules about whether and how the securities need to be registered. Second, if either the acquirer or target is a public company, the securities laws will require public disclosures about the transaction. See Chapter 5 for a discussion of securities laws in the context of the issuance of equity by a company.

5.   *Preparing Clients for an Exit*

There is considerable work in preparing a client for an exit. In addition to counseling a client about the advisability and timing of an exit, you will need to counsel them on possible structures for an exit and strategies for finding the right buyer or other partner. In addition, diligent, careful representation from the early stages of a business, including keeping up with government filings and maintaining good files, are essential. That said, it is not uncommon to take on a client where preparing for an exit requires considerable "clean up" of the files — finding executed versions of documents, organizing disorganized files, tracking down and verifying a capitalization table, and so on.

PREPARING YOUR CLIENT FOR A BUSINESS SALE
Terry Silver, The Legal Intelligencer (2014)

In your capacity as a corporate or transactional attorney, you have probably represented clients seeking your advice about the sale of their business. The first, and most important, question to ask: Is the business ready for sale? Business owners often decide to sell before they give thought about preparing for the sale. When considering this question, some of the issues to take into account include:

- Has the balance sheet been cleaned up of possible worthless and obsolete assets? From furniture and equipment no longer in use to outdated inventory, businesses must identify and get rid of worthless and obsolete assets.
- Are the business records in good condition, supportable and able to stand up to the buyer's due diligence? It is imperative the business records score a high grade in due diligence, as this promotes the buyer's confidence.
- Does the business have a mid- to long-term facility commitment? Having a fixed rent for a number of years will enhance value.
- Is there a plan to cut back on capital expenditures? Ownership should determine whether anticipated capital expenditures will be returned as part of the sale price. If not, holding the cash is probably preferable.
- Are all equity owners in favor of a sale? This question seems like a no-brainer, but you would be surprised. This question must be asked.
- Has the profit and loss statement been optimized? Preparing for sale may mean canceling planned expenditures and increasing revenue to the extent possible, in order to maximize current profit.
- Have extraordinary or non-recurring expenses been identified or controlled? Historical financial statements must be normalized to account for

any extraordinary items. Examples may be a casualty loss, litigation, bad debts or cost of moving.

- Have the owners considered those from the current workforce (including the owners) who are best suited to continue post-purchase, and for how long? Ownership needs to adopt a realistic timeline during which the buyer will require the continuation of employment of specific managers and owners.
- What housekeeping is needed, such as reducing nonproductive workforce and ensuring all business documents are up to date and fully executed? The devil is in the details.
- Are financial statements prepared by an independent CPA firm? The quality of the company's financial statements and the reputation of the CPA firm will have an impact on due diligence. Consideration should be given to upgrading the financial statement level to a review or an audit.

. . .

B. GOING PUBLIC — THE INITIAL PUBLIC OFFERING

An "initial public offering" is exactly what it sounds like: the first sale by a company of its shares to the public. Following the IPO, a company becomes a "public" reporting company with "publicly traded" securities — meaning that the company is required to make periodic public disclosures about its business and that its securities can be legally traded on the public market. Companies cannot just on their own decide to sell securities to the public and then sell them. Rather, the process is highly complex and is governed by federal securities laws.

A great challenge for lawyers representing entrepreneurs is the popular, but inaccurate, perception that an entrepreneur can "take my company public" shortly after founding the business and exit for a significant cash payment. Even when counseled that a company sale transaction is a vastly more common and practical exit strategy for most entrepreneurial ventures, clients continue to have stars in their eyes about the "IPO."

Clients often fail to see the drawbacks of going public. The IPO process itself is expensive and time-consuming, and the ongoing reporting and governance requirements are costly. Public companies lose the ability to keep many aspects of their business private due to securities law disclosure requirements. They are also a magnet for lawsuits (both baseless and meritorious), and the directors and officers of public companies are targets for suits alleging fault with their actions in running the business or compliance with securities laws. Board composition shifts to include more independent directors, which can annoy entrepreneurs who value control. There can even be a psychological effect, since the ever-present market reporting can shift management decision making in reaction to the increased emphasis on stock price, short-term earnings, and reported earnings. New realities and motivations may affect business decisions and allocations of resources.

There is, however, a significant and, in some cases, overriding legitimate business reason why a company might choose to "go public." As a general rule, public markets can provide larger amounts of money, with fewer strings attached, than investments from other sources. While venture capitalists may demand significant control over the business and preferred stock entitling them to a disproportionate share of company value, the public owns common stock with no economic or governance-based bells and whistles.

The rough timeline for an IPO is as follows:

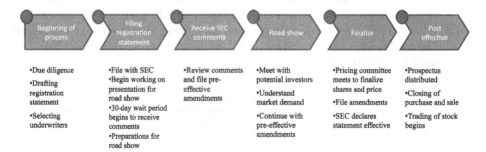

Once management decides that a company is ready for an IPO, it must find "underwriters" who agree. Underwriters are broker-dealers who buy the shares from the company and then sell them to the general public. The lawyer for an entrepreneur who hopes to have an IPO someday does well to make the company orderly from the start, so that by the time it seeks underwriters all the appropriate corporate documents (including board meeting minutes, documentation of all prior equity and debt transactions, and so on) are complete and in good order. As the time for seeking underwriters approaches, company counsel will work with the investors and their lawyers to simplify the capital structure as much as possible.

After underwriters are selected, the company will prepare the registration statement to be filed with the Securities and Exchange Commission. The key piece of the registration statement is the prospectus, which outlines information for potential buyers of the company's securities. The registration statement is typically amended many times in response to comments from the SEC, which are designed to ensure potential investors receive all information required under applicable regulations.

The underwriters next conduct a "road show," in which they travel around the country with management to convince investors they should buy securities as part of the initial public offering, and to gauge the market's view of the appropriate pricing for the securities. The SEC then declares the registration statement effective, and the securities are priced and sold to the public.

OPENTABLE INC. PROSPECTUS FILED PURSUANT TO RULE 424(B)(1)
Filed May 21, 2009

. . .

PROSPECTUS SUMMARY

This summary highlights information contained elsewhere in this prospectus and does not contain all of the information that you should consider in making your investment decision.

Before investing in our common stock, you should carefully read this entire prospectus, including our consolidated financial statements and the related notes included in this prospectus and the information set forth under the headings "Risk Factors" and "Management's Discussion and Analysis of Financial Condition and Results of Operations."

Our Company

We provide solutions that form an online network connecting reservation-taking restaurants and people who dine at those restaurants. Our solutions for restaurants include our Electronic Reservation Book, or ERB, which combines proprietary software and computer hardware that computerizes restaurant host-stand operations and replaces traditional pen-and-paper reservation books. Our ERB streamlines and enhances a number of business-critical functions and processes for restaurants, including reservation management, table management, guest recognition and email marketing. The ERBs at our restaurant customers connect via the Internet to form an online network of restaurant reservation books. Our solutions for diners include our popular restaurant reservation website, www.opentable.com, which enables diners to find, choose and book tables at restaurants on the OpenTable network in real time, overcoming the inefficiencies associated with the traditional process of reserving by phone. Restaurants pay us a one-time installation fee for onsite installation and training, a monthly subscription fee for the use of our software and hardware and a fee for each restaurant guest seated through online reservations. Our online reservation service is free to diners.

We initially focused on acquiring a critical mass of local restaurant customers in four metropolitan areas: Chicago, New York, San Francisco and Washington, D.C. These markets have since developed into active, local networks of restaurants and diners that continue to grow. We have applied and continue to apply the same fundamental strategy in developing and penetrating our other markets. As of March 31, 2009, the OpenTable network included approximately 10,000 OpenTable restaurant customers spanning all 50 states as well as select markets outside of the United States. Since our inception in 1998, we have seated approximately 100 million diners through OpenTable reservations, and during the three months ended March 31, 2009, we seated an average of approximately three million diners per month. For the twelve months ended December 31, 2007 and 2008, our revenues were $41.1 million and $55.8 million, respectively. For the twelve months ended December 31, 2007 and 2008, our subscription revenues accounted for 55% and 54% of our total revenues, respectively, and our reservation revenues accounted for 41% and 41% of our total revenues, respectively. For the three months ended March 31, 2008 and 2009, our subscription revenues accounted for 52% and 52% of our total revenues, respectively, and our reservation revenues accounted for 44% and 43% of our total revenues, respectively.

Market Opportunity

We target our solutions, by which we mean our ERB and the OpenTable website, to reservation-taking restaurants and diners, respectively. We believe based on our internal estimates that there are approximately 30,000 reservation-taking restaurants in North America that seat approximately 600 million diners through reservations annually, though this number fluctuates with economic and other conditions.

The ability of the restaurant industry to leverage the power of the Internet for reservation transactions has been inhibited by two key characteristics. First, the reservation-taking restaurant industry has been slow to computerize host-stand operations. Restaurant reservations historically have been largely handled by the traditional pen-and-paper reservation book, despite the inherent operational inefficiencies and potential for error. Second, the reservation-taking restaurant industry is highly fragmented, with independent restaurants and small, local restaurant groups comprising a significant majority of restaurant locations. The restaurant industry is also inherently local, making it time-consuming and costly to aggregate the breadth of local restaurant table inventory required to attract a critical mass of diners to make reservations online and create an online restaurant reservation network.

Historically, diners learned about restaurants through word of mouth and local print media, such as dining guides, newspapers and magazines. While diners continue to value personal recommendations, the Internet now puts a wealth of restaurant information at their fingertips. However, the ability to book restaurant reservations has largely been missing from online dining sources. Moreover, reserving by phone remains a highly inefficient and inconvenient process. In order for diners to fully embrace online restaurant reservations, they need real-time access to table inventory across a broad selection of local restaurants and the ability to instantly book confirmed reservations around-the-clock.

We believe the Internet can streamline operations and fill additional seats for reservation-taking restaurants and redefine the reservation experience for diners. In addition, we believe that there is a significant opportunity to provide solutions to reservation-taking restaurants and diners, as the network connecting the two groups is created and expanded.

Our Solution

Reservation-taking restaurants and diners have interconnected needs. Restaurants require cost-effective ways to attract guests and manage their reservations, while diners seek convenient ways to find available restaurants, choose among them and secure reservations. By creating an online network of restaurants and diners that transact with each other through real-time reservations, we have developed a specialized platform for addressing the needs of both.

Essential to this network is building a critical mass of local, computerized restaurant reservation books. We achieve this by offering software that provides important operational benefits for the restaurant, bundling it with computer hardware and installing this solution at the restaurant host stand, thereby creating a compelling solution for restaurants. We provide our solutions to individual restaurants within a market, one by one, via a direct sales force. We believe that we deliver a strong return on investment for our restaurant customers by streamlining their operations, filling additional seats and improving their quality of service. As a result, we have historically enjoyed high customer satisfaction and retention rates.

The OpenTable website gives diners real-time access to tables at restaurants on the OpenTable network. As more local restaurants are added to the network, the utility provided to diners increases and more diners discover the benefits of researching restaurants and making reservations on our website. The more diners who use our website to make their dining decisions, the more value we deliver to our restaurant customers and the more restaurants are attracted to our network.

Benefits of OpenTable to Reservation-Taking Restaurants

In response to the needs of reservation-taking restaurants, we offer the OpenTable ERB, a bundled solution consisting of proprietary OpenTable software, which is installed on a touch-screen computer system and supported by various asset-protection and security tools. Additionally, we provide restaurants with access to diners via our website as well as through reservation links on our partners' websites and on restaurants' own websites. Our solutions help restaurants participating in the OpenTable network to:

- fill seats that might otherwise remain empty and minimize "no-shows" by offering the convenience of online reservations directly through the OpenTable website as well as indirectly through the websites of our partners and restaurant customers;
- create operational efficiencies by replacing the restaurant's pen-and-paper system with a computerized reservation book and helping restaurants maximize seat utilization, facilitate server rotations and improve table turns;
- boost guest recognition and overall guest service by recording diner preferences and histories and by collecting and delivering feedback from OpenTable diners;
- computerize their host-stand operations by providing a solution that combines proprietary software and computer hardware and customized, on-site installation, training and technical support; and
- market to a targeted audience with measurable results by giving restaurants valuable marketing exposure during the diners' decision-making process and requiring payment by restaurants only for those diners whom they ultimately serve.

Benefits of OpenTable to Diners

In response to the needs of diners, we offer the OpenTable website, a destination website for those seeking a convenient way to research restaurants and make reservations. Our website enables diners to:

- find available tables by allowing diners to search for reservations by location, date, time and party size and view real-time table availability across a variety of restaurants;
- choose a restaurant by providing diners with restaurant information such as restaurant descriptions, photos and menus as well as lists of restaurants that are most highly rated by OpenTable diners in different categories; and
- book instantly-confirmed reservations for free by allowing diners to make reservations through the OpenTable website, which are instantly recorded in the ERB located at the restaurant.

Our Strategy

As our network of reservation-taking restaurants and diners grows, the value we deliver grows as well. Because the foundation of our network is building a critical mass of computerized reservation books, we enhance our offering to diners by adding new restaurant customers. In turn, as more diners use the OpenTable website to make their dining decisions and book their reservations, we deliver more value to our restaurant customers by helping them fill more of their seats. In this process, we grow the value of our business. The key elements of this strategy include:

Continue to Build the OpenTable Network in North America

The value of the OpenTable network grows as participation among restaurants and diners grows. Experience in our earliest markets provided a successful model that we have implemented while entering new markets, and, as a result, our newer North American markets have grown relatively predictably over time. We intend to continue to build our North American network in the United States, Canada and Mexico by employing this proven model, which includes the following elements:

- producing and maintaining superior solutions by continuing to evolve our ERB based on nearly a decade of in-field experience as well as feedback from our installed base of approximately 10,000 restaurant customers, and optimizing our website through insights gained from the experience of seating approximately 100 million diners through online reservations;
- providing excellent customer service and support by continuing to employ highly trained operational teams to provide installation and training services for our restaurant customers and continuing to augment our in-house support staff with contract support services to deliver superior customer assistance;
- leveraging our direct sales force, which is experienced in selling the benefits of OpenTable to reservation-taking restaurants, which operate in a highly fragmented industry; and
- continuing to attract diners to our website by offering the best reservation experience through enhanced ease of use and restaurant content, thereby increasing market adoption of our solutions, building our brand awareness and driving word-of-mouth referrals to our website.

Expand Internationally

We intend to augment our growing North American business by selectively expanding into countries outside of North America that are characterized by large numbers of online consumer transactions and reservation-taking restaurants. We currently have operations in Germany, Japan and the United Kingdom, each supported with a direct sales force and operational staff. We have approximately 1,000 restaurant customers in these markets. In general, our strategy internationally is to replicate the model we have successfully employed in North America. In particular, our initial focus in new international markets is to increase our restaurant customer base, and we believe the localized versions of our software solution will compete favorably against competitive software offerings, enabling us to expand our network of computerized reservation books across a broad selection of local restaurants.

Risk Factors

Our business is subject to numerous risks and uncertainties, including those highlighted in the section entitled "Risk Factors" immediately following this prospectus summary, that primarily represent challenges we face in connection with the successful implementation of our strategy and the growth of our business. Our limited operating history makes it difficult for us to accurately forecast revenues and appropriately plan our expenses. We expect a number of factors to cause our operating results to fluctuate on a quarterly and annual basis, which may make it difficult to predict our future performance. Such factors include deteriorating global economic conditions and our ability to maintain an adequate rate of growth, effectively manage our growth, retain and attract restaurant customers and visitors to our website, provide a high-quality customer experience through our website and ERB and successfully enter new markets and manage our international expansion.

Corporate Information

We were originally incorporated as easyeats.com, Inc., a California corporation, on October 13, 1998. On June 2, 1999, we changed our name to OpenTable.com, Inc. We subsequently reincorporated in Delaware on September 20, 2000 under our current name, OpenTable, Inc. Our principal executive offices are located at 799 Market Street, 4th Floor, San Francisco, California 94103, and our telephone number is (415) 344-4200. Our website address is www.opentable.com. Information contained on our website is not a part of this prospectus and the inclusion of our website address in this prospectus is an inactive textual reference only. Unless the context requires otherwise, the words "OpenTable," "we," "company," "us" and "our" refer to OpenTable, Inc. and our wholly owned subsidiaries.

. . .

Notes and Questions

1. The full OpenTable registration statement, including the complete prospectus, is available through the website of the Securities and Exchange Commission at www.sec.gov. To find it, search company filings for OpenTable, Inc., and look in the oldest available filings for the final S-1 Registration Statement.

2. In drafting the above prospectus, OpenTable and its lawyers would be careful to follow the regulations of the Securities and Exchange Commission. To avoid liability for securities fraud or other breaches of the securities laws, the prospectus must be entirely truthful and must highlight risky aspects of the investment. At the

same time, OpenTable will want to use the prospectus as a marketing piece to entice investors. Looking only at the summary section you read, what balance did the company and its advisors strike in summarizing the prospectus? Would it surprise you to learn that, in the full prospectus, the "Risk Factors" section (which is typically written by attorneys and is generally viewed by business people as a considerably negative piece that could be harmful to the offering) is a full 25 pages, followed by two pages of additional disclaimers?

3. The Securities and Exchange Commission gives the following description of so-called lockup agreements:

> Lockup agreements prohibit company insiders — including employees, their friends and family, and venture capitalists — from selling their shares for a set period of time. In other words, the shares are "locked up." Before a company goes public, the company and its underwriter typically enter into a lockup agreement to ensure that shares owned by these insiders don't enter the public market too soon after the offering.
>
> The terms of lockup agreements may vary, but most prevent insiders from selling their shares for a period of 180 days. Lockups may also limit the number of shares that can be sold over a designated period of time.

The SEC does not require lockup agreements, although it does require disclosure of any lockup agreements that exist. Some state securities laws do require lockup agreements in connection with an offering of securities to the public. Why might an underwriter seek a lockup agreement in an IPO? Why might the state have an interest in requiring lockup agreements?

4. In the "Use of Proceeds" section of the prospectus, OpenTable discloses that

> We currently intend to use the net proceeds to us from this offering primarily for general corporate purposes, including working capital, sales and marketing activities, general and administrative matters and capital expenditures. We may also use a portion of the net proceeds for the acquisition of, or investment in, technologies, solutions or businesses that complement our business. We have no present understandings, commitments or agreements to enter into any acquisitions or investments. Our management will have broad discretion over the uses of the net proceeds in this offering. Pending these uses, we intend to invest the net proceeds from this offering in short-term, investment-grade interest-bearing securities such as money market accounts, certificates of deposit, commercial paper and guaranteed obligations of the U.S. government.

The "Our Strategy" section you read above might provide more color on what "general corporate purposes" OpenTable management has in mind. If, in fact, the goal of this IPO was to raise money, can you speculate on why the company didn't seek additional capital through the means described in Chapter 5? What other benefits might you imagine management sought by doing an IPO?

5. Given the many options for business exit strategies you have read about in this chapter, why would OpenTable management have selected an initial public offering as the next step for the business, as opposed to, say, a strategic merger or company sale? Consider not only the path that best serves the enterprise as a whole, but also any self-interest officers or directors may have. Do you think there was a better option management should have considered, and if so, what about the other path do you prefer?

6. As noted earlier in this chapter, IPOs are relatively rare, and entrepreneurial clients need to be aware of the other available paths. How would you counsel a client who was focused on an IPO and saw OpenTable as an inspiring example?

PROBLEM

Your client, General Germ, Inc., has been a successful one-product venture for a few years. Knowing that General Germ must become part of a larger consumer products company to reach its full potential, Olivia and Andrew have met with you several times over the past few months to discuss ways the company can reach the "next level." The clients understand that they may need to give up control of the venture for it to continue, but are willing to do so as long as they continue to have an economic interest in the success of the business going forward. As it stands, General Germ has no debt, and your clients, plus one non-voting outside investor, are the only three owners.

Assume that, coincidentally and as far as you know unrelated to the conversations you have been having with your client, General Germ has received an unsolicited offer from a major consumer products manufacturer in the form of the following term sheet:

Term Sheet for Acquisition of General Germ, Inc.

Buyer:	Simple Corp., a Delaware corporation.
Company:	General Germ, Inc., an Illinois corporation.
Transaction:	Purchase of substantially all of the assets of the Company by Buyer.
Purchase Price:	$25 million, to be paid $10 million in cash at the closing, and $15 million in the form of a promissory note, payable over a ten-year period and bearing interest at the rate of 4.0 percent per annum.
Conditions Precedent:	Customary conditions precedent, including, without limitation, (i) due diligence satisfactory to Buyer in its sole discretion, and (ii) availability of financing acceptable to Buyer in its sole discretion.
Non-Competition:	Olivia M. Gold and Andrew Orlando will each sign a two-year Consulting Agreement in which he or she agrees to perform such reasonable services as may be requested by Buyer from time to time, which shall be performed at a mutually convenient time and which shall in no event exceed ten weeks per year. The Consulting Agreements will include an annual salary of $100,000 per year, and will include a seven-year non-competition agreement covering any position or investment in the antibacterial products industry in the United States and Canada.

Expenses:	Each party will bear its own expenses in connection with the Transaction.
No-Shop:	If Company agrees to pursue the Transaction, Company and its agents will not, directly or indirectly, (i) take any action to solicit, initiate, encourage, or assist the submission of any proposal, negotiation, or offer from any person or entity other than the Buyer relating to the sale or other disposition of the capital stock of the Company or the acquisition, sale, lease, license, or other disposition of the Company or any material part of the stock or assets of the Company, or (ii) enter into any discussions, negotiations, or execute any agreement related to any of the foregoing, and shall notify the Buyer promptly of any inquiries by any third parties in regards to the foregoing.

1. The proposed transaction is structured as an asset purchase. What advice will you give to your client about this structure, as compared with some of the other exit strategies described in this chapter? What additional facts do you need to know about General Germ or Buyer to determine whether this is the optimal structure?

2. Leaving aside the question of whether the aggregate purchase price is a good price for the assets being sold, what do you think of the form of the consideration? Is a promissory note the same as cash, and what might you advise your client as to negotiating the consideration? Are there other ways to pay purchase price or other types of consideration your client should seek? Assume your client thinks sales will grow significantly in the next five to ten years under the new owners.

3. What do you make of the heading "Non-Competition" being applied to a description of a consulting agreement? What advice might you give your client about the value being placed on the services they may be asked to provide? Is this arrangement fair to the outside investor in General Germ?

4. The "No-Shop" provision prohibits General Germ from soliciting competing offers or even having discussions with other suitors. In the corporate context, boards of directors are supposed to act in the best interest of shareholders. In this context where the target is a limited liability company, does agreeing to this provision represent a violation of a fiduciary duty by the controlling members? If it is a fiduciary duty violation, what will be the likely practical effect in this circumstance?

5. Assume your client decides not to proceed with the Simple Corp. transaction. If you could design the ideal exit strategy for your client, what type of buyer and what transaction structure would you choose? Does your answer change if your client's primary goal is (a) receiving the largest total cash proceeds at closing; or (b) propagating General Germ technology so that larger numbers of people can be helped; or (c) continuing to play a leadership role in the company while taking some "cash off the table"; or (d) walking away and never having to worry about product liability or any other kinds of lawsuits; or (e) preparing the company to be run by Olivia's son in a few years?

Afterword

FINAL THOUGHTS FOR ATTORNEYS REPRESENTING ENTREPRENEURS

Now that we have reached the end of this book, we hope that you have come to better appreciate the host of legal and business issues entrepreneurs must navigate during the course of launching and building a new venture. It takes a certain personality or personal attributes to successfully handle these unique challenges. Many entrepreneurs credit their own innate curiosity as an original catalyst to starting their venture. Their curiosity may be what initially leads them to explore ways to improve current situations, find solutions, and innovate new products. This trait is closely related to the rejection by many entrepreneurs of the "do it the same old way/business as usual" mentality. Many of the entrepreneurs we have encountered are visionaries who are able to see possibilities and pathways that most of us cannot imagine until they have been created and are concrete. Some people say entrepreneurs are risk-seekers or at least risk-takers. Others characterize this seeming appetite for risk as an acceptance of risk and ability to strategically minimize it. We have even heard entrepreneurs say that not starting the new venture would be the real risk. Perhaps most importantly, entrepreneurs do not simply stop in their tracks and retreat when they see potential barriers. Instead, they figure out how to get around the barriers and move forward.

We also hope that you have seen how lawyers can be important and crucial members of the start-up team. It is our job to help our clients spot issues, structure the business to minimize risk, handle challenges that arise, protect company assets, and best position the company from a legal standpoint to succeed. Start-ups that do not own key intellectual property, are inadvertently infringing on intellectual property rights of third parties, are misclassifying workers, or do not document important business deals in writing have the cards stacked against them.

We also hope you have learned that, as important as it is for the attorney to master this large variety of legal issues, it is equally important that an entrepreneur's lawyer understand her client and be able to effectively communicate legal analysis. When you work with entrepreneurs, understand that the entrepreneur is passionate and driven to make the venture succeed. Entrepreneurs do not want lawyers constantly shutting them down—they want lawyers who can identify risk, analyze the probability and consequences of various outcomes, and present strategies for minimizing legal pitfalls. At the same time, you must be clear with clients so they do not ignore legal hurdles. In addition, pay attention to the ways in which you communicate with entrepreneurial clients: do not assume they understand (or have any desire to understand) legal jargon. Speak plainly, be direct, but be sensitive to the client's passion for his venture and, of course, be empathetic.

In addition, you must stay informed about current trends in entrepreneurship. Nationally, new start-ups are being formed at an increasingly high rate. This should not be terribly surprising. The combination of significant changes in how we work and live, the explosion of the gig economy, increased state and federal governmental interest in job creation and development and worker classification, and the relative ease of launching a digital business has created the ideal climate. Lawyers should be focused on the fact that increased resources are being made available to entrepreneurs and keep abreast of developments to help ensure their clients do not miss potential opportunities. Staying well informed about the local entrepreneurship community is another valuable service a lawyer can provide to entrepreneurial clients.

One of the most important current trends in some regions is the recent proliferation of incubators and accelerator programs. Incubators, which may focus on traditional for-profit ventures or social entrepreneurs, are places where fledgling companies can share office space and resources while building their businesses. Accelerators are a new flavor of incubator, fashioned as limited-duration intense residencies for new businesses looking to develop quickly through workshops, mentorships, and ultimately prearranged pitch meetings with investors or other funders. Many incubators and accelerators also provide access to free or discounted legal services. Note the opportunity for lawyers building a practice area in this space to develop a client base. Lawyers representing start-ups should be well informed about the different incubators and accelerator programs in their communities and be prepared to discuss with clients the reputations, application processes, terms, and differentiators. Lawyers should be able to suggest programs that are particularly appropriate for a client and help clients compare options and make strategic decisions. As other trends emerge in the "entrepreneur support" industry, you should learn about those as well. Remember, providing excellent legal services to your start-up client is the base line. We should strive to also add value by understanding our clients' businesses, industries, and needs, and be a resource for non-legal information and good counsel.

Representing entrepreneurs is one of the most rewarding and entertaining ways to practice transactional law. Whether it is your main practice area or a side interest, it is a way for lawyers to directly and immediately support exciting new businesses, while at the same time contributing in ways that larger clients may prefer to handle on their own. Although entrepreneurs can, at times, be more emotional about business matters than large corporate clients, their passion and commitment is inspirational and incredibly enriching for practitioners. We wish you good luck in practice, and hope you enjoy the adventure that representing entrepreneurs can provide.

INDEX